The Social Context of Health and Health Work

The Social Context of Health and Health Work

Linda J. Jones

MACMILLAN

To Charles, and to the memory of Joyce,
my mother.

First published 1994 by
THE MACMILLAN PRESS LTD
Houndmills, Basingstoke, Hampshire RG21 2XS
and London
Companies and representatives
throughout the world

21385866

ISBN 0–333–55155–9 hardcover
ISBN 0–333–55156–7 paperback

A catalogue record for this book is available from the British Library

Printed in Great Britain by
MacKays of Chatham PLC
Chatham, Kent

Contents

List of figures

List of tables

List of useful terms

Standard mortality (death) rate – deaths per 1000 of the population, standardised for age

Standardised mortality ratio (SMR) – compares the standard mortality rate for the whole population with that of a particular region, group and so on, expressing this as a ratio

Potential years of life lost (PYLL) – compares life expectancy of the whole population with that of particular groups, regions and so on, expressing this as a ratio

Infant mortality rate (IMR) – deaths at all ages under one year (per 1000 live births)

Perinatal mortality rate (PMR) – stillbirths and deaths in the first week of life (per 1000 total births)

Neonatal mortality rate (NMR) – deaths in the first 28 days of life (per 1000 live births)

Maternal mortality rate (MMR) – deaths per 100 000 women in the population from complications of pregnancy, childbirth of puerperium

Stillbirths – foetal deaths after 28 completed weeks of gestation

Preface

List of useful terms

Many people have contributed to the realisation of this project, not least the health studies students and pre-registration nurses, midwives, health visitors and district nurses I have taught over the years. In particular, the pilot Project 2000 Diploma students of South Birmingham Health Authority in the later 1980s forced me to confront the problems of teaching health sociology and policy perspectives on health work courses. Students on the part-time nursing degree helped me to respond to this challenge and to demonstrate the practical value of social theory and research for health work.

Thanks are also due to the nurse tutors and to lecturers at the (then) Birmingham Polytechnic. In particular, Roswyn Brown, Course Director of the part-time nursing degree, gave me support at a critical time to develop the part-time sociology programme for nurses. Judy Hubbard, Course Director of the health studies degree, a physiologist and a long-standing friend and colleague, stimulated and challenged my thinking about health.

Colleagues in the Department of Sociology and Applied Social Studies gave me much sound advice and valued support over the years. In particular, I want to record my thanks to Peter Tetley, who introduced me to Michel Foucault's work, to Bob Kornreich, with whom I taught a sociology of health elective and from whom I learned a great deal, and to George Smith, for his wide knowledge and uncompromising defence of social policy.

My Open University colleagues have been generous to a fault. In spite of their own pressing deadlines Moyra Sidell and Stephen Pattison have read and commented on various drafts and have done their best to improve them. To Alan Beattie and Moyra Sidell, my fellow course team members on K258 *Health and Wellbeing*, I owe a tremendous debt. Working with them on the making of this course enabled me to review and relocate nursing within the broader context of formal and informal health work and to appreciate more clearly the significance of lay and alternative beliefs about health.

Graham Moon at Portsmouth and Margaret Miers and her colleagues at Bristol gave me detailed comments and constructive advice on every chapter, and undoubtedly improved the focus and flow of the text. Petra Kopp, my copy editor, has remained consistently cheerful and helpful, even when asked to do the near impossible. The book is much easier to read as a result of her efforts.

Finally, my love and thanks are due to Charles, Kate and Ellen for putting up with my tiredness and bad temper and for supporting and encouraging me when the writing was going badly and the deadlines were uncomfortably close. Without their help this book would never have been completed. Needless to say, the remaining mistakes and oddities, and the views expressed, are entirely my own responsibility.

Acknowledgements

The author and publisher would like to thank the following for permission to use copyright material:

The Controller of Her Majesty's Stationery Office for figures, extracts and tables from *Social Trends* (1993 and 1994), from OPCS (1994) General Household Survey, 1992. Series GHS No. 23, OPCS Longitudinal Study (1982), Perinatal and infant mortality statistics (1990), Working for Patients (1989), The Health of the Nation (1992); Kluwer Academic Publishers for a table from C. Helman (1978) 'Feed a cold: starve a fever' in *Culture, Medicine and Psychiatry 2*; Edward Elgar Ltd for tables from V. George and I. Howards (1991) *Poverty Amidst Affluence*; Elsevier Science Ltd, The Boulevard, Langford Lane, Kidlington OX5 1GB, UK for a table from C. Aakster (1986) 'Concepts in alternative medicine' in *Social Science and Medicine*, Vol. 22, No. 2; The Open University for figures and tables from K258 *Health and Wellbeing* and from K205 *Health and Disease*; Berg Publishers for a figure from A. Young (1986) 'Internalising and externalising medical belief systems' in C. Currer and M. Stacey (eds) *Concepts of Health, Illness and Disease*; Policy Studies Institute Publications for figures from J. Percy-Smith and I. Sanderson (1992) *Understanding Local Needs*; Churchill Livingstone for a figure from J. Bond and S. Bond (1986) *Sociology and Health Care*; Routledge Ltd. for a figure from A. Witz (1992) *Professions and Patriarchy*; Sage Publications Ltd for a figure from B. Hughes (1990) 'Quality of life' in S. Peace (ed) *Researching Social Gerontology*; Oxford University Press for a table from J.H. Goldthorpe *et al.* (1980) *Social Ability and Class Structure in Modern Britain*; The Macmillan Press Ltd for tables from C. Ham (1992) *Health Policy in Britain* (3rd edn) and a case study from E. Anionwu (1993) 'Genetics – a philosophy of perfection?', in A. Beattie *et al.* (eds) *Health and Wellbeing: A Reader*; NAHAT (National Association of Health Authorites and Trusts) for a table and figure from *Purchasing for a Healthy Population* (1993), and for tables from *The Health Service Yearbook* (1993) and *Action, Not Words* (1988); Blackwell Scientific Publications for a figure from J. Morse (1991) 'Negotiating commitment and involvement in the nurse–patient relationship', *Journal of Advanced Nursing*, **16**, pp. 455–7; Tavistock/Routledge for figures for M. Blaxter (1990) *Health and Lifestyles*, M. Jeffreys et al (eds) *Growing Older in the Twentieth Century* and G. Brown and T. Harris (1978) *Social Origins of Depression*; Wigmore Publications Ltd. for an extract from *Homeopathy for the Family* (1988) 8th edn.; Hodder and Stoughton for an extract from A. Brechin and J. Walmsley (1990) *Making Connections*; the National Extension College for material from *Health Care in Multiracial Britain* (1985); Open University Press for a table from C. R. Victor (1991) *Health and Health Care in Later Life* and a figure from M. Loney et al (eds) (1983) *Social Policy and Social Welfare*; Taylor and Francis for a figure from P. Abbott and G. Payne (eds) (1991) *New Directions in the Sociology of Health*; Equal Opportunities Commission for figures from *Men and Women in Britain 1993*.

Every effort has been made to trace all copyright holders, but if any have been inadvertently overlooked the publisher will be pleased to make the necessary arrangements at the first opportunity.

Introduction

Two main types of experience have helped to shape this book: face-to-face teaching work with nurses and other health students, and developing distance learning materials at the Open University. When the book was first planned it was to be a short text for nurses, harnessing the practical experience of planning and delivering health sociology and policy on a Project 2000 pilot course. So much has happened since then – to nurse education, to health care organisation and to health and welfare in general (as well as to the author) – that the finished book is rather more ambitious: larger, more reflective, more broadly based in health studies and more challenging to students.

Some students will always want a straightforward 'sociology textbook', and for them this book outlines key sociological concepts and theories and applies them to health work. But it also breaks new ground by linking together sociology of health and social policy perspectives, in the belief that students need both to reflect on the nature and meaning of their own practice and to tease out the relationships between social theories and health and welfare policies.

It is clear that the health sector is being transformed by market pressures and neo-liberal ideologies. Nurses and other health workers face new challenges from rapid changes in established training and work patterns. Primary and community care are growing and the hospital workforce is shrinking. Patients' charters, health targets, contracts and skill mix are the buzz words of the 1990s. At the same time relative poverty, health inequality and unequal opportunities are marked features of contemporary Britain. Demand for health care is growing, but so too are disenchantment with modern medicine and interest in alternative therapies.

The book seeks to explain why inequalities persist, why health work is in such a state of flux and why conflicts over welfare are growing. It does so not by narrowly focusing on health care but by encouraging students to understand how they themselves, as well as their patients and clients, are positioned within a broader social context. Debates about health policies are linked to wider conflicts over welfare. Trends in health and disease are explored in relation to contemporary social divisions of class, race, gender, age and disability. Changing practices and relationships in health work are also related to these broader patterns of social change.

Chapter 1 sets health in a social context, exploring how concepts of health, illness, disease and sickness have been shaped by lay beliefs and expert discourse. It introduces central themes in the book: the complexity and shifting basis of health itself, the scope and significance of inequalities in health, and possible uses of the 'social model of health' in contemporary health work.

Chapter 2 outlines major perspectives and theories in sociology and social policy which have influenced our thinking about health and health work. It introduces the main perspectives in social policy, in particular the influence of Fabianism and of the New Right in the 1980s. It briefly explores how the ideas of Marx, Weber and Durkheim have influenced current thinking about health and illness, reassesses the contribution of Talcott Parsons and outlines the work of social action and feminist theorists. The rise of social constructionism in medical sociology is set within a wider framework of postmodernist thought.

Chapters 3 and 4 focus on the family and on community, institutions which have become the focus of intense social and political pressure. Chapter 3 explores the changing structure and character of the family, relating this to broader economic and social change and reflecting on the implications for health work practice. It outlines the growth of state welfare provision for the family and the main structures of the welfare state. Chapter 4 examines the concept of 'community' and explores the scope and character of community health work, in particular the growth of community care.

Chapters 5–9 explore various dimensions of power and inequality in contemporary society. Theoretical insights from sociology and social policy are used to illuminate current features of health work organisation and practice. Class, race, gender, age and disability are examined both in terms of their relationship to health status and their impact on health work. Chapter 6 investigates why poverty persists in the affluent UK and why it has had such a profound impact on health.

Chapter 10 develops the analysis of health beliefs and health action begun in Chapter 1. It notes the wide range of offical ideas about health, from non-Western as well as Western cultures. Theories of health behaviour are reviewed and the role of the 'patient' within different health work systems is assessed.

The final three chapers explore in greater detail various aspects of health care organisation and delivery. Chapter 11 looks at power and control in health work, charting the rise to dominance of the medical profession and its influence over the division of labour in health care. Together with Chapter 13, it considers the establishment and growth of the National Health Service and changes in its structure and organisation.

Chapter 12 discusses the work of nursing, drawing on the analysis of class, race and gender offered in earlier chapters. Nursing is explored as a complex and ever-changing activity, influenced by both a medical and a social model of health, by new ideas about holism and empowerment and by changes in nurse education and training.

Chapter 13 reviews the contemporary politics of health care, the rise of managerialism, of contractualism and of the purchaser–provider split in health. The book concludes by reviewing prospects for health and health work in the future: for promoting health rather than treating disease, for broader evaluation of health care interventions, for increasing user participation and for the reformulation of health work itself.

How to use this book

The range of material in this book means that it can be used in several ways. Some students will choose to work through it chapter by chapter; others will dip into the book for particular purposes, to learn more about poverty and health, sociological theories or contemporary health policies. Those who have a grounding in sociology and social policy should find Chapter 2 a useful summary of perspectives and theories. Those who are coming new to these fields may find it more helpful to read Chapter 2 after having studied some of the other early chapters, such as those on the family and community.

However you use the book you will find help and guidance in every chapter. They all have summaries of major themes and issues at the start, together with learning outcomes so that you can check your progress through the text. Within each chapter there are comments, questions and ideas to set you thinking about what you are reading. You can, of course, ignore these and read on – the 'answers' are always provided for you – but the hope is that you will become an 'active reader' who reviews and evaluates the material presented. At the end of each chapter there are self assessment questions to enable you to check your understanding of the text. Frequent cross-references help you to review earlier sections of the book, and separate subject and author indexes enable you to track down ideas and references.

However you choose to use this book, I hope you find it as enjoyable and valuable to read as I found it stimulating and challenging to write.

Linda Jones, Moseley, Birmingham, May 1994

Chapter 1

Health in a social context

Contents

Themes and issues

Medical model of health: health as absence of disease – functional fitness – using mortality and morbidity to measure health

Social model of health: World Health Organisation concept of health – health field concept

Lay beliefs: private and public concepts of health and illness

Health chances: inequalities in health – environment, lifestyles and behaviour – government health targets – models of health work practice

Learning outcomes

After working through this chapter you should be able to:
1 Review different professional definitions of health, disease and sickness.
2 Demonstrate your understanding of the social model of health.
3 Compare and contrast behavioural and environmental explanations of health inequalities.
4 Review and evaluate lay accounts of health and illness.
5 Discuss the advantages and drawbacks of using a social model in health practice.

THIS chapter begins to explore what is to be gained by studying health in a social context. Health is a physiological and a psychological state but it is also, fundamentally, a *social* state. In other words, although health and illness may seem just to happen to us as individuals, we experience and make sense of them by drawing on a stock of current social beliefs, ideas and practices. From earliest infancy human beings are engaged in trying to interpret and negotiate the social world in which they find themselves, in processes of social learning and social action. In the social institutions of contemporary society, such as the family and the education system, people learn to understand 'what health is' and is not, and what are appropriate responses to disease and illness. In encounters with the structures of power in society – state welfare bureaucracies, professional groups, the class system and so on – people learn what it means to be 'sick', 'dependent' or 'disabled'. As they come into contact with organisations which provide health services they develop their understanding of how to be a 'patient' or a 'carer'.

It is the study of health and illness as *social products* – which become realised and understood only through exploring the social world in which they are embedded – that lies at the heart of this book. In this first chapter we begin the journey of exploration by questioning current ideas about health, sickness, disease and illness, and by exploring the definitions of health given by professionals and experts, and by lay people. But accounts of health and illness are not autonomous. As we have already noted, they are grounded in people's lived experience: of class, race, gender, age and disability, of poverty, of family and community life. Social factors such as these influence health professionals as well as lay people. So the chapter moves on to explore cultural and social influences upon health status, and then to consider their significance for health work. In doing so it introduces three major concerns of the book which will be developed in later chapters: the complexity of ideas about health, the social formation of health chances and current debates about health work.

1.1 Thinking about health

What is 'health'? Shouldn't a book about the social context of health and health work begin with a clear definition of health? This section investigates why health as a concept has proved hard to pin down and suggests that a preoccupation with definitions can obscure much of its complexity and shifting nature. All of us, whether we are professional health workers or lay people, create and re-create meanings of health and illness through our lived experience. By searching for the ultimate definition of 'health' we might fail to explore the intricate inter-relationships between meanings of health and changing social circumstances, experiences and values.

Health is a state of being that is subject to wide individual, social and cultural interpretation; it is produced by the interplay of individual perceptions and social influences. Undoubtedly there are widely accepted definitions which we'll return to later on – 'absence of disease', for example, and 'a complete state of wellbeing'. But your neighbour's notion of what constitutes 'health' will probably not agree with yours, and given different circumstances both of you might shift your ground. The definition you offer at fifteen (if you thought about it at all) will probably have changed considerably by the time you reach retirement age. You would find it surprising if a child – likely to be fit, active, with no serious impairment – viewed health in exactly the same way as an older person who may be coping with a chronic condition, limited mobility and several other moderate impairments. Recent studies of beliefs about 'what health is' suggest that people's perception of their own state of health influences how they define health (Cox *et al.*, 1987). Older people are more likely to view health in terms of function and coping: carrying out household tasks, managing to work, being able to get around. Young people frequently define it in terms of fitness, energy, vitality and strength, emphasising positive attainment and a healthy lifestyle (see Table 1.1).

○   Write down your own definition of health and compare it with the following definition from Mrs Brown, an 80 year old Yorkshire woman.

I've lived in the village all my life and there's rarely a day when I haven't been out. It doesn't feel right if we can't get out for a walk. You can see the hills from my window, we're the last house down the lane, you just step outside. Walking keeps you warm, getting around, that's what I call being well. I've never felt the cold except in the really bad weather, but now I can't walk like I used to, I need a stick. I always have the fire on and keep busy doing my jobs, tidy the house, cook the tea, but my legs go stiff and I have to stop, and then I do feel the cold. Rain's the worst, you can always be cheerful if the sun shines, can't you.

How far did you share Mrs Brown's view of health as the ability to 'get around' and 'keep busy'? Did you find yourself equating health with physical fitness and energy, like many respondents in the Health and Lifestyle Survey? You may have pointed out – as Mrs Brown implied – the emotional dimension of health. Mrs Brown's sense of contentment is threatened by her increasing lack of mobility, and other factors – like the weather – may significantly influence people's perception of their health as well as their physical and mental health state.

A person's age is only one of many factors that may influence their definition of health. The Health and Lifestyle Survey (Cox *et al.*, 1987) documented differences in responses between men and women. Younger women tended to link energy and vitality to undertaking household tasks, whereas younger men linked energy and fitness to

TABLE 1.1 Concepts used in the attempt to describe what health is. Source: Cox et al. (1987)

	Males			Females		
Concept of health used for describing someone else	Age					
	18–39	40–59	60+	18–39	40–59	60+
	Percentage					
Never ill, no disease, never see a doctor	26	39	37	45	51	37
Fit, strong, energetic, physically active	46	28	13	30	21	11
Able to do a lot, work, socially active	13	16	22	14	18	20
Has healthy habits (eg not smoking, taking exercise, taking care of health)	24	18	14	27	17	14
Psychologically fit (eg relaxed, dynamic, contented, able to cope)	9	9	6	11	8	5
In good health for their age (applied to an older person)	2	8	15	3	8	17
Mean no. of concepts used	1.2	1.2	1.1	1.3	1.3	1.1
Concept of health used for describing what it is to be healthy oneself						
Never ill, no disease, never see a doctor	15	17	16	12	10	11
Fit, strong, energetic, physically active	25	18	12	36	28	14
Able to do a lot, work, get out and about	18	18	27	18	23	31
Feel psychologically fit (eg good, happy, able to cope)	55	60	54	58	62	54
Can't explain, or don't know what it is to be healthy	8	7	8	6	6	10
Mean no. of concepts used by those offering any	1.3	1.3	1.2	1.4	1.4	1.3
Base = 100%	*1668*	*1240*	*997*	*2150*	*1596*	*1352*

Multiple answers possible

participating in sports. Having a traditional female role as a housewife influenced Mrs Brown's perception of health, in the sense that she measured her health partly in terms of her ability to cope with what she saw as her 'jobs' – that is, the housework. You may find already that your role as a 'student' and a 'nurse' or other 'health worker' plays some part in defining your view of health. You may also be realising that a straightforward definition of health – even if we could frame it satisfactorily – would not help very much in uncovering the variety of different experiences, beliefs and assumptions that make up people's views of health.

Many seemingly simple definitions – 'not being ill', 'an absence of disease', 'the ability to function normally', 'a state of fitness' among them – contain within them complex ideas about what it is to be healthy, whose responsibility it is to maintain health, how illness and disease should be interpreted. They may project officially sanctioned ways of viewing health which have passed into public circulation and become part of popular thinking. Consider 'absence of disease', for example, which appears as a category in many research findings (Herzlich, 1973; Blaxter, 1990). It has been the most pervasive official definition of health in the Western World. You may have encountered this definition already since it is associated with a 'medical' view of health.

○   Suggest what ideas and messages inform the definition of health as 'an absence of disease'.

The 'absence of disease' definition presents a rather negative view of health: as 'absence' rather than as a positive state. It is also a polarised view: you are either suffering from a disease or you are in health. Quite apart from the problems surrounding diagnosis – are you diseased if neither you nor your doctor recognise it? – there are clearly powerful signals in this definition about what health is and is not. Health is not about feeling well, at ease, energetic, or even necessarily about not feeling ill; it is about not having a disease. And since diagnosing disease is the specialist activity of medical doctors, it follows that all of us are healthy until diagnosed as diseased by our doctor. Indeed in Britain and much of the rest of Europe a person must be officially diagnosed in order to qualify for sickness pay beyond the first few days; so a state of health is what the vast majority of us are otherwise assumed to enjoy. And since many people in surveys offer this as one of their definitions of health, there is presumably quite widespread acceptance of such a view, which at least enables individuals of all ages and backgrounds to see themselves as being 'in health'.

From this seemingly simple definition of health we have begun to tease out a series of explanations which expose it as complex and multi-dimensional, highlighting certain issues and pushing others to the margins. Moreover, the popularity of 'absence of disease' as a definition offered by ordinary members of the public (not only professional health workers) suggests how people's definitions of health arise from the sifting of broader ideas and theories as well as from 'personal' beliefs and experiences.

○   Consider another 'official' definition. What ideas and messages inform this definition of health?

Health is not merely the absence of disease, but a state of complete physical, mental, spiritual and social well-being.

World Health Organisation (1974)

As a health student, you are probably already familiar with this World Health Organisation (WHO) definition, which seems to equate health with all-round wellbeing. You might have been influenced – as many have been – by its idealism and its positive message. Although in these terms almost all of us could be labelled 'unhealthy' – in a curious reversal of the 'absence of disease' scenario – this phrase has become a standard definition of health today. The WHO definition has been widely used within contemporary health care, particularly in community settings where professionals want to enhance people's health rather than merely to treat established disease. It highlights health as a positive goal rather than just a neutral state of 'no disease', and indicates that this is to be achieved by personal and social change as well as by medical advance.

As a definition, it contains almost as many new problems as it tries to solve. Its idealistic, even utopian nature has been commented upon by critics (Seedhouse, 1985). How is anyone to achieve a state of complete health? What would it feel like if we reached it? How can wellbeing be measured, and what kinds of individual and societal changes are required to realise it? In a similar way to the 'absence of disease' approach, the apparent simplicity of the WHO definition conceals a range of assumptions about what health should be. Freedom from disease is not health; real health is viewed as the transformation of 'no disease'-type health into all-round wellbeing. Health becomes a personal struggle and a goal to be worked towards on a community, national and global level.

This sense of health as action and adaptation is captured in the World Health Organisation Working Group report (1984) on health promotion, which conceptualised health as:

The extent to which an individual or group is able, on the one hand, to realize aspirations and satisfy needs and on the other hand, to change or cope with the environment. Health is therefore seen as a resource for everyday life, not the objective of living: it is a positive concept emphasizing social and personal resources as well as physical capabilities.

World Health Organisation (1984)

○ Reflect on this comment about health. Do you think it has any advantages over the two earlier definitions?

This later and less frequently quoted World Health Organisation comment emphasises that health is embedded in the processes and actions of everyday life. It relates health to our ability to cope and adapt within a particular environment. This deliberately avoids objectifying health; instead, health is viewed as 'a resource for living'. It also identifies health as a multi-dimensional and shifting concept which can't be easily analysed or measured: a view which for the last 150 years has not found favour with professional health workers.

1.2 Disease, illness and sickness

In the West health has been defined most often in terms of disease and death. Improved health is measured in terms of life expectancy, calculated from mortality (death) rates (see Figure 1.1). In recent years health standards have been measured in terms of potential years of life lost (PYLL), again using mortality statistics. Differences in health between various groups in society are calculated by means of the standardised mortality ratio (SMR), which measures the relative chances of death at a stated age. Mortality statistics began to be collected and published by governments in the 1840s, although official estimates of death rates go back long before this. All deaths (and births and marriages) had to be notified to the local registry office, so that the Registrar General's office in London was able to build up detailed information on death rates and causes of death. This work is still carried out today by the Office of Population Censuses and Surveys (OPCS) (see Figure 1.2).

By the 1890s medical officers of health in towns all over the country were producing quite sophisticated analyses of mortality by cause, and of the pattern of morbidity (sickness) in their populations. For example, the Medical Officer of Health for Birmingham, Alfred Hill, reported in 1896 on child mortality in different wards of the city. He demonstrated that the death rate in the 'unhealthy', inner area wards was nearly twice that of the 'healthy' wards and argued that diseases such as whooping

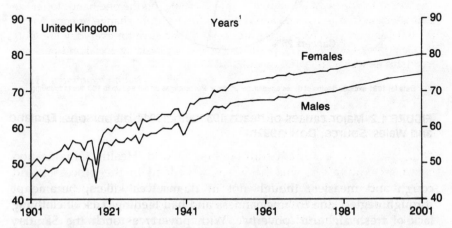

[1] The average number of years which a new-born baby could be expected to live if its rates of mortality at each age were those experienced in that calendar year.

FIGURE 1.1 Expectation of life at birth. Source: *Social Trends* (1994)

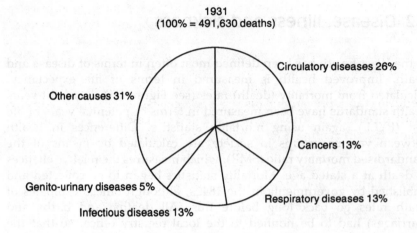

1931
(100% = 491,630 deaths)

Circulatory diseases 26%

Other causes 31%

Cancers 13%

Genito-urinary diseases 5%

Respiratory diseases 13%

Infectious diseases 13%

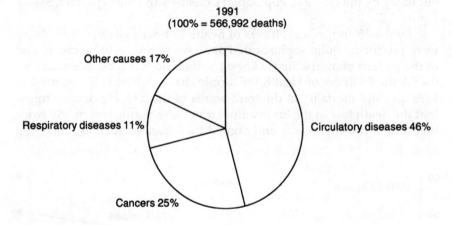

1991
(100% = 566,992 deaths)

Other causes 17%

Respiratory diseases 11%

Circulatory diseases 46%

Cancers 25%

* Data for 1991 exclude deaths of those aged under 28 days. Percentages do not add up to 100 due to rounding

FIGURE 1.2 Major causes of death 1931 and 1991*, all persons, England and Wales. Source: DoH (1992b)

cough and measles, though not in themselves killers, became so through neglect due to 'uncleanness and bad feeding, lack of clothing, lack of fresh air' and 'poverty'. 'With poverty as such the Sanitary Authority is, of course, not officially concerned' but 'with the provision of fresh air and removal of filthy conditions it is directly concerned' (Jones, 1993).

Mortality and morbidity are still widely used today as proxies for health, and lowering morbidity is equated with improving the nation's health. For example, in 1992 the goverment published a strategy for the English health service – called *The Health of the Nation* (DoH, 1992b) – which identified five key areas of objectives and targets for improving health (see Table 1.2). All of them were conceptualised in terms of 'reducing' and 'preventing' disease and sickness. For example, coronary heart disease and stroke were justified as a key area 'because of the scope for preventing illness and death from these conditions, and because reductions in risk factors . . . would also help to prevent many other diseases'. Cancers were selected 'because of the toll that cancers take in ill-health and death' (DoH, 1992b).

There are obvious advantages to measuring health in terms of mortality and morbidity, because it is generally relatively easy to record reported sickness and actual death. By contrast, recording 'health', as you may have begun to realise, is rather problematic. Given the historical predominance of the former approach, it is important to be clear about other terms subsumed under the concept of morbidity and therefore associated with measuring health; these are 'sickness', 'disease', and 'illness'.

○ Consider what you think are the differences between the three terms 'sickness', 'disease', and 'illness'.

You may have found it fairly easy to define illness, as a state of feeling ill or unwell. This draws our attention to the fact that illness is mediated through the individual: in other words, illness is about *how you feel*, not necessarily about the doctor telling you that you have a broken finger, or about getting a high blood pressure score or suddenly getting covered in measles spots. All these things *may* make you feel ill, but on the other hand they may not: the finger may have stopped hurting; you may feel just as well after your blood pressure test as you did before; and in spite of the spots you may feel fine.

Sickness is reported illness, when you go to the health centre for treatment of some kind and become a medical statistic. Hannay (1979) discussed what he termed an 'illness iceberg', in that only a proportion of illness ever gets reported and officially recorded. People treat themselves, ask advice from friends or just put up with feeling ill. We'll look at people's reaction to illness more closely (and to sickness and disease as well) in Chapter 10. Sickness rates are calculated from the use of health services and from absence from work records. Whitehead (1987) points out that neither are very reliable measures of the extent of disease because both are influenced by individual circumstances and different methods of recording and reporting sickness across the country.

TABLE 1.2 *The Health of the Nation* main targets. Source: DoH (1992b)

Coronary heart disease and stroke[1]

To reduce death rates for both CHD and stroke in people under 65 by at least 40% by the year 2000 (*Baseline 1990*)

To reduce the death rate for CHD in people aged 65–74 by at least 30% by the year 2000 (*Baseline 1990*)

To reduce the death rate for stroke in people aged 65–74 by at least 40% by the year 2000 (*Baseline 1990*)

Cancers[1]

To reduce the death rate for breast cancer in the population invited for screening by at least 25% by the year 2000 (*Baseline 1990*)

To reduce the incidence of invasive cervical cancer by at least 20% by the year 2000 (*Baseline 1986*)

To reduce the death rate for lung cancer under the age of 75 by at least 30% in men and by at least 15% in women by 2010 (*Baseline 1990*)

To halt the year-on-year increase in the incidence of skin cancer by 2005

Mental illness[1]

To improve significantly the health and social functioning of mentally ill people

To reduce the overall suicide rate by at least 15% by the year 2000 (*Baseline 1990*)

To reduce the suicide rate of severely mentally ill people by at least 33% by the year 2000 (*Baseline 1990*)

HIV/AIDS and sexual health

To reduce the incidence of gonorrhoea by at least 20% by 1995 (*Baseline 1990*), as an indicator of HIV/AIDS trends

To reduce by at least 50% the rate of conceptions amongst the under 16s by the year 2000 (*Baseline 1989*)

Accidents[1]

To reduce the death rate for accidents among children aged under 15 by at least 33% by 2005 (*Baseline 1990*)

To reduce the death rate for accidents among young people aged 15–24 by at least 25% by 2005 (*Baseline 1990*)

To reduce the death rate for accidents among people aged 65 and over by at least 33% by 2005 (*Baseline 1990*)

[1] The 1990 baseline for all mortality targets represents an average of three years centred around 1990.

Disease can be defined quite broadly as an 'unhealthy condition of body, mind, plant, or some part thereof, illness, sickness' (Concise Oxford English Dictionary, 6th edn, 1976). For our purposes the essential point about disease is that it refers to a specific condition of ill health in a patient; from a viewpoint of modern medicine this can be identified as an actual change (lesion) on the surface of, or inside, some part of the body. In theory a specific disease condition should characterise every episode of reported sickness; in practice, health workers sometimes treat patients and sign them off work where no disease can be identified.

The 'morbidity model' of health, as we might call it, has encouraged us to think of health as 'absence of disease'. There are many advantages in this: it has enabled us to take minor complaints in our stride; we can have aching feet, period pains, a bad cold, back ache and still see ourselves as healthy. On the other hand it has tended to label people with disabilities and chronic conditions of various kinds as inevitably 'sick' or even 'diseased', even if they are otherwise healthy. This kind of thinking, together with the measurement of health in terms of avoided or delayed death, has left lay people and professional health workers alike with a rather negative view of health which is only slowly being overcome.

1.3 The influence of official definitions of health

To a great extent official pronouncements have set the terms on which people talk about their health or lack of it – at least in public. By 'official' I mean those definitions produced by the medical profession and other health work agencies, by government reports and through legislation. Since the National Health Service began operation in Britain in 1948, successive governments have produced a mountain of reports outlining policy. In shaping health policy they have also influenced people's thinking about their own health and illness.

The notion of health as 'an absence of disease' and as 'a complete state of wellbeing' both have their origins in official medical publications. 'Absence of disease' derives from a medical concept of disease as a pathological state which can be diagnosed and categorised, or as deviation from measurable biological variables which represent 'normal' parameters in the 'healthy' body. This view of disease, which has come to dominate Western thinking about health during the past two centuries, is often termed the *medical model* (see Box 1.1). It is linked to the rise of clinical pathology and the scientific investigation of disease by a growing body of specialist doctors and researchers, and to the

BOX 1.1 The medical model

- Health is predominantly viewed as the 'absence of disease' and as 'functional fitness'.
- Health services are geared mainly towards treating sick and disabled people.
- A high value is put on the provision of specialist medical services, in mainly institutional settings.
- Doctors and other qualified experts diagnose illness and disease and sanction and supervise the withdrawal of patients from productive labour.
- The main function of health services is remedial or curative – to get people back to productive labour.
- Disease and sickness are explained within a biological framework that emphasises the physical nature of disease: that is, it is biologically reductionist.
- It works with a pathogenic focus, emphasising risk factors and establishing abnormality (and normality).
- A high value is put on using scientific methods of research (hypotheco-deductive method) and on scientific knowledge.
- Qualitative evidence (given by lay people or produced through academic research) generally has a lower status as knowledge than quantitative evidence.

emergence of health work as a formal, professionalised area of expertise (Freidson, 1970). Some evidence of the extent to which health is viewed as 'an absence of disease' is provided by the Health and Lifestyle Survey (Table 1.1), in which almost 40 per cent of respondents offered a definition of health as 'not ill' or 'no disease'.

As we noted earlier, the 1974 World Health Organisation definition builds a positive, idealistic vision of health as complete wellbeing, in which preoccupation with disease is replaced by a recognition of the broad social parameters of individual health. It reflects a more critical evaluation of the 'medical model' by researchers inside and outside medicine, and a questioning of how far diseases and 'norms' can be objective categories and measurements rather than reflecting social categorisations (Dubos, 1979; Engel, 1977).

The WHO definition connects to a *social model* of health, which emphasises the environmental causes of health and disease, in particular the dynamic interaction between individuals and their environment. Health is seen as being produced not just by individual biology and medical intervention, but by conditions in the wider natural, social, economic and political environment and by individual behaviour in response to that environment. An influential exponent of this approach was Marc Lalonde, who as Canada's Minister of Health and Welfare elaborated the *health field* concept (see Figure 1.3). Lalonde and his team argued that since prospects for improving health, and limitations upon it, arose in all four 'fields', interventions to promote health must also address all four. An overwhelming focus on health care organisation – and by implication on a 'medical model' of health – had obscured the

Human biology	Lifestyle
Environment	Health care organisation

FIGURE 1.3 The health field concept. Source: Lalonde (1974)

equally important environmental, behavioural and biological determinants of health (Lalonde, 1974).

Since then a number of studies have indicated that patterns of living
and social relationships are seen by people as being important in
maintaining health. Respondents in the Health and Lifestyle Survey
(Cox *et al.*, 1987) endorsed this view, although there was also strong
support for the idea that personal behaviour was a major influence.
Smaller-scale, more intensive contextual studies have provided stronger
evidence of people's belief that environmental factors influence their
health (Cornwell, 1984).

○ Some of the people in Jocelyn Cornwell's research in East London made
specific links between their work and state of health. Reflect on the ideas
about health and ill health that are highlighted in this comment by William
Cox, who worked as a lorry driver.

It's sending me deaf. The noise of the engine. I come home and I can't hear the telly.
If I've been out, not so much now because I am in the warehouse, but if I've been out all
day driving – say to Oxford and back which is like two, three hours out and two,
three hours back I come home and I can't hear the telly. I can hear it but not as loud
as I can . . . I don't really want to wear glasses, I don't know why, most drivers have to
wear glasses. Whether it's the strain on the eyes or something. The guy next door, he's
an ex-driver, and he's right deaf.

Cornwell (1984)

William Cox is well aware of his health problems: loss of hearing and
problems with eye-sight. He also highlights the work-related causes of
these conditions and is aware that they might get worse. Yet there is
little chance that he will be able to improve his health by changing his
occupation or that his current job will become healthier, and the view of
health that he conveys seems to be more about avoiding further
deterioration than about improvement.

Although Lalonde and others highlighted social and environmental influences on health – nutrition, public health measures, falling family size – it is lifestyle aspects that have received most attention from governments in recent decades. The British government published a White Paper entitled *Promoting Better Health* in 1987, in which behavioral change was highlighted:

Much distress and suffering could be avoided if more members of the public took greater responsibility for looking after their own health . . . family doctors and primary health care teams should increase their contribution to the promotion of good health . . . [they] are very well placed to persuade individuals of the importance of protecting their health; of the simple steps needed to do so; and of accepting that prevention is better than cure.

DHSS (1987)

In this respect government could claim to be reflecting public opinion. In spite of considerable research reported in the Black Report (1980) and *The Health Divide* (1987), which highlighted the relationship between poverty and ill health, there is widespread support from surveys for the view that personal lifestyle is the main influence upon health. Pill and Stott (1982) reported that women blamed themselves for their inability to modify their lifestyle – for example to eat a more 'healthy' diet – even though their failure was largely the result of material factors such as lack of money, time pressures and so on. Cornwell (1984) noted that although illness tended to be seen by people in East London as something outside themselves which 'happened' to them and for which they were not responsible, they believed that health (as an ability to function) was maintained by having 'the right attitude':

The moral prescription for a healthy life is in fact a kind of cheerful stoicism, evident in the refusal to worry, or to complain, or to be morbid.

Cornwell (1984)

On the other hand it is difficult to tell how far people's responses to researchers represent what they feel they *ought* to accept or what they *really* believe. How far are people offering a public, officially sanctioned view of health and keeping their real opinions to themselves? Mildred Blaxter commented:

There is a high level of agreement within the population that health is, to a considerable extent, dependent on behaviour and in one's own hands . . . at least it is recognised that these are the 'correct' and 'expected' answers to give.

Blaxter (1990)

○   Look back at your own earlier definition of health. How far was it related to being a nurse or health work student? Was your response influenced by what you considered was the proper attitude for you to take? You might like to ask non-health students for their views and compare their responses.

Most student nurses, when asked to define health, give an official answer. But many lay people do as well, as you may have found. This doesn't necessarily mean that we simply swallow official versions wholesale. 'Official' and 'professional' health definitions clearly influence public opinion, but they are also shaped and modified by public opinion. It is unclear how far government health policy is itself involved in creating (rather than reflecting) a public consensus which explains health in terms of personal behaviour. It is also difficult to discern – but very important to try and discover – whether people (consciously or unconsciously) offer acceptable, public definitions of health which are different from their privately held views. All this suggests that it would be misguided to assume a simple correspondence between public responses and private thoughts.

1.4 Lay definitions of health

The unpicking of definitions of health and illness reveals an underlying complexity and ambiguity. Although phrases such as 'absence of disease' and 'ability to cope' are widely endorsed in health research, they may not reveal much about what people really think: what they privately believe, what public explanations they give, what stories they tell and to whom. In subsequent chapters we'll be considering in some detail how material factors and cultural and social differences can influence people's accounts of health and illness. This section introduces the notion of *lay definitions* of health and illness – that is, of views held by ordinary people who are not health professionals, experts or official exponents of health policy.

During the last decade or so research into lay ideas about health and illness has gathered pace. The assumption that medical-derived definitions of health had colonised people's thinking and driven out non-medical explanations has been increasingly questioned. Researchers have uncovered complex narratives about the causes of illness, about responsibility and blame, and about the maintenance of health. Whereas earlier studies by anthropologists focused upon the health beliefs of 'primitive cultures' in exotic settings, more recent research has indicated that 'lay belief systems' co-exist with official medical modes of thought in Western industrialised societies as well.

Stimson and Webb (1975) highlighted differences between people's 'private' comments on their own ill health and what they chose to tell their doctors. Their research indicated that the stories people tell their family, friends and neighbours revealed private beliefs about the causes and nature of their complaint that they would not tell their doctor.

Patients selected information that they felt was relevant, or that they wanted the doctor to hear, and censored details they felt were private or unlikely to be taken seriously. They did not necessarily believe or accept the medical explanation for their condition.

Such 'private' and 'public' explanations may to some extent reflect quite different ways of thinking about illness. Cecil Helman (1986) investigated popular beliefs about colds and fevers in a suburban general practice. His research demonstrated how the popular phrase 'feed a cold, starve a fever' is underpinned by a more elaborate classification of colds and fevers in terms of 'hot' and 'cold', 'wet' and 'dry' symptoms (see Table 1.3).

Colds were seen as caused largely by personal behaviour, by 'carelessness, stupidity or lack of foresight', and once you had 'caught' the cold it might attack various parts and organs. A cold might present as a cold, wet condition with cough and congestion, or as a shivery, dry cold. In a similar way fevers might be dry or accompanied by discharge and diarrhoea. Unlike colds, however, they were not seen as the sufferer's fault. Fevers were caused by 'germs' external to the individual, a result of social relationships which people could not avoid. The patient

TABLE 1.3 Lay classification of colds and fevers. Source: Helman (1986)

	HOT	COLD
	(1) *Ear, Nose, and Throat* Fever + nasal congestion or discharge	(1) *Ear, Nose, and Throat* Cold + nasal congestion or discharge, watery eyes, 'sinus' congestion
	(2) *Chest* Fever + productive cough	(2) *Chest* Cold + non-productive cough
WET	(3) *Abdomen* Fever + diarrhoea and abdominal discomfort	(3) *Abdomen* Cold + loose stools and slight abdominal discomfort
	(4) *Urinary System* Fever + urinary frequency and burning	(4) *Urinary System* Cold + slight urinary frequency but no pain
	(5) *Skin* Fever + rash + nasal discharge or cough	
DRY	Fever + dry skin, flushed face, dry throat, non-productive cough	Cold + shivering, rigour, malaise, vague muscular aches

gets sympathy as 'the passive victim of a Germ that is "going around" and his illness is not in any way linked to the moral order'. Helman called this a 'folk' model: that is, a systematic and well-established set of popular beliefs about the causes of health and illness.

○   Try to collect some comments about the causes of health and illness or reflect on explanations you have used yourself. How far do they agree with, or differ from, the views that Helman uncovered?

Responsibility for colds often seems to be accepted by the sufferer, on the grounds that they have taken risks. Were you told as a child to keep your head and feet dry, not to go out with wet hair, not to bath in the morning? Fevers were seen as more serious and out of one's control; colds were viewed as minor, uninteresting and perhaps for these reasons one's own fault.

Lay beliefs, it appears, include both the more personalised sets of ideas about health that Stimson and Webb uncovered, and the folk model of explanation reported by Helman. Both draw upon, and help to create, social and cultural beliefs and practices in the wider society, and neither is untouched by official explanations from professional health workers. Helman discussed this inter-penetration of folk beliefs and official beliefs. He argued that they are not necessarily in conflict with each other, and that neither folk nor official ideas remain static. For example, Helman and others noted that people's explanations alter with age. Older people who grew up before the establishment of the National Health Service in Britain were more likely to cope with colds and fevers without medical assistance; younger sufferers were more likely to visit their doctor and to explain their illness in medical terms. In their turn, general practitioners incorporated elements of the folk model into their explanations to patients:

A patient who presents a list of symptoms is often given a diagnosis couched in . . . everyday idiom: 'You've picked up a germ', 'You've got a flu bug'. 'It's a viral infection', 'It's just a tummy-bug – there's one going around', 'You've got a germ in the water', 'I'm afraid it's gone to your chest', or 'Oh yes, is that the one where you've got a runny nose, watery eyes, and you lose your voice? I've seen a dozen already this week'.

Helman (1978)

People's explanations of health and illness influence the action they take as sufferers. Michael Calnan (1987) noted the often intricate personal process of assessment and negotiation that takes place before someone decides to consult their doctor, a process which draws upon lay ideas about health and illness from family and friends, experience, the media, current reading and so on. Social position, material and psycho-social interests also influence people's perception and action regarding health (Stacey, 1986).

1.5 The formation of health chances

People's beliefs about health and illness are connected to wider social, cultural and material factors. Your own definition of health and other views you may by now have collected will have been influenced to varying degrees by age, sex, occupation and so on. Social background, education, material circumstances and cultural affiliations may be important too. When asked to describe what it is to be healthy, many people respond with evidence about their life situation – having a healthy diet, taking enough exercise, participating in leisure activities, having reasonable working hours and conditions, having a decent roof over your head, getting through the day without feeling tired or depressed. Comments like these from health surveys remind us that health is contingent, that to realise good health depends not just upon genetic inheritance and personal behaviour but upon how 'personal behaviour' (or 'lifestyle' as it is generally termed today) is influenced by social and economic factors. People's *health chances* – the likelihood that they will enjoy better or worse health – depend on a wide range of factors (see Figure 1.4). Although 'having a healthy diet' and 'taking enough exercise' can be partly realised through personal decision making, other decisions – about food pricing, marketing, transport

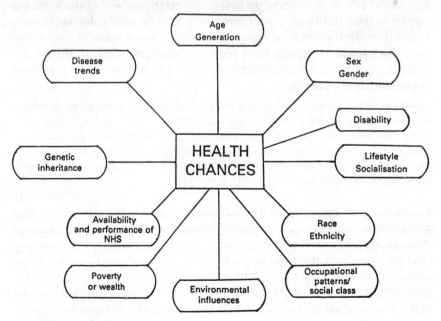

FIGURE 1.4 Health chances

provision and access, pedestrian safety, provision of open spaces and so on – are made at an institutional level, largely beyond the control of individuals.

○   Consider the following extract from the Trades Union Congress response to the Black Report of 1980. How and why do you think the health chances of the two families would differ?

Mr Smythe is the financial director of a large company. Mrs Smythe does not work and she is soon to give birth to her third child. They live in a pleasant suburb on the edge of the green belt with their two children, Emily aged five, and Rodney aged 10. They own their own home and the area where they live is mainly populated by professional people. There are plenty of recreational and sporting facilities, good schools and a brand new health centre in the locality.

Mr Jones is an unskilled labourer at a factory. His wife supplements the family income by working as an office cleaner. They live in a high rise block of flats in the centre of the city. The flats were built in the fifties and are poorly serviced with play areas and parks. The Jones's also have two children, Janet aged five and John aged 10. Mrs Jones is also expecting her third child. The family is registered with a local GP whose list of patients is already oversubscribed.

Trades Union Congress (1981)

Using the findings of the Black Report, which documented inequalities in health, the commentary highlighted the contrasting health chances of the two families. These included differences in access to and take-up of health services, in nutritional status, in the risks of suffering from major diseases like cancer, in the adequacy of the primary health care available. For example:

Mrs Jones's poorer living standards will probably mean her standard of nutritional diet is poor. She is nearly twice as likely as Mrs Smythe to die in childbirth, or her baby to be still-born or die within the first few months of life.

If her baby is a boy and survives birth, he is still four times more likely to die before his first birthday than Mrs Smythe's new born son. Like his brother John, the new-born Jones boy is ten times more likely to die, before he is 14, through an accident involving fire, a fall or drowning, than his counterpart Rodney Smythe. John is seven times more likely to be knocked down and killed in a road accident.

Trades Union Congress (1981)

You may have pointed out that there were some risks for the Smythe family too, such as asthma, of which there is a rising incidence in middle class children (Read, 1991). Mrs Smythe might find herself isolated on a new executive estate. Executive stress is often mentioned, although statistically there is a greater incidence of stress-related sickness among semi-skilled and unskilled workers (Townsend *et al.*, 1988). You might also have wanted to argue that a healthy diet is a matter of 'good housekeeping' as well as income level, and that children's health depends partly on parental care: in other words, that personal as well as material factors may influence health status.

This highlights the two major lines of enquiry into the formation of health chances that have developed alongside each other in recent years – one focusing on structural health inequalities, and the other on personal behaviour. There have been considerable tensions between them, but there is an increasing recognition that they are not mutually exclusive but interdependent (Whitehead, 1987). Research into health inequalities has a long and distinguished record linking back to investigations of poverty at the end of the nineteenth century (see Chapter 6) and to the work of the medical officers of health, health visitors, midwives and district nurses. But these observers have sometimes explained the causes of poverty in terms of personal behaviour, emphasising the part that lifestyle and fecklessness played in both poverty and ill health (Jones, 1993). Let's look briefly at both of these approaches.

1.6 Research into health inequalities

With the coming of the welfare state in Britain in the 1940s, and the right to free, needs based medical treatment in the new National Health Service, it was thought that health chances would gradually be equalised. But following soon after new evidence about the widespread incidence of poverty in prosperous post-war Britain came the Black Report (1980) which indicated, at the extreme, that the death rate for adult men in occupational class V (unskilled workers) was nearly twice that of adult men in occupational class I (professional workers) (see Figure 1.5).

The report pointed to the existence of a growing occupational class gradient in all the major diseases. In particular it reported that between the 1950s and the 1970s the mortality rates for both men and women aged 35 and over in occupational classes I and II had steadily declined, whereas those in classes IV and V were the same or marginally worse. In addition there was some evidence that black and minority ethnic groups suffered differentially high rates of heart disease, evidence of regional variations, evidence of sex differences and evidence linking disease risks to household type, with houseowners having the lowest risk of premature death.

Occupational class represented the major, though not the only, means by which health inequalities were measured in the Black Report. As the report commented, 'undoubtedly the clearest and most un-equivocal – if only because there is more evidence to go on – is the

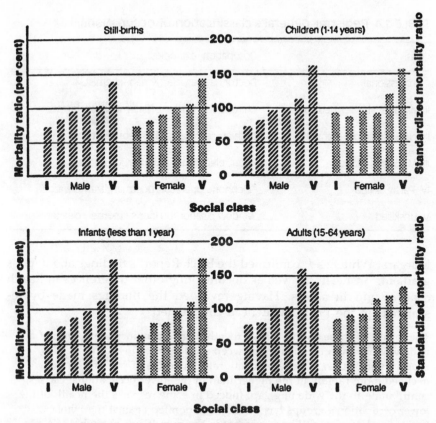

FIGURE 1.5 Mortality by occupational class and age. Source: The Black Report (1980) in Townsend *et al.* (1988)

relationship between occupational class and mortality' (Townsend *et al.*, 1988). As you can see from Table 1.4, the Registrar General classifies every male and every unmarried female worker 'in gainful employment' in one of six categories, ranging from higher professional (class I) to unskilled (class V). Although this classification tends to marginalise women's work and creates various other distortions that we'll investigate in later chapters, it is a widely used and relatively reliable indicator not only of differences in income, occupational status and living standards but also of relative levels of deprivation. Because researchers are able to draw on a long run of roughly comparable national data on death rates and causes of death, they can highlight the relative fortunes of the different classes over time; indeed, it was the discovery that class V death rates were not declining relative to other classes that caused major concern in the report.

The Health Divide (1987), a second survey of research carried out by

TABLE 1.4 Registrar General's classification of occupations

Class	Occupation (examples)
I Professional	Doctor, lawyer, clergyman, chemist
II Managerial/Intermediate	Chiropodist, nurse, office manager, farmer
III (N) Skilled Non-manual	Cashier, secretary, sales representative
III (M) Skilled Manual	Fitter, electrician, plumber, carpenter
IV Partly Skilled	Telephone operator, postman, traffic warden
V Unskilled	Window cleaner, builder's labourer, cleaner

Margaret Whitehead, confirmed the Black Report's findings about 'class gradients' in health as well as documenting other differences in health chances and in access. Having reviewed the findings made by researchers in the 1980s, Whitehead commented:

The results of these studies, taken together, give convincing evidence of a widening of health inequalities between social groups in recent decades, especially in adults. In general, death rates in adults of working age have declined more rapidly in the higher than in the lower occupational classes, contributing to the widening gap. Indeed in some respects the health of the lower occupational groups has actually deteriorated against the whole background of a general improvement in the population as a whole. While death rates have been declining, rates of chronic illness seem to have been increasing, and the gap in the illness rates between manual and non-manual groups has been widening too, particularly in the over-65 age group.

Whitehead (1987)

During the 1980s there was a considerable amount of new research which focused on health status and inequalities at a local and regional level, and which demonstrated that there were often wide variations within quite small areas. Researchers began to develop social indicators which could be used to assess health by measuring levels and risks of deprivation (see Box 1.2).

O   Look at the Jarman Index in Box 1.2, a set of indicators which has been used by health authorities to measure the extent of deprivation in localities with a view to taking action to improve health. Have you any comments on the indicators chosen by Jarman?

The Jarman Index combines direct measures of deprivation – overcrowding, poor housing, unemployment – with indirect measures of numbers of people 'at risk' of deprivation – ethnic minorities, children

BOX 1.2 The Jarman Index of Deprivation. Source: Whitehead (1987)

Jarman (1983, 1984) Underprivileged Area Score

Children aged under 5
Ethnic minorities
Single-parent households
Elderly living alone
Lower social classes
Highly mobile people
Non-married-couple families (indicating less stable family groups)
Overcrowding factor
Poor housing factor
Unemployment

BOX 1.3 Social indicators used to assess health in other area based studies. Source: Whitehead (1987)

Scott-Samuel Score (1984)

Persons aged over 15 with temporary sickness
Households overcrowded
Households severely overcrowded
Households owner-occupied
Households rented from local authority
Households lacking a car
Men aged 16–64 out of employment
Women aged 16–59 out of employment
Private households with 3 or more dependent children
One-parent families
Working-age people permanently sick

Townsend et al. (1985) Bristol Study

Households with fewer rooms than persons
Households lacking a car
Economically active persons seeking work (or temporarily sick)
Children aged 5–15 who receive school meals free
Households experiencing disconnection of electricity

under five, single-parent households, elderly living alone and so on. The indirect measures have been criticised on the grounds that not all people in such 'at risk' groups are deprived, so that too great a reliance on indirect measures can produce a distorted outcome. For example, the Jarman Index indicates that seven out of ten of the most deprived local authority areas are in London. But Colin Thunhurst (1985) has argued that this arises largely because of the disproportionately high numbers of one-parent families and ethnic minority households in London,

which skew the figures. The greatest concentration of material deprivation can be found in the north of England and Scotland (Whitehead,
1987). Another index of deprivation, developed by Townsend and other
researchers (1987) tried to avoid this criticism of indirect indicators by
using direct measures (see Box 1.3). It calculated deprivation in terms of
levels of unemployment, overcrowding and ownership of key household goods. The research team argued strongly that 'it is we believe
mistaken to treat being black, or old and alone, or single parenthood as
part of the definition of deprivation . . . the point is to find out how
many are deprived rather than operate as if all were in that condition'
(Townsend et al., 1986).

1.7 Investigating personal behaviour

In Section 1.5 we noted that the other, linked, line of enquiry into how
health chances are formed has emphasised personal behaviour, suggesting that individual attitudes and lifestyles are at least partly responsible
for differences in health chances. *Lifestyle*, the term currently used to
describe a bundle of linked attitudes and behaviour patterns, is now a
central focus for health education and health promotion. The targeting
of individual lifestyle 'deficiencies' is widespread. Smoking behaviour,
eating habits and exercise routines, which were hitherto thought of as
private concerns, are now public issues and the focus for professional
health action. As we noted earlier in Section 1.3, lifestyle formed one of
the four 'health fields' of the Lalonde Report, and the one in which
intervention by health professionals seemed most possible.

The 'lifestyle' approach

Lifestyle approaches have received support from the World Health
Organisation (see Table 1.5, targets 13–17) and have been endorsed by
recent UK government reports. *The Health of the Nation* (DoH, 1992a)
identified several aspects of individual behaviour – smoking, diet,
alcohol consumption and drug use – as risk factors and set 'risk factor
targets' for the reduction of unwanted types of behaviour and
consumption. Most health professionals welcomed the idea of a strategy
and the setting of health targets (Delamothe, 1991). Individual behaviour
plays some part in many diseases; the connection between lung cancer
and smoking is well established, for example, and dietary factors are
now thought to be significant in relation to circulatory disease and in
some cancers. So persuading people to change risky aspects of their
lifestyle seems highly appropriate. If clear targets and priorities are set,

TABLE 1.5 WHO Health For All targets for Europe, 1985. Source: K258 (1992)

Targets 1–12

Health for all in Europe by the year 2000

1   Reducing the differences

The actual differences in health status between countries and between groups within countries should be reduced by at least 25%, by improving the level of health of disadvantaged nations and groups.

2   Developing health potential

People should have the basic opportunity to develop and use their health potential to live socially and economically fulfilling lives.

3   Better opportunities for the disabled

Disabled persons should have the physical, social and economic opportunities that allow at least for a socially and economically fulfilling and mentally creative life.

4   Reducing disease and disability

The average number of years that people live free from major disease and disability should be increased by at least 10%.

5   Elimination of specific diseases

There should be no indigenous measles, poliomyelitis, neonatal tetanus, congenital rubella, diphtheria, congenital syphilis or indigenous malaria in the Region.

6   Life expectancy at birth

Life expectancy at birth in the Region should be at least 75 years.

7   Infant mortality

Infant mortality in the Region should be less than 20 per 1000 live births.

8   Maternal mortality

Maternal mortality in the Region should be less than 15 per 100,000 live births.

9   Diseases of the circulation

Mortality in the Region from diseases of the circulatory system in people under 65 should be reduced by at least 15%.

10   Cancer

Mortality in the Region from cancer in people under 65 should be reduced by at least 15%.

11   Accidents

Deaths from accidents in the Region should be reduced by at least 25% through an intensified effort to reduce traffic, home and occupational accidents.

12   Suicide

The current rising trends in suicides and attempted suicides in the Region should be reversed.

Targets 13–17

Lifestyles conducive to health

13   Healthy public policy

By 1990, national policies in all Member States should ensure that legislative, administrative and economic mechanisms provide broad intersectoral support and resources for the promotion of healthy lifestyles and ensure effective participation of the people at all levels of such policy-making.

14   Social support systems

By 1990, all Member States should have specific programmes which enhance the major roles of the family and other social groups in developing and supporting healthy lifestyles.

15   Knowledge and motivation for health behaviour

By 1990, educational programmes in all Member States should enhance the knowledge, motivation and skills of people to acquire and maintain health.

16   Positive health behaviour

By 1995, in all Member States, there should be significant increases in positive health behaviour, such as balanced nutrition, non-smoking, appropriate physical activity and good stress management.

17   Health-damaging behaviour

By 1995, in all Member States, there should be significant decreases in health-damaging behaviour, such as overuse of alcohol and pharmaceutical products; use of illicit drugs and dangerous chemical substances; and dangerous driving and violent social behaviour.

Targets 18–25

Healthy environment

18   Multisectoral policies

By 1990, Member States should have multisectoral policies that effectively protect the environment from health hazards, ensure community awareness and involvement, and support international efforts to curb such hazards affecting more than one country.

19   Monitoring and control mechanisms

By 1990, all Member States should have adequate machinery for the monitoring, assessment and control of environmental hazards which pose a threat to human health, including potentially toxic chemicals, radiation, harmful consumer goods and biological agents.

TABLE 1.5 *Continued*

20 Control of water pollution
By 1990, all people of the Region should have adequate supplies of safe drinking-water, and by the year 1995 pollution of rivers, lakes and seas should no longer pose a threat to human health.

21 Control of air pollution
By 1995, all people of the Region should be effectively protected against recognised health risks from air pollution.

22 Food safety
By 1990, all Member States should have significantly reduced health risks from food contamination and implemented measures to protect consumers from harmful additives.

23 Control of hazardous wastes
By 1995, all Member States should have eliminated major known health risks associated with the disposal of hazardous wastes.

24 Human settlements and housing
By the year 2000, all people of the Region should have a better opportunity of living in houses and settlements which provide a healthy and safe environment.

25 Working environment
By 1995, people of the Region should be effectively protected against work-related health risks.

Targets 26-31

Appropriate care

26 A system based on primary health care
By 1990, all Member States, through effective community representation, should have developed health care systems that are based on primary health care and supported by secondary and tertiary care as outlined at the Alma-Ata Conference.

27 Rational and preferential distribution of resources
By 1990, in all Member States, the infrastructures of the delivery systems should be organised so that resources are distributed according to need, and that services ensure physical and economic accessibility and cultural acceptability to the population.

28 Content of primary health care
By 1990, the primary health care system of all Member States should provide a wide range of health-promotive, curative, rehabilitative and supportive services to meet the basic health needs of the population and give special attention to high-risk, vulnerable and underserved individuals and groups.

29 Providers of primary health care
By 1990, in all Member States, primary health care systems should be based on co-operation and teamwork between health care personnel, individuals, families and community groups.

30 Co-ordination of community resources
By 1990, all Member States should have mechanisms

by which the services provided by all sectors relating to health are co-ordinated at the community level in a primary health care system.

31 Ensuring quality of care
By 1990, all Member States should have built effective mechanisms for ensuring quality of patient care within their health care systems.

Target 32

Research

32 Research strategies
Before 1990, all Member States should have formulated research strategies to stimulate investigations which improve the application and expansion of knowledge needed to support their health for all developments.

Targets 33-38

Health development support

33 Policies for health for all
Before 1990, all Member States should ensure that their health policies and strategies are in line with health for all principles and that their legislation and regulations make their implementation effective in all sectors of society.

34 Planning and resource allocation
Before 1990, Member States should have managerial processes for health development geared to the attainment of health for all, actively involving communities and all sectors relevant to health and, accordingly, ensuring preferential allocation of resources to health development priorities.

35 Health information system
Before 1990, Member States should have health information systems capable of supporting their national strategies for health for all.

36 Planning, education and use of health personnel
Before 1990, in all Member States, the planning, training and use of health personnel should be in accordance with health for all policies, with emphasis on the primary health care approach.

37 Education of personnel in other sectors
Before 1990, in all Member States, education should provide personnel in sectors related to health with adequate information on the country's health for all policies and programmes and their practical application to their own sectors.

38 Appropriate health technology
Before 1990, all Member States should have established a formal mechanism for the systematic assessment of the appropriate use of health technologies and of their effectiveness, efficiency, safety and acceptability, as well as reflecting national health policies and economic restraints.

progress can be closely monitored and strategies adjusted if the desired changes fail to materialise. The strategy also urges central and local government, individuals, statutory and voluntary agencies, and health professionals to work together to meet these targets.

Yet some health professionals have practical and ethical doubts about an approach which mainly targets personal lifestyles (Delamothe, 1991). First, how far can health really be improved through targeting personal behaviour? Recent health campaigns warning young people to modify their sexual behaviour in the light of the HIV/AIDS danger seem to have had some immediate but far fewer lasting effects (Weeks, 1991). Making changes in personal behaviour is very difficult. A five year study of working class mothers in South Wales indicated that, although half of the women had made a change in their behaviour at some point in the study, most fairly quickly relapsed (Pill and Stott, 1982; Pill, 1990). Although the women tended to blame themselves for their relapses, many of the reasons for failure were actually to do with pressure from domestic or work circumstances and from partners and children.

This raises a second point, about the ethical basis of a lifestyle approach. If many of the impediments to change are related to social circumstances, to the constraints imposed by income, housing, childcare demands or social pressure from partners or peer group, how justifiable is it to target personal behaviour? Targeting individual lifestyle can come close to 'blaming the victims' if people are in a position where change is very difficult or even impossible, and yet are made to feel guilty for not making a change. Pill (1990) commented that 'some were only too ready to blame themselves' and their 'lack of willpower', and for a few 'this led to loss of self-esteem and strong guilt feelings'.

Environmental influences on lifestyles

Health research findings increasingly suggest that behavioural and cultural factors on the one hand and material, environmental and structural factors on the other are inter-related and interdependent. If behaviour cannot easily be separated from its social context, then an attack targeted at people's behaviour will have little chance of success unless it also addresses the social, material and cultural environment in which that behaviour takes place. Hilary Graham's work on young working class women who are regular smokers and have children under five indicates that their smoking behaviour arises largely from their social circumstances (Graham, 1976; 1988). Smoking became the one activity that the women could choose to do 'for themselves'; it gave them a little time and personal space during a day filled with housework and responding to children's demands. This suggests that wider material and structural changes – perhaps in childcare provision, the availability of part-time work, educational provision – might be as useful, or more useful, in improving health as targeting individual behaviour. Margaret Whitehead (1987) gives another example, that of child accidents. The higher incidence of childhood accidents in lower social groups could be explained, she suggests, in terms of personal risk-taking and parental neglect, but it could equally well be seen as the result of unsafe local environments which create supervision problems for parents. 'In the latter view, the environment is dictating the behaviour of both mother and child' (Whitehead, 1987). It does not follow that because of individual-cultural factors influence health, life-style modification is necessarily the way forward.

○   At this point, note down your own views about the relative importance of behaviour and environment in creating health chances.

It remains difficult to disentangle the relative importance of behaviour and environment in creating health chances. For example, there is evidence that middle class households consume more of what are considered to be healthier foods than do working class households (Townsend *et al.*, 1988). It may be argued that this is due to their greater willingness to modify their behaviour, to 'act responsibly' and rationally and to think more seriously about their health. In this view it is the attitudes and behaviour of working class people which need to be modified so that they too 'act responsibly'. On the other hand it is clear that in some respects middle class people, with higher living standards and greater material security, are able to make 'healthy choices' more easily than people from poor working class backgrounds. A diet that meets national nutritional guidelines (NACNE, 1983) by including brown bread, lots of fresh vegetables and fruit, low fat spreads and lean meat is more expensive to maintain than a nutritionally unsatisfactory diet of white bread, sugary foods and potatoes (Graham, 1986). It may be that working class women are acting responsibly and rationally – by buying the cheapest, most filling foods available to feed their families.

Claims about what is rational behaviour also seem to be class biased; it is the lower social classes who are seen as the problem. But it is likely that middle class people are just as liable to be influenced by 'peer group pressure' as others; witness the spectacular spread of jogging, aerobics, health clubs and fitness training with the attendant mass middle class consumption of appropriate clothing and footwear. Is this a result of individuals making 'healthy choices', or is it the consequence of multi-million pound advertising campaigns and promotions which create fashions and persuade people that they must jog and work out to keep up with their peers?

1.8 Working for health

The earlier sections of this chapter have encouraged you to investigate health beliefs and health chances and to review some of your own taken-for-granted ideas about health and illness. You will have begun to appreciate the complexity of lay and professional thinking about health, and to understand some of the ways in which health may be viewed as 'a resource for everyday living' rather than as 'the objective of living'. Health, it has been argued, should not be studied simply as an abstract concept; it is embedded in people's lives and their understanding of it will be influenced by their different social circumstances and life experiences. If health chances are shaped by social, economic and cultural factors, those who work for health will need to intervene actively in the wider society in order to protect and promote it.

As we have noted, there has been a long tradition within health work of concern for social interventions. After all, the National Health Service was set up in 1948 because it was recognised that sickness and disease could only be tackled by a collective effort, through a comprehensive health system which could respond to individual needs for treatment and care. Even earlier some of the work of the medical officers of health was directed towards improving local environmental conditions by improving slum housing, clearing rubbish and so on. Health visitors began to teach principles of hygiene and 'good housekeeping' and to offer support to inexperienced mothers (Lewis, 1980). Community health services have always undertaken some preventive health work.

However, since its inception the National Health Service has been concerned mainly with the 'disease and sickness' dimension of health. Over the years the demand for hospital treatment has grown considerably and most of the resources and staff are still concentrated in hospitals. Nurses and most other health professionals, especially those working in hospital settings, spend most of their time treating disease and sickness. Although all health workers today are being encouraged to develop a role in educating people about health, the opportunities for carrying out this role may be quite limited. Work which involves enhancing the health of patients, rather than treating sickness, is generally viewed as of marginal importance. Changes in staffing levels, the wider use of sophisticated technology and the increasingly swift turnover of patients have meant that many nurses feel they have less time to teach the skills and 'healthy habits' that could help their patients once they leave the hospital (Mackay, 1989).

Prevention and health education

The medical profession has played a central role in determining priorities in health work, and this has meant that when strategies to improve health have been developed they have been mainly, though not exclusively, medically-driven and clinically-oriented. *Prevention*, for example, involves a set of strategies which depend on clinical interventions and treatments (see Box 1.4). *Primary* prevention involves strategies to prevent the onset of disease, such as childhood immunisation against measles or screening to find and control risk factors. *Secondary* prevention aims to detect and cure a disease at its onset, as in screening for early stage cervical cancer. *Tertiary* prevention involves minimising the effects of an already established disease; an example here would be hip replacement surgery. Clearly policies for prevention are very important, but their focus is on clinical treatment at an individual level.

Most health workers will, at some point, adopt a *health education* role. This usually involves giving health advice at a secondary or tertiary stage on a one-to-one basis, or in small group sessions, for example counselling patients about diet or giving advice about coping with a disability. Health education directed at healthy people, such as education about hygiene or contraception, could also be viewed as one aspect of primary prevention (Lambert and McPherson, 1993, and see Box 1.4). Once again, although not exclusively so, the focus of health education is at the individual level. Health education, it has been argued by critics, developed within the National Health Service and has been constrained within 'the medical model, founded on the principles of behaviourism and individualism . . . The medical profession has determined the ideological imperatives for health education, and continues to attempt to do so' (Rodmell and Watt, 1986). Health

BOX 1.4 Primary, secondary and tertiary prevention

Primary prevention	Secondary prevention	Tertiary prevention
Aims to prevent the onset of disease	Aims to detect and cure a disease at an early stage before it causes serious irreversible problems	Aims to minimise the effects or reduce the progression of an already established irreversible disease
Example: Immunisation	**Example**: Cervical cancer screening	**Example**: Hip replacement surgery

education remains committed to individualist philosophy and strategies, to an assumption of 'individual free choice as both an accurate account of the status quo, and as a desirable goal for which to aim'. Yet evaluation studies show that this approach is not very effective in modifying behaviour or encouraging the adoption of healthier lifestyles (Naidoo, 1986).

○ Prevention and health education are both positioned within a 'medical model' of health. Note down your own definition of the medical model before you continue.

In Section 1.2 you encountered the medical view of health as 'an absence of disease', and this was discussed further in Section 1.3, so you will probably have noted the biological basis of modern medicine, and the preoccupation with disease – conceptualised as a pathological state represented by deviation from 'normal' parameters in the body.

The dominance of this medical model means working within an overwhelmingly biological framework, with a concept of health as 'no disease' which arises from a preoccupation with normality (and abnormality), with 'risk factors' and 'at risk' groups, and with a focus on prevention, identification and treatment of disease and sickness. In doing so it emphasises individual, behavioural factors rather than structural and material influences. The medical model of prevention, like the medical model of health itself, tends to marginalise wider issues about how health chances are formed and pays little attention to environmental and social change. For example, although there was widespread interest at the time in the Black Report (1980) and *The Health Divide* (1987), this did not mean that health authorities made the reduction of health inequalities a higher priority (Castle and Jacobson, 1988).

The medical approach to prevention, linked with an emphasis on health education, underpins current official health policies and strategies. The targets identified in *The Health of the Nation* (DoH, 1992b), which we noted earlier, emphasise this approach to prevention and focus on a lifestyle approach. Although prevention has become a more recognised and indeed prescribed dimension of health professionals' work, it remains difficult to incorporate into it a broader structural view of health. The objectives to be met in prevention are already fixed and the opportunity to explore new health needs has been limited.

In community settings, for example, primary health care team members are increasingly working on a contract basis, carrying out specified duties and types of interventions, such as annual standardised health monitoring of all people over 75. General practitioners and district nurses have not generally welcomed this contractual require-ment, set out in the government's 1986 White Paper *Promoting Better*

Health. Critics point out that such screening is expensive and time-wasting; it makes assumptions that all older people are 'at risk', when they are not, and that the primary health care team will have not picked up those at risk already (Marks, 1988). Another significant shift of emphasis has been in health visitor contracts. The first principle of health visiting is 'to search out health needs' in the community, but new contracts require standardised interventions at the health centre. Mothers who find it difficult to visit health centres are unlikely to get their needs identified (Dingwall and Robinson, 1990).

1.9 Towards a 'social model' of health

Until recently nurse training and education very much reflected this medical model, and the medical approach to prevention and health education was accepted as official and 'normal'. It structured health professionals' thinking about practice – about their patients and their needs, and about health services – and marginalised other approaches. For example, nurse tutors could cover the 'social dimension of health' largely by focusing on the individual patient's 'social history'. Socio-economic influences on health, such as poor housing conditions or lack of heating, remained hidden from view. Wider issues about patient care, such as the poor nutritional status of many patients in hospitals, have until recently been overlooked because of the preoccupation with clinical interventions. The care of nursing staff themselves, who frequently suffer from poorly designed equipment and physical and mental stress, has often been neglected (Mackay, 1989). Perhaps this is because nurses have traditionally been seen as adjuncts to the doctor rather than as practitioners in their own right. In a similar way, the contribution and views of informal carers have until very recently been grossly undervalued, because the focus of concern was on formal, medical-led treatment and cure (Ungerson, 1987).

The medical model has come under heavy fire in recent years. Hospital and community nurses have sought to distance themselves from medical control and to identify the particular skills, knowledge and underpinning philosophy of nursing. One main impetus for Project 2000 and for numerous diploma and degree programmes has been the growing realisation that, as long as nurses were trained to work within the medical model, the skills required in contemporary nursing practice – to work in teams, to control sophisticated technology, to advise on drugs, to take an 'extended role' and so on – would not receive much public recognition or occupational reward. Professions allied to medicine have been critical of the medical model's narrow disease focus;

speech therapists, for example, find it difficult to work within its constraints. Doctors themselves, particularly public health physicians and some general practitioners, have called for a reorientation of health services – and a redistribution of resources – towards public and community health.

The primary challenge to the medical model has been on the grounds of its failure to share power with other health professionals rather than its preoccupation with health as absence of disease. There is certainly evidence that critics within and outside the health service have contested its narrowness of vision – terming the health service the National 'Disease' Service – and that calls for more 'holistic' and humanistic treatment for patients were to be heard even in the early days of the service (Morris, in Oakley, 1984). But until recently there has been little support for a *social model* of health which would view health and health work in broader social and structural terms.

○ This term, the social model of health, is widely used today in the field of health. Note down what you understand it to mean.

You may have found some difficulty in pinning down the social model of health. It is a broad 'umbrella' concept underneath which several different sets of priorities have sheltered, variously emphasising large-scale statutory intervention, small-scale self-help, lay power and shared lay and professional leadership. Health promotion projects, public health programmes, community health projects and campaigning groups have all used its rhetoric (Beattie *et al.*, 1993). The term has been used to describe a set of underlying values – a philosophical approach to health, a set of guiding principles to orientate health work in a specific way and a set of practice objectives. In this sense it mirrors the medical model, which is about practice (ways of doing) and about theory (ways of seeing).

The underlying philosophy of the social model of health is that the health of individuals and communities is the result of complex and interacting material-structural and behavioural-cultural factors. Whereas the focus of the medical model is on pathologies, clinical interventions and patient behaviour, the social model also focuses on environment and collective measures. The most frequently stated guiding principles are a commitment to empowerment, to community participation, to equity in health, to accountability and to co-operation and partnership with other agencies and sectors (K258, 1992). This in turn creates distinctive objectives: to work to improve adverse features of the environment, such as pollution, bad housing or poor working conditions; to reduce health inequalities; to work with groups such as older people and women, whose health needs may be overlooked. Again priorities vary, and in most programmes which claim to project a social model of health you will find that targets for disease reduction are included as well. In other words the social model does not abandon a medical model but adds to it a greater concern for the social and environmental framework within which health and ill health arise (see WHO targets 18–25, Table 1.5).

The social model places a greater emphasis on *health promotion*: that is, on broader structural and strategic interventions to improve people's health. It emphasises the need for health authorities, government agencies, voluntary and commercial organisations to work together to promote healthy lifestyles. For example, reducing excessive and in-appropriate consumption of alcohol could be a goal not just for health authorities but for the Department of Transport, for local planners and road safety units, for employers – who might organise screening or prevention initiatives – and for pressure groups such as motorists' organisations or community health groups.

You may agree that the social model as described here is of value to nurses and other health workers, in that it offers an approach to health work which moves beyond an exclusive focus on disease treatment and behaviour modification. As a student of nursing or health studies, or as a trained professional, you may think that elements of the social model already inform your studies or your practice.

○   Reflect on the extent to which the social model of health connects to your experience as a health student or practitioner.

Whether you are training to be a hospital nurse, a community nurse or a health practitioner of some other kind, it is very likely that your analysis of health will embody several features of the social model, and the same may well be true for trained practitioners. It is less likely that the interventions you are able to make will do so, and this has sometimes been a source of frustration for community based practitioners such as health visitors. If you use the nursing process, you may well find it easier to make a broadly based, social and environmental assessment of your patients and households than to instigate interventions that take social and material factors fully into account. To some extent – and critics would say to a great degree – the analysis of the causes of ill health, and assessment of the action required to reduce ill health and promote good health, do not match the intervention. Moreover, this is not always reflected in the evaluation process, so that failure may be attributed to individual incompetence or backsliding rather than to unchanged structural features of the environment (see Table 1.6). Indeed, we noted in Section 1.3 that individuals may blame themselves for their failure even if material or environmental factors were largely responsible.

The causes of ill health, as we noted in earlier sections, may lie partly outside individual control, as in the case of damp housing or a

TABLE 1.6 Health problems and health work interventions

'External' influences →	Issue/problem →	Possible health outcome →	Implications for health work interventions	
			→ Work with family	→ Work outside family
- Socialisation patterns and cultural influences - Standardised 'nuclear' family style housing - Close relationship of housing size and cost	- Large family → - Overcrowding - Inadequate housing	For example: - Respiratory diseases - Mental health problems - 'Backwardness' of children	- Contraceptive advice (prevention) - Try to get family rehoused/get improvement grants etc.	- Liaison with local schools over sex and health education - Campaign for improvement in local housing/ pressure to build adequate sized houses - Publicise evidence showing links between overcrowding and respiratory disease
- Growth of low wage sector of economy and casual working - High levels of unemployment - Low wages of women workers - Great inequality in distribution of income (and wealth)	- Man, breadwinner, brings in sole family income → - Family poverty	→ Possible problems from inadequate diet For example: - Obesity - Undernutrition - Low resistance to disease (immune system impaired)	- Help with family budgeting - Try to get all benefit entitlements paid to family	- Plan local 'take-up' campaign for low earners - Campaign for local crèche/nursery facilities - Join with other health workers to publicise evidence on 'social costs' to NHS of low wages
- Cultural influences and socialisation patterns - Class influences - Impact of work patterns, conditions, environment	- Parenting influences - 'Unhealthy' lifestyle	→ Effect on infant feeding and health attitudes and smoking For example: Diet Alcohol consumption and so-on	→ Giving knowledge and advice to immediate family circle (parents and grandparents)	- Campaign for government action on Health Divide, and Nacne Reports/for tougher laws on drink - Set up self help groups - Produce your own health education literature geared to your clients' own priorities and defined needs in a locality

poor diet. Any intervention would need to respond not just by treating the resultant ill health and by giving advice and support to individuals and households, but also by taking wider action: alerting the primary health care team, networking with other community workers, tackling housing departments, organising a residents' campaign, helping to start a self help food co-op, encouraging residents to bulk buy from supermarkets so that more healthy foods can be afforded and so on. Thus the social model of health may require action at a number of different levels: individual, household, local, national, even international.

Clearly some aspects of this will not be easy and perhaps it is not surprising that health workers sometimes argue that this is 'not the job of the NHS'. Ewles and Simnett (1985) suggest that this wider dimension of the social model, which they call the 'social change approach', usually involves political or social action to change the environment and 'to make healthy choices easier choices'. They go on to comment:

The contentious nature of the social change approach is its chief limitation.
Many of the issues are politically sensitive (eg. unemployment) and the health
educator is likely to fall foul of powerful vested interest groups and financial
considerations . . . The approach is also contentious because it is markedly
different from traditional individual health education directed at clients. Its aim
of effecting social change is difficult for some people to justify as 'education',
but we believe that raising awareness of the health aspects of policy decisions
can be considered as valid education of policy-makers and the public.
Ewles and Simnett (1985)

There are examples of practical interventions of this kind both inside and outside the formal health sector. These range from large-scale multi-agency programmes, such as health promotion initiatives, to small-scale community health projects. By the mid-1980s the National Council for Voluntary Organisations had recorded information about 10 000 local health projects. Individual nurses can have an impact too. One health visitor in Oxford described her work on an outer ring housing estate in a recent seminar (Slavin, THSG seminar 1992). She helped to start a community centre on the estate, organised keep fit sessions and a playgroup and worked to get a dangerous road through the estate fenced off. Hospital based health workers can also use a social change approach, even though their work is largely with individual patients. This might involve networking with community health workers to raise awareness of how presented sickness reflects levels of housing need, unemployment and poverty. It might also include challenging hospital policy – for example on the range of diets catered for or whether hospital catering supports dietary advice on 'healthy eating'.

1.10 The contribution of sociology and social policy

In this final section of Chapter 1 we will draw together the work we have done so far on using a sociological approach to highlight issues and raise questions about health and health work. In Chapter 2 we will be taking a much closer look at sociological and social policy perspectives on health and health work, and in Chapters 3 and 4 we'll look at two important contexts for contemporary health work: the family and the community.

○ Review the work you have done in earlier parts of the chapter, noting down what you have learned about lay and official health beliefs, the formation of health chances and health work.

Sections 1.1–1.4 discussed definitions of health, disease, sickness and illness, and social research demonstrating the complexity and diversity of lay health beliefs. We explored official definitions in more detail, noting the contrast between the 'absence of disease' definition of health, rooted in the 'medical model', and World Health Organisation definitions which emphasised wellbeing and social and psychological health as well as physical health. This was nearer to a 'social model'. We noted that private ways of explaining health and illness were rooted in intricate lay belief systems. In Chapter 2 we consider what sociological theory has to say about the nature of health and illness. In Chapter 10 lay beliefs about health and illness will be explored in some detail. In addition, we'll consider how people behave when they do fall ill and become 'patients'.

Sections 1.5–1.7 raised the idea of 'health chances' and began to explore different accounts of how health chances were produced. We noted the persistence of health inequalities and conflicts between explanations that emphasised material and cultural influences on health and those that focused on behavioural features. The former linked more closely to a social model, the latter to a medical model. Chapters 5–9 will investigate contemporary social divisions, not only considering their impact on health status but also exploring their signficance for health work.

Finally, in Sections 1.8–1.9 we addressed some of the implications for health work. We noted the dominance of the medical model and its approach to prevention. We noted that nurses and other health workers had been generally trained within a medical model, but increasing criticism of its narrowness and limited effectiveness in relation to health has brought the social model into focus. The social model, when examined, was found to be wide-ranging and multi-faceted; it worked for social change at one level, but could also be applied to individuals and households. It offered prospects for reconciling behavioural-cultural and material-structural approaches. We will consider the rise and contemporary character of professional health work in Chapters 11–13.

The research which is reported in this chapter reflects the contribution sociology and social policy have made to the field of health and illness. In particular, sociologists and social policy researchers, while demonstrating how socio-economic and cultural factors influence health, have highlighted how the medical model of professional health work has shaped our perceptions of health and illness. They have also placed this analysis of health work in the wider setting of welfare politics. Together with psychologists, biologists and other health analysts they have played an important role in developing our understanding of the health field.

Suggestions for further study

Lay beliefs about health and illness are well documented in M. Blaxter (1990) *Health and Lifestyles*, London, Tavistock, which discusses the findings of the 1987 Health and Lifestyle Survey. Health inequalities are discussed in P. Townsend, N. Davidson and M. Whitehead (1988) *Inequalities in Health: The Black Report and The Health Divide*, Harmondsworth, Penguin. The social model of health can be explored in A. Beattie, M. Gott, L. Jones and M. Sidell, eds (1993) *Health and Wellbeing: A Reader*, London, Macmillan.

Self assessment questions

1 Discuss why health is a difficult concept to define.
2 Distinguish between 'disease', 'sickness' and 'illness'.
3 Assess the evidence for the existence of 'inequalities in health'.
4 Compare and contrast the 'medical model' with the 'social model' of health.
5 What might be the advantages and disadvantages of using the 'social model' of health in practice?

Chapter 2

The scope of sociological enquiry

Contents

Themes and issues

Structural and social action approaches: consensus and conflict – Durkheim, Marx and Weber – a social perspective on health

Scientific and interpretive sociology: scientific method – empiricism, positivism and phenomenology – objectivity and subjectivity

Social policy: collectivism and anti-collectivism – universalism and selectivism – Fabianism – the New Right – feminist and socialist critiques

Rise of medical sociology – Talcott Parsons and structural functionalism – conflict theorists: interactionism and ethnomethodology – feminist perspectives – postmodernism – social constructionism – Giddens and structuration

Learning outcomes

After working through this chapter you should be able to:

1 Compare and contrast structural and social action approaches to sociology.
2 Assess the strengths and limitations of the positivist research tradition.
3 Suggest why and how theories of 'modern industrial society' have been challenged.
4 Explain the grounds on which feminist theories have attacked mainstream sociology.
5 Discuss the significance for health work of a social constructionist approach to the body.

THIS chapter introduces you to the disciplines of sociology and social policy, indicating their particular areas of concern and explaining important concepts and specialist language. It reviews how different traditions in sociology and social policy have explained health and illness and considers how these insights can be of value to health workers. It highlights some important distinctions between sociological theories and methods of enquiry, in particular between approaches which are more abstract and 'scientific' and those which stress the importance of studying people as subjects rather than as objects.

Social investigators have developed systematic theories about the nature of the social world, and these have often been fiercely debated. The theories advanced by some writers are questioned by others; indeed the complexity of social life and the challenging nature of social research make for controversy. So this chapter cannot offer you a tidy set of 'right answers' about how to view health and illness. Instead, by presenting the different strands of sociological thinking about health, it can encourage you to question and review your own taken-for-granted views and attitudes.

Parts of this chapter may be familiar to you, but other parts will be new and less accessible. You may want to reread some parts at a later stage. Remember that subsequent chapters will refer back to the ideas outlined here, encouraging you to review your understanding of particular concepts and theories. So don't feel concerned if some of the rather abstract ideas discussed here are difficult to grasp. Take your time and review your progress in a systematic way, using the questions in the text and the self assessment questions at the end of the chapter.

2.1 What is sociology?

Sociology is the systematic study of human society. It provides us with evidence and explanations of how society works, of the actions of individuals and groups, of patterns of similarity and difference between people (within a single society and between societies), of the distribution of social resources and economic and political power. Sociology is concerned both with studying individuals (social actors or agents) operating in the social world and with trying to understand how the social world 'works' by investigating how social structures and relationships develop, persist and change.

A sociological explanation of inequalities in health, for example, emphasises the impact of economic, social and cultural structures and relationships within the wider society on people's health chances as well as the actions and attitudes of individuals (Whitehead, 1987). In fact it has been argued that, to the extent that health and illness were recognised at all as being appropriate topics for sociological study before the 1930s, it was the impact of social structures on people's health that was noted rather than how a person's physical and mental state might influence their actions (Gerhardt, 1989).

This does not mean that sociologists do not study individual actions and see them as significant. Some of the most compelling research in sociology has taken as its focus the exploration of human action and has highlighted the role of individual 'social actors' in influencing the social environment (see Section 2.6). But a sociological approach to the problem of health inequalities would reject any account which focused merely on 'individual behaviour', and saw health choices as entirely 'free' and autonomous (and therefore not influenced by work or family or the media and so on). This is an important point to remember, because we use other frames of reference and explanation, such as moral frameworks, which are not sociological.

○ Note down some other frames of reference which could be used to explain the fact of a person's unemployment or illness.

You might have suggested 'expert' frames of reference: for example, explanations arising from psychological theories of behaviour or biological theories about genetic inheritance. But you might also have mentioned 'common sense' frames of reference which emphasised 'character', or explanations which were grounded in moral judgements. It is not uncommon to explain a person's unemployment in terms of individual moral failings: laziness, lack of motivation and so on. In the same way, people explain ill health by reference to an individual's defective lifestyle – unsuitable diet, lack of exercise, smoking, drinking and so on – or explain suicide in terms of a particular individual's 'unstable personality'.

None of these is a sociological account. Sociological accounts do not conceptualise the individual as autonomous – completely independent in their actions and choices. They look beyond the individual to take into account wider *social* causes of individual behaviour. Explaining un-employment in individual terms overlooks a number of what might be crucial factors: the 'social class gradient' in unemployment – that is, its uneven distribution in the population (7 per cent of the population experience nearly 70 per cent of unemployment); the relative vulner-ability of various types of work; the ability of higher occupational groups to protect themselves; the social isolation, poverty and marginalisation of the unemployed. Similarly, we would gain a very one-dimensional view of health inequalities if social influences on individual lifestyle were not studied, such as the influence of peers, the effect of upbringing, the distribution of work, access to education.

Sociologists are interested in exploring 'what is going on' under the surface of society as well as investigating the character of its visible structures and institutions. You might say that their motto is 'things are not what they seem'. They are interested in the structures within a society that reflect particular types of social relationships. They investigate not just what social actors 'do' but the hidden aspects of their actions and their unintended consequences. Actions frequently have effects that people can't know about or control, and people act with incomplete awareness of their situation. The task of the sociologist is to try to unravel and to interpret action as well as structure. As Berger (1966) has commented: 'The fascination of sociology lies in the fact that its perspective makes us see in a new light the very world in which we have lived all our lives'.

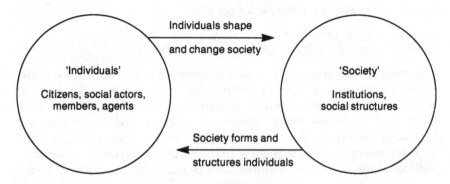

FIGURE 2.1 Sociological approaches: a simple model

Distinctive approaches in sociology

It is important to realise that sociologists have widely differing interests and perspectives, and that over the years they have advanced very different theories about the relative significance of individual social action and social structures (see Figure 2.1). For example, some sociologists would explain health inequalities almost entirely in terms of structural forces beyond the control of the individual, whereas others would acknowledge the importance of behavioural factors. The Black Report (1980) emphasised what it termed *structural/materialist* explanations: that is, it discussed the significance of occupational class, poverty and unemployment in determining health status and concluded that 'it is in some form or forms of the "materialist approach" that the best answer lies' (published in Townsend *et al.*, 1988). But after a decade of further research Whitehead in *The Health Divide* (1987) observed that:

Several commentators are beginning to question whether the distinction between the two approaches is artificial, as behaviour cannot be separated from its social context . . . The behavioural and the structural/materialist explanations . . . are interrelated rather than mutually exclusive.

Whitehead, published in Townsend et al. (1988)

The study of human society is such a complex task that it is perhaps no surprise to find conflicts of view amongst sociologists. Natural science, by contrast, has tended to bury controversy and emphasise orthodox explanations. You would be unlikely to find a full-scale debate about the structure of the liver in your biology textbook, for example; the most recent generally accepted account of its structure would be what was reported there. In sociology textbooks, particularly in recent years, conflicts have been highlighted and perspectives have been presented as entrenched and irreconcilable accounts of the social world.

This preoccupation with conflicts between sociological perspectives has obscured the extent to which the whole basis of social thought has been shifting as it struggles to interpret deep-seated political and contemporary cultural change. Sociology has entered a new phase of turbulence and dissarray, in which many of its characteristic assumptions and debates are being revalued. This is a useful point at which to review the contribution sociology has made to our understanding of the social world and of the nature of health and contemporary health work.

2.2 Theoretical dilemmas

In this section we will highlight three important sets of theoretical distinctions in sociology: between *positivist* and *interpretive* approaches; between *social action* and *structural* theories; and between *consensus* and *conflict* accounts. They represent different ways of 'seeing' and 'knowing' the social world, and they draw our attention to important dilemmas in the business of 'doing' sociology.

Sociology as the science of society

The first distinction to be made is between positivist and interpretive approaches. Sociologists concern themselves with the investigation of social relationships and social behaviour. They explore fundamental social processes and organisational structures and interpret the behaviour of social actors in the social world. In doing this, they have generally claimed to be engaged in the 'scientific study of society'. Sociology emerged as a discipline with this specific focus and with a set of research methods and procedures in the nineteenth century. Many of the concerns which sociologists began to investigate – such as the problem of order in society – had been studied in earlier centuries by philosophers and historians. The claim made by the first sociological thinkers, such as Durkheim, to be founding a new discipline was based not so much on subject matter as on approach and *methodology*: that is, on the research methods being used to investigate the social world.

To the first sociologists the overarching purpose of sociology, the vision and grand plan, was to uncover the nature of human society and the *general laws* governing human behaviour. To do this they needed to observe and investigate the character of social relationships, looking for patterns and regularities. Although atypical and 'deviant' behaviour was not ignored, the main thrust of sociological research was to demonstrate the predictability of much of human behaviour – the patterned regularities which arose from shared social relationships and common experiences.

○ Consider this description of sociological research. What does it have in common with other research traditions you have encountered?

You may have been reminded of lessons at school or at college about scientific method, which proceeds by means of observation, hypothesis and testing. The *observation* of phenomena (such as changes, reactions, movements) gives rise to the construction of a *hypothesis* or set of predictions about why these phenomena may occur. The hypothesis is *tested* to see if the predictions hold or are disproved, and the longer the hypothesis withstands testing the more likely it is be seen as satisfactory. The building up of general theories in biology, physics, chemistry and other disciplines has proceeded on this basis.

In this view the character of sociology is that of a science, analogous to natural science but with the social life of human beings as its object of study rather than, say, the human body or the nature of the universe. Both natural scientists and social scientists observe material phemonena; they make *empirical* (fact based) observations and record these. They develop hypotheses and collect data to test their soundness. In both cases observation and systematic testing of conclusions is a central activity. Both methodologies are rooted in two assumptions: that there are phenomena or facts 'out there' to be collected; and that reality can only be studied through observable phenomena. Both distance themselves from the world they study and claim to investigate it in an *objective* way.

This approach is associated with the philosophical stance of *positivism*, the intellectual bed-rock on which much of social research has been built. Positivists claim that the social and natural sciences share a common logical framework; in their research methods, they argue, all sciences are guided by empiricism and by the hypothetico-deductive method. This has given rise to counter claims by philosophers of social science that sociology cannot be regarded as a science, and to a questioning of the claims of natural science to be 'objective' and 'value-free'. This *anti-positivist* account has been influential in recent years. But it is the positivist tradition that has been most influential in the development of sociology, and in science and medicine as well (see Box 2.1).

BOX 2.1 Positivist and anti-positivist research

Positivist research methods	Anti-positivist research methods
1 Phenomena can only be termed 'real' if their existence can be demonstrated through empirical evidence: in other words, phenomena are seen as linked to each other in a 'cause and effect' way.	1 Social reality is a product of meaningful social interaction. Investigating social life involves trying to understand the meanings which people attribute to their actions and behaviour and the unintended consequences of people's actions. It involves exploring people 'through their own eyes': in other words, there is no observer role or objective category outside social interaction.
2 Positivist research involves the investigation and uncovering of enduring cause and effect relation-ships. The positivist sociologist observes, defines and 'objectifies' the variables being tested as clearly as possible and examines whether there is a relationship between them. To do so may mean that some variables need to be held constant so that relationships between the two variables can be measured.	2 An anti-positivist view accepts the need for a systematic and objective 'scientific' approach to sociology, but contends that studying human beings in society is different from studying the physical world. It questions the value of pre-conceived hypotheses and objectification and emphasises qualitative research which describes and explains human action and meaning.
Example: To measure the impact of damp housing on health means holding constant other variables – such as smoking, occupation, sex and age – which might also influence health. If one variable increases or decreases when the other does, this denotes a positive or negative **correlation**. But in order to establish a **causal relationship** the researcher must demonstrate that one variable changing actually causes the other to change.	**Example**: In assessing the signifi-cance of damp housing, the views of residents about its effects would be seen as important evidence. Their experiences and other people's views (for example doctors', social workers') would be used to construct an account of what damp housing 'means' to them.

Although this is a very simple account of both sociology and natural science, it does serve to remind us that sociology developed historically within a framework of scientific enquiry. A dominant tradition in sociology was that of abstract generalisation (hypothesising, theory building) on the basis of quantitative (usually statistical) research. Durkheim's research into suicide is a good example of this kind of approach (see Section 2.3). This classic nineteenth century study concluded that, although suicide seems to be the ultimate 'individual act', it is in fact 'determined' by social factors. It explained the actions of individuals in terms of features of social structure and levels of social integration.

The notion of social science as the 'natural science of society' became deeply entrenched in sociology, particularly in Britain and the United States. In the first place it led to increasingly abstract theorising about the nature of 'man and society'. Another result of the dominance of 'natural science' methods was an increasing preoccupation with *empiricism*: that is, with fact-driven studies of social issues and social problems. Such studies were invariably preoccupied with gathering and analysing statistics, and they were concerned to demonstrate objectively some aspect of social life. Sociology was projected as scientific in another sense too: as being objective, value-free enquiry in the tradition of the natural sciences. In a similar way to natural scientists, it was suggested, sociologists stood outside society and could investigate it objectively.

Interpretive approaches

Interpretive sociological research, so called because it is concerned with understanding how people themselves see and interpret the social world, has tended to be more descriptive and intuitive. Instead of engaging in quantitative analysis of social facts, in an attempt to uncover causal relationships and social laws, interpretive research relies on interviewing and observing people engaged in social action. The idea is to observe and carefully record the quality of human experience – people's ideas, thoughts and feelings – rather than impose the researcher's own categories of meaning (see Box 2.2). Interpretive research is associated with social action theories and with an anti-positivist philosophy.

Interpretive researchers reject the scientific model of sociology, or at least its abstract and quantitative treatment of human experience. However, the distinction between abstract, quantitative and 'scientific' sociology and humanistic and qualitative sociology is not hard and fast, and at times researchers may make use of both approaches.

BOX 2.2 Approaches to research: a summary

'Scientific' orientation	'Interpretive' tradition
Quantitative emphasis	Qualitative emphasis
Object-focused	Subject-focused
Interest in 'hard' data: – surveys – structured interviews – statistical analysis	Interest in 'soft' data: – open, unstructured interviews – observations – documentary material

Theories of social action

Within sociology there have also been debates between social action theorists and structural theorists. Sociologists have always been aware of the need to probe human creativity and diversity, to understand the ways in which individuals and groups relate to society, and what meanings they themselves attach to events and situations. This approach is generally called *social action* theory. C. Wright Mills (1970) comments that the essence of the sociological enterprise is the attempt to interpret the complex inter-relationship between social structures and human actions: 'The sociological imagination enables us to grasp history and biography and the relations between the two within society'. In other words, the dilemmas and uncertainties of human action as well as the regularities of social structure must be kept in the frame.

Wright Mills has argued that in all classic social analysis a concern to uncover social structures was related to a concern with 'urgent public issues and insistent human troubles'. In the work of Max Weber there is a strong interest in the interpretation of human action as well as in the investigation of social structures, and in the relationship between the active 'social actor' and historically changing social structures (see Section 2.3). Weber was influenced by philosophical and historical ideas as well as by a natural science approach, and he remained sceptical about whether sociology could establish 'social' laws akin to 'natural' laws.

Social action approaches are less concerned with 'macro' theories of how society works and are sceptical about the existence of general social 'laws'. Instead they focus on 'micro' theories of human action. *Interactionism*, associated with the work of Howard Becker and his colleagues, is one example of social action theory. It has concerned itself with the way in which people perceive and interpret different social situations (see Section 2.6). In interactionism there is an emphasis on the role of the self (individual social actor) as the starting point for sociological study. Society is seen as being mediated through the self, and it is by developing shared language and meanings that individuals are able to co-exist in an ordered way. The interactionist tradition has focused on individuals as 'actors', presenting and managing themselves in social roles and negotiations.

Theories of social structure

Structural theories emphasise the way in which society shapes and constrains people by means of norms and values which they internalise as they grow up, and which direct and determine their behaviour. Durkheim and Marx can both be seen as structural sociologists (see Section 2.3). It is 'behaviour' – largely responding to pre-set rules – that is stressed rather than 'action', which would suggest a greater freedom to choose what we do. In a broader sense, people's social behaviour, values and attitudes may be seen as the result of the types of social organisation, processes and structures that exist in the society in which they live. In other words, what we are as individuals is largely determined by the particular society in which we live and, within that society, by the particular social groups in which we operate. Structural sociologists (although not arguing that people's behaviour is totally determined) put much more emphasis on how people have their choices circumscribed by the norms (unwritten rules about behaviour and attitudes) and values (fundamental ideals) of their social world.

○   Reflect on this description of structural sociology. Can you think of instances in your own experience where social structures (in the shape of social organisations and processes) seemed to be shaping or directing your behaviour?

You may have thought of your experience as a health work student and the rules and regulations that governed your behaviour in your college and in the hospital. Educational institutions have developed elaborate rules about attendance, essay writing, examinations, using the library and so on. Hospitals, in a similar way, have developed codes of practice for their workers (and for the patients). These codes control people's behaviour and shape their attitudes to the work. Some are explicit rules – such as the wearing of uniforms for staff or night attire for patients – and others are informal and 'hidden' – such as the traditional deference of nurses towards doctors. The family is a social institution, and you may have thought of your childhood and the way in which adult family members demanded certain types of behaviour from you: going to bed at a set time, not interrupting adult conversation, eating your food 'properly' with a knife and fork and so on.

   You may have found some (or all) of these demands oppressive, or you may have felt that they were perfectly reasonable and necessary in order for things to run smoothly. Either way, it would be hard to argue that we aren't subject to a large number of social rules, which go beyond the formal codes set out in the law and enforced by the police, law courts and prisons. Structural sociologists often refer to these collectively as 'mechanisms of social control'.

One example of an account grounded in structural sociology was mentioned in Section 2.1. The 'structural/materialist' account of health inequalities in the Black Report emphasises that it is some people's deprived material circumstances and resources – their unemployment, poverty, poor housing and so on – that causes them to experience higher rates of disease and death (Townsend *et al.*, 1988). In this view social structures – work organisation and distribution, social welfare policies – are not the result of a shared ideology but of the unequal distribution of power and resources. Some groups in society are able to exercise considerable power and influence over the shaping of social norms and values (although they are also constrained by them) whilst others find themselves virtually powerless.

Consensus theories

The third set of distinctions is between consensus and conflict approaches. Sociologists have explained order and change in society in very different ways. *Consensus* theorists argue that society survives because all citizens broadly acknowledge the benefits of reciprocity and class co-operation, and at least tacitly accept the regulatory mechanisms needed to deliver such benefits. A consensus account suggests that power differences and structural constraints on individual action flow from moral agreement between members of a society. The natural state of society is one of dynamic equilibrium; it is open to change, but able to resolve difficulties and restore a state of balance and harmony.

Consensus theorists have made use of organic analogies, in which the social organism is compared to the biological organism. By implication the ideal society is one in which a state of balance or equilibrium exists. The malfunction of part of the social body can cause damage across the whole system in a similar way to disease striking the human body. For example, Durkheim emphasised that human societies (like human bodies) can adapt and transform themselves to cope with new conditions; the emergence of industrial society in nineteenth century Europe was seen as a good example of this process at work (see Section 2.3). Class conflict and the threat of social disintegration were evidence of the strains within the emerging industrial society, but Durkheim thought that a mature industrial order would develop, characterised by organic solidarity.

Conflict theories

Conflict theorists, as their name implies, would question the presumption of consensus, arguing that if social order was maintained it was because dominant social groups had persuaded or coerced weaker groups into accepting a subordinate position and an unequal society. Conflict theorists assume that society is composed of individuals and groups with diverse and often conflicting interests. For example, Marx argued that in nineteenth century industrial society there was a fundamental conflict between the capitalist class and the working class (see Section 2.3). In every society some groups have access to more knowledge, power and economic resources than others, and conflict structuralists explore why and to what extent these imbalances exist, theorising them as conflict-derived 'inequalities' rather than consensually-grounded 'differences'. A conflict account emphasises how individuals are constrained and coerced into acquiescence, and often seems to suggest that subordination and powerlessness are the inevitable outcomes of an unequal society.

Conflict theorists have worked with a 'fixed sum' view of power in society: that is, if some groups disproportionately exercise power and privileges, this means that the power of the remaining citizens has been proportionately decreased. The means used to achieve this may be physical force, but in modern industrialised societies peaceful persuasion – by projecting suitable values and laying down appropriate norms of behaviour – would increasingly be substituted. The mass of society would find their consent 'engineered' by dominant groups. Informal mechanisms of social control, embedded in a dominant value system, could be enforced through the family and the group. More formal sanctions – the law, police, prisons – were called into play if the informal mechanisms failed to produce compliance.

2.3 The sociological tradition: Durkheim, Marx and Weber

Sociology developed as a separate field of enquiry in the nineteenth century, when industrialisation and urbanisation were transforming the Western world. It is important to remember that the human and social sciences (including social medicine) were inextricably involved in the surveillance and control of the new urban populations (Foucault, 1983). Much of the work of the early sociologists focused on documenting and interpreting the massive shifts in social structure and social organisation which characterised industrial capitalism; in particular, there was a

BOX 2.3 Founders of sociology

Auguste Comte	1798–1857	Defined 'sociology' as a scientific, theory building approach
Karl Marx	1818–1883	Combined political and social theory in a 'materialist' analysis of society
Emile Durkheim	1858–1917	Saw modern society as a progression to 'organic solidarity'
George H. Mead	1863–1931	Developed theories of social action and the social construction of the self
Max Weber	1864–1920	Highlighted rationalisation in modern society, but also emphasised social action
Talcott Parsons	1902–1979	Analysed society as an organic social system

concern with the problem of social order. *Emile Durkheim* (1858–1917) writing in France, *Karl Marx* (1818–83) observing change in Britain – the first industrial nation – and *Max Weber* (1864–1920) in Bismarck's post-1870 unified Germany were all concerned with analysing contemporary social upheaval and change, although they responded in different ways (see Box 2.3). We'll briefly consider these different approaches and review their implications for health status and health work.

Theories of industrial society

All three writers were concerned with analysing the new social conditions and structures being created by the growth of industrial capitalism. From their research emerged a theory of industrial society which remains very influential even in the 1990s. The theory contrasts *agrarian society*, based on religion, a settled social hierarchy and military power, with *industrial society*, based on democracy, social mobility and written contracts between individuals, organisations and the state. Whereas in agrarian society social status was 'ascribed' – a product of birth and breeding – in industrial society it was 'achieved' through individual merit. Thus industrial society was more efficient and *rational* – based on reason and the exercise of law – than agrarian society (see Box 2.4).

Durkheim and structural functionalism

The central importance of *structural* influences on individual behaviour is highlighted in the work of Durkheim. In his view the transition to

BOX 2.4 Traditional and industrial society

Dimension	Traditional	Industrial
Ties based on	Kinship Loyalty	Contracts
Social position	Given at birth Ascribed	Achieved Class
Social relations	Mutuality Personal intimacy	Instrumental
Authority	Traditional Charismatic	Rational

industrial society was beset by structural problems, class conflict and the dangers of *anomie*: that is, social disintegration following the breakdown of established patterns of behaviour. But Durkheim predicted that this stage was transitory and that a mature industrial society would emerge, which was classless, co-operative and more equal. Modern industrial society would be characterised by *organic solidarity*: that is, by a moral consensus based on a recognition by its members of their different but complementary roles. Social harmony and balance derived from *norms* (shared patterns of behaviour) and *values* (shared attitudes and beliefs) and from the open acknowledgement that individuals have different abilities and roles, and therefore that not all people will possess the same resources or exercise the same degree of power in a society. Since people accepted that all parts of society were interdependent and that co-operation helped everyone, social order would be maintained.

   This way of looking at the social world has been termed *structural functionalism*. Functionalism conceptualises society as a system made up of different, inter-locking parts which each have their own function and role and which together create stability and order. Social change only comes about when it is functionally necessary, either by adaptation – for example of institutions – or integration – perhaps of new ideas or values. Functionalism has been a very influential approach and is also as-sociated with the work of Talcott Parsons (see Section 2.5).

○   Durkheim has also been seen as a consensus theorist. Suggest why this might be.

You probably noted down several ways in which Durkheim's ideas link to consensus theory, such as his emphasis on organic solidarity and shared norms and values, his view of society as an interdependent whole and his prediction that mature industrial society would be more classless and co-operative. It is the emphasis on social harmony and stability in Durkheim's work that has resulted in him being placed in the category of consensus theorists. Durkheim considered that equilibrium and integration were the normal conditions of a society; disruption was seen as abnormal and dysfunctional.

Nevertheless, you may have had one or two doubts. After all, Durkheim did discuss change and adaptation, and he did draw attention to class conflict and anomie (though he thought they would be resolved). He did say that the resolution of class conflict would come through greater equality and participation, not just through individuals 'knowing their place'. Giddens (1982) has commented that Durkheim was a social reformer, not a conservative. He did not regret the passing of pre-industrial society and 'mechanical solidarity' because he welcomed the growth of individual freedom.

Durkheim's research into suicide

Durkheim argued that sociologists were scientists who should explain the relationships between social facts and work to establish general laws of society in much the same way as natural scientists. His research into suicide demonstrates both his scientific approach and his structural outlook. Durkheim's theory of suicide emphasised that when shared values disappeared and norms of behaviour began to disintegrate, people felt alienated from society. He interpreted the act of suicide in terms of social anomie rather than as an unpredictable individual act. The rate of suicide, he argued, 'varies inversely with the degree of integration of social groups of which the individual forms a part' (Durkheim, quoted in Atkinson, 1978). Durkheim demonstrated that there was a statistical relationship between suicide rates and a range of social variables, such as religious affiliation and marital status, which he used as measures of social integration (see Box 2.5). Note how this account suggests that social structures may provide safeguards for individuals and may be the result of a general acceptance of the need for regulation in society. In other words, Durkheim saw social order and control as beneficial and generally protective of the health of the individual. To be healthy was to be integrated, to be able to function effectively and to contribute to society. Social fragmention undermined people's health.

Durkheim's research findings have been questioned, partly because of his preoccupation with structural influences. Gerhardt (1989) comments that Durkheim makes no mention at all of the physical or mental state of individual actors in discussing variation in suicide rates. Durkheim also makes use of official data on suicide rates, thus accepting the act of suicide and definition of 'a suicide' as unproblematic. Other writers have argued that suicide is not a social 'fact' but a particular

BOX 2.5 Durkheim's research into suicide

Underlying assumption:
- That society has an independent existence and that social facts (phenomena) about a society can be observed at a societal level
- That the *laws* governing the rate of suicide can be discovered by using a social science method

Lines of research:
- Definition of suicide: 'every case of death resulting directly or indirectly from a positive or negative act performed by the victim himself which he knows will produce this result' (Durkheim)
- Definition of his concept of *social integration*: degree to which individuals share the norms, values, attitudes and beliefs and follow the prescribed rules of behaviour in their group

Statistical analysis to demonstrate that:
- The suicide rate is constant over time within single societies
- The suicide rate varies between different societies
- The suicide rate varies between different groups within the same society and cannot be explained by reference to the mental states of individuals: no significant correlation between number of suicides and individuals' mental states can be found

Examples of statistical patterns of variation:
- city dwellers tend to have a higher suicide rate than rural dwellers
- male suicide rate is higher than female
- unmarried is higher than married

Hypothesis building from statistical correlations:
Suicide varies inversely with the degree of integration of
- domestic society
- religious society
- political society

General hypothesis:
Suicide varies inversely with the degree of integration of social groups of which the individual forms a part

Conclusion:
Social phenomena beyond the level of the individual and the degree of social integration of the individual do influence the rate of suicide

social interpretation of an event (Atkinson, 1978). Another way of thinking about suicide might be to ask why a particular death became classified as a suicide in the first place (see Section 2.6).

Marxism

For Marx the emergence of industrial capitalism was inevitably accompanied by bitter class conflict, as new technologies and new methods of production threatened established patterns of work and traditional social relationships (see Chapter 5 for a discussion of class structure). Marx predicted that the contradictions between the interests of the workers and the capitalists would result in growing working class consciousness and increasing resistance. Social conflict would not disappear until capitalism was finally overthrown. He was optimistic, not about industrial society as such but about the prospects for change that it offered. Democracy, equality, education, contracts and social mobility were snares for the working class – the products of *bourgeois ideology* – but they also provided the means whereby the working class could organise and challenge capitalism. By overthrowing traditional agrarian society capitalism could operate as a force for progress.

Marx argued that it was the *economic substructure* – the particular technologies and processes of the economy and the work relationships they required – that caused social change. Industrial capitalism, by causing profound changes in the economic substructure, created fundamentally opposed classes of workers and capitalists whose interests could never be reconciled. Thus it was an economic shift which laid down the conditions for future social and political change (see Figure 2.2).

Capitalism and ill health
Marx saw industrial capitalism as largely to blame for the unequal distribution of illness and disease, for the premature death of the

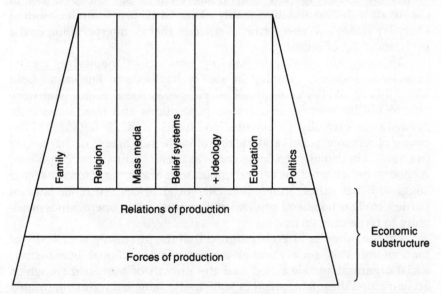

FIGURE 2.2 Marx's theory of society. Source: Cuff and Payne (1979)

labouring classes and for unequal access to health-protecting social conditions, such as decent housing, diet and wages. He and his fellow writer Friedrich Engels, who published *Condition of the Working-Class in England* in 1847, had no doubt that the poverty and immiseration caused by early industrial capitalism was responsible for the heavy burden of working class sickness:

When one . . . thinks how crowded their dwellings are, how every nook and corner swarms with human beings, how sick and well sleep in the same room, in the same bed, the only wonder is that a contagious disease like this [typhus] does not spread further . . . The food of the labourer, indigestible enough in itself, is utterly unfit for young children, and he has neither means nor time to get his children more suitable food.

Engels, quoted in Gerhardt (1989)

The analysis of illness as caused by economic processes and exploitative social conditions is still a strong theme in writing about ill health today (Townsend *et al.*, 1988).

Weber and social action theory

Weber argued that people operated as creative agents in society rather than just responding to economic stimuli. For Weber sociology needed to work at two levels: building theories about how society worked and how people fitted into it, and piecing together an understanding of society by exploring how individuals went about the business of constructing inter-subjective reality. This latter task – understanding everyday reality – Weber termed *Verstehen*: that is, interpretation or the understanding of meaning.

This emphasis on understanding how actors themselves create, experience and find meaning in society has become known as *social action* theory. Weber conceptualised people as social actors who were able to initiate change, and whose perceptions and lived experience needed to be carefully documented and interpreted. He highlighted the power of religious beliefs and the role of individual agents of change: for example, charismatic leaders such as Jesus Christ or Napoleon. Although he accepted the central importance of economic forces, Weber suggested that other, quite different social forces, such as political parties, trade unions and professional groups, could operate independently to transform society.

On the other hand Weber argued that the increasing complexity of modern industrial society was giving rise to more rational, bureaucratic social organisation. He noted that the growth of bureaucracy, which accompanied the enlargement of scale in the state and industry, offered considerable advantages to individuals. They would be selected for posts in which they could use their skills, in a system based on merit and which encouraged social mobility. Although he was convinced that the trend toward rationalism in modern industrial society was inevitable and in many ways progressive, he was less than optimistic about some aspects of change. He highlighted the stifling effects of bureaucratic organisation on innovation and radical ideas and noted the de-personalising anonymity of the worker trapped in a soulless and remote bureaucracy.

Social theories and health

In their theories about industrialisation and social change the early sociologists did not discuss health and illness directly. They did not explore medicine as a set of social practices or analyse the social role of the patient, as medical sociologists were to do in the twentieth century. Uta Gerhardt (1989) notes:

How remote in nineteenth century sociology was the idea that a person's normal organic or mental functioning was not to be taken for granted. Equally remote was the idea that medicine or medical practice might be seen as a social institution with integrative functions for society . . . Classical sociological thought attributed little significance to the physical or mental state of the person, while problems of social organisation and structure were prominent.

Gerhardt (1989)

Nevertheless, Marx, Weber and Durkheim were interested in the re-lationship between disease and social stability. They viewed disease and illness as social facts which were inextricably bound up with the problem of social order (Turner, 1987). The incidence of illness reflected the state of society. Diseases were in part produced by the economic and social conditions of industrial capitalism – such as poverty, social deviance and the social anomie arising from rapid change.

The theories of Durkheim, Marx and Weber offer valuable insights into contemporary issues in health work, such as the relationship between social structure, health status and health inequalities, and the nature of power relationships in health work organisations. For example, Weber's ideas about bureaucracy have influenced current thinking about the nature of power relationships in health work organisations, which we explore in Chapter 11. Their theories of economic and social class cast a long shadow over most discussions of poverty, class and inequalities in health status, and we'll consider these in Chapters 5 and 6.

In broad terms many of the issues raised by the first sociologists are still relevant today. In spite of the growth of democracy, rationality and bureaucracy, educational opportunities and greater equality, concern about how to maintain social order is still widespread. Politicians in the

1990s have highlighted a crisis in law and order, in social solidarity and in democratic institutions. Class is still a live issue in contemporary society and in health work, even if class barriers and class conflict are much less pronounced now and social mobility is much greater.

2.4 The social policy tradition

Throughout this book we will also be drawing on concepts and findings from social policy. *Social policy* – the study of welfare principles and policies – is concerned (like sociology) with the relationship between the individual and society, but it focuses on the investigation and evaluation of public and private provision of social welfare. Since the identification of 'social problems' and 'social needs' depends crucially on perceptions of what are appropriate levels and types of welfare provision, social policy will always remain a highly contested issue. The allocation of scarce resources, in the form of social security benefits, housing subsidies, education grants or health sector funding, will always involve the exercise of *power* and judgements about *values*. Social policy asks questions about what should be, and what is, more highly valued: the building of a new hospital or of another school, support for community care work or secure provision for psychiatric patients, more sheltered housing or more long-stay beds? Policy makers (politicians, civil servants and so on) are inevitably involved in relating needs to resources, in resolving what are seen as the most urgent (or dangerous) social problems; social policy researchers seek to analyse and influence this process.

The Fabian contribution

Social policy emerged as a distinct discipline in the UK in the early twentieth century and is associated with the work of social reformers such as Sidney and Beatrice Webb of the Fabian Society. Fabians argued that social problems (for example poverty) and economic inefficiencies (such as unemployment) could be solved through *collectivism*: that is, state intervention and collective provision of welfare services. This envisaged extensive but benign and paternalist state control over people's everyday lives and was grounded in a rather elitist approach, aimed at influencing top policy makers and prescribing policies for people's 'own good'.

The growth of state welfare provision in the UK, which owed much to Fabian influence, culminated in the creation of the welfare state in the 1940s. This established a fairly comprehensive welfare system to maintain income, relieve poverty and sickness, and begin to provide decent public housing as well as health, social and education services. Many of these services were provided on a *universalist* basis: that is, they were available to all who had need of them, without exceptions and qualification. Some other services and benefits were *selectivist*: that is, they were provided only to certain categories of people who fulfilled specific conditions.

○ Drawing on your own knowledge of welfare state services, give examples of universalist and selectivist services/benefits.

Universalist benefits which exist today include health and education. Everyone can gain access, in theory on an equal basis, to almost all services provided by the National Health Service, without payment at the point of use. Under the 1944 Education Act all children became entitled to free, full-time education up to the age of 15, and the school leaving age has since been raised to 16. A good example of a selectivist benefit is Family Credit, paid only to families on very low incomes. The Independent Living Fund gives selective, discretionary benefits to specific groups of people to help them live in private households in the community. Unemployment Benefit is only paid to those out of work who can satisfy the regulations for entitlement, so that many part-time workers as well as school leavers and 'housewives' do not qualify (see Chapters 3 and 6 for a discussion of welfare provision and entitlement).

Theoretical tensions in social policy

The establishment of a strong welfare state also entrenched social policy as an empiricist (fact-driven) study of the administration of welfare. By the 1960s R.M. Titmuss defined the purpose of social policy as being to investigate 'the structure, history, organisation, practices and principles of collective action falling within the area of social welfare'. It was argued that the welfare state reflected and reinforced concepts of citizenship, altruism and social justice, and that its triumph represented the 'end of ideology': in other words, provision of welfare by the state had become acceptable to all major political parties and groupings. The main concern of social policy analysts should therefore be to evaluate service provision and highlight deficiencies.

This anti-theoretical stance in social policy has been challenged in recent years, and researchers now draw much more freely on socio-logical theories and traditions to inform their work. From the 1970s feminist and anti-racist commentators on the welfare state have highlighted the sexist and racist assumptions on which it was constructed (Williams, 1989; see also Chapters 7 and 8). The dominance of the Fabian tradition and of the 'Titmuss paradigm' (Donnison, 1979) – which

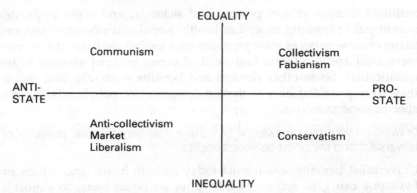

FIGURE 2.3 Traditions in social welfare theory. Source: adapted from Lee and Raban (1983)

viewed collective welfare provision as inherently progressive and civilising – was challenged, though not strongly at first, by both anti-collectivist and socialist traditions (see Figure 2.3). *Socialist* critics of state welfare provision in the Marxist tradition saw it as an attempt by the capitalist state to 'buy off' working class protest and control labour more effectively (Ginsberg, 1979). *Anti-collectivists* (the *New Right*) attacked the growth of state power as undermining individual liberty and argued for free market provision of welfare (Harris and Selden, 1979).

During the 1980s traditional welfare state and collectivist values came under considerable pressure from anti-collectivists on the political right, who issued a fundamental challenge to collectivism. The dis-mantling of state organisations, cutbacks in welfare and attacks on the 'nanny state', which kept its citizens in welfare 'chains' and undermined their personal freedom, are particularly associated with Thatcherism (Dean and Taylor-Gooby, 1992). (We will explore the implications of this debate for health and health work in Chapters 4, 6 and 13.) But disillusion with state welfare is not confined to the political right or to the political arena. A general crisis of confidence in collectivism has led to a wider questioning of the empiricist, anti-theory tradition in social policy.

Social policy and sociology

Researchers in social policy now draw much more widely on sociological theories – not only those of Marx and Weber but also more recent feminist and post-structural accounts (see Sections 2.7 and 2.8). Many of the tensions and conflicts that have already been identified in sociology can be traced in social policy as well. Structural approaches to social policy focus on the way in which individuals are shaped and constructed by welfare – into state dependants, such as 'old age pensioners' or 'the unemployed' or 'welfare scroungers', for example. Social action approaches celebrate the diversity of people's lived experience and the active engagement of people in influencing policy making and contesting welfare provision. Empiricist and quantitative research was until quite recently the dominant tradition in social policy. Now this tradition has been supplemented by qualitative and interpretive research, which is concerned to uncover people's own perceptions of their welfare needs and social circumstances.

New theoretical insights in social policy link to urgent new concerns in sociology: how to explain fragmentation, instability and uncertainty in contemporary social life (see Sections 2.8 and 2.9). As welfare systems have come under increasing attack, the attempt to rethink welfare in terms of theories of social needs and values has been a marked feature (Taylor-Gooby, 1991). In addition, there has been concern to acknow-ledge the negative features of universalism – particularly its association with uniformity, bureaucracy and state control – and to consider the positive aspects of a *mixed economy of welfare*, to which state, market, employers, households and individuals all contribute. Recent theorists have argued for welfare frameworks which retain the security and protection offered by universalism while providing opportunities for diversity, autonomy and empowerment of users (Williams, 1992). These new theoretical insights have an important bearing on health and health work, and we will explore them in more detail in Chapter 13.

2.5 Debates in medical sociology

In the sociology of health and illness two traditions have been prominent: the functionalist approach and social action theory. In addition, conflict theories have questioned the whole interpretation of medicine and health work as naturally beneficent and Marxist critics, for example, have highlighted the links between capitalism and ill health. Until the 1960s the functionalist theories of Talcott Parsons (1902–79) dominated the field of health and illness, but this consensus approach was increasingly challenged. In this section we will examine the contribution of Talcott Parsons and the criticisms mounted by conflict theorists, and in Section 2.6 we'll consider the work of social action theorists.

The contribution of Talcott Parsons

Talcott Parsons has a central place in medical sociology because he carried out major empirical research into the role of the medical profession in society. In particular he explored relationships between doctors and their patients, and his findings informed his work on social structure. Parsons conceptualised medicine as a professional role – that is, a non-market based, person-focused, knowledge based and rational occupation – which had developed to serve people in difficult and complex areas of social life. Together with law, technology and education, medicine operated across society to help people fulfil social goals and remain integral members of society.

Parsons worked within a *functionalist* framework: that is, he saw society as a social system of different, interdependent parts each having a particular function and role, which together operate smoothly to maintain stability. In his work, much more than in Durkheim's, concepts of adaptation and change almost disappear and the emphasis on maintaining the status quo is very strong. Wright Mills (1959) comments that in the work of the early sociologists like Durkheim balance is used as a metaphor, but Parsons uses it in a literal way – as if society itself had a set of 'needs' and functional requirements of overriding importance which are separate from those of the people within that society.

In *The Social System* (1951) Parsons interpreted the role of medicine as a mechanism that was crucial to the smooth running of society. He conceptualised society as a system which had both 'instrumental' and 'expressive' needs. In *instrumental* terms there were evident economic and political imperatives: to continue to produce enough to satisfy people's physical needs and to create and maintain accepted authority systems. In *expressive* terms there existed social integration and cultural imperatives: to bind the 'societal community' together and to reproduce culture and tradition. Together these produced the four subsystems (see Figure 2.4) of modern, rational, achievement-oriented industrial society, a society in which role fulfilment and goal attainment were crucial for survival. The central role of medicine was to keep people healthy or, if they fell sick, to heal and reintegrate them into society as quickly as possible. It is possible to see the foundation of the National Health Service in the UK in the 1940s as a triumph for consensus values, and to argue that health work has played a significant part in maintaining 'organic solidarity' by promoting class co-operation and a more even sharing of resources.

Parsons' 'sick role' theory is examined in Chapter 10, but it is worth noting at this point that he conceptualised medicine as a form of *social control*: that is, as a means by which individual behaviour was modified and adapted to fit wider societal needs. Only by being healthy – fit enough to function – could individuals participate in society, and on their efficiency depended economic production and ultimately the society's survival.

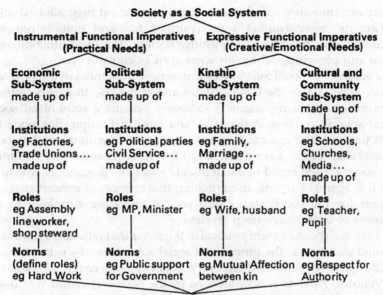

FIGURE 2.4 Parsons' social system. Source: O'Donnell (1981)

○ Reflect on the idea of health as 'fit to function' and suggest which model of health it links to (you might like to look back at Sections 1.1–1.2 at this point).

Health as functional fitness connects to the medical model of health that we discussed in Chapter 1. As Parsons noted, doctors make the decision about whether someone is fit or unfit to work; they have a crucial role in determining the level of 'health' (as ability to function) in a society. Although organic and socio-cultural factors undermined people's health and entitled them – quite legitimately – to enter the 'sick role', Parsons also noted that retreat into illness could be a form of deviant or aberrant behaviour. Doctors needed to police the boundaries of the sick role because 'illness, in so far as it is motivated, is a form of deviant behaviour' (Parsons and Fox, 1952).

In building theories Parsons used new ideas from science; in particular the physiological concepts of 'homeostasis' and equilibrium were applied to the social world. He incorporated the theory of homeostasis into his social theory, suggesting that social, cultural, psychological and organic mechanisms operated to rectify deviance and restore equilibrium in society in a way analogous to the operation of homeostasis in the human body (Gerhardt, 1989). Homeostasis in social terms was transformed into a social control mechanism ensuring that society ran smoothly and that everybody carried out their allotted roles. In Parsons' view conflict was dysfunctional and equilibrium was functional and 'healthy'. The healthy society, the fit-to-function individual and physiological health were seen as equivalents.

Parsons' *The Social System* was immensely influential in the post-war period, especially in the United States and in the UK. In part because of his work on medicine, medical sociology became a recognised sociological specialism, first in the USA and later in Europe. But since the 1960s the backlash against Parsons' version of functionalism has been considerable. Critics have pointed out that it reifies society by assuming that 'society' itself could make demands and have discrete 'needs' to be met. It is against Parsons, in particular, that charges of conservatism, of support for the social status quo and of shackling sociology to the 'problem of order' have been levelled.

Parsons' theories were political in the sense that rational, attainment-oriented society – as the pinnacle of social achievement – is unproblematically equated with contemporary America. Moreover, as Gerhardt (1989) notes, Parsons was influenced by the Nazi era, World War II and by the revelations about Nazi treatment of the Jews. He defined health and the healthy society as one in which there was a 'reciprocity of social exchange' and equated this with democracy; the failure of democracy then became a state of illness equated with the sick society of Nazism. Parsons' social theories thus represent a defence of liberal against fascist values; in a real sense they are a product of their time. To this extent it may be argued that they are no more (or less) political than the work of the founders of sociology that we noted in Section 2.3. They continue to offer valuable insights into health and illness.

Conflict theories of health and illness

Conflict theorists have attacked consensus theories of the role of medicine in society on two main grounds. First, the characterisation of medicine as a benign and supportive social institution was questioned. Instead of seeing medicine as a profession which helped people in difficult areas of social life, doctors could be viewed as a self styled 'expert' group which monopolised not only the production of health and illness but also the terms on which illness was experienced. It could not necessarily be assumed that medicine policed the boundaries of sickness with social consent.

A medical monopoly
Freidson (1970) argued that the medical profession had extended its monopoly over health and illness both through subordination or exclusion of other health work occupations such as nursing, and

through control of the process of diagnosis, treatment and hospitalisa-tion. In consensus theory medical knowledge about illness was seen as paramount: people took their symptoms to be diagnosed, and doctors claimed neutral and objective status for their theories and classifications of disease. But Freidson argued that illness was actually negotiated initially through lay culture. People consulted with family, friends and neighbours through a 'lay referral system'. Moreover, when patients presented themselves, doctors did not just diagnose disease (which he accepted was a biophysical state); they were also involved in treating illness and therefore in creating meanings and frameworks of social knowledge which they could impose upon patients.

Marxist theories

A second, broader critique of functionalism related to its conception of the role of medicine in capitalist society and in the social production of health and illness. Marxists claim that, although capitalism and professionalised medicine have improved standards of living (at least in industrialised countries), there are still glaring global and local in-equalities in health – the 'social class gradients' – and there is still evidence of class conflict in health work. Lesley Doyal (1979) has argued that 'the way health and illness are defined, as well as the material reality of disease and death, will vary according to the social and economic environment in which they occur'. This does not mean, of course, that biology plays no part in health, but that it operates within a social and economic context:

Thus, the historical development of the capitalist mode of production has had extremely far-reaching effects on health. On the one hand, the develop-ment of the productive forces on an unprecedented scale has meant that the standard of living of the entire population in developed capitalist countries has been improved, with a consequent amelioration in standards of physical health. This same process however has simultaneously underdeveloped the health of many third world populations. Moreover, new hazards to health have been created in the developed world by the large-scale economic, social and technological changes which were a necessary part of this development.

Doyal, with Pennell (1979)

Doyal comments that, while today's National Health Service provides a very much better system of health care than in earlier stages of industrial capitalism, it is by no means 'a socialist health service'. Rather it was 'an important part of the post-war settlement between capital and labour' which institutionalised class, race and gender inequalities for patients and workers. Working class patients still suffer more death and disease and poorer standards of treatment. The lowest paid and lowest status workers in the health service are migrant workers, women workers and those in the lowest social classes.

The National Health Service was created on a basis not of moral consensus but of economic determinants and class bargaining – in which capital retained the upper hand. The medical profession gained a monopoly position within health work, but only on the basis of protecting the interests of capital by controlling the production of health and ill health and maintaining a productive workforce. In this view the operation of medicine as an institution of social control serves the interests of the ruling capitalist class, not of society as a whole. Although medicine has projected itself as a technical and neutral activity, it is an ideological enterprise which controls and persuades populations.

2.6 Social action theories and medical sociology

Social action theory, as we noted earlier, seeks to explain social action first and foremost by understanding the ideas, values and 'social world' of individual actors themselves. Weber pointed out that, in order to understand how society develops and changes, we need to disaggregate it, to study the motives and goals of social actors and not just to build grand theories. Parsons' general theory of society seemed to focus exclusively on how social subsystems controlled individual action, and this produced a humanistic backlash, in which the attention of sociologists became refocused upon the 'actor' as a human subject rather than as an object of enquiry.

Interactionism

There were several strands to this attempted reformulation of sociology, and in most of them issues related to health and health work achieved considerable prominence. *Interactionism* represents one of the most important and influential attempts to study human action 'in and on its own terms' rather than within a tradition of scientific positivism. The writings of George H. Mead (1863–1931) and Charles Cooley have been seen as important in formulating some central interactionist concepts. Mead drew attention to the reflexive character of symbolic reality: in other words, the human capacity for self-consciousness and self-reflection in and on action, which enabled human actors (unlike other species) to be both subjects and objects of themselves. Cooley explored this in the notion of the 'looking-glass self'; the gazers view themselves in the glass, but transformed – as in a mirror image – by their perceptions of the views that other people have of them and of their actions. The meanings that an individual attributes to particular situations will never be fully shared by others, because that individual will have a unique set of experiences. But through the medium of language, Mead suggested, human beings learn to share symbols and attribute common meanings to actions and situations.

It is through the careful study of these social exchanges – of the process of social interaction as it has been termed – and by 'getting inside the defining process of the actor' that sociologists can begin to understand the complexities of social action (Blumer, 1969). This has required the adoption of an *anti-positivist* approach to research, where the researcher adopts as far as possible the stance of the human subjects being studied. A great deal of interactionist research has involved studying small groups or human interaction in particular settings, where the researcher can 'get inside the skin' of the subjects and understand their attitudes and values.

In one sense this emphasis on the complexity of human interaction and the myriad different negotiations and outcomes that it contains offers a humanistic and 'progressive' view of human action, a vision of diversity and creativity in which (although individuals may not have equal power) everyone gets a chance to help make the rules. The rising popularity of interactionist research in the 1960s and 1970s (and possibly the rise of interactionism as a perspective) owed much to its view of human beings as creative social actors. This approach resonated with new social movements and with liberation struggles in the political sphere. Interactionism seemed to liberate individuals from the dead weight of the 'social system'; it would also liberate nursing research, it was hoped, from domination by abstract and quantitative research traditions of natural science (Dingwall and McIntosh, 1978).

Anselm Strauss (1963) developed the concept of 'negotiated order' to describe the management of interactions between patients and staff in modern hospitals, and Strong (1979) has written of the 'ceremonial order' that exists in clinics. Acknowledging the ideas of G.H. Mead, Strauss comments on the fluidity, bargaining and conflict in human interaction:

The Meadian emphasis on the endless formation of universes of discourse – with which groups are coterminous – is extremely valuable, yielding a metaphor of groups emerging, evolving, developing, splintering, disintegrating, or pulling themselves together, or parts of them falling away and perhaps coalescing with segments of other groups to form new groups, in opposition, often, to the old.

Strauss (1978), quoted in Gerhardt (1989)

Erving Goffman in *Stigma* (1964) explored how individuals understood and came to terms with their particular disabilities, and how they 'managed' and presented themselves in their relationships with others so that the dangers to self were minimised. In *Asylums* (1961) Goffman paints a grim portrait of a rigid and hierarchical 'total' institution for mental patients, but he also highlights how inmates adapted to and sometimes 'psyched out' or sabotaged the system (see Chapters 10 and 11).

But interactionists also throw up difficult issues about relativism and human action which underline the individual's lack of freedom. They argue that meanings and understandings are products of particular social frameworks, and that societies will differ (and the same society may change over time) in the way they define and interpret human behaviour. What is 'normal' and what is 'deviant' behaviour is not fixed and immutable. Howard Becker (1963) argued that in some situations behaviour may be labelled as deviant when in other circumstances the same behaviour is seen as normal: the murderer and the soldier both kill, but their action is judged very differently. In the case of illness it is not the existence of biological disease as such that is significant, but how this is perceived, explained and responded to within a society, because this influences how people will live their lives. Although there may be international agreement on what a case of tuberculosis looks like, many other areas of illness – most evidently mental illness – are not so easily defined.

For example, social action theorists would not treat suicide as a 'social fact', as Durkheim did. They would be more concerned to ask why a particular death became classified as a suicide in the first place. This would lead on to thinking about what meanings the social actors in the drama – the police officer, the relatives, the coroner, for example – attached to the event. In his study of categorisations of death as suicide Atkinson (1978) suggested that coroners held a common sense theory of 'what suicide is'. The theory of what constituted a 'typical suicide' influenced the type of evidence gathered about each suicide and the interpretation that was made.

It follows that illness is what a given society defines and treats as such. In an interactionist approach illness is viewed as 'the culturally variable product of deviancy labelling' (Gerhardt, 1989). What is identified as illness will depend on the judgements made in a particular society by those empowered to define and label it, and in Western society it is the medical profession that has the power to label and that exercises a social control function.

The medical profession plays the central role in such labelling, and interactionists do not assume – as Parsons did – that doctors are beneficent or impartial in their judgements. Interactionist research into labelling suggests that a whole range of behaviours, from marijuana use and homosexuality to political radicalism and epilepsy, have been at times labelled as illness largely on 'political' grounds, to maintain the status quo. Labelling theory thus tends to emphasise the *lack* of power of individuals when faced with the diagnostic and labelling power of doctors. But by highlighting the social relativism in illness labelling interactionists also cut away at the moral basis upon which labelling might be condemned. Interactionists left themselves no theoretical grounds for claiming that one society's judgements were 'better' than another's; they were just 'different'. Becker's call for sociology to support the underdog was a political one.

○   Symbolic interactionism is a very different approach to studying the social world. On what grounds might structural sociologists criticise the interactionist approach?

Although interactionists have seen themselves as social reformers, their preoccupation with individuals and deviant subcultures has been criticised on the ground that it has led to a neglect of structural organisation and power distribution. Structural theorists argue that, in the absence of a theory of how society as a whole operates and changes, the very real constraints on social action are ignored. They also criticise the research methods used by interactionists on the grounds that they do not follow the lines of objective, scientific enquiry.

Interactionists, however, argue that social life is produced by the processes of social interaction; there are no social structures 'out there' determining people's behaviour. A range of factors influences how people act, but there is no immutable social order; everything is up for negotiation. Hence their emphasis on interpretive research and 'particip-ant and non-participant observation': that is, on methods which involve the researcher in close-range investigations of – and even involvement in – specific bouts of interaction. This does not mean that interactionists abandon the scientific method; they are still concerned with hypothesis building and testing, but within an action and observation framework. The emphasis on this as the major means of 'coming to know' about the particular relationships under study distinguishes interactionism from the more abstract and quantitative research tradition of structuralism. Its humanistic, qualitative approach has been criticised as 'soft' and lacking in rigour.

Other social action approaches

There are other interpretive approaches to problems in health work. *Ethnography* is a research tradition which attempts to study human subjects in and on their own terms by using unstructured interviews in which people are encouraged to set the terms and ground rules. Donovan's (1986) research into the health beliefs and actions of black and minority ethnic groups was grounded in ethnography, and she describes how she worked on a basis of equality and openness with each research subject, and how she followed the leads given by them in order to find significant new people to interview. In addition research subjects were involved in reviewing, commenting on and evaluating the findings. The research subjects as well as the researcher herself greatly influenced the direction and outcomes of the research process.

Probably the most controversial approach is *ethnomethodology*: that is, is the study of the methods (methodology) used by people (ethno). Ethnomethodologists explore the everyday ways and means by which people sustain their everyday social life. This involves researchers in detailed observation and 'micro-analysis' of social transactions, in an attempt to see in the details of everyday acts and utterances the underlying, unacknowledged 'patterns' which make up social inter-action. Gerhardt (1989) suggests that health is conceptualised in ethnomethodology as 'competence' – what each member needs to have to manage transactions and accomplish social action. In contrast, illness is 'trouble' – a broad concept of unease, disruption, breakdown – which interrupts members' daily lives and requires them to respond, perhaps by seeking medical advice. When this happens, problems can arise if doctors and patients have different frames of knowledge and language and different degrees of competence in the encounter.

Social interaction is viewed in ethnomethodology as a complex process – of juggling with codes of language and ways of communicating (verbally and non-verbally) and acting in different situations – that enables social life to continue. The task of the sociologist is to find out how this whole dynamic interplay works, by studying how 'members' of social groups go about their social transactions. Researchers in the health field have focused on situations where such 'juggling' can have crucial outcomes, in particular on doctor–patient communication. For example, Heath (1981) engaged in micro-analysis of the form and function of medical consultations. The ethnomethodological contribu-tion to health was launched through studies of suicide, although it was not the fact of suicide itself that was studied but the methods (medical records, verbal reasoning and so on) used by officials to reach decisions about doubtful cases (Garfinkel, 1967).

An anti-positivist approach

The notion of social science as a project standing apart from everyday life is challenged in social action theories. Researchers need to know the 'facts of life' that any person in the group knows. This will involve very detailed recording of interviews with people, or of transactions between people, so that researchers understand and reflect using the same everyday methods – language and understanding – as the subjects they study. Social action theories are *anti-positivist*, rejecting the idea that only positive facts and observable phenomena are real and that only these can be studied (see Boxes 2.1 and 2.2). Instead they put into practice the ideas of *phenomenology* – that is, that all sense data (thoughts, feelings, meanings and other cognitive processes) are real and can be interpreted by the researcher. They see the interpretation of meaningful action (a task completely different from scientific enquiry) as the proper sphere of sociology.

At the extreme, social action theories reject not just the abstract and quantitative research tradition associated with positivism but the whole 'social science' project itself. Researchers must not just observe but must experience and use the everyday methods of people's transactions, because there is no other way of understanding the acts, meanings or underlying patterns and accounts. This raises the criticism that, since researchers are using the same everyday frameworks as those they study, disentangling their meanings and interpretations from those of their research subjects will be difficult – perhaps impossible.

2.7 The problem of gender

Theories of gender represent a challenge to mainstream sociology and its application to health and health work. The 'founding fathers' of sociology, Durkheim, Marx and Weber, and most sociologists up to the 1960s, saw gender issues as largely unproblematic. The public world of work and politics, which was their main focus of attention, was almost exclusively controlled by men. In the nineteenth century and for much of the twentieth century women were effectively excluded from higher status occupations, such as the professions, political life and business. Working class women who worked in industry, and poor but 'genteel' women who worked as nurses, housekeepers, nannies and teachers, occupied a marginal position in the public sphere. Women remained in the private domain of the home, largely subservient to male control and dependent on male wages.

Although sociologists wrote about citizenship and society, they did not remark on the fact that women were excluded from many aspects of citizenship, such as political rights and equal access to welfare benefits. Citizenship itself was predicated on an idea of individual male rights and freedoms (Dalley, 1988). The division of labour in Western society was accepted as a 'natural' order in which women's position in the labour market merely reflected their domestic responsibilities. Women's role in biological and social reproduction, as childbearers, house-keepers, mothers and obedient wives, were largely 'read off' from their biological make-up. In Durkheim's study of suicide he argues that a man is 'almost entirely the product of society' but a woman is far more 'a product of nature' (quoted in Giddens, 1989). Margaret Stacey (1981) has commented that in the 1950s there still existed two unrelated theories about the division of labour, one originating in the writings of the eighteenth century political economist Adam Smith on the division of labour in industrial capitalism (in *The Wealth of Nations*) and the other in the creation myth of Adam and Eve:

The first has to do with production and the social control of the workers and the second with reproduction and the social control of women. The problem is that the two accounts, both men's accounts, have never been reconciled. Indeed it is only as a result of the urgent insistence of feminists that the problematic nature of the social order related to reproduction has been recognised.

Stacey (1981)

The preoccupation of sociologists with problems of production – markets, paid labour, industrial organisation, state power and so on – contrasted sharply with their relative neglect of reproduction and their lack of interest in theorising the relationship between the two.

Gender in medical sociology

The same kind of myopia applied to conceptions of health and illness. Medical sociology has been accused of being 'gender blind'. Early analysis of the relationships between doctors and patients did not at first take into account the fact that most doctors were male – or that their descriptions of the ideal patient were of a young, physically ill male (Miles, 1991). Feminist sociologists highlighted how medical accounts of women as patients focused on their biological weakness and depend-ence. It was claimed that women consulted more frequently, and with more mental health problems, because they were naturally fragile and emotional. Doctors treated these manifestations of sickness with less seriousness than similar complaints voiced by male patients (Lennane and Lennane, 1982). In pregnancy and childbirth these natural charac-teristics were heightened, and women were portrayed in medical literature as essentially unstable, present-centred, even childish (Graham and Oakley, 1981).

At the same time women's fundamental role as unpaid health worker was largely overlooked (Graham, 1984a). Although most health work takes place outside the formal health sector, and most of this informal labour is undertaken by women, it was the paid professional labour of health workers that was the 'visible' part of the iceberg. In the public sphere control rested conclusively with the mainly male medical profession, and it was this group on which medical sociologists overwhelmingly focused. In 1990 some 12 per cent of nurses were male and around 70 per cent of all health professionals were women. Yet nurses and other female health professionals, although forming the vast majority of the workforce, are still rarely studied by medical sociologists (Oakley, 1986).

The challenge of feminist accounts

Feminist critiques can be characterised as conflict theories both attacking the 'malestream' tradition of mainstream sociology (O'Brien, 1981) and seeking to revise theories of social structure so that women are no longer 'hidden' from view. But beyond this, as Chapters 3 and 7 demonstrate, feminist theories have challenged 'malestream' sociology by addressing a range of issues of interest to health workers. Some feminist accounts are structural in orientation. Feminists have particularly focused on revising theories of the private/public division of health labour and family health work, and more recently they have turned their attention to caring (Finch and Groves, 1983). Marxist feminist theorists tried to use Engels' theory of the family and patriarchy to propose that partnership and equality had characterised early social relations. Engels had argued that women's oppression arose only with the emergence of private property and early capitalism (Williams, 1989). But they have also attempted to blend Marxist theories of class with feminist and anti-racist theories, for example to demonstrate the triple oppression of black female workers in the health service (Doyal, 1979). Other accounts are closely linked to social action theory and post-structuralism (see Section 2.8).

The emergence of a feminist research methodology which is humanist and qualitative reflects the attempt to recapture women's lives; these, it is argued, have been 'hidden from history' and are still difficult to record today (Rowbotham, 1973). Much of feminist research is strongly anti-positivist and emphasises the need to rethink the researcher–research subject relationship and to revalue their relative roles and statuses (Roberts, 1981). In particular, feminists have questioned the much vaunted objective stance of the researcher in the research interview and have suggested that a more appropriate relationship when dealing with sensitive issues in health and illness – such as childbirth or hysterectomy – would be a reciprocal one, in which both parties were able to participate and contribute on a more equal basis.

Graham (1984b) discusses the importance of personal accounts – story-telling, letters and diaries – in constructing women's lives. Fundamental to story-telling, she argues, is:

The idea of a 'sociology for women' [as] contrasted with the sociology of women . . . a sociology in which women are subjects and not objects in the research process; a sociology which enlightens and emancipates . . . with the sociologist constructing 'new meanings' so that women can become 'more intelligible to themselves', can oppose their social condition more effectively; a sociology which places a particular emphasis on experience and subjectivity as the route to theory.

Graham (1984b)

○   Reflect on the implications of this approach for your own personal and professional experience.

This approach to research may lead you to revalue your own and other people's personal and professional experiences. It may make you bolder in your use of (relevant) personal experience in your professional role and may encourage you to engage in research which is qualitative and person-focused. Much of what Graham says about research is relevant to relationships between health workers and their patients as well. The pressure of work may mean that patients are treated rather like 'objects' of care and treatment, whereas a feminist approach would emphasise patients as 'subjects'. Feminist ideas often challenge taken-for-granted views and encourage women to rethink issues which have been seen as natural and normal, such as definitions of 'full-time work' or of men as 'natural managers' (see Chapter 7).

2.8 Social constructionism and medical sociology

The next part of this chapter introduces new ideas and perspectives which have influenced health and illness research: postmodernism and social constructionism. These challenge existing accounts of the social world but, instead of proposing new 'grand theories' about how society works, they have questioned whether any one explanatory model can make sense of the world (Featherstone, 1991). In sociology they have directed attention to the social uses and power of language, focusing on how 'truth' is constructed and how meaning is culturally defined, socially learned and fluid. In particular, human subjectivity is seen as shifting and fragmentary rather than fixed for all time. What it means to be male or female, for example, is learned by people within a particular society and is relative to that society, so ideas of masculinity and femininity will always be changing.

Postmodern perspectives

Postmodernism is a broad term, used in a range of academic disciplines to describe and define trends in contemporary highly industrialised society towards greater diversity, fragmentation, conflict and pluralism. The postmodern view is that many key features of modern industrial society, such as industrial organisation, class systems, cultural and religious allegiances and political institutions, have been transformed over recent years. At the same time, intellectual traditions which underpinned modern industrial society, such as the idea of progress, the notion of society as an 'organic community', the autonomy of the individual and the supremacy of science and of rational thought have been under-mined. It is partly that we are now not so convinced that industrialisa-tion, science and modernism are unalloyed forces for progress. But it is also that highly industrialised societies are becoming fragmented, as the 'electronic revolution' and the 'commodity revolution' transform habits, attitudes, and styles of life (Willis, 1991).

In sociology, it is argued that overarching structural explanations and models of society, such as those proposed by Durkheim, Marx and Parsons, cannot be sustained. Such attempts to create 'meta-theories' which explain how a whole society works are doomed to failure, not just because they are always being challenged by counter-theories but because they represent particular and limited 'ways of seeing', which are inevitably rooted in the social relationships and processes of particular societies in particular historical periods. For example, Talcott Parsons' *The Social System* (1951) still offers us important insights into health and health work, but as an attempt to produce a grand theory of society it has been discarded. Its *cultural relativism* – that is, its projection of contemporary United States society as the normal and healthy social system – must be viewed with scepticism. It makes intellectual claims to have uncovered the 'truth' about society but, as we have seen, such claims have also been made by other sociologists. In other fields, too, experts have made 'truth claims': about the nature of the physical world (science), about human bodies (biology and medical science), about human nature (psychology) and so on.

Postmodernism can best be seen in sociological terms not as a unified theory but a search for new possibilities. In social theory it is characterised by a renewed emphasis on Weber's concept of *Verstehen* – the understanding of meaning – and on the anti-positivist philosophical tradition of *hermeneutics* – the problem of interpretation. These approaches (together with phenomenology) emphasise the ways in which social life is constituted by means of people's everyday trans-actions and taken-for-granted beliefs and interpretations. A postmodern perspective takes this as its starting point and seeks to solve the problem of how human subjects engaged in meaningful social action may be understood – not simply described and reported on, but *interpreted* – without becoming objectified in the process.

One concept which is central to the work of sociologists working within a postmodern framework is that of 'agency'. This emphasises a concern to go beyond the science based objectivism of structural theories and the liberal subjectivism of social action theories, and to develop a theory of the subject. In other words, it is hoped to avoid not only positivist 'social structure' accounts but also a collapse into subjectivism. Social action theory, as we have seen, celebrates the creativity of social actors (members, human subjects) in and on their own terms as individuals. But from a postmodern perspective we need to question this assumption.

Why do we see ourselves as 'individuals'? It is because we have constructed ourselves as such. The notion of individualism is not a 'natural' idea; it is derived from a particular way of conceptualising human beings in modern liberal thought. It is also one in which some people (men) have been seen as full individuals with voting and property rights and political power whereas others (women and children) have not (Dalley, 1988). So a new account must try to theorise the human subject from outside, as the object of sociological enquiry. These concerns with agency and the rejection of structural sociology reflect the disintegration of industrial capitalism and the fragmentation of social relations based on class:

We think that with the increasingly post-industrial structuring of contemporary capitalism, the seemingly never-ending round of economic and legitimation crises, theories of structure have lost some of their plausibility. The disorganization of capitalism and the theoretical dissolution of the social appear – in some sort of elective affinity – to be proceeding apace hand in hand.

Lash and Urry (1986)

Agency directs our attention away from structures and towards human action – not just to 'rational choice' but to passionate and intuitive concerns (Lash and Urry, 1986). In other words, it is definitely not about people as individual, conscious social actors and decision takers (as in social action theory). Instead the focus is on 'free-flowing, aesthetic and sensual notions of subjectivity', on the body as agent of conscious and unconscious senses (pleasures, desires, fantasies) and on their (intended and unintended) effects. The theory of the 'human subject' is of a shifting and fragmented being rather than the autonomous, 'whole individual' of liberal ideology.

This attempt to piece together a theory of the human subject has led to the broadening out of sociological enquiry into fields hitherto seen as distinct and distant, such as psychoanalysis and linguistics. It has drawn on post-structural literary theories about interpreting social talk, practices and beliefs as 'texts' or stories about the social world told by social actors and presenting multiple and conflicting accounts of social reality. Each 'text' has a multiple reality, each one can be interpreted in a number of ways, each plays a part in framing our relationships with other actors;

some 'texts' have even succeeded in persuading us (just as a film may convince us that what is happening on screen is real) that their versions are 'the truth'.

Social constructionism

Social constructionism can be seen as one strand in the postmodernist enquiry into meaning, subjectivity and the rest of social reality. The question of 'how we know what we know' and the focus on social reality as essentially contested have become marked features of accounts in medical sociology. In particular there has been increasing questioning of scientific positivism and, along with this, of the status of medical knowledge. Whereas Freidson (1970) demonstrated that illness was 'socially constructed', critics of scientific claims to objectivity and privileged status have claimed that disease, bodies and nature are social constructs as well.

Social constructionism treats all medical knowledge as problematic: what have been thought of as biological realities, such as diseases, come under review. Reality is seen to be far from self evident. For example, diseases do not exist 'out there' waiting to be discovered but are the product of human cognitive activity. The question to be asked shifts to why disease should be conceptualised in particular ways in particular historical periods, or why the field of medicine should be constituted in a particular way. As Wright and Treacher (1982) comment, we then go on to ask 'how should it be that certain areas of human life come – or cease – to be regarded as "medical" in particular historical circum-stances'. Some researchers have answered this by exploring how the fabrication of disease categories or other types of medical knowledge have served the interests of particular groups in society. For example, Figlio (1982) argues that the battle to construct 'miners nystagmus' as a disease category mirrored the class struggle in early twentieth century Britain.

Social constructionists have also explored the emergence of expert *discursive practices*: these are not only 'ways of seeing' and 'ways of knowing' – that is, theories about the social world – but also 'ways of doing' – interventions and techniques of discipline and control (Foucault, 1971). These are not seen merely as repressive but also as creative; they construct new configurations of social reality and new types of human subjectivity.

Foucault's theory of the body

Michel Foucault's account of the fabrication of the human body has influenced sociologists in the field of health, particularly in relation to thinking about the role of science and the development of medical practice. Because of this, we'll use some of his ideas to illustrate aspects of postmodernism and social constructionism and to illustrate some problems with these ideas.

Foucault focuses on how the human subject becomes 'embodied'; in other words, on how bodies are and have been conceptualised and on how people's views of their own (and other people's) bodies have emerged. He notes how, in industrial society, the human and social sciences increasingly developed techniques to discipline and monitor the human body, individually (through a new account of the physical and mental body) and at the level of regulating populations. New explanations of madness, disease, punishment, idleness, intelligence and sexuality gave rise to new interventions (disciplinary technologies), which together created our modern notions of identity and behaviour. Through a vast enterprise of measuring, examining, analysing and training the human and social sciences helped to create the 'docile body' and the 'therapeutic state' – with its new conceptions of what was normal/abnormal, sane/insane, healthy/sick and so on. In this account sociologists were not detached observers of society but producers (with others), through social science 'discourse', of this disciplinary society.

Let's look at the area of health and health work in more detail. In *The Birth of the Clinic* (1973) Foucault argues that the human body as we know it is not natural but has been fabricated through a 'clinical gaze'. By this he means a particular way of 'seeing and knowing' the body associated with modern biomedicine. The clinical gaze, Foucault argues, obliterated earlier ways of seeing and knowing the body, but it is only one way (albeit very persuasive and all-encompassing) of conceptualising bodies. It might itself be replaced in the future by some new 'truth':

For us the human body defines, by natural right, the space of origin and the distribution of disease: a space whose lines, volumes, surfaces, and routes are laid down, in accordance with a now familiar geometry, by the anatomical atlas. But this order of the solid visible body is only one way – in all likelihood neither the first nor the most fundamental – in which one spatialises disease. There have been, and will be, other distributions of illness.

Foucault (1973)

Two important points emerge from this theory and we will look at each in turn. First, the gaze 'created' the body we know. Its form, structure, relationships and so on we can only see and know because the anatomical atlas tells us they exist. In other words this new reality is viewed as being produced by an *epistemological shift* – a reconceptualisation of knowledge and the meaning of language. It is rooted in agency, in thought, not in changes in economic or political structures.

Second, the 'clinical gaze' when it established itself in the early nineteenth century represented not just knowledge and truth claims, but also power. Only by being trained in the use of the 'anatomical atlas' could medical students learn what they were looking at and what significance to attach to different signs, symptoms and lesions on the body. Specialist language and culture distanced the patient, and doctors developed treatment regimes ('disciplinary apparatus') to monitor and control bodies in hospitals.

○ Reflect on what you know of the rise of 'scientific medicine' in the early nineteenth century. How far does Foucault's theory fit in with this?

You may have seen things differently – as modern medicine stripping away doubts, mysteries and wrong ideas and reaching a better understanding of how the body worked. Foucault doesn't deny that pathology (and biochemistry, physiology and so on) explained the body in a way hitherto impossible; what interests him is that the body was transformed by this new account (the *'discourse'* as he calls it) into something quite different. Far from being a fixed biological entity 'waiting to be discovered', the body as we know it came into being only when the anatomical atlas allowed us to see and know it.

The account raises other issues too. The postmodernist thrust of Foucault's account is clear enough: the emphasis on ways of seeing and knowing; on shifts in knowledge and ideas; the text as a regime of 'truth'; and the absence of interest in social structures (such as class relations, professional status or industrialisation). But the apparatus of surveillance seem to leave little space for people, who become the objects of the clinical gaze. The body may have moved centre stage, but it doesn't have much freedom of action.

○ Think back to the categories we used earlier on: do these ideas link to consensus theory or to conflict theory?

You probably suggested conflict theory, but may have had some doubts about how power is exercised by ordinary people in society. Anthony Giddens (1982) argues that this type of account is in danger of being 'an objectivist type of social theory, in which human agency appears only as the determined outcome of social causes'. But Foucault himself has argued that the exercise of power is a *relationship*; power is not fixed but fluid, and where power is exercised so too is resistance. Social surveillance is not just about repression but about social construction and creativity. The modern way of thinking about ourselves – as individuals, free agents, autonomous human beings – has been brought into being by the human sciences. David Armstrong (1983a, 1993), who has applied Foucault's ideas about medical knowledge to the twentieth century, notes that patients came to participate much more in monitoring and treatment. Indeed, by the 1950s patients had become partners (subjects, not objects) in health work, which moved beyond the hospital into the whole community.

The position of science

Perhaps the most interesting aspect of Foucault's theory from the point of view of health work concerns the position of medicine in society and its relationship to science. The idea of science as linear progress and scientists as detached experimenters has increasingly come under attack. Thomas Kuhn (1970) argued that science operated within dominant frameworks of knowledge (paradigms), resistant to change, and that most research reinforced current orthodoxies. Only when the anomalies in official thinking create too many contradictions did 'scientific revolutions' force new paradigms to be adopted. Other writers have suggested that science advances as much by guesswork and backing hunches as by the orthodox experimental method (Medawar, 1985).

For Foucault the progress-focused view of medicine, its association with science and claims about the scientific method, is merely part of its claim to 'truth'. Medicine, and science itself, are successful 'ways of seeing and knowing' which have come to dominate – indeed, set the terms of – our thinking about bodies and about the natural world. But there is no reason why other 'ways of seeing and knowing' should not replace them. Medicine and science do not exist outside society – quite the reverse; they are fabricated through gazes which tell us what to look for, what to see and what 'reality' is.

○   What implications do these ideas about science and medicine have for sociology itself?

They draw our attention to the fact that sociologists, like doctors and scientists, are part of the social world about which they build theories. The sociological gaze (as other gazes, such as the medical and psychological) has played a part in fabricating the 'human subject'. David Armstrong (1983a) has argued that the notion of the human subject appeared in sociology (in social action theories) as well as in medicine (the active patient); the shift from objectivism to subjectivism in medicine was paralleled in sociology. You may have noted that in other disciplines, for example in psychology, the human subject became revalued; think of the rise of humanistic psychology associated with Abraham Maslow and Carl Rogers in the 1960s. Again, as with interactionist and ethnomethodological research approaches, nurses have been increasingly attracted to these more qualitative and subject-focused methodologies.

You might also have begun to think again about the problem of relativism. If we accept the idea that forms of knowledge are cultural products ('discourses', 'paradigms' or frameworks) made within societies, which configurate bodies, the natural world or human subjects in particular ways (so that people within a given society can no longer 'see' or 'know' them in other ways), we must admit the possibility that other, equivalent, discourses can exist as well. In the field of health it helps us to recognise the cultural specificity of Western biomedicine and to think again about alternative, non-Western systems of thought about health. Indeed, the rising interest in alternative therapies and theories about health and the body provide evidence that some revaluing of health discourses is taking place (K258, 1992).

It is important to remember that postmodernism offers possibilities, but not many answers. It is not a unified theory but a possible way of continuing the sociological project which started with Durkheim, Marx and Weber and which is heading along a number of different routes. Social constructionism is perhaps most usefully seen as one of these lines of development, although it also has its critics: recent feminist theory, for example, has challenged the ideas of Foucault on the grounds that knowledge and truth are conceptualised in terms of a masculine subject and the repression of the feminine. The sociology of the body is an important area for health workers to investigate, but postmodernism is much broader than this.

2.9 The fragmentation of social theory

Sociology is in a state of flux, brought about not just by the challenge presented by new sociological theories but also by social and political transformations. As we noted in relation to the theories of the 'founding fathers,' sociology acts upon and is influenced by the society it seeks to explain. Economic and political movements associated with industrial-isation, democracy, fascism and 1960s liberation philosophy have helped to frame the questions that sociologists have asked and to shape the answers. In the late twentieth century, fractures in 'industrial society' and the emergence of post-industrialism, and cultural and political transformations such as the collapse of Soviet communism, have helped to focus the interests of sociologists on the diversity, fragmentation, even chaos of the social world. In many ways this mirrors the flux and chaos in other domains of knowledge.

We'll be returning to many of the theories sketched here in greater detail later. So if you feel overwhelmed by sociological theory at this point, remember that you'll be directed back to this chapter at various points in the book so that you can make connections between the broad theories and perspectives discussed here and particular problems and issues in health and health work.

The uses of sociological study

There are three comments to make by way of conclusion, to direct your attention to the potential of sociological study. First, the postmodern emphasis on stories (texts) and human creativity (agency) offers a way in which sociology might assist health work in acknowledging diversity and empowering users of health services. The view of social interaction as one of people engaged in a complex process of telling and retelling, adapting and changing texts offers useful insights into how lay attitudes and values regarding health and health services are constructed (and those of health workers as well). It situates patients as creative and dynamic agents in the process of developing and changing health work. The insights to be gained in this respect provide one reason why interpretive research methods (and other approaches, such as ethnography and oral history) have recently become more widely used by health sociologists and health professionals engaged in research.

Second, it is important to realise that in many ways the current flux and controversy in sociology offers opportunities to rethink health and health work. The range of theories of different ways of coming to know about the social world offers a rich choice to the students of health. In this respect it is worth considering the implications of introducing the notion of *relativism* into the debate about knowledge. An important consequence of adopting the view that science – and any discipline which claims to be scientific – is a social activity rather than a timeless, abstract and objective method for discovering empirical facts and irrefutable laws, is that no form of knowledge has a privileged position in relation to the rest. The natural sciences, sociology and modern medicine (and other disciplines as well) have produced very successful accounts (truth claims), but they are no more special or 'true' than the claims of other disciplines and theories. Each discipline or set of theories has to be evaluated in terms of whether it does or does not convince others of its validity. We judge them on whether they are systematic and rational, consistent and soundly based, good or bad at persuading us of their validity.

This suggests a future of pluralism and conflict in sociology, but it does not mean that we have to abandon the search for truth (although we make our acceptance of any truth claim provisional). It means that we need to think about the normative (and perhaps the ethical) grounds on which we accept or reject truths, and therefore about what our vision of the 'just society', or the 'ideal future' might be. In the health field, dominated for so long by the truth claims of modern medicine, this is especially refreshing. It leads us on to think about how health may be reconceptualised, in sociological (and other) terms, to become much more than just 'an absence of disease'.

Third, this chapter points to the need to pursue a balancing act between theories of social structure and theories of social action. On the one hand social action theorists are celebrating subjectivity and postmodernists are claiming that 'all that exists' is a range of competing accounts (texts) which, at a variety of levels, individuals create and on which they draw to explain the social world. On the other hand it is difficult not to accept the existence of social constraints on individual actions. The impact on individuals and groups of various kinds of inequality or social differentiation – class, poverty, a sexual division of labour and so on – is tangible and 'real' in its effects. It is difficult to accept that society is a mental event sustained only by the interactions of agents and the patterns they share.

Social structure and social agency

When structural theorists conceptualise society in terms of social structures we need to be clear about what is and is not being claimed. Social structures do not exist other than through their manifestation in human social action; there is no society 'out there' that oppresses or protects us. As human beings we oppress or protect each other. The patterns of difference or inequality that exist are reproduced through social agency and, just as social transactions continually throw up new meanings and outcomes, so the patterning of differences continually shifts and gradually becomes transformed. Social structures, argues Anthony Giddens (1982), are never entirely static; actions to maintain social institutions do not simply reproduce but may also transform patterns of control:

In the theory of structuration, I argue that neither subject (human agent) nor object ('society', or social institutions) should be regarded as having primacy. Each is constituted in and through recurrent practices. The notion of human 'action' presupposes that of 'institution', and vice versa. Explication of this relation thus comprises the core of an account of how it is that the structuration (production and reproduction across time and space) of social practices takes place.

Giddens (1982)

This offers a way forward which enables us to bring into focus both people's everyday transactions and the on-going development and transformations of social structures. 'The most casual exchange of words', Giddens (1982) comments, 'involves the speakers in the long-term history of the language via which their words are formed, and simultaneously in the continuing reproduction of that language.' The approach exemplified in Giddens' comment gives due weight to human creativity without undervaluing the power exerted on human agents by human agency as it (re)constitutes social institutions – the family, community, class system, economic institutions, political groups and so on. In the field of health and health work it draws us on to investigate how human agency creates and transforms social institutions, and what influence this process has on users and providers of health services. But it also leaves centre stage the raw ingredients which constitute those institutional frameworks: that is, the transient encounters and personal troubles of people's everyday lives.

Suggestions for further study

To find out more about sociological theories dip into A. Giddens (1989) *Sociology*, London, Polity Press, or T. Bilton *et al.* (1987) *Introducing Sociology*, London, Macmillan. Aspects of medical sociology are discussed in B. Turner (1987) *Medical Power and Social Knowledge*, London, Sage, and social constructionism is reviewed in M. Bury (1986) 'Social constructionism and the development of medical sociology' in *Sociology of Health and Illness*, Vol. 8, pp. 137–169.

Self assessment questions

1 Define the terms 'sociology' and 'social policy'.
2 Distinguish between sociological theories of social structure and social action.
3 Explain what is meant by a 'positivist' approach in sociology and comment on its limitations.
4 What is the 'problem of gender' in sociology?
5 Discuss the main features of a 'social constructionist' approach to medical sociology.

Chapter 3

The family and health

Contents

Themes and issues

Family structure and types: normal and deviant – nuclear and extended – residence, parenthood, marriage – the traditional, modern and conjugal family – symmetrical family

Socialisation: looking-glass self – social action – social roles – gender socialisation

Social change: ideologies of the family – familism – industrialisation – family wage – gendered parental roles – gendered division of labour – double shift – the welfare state and the family: family policies – Income maintenance – benefits system

Health work in families: coping with illness – health education – family–professional relationships – the social construction of health work

Theoretical perspectives: interactionism – conflict and consensus structuralism – feminist theories – social constructionism

Learning outcomes

After working through this chapter you should be able to:
1 Comment on the role of the family in socialisation.
2 Compare and contrast functionalist and feminist accounts of family life.
3 Review the different ways in which women act as unpaid health workers.
4 Assess the value for health work of using sociological ideas about the family.

THE family is still, despite major change and challenge, a fundamental social institution with a major role in informal health work. Most children are reared in families and most caring work is undertaken by families. The family is also a complex social institution; it is both a private world and a public target. Families are at the receiving end of a great deal of offical advice and legal control: from health workers, social workers, politicians, the courts and so on. Economic and social changes – unemployment, war, migration, welfare, poverty, and the health effects of these changes – are mediated through the lived experience of family members. For all these reasons the family is an important element of the 'social context' of health work.

This chapter introduces the sociology of the family and its relation to health, and in doing so invites you to identify central theories and concepts in sociology which have been discussed in Chapter 2. It also extends your knowledge of social policy by exploring how shifting social policies and values have shaped family life. The chapter can be thought of as a 'can opener' – for investigating the family raises the lid on many important debates in sociology and social policy and enables you to sample the diversity of sociological ideas. Important concepts in sociology are introduced here: socialisation, social roles, norms and values, social change. You are also encouraged to consider different ways of 'seeing and knowing' the family and the social world. For example, some sociological theories emphasise tensions and conflicts within the family (and society) whereas others see family structure and roles as the product of social consensus. The chapter ends by noting the value of a sociological approach in illuminating the relationship between the family and health.

3.1 Studying the family

Most people spend their lives in families of one kind or another. Their experiences of family life vary considerably but, whether good or bad, they generate strong feelings about what a real family should be and how it should operate. In newspapers, television, soap operas, political meetings and pubs, discussions about values and attitudes use family relationships as their raw material for creating frameworks of social meaning and generating social ideologies.

○   Begin by defining what the term 'family' means to you.

You may well have given a description of your own family or a generalisation based on your experience of family life. You might have suggested that families usually consist of parents and children. But it might be a larger family of more than two generations, or just adults living together. You might have focused on the importance of relation-ships in family life: legal relationsips such as marriage or blood ties; or on family responsibilities, for example bringing up children, creating a home, providing a family income, 'keeping up with the Joneses'.

These points are a reminder that families are complex and tricky to investigate, and that individual experiences may create barriers to a wider and more systematic understanding of family life. People often see their own family background as 'normal' and that of others as 'deviant' or less desirable, and in health work this might lead to a lack of sympathy or a readiness to make judgements which could be prejudicial to effective patient care. As in other areas of social analysis, personal experience of family relationships provides raw material which has to be questioned and modified in the light of research findings.

This does not mean that personal experience should be ignored, but it needs to be channelled and evaluated. Our feelings and consciousness represent the means by which we confront and make sense of the social world. Inter-subjective relationships generate wider social meanings and frameworks. Both are influenced and shaped by broader social trends and ideologies, and the development of the modern family demonstrates the complex inter-relationships that result.

3.2 The family in sociology

A sociological account focuses on the family as a *set of social relationships* and investigates the range of forces that influence the interaction of the family with the wider society. Diana Gittins (1985) commented that 'families are not clear-cut, but are highly complex and often confusingly fluid social groupings'. We need to explore the cultural patterning of family life and its reproduction through socialisation, the complex interaction between class, race and gender divisions and family structures and relationships. Sociologists acknowledge the significance of internal family dynamics, but their interest lies in understanding the ways in which these are socially influenced and constructed. As we shall see, there is considerable disagreement about the nature, extent and significance of the impact of social change on the family, about how the family has mediated such change and about the survival of the family in the future.

Family structure

A useful and well-established starting point is an analysis of contemporary family structure. The mix of family types – large and small, one- or two-parent, one, two or more generations, all male, all female or of mixed sex, childless or with child(ren) – seems bewildering. But a broad distinction can be made between the *nuclear* family of two or less generations and the *extended* family of three generations and possibly

BOX 3.1 Nuclear and extended family structure

Nuclear family	Extended family
A two generation family of parent(s) and child(ren) living together. The nuclear family is seen as partly the product of industrialisation which broke up the extended family network and created the 'breadwinner' man, the dependent woman caring for/servicing her man/children and the home. (Man = producer, woman = reproducer). Nuclear families are seen as encouraging gender socialisation, though Willmott and Young researched symmetrical families: dual career families where roles were changing. The nuclear family need not be based on kinship and need not include two parents, or any children.	An extended family is where more than two generations live under the same roof, for example grandparent(s), parent(s) and child(ren). Extended families still flourish in many parts of the world, especially where the family is still the basic unit of production, for example as peasant-farmers on a patch of land, largely self sufficient and subsistence based.

other kin living together (see Box 3.1). Nuclear families predominate in industrialised or Western societies, and extended families predominate in most other parts of the world.

The apparent clarity of this distinction cannot be easily sustained, however, if we think about roles and relationships. Many conventional two-parent, two-child families have extensive local kinship ties which indicate an extended family type of relationship. Mother-in-law collects the children from school and gives them tea three times a week; grandparents regularly baby-sit in the evenings; sister-in-law (at home with small baby) looks after the children in the holidays; kin meet for family dinner on Sundays. In Graham and McKee's (1980) study of 200 mothers over 60 per cent saw their parents or their in-laws at least once a week. Roles and responsibilities in a lone-parent family may be shared out quite differently in a two-parent family; conversely the two parents may carry such unequal loads that one parent keeps the family afloat in much the same way as a lone parent might do. In some families unemployment has created an opportunity to redistribute the family labour, and in some women carry the double burden of labour in the home and in the wage economy (Graham, 1984a).

In addition, in a multi-racial society such as Britain, black and minority ethnic groups have to varying degrees upheld traditional family structures and culture. For example, many Jewish, Greek and Italian households continue to operate as extended families themselves, and family is the basis of extensive neighbourhood networking, based on religious worship and voluntary aid. On the other hand many nuclear type families can be found in such minority groups. Jocelyn Barrow (1982) suggests that Afro-Caribbean families take several different forms, ranging from 'Christian marriage' – based on the model of the Victorian family – to the 'common law family' of unmarried partners, to the 'mother household' – in which a mother or grandmother is the sole household head and manager.

It is also difficult to generalise about British Asian households; the term covers diverse population groups, such as Sikhs and Bengalis, with disparate cultural norms – concerning the social role of women, for example. In its traditional form the 'Asian marriage' is an alliance between families rather than just a union between partners, and it represents a complex blend of worldly and spiritual concerns. Education and occupational class, among other factors, have encouraged a shift to a nuclear type structure (Rapoport *et al.*, 1982). But over 10 per cent of Asian households contain more than one family, compared with only 2 per cent of Afro-Caribbean households and 1 per cent of white households (Jackson, 1993). Parmar (1988) warns against projecting damaging stereotypes of family life, commenting that 'the Afro-Caribbean family is seen as being too fragmented and weak and the Asian family seems to be unhealthily strong, cohesive and controlling of its members'.

In spite of the diversity of family arrangements among minority ethnic groups they are often presumed by health workers to live in extended families with adequate support networks for elderly dependent relatives. Recent research findings suggest that this may be an ethnocentric view. In a major study in Birmingham Cameron *et al.* (1989) discovered a high degree of felt, but unmet, need for domiciliary and day care services among older people living in black and minority ethnic households.

The distinction between nuclear and extended family structure relates to sociological investigation of the impact of social change on families. It prompts other questions: how do families organise and experience their lives? How is the work divided between the adults, and between adults and children? Does this division reflect differences in power between family members? How do families negotiate the division of roles and responsibilities? How much choice and scope for change do families have? To begin to answer these questions draws us on to an analysis of the dynamic social, political and economic context of contemporary nuclear family life.

Residence, parenthood and marriage

A second overlapping approach is to establish the significant social and legal relationships that characterise families. *Residence, parenthood* and *marriage* are frequently seen as central, indeed necessary, features (Gittins, 1985). This is a reminder that family may be a biological linkage, a legal tie or an informal agreement about common housekeeping; it may well be a combination of these, and a quick survey of your friends and neighbours would probably reveal a number of variations. While marriage is still very popular as an institution, divorce and common law marriage are increasingly widespread, and growing numbers of children are born outside marriage (see Figure 3.1). Common residence and shared housekeeping may become the 'bottom line' of definition in the future. Whereas Afro-Caribbean 'mother household' types are some-

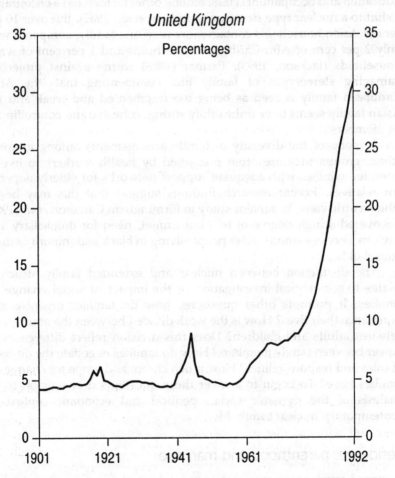

FIGURE 3.1 Live births outside marriage as a percentage of all births.
Source: *Social Trends* (1994)

times viewed as 'deviant' by local authority housing departments – and by some health and social workers – this all-female household pattern has now become much more common.

But even if families decreasingly display all three characteristics, it is still difficult to conceive of a family which has none of them. What about the six million people who live alone? These individuals may have strong family and kinship ties but they aren't families. To avoid excluding them sociologists increasingly use the word 'household', a more neutral yet less definitive term (Graham, 1984a).

The role of the family in society

A third approach to defining the family is to focus on what families do in contemporary society: their perceived *social roles* and actions. Perhaps the most significant of these is the regulation of sex and sexual expression through formal legal constraints and informal sanctions and rituals. Adultery and cruelty are well established grounds for divorce, but until very recently the law made an important distinction between sexual behaviour in- and outside marriage. Rape within marriage was only established as a criminal offence in 1991.

Families have generally been, and still are, the channel through which property and wealth are accumulated and inherited. They perform a vital economic role in supporting the present workforce and in its reproduction, and they are major consumers of the goods and services produced. Families also play a major part in maintaining and restoring the health of their members, as well as in taking on new responsibilities for the care of dependent relatives. Family members mediate between the dependent sick and formal health care services, and they perform other informal health work, such as seeking advice from doctors and visiting people in hospital (Graham, 1992, and see Section 3.3).

As in earlier times, families today play a major part in shaping the attitudes and values of children in their early years and continue to be influential in the upbringing of older children. Sociologists speak of the *conjugal* family as shorthand for the private, intimate family grouping of parents and children, so that 'mothering', 'fathering' and 'parenting' represent key family roles and notions of affection, intimacy and caring become attached to them. It is worth remembering that such notions, like that of 'romantic love' or 'partnership', are of fairly recent origin compared with the historic predominance within marriage of concern for ownership and inheritance (Shorter, 1975). Studying the family by means of its social roles is therefore very rewarding, because it emphasises hidden aspects of the family, and links it emphatically to economic and political structures. But investigating 'roles' has its drawbacks; traditional ideas about 'normal' and necessary roles in the family tend to emerge, as do ideas about 'abnormal' and unnatural ones.

Sociological debates

For a long time functionalist accounts were dominant, characterising the family as an unproblematic 'building block' in society. In functionalist analysis the universality of the family has been emphasised – a phenomenon which seems to exist in every known society. Parsons (1951) saw the family as serving universal human and social needs. This universalism has often been linked to biological factors: in particular the different reproductive roles of men and women, the lengthy depend- ence of infants upon adult nurturing and the consequent need for a division of labour so that care and material resources – food, shelter, clothing – can be provided. This type of analysis has produced a rather static account, emphasising the family's roles in modern society and the efficiency of the nuclear family structure in meeting the needs of individuals for intimacy, security and sexual expression as well as the needs of the wider economy and society. In recent years this approach has been criticised because it tends to make fundamental assumptions about what the family is, and what its essential roles and functions are, without enough acknowledgement of definitional problems, hidden assumptions and social change (Gittins, 1985).

Feminists in particular have challenged the stereotype of the 'cereal packet' family which appears in advertising – breadwinner husband, dependent wife and two children. This accounts for only about a quarter of British households today. The projection of this as 'normal' family life has helped to underwrite the subordination of women and other dependants and the domination of men (Moore, 1988). In social policy the New Right has viewed the decline of the 'normal' family as linked to – and largely responsible for – a wider moral crisis involving increasing lawlessness, deviance and welfare dependency (Fitzgerald, 1985). Feminists, in contrast, have emphasised the heavy emotional and financial price paid by women in families with traditional gender roles, where they have little autonomy or emotional support and are responsible for all domestic labour (Finch and Groves, 1983). Most sexual and physical violence towards women, and most abuse of children, occurs within the home. The rising divorce rate, and the fact that 73 per cent of divorces are initiated by women, suggests that more and more women are escaping from marriages in which they do not feel loved and valued, and perhaps 'a growing disillusion with the institu- tion' itself (Jackson, 1993).

Feminist accounts have also highlighted the enormous variation of family forms and the varied meanings attached to the term family in different cultures (Edholm, 1982). The use of anthropological findings demonstrates that what seems natural and biological is culturally constructed within a given society. Ideas about fatherhood and motherhood, about conception, birth and child-rearing, and about relationships between parent(s) and children, have changed over time and across cultures (Moore, 1988). This raises questions about the assumed 'fit' between family structure and roles on the one hand and society's needs on the other, and draws attention to instability and oppression in family life. In particular the pervasiveness of the ideology of *familism* has been noted in debates about the family: that is, the assumption that a gendered division of labour and the continued separation of public and private spheres is 'natural' and proper, and that the family should be the locus of caring (Dalley, 1988, and Box 3.2). Such a claim reinforces and reproduces women's oppression at home and at work (Barrett and McIntosh, 1982).

The cultural relativism of accounts of mothering and child-rearing has been noted in social constructionist research as well. Not only has expert advice about mothering shifted dramatically over the last 150 years, but the intellectual and scientific conception of the child has constantly changed. Children have been seen as 'biological blueprints', as 'a seething mass of unconscious sexuality and aggression' and as 'almost infinitely flexible receptacles of specific socialisation practices' (Rex Stainton Rogers, 1993). Although the traditional explanation for such differences of interpretation has been that science is steadily 'moving closer to the truth', another way of looking at the issue is to see all accounts as social constructions 'fabricated' (in Foucault's term) by interested and powerful voices. In the same way as medical science fabricated the body, the science of child-rearing 'constructed' the child.

BOX 3.2 Familism. Source: Dalley (1988)

The ideology of *familism* (Dalley, 1988) or *familialism*, as Barrett and McIntosh (1982) have termed it, projects a particular view of the family and of the roles of its various members. It is based on the assumption that the family, and in particular the nuclear family, with breadwinner male and dependent female and child(ren), is the normal and natural unit for nurturing and caring. 'It is the standard against which all forms are measured and, importantly, judged. Thus within, and according to, the ideology of familism, non-family forms are deemed to be deviant and/or subversive' (Dalley, 1988).

Familism is projected as an ideology: that is, as a set of dominant ideas and values which persuade individuals to think and act in certain ways. Its success means that it is internalised and defended by many individuals 'even though its dominance may, objectively, run counter to their interests. And if they fail to achieve the required standard, then they perceive themselves as deviant' (Dalley, 1988).

In this view Sigmund Freud's discovery of the 'Oedipus Complex' (every little boy's secret wish to kill his father and possess his mother) is not so much a discovery as an invention which reflected and reinforced cultural processes and interactions between experts and lay people.

3.3 The family and socialisation

In all ages and in most societies families have been largely responsible for the rearing of children. One key aspect of this is the *socialisation* of children: that is, their internalisation of social *norms*, *beliefs* and *values* which enables the transmission of culture between generations (see Box 3.3). Sociologists distinguish between processes of *primary* socialisation and of *secondary* socialisation, between the first few years of a child's social life and the experiences of the older child moving toward adulthood (see Box 3.4). But they hold different views about how socialisation processes operate. Broadly speaking the distinction is between theories which emphasise socialisation as a negotiated process in which norms and values are voluntarily internalised, and theories which focus on the coercive dimension of socialisation. In this latter view people are socialised into social conformity by the demands and persuasion of (more powerful) others.

A social action approach

Investigation of primary socialisation processes was an important aspect of the work of social action theorists, such as Mead and Cooley (see Section 2.6). They suggested that very young children have to learn social selfhood and that this is constructed in terms of negotiation between the child, the immediate family and significant others. The child learns appropriate patterns of social action by observing and absorbing how other people act in various situations, and by how they respond to the child's actions. This negotiation within the child, between the assertion of self and the maintenance of individuality on the one hand and the building of social self through the reflected impressions and responses of significant actors on the other, creates a third dimension: the *looking-glass self* suggested by Cooley (Cuff *et al.*, 1992). In other words young children receive an impression of how others see them (the mirror view of themselves) and begin to learn how to manipulate this identity to project selective images. For example, children who learn that parental anger may be defused if conciliatory gestures and language are used at once, or if they can make their parents laugh, might adopt such action as a regular strategy to enable them to

BOX 3.3 Norms, beliefs and values

Norms	Beliefs	Values
Norms define appropriate behaviour and attitudes for particular social situations and social roles. Thus the social role of the nurse requires conformity to certain unwritten rules about dress, hygiene, punctuality, behaviour on the ward and so on. These are internalised during nurse training so that the nurse carries them out without having to think about them. Norms may be constructive, but also destructive of a person's individuality and of her attitude to others, such as patients. Norms often relate to particular subcultures, and conflicting norms may exist in society about how certain situations should be viewed or what behaviour is appropriate: for example, football match violence may be accepted/condemned/ seen as an essential part of the game.	Beliefs are sets of ideas (religious, political, racial) which individuals or groups – or a whole society – accepts and regards as centrally important and which rest upon a basis of faith rather than rationality. Religious belief is perhaps the best example, but beliefs about the superiority of one race over another or in one political party as holding the real political truth are also based ultimately on faith by the individual or the group.	Values are ideas/ideals which individuals, groups or a whole society sets up as being of supreme importance. 'I have my own values' often means that the individual has her own moral code of conduct, set of priorities and so on, which may set her apart from other groups and enable her to identify with one particular group. Values underlie norms and give them their particular characteristics. For a whole society particular values may exist. In our society, for example, a high value is placed upon work and productivity – measured by wages and output, so women (who don't get paid if they are housewives and don't produce goods for sale) or the unemployed often seem to be viewed as of lesser value. Values may be seen as general social attitudes/ideas which are difficult to change.

continue a censored activity – like throwing their dinner out of the highchair on to the kitchen floor.

Children are seen as social actors who can express and build their own individuality rather than merely modelling their behaviour upon the examples and responses of others. This 'psyching out' or 'learning to

BOX 3.4 Socialisation

Primary socialisation	Secondary socialisation
The early stages of the child's life when she/he begins to relate to the family and to significant others. Through the use of language/actions by itself and others the child learns appropriate behaviour/verbal response/attitudes for particular situations and gradually learns to generalise these situations and the other people it meets. The child sees itself increasingly through the eyes of other people – through others' reactions to itself (the looking-glass self) – and this conditions (to some extent) its behaviour.	Begins when the child's immediate family circle is expanded – through playgroup, school and so on – at around four or five years. The child is now influenced by the school environment, by teachers, by peer group. Gender socialisation is particularly strong at this stage; a 'pecking order' for classroom and playground develops. Secondary socialisation can be used to explain further socialisation throughout life – for work, changing jobs, new roles (husband, grandfather, widower, retired and so on). Most of these states require the learning of new habits/attitudes/behaviour/beliefs and values which is what happens in the process of socialisation.

play the game' enters a new stage in secondary socialisation when children begin to act upon a wider stage: at school, within a peer group and with a growing circle of significant others. They play an increasingly large number of different social roles, but these roles are negotiated in a complex sequence of interaction so that the same social role – say that of a nursing student – may be interpreted in many different ways. Individuals have an array of different roles – daughter, girl, sister, student nurse, granddaughter, lead guitarist in a rock group, girlfriend – but what they make of these roles and how they choose to 'play' them depends on how they 'write the script' (Goffman, 1959).

In relation to gendering and inequality in family life, social action theorists emphasise the diversity of social interpretations made by individuals of the role of daughter, student nurse, girl, sister and so on, and your student peer group might provide considerable evidence to support this view. 'Being a good daughter' might be constructed by one student as becoming socially and financially independent and accomplished by means of a yearly visit home and a few phone calls, but be seen as an active caring role by another. A whole process of negotiation conducted from childhood, not just the immediate circumstances, will influence how the role is performed. The influence of families, peer groups and subcultures will be negotiated in different ways by different individuals, so that generalised social ideologies of femininity and masculinity mask the myriad ways in which people actually act, think and feel. Even if people outwardly conform to 'accepted' patterns of behaviour, they will do this selectively and their real thoughts and feelings will emerge in their other social actions. This suggests that gendering may be less complete or constraining than it appears, and that families may create a negotiated order that does not necessarily mirror formal social relationships.

A structural view of socialisation

In contrast to this, we might highlight the ways in which individuals are influenced and moulded to fit into a given culture and society (see Section 2.5). The thoughts and feelings people have, the way these are expressed in social behaviour and their underlying motivations are slowly and carefully constructed or constrained through socialisation. This isn't a conscious process of negotiation; indeed, its success and power lies in people's lack of awareness that it is taking place at all. Norms, values and beliefs are largely imposed, either with the consent of the individual or by coercive means. For example, higher status and material rewards may follow as a consequence of certain types of behaviour and conformity to particular views and values, and this may persuade people to internalise norms.

Without some kind of shared value and belief system and some degree of agreement (forced or willing) on the limits of acceptable behaviour social life would be impossible. Key social institutions – government, family, schools and so on – create and reproduce dominant values and beliefs. There may be disagreement as to whether this is achieved through a process of coercion and conflict or delegated authority, but the view that each social actor is able to negotiate within society is met with scepticism.

A structural approach emphasises ideological or material influences and constraints on individual behaviour and suggests that the patterning and gendering of family inequality derives from the wider society. People have relatively little room for manoeuvre; most of their choices turn out to be predictable from their social background and upbringing. Perceptions of the 'good daughter' role, for example, will derive from a particular combination of class, race and gender influences upon socialisation which leave the individual with a sharply restricted range of possible action.

Nevertheless, there are problems with this view. For example, primary socialisation has been viewed as the crucial stage in which children learn maleness or femaleness. These definitions are socially produced and are mediated through the actions and attitudes of adults and other children. People are 'socially conditioned' into masculinity and femininity. In secondary socialisation these images are reinforced and elaborated. In this way gender socialisation plays a part in maintaining the unequal distribution of power and labour within the family. But as Stacey (1993) comments:

How do we account for the many different forms of femininity which exist in society; how do we explain changes within the lives of individual women and in broader historical terms; and finally, how do we explain the emergence of resistance movements such as feminisim if we have all been successfully socialised to accept our subordination?

Stacey (1993)

One way has been to suggest that femininity or masculinity have meant different things at different times in history and in other cultures. Although we perceive being a 'woman' or a 'man' as a stable experience, they are really fluid and changing identities and meanings which have been socially produced. These ideas, which are associated with a social constructionist approach, draw our attention to the extent to which particular accounts – ideologies, media images, expert theories, official views – shape our thinking about ourselves and our bodies.

3.4 Social change and the family

How 'modern' is the modern family? How did current perceptions of normality – in terms of size, roles, structure, values – come to exist? To what extent, and why, have family structures and roles changed? These questions are still being hotly contested by sociologists, historians and anthropologists, among others, and in this section we'll review the current state of the debate. If the answers remain inconclusive, it is because questions of interpretation and of ideology continue to be important, as they have been in the past.

Certain trends in family size and structure are fairly well established, for example the rapid decline in the birth rate from the 1850s, in adult

TABLE 3.1 Changing family size. Source: Lewis (1980), GHS (1987)

Date of marriage	Number of children	
	Non-manual	Manual
1900/9	2.79	3.94
1935/9	1.73	2.94
1971	2.43*	
1992	1.80*	
(* = n/m and manual combined)		

mortality from the 1870s and in infant mortality rather later, from the 1890s. By the 1940s completed family size was down to more or less its present level among non-manual workers and only slightly higher among manual workers (see Table 3.1).

○ Comment on how you would interpret the trends shown in Figures 3.2 and 3.3.

It would be tempting to argue that, as fewer babies died, so fewer live births were needed to create the same population, and this explains the falling fertility rate. But fertility was falling erratically before infant mortality rates fell, suggesting a response to other factors; the spread of contraception and the rising standard of living of the mass of the population have been the most popular explanations. Political concern over declining fertility in the late Victorian era, when infant deaths were still high, was a major factor in the growth of infant and maternal welfare services like health visiting, and parents were denounced as selfish and worldly for enjoying their prosperity and limiting their family size (Lewis, 1980). Later in the 1910s and 1920s, as more babies survived, the fertility rate dipped more sharply, suggesting that parents were responding to the higher survival rates of their offspring.

Another dramatic shift was the result of enhanced survival beyond infancy, resulting in a larger adult population forming more families and producing children. Although individual family size fell, the UK population rose as the effects of survival worked as a kind of multiplier

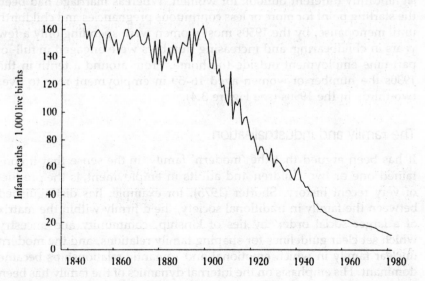

FIGURE 3.2 Infant mortality rates, England and Wales 1846–1982. Source: Oakley (1984)

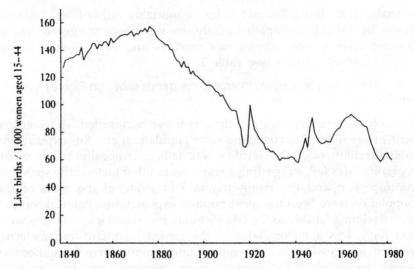

FIGURE 3.3 Fertility rates, England and Wales 1838–1982. Source: Oakley (1984)

in society. The existence of larger numbers of elderly people in the 1990s is largely explained by falling infant mortality and the multiplier effect, rather than by greater life expectancy in old age.

A third implication is more difficult to tease out. As the birth rate, infant death rate, and completed family size fell, they created a significantly different outlook for women. Whereas marriage had been the starting point for more or less continuous pregnancies and childbirth until menopause, by the 1950s most women were spending only a few years in childbearing, and increasing numbers were engaged in full- or part-time employment outside the home. From around a tenth in the 1930s the number of women aged 16–59 in employment rose to over two-thirds in the 1990s (see Figure 3.4).

The family and industrialisation

It has been argued that the 'modern' family, in the sense that it con- tained one or two children and adults in employment, is the product of very recent history. Shorter (1975), for example, has distinguished between the family in traditional society, 'held firmly within the matrix of a larger social order' by ties of kinship, community and ancestry which set clear guidelines for shaping family relations, and the modern nuclear family in which emotional and romantic relationships became dominant. His emphasis on the internal dynamics of the family has been questioned, but the link between the nuclear family and modern in- dustrial society is an important one.

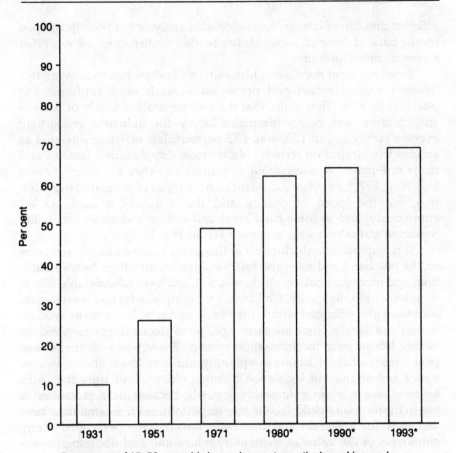

Percentage of 15–59 year olds in employment or actively seeking work
* 16–59 year olds

FIGURE 3.4 Women in employment. Source: *Social Trends* (1994)

There are two conflicting accounts of the origins of the nuclear family in the West: the first claims that it evolved as a response to the needs of industrial capitalism; the second argues that it has a much longer, pre-industrial history (Dalley, 1988). One account suggested that the nuclear family came into prominence in Britain on the heels of industrialisation and mechanisation within a capitalist mode of economic organisation (Parsons and Smelser, 1959). This view contrasted the modern nuclear family with the traditional extended family of several generations living together in pre-industrial societies in the contemporary world. The nuclear family was seen as representing an efficient adaptation of family structure to social needs: to raise the next generation, support the wage earner, create a home. The nuclear family was functionally superior: mobile, more adaptable, with a highly efficient division of labour. A considerable analysis has been developed on the back of these ideas which has tended to disparage the extended family as more 'primitive'.

Evidence from population historians and others has challenged this 'linear progress' model and presented a much more confused and puzzling picture. They claim that the two generation family of parents and children was very widespread before the industrial revolution: average family size in 1750 was 4.75 persons; late marriage operated as an effective control on fertility; higher mortality denuded families and made one-parent families about as common as they are today (Laslett and Wall, 1972). Families did adapt to new types of industrial organisation, but the speed of change and the demands it made varied enormously, and in some rural areas and cottage industries family life remained virtually unchanged until World War I.

It is important to distinguish at this point between family structure on the one hand and roles and relationships on the other. Industrialisation, and more particularly mechanisation, did have considerable effects on roles within the family. Children, for example, who had been largely socialised and educated within the family and who had usually worked within the family from an early age, were decreasingly required as factory labour once mechanisation spread. There was widespread use (and abuse) of child labour in spinning mills, in chain shops, in coal mines and so on, but legislation banning child labour from the 1840s became slowly more enforceable – partly because new processes in many trades made child labour less important. At the same time new demands for a literate and numerate labour force persuaded many employers of the value of elementary education, and declining opportunities in many industries convinced parents that child wages could be dispensed with. Indeed, there was active hostility in many trades to child labour because of its cheapening effect on adult wages. The concept of 'childhood' had been invented, a vital aspect of the contemporary family carrying with it a notion of dependence and an ideology of innocence that played a major part in shaping twentieth century welfare policy.

The position of women and their role within the family was also massively influenced by industrial change. Before the industrial revolution women had been constrained in many ways, by legislation and ideology. Many skilled trades, most education and much of public life was closed to them, but as widows women could continue their husband's trade (Davidoff and Hall, 1987). Single women and poor women had always worked in the narrow range of domestic and caring jobs open to them. The predominance of domestic employment gave women considerable opportunities to combine housekeeping and child-rearing with paid work as weavers, spinners, knitters, lacemakers and so on. In the nineteenth century the mechanisation of these trades pushed women out of employment, changes in business organisation pushed them out of business life and legal changes prevented them entering the professions.

Middle class women were increasingly constrained by an ideology which constructed them as 'angels of the hearth' keeping the home as 'the haven in a heartless world' for their husbands and supervising the proper upbringing of their children (Hall, 1989). Working class women, feared as cheap labour by men, were increasingly segregated into a narrow range of low paid industrial jobs characterised as semi-skilled and unskilled, complementing the poorly paid 'domestic' work that had always been open to them. This domestic sector grew enormously; in the 1880s one in five of all women workers were employed as servants. For these women too the ideology of motherhood and homemaking was a powerful influence. The symbol of Victorian respectability was a clean and ordered home and a full-time wife and mother to run it.

The family wage earned by the 'breadwinner' man was the third dimension of this redistribution of roles and relationships within the family. Unionised labour, employers and the state co-operated to restrict women's work and redefine wives and children as dependants; the corollary of this was the necessity for a wage sufficient to keep the nuclear family afloat. The concept of the breadwinner, arising in middle class households in the eighteenth century, was a widespread demand voiced by skilled workers in the nineteenth century (Gittens, 1985). Employers and state legislation acknowledged and increasingly accepted it, though there were always many insecure, poorly paid and unskilled jobs for men as well as women, where the idea of a family wage clearly didn't apply; dockyard work and agricultural labour are two examples.

These changing roles created new relationships within the family. Men in most societies most of the time have been dominant within the family, and this male control in private relationships has been reinforced by male control of public life from earliest times. This more recent exclusion of women from much of paid work, their reorientation as exclusively domestic workers and the dependence of children increased the private and public power of men. In the family, as in all work and public life, men ruled and women and children obeyed, a position reinforced by their legal control over property and their wives' and children's bodies.

Power and control in family life today

This social production of exclusive male and female roles within the family was reinforced by the elaboration of an ideology of *biological essentialism*: that is, of a notion of 'natural' biological differences between the sexes determining their distinct social roles. This was underpinned by a grim reality of legal and political inequality and is still reflected in the gendering of roles and distribution of power within many nuclear families today. But how widespread and significant are these features in contemporary Britain? It might be argued that industrialisation, in the longer run, has brought women considerable opportunities for access to paid work and higher status, and legislative changes have created much greater equality of opportunity between women and men. Researchers have detected the emergence of a *symmetrical* family, nuclear in structure, with men and women workers sharing household tasks and taking joint responsibility for children (Wilmott and Young, 1973). This might suggest that discussion of nineteenth century change is largely irrelevant to an analysis of late twentieth century British society.

○   Suggest some other reasons why past social change might not be helpful in explaining the position of the family today.

In the first place, many features of earlier industrialisation are no longer significant today. The largely male industrial labour force has been transformed, and women now form 41 per cent of the workforce. Male strongholds in the core industries of Victorian industry – coal, iron and steel, shipbuilding, textiles – have been transformed or marginalised, and their once skilled and strongly unionised workforces have shrunk in numbers, prestige and power. Old ideologies justifying job segregation on the basis of biological differences in strength or dexterity can no longer be sustained, and the greater integration of men and women as workers has greatly influenced work sharing in the home as well.

   In addition, professional careers from which women were excluded by social pressure and legislation are now open, and increasing numbers of women are entering medicine, law, accountancy, finance and management and even the church. In all kinds of work women are becoming equal earners and equal contributors to family income. If women as well as men can earn a family wage, the concept of the breadwinner must be undermined, and women will increasingly expect equal control of finance and resources in the home. Pahl (1981) commented that women could use their position in the formal economy:

To renegotiate their previously subordinate position in the domestic economy. Socialising their husbands into their role as partners in the reproduction of labour power is easier when, at a pinch, they could manage without their husbands altogether.

Pahl (1981)

The rise of welfare services in the twentieth century has provided support for the family in raising children and caring for dependent relatives. Birth control and the reduction in family size have made mothering an activity more compatible with paid labour. Domestic gadgetry, slum clearance and the imposition of national standards in house building, improved transport and supermarket shopping have made housekeeping less onerous and more acceptable as a responsibility shared between men and women. For example men, accompanied by their children, are increasingly taking responsibility for the weekly expedition to the supermarket.

At the same time, as industrial and social change has made gender segregation a thing of the past, so legislative change has enforced the equality of women in the workplace, enabled women to claim legal status as heads of household, reformed the bias against women in the tax system, made divorce easier and enforced the rights of women and children to property and personal choice. In short the family as a whole, and especially its dependent members, could be argued to have evolved to a position today in which power, resources, rights and responsibilities are far more equally shared. This has been reflected in the changing ideology of the family to an emphasis on mutuality, companionship and democracy rather than obedience, subordination and hierarchy.

Inequality in family life

But how much significance should be attached to such changes? How complete are they, and have they been accompanied by a revolution in public ideas about what 'normal' families should be like? It might be argued that in spite of twentieth century social changes, and not denying their importance, many of the characteristic features of the old style nuclear family – role segregation, inequalities in power and in control of resources, differential access to the job market and unequal social status – still remain largely intact in late twentieth century Britain. In addition the rhetoric of equality within families is just that; rhetoric unmatched by deeper changes in family structure or social attitudes.

○   Reflect on this argument. What evidence might be used to demonstrate that resources, power and responsibilities are still unequally distributed within families?

The findings of the General Household Surveys (which investigate patterns of family life and are published in the form of an annual report) might be used to demonstrate that *gendered parental roles* are still a common feature of family life. In families with children the vast majority of housekeeping and childcare is still undertaken by women. Men may do the supermarket shopping – far more men than women have access to a car – but women still do most of the shopping, and the cooking, washing and ironing and cleaning too. Women take and fetch children

TABLE 3.2 Domestic division of labour. Source: Social Trends (1985)

	Married people[1]		
	Actual allocation of tasks		
	Mainly man	Mainly woman	Shared equally
Household tasks (percentage allocation)			
Washing and ironing	1	88	9
Preparation of evening meal	5	77	16
Household cleaning	3	72	23
Household shopping	6	54	39
Evening dishes	18	37	41
Organisation of household money and bills	32	38	28
Repairs of household equipment	83	6	8
Child-rearing (percentage allocation)			
Looks after the children when they are sick	1	63	35
Teaches the children discipline	10	12	77

[1] 1 120 married respondents, except for the questions on actual allocation of child-rearing tasks which were answered by 479 respondents with children under 16.

from school, take time off work if children are sick, nurse children and care for dependants (see Table 3.2). In particular, they undertake most of the intimate and 'dirty' caring jobs.

Most female work is either part-time or is negotiated to enable women to combine housekeeping and mothering with paid labour. This *double shift* of paid labour and unpaid household labour is still normal in the vast majority of nuclear families; indeed the predominance today of the nuclear family (in spite of the variations in form that have been mentioned) reinforces the double shift. There are no other female family members to help out. Thus women negotiate and enter the job market with family responsibilities foremost in their minds. A *gendered division of labour* within the home is reinforced by paid work. Women may go out to work to provide the crucial extra money to keep the household going, but that job must be made compatible with family roles and responsibilities (Graham, 1984a). Note that the ideology of 'familism' (Dalley, 1988) reinforces this situation by emphasising that family care is best and that it is also one of the integral 'functions' of the family – whether nuclear or extended. Diana Gittins (1985) has argued that:

For women . . . the family household never can be a refuge from the demands of work and society. Arguably, a women's only 'refuge' in contemporary society is escaping domestic drudgery by entering the labour market – but that is only an escape from one set of demands to another . . . The way in which concepts of 'work' and 'family' are treated as totally separate categories and spheres is fallacious.

Gittins (1985)

Women's wages are currently an average two-thirds of male wages, and most wives or female partners are taking home less money than their men. This 'secondary' labour for 'extra' family income still contrasts with the 'primary' labour and 'breadwinner' wage of most men. We'll explore these issues further in Chapter 7.

Divorce and separation may be easier nowadays, but women are far more likely to end up in poverty as a result of the process than men. The ideology of mothering and women's role in childcare means that far more women than men get custody of the children, and their lower earning power means that women are more likely to have to depend on social security payments from the state while their children are young, rather than being able to continue working and pay a nanny or housekeeper. Over 50 per cent of fathers fail to keep up their maintenance payments to their children and ex-wives and nearly 50 per cent lose touch with their ex-families within two years.

Women are, of course, much less likely to be working when their children are very young anyway. The lack of state nursery provision reinforces the dominant view that young children should be looked after by their mothers at home; if they do work, provision for childcare remains largely a private responsibility to be met out of net income after taxation. The emerging labour shortages in some skilled work, which has enticed a few employers like Lloyds Bank to provide workplace crèches, have not changed this position, except that the employer is taxed instead.

The realities of work and pay and the distribution of domestic labour reinforce an ideology of gender segregation built on a basis of biological essentialism. Legal and economic change has not produced a widespread restructuring of family roles and power because the ideology is so difficult to shift at a grass roots level: that is, through negotiation within individual families. The reproduction of attitudes and values initially takes place, by and large, in families through the process of socialisation, though the construction of norms and values is the result of conflict and negotiation within the wider society.

3.5 The impact of the welfare state on family life

Modern welfare policies have had a dramatic impact upon families, in spite of the fact that the family has always been idealised as a private territory. Sayings like 'The Englishman's home is his castle' and 'I can do what I like in the privacy of my own home' express this sense of the social autonomy of family life. The reality has been increasing constraint; the shaping of family life that accompanied factory legislation, public health acts and the rise of elementary education was reinforced fairly rapidly by maternal and child welfare provision, the regulation of midwifery, the emergence of health visiting, of social case work and the growth of a breadwinner-focused social security system. The fierce arguments that raged over these interventions in family life were stilled by the particular construction of such policies. The responsibility of parents to provide for their families was re-emphasised; to avoid the danger that parents might shirk their role, early welfare work was largely directed at educating women to become better mothers. They were exhorted to stay at home, improve housekeeping and budgeting, follow expert advice and improve the health of the next generation by breastfeeding their babies (Lewis, 1980).

Indeed the 'new Liberalism' of the period from 1906 to 1914 acted boldly in relation to children. Children were the citizens, workers and soldiers of the future, but almost 50 per cent of volunteers for the Boer War (1899–1901) were found to be medically unfit. A Royal Commission report of 1903 detailed what it termed the physical and mental deterioration of those living in the inner areas of the great cities, and there was considerable alarm over the falling birth rate, in particular because this was more dramatic in middle class families than in the working class. *Eugenics* – the science of breeding to create a 'healthy' population – became, not for the first or last time, a fashionable intellectual talking point. After 1908 children were regularly submitted to medical inspection in schools, the poorest children could obtain free school meals, child abuse became a punishable offence and the school leaving age was raised to 13. Childhood was being redefined as a separate and special sphere where legal protection was appropriate.

This official concern for mothers and children was matched only slowly and grudgingly by income maintenance policies for families, although the surveys of Charles Booth and Joseph Rowntree in the 1890s had demonstrated that it was lack of income (through ill health, age or unemployment) and not drink or fecklessness which was the major cause of poverty (see Section 6.2). The 1908 Old Age Pensions Act provided an income supplement which, if added to savings or income, would prevent recourse to the workhouse. It was paid to men over 70 and women over 65 and saved local boards of guardians more in poor law charges than it cost the Exchequer in hard cash. The 1911 National Insurance Act was the second tentative policy acknowledgement that factors beyond individual control might require state intervention; it created a legal framework requiring a limited number of low paid or vulnerable groups of workers to contribute, along with their employers and the state, to a sickness, unemployment and pension scheme.

Only after 1945 was this modest initiative translated into a general National Insurance Act which aimed to provide a 'safety net' of standard individual contributions and benefits for sickness, old age and un-employment, although mass unemployment and unrest in the 1920s and 1930s did encourage the extension of the means-tested 'dole'. The 1946 National Insurance Act created a comprehensive system of income maintenance, but the aim was to underwrite, not supersede, the ability of breadwinners to provide adequately for their families. It did not provide a full replacement wage in time of sickness or unemployment, because responsible earners were expected to be able to supplement state benefits from savings and insurance. The families of 'irresponsible' breadwinners might suffer considerable privation, but this was a necessary feature of the act. Set within a framework of economic policies designed to deliver 'full employment', the act assumed that unemploy-ment and sickness were temporary states. For the permanently disabled, chronic sick and for war widows long term pensions and allowances were available. The scheme began as a strictly actuarial one; incomings balanced outgoings, and if individuals ran out of entitlement they had to apply under the National Assistance scheme. They then received *means-tested* benefits: that is, benefits which were given only if people's income and savings were deemed to fall below a certain threshold.

Brian Jackson (1982) pointed out that in the post-war welfare system the state treated different types of families in very unequal ways:

State support for widows was built into the very fabric of the welfare state. Support for one parent families was not . . . There was a general reluctance to become involved in difficult questions of illegitimacy, marriage breakdown and divorce. As a consequence, unmarried mothers, divorced, deserted or separated wives were left entirely out of the new policy which shapes today's world. That is one major origin of their poverty today.

Jackson (1982)

Much of this framework of benefits is still visible today. There are still distinctions between national insurance and means-tested benefits, but the system has been modified in several significant ways.

○   Note down what you see as being the main elements of the income maintenance system today.

Your comments probably included some of the following key contem-porary features: Child Benefit; Family Credit, Income Support; Housing Benefit; Community Care Allowances. You may also have noted other, less obvious, aspects of income maintenance, such as mortgage relief.

National Insurance is still paid by almost every worker, but contributions are graduated according to earnings. National Health Service treatment does not depend upon insurance contributions, but state old age pensions and unemployment benefit require a sufficient contribution record and provide a standard benefit.

Child Benefit was developed in the 1970s to replace child tax allowances and give all families with children – in particular the prime carer, usually the mother – a small income which was independent of the breadwinner wage, and thus combat child poverty. *Family Credit* is a means-tested benefit which was developed in the 1970s for low earning families with children. It was designed to combat family poverty by supplementing family income. In 1993 single parents (who are mainly women) were encouraged to return to work by the raising of the disregard on earned income.

National Assistance is now called *Income Support* and is still available as a range of means-tested benefits for part-time workers and non-earners, not only the long term unemployed but also pensioners, carers and lone parents. It has expanded massively, far outstripping the residual role envisaged for it in 1945, partly because of the growth of long term unemployment and the increasingly large number of poor elderly people.

Housing Benefit was developed as a separate means-tested system to provide support for council and private tenants, but it also supports many old people in private and local authority residential and nursing homes through the board and lodging allowance. The cost of providing housing benefit to council and private tenants is still considerably less than the cost to the government of tax relief on house mortgages. This is income maintenance too, as are fringe benefits at work, such as company cars and lunch vouchers, although they aren't usually seen as such (Titmuss, 1968).

There are several important additional allowances and pensions available for disabled and chronically sick people, designed to provide help for them and their carers. These include the Disability Living Allowance and the Attendance Allowance paid to people with disabilities to enable them to live independently in the community (see Chapter 4). There are also Community Care Grants to enable dependent people to adapt their homes and purchase special equipment. Most carers, of course, are women and a 1986 European Court ruling has enabled them to claim Invalid Care Allowances even if they are 'housewives'. The British government had argued that care was a normal part of housework and therefore needed no financial reward. You'll find a more detailed discussion of the 1945 Beveridge system and of the contemporary benefits system in Section 6.4.

These are by no means the only benefits, but they are the backbone of the current system and demonstrate the degree to which the state is still committed to supporting families, although some of the attempts to eradicate family and especially child poverty were radically pruned in the 1980s. By contrast support for home ownership through mortgage relief has become one of the major income maintenance weapons of the government in spite of recent pruning.

Income maintenance policy is, of course, not only about state aid for families; it serves many other purposes and it does not straightforwardly underpin family life. Indeed it has been seen by right-wing politicians as the great betrayer of the family insofar as such a policy supports single parents. Since 1983 women have been able to claim breadwinner status for social security benefit purposes. The state is still not even-handed in its allocation of benefits to lone-parent families, but the 1983 changes considerably improved the situation for those groups which Jackson noted had been completely ignored in the Beveridge system. Rising divorce rates and ineffective maintenance arrangements have left the state to pick up a huge bill for state support of lone parents and children. The recent establishment of the Child Support Agency which pursues ex-partners through the tax system is a political reaction of alarm at the rate of break-up of families, and of anger at increasing evasion of responsibility towards children. Underlying it is an ideology which applauds family stability and emphasises the social dangers of family disintegration, views men and women as having significantly different roles in the family, with men as the major breadwinners and women the natural carers, and links the decline of morality and rising crime rates to what is seen as the family's abdication of its role in discipline and in teaching morality (Fitzgerald, 1985).

Other welfare policies influence and shape the family too. For example, the provision of certain types and sizes of housing by the state, and by the private sector to some extent as well, may reinforce certain notions of normality and make life quite difficult for those who do not conform. So large families find their choice limited in both public and private sector housing unless they have a high income, and they may be seen as deviant if they have large numbers of children or live as an extended family. The state has played an increasingly important role in the education and socialisation of children, and critics highlight the way in which middle class norms and values are the predominant ones in schools, making the language codes and culture of working class children seem inferior or at least marginal. Other research, including government reports, has demonstrated how black and minority ethnic children as well as girls can find their needs ignored and their values questioned (Swann Report, 1985; Stanworth, 1983). In almost every area of state welfare policy there are hidden assumptions and approaches which have a real impact on family life.

3.6 Health work and the family

Most health work takes place in families. Although in the twentieth century governments have increasingly intervened in the family, providing greater material and professional support and shaping family life, the everyday work of nurturing and caring for the health of dependants has been largely undertaken by families – and in particular women. The work of paid health visitors in the early twentieth century, for example, depended on securing the active help of mothers. Mothers were the targets of a great deal of health advice about hygiene and adequate nutrition, but they were also the unpaid workforce who implemented this advice (Stacey, 1988). Although from the 1920s women were increasingly able to count on support from professional health services in relation to childbirth and infant health, the development of these services was sporadic and health clinics and preventive health services were not seen as a priority by most doctors (Lewis, 1980). In relation to the care of other dependants there was little help available, apart from the last resort of the workhouse for those unable to pay for care.

In the post-war years the development of hospital services increased the numbers of available beds for the elderly, mentally ill and chronic sick. Welfare services, as we have seen, were designed to maintain the incomes of those too feeble, sick or old to work. With the growth of hospitalised maternity care and primary health care services it was assumed that the 'cradle to grave' welfare state was in place. But as Finch and Groves (1983) have argued, welfare structures depended on the unpaid work of women. They were grounded in assumptions that care-giving by families was normal and that caring was a 'natural' role for women. The costs to women of giving up paid work to care for dependent relatives were not seen as real costs, so the shift towards community care policies in the 1970s and 1980s was initially seen as unproblematic. For example, the White Paper *Growing Older* (DHSS, 1981) stated that 'care in the community must increasingly mean care by the community'. Work by the Equal Opportunities Commission in the 1980s highlighted the fact that the costs of policy shifts were 'borne individually and do not figure in any public expenditure account. The price is paid in restrictions on women's opportunities' (quoted in Stacey, 1988).

In later chapters we will explore community care policies and the ideology and nature of 'caring' as an activity, and investigate the position of older people as care-givers and receivers and of women as the main care-givers at all ages (Chapters 4, 7 and 9). At this point we'll focus on the extent of the family's involvement in such health work. Two types of informal health work will be briefly considered: care of dependants and health education in the family.

Care of dependants

Around 1.3 million people act as primary unpaid carer to a disabled child or adult, and the vast majority of those carers (1.2 million) actually live with the disabled person (Graham, 1986). Three-quarters of the carers will be female relatives and, in the case of caring for sick or physically or mentally disabled children, almost all the main carers will be the mothers. In cases of chronic illness, there are studies indicating that the greater the degree of help needed from friends and relatives, the smaller is the amount of external help likely to be offered (Nissel and Bonnerjea, 1982). Much of this work will be unpleasant, heavy and 'dirty' work: lifting, toileting, bathing, dressing and feeding. It will be almost indistinguisable from what nurses term 'basic nursing' (Melia, 1987). In a recent study one mother of a disabled child described her routine as follows:

First of all, in the morning, Andrew's got to be got up and dressed and fed and toileted, and you know he's got to be held on the toilet – you can't leave him. It's a couple of hours really. And you can't do anything else while you are feeding him. If you turn round, it's spat out. It's a couple of hours getting him ready for school. And then when he comes home at half past three, your time is devoted to him. Someone has to be there. And when he goes to bed, you're constantly turning him. He has to be turned so many times before he goes to sleep. And he can be sick three times a night.

Read (1991), quoted in Graham (1993)

There is now much more general understanding of the implications of care by the family, in terms of the physical 'daily grind' and the emotional burdens shouldered by carers (Bayley, 1973; Ungerson, 1987). A survey in the early 1980s demonstrated that this burden is borne unequally. In a sample of 44 married couple households who cared for an elderly dependent relative, the wives spent an average of two to three hours per day in caring tasks whereas the husbands spent eight minutes (Nissel and Bonnerjea, 1982). Although it is likely that care-giving by male relatives is growing, and that men are well represented in one group – caring for the dependent spouse – this imbalance in caring work is still significant. It reinforces the *gendered division of labour* in the family that we noted earlier, because women become even more constrained by their caring duties. Unpaid caring frequently determines the type of employment women can seek and it binds them to the home. A range of surveys in the 1980s indicated that women (and dependants, and men) are well aware of the costs of family-only care and favoured much more support from professional health workers, social services and residential care (Ungerson, 1987). Ungerson commented on these findings:

It is ironic and paradoxical that the alternative to care organised and provided by that most hierarchical and task-divided set of professions – namely, health-care personnel – should be devolved on to the single carer working alone in her own home carrying out, all day and every day, all the tasks akin to those of the nurse, the home help, the care assistant, and the 'social care manager'.

Ungerson (1987)

Health education in the family

Health education in families has been seen as an unproblematic part of women's domestic role. In the late 1970s the government White Paper *Prevention and Health, Everybody's Business* (DHSS, 1976) commented on the 'simple steps' that families could take to safeguard their health. Whilst the protection of health undoubtedly deserves a high priority, critics argued that the main business of preventing ill health fell on women's shoulders (Graham, 1979). It was women who must purchase healthier foods, encourage their husbands to exercise and help to reduce their stress levels, set a good example to the family by giving up smoking and so on. In relation to children women are the main 'teachers' for health – checking up on tooth brushing, on sweet eating, on diet, taking children to the clinic and to the doctor when sick.

Professional health workers regard *women* as the principal guardians of family health, but it is women in their role as *mothers* who are the major target for advice. An investigation of the work of health visitors, educational welfare workers and social workers concluded that they operated by targeting mothers and persuading them to modify their own behaviour and that of the children and men in the family (Mayall, 1990). Health visitors emphasised various aspects of health education that mothers should teach their children: teaching children 'good habits'; instilling routines and social norms; regular mealtimes and bedtimes; preparing children for school. But they had no model of the 'caring father' beyond that of the breadwinner, and no health education messages were directed at men in the household, even though men and women parents themselves were engaged in more complex and shifting negotiations about the domestic division of labour.

In a broader sense Graham (1985) has commented on the lack of attention given to the issue of the maintenance of good health in families: 'The routine business of keeping individuals alive and functioning has gone uncharted . . . [and] we can only guess at the division of resources and responsibilities within the community on which this health work rested'. What studies there are suggest that women's unpaid labour has been crucial, to the point of safeguarding the family's health by risking their own (Llewelyn Davies, 1978; Blaxter and Paterson, 1982).

The family as the recipient of health work

Families do not only provide care; they also negotiate with the formal health sector and they are the recipients of health care provided by a range of specialist health care professionals and care assistants. Orr (1987) points out that health services have not always responded to women's felt needs as wives or mothers, and it has sometimes been lay action which has triggered an official response. The women's health movement itself, self help groups and refuges for battered women were all lay initiatives, for example. Whereas much health literature has been preoccupied with problems of non-compliance, recent interpretive research into the perceptions and attitudes of users of health services has highlighted the ambiguities and tensions that can arise between family members and health professionals.

This tension can be particularly evident where there are no shared cultural values and norms. In a study of 43 Pathan mothers living in the North of England Currer (1991) noted that women saw themselves as the 'experts' in child-rearing and had most respect for women's learning which derived from their experience: 'An unmarried white health worker might therefore command little respect as an adviser concerning child care'. On the other hand, in relation to illness as opposed to 'routine care', the mothers consulted their husbands or a doctor, 'having a high regard for the power of biomedicine to heal, although sometimes a poor opinion of particular doctors'. A study of mothers and daughters in Scotland found that, although lay referral was indeed evident, daughters were more likely to consult health professionals about illness in the family (Blaxter and Paterson, 1982). Other researchers have found a similar ambivalence towards health workers in relation to child care and evidence of resistance to professional advice and scrutiny (de la Cuesta and Pearson, 1993). Bloor and McIntosh (1990) used Foucault's notion of power as a shifting relationship between those who engage in surveillance and their clients to explore patterns of resistance. In a case study of health visiting, mothers used various devices to resist expert surveillance, for example non-response to questions, concealment and absence (leaving the house by the back door as the health visitor arrived at the front!).

Families, and in particular mothers, wives and daughters, also play an important role as mediators at the frontier of paid and unpaid health work. As we have noted, it is women who negotiate with doctors, nurses and other health professionals:

Their caring role places them at the interface between the family and the state, as the go-betweens linking the informal health care system with the formal apparatus of the welfare state.

Graham (1985)

This may sometimes be an uncomfortable position to be in, if professional workers resent their presence or pay little attention to their views. On the other hand many mothers and some fathers are now able to stay in hospital with their children and share care with nurses, even though there have been problems in finding a role for the parent (Stacey, 1988).

Health professionals and the sociology of the family

A sociological analysis problematises the family in health work by questioning preconceptions and ideas about family life. As with their clients, health workers create meaning and rationality in their lives through reflecting on their own lived experience. Cultural and gender socialisation within a family will almost certainly have formed an important part of that experience. Health workers, who are frequently required to modify their clients' behaviour, may welcome an opportunity to reflect on their own assumptions about family life. Like other people they are likely to operate within frameworks of views and attitudes about family roles and responsibilities which remain largely hidden: they will have their own taken-for-granted assumptions about what these should comprise. Professional socialisation into a health work role is a central mechanism by which processes of health work practice are reproduced (see Chapter 12). Health workers are not just 'learning how to do the job' but 'learning how the job is done (and not done)' (Davis, 1975; Dingwall, 1977). These ideas and preconceptions, as well as clinical knowledge and experience, will influence how health workers interact with families and how they assess, intervene and evaluate the particular situation that is presented.

The example of health education work illustrates this point. The growing emphasis on health education in nurse training is a notable example of the attempt to move nursing from a medical and disease orientation to a health focus. Nurses are encouraged to learn the skills of counselling and supporting clients to modify or change unhealthy habits, with the implication that such changes will enhance their clients' health status. There is a growing body of consensus science which supports this approach, for example in relation to fat consumption, salt intake and smoking. Since people in the higher occupational classes seem to have responded to such advice and lower classes do not, there is a tendency to categorise lower class people as less rational, less intelligent, less educated or perhaps as more feckless and present orientated than the higher classes (Graham, 1984a).

Hilary Graham's research into smoking behaviour in young mothers, however, suggested that smoking might enhance the well-being of the whole family even though it had an adverse effect on the health chances of the mother. Smoking enabled young mothers to 'get by', keeping them calm and raising their self-esteem. It was the only activity they undertook entirely for themselves and represented a vital ten minute break from family toil (Graham, 1988). If health work interventions deny or ignore the possibility of rationality in their patients' habits and priorities, then practice will either become increasingly ineffective or increasingly coercive. If, on the other hand, health professionals listen to their patients they will end up in horrible dilemmas – do you counsel young mothers to give up or continue to smoke? But they will help to find new solutions and in the process they will modify health work practice and make it more effective.

Some groups of health workers, such as psychiatric nurses, still smoke in quite large numbers (Spencer, 1982). A possible explanation for this could be that their behaviour is also a rational response to lived experience. After all, nursing is a very stressful occupation, physically exhausting and emotionally draining. Around 40 per cent of nurses experience persistent bouts of lower back pain, and several recent surveys have reported on low morale as staffing levels fall (Mackay, 1989). These situational factors together with professional socialisation and occupational experience – such as the organisation of nursing as shift work – could explain the persistence of smoking among some groups of nurses.

The individualist focus of health work

A sociological analysis looks behind the taken-for-granted face of health work and draws attention to its social and ideological construction. For example, the mode of health work practice directs most health workers towards interventions in individual health rather than to family, community or wider social interventions. In spite of other approaches (notably the public health model) this professional–patient model is still the dominant mode of production of health care. This model has been projected as 'natural' and 'normal' health work, whereas community development models or health promotion frameworks, which attempt to develop 'intersectoral' collaboration between health work and other sectors (such as planning or housing), are dismissed as marginal or misguided.

But the professional–patient model is not natural or normal. It was developed in particular social and historical conditions and reflects the power of the medical profession and its ability to control the mode of production of health (see Chapter 11). Other ways of doing health work – for example the public health approach of Victorian times – became more marginal. In practice this produces significant outcomes for families. For example, a focus upon patients as individuals will almost certainly involve making considerable assumptions about family attitudes and support – that a family can cope, is able to take up a caring role and so on. If most health work interventions are about providing care, advice and support for particular individuals at times of stress or sickness, they will also marginalise consideration of the wider social patterns, issues or problems of which these individuals provide examples, and they will largely ignore social health intervention at a family, community or organisational or macro-social level.

For example, it is clear that a small bronchitic baby living in a poor quality rented flat with her young, depressed mother who depends entirely on Income Support can only benefit from a careful and particular assessment of her health needs and from expert care and treatment, sympathetic advice and practical assistance. A serious study of sociology and social policy seeks to assist the health worker in moving beyond this essential first stage of treatment, to ask why the baby gets bronchitis and the young mother is depressed. This may lead to questions about why the housing is inadequate, why social security support is low, why the mother is unable to work, why nursery provision is so scanty. And it may lead further still, to ask why single mothers as a social group are among the poorest in contemporary Britain, to consider why women on average earn much less than men, why the state makes it easier for men to go out to work if they have dependent children than for women, and why women feel obliged to stay at home and care for young children. From our earlier investigation of the family and the welfare state it is clear that (however interpreted) the state has intervened widely in family life. It has shaped motherhood, parental obligations and their limits, and the experience of childhood. If family life is socially constructed in this way, then attempts to intervene must acknowledge this.

This means challenging the boundaries of health work practice, and this challenge is being increasingly undertaken by health professionals in health projects and campaigns. Health visitors, for example, have a long tradition of involvement in community based activities such as setting up crèches and playgroups, helping to develop well women clinics, encouraging self help groups, campaigning on housing and benefit issues and so on. Some projects, such as the Pilton project in Edinburgh, have developed as a result of close co-operation between local residents and health professionals, who have acted mainly as facilitators – to help establish groups and structures but to leave local residents in control. The Pilton project has a Health Hut, a Food Co-op, a 'Big Women' fitness group and self help groups for young, depressed mothers and local people with mental health problems. Other projects are professional-led, but aim to involve local people and to work within a social model of health. In the Right Angle project, for example, public health doctors and paid local workers have helped young, socially isolated mothers in Northamptonshire villages to organise a playgroup and have provided educational and craft activities (K258, 1992).

3.7 Theories of the family

By now it should be clear that sociological theories are not abstract 'isms'; they are active and dynamic ways of trying to make sense of human social experience and activity. From this point of view this whole chapter has been about theory, because it has tried to investigate and explain aspects of debates about the family in several different ways. This final section of the chapter encourages you to reflect on these different accounts and to consider their relevance to health work.

○ Identify at least two contrasting sociological approaches to 'the family' that have been discussed in this chapter.

One identifiable approach was that of *structural functionalism*, a *consensus* account associated with Durkheim and Parsons. This emphasises the universality of the family, which was linked to biological factors, especially reproductive differences, to explain male and female roles and the gender division of labour. A functionalist account suggests that the predominance of nuclear families in modern society was largely a functional response to industrialisation, and that the nuclear family was (and still is) the structural type that provided the best functional 'fit' between the instrumental requirements of industrialised Britain (for mobile, full-time, disciplined, adaptable labour) and the expressive needs (for nurture, love, security) of adults and children. It sees an ultimate harmony of interests between families and economic and political institutions.

Functionalist theory emphasises the consensual basis of socialisation and the vital importance of the success of this process for social stability. In this respect the family is seen as a vital subsystem in society, meeting expressive needs and successfully adapting children to execute roles in adult society. If the family does not perform this task successfully, dangers may result: deviant adults, inter-generational problem families, non-conformity and criminality.

From a functionalist viewpoint the family serves the interests of the whole society; its emergence depended upon consensus, and as that consensus has slowly shifted so the character of the nuclear family has altered. Greater equality between men and women in the workplace and in public life has been reflected in the redistribution of household labour, income, decision making and in the rise of the 'symmetrical' family. So this kind of consensus account does not have to present a static analysis, although it is often linked to a defence of traditional family roles and responsibilities. It attempts to explain adaptation and change, although this is rather difficult; there is inevitably tension within an analysis which emphasises the functional necessity of family stability on the one hand, yet on the other hand theorises a consensual basis of change. How far is it possible to reconcile the implication that social change is inevitable if enough people see the need for it with an approach which emphasises that stability requires unchanging support for the status quo in family life?

By contrast, a *social action* approach emphasises socialisation as a process of negotiation between social actors and the wider society. The creativity of social action is the focus, viewed as the product of complex and often conflictual interaction between individuals, groups and subcultures. Class, race and gender divisions may influence socialisation within the family, but in the final analysis individuals adopt attitudes and develop roles that hold meaning for them. Two individuals from very similar social backgrounds may hold very different ideas and values.

Another identifiable approach was *conflict* theory, which questioned the universality of the family and suggested that what seems to us to be universal is a particular biological and social construct that has become so natural and normal that we 'find' it in other contemporary societies we investigate. This account has been associated with *social construc- tionism*. Other theories – *conflict structuralism* and, above all, *feminist* theories of the family – have questioned the presumed coincidence of interests between the family and society and suggested that families may suffer considerably from the ideological and social pressures of the wider society.

Conflict structuralist theories see socialisation mainly as one-way adaptation by individuals to the wider society. There may be resistance by individuals and groups – women resisting male power, black people resisting whites – but dominant ideologies, forces or structures possess considerably greater power to persuade or enforce conformity.

Marxist theorists would argue that industrial capitalism exploited the family by shaping it to serve the productive needs of capital and to bear the social costs of the reproduction of labour power; in other words, family relationships are seen as an outcome of the mode of production. But it has also been argued that the nuclear family structure was not a straightforward product of industrialisation, but may have roots in pre-industrial society. Feminist theories have highlighted 'familist' ideology based on individualist assumptions and have called for the development of collectivist alternatives, based on collective responsibility and provision for welfare and social support for citizens at a state or community level (Dalley, 1988).

The feminist contribution

From the 1970s feminist theories highlighted the crucial importance of theorising the family in relation to the wider society. They focused on the social implications of industrial change for the division of labour and the distribution of power within the family. They saw women as the major casualties: systematically excluded by men from public life and most well paid employment, constrained by a sexist ideology to domesticity and motherhood, financially and legally in thrall to their husbands and fathers. Women today still bear the scars of this oppression, witnessed by their segregation in lower paid jobs, their continuing responsibility for homemaking and child-rearing, their sexual and financial subordination within marriage. By no means all 'women's oppression' should be explained in terms of 'the family', but it has been a significant and continuing influence on women's lives.

A major contribution of feminism has been to position the family centre stage in sociology, by drawing attention to the connections between the *public* world and the *private* world of the family. Feminist writers have emphasised that personal, private relationships and troubles are intimately and potently bound up with political and public issues (Ungerson, 1987). The systematic exclusion or subordination of women in the public sphere is constructed upon an ideological and material foundation of patriarchal control in family life. This theory of *patriarchy* – the domination by older men of women, children and young men – is a key explanatory device for many conflict analysts (see Chapter 7).

Feminists differ in their approach to patriarchal power. Some feminists emphasise that patriarchy has been the fundamental and universal form of oppression throughout history; it may have appeared in various guises and with different emphases, but it has retained ideological predominance, and this has always resulted in the sexual subordination and exploitation of women by men, for example in marital violence and rape, child abuse, prostitution, fertility control and medical intervention. Other feminists would draw attention to the considerable differences in the power and ideological control which patriarchy can exert in different historical periods and in different kinds of societies. They suggest that its form has changed fundamentally as

women have gained greater legal equality, votes, more equal opportunities as workers and carers, and greater consciousness of the web of
ideology. A male gender order still persists, and there is still plenty of
inequality and exploitation, so conflict will continue, but there has been
significant recasting of relationships between men and women. This has
led some feminist researchers to an investigation of female sexuality,
femininity and the female unconscious, to uncover the hidden origins
and bases of social emotions and feelings.

The uses of theory

Reflecting upon theory can be immensely useful in two respects. First, it
demands an acknowledgement of our intellectual, experiential (and
emotional) preconceptions and enables them to be measured against
systematised and tested theoretical frameworks of explanation. Second,
it generates an evaluative approach to theory itself and to health work
practice. If health workers find that some dimension of theory is
consistently contradicted by practice, it may be that the theory needs
modifying! Health workers can begin to develop 'grounded theory', in
which the feedback loop of reflection leads to evaluation, systemisation
of thought and finally to the generation of new theory. Interesting
examples of how this might work are provided by feminist research.
Jean Orr (1986), in her reflections on health visiting practice, pointed out
how feminist health visitors might perpetuate stereotypes of male and
female family roles because of their imprisonment inside traditional
modes of health visiting practice. Orr argued that health visitors need to
adopt a practice model which enables all family members to participate
in health work. This implies a modification of feminist theories, which
emphasise the marginality of men in early parenting. If men are not
encouraged to participate in early parenting by the largely female
'experts', they cannot then be blamed for feeling that parenthood is
'women's work'. So here reflecting on practice feeds back into reflecting
on an aspect of feminist theory.

It should be evident by now that any analysis of the family in
contemporary society requires sceptical interpretation of a bewildering
mass of evidence, and that this has meant that sociologists have reached
contrasting and often sharply conflicting conclusions. As we have noted
already, sociologists are also social actors in the society they are
investigating, however much they detach themselves and try to act as
objective observers. Sociological theories – like other scientific theories –
are attempts to explain some aspect of the world, but no researcher
stands outside the world to do this. This makes sociologists acutely
aware of the need to ask questions about what is seen or remains

unnoticed, what patterns are created, what interpretations are made, what conclusions are drawn.

Some will argue that theories are too remote from the 'real world' of practice to be worth spending much time on. But we have seen that it is scarcely possible to engage in health work with families without getting involved in judgements about what a 'normal' family is, what roles we expect men and women to fulfil, how childhood should be defined, in what ways the state should intervene and so on. Without reflection and detached evaluation uncritical judgements about such issues become unacknowledged assumptions at the basis of health work with families. This is a challenge for sociological theory: to demonstrate that practice and theory are not separate spheres.

An example of child abuse

Let's illustrate this with an example of a not uncommon dilemma in health work: how to come to terms with – that is, explain and 'theorise' – a situation in which the sexual abuse of a little girl by her father is suspected (Box 3.5). There will be considerable conflict between the type of explanation put forward in a consensus theory, such as funtionalism, and that highlighted in a conflict analysis, such as feminist theory.

○ You may have been involved in a similar situation yourself. If not, you will certainly have read about such cases in the press. What are likely to be the main differences between a consensus and a conflict account of child sexual abuse?

A *consensus* approach such as *functionalism* would operate with a 'dysfunctional family' model, in which child abuse is viewed as the consequence of the breakdown of family relationships within a wider social framework of social deviance. The social roles of mother and father have not been successfully fulfilled. The mother is physically or emotionally absent; as a wife she is unresponsive to her partner's emotional and sexual needs. The father is emotionally immature, perhaps a product of an emotionally deprived childhood. A cycle of deprivation may have become established. At any rate, the family is not a successful social unit. It is not adapting the children to adult life in appropriate ways; indeed it is a source of social danger, providing an unhealthy glimpse of adult sexuality to a child at an inappropriate stage of development. If the family is viewed as a vital subsystem which has a set of roles and responsibilities in ensuring the stability of the wider society, then this family has surely failed. Treatment often involves removing the child, prosecuting the father, with a longer term hope of therapeutic help to rebuild the shattered family into a functional unit.

BOX 3.5 Child abuse: a case study

Maria and her three children lived on a council estate in East London with Maria's boyfriend Jack Clark. Maria had a three bedroomed flat on the fourth floor of a tower block, and Jack had been living there for nearly three years. He worked as a machinist in a factory but had been on short-time working for the last six months and was only bringing home half his usual pay. Maria had found evening work as a cleaner to help out. She was constantly tired and had sought help from her GP for back pain. He prescribed pain killers, but Maria's job made her condition worse.

Maria's elder children, Shane (14) and Emma (10) were by a previous relationship; two year old Robert was the son of Maria and Jack. The couple got on quite well, although Jack had a bad temper and neighbours reported that he 'knocked Maria around a bit' when drunk. However, Maria did not complain, and the children seemed well cared for in spite of the difficulties of managing on very little. Jack was very fond of Robert, but also treated the other children quite well. Shane did not get on with his 'stepfather' and stayed out of his way as much as possible.

Maria's previous relationship had ended when her partner left her for another woman. She lacked confidence and had no close friends. Jack was an only child, brought up by his grandfather after his mother had died. He had been in several previous relationships, but none had lasted very long. He was also something of a loner, but he did go out for a drink most evenings. When he came home, Maria was sometimes still at work.

Jack had first sexually abused Emma when she was eight years old by touching her genitals and exposing himself to her. He warned her not to tell her mother because she would be upset and angry with Emma, and said that it was 'their little game'. Emma was frightened, but not physically hurt and said nothing. After Maria started work as a cleaner, Jack began to abuse Emma about once a week, moving from touch to full penetration.

One or twice Emma tried to talk to her mother, but was too frightened. She started to behave differently, being rude to Maria and staying at her friend's house until Maria had to go and fetch her. Her school work deteriorated. Maria knew something was wrong and became worried. Finally, Emma told her best friend Tracey about what Jack had done. Tracey told her mother, who called the police.

A *conflict* approach such as *feminism* would argue that child sexual abuse needs to be considered within the broad context of the social construction of the family and predominant ideologies about the nature of contemporary family life. The family represents private territory in society, in spite of increasing legislative intervention in this century, and there is still considerable ambivalence in public and political attitudes toward professional 'interference'. The small 'private', nuclear family may have little social support from kin, friends and neighbours or from overstretched social services. More fundamentally, the family is the arena within which contests about power and control take place between men, women and children. Men still hold considerable power over women and children, physically, financially and emotionally. The legal basis of that power has been eroded, but the low pay and status of many women workers and the continuing expectation that women are primarily wives and mothers and only a secondary labour force perpetuates inequalities of power, responsibilities and rights within the family. Gender socialisation reproduces norms of behaviour and attitudes which are underpinned by social values and a widespread continuing belief in biological essentialism.

An analysis of child sexual abuse must first acknowledge that most sexual abuse is by men and most victims (about 80 per cent) are girls. An assessment of 'family dysfunction' and inadequate socialisation does not consider this; by sustaining notions of male sexual drives and female physical or emotional inadequacy it may avoid focusing at all upon the social construction of these male and female images. It may even suggest that men can be excused because they 'need sex' (think of recent pronouncements still made by some judges), and that women are failing in their family duty if they don't provide this. Feminist research suggests this approach may leave women and children feeling more guilty than men. This may be reinforced by removing children from the family if abuse is suspected; the child may think it has destroyed the family.

Feminists suggest that change can only come through dissecting and challenging the inter-related ideologies of maleness and femaleness, perpetuated not just through socialisation, but by media stereotypes, pornography, political and legal discrimination and continuing unequal treatment of men and women at work and in the home. This does not mean that there should be no intervention in cases of child sexual abuse, but that without a public and sustained discussion about male and female sexuality, the rights of children and the relationship between popular ideology and abuse there will be no real change where it is needed – in the attitudes and actions of men.

If we reflect on the implications for health work practice, it is clear that the two approaches differ very considerably in their assessment of what the problem is really about: a dysfunctional family, or structural and ideological oppression. They would differ in their planning and intervention, though there may be short term similarities such as the removal of the endangered child. A consensus functionalist approach would focus on returning the family to social health and normality, whereas the priorities of the conflict feminist approach would be to ensure male exclusion from the family, and to raise the debate about sexuality and male power at a social level. A consensus approach would intervene to uphold consensus based family values, a conflict approach would see 'family values' as part of the problem. Any evaluation of a feminist approach would need to reflect on change promoted outside the family as well as inside that particular family.

Implications for health work

A sociological analysis of the family may provide useful insights into practice, but what kinds of sociological theories are most valuable to health workers? Should nurses use a functionalist, feminist, Marxist, interactionist or some other approach? And which kind of feminist or Marxist approach? The social constructionist approach that was outlined in Chapter 2 may be helpful in this respect. It questions the attempt to produce monolithic sociological meta-theories that explain society as 'a social system', 'the consequence of a mode of production', 'a patriarchy' and so on, and in doing so suggests that disjunction and fragmentation have a creative logic of their own. Social constructionism suggests that 'all there is' is a range of conflicting accounts – truth claims – from which a selection must be made. In this view health workers need to be open minded and eclectic, piecing together theory from different perspectives to suit their purposes. Since the family itself is becoming more fragmented and diverse in character in the late twentieth century, a multi-theory approach offers one way of dealing with this complexity. Moreover, in emphasising the role of language and thought – human agency – in creating frameworks of knowledge which influence and constrain action, social constructionists draw attention to the connections between 'doing' and 'seeing'. This signals the importance of theory: 'doing' involves not just action but interpretation, which leads on to the business of theory building.

Sociological research can assist health workers in questioning and revaluing practice in relation to the family. Health work has often been obsessed with product innovation – new machines, new drugs and so on – rather than with rethinking ways of working: process innovation. That is to say it has focused on the easier option of 'having something new' rather than adopting a slower, more painful, messier, rethinking of practice. Health workers themselves have acknowledged this. In relation to family violence Jean Orr (1987) has commented that 'professionals have been prepared to ignore issues of violence against women because it disturbs the accepted view and values of family life'. We noted earlier that health professionals who work with fixed assumptions about 'normal families', 'motherhood', 'fatherhood' and 'parenting' may not provide the type of health work that best serves or empowers the family. A radical process change involves giving health workers time and space to evaluate their practice, encouraging them to get involved in grass roots criticism and experiment and making sure that the results are assessed and fed back to modify the theoretical framework within which modes of practice are developed.

Suggestions for further study

H. Graham's (1984) *Women, Health and the Family*, London, Wheatsheaf, is informative and illuminating in its discussion of family life, and health issues are addressed in a helpful way. D. Gittins (1985) *The Family in Question*, London, Macmillan, offers a useful and detailed discussion of changing households and familist ideologies from a feminist standpoint, as does S. Jackson (1993) *Family Lives: A Feminist Sociology*, Oxford, Blackwell.

Self assessment questions

1 Discuss the advantages and drawbacks of studying the family in terms of its structure and roles.
2 In what ways have welfare policies influenced family life?
3 In what ways are women 'unpaid health workers'?
4 What insights does a sociological approach to the study of the family offer to health workers?

Chapter 4

Community and health

Contents

Themes and issues

The problem of community: locality in health work – community social work models – patch system

Community care: formal and informal care – lay carers – private and voluntary sector care – consumer sovereignty – market models

Theorising community: community and association – community as ideology – breakdown of community – networks – caring

Learning outcomes

After working through this chapter you should be able to:

1 Explain the different meanings of 'community'.
2 Discuss the factors that have most influenced health work in community settings.
3 Assess the implications for health work of the 1990 changes in community care.
4 Evaluate the evidence about the impact of social networks and ties on health status.

THIS chapter will explore the problematic relationship between community and health, as it is highlighted in local health and welfare work. Community care policies will be discussed and evaluated in the context of broader debates about welfare. In particular, the chapter will investigate how the ideology of community has shaped not only lay and professional thinking but also sociological research. The 'disappearance' of community as a live issue in sociology has been matched by its growing importance – in rhetorical terms, at least – in social welfare and politics. This suggests there is a need to rethink and redefine what is meant by community.

4.1 The language of community

Health work today proclaims to be focused on the community. Community health care achieved prominence in the 1970s, creating 'community' health teams, 'community' nurses and other community specialists. For some groups, such as community psychiatric nurses and mental handicap nurses, the term also served to underline their distance from institutionally based work. During the 1980s a great deal of health research investigated health and disease at a community level and developed strategies for community health promotion. Most Project 2000 students now go out 'into the community' before they work in hospital settings.

What, we may ask, is the significance of this language of community? Why are we now attended by community nurses and in receipt of community care? Is the growing use of the term an accurate reflection of current priorities and services? Does it denote a substantial shift in health sector priorities away from hospitals? Or is it being used to persuade us that health care has a more local and user friendly focus, while everyday work remains much the same?

In order to begin to answer these questions, stop and think about some of the phrases that have slipped into everyday usage over the past two decades.

Make a list of phrases or job descriptions which include the word 'community'. Reflect on why these terms came into use.

Here are some examples: community policing, community theatre, community social work, community care, community health councils and the community charge.

One explanation for the popularity of the word 'community' might be that it provides a shorthand way of emphasising that services or amenities are local and accessible. They might not be, but 'community' suggests they are under local control, meeting local needs, serving the common interests of local people. This reminds us that the term has often been used to persuade the public that significant changes are being made. The use of the term 'community policing', for example, was linked to a call for the revival of 'the bobby on the beat' policy and to the growth of 'neighbourhood watch' schemes, designed to show that localities were being policed more effectively, and to counter popular images of a remote, invisible, car-bound police force. Yet as Paul Ekblom (1986) has suggested, fundamental obstacles exist both in police (1986) has suggested, fundamental obstacles exist both in police organisation and in public expectations of 'a fast patrol response to their more than a PR job – superficial and nostalgic . . . Real police work would continue as before'.

The choice of the title 'community charge' (as opposed to 'poll tax') for the local tax which briefly replaced the rates in the late 1980s was meant to emphasise local autonomy and responsibility for the charge – even though central government manipulated it through charge-capping. The phrase also conveyed the idea of shared benefits and common interests for the people who made up this 'community'. In reality a recent analysis of the community charge suggested that it was regressive, not just because everyone paid the same amount irrespective of their means, but because local government spends a disproportion-ately high percentage of its revenue on services which are much more widely used by the better-off, such as education, roads and leisure services: 'Overall we can say that the better-off use services costing 45–70% more than those used by the least well off' (Bramley *et al.*, 1989). In other words, the term 'community' helps to disguise such unequal outcomes.

The use of the term 'community' in health work carries a similar subtext: that health care is local, accessible, autonomous, meeting local needs, reflecting common interests and offering shared benefits. This picture is a cosy one, but it is not necessarily very accurate.

○   One example given earlier was 'community health council'. What do you know about the role of community health councils (CHCs)?

CHCs were established in the health service reorganisation of 1974 to represent the 'people's voice' in a service which controlled huge budgets yet was subject to little public scrutiny (Levitt, 1980). CHCs are local bodies in that their members are local people, drawn from local organisations like colleges and trade unions, but they are almost entirely unknown to the general public and work with the added constraint of tiny budgets and usually just two full-time members of staff. They rely heavily on the work of unpaid, lay members of the council. Although they carry out important work in scrutinising district health authority decisions, monitoring policies and putting the lay viewpoint on health, they in no way – and do not claim to – represent 'the community'. Since the 1990 health service reforms CHC members have had no automatic right to attend health authority meetings. Yet the use of the term 'community' in the title implies, and was meant to suggest, that the views of the people in that district health authority are being heard.

4.2 The 'problem' of community

This dual use of the term 'community' is problematic; it is used both as a shorthand term for services and organisations which are 'locally based and organised' and as an ideology conveying notions of accessibility, local autonomy, responsiveness, social solidarity and shared benefits. In fact the range of meanings associated with the term is wider still (see Box 4.1). It may refer to groups with common interests, values, beliefs, experiences, on whatever scale they operate – for example, think of the very different focus of a local community group, 'the farming community', the European Community. Wilmott and Thomas (1984) reviewed the increasingly extensive literature on the concept of community in social policy, commenting that its meaning was still vague:

Clearly the essence is 'having something in common'. There is general
agreement about one distinction: the word can refer either to the population of
a particular geographical area – a territorial community – or to people who
share in common something other than physical propinquity . . . The two
concepts – local community and interest community – are not mutually
exclusive.

[Community] refers also to feelings or sentiments, and to the social networks
and patterns of behaviour that sustain and reflect such sentiments and
feelings. The extra dimension, which can be present in varying degrees and in
both territorial and interest communities, can probably best be summarised as
'community sense'.

                                                                    Willmott and Thomas (1984)

Nicholas Deakin (1987) tells the story of an industrial review procedure which a prominent industrialist claimed was good for the 'community'. When asked what he meant by 'community' the industrialist replied, 'I mean beneficial to the community of those who work in the industry, beneficial to the mining communities, beneficial to the community of the people who live in Britain'. Here are the three different meanings of the term 'community' identified by Willmott and Thomas (1984) being used together – community of common interests, community as local inter-personal relationships (community sense), community as place – all with different hidden messages about what the community is.

In addition, other terms with similar and overlapping meanings are also widely used by those seeking to escape the problems surrounding the use of the term 'community'. Some sociologists have suggested 'local social systems', a definition which focused attention on social interaction, on local stratification systems and on the dynamics of

BOX 4.1 The range of meanings of 'community'. Source: Willmott and Thomas (1984)

• As a synonym for 'the public', 'everybody' or 'the British people' (for example 'This White Paper is . . . addressed to the whole community', 'Foreword' by Secretaries of State, in Department of Health and Social Security, 1981).	• To refer to an ethnic or other minority whose interests might be taken into account locally or nationally (for example 'the Asian community', 'the gay community').
• To signal a new approach or soften the public image of an institution (for example 'community homes' instead of 'approved schools').	• When a public service is locally based and organised in order to serve people locally and to provide care in a familiar setting (for example community care).
• When a service or activity, whether public or voluntary, is run with the participation of local people (for example community arts).	• When an activity or a protest movement is organised by and for local people (for example play-group, residents' action group).

change (Stacey, 1969). The use of 'locality' has also been argued for, on the grounds that this avoids the ideological overtones of 'community'. In social work, and to some extent in nursing, the term 'neighbourhood' has been used instead, although as Willmott and Thomas (1984) comment, 'it suffers from some of the slipperiness of community; applied to both a place and the residents, it too can suggest nostalgia and exhortation'. It seems unlikely that any of these terms will replace 'community', however. The social and historical associations of the term are very strong, and sociological analysis has tended to obscure rather than to clarify the issues.

Sociological approaches to community

The sociological debate about community has also been marked by a degree of conceptual confusion. At one level there is relatively clear evidence that community, in the pre-industrial sense of the word, largely disappeared in the nineteenth century as a result of industrialisation and urbanisation. Whereas in pre-industrial society community had great significance in people's lives, with towns and even villages often having a high degree of self sufficiency and political autonomy, industrial society became marked by increasing division of labour and growing central state authority. There was a steady, if gradual, shift from social relationships based on close personal ties of loyalty and deference to relations based on formal and legal contracts (see Section 2.3).

By the late twentieth century few communities in any part of the world remain untouched by external market pressures or the effects of industrialisation. Retail chains, brand name goods, mass advertising, multi-national manufacturing corporations and nationwide banks all bear witness to increasing international and global economic inter-dependence. Our socks come from Korea, our books are printed in Hong Kong and India, our coal comes from Poland, our yoghurt from France. Few local products remain; the most successful, like Melton Mowbray pork pies and Cheddar cheese, can be found on every supermarket shelf. Test this out for yourself when you next go shopping: what proportion of the goods you buy are made in your local area or region?

The enlargement of scale in industry has been matched by the growth of the state. At a central and local level government has taken on wider responsibilities: for law and order, public health, industry, economic strategy, transport, wage levels, welfare and so on. Some of this executive power is vested in international organisations such as the European Community (EC). Most economic and political decision making now takes place at a level far above the individual town or village, even if they are still left with some political responsibilities. At the same time the modern privatised nuclear family has become more home-focused – encouraged by the acquisition of private consumer durables, in particular television (Willmott and Young, 1973). Increasing mobility has also served to weaken local social ties and the sense of belonging to a discernible community.

Sociologists, as we noted in Chapter 2, have been observers and investigators of these changes. Durkheim's (1987) study of suicide, for example, was a careful, empirical account of a range of social variables that influenced individual action, and he saw a significant correlation between lack of social cohesion and the suicide rate. But he and other sociologists were also interested parties; they were not just 'detached observers' but interpreters of what they thought was happening. To some other early sociologists, such as Auguste Comte, community was fundamentally associated with social stability and traditional values, with a vision of the 'good life'. The passing away of pre-industrial society spelled the death of community and its profound significance in people's lives. Industrial society became marked by increasing impersonality and anonymity. Bell and Newby (1971) commented that Comte conveys 'an anguished sense of the breakdown of the old . . . the traditional form of association. The community, in other words, was viewed as man's natural habitat'.

Gemeinschaft and Gesellschaft

Ferdinand Tonnies, writing in the 1880s, was also pessimistic about the future of community (Bell and Newby, 1971). He developed the concepts of *Gemeinschaft* (community) and *Gesellschaft* (association or society). *Gemeinschaft* was characterised by kinship loyalties (blood), a sense of place or belonging (land) and ties of mutuality and friendship (mind). *Gemeinschaft* described the traditional style of living in a pre-industrial age, characterised by small, largely self sufficient, kinship and friendship based social systems, in which relationships were founded on a clear understanding of each individual's status and local standing. It was a community of support and mutuality and above all of place (see also Box 4.2):

Community makes for traditionalistic ways and at the very core of the community concept is the sentimental attachment to the conventions and mores of a beloved place. Community will reinforce and encapsulate a moral code, raising moral tensions and rendering heterodoxy a serious crime, for in a community everyone is known and can be placed in the social structure.

Bell and Newby (1971)

Gesellschaft was the opposite of this, a society characterised by individualism, in which impersonal ties were based on contract not on kinship or mutuality, and in which the rational pursuit of self interest ensured that social relationships were functional rather than altruistic. Tonnies argued that in *Gesellschaft* all activities were instrumental, geared to definite ends and means, so that a sense of mutuality and any disinterested concern for others withered away. This was the community of interest, preoccupied with status and embracing co-operation only in the limited sense of identifying particular common interests. For Tonnies capitalism was the result of the loss of *Gemeinschaft*.

BOX 4.2 *Gemeinschaft* and *Gesellschaft*

Gemeinschaft	*Gesellschaft*
Community	Association (society)
Kinship (blood ties)	Rootless nuclear family
Neighbourhood (sense of place)	Atomistic society (impersonal, mobile)
Mind (intimacy, friendship)	Instrumental relationships (for particular ends)

See also Chapter 2 for related ideas about 'traditional' and 'industrial' society.

O Review the ideas of Durkheim, Marx and Weber about the rise of 'industrial society' that we noted in Chapter 2. Were they as pessimistic as this?

Durkheim took a more optimistic view of the potential of industrial society. He did fear the disintegration of social relations into *anomie* (normlessness), as relationships marked by mutual support and deference based on kinship, ascriptive status and geographical intimacy – which he termed *mechanical solidarity* – gave way before rampant self interest and individualism. We have noted his research findings: that suicide was more common in large cities experiencing rapid industrial change, where rootlessness and individualism had undermined traditional morality and social ties. But he saw this as a transition stage in the shift to mature industrial society.

Durkheim looked more optimistically to the growth of *organic solidarity*: that is, relationships based on an emerging moral consensus, and on people's growing realisation of their social interdependence. Out of this would grow the classless society, built on new forms of mutuality and on formal contract, which would give individuals much greater freedom than had the enforced conformity of traditional society. As Bell and Newby (1971) put it, 'Durkheim was gratified to conclude that, far from community disintegrating, society was becoming one big community'.

Marx saw capitalism as the economic driving force behind changing social relationships. It was ordinary people's 'alienation' in the face of new working practices and the destruction of traditional skills and crafts that spelt the loss of community. Industrialisation, which uprooted people and transformed their ways of life, inevitably undermined their identity, intimacy and traditional ties of loyalty. Weber shared some of these doubts; on the other hand he saw modern industrial society as more liberating for the individual. 'Rational-legal' authority was more likely to create a just and meritocratic society than 'traditional' authority, based on ascriptive status. Marx himself was optimistic that in the long term rapid industrialisation would result in the total transformation of society, because the contradictions of industrial captialism and the 'emiseration' of the industrial workforce would act as powerful forces for proletarian solidarity and social change.

4.3 Community in current sociological debate

Community did, and still does to some extent, provoke strong feelings among sociologists as well as lay people. Bulmer (1987) has commented that romanticism still pervades the discussion of community, and in so doing conjures up a mythical golden age. It is also important to acknowledge the impact of other myths. The myth of the 'traditional community', for example, ignored evidence of the disparate nature of pre-industrial society, and the elaborate and oppressive social hierarchy and social round. The typification of urban industrial society as impersonal and rootless overlooked the degree to which mutuality and kinship ties have continued to form the basis of urban life.

In the new industrial towns working people developed strong informal ties based on kinship, friendship and proximity, and these provided a basis for quite elaborate systems of mutual aid and neighbourly support. The nature of the community was transformed from that of the traditional town or village, but some of the characteristics associated with those patterns of living – a sense of belonging to a social group, mutual aid, attachment to place, feelings of mutuality, shared rituals – were reflected in the urban working class neighbourhood. Several autobiographical accounts and reminiscences of life in urban working class neighbourhoods, such as Richard Roberts' study *The Classic Slum* (1951), remind us of this solidarity. On the other hand they highlight the fact that oppression and hierarchy existed side by side with these more acceptable and cosy features of working class neighbourhoods.

The 'working class' community

Post-war sociological research into urban communities also tended to focus on working class neighbourhoods. Michael Young and Peter Willmott (1957) investigated family life and kinship patterns in the East End of London in the 1950s, at a time when this area was experiencing rapid social change due to slum clearance and rehousing policies. Their research emphasised the existence of a dense mesh of friendship and kinship links, underpinned by shared values and sustained by ritualised conviviality, and they highlighted the destructive impact of post-war housing relocation policies. Community had survived in Bethnal Green, they argued, both as a form of collective social life and as a set of social relationships ordered not by status but by reputation (being known within the group). Young and Willmott's study and others like it (such as Rosser and Harris (1965) *The Family and Social Change*), which mapped the social relationships underpinning working class urban life, also projected powerful images of community. Martin Bulmer (1987) suggests that such studies have mingled uneasily with ideas of the classic *Gemeinschaft* to give an almost mythical status to 'the solid, tightly-knit urban working class "community" '.

Jocelyn Cornwell (1984), who has explored aspects of working class life in Bethnal Green, is critical of Young and Willmott's account of working class community on both empirical and ideological grounds. She argues that their 'romantic vision of harmony and friendliness in Bethnal Green is not supported by reports of social life in "face-to-face" communities, either in our own society in the past, or in other societies'. Enmity, flattery, one-upmanship and ostracisation, she suggests, all figure largely in such ethnographic, face-to-face studies. But the strength of the dominant ideology of community, which Willmott and Young helped to create and project, was reflected in the public statements about community made by local people in Cornwell's study – even though their private accounts echoed those recorded in ethnographic studies. Whereas in public accounts of the neighbourhood as it used to be local people emphasised friendliness and concern for others, their private accounts highlighted 'the over-riding importance of looking after oneself and one's own' and underlined the diversity of community. Men and women, young and old, shared no common vision or experience of what community was in the past, or what it had become in the 1980s.

The picture of diversity and contradiction documented by Cornwell led her to comment unfavourably on Young and Willmott's 'romantic vision' of community:

The definition of community became stronger and more exaggerated in the course of their research careers. Originally Young defined 'community' simply as 'a sense of solidarity with other people sharing a common territory' (Young, 1955). In *Family and Kinship*, Young, with Willmott, began to develop the idea that 'community' is collective life, lived on the streets and in public places, but at the same time they acknowledged the central importance of privacy and of 'your home being your own' to people surrounded at very close quarters by many others . . . By the time they wrote *Family and Class in a London Suburb* (Willmott and Young, 1971), they were making the straightforward assertion that collective life was more important than life in the home.

Cornwell (1984)

Social network analysis

Magaret Stacey (1969) has argued that community is a 'non-concept' and in her research on Banbury in the 1960s used the term 'local social systems', as we noted earlier. The difficulty of reaching a shared view of community has persuaded other sociologists to avoid the term altogether and to focus instead on local social networks and caring relationships. The focus on social networks – that is, local webs of inter-personal relationships and mutual support – underpins attempts to theorise local social systems. Social network analysis offers one approach to 'understanding the patterning of social ties which pertain neither to a group nor to an institution' (Bulmer, 1987).

Network analysis involves the mapping of the frequency, duration and durability of social contacts, of the extent to which 'everyone knows everyone else'. Obviously proximity, and therefore locality, is important; accessibility – 'reachability' – appears to be crucial in maintaining supportive social networks (Willmott, 1989). The mapping approach sidesteps some of the problems of conceptualising community by focusing on the actual social ties around an individual (which may be local or non-local) rather than the rhetoric. It also enables us to begin to determine the extent to which territorial community, interest community and community sense might in fact exist in any particular locality.

Familist ideology

The other important line of research has drawn on a feminist critique of familist ideologies (Dalley, 1988, and see Section 3.2). Since the early 1980s feminist researchers have drawn the attention of policy makers to the central role of women in informal social support networks: 'In practice community care equals care by the family, and in practice care by the family equals care by women' (Finch and Groves, 1983). You'll have an opportunity to read about this research in Chapter 7, but it is important to be aware that theories of community have largely overlooked the crucial role of women. Cornwell (1984) points out that today, as in the past, women's experience of community life is radically different from that of men. As local employment declined, the men of Bethnal Green found work further afield:

Most of their sense of community comes from the atmosphere of the local pub . . . Women, on the other hand, occupy a much wider range of communal spaces – the shops, the street, the school gates, their relatives' houses – and they have a much wider variety of contacts, not only with the shopkeepers and other mothers, but also in the schools, pubs and blocks of flats where many of them are employed as cleaners.

Cornwell (1984)

This raises another point. A preoccupation with the fragmentation of community in the twentieth century – because of residential mobility, increased travel, rebuilding and so on – may mask the extent to which some groups in the population remain fairly immobile. This might include not just women with young children, but also older people and those with chronic sickness or disability. Their perceptions of community – as place, common interests or feelings – are likely to be rather different, although there is hardly any research to demonstrate this claim.

A social constructionist view

From a social constructionist perspective the supposed discovery of community can be seen as a fabrication arising from current concerns and linked to contemporary social practices. Community is not to be seen as a 'social fact' waiting to be discovered, but as a concept which has been 'brought into being' by human thought and activity. The rediscovery of community in official knowledge and practice coincides with the growing fragmentation of contemporary industrialised society and despair at the threatening anonymity of urban life. Community operates as an ideology conjuring up the notion of that older, safe and intimate 'traditional community'. In health and welfare work today it is most often this latter vision that is invoked rather than Durkheim's 'community-as-society' version with its notion of organic solidarity and its essential optimism about the progressive nature of industrial society. Yet as we noted earlier, the self sufficiency, political autonomy and social relations based on close personal ties that characterised the 'traditional community' are precisely the forms of life that gradually disappeared as Western industrial society emerged. We'll return to consider the implications of these various lines of research for the rethinking of community in Section 4.8.

These problems and reservations do not necessarily mean that 'community' as a term should be abandoned, but they do suggest that it should be used with caution. First, there is a need to be aware that it is a shifting concept which has been characterised in different ways in different historical periods. The multiple meanings of community today do not equate with traditional community. Second, the use of community as an *ideology* – which projects a vision of homogeneity and neighbour-liness, of a sense of belonging and of security – is an increasing feature of late twentieth century life. In a rapidly changing world the promise held out by community is not dissimilar to that held out in Comte's day, a nostalgic longing for the lost 'good life', reflected in television commercials and other media images. This needs to be borne in mind as the discussion of health work is developed; community has not just signified 'local area' but also, in recent years, a particular ideology of health care.

4.4 Health work and the community

There has always been an ambivalence in the relationship between health and the community. Health workers have served 'the community' by providing services locally to meet people's needs. Most hospitals were built with local support to serve specific geographically or socially defined communities. Midwives, general practitioners (GPs) and later on district nurses and health visitors provided health care for individuals and families in specified areas. Health visiting, for example, grew out of local initiatives in home visiting of mothers and young children in Liverpool and Birmingham and gradually became a nationwide service to seek out the health needs of ordinary 'healthy' children and families (Dingwall, 1976). In recent decades primary health care teams have been developed to meet the health needs of local people more effectively by using an inter-professional, teamwork approach. As we noted in Chapter 1, a whole series of local health studies have investigated the health status and analysed the health needs of 'local communities' across Britain, and 'Health for All' strategies and health promotion initiatives are firmly based 'in the community'.

On the other hand health work outside hospitals has generally been the poor relation in terms of status and resource allocation, and the term 'community' has been more of a convenient shorthand for 'outside the hospital' than a positive vision of health work. It is generally used to refer to the provision of services to meet people's needs in a given locality. Even so, this is still not very accurate; for example, health visitors have worked within specified localities, but GPs have not. They have provided a service to their registered patients, who may all live in the same area (although this is rare) but who certainly don't constitute the entire population of that locality. The shift towards 'community trusts' means that some primary health services are being provided by non-local teams, because they have made successful bids for the service contract.

These examples are a reminder that words are not just words, but codes of persuasion and the tools of ideology. It can be argued, for example, that during the last two decades, while the term 'community' was becoming increasingly popular, the focus of health work – measured in terms of budget and staffing – did not change (Figure 4.1). Not only have hospitals devoured most of the health budget, they have also become increasingly detached from their local area. The rationalisation of the hospital service has involved the closure of many small units and the concentration of services into district general hospitals (DGHs) serving populations of up to 500 000. These DGHs are now moving to hospital trust status and are signing contracts to supply treatments and services to purchasers of all types (see Box 4.3 and Chapter 13). Links between local populations and their local secondary health care institutions have been decidedly weakened.

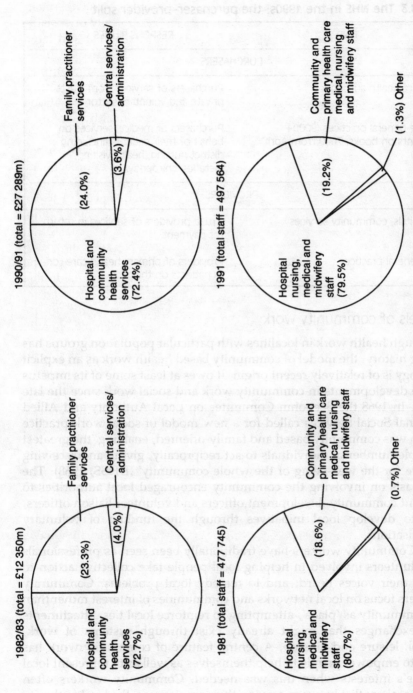

1982/83 (total = £12 350m)

Family practitioner
services

Central services/
administration

(23.3%)

(4.0%)

Hospital and
community
health services
(72.7%)

1990/91 (total = £27 289m)

Family practitioner
services

Central services/
administration

(24.0%)

(3.6%)

Hospital and
community
health
services
(72.4%)

1981 (total staff = 477 745)

Community and
primary health care
medical, nursing
and midwifery staff

(18.6%)

(0.7%) Other

Hospital
nursing, medical and
midwifery staff
(80.7%)

1991 (total staff = 497 564)

Community and
primary health care
medical, nursing
and midwifery staff

(19.2%)

(1.3%) Other

Hospital
nursing,
medical and
midwifery
staff
(79.5%)

FIGURE 4.1 NHS expenditure and nursing and midwifery staff. Source: NAHAT (1993a), NHS Statistics for England (1984, 1993)

BOX 4.3 The NHS in the 1990s: the purchaser–provider split

UNIT	RESPONSIBILITIES
PURCHASERS	
District health authorities	Purchasers of services from trusts, private and voluntary sector
Some general practices (9000+ patients on books; 7000 from April 1993)	Purchasers of medical services on behalf of their patients (including district nursing, health visiting, dietetics, chiropody)
PROVIDERS	
Hospitals, community services	'Trust' providers of services in return for payment
All general practices	Providers of primary health care for all patients on their lists

Models of community work

Although health work in localities with particular population groups has a long history, the model of community based health work as an explicit ideology is of relatively recent origin. It owes at least some of its impetus to the developments in community work and social work since the late 1960s. In 1968 the Seebohm Committee on Local Authority and Allied Personal Social Services called for a new model of social work practice which was community based and family-oriented, enabling 'the greatest possible number of individuals to act reciprocally, giving and receiving service for the well-being of the whole community' (DHSS, 1968). The emphasis on involving the community encouraged local authorities to appoint community development officers and volunteer liaison officers, and to develop local initiatives through the funding of voluntary organisations.

Community workers have traditionally been seen as professionals or volunteers involved in helping local people take collective action to make their voices heard, and to remedy local problems. Community workers focus on local networks and communities of interest rather than on community as 'place', attempting to reinforce local ties, attachments and exchanges that might already exist through systems of work, school, leisure and kinship. A central feature of community work has been to empower people to help themselves as well as to represent local people's interests when this was needed. Community workers often face a real conflict between serving their employers – the local authority

– and encouraging local people to fight for their rights, say, for prompt council housing repairs or better local facilities from the council (Derricourt, 1985).

The 'caring sharing' community – homogeneous and united, with common values and goals – has rarely existed, even in the past. Communities have almost always been divided: along lines of class or race, because of ethnic or religious loyalties, and in other less obvious ways, such as by age, sex, disability and so on. Derricourt has pointed out that these divisions are often ignored by using terms such as 'multiracial community', which gloss over contradictions and potential conflicts. In effect we cannot assume that any change will benefit the 'community', but only that changes and initiatives will be welcomed by some groups within the community.

There are several different models of community work. The most significant early initiative was the Home Office Community Development Project (CDP) scheme set up in 1969 by the Labour government and eventually covering twelve inner-city project areas. The objective in setting up the CDPs was to regenerate inner-city communities through self help and local financial support. The CDPs were essentially neighbourhoods of 10–20 000 people, but local workers challenged the limitations imposed by place and moved to a more radical, structural analysis of local problems (Henderson and Armstrong, 1993). Project officers made it clear that in their view both the causes of material deprivation in their areas and the solutions to these problems lay outside particular communities – in the wider structures of inequality and uneven distribution in the wider economy and society (Loney, 1983). They provided considerable evidence to reinforce the argument that 'community', in terms of any traditional meaning of the word, was dead. Many of the economic and social problems which local areas exemplified were, by and large, bound up with national economic policies.

The political implications of this critique led to the piecemeal abandonment of CDPs in the later 1970s, although much of the work of community development workers continued. To some extent it also fuelled the attack on monolithic and bureaucratic systems of welfare and on the enlarged-scale social services departments that emerged in the 1970s. Critics argued that community-oriented welfare systems should be encouraged which were sensitive to local needs, whereas social services were actually becoming more remote and difficult to access (Hadley and Hatch, 1981).

'Going local'

In a critique entitled *Social Welfare and the Failure of the State* Hadley and Hatch called for the development of 'patch systems' of social work: that

BOX 4.4 The 'patch' system in social services. Source: Hadley and Hatch (1981)

Organisation and operation
To re-capitulate, the essential features of the alternative community-centred model of organisation were:
(a) locally based teams, focusing on small areas or patches;
(b) the capacity to obtain detailed information about the patch;
(c) accessibility and acceptability to the patch population;
(d) close liaison with other local agencies and groups;
(e) the integration of all field and domiciliary workers within patch teams;
(f) participative forms of management in patch and area teams;
(g) the exercise of a substantial degree of autonomy by patch and area teams.

---

is, a locally based team serving a population of under 10 000, which liaised closely with other local agencies and voluntary groups, developed integrated systems of support and were able to exercise quite a high degree of control over their work (see Box 4.4). This process of 'going local', it was argued, would enable social workers to know their local areas, support local social networks and maximise the potential for informal caring in a given locality.

In 1982 the Barclay Report proposed the development of community social work, to underpin and 'tap into' the informal networks that had always provided the bulk of non-medical care. The report commented that since relatives, friends and neighbours provided the bulk of care for dependent people, the role of social services should be to work in a close relationship with these carers. Social workers should develop a partnership in which local communities and mutual help and self help groups would have some share in decision-making.

The report suggested two approaches, one focused on work with particular client groups and the other on locality, and this second option – called neighbourhood based social work – owed a great deal to the patch idea. Variants of the patch system of working have been developed in social work, for example the Normanton project, and have also influenced health work thinking, for example the 1986 Cumberlege Committee Report (see below). But the Barclay Report has also been criticised, particularly on the grounds that it overestimated the extent of 'untapped sources' of informal care.

In the 1980s local community work was given new impetus by the development of neighbourhood offices, where local people could bring a whole range of welfare problems to one office and be referred on for specialist advice and support. Many local authorities have now divided up their areas into 'neighbourhoods' of a few thousand people and have de-centralised services such as housing allocation, building works, rent collection and environmental services. In addition, local authorities are setting up systems of local representation: planning committees, area subcommittees or even neighbourhood councils. Nor are these the only recent initiatives to focus on underpinning (or reviving) community; Inner City Partnerships and the most recent City Challenge projects are aimed at the economic regeneration of inner-city areas and at offering support to the most deprived populations.

Lay initiatives

The other major influence on professional community health work has come from lay and self help initiatives. Beattie (1991) suggests three different strands here: those originating in community settlements and charitable outreach projects; grass roots mutual aid organisations in poorer areas; and 'civil rights' activists, for example women, black and minority ethnic people, lesbians, gay men and disabled people. He also adds a fourth, which has been developed in some detail already: the community work and development initiatives led by professional workers but aimed at involving local lay people.

These groups, and in particular the women's movement and black and minority ethnic initiatives, have had a triple impact on professional health work. First, they have raised specific issues in the area of health and welfare and pushed to get these on to the health agenda: for example, the campaign to get information about sickle cell anaemia made freely available to black sufferers and black people in general (Anionwu, 1989). Second, they have developed self help groups and initiatives to support sufferers (for example with mental health problems) and carers (such as young mothers), and this has encouraged professional health workers to recognise and respond to unmet needs. Third, they have led to professional health workers becoming involved in lay projects, both as advisers providing expert support (and financial backing) and in more egalitarian partnerships with lay people.

Working for health in community settings

Now let's consider the ways in which these various models have fed into community health work initiatives. First of all, it is worth noting that several government reports in the 1980s put a greater emphasis on locally based primary health care services. *Primary Health Care* (DHSS, 1986a) and the White Paper *Promoting Better Health* (DHSS, 1986b) both envisaged a much wider role for family doctors (GPs) in monitoring local populations. Contractual changes have encouraged GPs to provide a more ambitious local service, including health promotion work and small scale surgical treatment, and led to the setting of area based targets for screening 'at risk' groups (see Box 4.5). There is also the evidence of rapid expansion in local health projects and of attempts to develop a

BOX 4.5 The new general practitioner contract

From 1 April 1990 a new contract for GPs was introduced by the government. This changed the balance between allowances (paid to all family doctors), capitation (fee per patient) and service fees (paid for specific work carried out). Some of the changes were:

1 Capitation per patient was varied. Doctors were paid more for 65–74 year olds, for over 75s and for patients resident in 'areas of deprivation'.

2 New service fees were given for health promotion work, for new patient check-ups, child health surveillance and minor surgery. GPs were required to do more health promotion work, including annual check-ups and home visits to over 75 year olds, more assessment of young children and regular 'life-style' check-ups for adults.

3 Target payments were offered for cervical cytology and infant immunisation. Lower and higher targets were set – 50 and 80 per cent of those eligible for cervical smears and 70 and 90 per cent of infants.

4 GPs were able to advertise and provide more information for patients. They should hold surgeries at times convenient for their patients.

5 All doctors were given a basic 'practice allowance' and payment for practice expenses such as rent and practice nurses. Doctors were encouraged to employ more practice team staff and carry out minor operations.

better focused 'neighbourhood' approach to nursing care (Cumberlege Committee Report, DHSS, 1986c). During the 1980s the community has increasingly become the focus of health work. Most obvious is the growth of community care, which we'll explore in Section 4.5, but a wide variety of other health services and activities directed at groups within the community has been developed too.

○ Make a list of all the groups you can think of in your locality which are targeted by health workers, and the kinds of group activities that exist. Is there anything significant about the list you have made?

Here is a list to compare with your own: well woman clinic, mother and toddler group, keep fit class, antenatal class, relaxation group, alcohol advice centre, patients' committee, outreach clinic, advice session, health shop, community health project. This would represent the work of a well-organised and ambitious primary health care team, although many GP practices would certainly not offer this range of facilities. Marylebone Health Centre in London is one example of a GP group practice which does provide a wide range of services and support. It

encourages patient participation in user groups and offers complementary therapies, counselling, stress management and an outreach
scheme to the local multi-ethnic community (K258, 1992).

Much health work is directed towards women, especially young
mothers with pre-school children, and much less is specifically aimed at
black and minority ethnic groups or at older people, another group that
might be socially isolated within the community. This reflects the
historic priorities of community based health work: tackling high rates of
maternal and infant mortality (Lewis, 1980). Some health work targets
particular 'problem' groups, such as those with drug or alcohol
problems. Perhaps not suprisingly, hardly any targets the whole
community.

You may have been struck by the diversity of local groups working
for health. The range reflects the growth of 'fringe' health services which
are not statutory requirements in primary health care. There is no
obligation to seek patients' views by running a patients' forum, for
example, although the British Medical Association has given them a
cautious welcome and no longer sees patient participation as necessarily
a threat to medical authority (Watkins, 1987). There is similarly no
requirement to run well women clinics, yet the numbers of clinics grew
rapidly during the 1980s (Thornley, 1987). The list also reminds us of
how health work is responding to changing needs in very different
ways. Almost all of the groups listed could meet locally, at the clinic,
health centre or in a nearby hall, and most are run by nursing staff:
health visitors, midwives and practice nurses. Indeed these categories of
health worker may be the key players in developing GP practice based
groups, even if the initial decision is taken by the doctor.

As we noted earlier, health professionals have variously been
experts, advisers and co-partners in lay–professional initiatives. Thornley
(1987) identifies three contrasting models among well women clinics: a
'medical model' based on the preventive health check by an expert; the
'holistic model' based on expert–lay co-operation; and the 'self help
model' in which volunteers, with and without health work training,
share knowledge and responsibility. Clearly there are tensions as well as
advantages when the holistic model of co-operation and equal partnership is chosen. In one well woman clinic in South Manchester, for
example, local health professionals made no response and gave little
support to the initiative, although individual, highly committed health
workers joined with the local women's group and the CHCs to launch
the scheme (Williams, 1987). Particular problems were over relations
between professionals and volunteers, and the fear that 'the majority of
health workers we had made contact with wished to change or control
rather than help or join the team'. This problem was overcome when a
new nursing officer based herself at the clinic and made it her business

to draw in local professionals. By contrast, another South Manchester well woman clinic was started by three local health visitors who deliberately developed it on a holistic, partnership basis with lay helpers.

Several high street 'health shops' now exist, run by health promotion professionals with volunteer support. They enable people to call in and get immediate advice and help, as well as to find longer term support through local networks. The health shop initiative complements the 10 000 community health projects (as we noted in Chapter 1) in the UK today, many of which have health professional support but are run to a considerable degree by lay people. There are markedly different models here too, but this lay–professional collaboration and the whole effort to encourage 'community' participation (at least among some groups in the community) are striking features of contemporary community health work.

○   Suggest how the concerns of health professionals working in community settings echo those of community workers.

First, notions of power-sharing between lay people and health professionals, and of empowering local groups to take action on their own behalf, are prominent in current community health work. Health promotion campaigns such as the Healthy Cities network and Health For All 2000 also emphasise the importance of involving local people and groups. The Healthy Cities Project in Liverpool, for example, stresses community participation and intersectoral collaboration: that is, working 'with all agencies and groups whose activities are relevant to the promotion of the public health' (Ashton and Seymour, 1988). Second, in community health projects, in some outreach and well women clinic work and in local health surveys there is considerable evidence that area poverty and deprivation reflect wider inequalities of income, choice and access which require a response at regional or national level as well as in terms of local initiatives (Townsend *et al.*, 1987). In other words, community based health work is not a panacea, as community workers and patch teams have already discovered.

Alison While and other researchers (1989) demonstrate some of the problems inherent in using an area approach to health issues, and indeed their analysis draws on the urban deprivation research of the 1970s. *Health in the Inner City* explores the health issues and problems facing different groups in inner-city areas – children, youth, families, people in old age and those with mental health problems. The authors acknowledge the difficulties in identifying and focusing on place as the crucial determinant of health needs. They comment on the danger of 'labelling and stigmatizing certain areas and the families who live there' and argue that:

The evidence does not support the thesis that inner cities throw up a unique pattern of problems, but rather there is an excess of disadvantage which varies from one location to another and, indeed, . . . outside inner city areas . . . Not only are there major differences between different inner city areas, but also enormous contrasts in the circumstances of different inner city residents.

While (1989)

This is a timely warning in view of the growing enthusiasm for community based forms of health work and the government's recent interest in health targets, because it highlights important issues about patterns of health disadvantage and inequality. You can read about definitions of poverty and its relationship to health status in Chapter 6.

The impact of health policy shifts

Some of the tensions and contradictions of health work in community settings can be demonstrated by reviewing the fortunes of the Cumberlege Committee Report. This envisaged a nurse manager-led 'neighbourhood nursing service' for each local area, in which all specialist nurses outside hospitals would work. Wisely side stepping the confusion about community, the report argued that evidence of neighbourly feelings and lay people's willingness to care for dependent people justified a 'neighbourhood' focus. Each nursing team was seen as serving an area of 10–25 000 people; in other words, the neighbourhood was seen as a geographical area, with no autonomy but with its own networks and mutual support. The aim was to provide a better trained, co-ordinated and more independent nursing service which was orientated to client needs, instead of one which was largely geared to meeting general practitioners' needs. The report was welcomed by nurses working in community settings but implementation (at nil cost) has been left to district health authorities (see Box 4.6). The more radical changes proposed by Cumberlege, such as the phasing out of payments to GPs to employ practice nurses (which would have funded the creation of the neighbourhood nursing service) and the creation of written contracts between GPs and nurses, were quietly shelved.

Instead recent changes in health service structures have had the effect of strengthening GPs' independence. Their controlling bodies, the family health services authorities (FHSAs), were given greater independence and higher status. The White Paper *Working For Patients* (DoH, 1989a) announced plans to encourage GPs in larger general practices to become independent 'fundholders', with an annual budget from which they purchased treatments for their patients (see Box 4.5). By the end of 1992 evidence from the first wave of fundholders suggested that some had amassed a considerable budget surplus,

BOX 4.6 Cumberlege Committee Report: main recommendations. Source: DHSS (1986c)

1 Each district health authority should identify within its boundaries neighbourhoods for the purposes of planning, organising and providing nursing and related primary care services.

2 A neighbourhood nursing service (NNS) should be established in each neighbourhood.

3 Each neighbourhood nursing service should be headed by a manager chosen for her manage-ment skills and leadership qualities, and she should be based in the neighbourhood.

4 Community midwives, community psychiatric nurses and community mental handicap nurses should ensure, through their respective managers and the neighbourhood nursing manager, that their specialist contributions are fully co-ordinated with the work of the neighbourhood nursing service.

5 All other specialist nurses who work outside hospital should be based in the community and managed as part of the neigh-bourhood nursing service. Each specialist nurse should be assigned to one or more neigh-bourhood services and have the commitment of her time to each service specified.

6 The principle should be adopted of introducing the nurse practitioner into primary health care.

7 The DHSS should agree a limited list of items and simple agents which may be prescribed by nurses as part of a nursing care programme, and issue guidelines to enable nurses to control drug dosage in well-defined circumstances.

8 To establish and be recognised as a primary health care team, each general medical practice and the community nurses associated with it should come to an under-standing of the team's objectives and individuals' roles within it.

That understanding should be incorporated into a written agree-ment signed jointly by the practice partners and by the manager of the neighbourhood nursing service on behalf of the relevant health authority.

The agreement should name the doctor and community nurses who together form the primary care team and should guarantee the right of the team members to be consulted on any changes proposed in its composition.

The making of such an agreement should be a qualifying condition for any incentive payments which may be introduced to improve quality in general practice (as suggested in the recent policy statement of the Royal College of General Practitioners).

9 The Government should invite the Health Advisory Service, with its established reputation, credibility and acceptance by the professions, to take on responsibility for identifying and promoting good practice in primary health care.

10 Subsidies to general practitioners enabling them to employ staff to perform nursing duties should be phased out.

11 Within two years the United Kingdom Central Council for Nursing, Midwifery and Health Visiting and the English National Board should introduce a common training course for all first-level nurses wishing to work outside hospital in what are now the fields of health visiting, district nursing and school nursing.

12 The provision of nursing services in the community should remain the responsibility of district health authorities. We would urge, however, that in due course the Government should give consideration to amalgamating family practitioner committees and district health authorities and so bring all primary health care services under the control of one body.

13 A short but thorough manpower planning exercise on a practical (as distinct from purely academic) basis should be undertaken to ensure that the training and supply of community nurses is, and remains at, the appropriate level. The study should be supported by the NHS Management Board as an essential task in reviewing the adequacy and consistency of Regional plans.

14 Health care associations should be formed, each covering one or more neighbourhoods.

which they could spend on private surgery extensions and improvements and on staffing. There was also some evidence that GPs were selecting their patients more carefully and not accepting those with chronic, expensive-to-treat conditions, even though in theory patients had now more freedom to change their doctor.

It now seems that the effect of health service changes has been to strengthen the position of GPs as opposed to the independence of patients or nurses, although nurses are being given powers to prescribe a limited range of medicines (Calnan and Gabe, 1991). GPs are now accountable to a fully independent FHSA rather than (as pre-1985) to the regional health authority. The model of primary health care being projected in the 1990s is firmly focused upon the budgetholding group practice with its primary health care team of doctors, practice nurses and community nurses, its social work and counselling, its monitoring, health promotion and minor surgery and its patient participation groups. This might bring considerable benefits to local communities if it can be generalised across the health service. At present, particularly in large cities such as London and in poorer inner-city areas, only a small minority of practices conform to this model. Many GPs still work single-handed in practices in inadequate premises (Tomlinson Report, DoH, 1993b).

To move beyond a 'medical treatment' model and develop community based health work, which picks up on and responds to the range of primary health needs in local communities, requires not only adequate resources but also a reconceptualisation of what community means. Much of the impetus of recent community health initiatives has come from outside the formal health service – from lay users of services, women's groups, black and minority ethnic groups and so on – and from the intellectual and practical contribution of community and social work. It is rooted to some extent in the idea of 'community of place' – the neighbourhood or local area where interaction already exists and can be encouraged. It is also rooted in 'community of interest' – in assisting groups of patients with common interests (for example an illness or a caring responsibility) to work together to their common advantage.

Finally, there is a less tangible 'community sense' dimension: that the interaction and self help will develop or reinforce belonging, mutuality and shared rituals. A wide range of voluntary groups – religious organisations, charitable bodies, school based associations and so on – are now involved alongside health professionals in local projects; to that degree 'community sense' does exist. On the other hand, the growth of 'community care' in the 1980s, as we shall see, has overwhelmingly meant either professional or commercially based services or family care. This suggests that community continues to be a useful ideological construct and for that reason should be intensely scrutinised.

4.5 Care in the community

The most influential current use of the term 'community' is in 'community care'. Community care has had a long and confusing history, and this makes it particularly important to think about the significance of the term itself, and about the pairing of 'care' with 'community', before we look at the policies themselves.

○   At this point note down your own definition of the term 'community care'.

You might well have referred to treatment and professional assistance provided outside hospitals, in people's own homes or in local, accessible centres and clinics. You could equally well have described a network of voluntary and informal support provided for people who need help in their local areas. In other words, you could have defined the 'care' as treatment provided by professionals or as support given by lay people. You could have defined 'community' as a locality in receipt of non-hospital services and as the object of professional activity, or you could have defined 'community' as a local self help system. Philip Abrams (1977), in an authoritative review of the issues, emphasised that community care meant care provided by 'lay members of societies acting in everyday domestic and occupational settings': that is, care *by* the community operating through informal networks. But the widespread use of the term to describe professional services in specific localities outside institutions – care *in* the community – has produced a new and completely different set of meanings.

Women and caring

The fact that both sets of definitions have at times been associated with community care alerts us to the politics of the issue and the deliberate ambiguity of the term. The phrase seeks to persuade us that an identifiable area and web of relationships exists and represents a legitimate subject for the activity of caring, but it leaves unclear who should be doing the caring and with what resources. As critics have pointed out, in reality the burden of community care has been borne not by the community, not even by the family, but by women. In the case of families caring for an infirm elderly person, or for someone who is severely handicapped, this work can become onerous and even crippling in its demands: 'the daily grind' of dressing, feeding, washing, fetching and carrying (Bayley, 1973). Normative assumptions about caring have romanticised its burdensome nature and enabled policy makers to ignore the implications for women of undertaking this private, unpaid, largely unsupported labour (Finch and Groves, 1983).

Gillian Dalley (1988) has argued that the nuclear family model, although it is in decline in practice, still has immense ideological force. The sexual division of labour in the nuclear family – male breadwinner in the public sphere and dependent wife caring for husband and children in the private home – structures the ideology and practice of caring. It is intimately connected to an ideology of 'familism' (see Section 3.2). Women are expected to be altruistic, to care; they are socialised into caring roles in the family and into caring jobs if they enter the public sphere. They are not expected to have negative feelings about those they care for:

The ambivalence frequently felt by those involved in the process of caring is made more problematic because public discourse insists that there can be no separation between caring for and caring about. Those who care 'about' are expected always to care 'for' and vice versa. Official and lay commentaries on community care policies all assert the conjunction of the two: chronically dependent people are best cared for at home or in home-like surroundings because this is the only location where the two processes coincide.

Dalley (1988)

Dalley suggests that men, because they work in the public sphere as 'breadwinners', are allowed to *care about* – that is, to be responsible for – dependants without *caring for* (tending) them. This ideology underpins the drive for community care. The policy is seen as unproblematic, but in fact it reinforces the subordinate role of women and the ideology of women as altruistic, 'natural' carers. It is the reverse of what it claims to be; community care is in reality privatised female care.

Richard Titmuss, a major writer on post-war social policy, warned long ago that the phrase 'community care' conjured up visions of 'warmth and human kindness, essentially personal and comforting'. He belittled the idea that 'statutory magic and comforting appellation' could somehow create a 'community' where it didn't exist before, let alone one that 'cared' (Titmuss, 1968). Over the years community care has become an ideological battleground, an arena in which very different and often conflicting policy claims have been staked out. As Alan Walker has commented:

The amalgamation of two terms –'community' and 'care' – both of which are so overladen with ambiguity, idealistic values and connotations, has proved particularly irresistible to politicians. In their hands community care has been elevated to almost mystical status and, in the process, has lost touch with reality . . . The problem for those seeking conceptual clarity is that policy makers requisitioned the term community care in the immediate post-war period and developed a completely new meaning for it when they started applying it to the delivery of services.

Walker (1986)

The shifting basis of community care

Community care has figured as part of social care and health care policy since the 1950s. The major goal of community care policy, filtered through 40 years of government reports and recommendations, has been to maintain individuals whenever possible in their own (or their families') homes or in 'community' settings, as opposed to providing care in institutions. As a broad policy goal this has received support from right across the political spectrum, on economic and humanitarian grounds. Erving Goffman's (1961) powerful academic critique of the dehumanising effect of institutions was driven home by a series of shocking revelations about conditions in long-stay hospitals which climaxed in the inquiries into substandard hospital care in Ely and Whittingham hospitals at the end of the 1960s. Social researchers provided powerful intellectual support for community care policy by exploring the dehumanising effects of institutional care, and only a few dissenting voices pointed out that there would be possible hidden costs unless the financial implications of providing adequate care in the community were accepted. It is in the interpretation of this goal of community care – in terms of specific policy objectives and priorities for service provision – that conflicts have arisen.

○   Make a list of all the individuals and groups who you think might be eligible for community care and of the care they would receive and the types of workers who would deliver this care.

Box 4.7 shows a list compiled by two nursing students in 1989, and it demonstrates the multiplicity of groups, services and workers involved. You might like to compare it with Table 4.1, which is the Audit Commission's 1986 diagram of the agencies involved in community care for elderly people.

From the 1950s onwards the term 'community care' was used to refer to care services for dependent groups – mainly people with disabilities, older people, children and those with mental health problems or with learning difficulties – provided by professional and domiciliary staff in non-institutional settings. Until recently, therefore, it referred more to services provided by the personal social services than by the health service, because health care was focused on the hospital. In the 1950s and 1960s the major focus was the provision of treatment by professional health workers in local settings, and it was acknowledged that these might need to be residential, even if they could be mainly clinic based, or domiciliary (Allsop, 1984). In the mid-1970s, to add to the confusion, hospitals, hostels, residential homes and day centres were brought under the community care banner. Community care now ranged from care in residential settings (such as older peoples' homes),

BOX 4.7 Community care agencies and recipients: the students' list

People who receive community care	Community care agencies
- Elderly people - The chronic sick and disabled - People with mental health problems - People with mental disabilities - Children	- Health authority community nurses – psychiatric nurses, mental handicap nurses, district nurses, health visitors - Other health staff, for example bath nurse - Social services departments – social workers - Home helps - Meals-on-wheels - Local authority residential homes - Sheltered housing (local authority) - Day centres - Voluntary provision such as St John's Ambulance and Red Cross - Self help groups and community centres

TABLE 4.1 Community care: main care and accommodation services. Source: Audit Commission (1986)

Agency	Form of care	Service	Variations
Health Authorities	Hospitals	- In-patients	- Long-stay - Short-stay/respite
	Residential	- Day - Community units - Nursing homes	
	Community Services	- Nurses	- Qualified - Auxiliary
		- Health visitors - Therapists	- Physiotherapists - Chiropody
Family Practitioner Committees	Primary Health Care	- GPs - Nurses - Dental and opthalmic services	
Social Services	Residential	- Residential homes	- Long-stay - Short-stay/respite

TABLE 4.1 *Continued*

Agency	Form of care	Service	Variations
	Accommodation	– Staffed group homes	
		– Unstaffed group homes	
		– Sheltered lodgings	
	Day Care	– Workshops	
		– Day centres	
		– Training centres	
		– Drop-in centres	
	Domiciliary	– Social workers	
		– Good neighbours	
		– Home helps	
		– Therapists	– Occupational
Housing Authorities	Housing	– Sheltered housing	– Wardens
			– Alarm systems
		– Hostels	
		– Group homes	
		– Flats/houses	– Improvement grants
Education	Training facilities for adults		
Voluntary Sector and Housing Associations	Residential Housing	– Residential homes	
		– Group homes	
		– Sheltered housing	– For special needs
		– Flats/houses	
	Day Care	– Luncheon clubs	
		– Drop-in centres	
	Domiciliary	– Care attendant schemes	
		– Volunteers/good neighbours	
Private Sector	Residential	– Nursing homes	
		– Residential homes	
	Housing	– Sheltered housing	
	Domiciliary	– Domestic agencies	

through provision of services in day centres (such as chiropody and occupational therapy), to the domiciliary work of home helps. Essentially, client groups were seen as more or less passive recipients of expert care; on the other hand these services were seen as vital in helping individuals to maintain their independence.

Unfortunately, compared with the resources devoted to hospitals and institutional care, they were also 'Cinderella' services, which were often understaffed and perennially underfunded. By the late 1970s, in spite of two decades of unprecedented growth, official targets were not being met in a number of services: for example in day care places for elderly people and those with mental health problems and disabilities, in the provision of home helps or of meals-on-wheels (Townsend, 1981).

Care by the community

Government reports up to the late 1970s emphasised community care as care *in* the community, but thereafter the emphasis has increasingly shifted to care *by* the community. In 1981 Margaret Thatcher, then Prime Minister, commented in a complete reversal of policy that 'the statutory services are the supportive ones, underpinning where necessary, filling the gaps and helping the helpers'. A succession of reports from the late 1970s onwards signalled this new orientation towards voluntary and informal caring, and towards private instead of public sector provision (see Table 4.2). Financial pressures, caused by political pressures to cut costs and by the rising numbers of very elderly people, have encouraged

TABLE 4.2 Growth of private sector care. Source: NAHAT (1993c)

1 Elective surgery in private sector

1981	13.2% of elective surgery in private sector
1986	16.7% of elective surgery in private sector

2 Private medical insurance

1981	1.87 million policy holders
1986	2.82 million policy holders
1989	3.43 million policy holders, covering 7.24 m people

3 Total share of UK hospital based treatment
(as a percentage of total revenue/capital costs of UK hospital services)

1984	7.5
1986	9.6
1988	12.0
1989	15.3 (total value of £2 699m)

slower growth and therefore increased dependence on informal carers. As we noted earlier, much of the everyday work of caring is, and always has been, carried out largely by women – in families, or as neighbours and friends.

Such unpaid labour was recognised in official reports, such as the Wolfenden Report of 1977, but largely in the sense of being included in the balance sheet of resources available. The report identified statutory agencies, the commercial sector, voluntary provision and the 'informal' sector as the constituent elements of community care (Allsop, 1984). Indeed the existence of the informal sector was used to justify cuts in personal social services, because of the 'continuing growth in the amount of voluntary care, of neighbourhood care, of self help' (Social Services Committee, 1980, quoted in Walker, 1986).

In addition, the contribution made by the private sector became increasingly significant in the 1980s. Both in the negative sense of restricting the resources available to local authorities, and in the positive sense of covering the costs (for those on income support) of private residential and nursing homes, Conservative governments have encouraged the rapid expansion of private sector care. The costs to the then Department of Health and Social Security (which became two separate departments covering health (DoH) and social security (DSS) from 1988) have been very high. In spite of the imposition of national cash limits in 1985, which ranged from £150 to £215 for weekly board and lodging payments to older and mentally handicapped people in residential and nursing homes, costs rocketed from £6 million in 1978 to £1.3 billion in 1991 (NACAB, 1991).

Until the 1980s powerful vested interests, particularly in the hospital sector, resisted change, and community care was only slowly implemented. The government itself accepted that the pace of change must be determined by the level of community provision and that 'hospitals should not encourage patients to leave unless there are satisfactory arrangements for their support' (DHSS, 1976). In the 1980s, as political pressure for the discharge of people with mental health problems into the community increased, thousands of individuals were discharged from hospitals and many ended up in bed and breakfast accommodation with little or no community support. Among mentally handicapped people increased rates of discharge in the 1980s have resulted in large numbers entering private residential homes: a shift, in effect, from one institution to another.

In 1986, in a hostile and influential report, the Audit Commission (the Government's independent watchdog on public expenditure) attacked the high costs and widespread inefficiencies of policies for community care. It singled out for criticism the estimated £500 million cost of private sector care and commented that:

If all residents now in local authority care or NHS geriatric and mental health hospitals were to be transferred to private residential care, Supplementary Benefit [now Income Support] payments for board and lodgings would increase up to a theoretical upper limit of more than £2 billion a year.

DHSS, Audit Commission (1986)

The Commission also drew attention to the lack of redistribution of resources from hospital based services to locally based local authority and health services, and to the lack of funds (and lack of will) to ease the transition of patients to community care settings. It pointed out that people were being cared for in inappropriate, institutional settings in the community when they could be given more appropriate, and less expensive, assistance in their own homes (see Figure 4.2). In particular, the lack of financial resources and support for those with mental health problems was criticised.

In these comments the Commission was echoing the widespread findings of social researchers that community care policies were often not working in the best interests of clients. A number of reports indicated that there were too few controls over standards in private homes, some of which offered poor quality care and were inadequately staffed (Holmes and Johnson, 1988). Increased choice has proved a chimera since most admissions to residential care have been the result of a crisis in care in the informal sector (Walker, 1993). The reality is that private mini-institutions in the community have been replacing larger-scale public sector institutions.

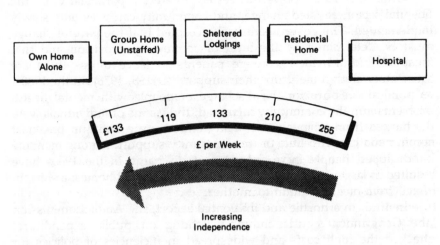

FIGURE 4.2 Cost estimates for different types of care. Source: Audit Commission (1986)

4.6 Current policies for community care

In the late 1980s mounting criticism of current policies and the rising cost of care persuaded the government to appoint Sir Roy Griffiths to report on future policy directions. He was a private sector executive who had already headed a management enquiry into the NHS in 1983 (see Chapter 11). Griffiths was specifically asked to investigate:

The way in which public funds are used to support community care policy and to advise on the options for action that would improve the use of these funds as a contribution to more effective community care.

DHSS (1988)

In his report *Community Care: Agenda for Action* (DoH, 1988) Griffiths echoed the views of previous investigators that 'community care is a poor relation; everybody's distant relative but nobody's baby', noting that there were few areas where 'the gap between political rhetoric and policy on the one hand, or between policy and reality in the field on the other hand have been so great'. His emphasis was on creating practical policy 'in the context of available resources and timescales for action' and on promoting consumer satisfaction and choice. As you can see from his proposals for action (Box 4.8) it contained a number of quite radical recommendations for changing community care policy.

Reflect on the Griffiths proposals in Box 4.8 in the light of the discussion in Section 4.5. What do you think are the most significant changes suggested in his report?

The most radical changes proposed are perhaps the creation of a ministerial post with clear responsibility for community care and the use of local social services authorities as the lead agencies to design, organise and purchase care, though not primarily to provide it themselves. Both these proposals were designed to overcome what was seen as confusion about roles and responsibilities and the conflicts inherent in multiple agency provision. Other parts of his report, such as the increased role for voluntary and private sector agencies, are more familiar and closely reflect the reorientation in community care policies in the 1980s that we have already noted. The transfer of board and lodging funds to what he hoped would be ring-fenced social services budgets was seen as putting an effective ceiling on statutory expenditure; central government would have controlling powers both to monitor local plans and to regulate resources.

BOX 4.8 The Griffiths Report: main findings. Source: DoH (1988)

1.1 I recommend that the following steps be taken to create better opportunities for the successful and efficient delivery of community care policies for adults who are mentally ill, mentally handicapped, elderly or physically disabled and similar groups.

1.2 Central government should ensure that there is a Minister of State in DHSS, seen by the public as being clearly responsible for community care. His role should be strengthened and clarified in the light of the other recommendations.

1.3 Local social services authorities should, within the resources available:
1.3.1 assess the community care needs of their locality, set local priorities and service objectives, and develop local plans in consultation with health authorities in particular (but also others including housing authorities, voluntary bodies, and private providers of care) for delivering those objectives;
1.3.2 identify and assess individuals' needs, taking full account of personal preferences (and those of informal carers), and design packages of care best suited to enabling the consumer to live as normal a life as possible;
1.3.3 arrange the delivery of packages of care to individuals, building first on the available contribution of informal carers and neighbourhood support, then the provision of domiciliary and day services or, if appropriate, residential care;
1.3.4 act for these purposes as the designers, organisers and purchasers of non-health care services, and not primarily as direct providers, making the maximum possible use of voluntary and private sector bodies to widen consumer choice, stimulate innovation and encourage efficiency.

1.4 To enable this to happen, local social services authorities must be put into a position to take a more comprehensive view of care needs and services.

1.5 Equally to enable action to be taken, local social services authorities will need confidence that their resources can match their responsibilities. Therefore:
1.5.1 central government should arrange for the necessary transfer of resources between central and local government to match the defined responsibilities.

1.6 It is further recommended that:
1.6.1 health authorities should continue to be responsible for medically required community health services, including making any necessary input into assessing needs and delivering packages of care;
1.6.2 general medical practitioners should be responsible for ensuring that local social services authorities are aware of their patients' needs for non-health care;
1.6.3 public housing authorities should be responsible for providing and financing only the 'bricks and mortar' of housing for community care;
1.6.4 authorities should have the power to act jointly, or as agents for each other;
1.6.5 distribution of specific grant should take account of the extent to which consumers in a local authority area are able to meet the full economic cost of services;
1.6.6 the functions of a 'community carer' should be developed into a new occupation, with appropriate training, so that one person can, as far as possible, provide whatever personal and practical assistance an individual requires.

A new framework for community care

The Griffiths Report was followed by the government White Paper *Caring For People* (DoH, 1989b) and by the National Health Service and Community Care Act of 1990. Most of the recommendations of the Griffiths Report were reproduced in *Caring For People*, which once again emphasised the role of the voluntary and informal sector and the aim of promoting choice and independence – the key refrains of 1980s Conservative policy. The notion of a 'purchaser–provider split', implicit in Griffiths, was made explicit in the White Paper. Social services departments were to be the purchasers of packages of care, but they were no longer to be major providers; indeed the 1990 Act ensured that there were financial disincentives for local authorities in continuing to run their own residential homes. One major difference, however, was that the government refused to ring-fence the community care budget, so that the monies remained part of the general revenue support grant given to local authorities and risked being diverted to support other local authority services. After a fierce battle Virginia Bottomley, the Health Secretary, agreed in 1992 to protect some resources, but only those provided for services to people with mental health problems.

The legislative framework for community care was in place by April 1990 and was at first due to come into effect in April 1991. But its implementation was then delayed for two years, almost certainly because of financial pressures. Meanwhile local authorities began the task of creating the framework which was to deliver choice in options and services, flexibility and active participation by the user and carer.

Social policy responses

On the whole the response of social policy analysts to these changes can be described as one of optimism overlaid with doubt. Commenting on the Griffiths Report, Sally Baldwin and Gillian Parker (1989) criticised its political naivety but welcomed the recommendation to give social services departments the lead role. Other commentators have focused on problems of choice, the role of carers and finance, issues which are central to the provisions of the 1990 legislation. There is potential conflict, for example, between enlarging consumer choice – enabling people to select packages of care to suit them – and meeting priority needs – providing care in line with professional assessment of need (Pollitt, 1988). If those people with independent resources buy up the best care services, others who are dependent on more meagre state benefits might end up with second class services, even if their needs are greater. Although consumer choice is encouraged, public sector residential care will be cut back (and local authority homes may be privatised), so that increasingly choice will only be between different private sector options. There is also the possibility of tension and conflict between the views of professionals and lay people, and between carers and their dependent relatives.

Carers were acknowledged by Griffiths and in the White Paper to be in need of 'help and support if they are to continue to carry out their role' (DoH, 1989b). But although carers are to play a part in helping to decide the most appropriate package of care, there is no evidence of extra resources being provided for them. There is also a central assumption that the family (or friends and neighbours) will carry out the 'great bulk' of care, despite evidence that conflicts and tensions frequently exist in caring relationships (Qureshi and Walker, 1989). We noted earlier that the feminist critique of community care highlights how the nuclear family-derived (familist) model exploits women as 'natural' carers.

Alan Walker (1993) has pointed out that the Griffiths Report itself, the White Paper and the subsequent legislation were products of a top-down managerial approach in which the views and needs of users and their informal carers were not given priority. Participation in decision-making about the packages of care and about the quality of services might well be restricted to the occasional survey among users, a model proposed by private management consultants.

Several critics have highlighted the financial implications of community care policies, since it is clear that good quality community provision is not much cheaper than institutional care (Challis and Davies, 1986). Some have questioned whether resource constraints in general will prevent these new policies for community care from ever being fully implemented, unless the cheapest solution of informal care is expanded to breaking point.

4.7 Community care and consumer sovereignty

At the root of the community care policies being implemented in the 1990s lies the concept of 'consumer choice'. It is a powerful and persuasive rhetoric associated with the rise of the New Right in British politics. As we noted in Section 2.4, the New Right espouses an anti-collectivist, free market approach to welfare and emphasises the overarching importance of personal freedom. The notion of the 'sovereign consumer' expresses this market-orientation, and it currently informs many other contemporary policies in and beyond the field of welfare. We'll be looking in some depth at the politics of welfare in

Chapter 13, but it is useful to review the ideas associated with the term at this point since it resonates powerfully with 'community'.

Reflect for a few minutes on the concept of 'consumer choice'. What do you see as its main characteristics, and what other examples of the use of this term can you recall?

Consumer choice, or 'consumer sovereignty' as it is often termed, focuses on ways of extending the range of available options and services so that individuals can select what they want for themselves. Since the early 1980s promoting consumer choice has become associated in political terms with contracting out and privatisation of public services, and the public sector has been castigated as monolithic, bureaucratic, inefficient and dependency-creating: the 'nanny state' of Conservative demonology. The premise is that of 'free market' economics: that consumers will ensure through their purchasing power that an appropriate range of goods and services is always available at reasonable prices, and that this will work as well for what have been 'public sector services' as it has for private sector goods and services. There is no essential difference, in other words, between purchasing a package of care and buying a washing machine.

You may have noticed that the 'privatisation' of hitherto public sector services has been advocated on the grounds that individual choice would be widened by market competition, and that competition would create more sensitive and consumer-oriented services, whereas public sector monopoly offered no freedom of choice and often provided poor quality service. Public monopolies, such as gas, water, electricity and latterly British Rail have been broken up into separate companies and sold to the private sector. Other public sector services, which can't be easily privatised, have been persuaded to become 'more competitive' by the introduction of 'competitive tendering' and 'internal markets', as in the National Health Service.

It is useful to pick up Gillian Dalley's (1988) analysis at this point. You will recall that she saw community care arising from the ideology of familism and the nuclear family. She goes on to argue that both are rooted in *possessive individualism*: that is, in the idea of the individual as a free and autonomous agent in society. But the free individual is conceptualised as the man, historically the property owner, income earner and owner of wife and children. This leads us to the conclusion that individualism has largely been a celebration of men's freedom; men were natural sovereign consumers whereas women were naturally dependent.

The 1990 community care legislation should be viewed as part of this much wider ideology of consumer sovereignty and individualism. The shift in community care towards voluntary and informal caring and

private sector provision has been above all else an ideological reorientation. It reflects a clear conviction that the state (in this case local
government and its statutory social services departments) holds
monopoly powers that restrict the individual enterprise of both carers
and dependent individuals. By creating a situation in which local social
services departments create packages of care, but decreasingly provide
them, power will be handed back to individuals. They will operate as
consumers of care just as they do in relation to the purchase of other
market goods, by making rational choices based on their preferences
and resources.

A supermarket model of community care?

Several years ago, in relation to health service changes, Fedelma
Winkler (1987) coined the phrase 'the supermarket model of health' to
suggest that consumer choice went only as far as largely reactive
decision-making about which branded goods to buy or the right to make
a complaint. There was no provision for proactive choice, in which
people could genuinely participate in decisions about the services to be
provided and about allocating resources. Community care legislation
can be criticised in very similar terms. It has been argued that
community care is being deliberately subjected to fragmention, 'market-
isation' and to de-centralisation of administration accompanied by
centralisation of power (Walker, 1993). Although it appears that more
choice is being offered, the run-down of public sector residential care
means that a whole area of choice will disappear. Although local social
services' lead role appears to bring services nearer to the consumer and
to make services more responsive to consumer demands, strategic
decision-making power, exercised through financial and planning
controls, remains firmly at central government level. Local authorities
will increasingly have to ration services and may be forced into
purchasing quantity, not quality care. Moreover, there is no certainty
that consumer choice will be enlarged. Professionals and bureaucrats in
local authorities, who make the final decisions about appropriate forms
of care, may continue to value their own expertise above that of the
consumers with whom they negotiate; there are no rights of appeal for
users in the 1990 Act.

More fundamentally it might be argued that choice in the public
sector differs from private market transactions in several ways: many
consumers cannot 'shop around' for bargains, they often know fairly
little about the relative merits of services and they often lack the
resources to make their views count. Wealthier consumers may gain
greater choice, but this may be at the expense of those who lack
resources, even if their need is greater. The 1990 Act will not create a real

market system but a 'quasi-market': there will not be a range of suppliers with similar goals, there will not be consumers with cash and there will not be a free interplay of buyers and consumers (Hoyes and Means, 1993).

Clearly the policy of community care takes on a particular significance when linked to the ideology of consumer sovereignty. This ideology reinforces the notion of services that are sensitive and well-attuned to consumer needs, that take consumer preferences into account, that encourage active choice and individual participation in decision-making. Yet as we have seen, the 1990 Act may not deliver any of these promises to consumers. It remains an open question whether the legislative changes really intend to create (and if they do, whether they can deliver) consumer sovereignty in community care.

4.8 Rethinking community?

It is time to stand back from debates about specific policies for community and reflect once again on the broader significance of the concept itself. At one level it is clear that community is used as a synonym for 'local' or 'area'. But it is rarely used simply for convenience and without purpose. An ideological objective underpins its use; the rhetoric of community is projecting at a deeper level messages about boundaries, common interests, identity, membership and participation. Even more important, it is mediated through other ideologies which shape and inform it: the notion of consumer sovereignty and the ideologies of familism and possessive individualism.

Can you think of any ways in which 'rose tinted' visions of traditional community are still influential today?

Contemporary interest in country pursuits, in a pre-industrial heritage (stately homes, theme parks, museums of rural life and so on) and in escaping to the intimacy of village life indicate at least a romantic interest in community living, and a continued ambivalence toward the anonymous and impersonal world of the city. The 'flight to the suburbs', which began among wealthier groups in urban society in the later nineteenth century, spread to middle class and skilled working class households thereafter and still persists in the 1990s. Almost all big old industrial cities have experienced a decline in their inner and middle core populations; at the same time 'garden cities' and new towns have tried to capture the ideal of the 'village in town' through a deliberate recreation of neighbourhoods and of the supposed intimacy of village community life (Elkin *et al.*, 1991).

We have noted in this chapter that this results in an inevitable confusion between 'community' as ideal and its reality. The sociological contribution to this debate, while it has advanced our understanding of community in a number of ways, has muddied the waters in others. Its early critique of the demise of community and of traditional lifestyles in the face of rapid social and economic change in nineteenth century Europe gave way to a preoccupation with cosy working class communities. This created a series of myths – given substance and academic respectability by theorists – of earlier 'golden ages' of small, tightly-knit organic communities. It prevented us from investigating the complexity and heterogeneity of local communities and made the term itself almost redundant: the ultimate 'hooray' word which should be profoundly distrusted.

Some recent research into social networks and caring relationships has begun, in a sensibly modest way, to reconceptualise community. Recognising that the dispersal and internal migration of population in contemporary society has undermined the logic of investigating community of place in any traditional sense of the term, the focus is now on the connections between the individual and local activity. Peter Berger (1977) defined these as 'mediating structures': 'that is, those institutions which stand between the individual in his [sic] private sphere and the large institutions of the public sphere' (quoted in Willmott and Thomas, 1984). Among these intermediate institutions – 'family, church, voluntary association, neighbourhood and sub-culture' – some are long-standing, if continually changing, such as the family and the church. Others have been consciously planned, for example the attempt to support and empower deprived inner city populations by means of community based projects. Bulmer (1986) has argued that growth of community centres and activities demonstrates an attempt, predominantly in middle class neighbourhoods, 'to create a local social world through political or quasi-political action'.

Willmott and Thomas (1984) point out that the decline of community, in all three senses of the term, could be gradually reversed by changing work patterns, early retirement and the forced outcome of unemployment. In addition, James Robertson (1993) outlines a future for work in which the home increasingly becomes the workplace, and in which small-scale industries (which local authorities have attracted to revitalise run-down inner areas) become more widespread. It is possible that these shifts might begin to break down distinctions between work and leisure, and between formal, paid work and local voluntary action.

Health work practice and community

Enough has been said to indicate the dangers of adopting an uncritical stance towards community. The concept, however, still remains a central one in health work, not least because it is so widely used by health workers themselves. As we have seen, it is increasingly being claimed that services are delivered 'at a local level' to meet 'local community needs' and to 'empower the community'. The example of community care – the most important current development in the local health arena – offers striking evidence that ideologies surrounding community are powerful and persistent.

It is worth recalling the ideas of Dalley at this point. She argues that it is important to separate the idea of community care as a reforming approach from its oppressive policy outcomes. It is not community care as such that should be criticised, but the ideological constructs of familism and possessive individualism that underpin and influence it:

To be critical of community care is not to be critical of the importance of caring for and caring about, or of the necessity of enabling disabled and chronically dependent people to live 'normalised' and 'ordinary' lives . . . To question the nature of community care is to seek solutions which are equitable, comfortable and acceptable for chronically dependent people as well as for women as (potential) carers.

Dalley (1988)

We shall return to the debate about caring in Chapter 7, but it is important to bear in mind that these remarks relate to professional health work as much as to the work of informal carers. Most paid carers are also women, and the ideology of caring influences their perceptions of their work.

Another lesson of community is that is it experienced differently by men and women, children and dependent individuals. There are no homogenous communities, and health workers involved in 'community surveys' – as many students are at the start of their course – need to recognise that the collection of a few statistics (important though these are) is not likely to provide an adequate picture of their local health work area. On the other hand, some careful mapping of social networks within a defined locality, with due attention to the class, race and gender composition of the individuals who provide the (professional and lay) care, as well as to the characteristics of those who receive the care, could be immensely revealing.

There is much research still to be done. Several studies in the health field suggest that it is possible to use the mapping techniques of social network theory to identify and document local informal social support systems. Bulmer (1987) comments that, whereas there is little evidence from the social care field, research into health demonstrates that social support and a stable social environment may enhance people's resistance to disease. A study of depression in working class married women in the East End of London demonstrated that, among other things, lack of social support was a 'vulnerability factor' which, together with 'background social factors', determined the individual's response to 'provoking agents' or stressors (Brown and Harris, 1978). But this does not reveal much about the precise ways in which social support might act as a safeguard.

However, an influential longitudinal study of residents in Alameda County, California indicated that individuals who lacked social and community ties were at greater risk than those with more extensive social contacts (Berkman and Syme, 1979). During the nine years between their initial and follow-up survey the mortality rate among those lacking close social ties was significantly higher. Clearly the relationship between social ties and stress levels, and the implications for ill health or wellbeing are difficult to unravel. People experiencing greater stress and ill health are perhaps less likely to be able to develop social ties.

These lines of research suggest that health workers will continue to find a use for some kind of concept of community, however much it differs from the rose tinted visions of the past. They also suggest that community cannot be operationalised without some discussion of wider social inequalities and of how an analysis of community connects to wider social divisions along class, race and gender lines, and it is these issues that are addressed in the chapters that follow.

Suggestions for further study

J. Bornat *et al.*, (1993) *Community Care: A Reader*, London, Macmillan, is a splendid introduction to a range of issues in community care politics and practice. P. Willmott and D. Thomas (1984) *Community in Social Policy*, London, Policy Studies Institute, remains the best, short exposition of the different meanings of community care. Community health work is explored in J. Orr (1987) *Women's Health in the Community*, Chichester, Wiley.

Self assessment questions

1 Discuss the problems in defining the concept of 'community'.
2 Discuss how far, and how appropriately, health work in community settings has changed in recent years.
3 Make an assessment of the 1990 changes in community care policies.
4 Suggest how social networks and close community ties may protect people's health.

Chapter 5

Stratification, class and health

Contents

Themes and issues

Social stratification – class, race, gender – caste, feudalism, class

Industrialisation: class conflict – economic and social class – status and party – the classless society – functional inequality – social closure – social mobility – class consciousness

Class gradients in health: occupational class – work patterns and health inequalities – class consciousness and attitudes to health

Postmodernist perspectives and 'lifestyle' choices

Learning outcomes

After working through this chapter you should be able to:
1 Outline the concept of stratification and comment on the dimensions of social divisions.
2 Demonstrate your understanding of how class might influence health work interventions and negotiations.
3 Assess the significance of class gradients in health.
4 Review the evidence for and against the existence of a 'classless society' in contemporary Britain.

SOME of the central questions in sociology are about the nature and significance of social divisions: about why people's social resources and opportunities differ, why some individuals and groups are more powerful than others, and how structures of power are created and reproduced through social institutions such as the family and the state. In particular, why and how have some differences – such as those between men and women, black and white people or older and younger people – given rise to such pervasive forms of structured social inequality? This is the first of five chapters which explore the impact of social divisions on health and health work. The chapter opens up the debate about social divisions by examining the sociological concept of stratification and notes the variety of stratification systems that have existed. Class is then examined in greater detail and its complex relationship with health established, and this is followed by an investigation of debates about poverty and health (Chapter 6). In Chapters 7–9 we will consider the impact on health and health work of other social divisions – along lines of gender, race, age and disability.

The contribution of structural sociology

There is no immediate agreement among sociological theorists on the nature and significance of social inequality. Whereas *structural* sociologists emphasise how social institutions shape and constrain social behaviour, *social action* theorists are more concerned with the creativity of social interaction and the fluidity of social situations. In some social theories everyday transactions themselves constitute the sum of constraining pressures on individuals. But in structural theories society is more tangible than this. Patterned social inequalities are both created and reproduced (reinforced or modified) through social transactions. The pressure on individuals of such inequalities, expressed through social institutions and structures of power, is seen as formidable, though varying in nature and extent.

This is why structural theorists have provided much more wide-ranging accounts of social inequality than social action theorists, who have concentrated on how social differences are perceived and handled at an inter-personal level. It is writers on social structure, most notably Durkheim, Marx and Weber, who have produced the main theories about stratification and class. They have asked the questions about why some groups are more wealthy and powerful than others, how far social mobility exists in different societies and why inequalities and poverty persist. It is these accounts that we focus on in this chapter, although we will also reflect on the implications for health of adopting a postmodern perspective on social inequality.

5.1 Social stratification

The concept of stratification provides a useful point of entry to the debate about social inequality. *Social stratification* refers to the structured inequalities that exist between different groups of people in a given society. In geology strata are layers of deposits, as in rock formations, and this notion highlights a main assumption in theories of stratification: namely that some groups in society are higher up the social scale than others. The geological analogy, which emphasises a correspondence between the social and the natural world, also implies that groups are to an extent discrete.

Although dislocations and eruptions in strata may occur (as people move up or down the social scale, or as social revolution transforms the stratification system) there always exist identifiable social layers. Within these social layers people will have features in common, such as income levels, cultural traditions and social values, which will differentiate them from other strata; these features, and the strata themselves, will tend to persist across the generations. However, this social patterning and layering will itself be subject to stress and change. Like geological formations, the relationships between the strata may be modified or transformed.

Of course, in geology rocks are not ranked in importance according to their position in the strata, whereas in human society the social influence of different groups generally reflects their social position. Stratification implies that groups are in an unequal relationship with other groups; some are more powerful, others less. Thus, some degree of structured social inequality is a major feature of such systems. Such inequality might be of a material nature, and here we might think of income, housing or health chances. We noted in Chapter 1 that health inequalities are still quite widespread in the 1990s, in spite of the work of the National Health Service. Inequality might also be of a social or political kind, with some groups enjoying much higher status and decision-making power than others. The central concern for theorists of social structure is why this should be the case; they build theories about how stratification systems came to exist, what form they take, what their key features are, and how and why they change over time.

Forms of stratification

Class is the form of stratification which has been most pervasive in industrialised societies such as Britain. A class system is based primarily on economic differences between groups: that is, groups have unequal access to and control over possessions and material resources, and members of each class have similar levels of resources. Because economic achievement is a main determinant of class position, people can move up and down the social scale to some extent; their class position is not fixed for all time. But class is by no means the only form of stratification identified by sociologists, and you may yourself have learned in school history or geography lessons about other types of social hierarchy.

○ Can you suggest any other (perhaps earlier) forms of stratification?

You might have recalled learning about *slavery* and citizenship in the Roman Empire, and perhaps about more recent examples of slavery in the British Empire and in the American South before the Civil War. These stark forms of stratification made dramatic distinctions between slaves and 'free men'; slaves had no civil rights and could be bought and sold at will by those who were free. Some of you might have mentioned the *caste* system in India, a much less rigid and extreme form of stratification, but one in which status and role is largely fixed at birth. Caste has a basis in religious beliefs. Brahmins, for example, continue to be the priestly caste whereas untouchables – at the bottom of the hierarchy – still perform menial and dirty jobs.

The *feudal system*, which was widespread in medieval Europe, represents another type of stratification. In feudal society most people were peasants or serfs who laboured to make a living from their plots of land, as well as performing services for the lord of the manor and giving tithes to the church. Small numbers of shopkeepers, merchants and craftsmen lived by their skills, but a tiny minority – the king, barons, lords, knights and squires – held almost all power. This, then, was a highly elaborate, largely static hierarchical society in which people's position and status was ascribed (fixed) at birth and very unlikely to change. It is a type of society delineated by sociologists as pre-industrial or agrarian, based on military power, religious conformity and a settled social hierarchy (see Section 2.3). Under slavery and feudalism people's health status was likely to depend cricially on their place in the social hierarchy. The basic necessities for life – food, shelter, clothing and warmth – were systematically denied to some groups. The poorest groups were unlikely to have access to adequate health care, life expectancy was low and death from starvation or epidemics was the fate of quite large sections of the population in medieval Europe (Cippolla, 1973).

Agrarian society was not unchanging, but it presented a decided contrast with the industrialised society which gradually displaced it. Whereas in agrarian society social status was ascribed, industrial society offered new opportunities for social mobility, based on the acquisition of wealth through manufacturing and on the possession of valued skills.

The theories of 'industrial society' which were developed by Durkheim, Marx and Weber attempted to explain (and predict) how social structure was changing. There was considerable disagreement between them about the social consequences of industrialisation, but a general acknowledgement that class – in some form – was emerging as the characteristic type of stratification system of industrial society.

5.2 Class as a form of stratification

Since the nineteenth century, if not before, class has dominated our thinking about social relationships. The powerful theories of Marx and Weber about economic and social class formation were grounded in their analysis of the impact of industrialisation. In Britain the process of class formation was rapid and disruptive. In parts of continental Europe the old structures and the new sat uneasily together. In France, for example, a solid peasantry of independent, very small-scale farmers continued to exist well into the twentieth century. In many parts of the world today, even where industrialisation has taken root to some degree, subsistence peasant farming provides an important economic contribution and still influences social relationships – at least in rural areas.

Can you recall what Durkheim, Marx and Weber had to say about class? Look back at Section 2.3 for some help with this.

Durkheim saw class and class conflict as part of a transitional stage towards mature industrial society in which a moral consensus would prevail. Class conflict was not inevitable but was the result of industrialisation and social dislocation. The old social order, the settled hierarchy of small towns and rural villages, was challenged and upturned by mass population shifts and rapid urbanisation. Anomie and class antagonisms characterised this period of upheaval, but the triumph of rationality, marked by the emergence of more democratic forms of government and by regulatory frameworks binding employers and workers, would result in a more just and equal society. As employers and workers came to recognise that they had different but complementary skills and a shared interest in the peaceful development of industrial capitalism a 'classless' society would evolve. This would be marked by class co-operation and the development of inter-class organisations (corporations).

This theory, that class as a form of stratification would be superseded by a classless society, assumed that in a mature industrial society individuals would acknowledge that they had different kinds of skills and abilities, which all needed harnessing in order for society to work efficiently. Inevitably, some skills and roles would be more specialised and useful than others, and the higher status accorded to some citizens would reflect the value to the whole society of their specialised training and skills. In other words, a degree of inequality would remain, in spite of moves toward greater equality, but this would reflect the social value of different roles in a society rather than domination by a particular economic class or social elite. The degree of stratification that existed would only be that which was consistent with the needs and goals of a society as defined by its members; the resultant inequalities would be, as it were, the product of 'moral consensus'.

Marx and Weber developed conflict theories which questioned Durkheim's prediction of the emergence of the mature industrial, 'classless' society. Although Marx predicted that a classless society would finally come into being, he argued that this would be produced only by escalating class conflict, leading to the overthrow of industrial capitalism by the organised working class. Until this resolution of the internal contradictions of capitalism was achieved class conflict would predominate, since the goals of the working class – a fair return for their labour, better wages and working conditions, a share in wealth they had created – would always be diametrically opposed to those of capitalists.

Economic class

For both Marx and Weber *class* was the central mechanism of social stratification in industrial capitalist society. Material, social and political inequalities were an integral part of industrial capitalism, and class conflict of some kind was inescapable. In Marx's view it was the mode of production – the economic substructure and infrastructure – that determined social and political relationships. Class was *economic class*, a group of people sharing a common relationship to a mode of production. Class structures and conflicts, whatever form they took, were primarily economic in origin. Marx argued that in pre-industrial society agrarian modes of production had determined the basic two-class society of landlord and peasant. In industrialised society industrial capitalist technologies and work relationships forced the mass of the non-capital owning population to sell their labour power and created the two-class society of bourgeoisie (capitalists) and proletariat (working masses). In each case the profits of the dominant class derived from the surplus value of the labour of the oppressed class. In other words, the extra wheat grown or cotton goods manufactured over and above what was needed to cover the costs of production (including wages) went as profits into the hands of the dominant class. Just as the bourgeoisie attempted to maximise profits by driving down wages to their lowest possible level, so the proletariat would begin to develop collective strategies to advance their bargaining power and secure social and political rights. The capitalist pressure towards 'emiseration' would be increasingly challenged by working class organisation within a polarised two-class social system.

Class, status and party

In Weber's view a wider range of economic factors influenced class formation; for example, the possession of highly valued specialist skills would improve an individual's class position. Weber also emphasised the importance of *status* distinctions – inter-subjective judgements about a person's social worth and prestige – and *party* – the power exercised by organisations (such as religious groups or political parties) which cut across class boundaries. Weber distinguished between class as an economic concept and *social class*: that is, groupings sharing a similar economic and social position in society with similar chances of social mobility. The accumulation of capital represented only one of the determinants of the class system in modern industrialised society. As the scale of industry grew the demand for skilled 'white-collar' and professional workers increased and created ranks of property-less workers selling their specialist labour: civil servants, clerks, doctors, craftspeople, surveyors, accountants and so on. Their training and expertise gave some groups a position of power in relation to the capitalist class, a power not derived from the possession of property (capital) but from their intellectual skills and special kinds of expertise, for example a law degree or medical qualification. Far from being subsumed into the proletariat, Weber noted that intermediate workers were becoming increasingly socially distinct as the 'middle classes'. They shared with the working class their property-less state, but their conditions of work and degree of autonomy were much better.

Status and party provided other, independent avenues through which individuals and groups could improve their social position, and this was particularly the case for the higher grades of intermediate workers created by industrialisation. The social prestige attached to some occupations – particularly the professions – provided one example of this; the high status accorded to those considered to be 'gentlemen', even if they were poor, offered another. In addition, Weber noted the continuing importance of other non-economic influences on social position, based on party. Although some organisations grew out of class relationships – for example trade unions and employers' organisations – others had no clear economic class basis, yet might have considerable socio-political (and economic) influence. For example, political parties and religious organisations in the nineteenth century (and today) did not divide neatly across class lines in terms of membership or objectives. Social change might be brought about by social and political forces, Weber argued, and not just by economic influences. The concept of social class draws our attention to what Weber saw as the social as well as the economic influences on class formation and social mobility. The class system in mature industrial society was becoming more complex, not less, and possibilities for alliances and conflicts between classes were becoming greater.

5.3 Changing patterns of stratification and inequality

How relevant are these ideas about class in late twentieth century Britain? It might be argued that nowadays we live in a *classless society* in which individuals make their own 'life chances' through education and hard work in a 'meritocracy' in which anyone with ability can rise to the top. Rising living standards and mass consumption have eroded the vast differences between consumers that were so marked in Victorian times. Now almost everyone under 40 wears blue jeans; almost everyone has a fridge, a hoover, a television and a washing machine; all social groups shop at Sainsbury's and Marks and Spencer; two-thirds of households have cars and own their own homes and so on. Lifestyles and consumption patterns have converged, it has been argued, and have blurred class divisions to such an extent that the concept itself has become redundant; everyone has become 'middle class'. From another angle, it could be argued that a preoccupation with class has obscured our understanding of other social divisions – along lines of race and gender, for example – which may be more fundamental in sustaining social inequality.

Critics on the political right have argued that what now exists is unavoidable inequality; a social patterning of difference that largely reflects the natural, innate differences between individuals that no amount of social legislation will overcome. Hayek (1944), who became the guru of the 1980s New Right, anti-collectivist revival in British politics under Margaret Thatcher's Conservative administration, has claimed that the efforts of the state to end poverty and engineer equality have only served to lead all citizens along the 'road to serfdom'. The state should retreat from social engineering and allow people to be free – and naturally unequal – in a market system (see Section 2.4).

Here's a chance to take stock of ideas about class in a practical way, by making some provisional judgements about stratification and inequality. Begin by taking a snapshot of Britain in the mid-nineteenth century and noting the vast material disparities that existed. If you have studied the economic and social history of Britain at any time, you can sketch the outline yourself.

Note down the types of material inequalities which existed in the 1840s. What evidence of class divisions can you recall?

Massive wealth was accumulated by the few, mass poverty (and the threat of the workhouse) was suffered by the majority (see Table 5.1). A class based stratification system reinforced and reproduced economic and social inequalities. Industrialisation and urbanisation had brought about widespread social dislocation and class conflict. There was little social mobility, little protection of workers by the state and few civil rights. A sense of class consciousness – of belonging to a particular social group and experiencing a common lifestyle and culture – was the product of this gross inequality and social rigidity.

TABLE 5.1 Britain in the 1840s. Source: Rose (1972), Mitchell and Deane (1962), Hobsbawm (1964)

Pauperism
(per 1000 population, 1850 estimates)

England and Wales	57.4 per 1000
Scotland	41.8
Ireland	72.5

Life expectancy at birth (1850)

Males	40 years
Females	42 years

Death rates (per 1000)

Year	Adults	Infants
1840	22.9	154
1850	20.8	153
1860	21.2	162

Unemployment in some towns

Town	Numbers fit for work	% Fully employed	% Partly employed	% Unemployed
Liverpool (Vauxhall)	4 814	38	12	49
Stockport	8 215	15	35	50
Colne	4 923	19.5	32.5	48
Oldham	19 500	49	25.5	25.5
Wigan	4 109	24	62	38

Since that time, it must be argued, there has been considerable social change and upheaval. There have been two world wars, a considerable rise in general living standards, the extension of political and social rights, a growth in social mobility. If we take another snapshot of Britain in the 1940s, the picture will be quite different. Whereas society in the 1840s was basically hierarchical and grossly unequal, it might be argued that Britain by the 1940s had become basically democratic and egalitarian.

○   What evidence would you put forward to support the view that by the 1940s class stratification had become less rigid and material inequalities had been reduced?

You might have mentioned the setting up of the welfare state in the 1940s, in particular the National Health Service with its 'free at the point of use' services paid for by all taxpayers and insured workers. The notion of sharing risks by setting up a nationally organised benefits system for vulnerable groups, such as families with young children, widows and unemployed workers was radically different from the mass poverty of the 1840s. By the 1940s income had become more evenly distributed, and income tax had a redistributive impact. General living standards had risen considerably; decent council-built housing was increasingly available. A free national education system provided a ladder of educational opportunity for all children with ability, and a democratic political system existed in which all citizens could participate at local and national level (see Table 5.2). Class consciousness and loyalties, shared cultural forms and lifestyles still existed, but so did a much greater degree of social mobility.

There is little doubt that class based stratification was far more rigid in the 1840s than it was in the 1940s, or that inequality was far more

TABLE 5.2 The extension of voting rights (UK)

Date	Appr. number of votes	Appr. total population
1830	440 000 = adult men	16 300 000
1832 (after First Reform Bill)	717 000 = adult men	16 300 000
1886 (after Third Reform Bill)	4 940 000 = adult men	30 000 000
1918	21 000 000 = men over 21 and women over 30	44 000 000
1928	29 000 000 = all adults over 21	46 000 000
1970	40 000 000 = all over 18s	55 000 000

widespread. By the 1940s a safety net of state welfare services was specifically designed to keep households above the poverty line, and full employment policies were in place to keep people in work (see Chapter 6). Inter-class mobility was greater, disparities in income and wealth significantly smaller.

Does this mean that the ideas of Marx and Weber about class stratification had become outmoded? Before plunging into the sociological debate, let's take some final snapshots of Britain in the 1990s – the period that you know most about. Think about the extent to which material inequality and social stratification are features of the contemporary social landscape. Consider how far class still pervades British society in the 1990s. As we noted earlier, there are a range of different views about class, so take some time to consider where you stand.

○   To what extent do material inequalities exist in British society in the 1990s? Do you think that they point to a stratification system based on class?

There is considerable evidence of material inequalities in contemporary Britain. You may have noted the high level of unemployment and the large numbers of people who depend on social security benefits of some kind (see Figure 5.1). The distribution of income and wealth is still very uneven, and there is also evidence from official reports that material inequality is growing. The poverty gap widened in the 1980s; the wealthy improved their position while the incomes of the poorest groups in the population declined in real terms (see Chapter 6).

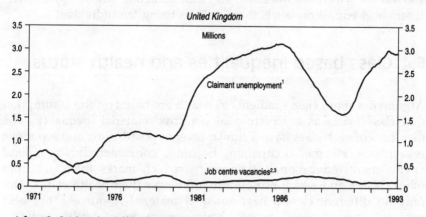

1 Seasonally adjusted unemployment (claimants aged 18 and over).
2 About one third of all vacancies are listed by job centres.
3 Data before 1980 are not consistent with current coverage.

FIGURE 5.1 Unemployment and vacancies 1971–93. Source: *Social Trends* (1994)

Although spending on the welfare state grew in the 1980s, much of the extra money was used to pay out unemployment benefits, Income Support and other means-tested benefits to the growing numbers of poor families.

It is more difficult to 'prove' scientifically the existence of class. However, you probably mentioned *occupational class gradients* in health: that is, the evidence from Section 1.6 that mortality and morbidity is not evenly distributed in the population but varies in relation to peoples' class position. The Black Report (1980) and *The Health Divide* (White-head, 1987) demonstrated that classes IV and V had not improved their health status relative to classes I and II. Whitehead reported that between the 1950s and the 1980s mortality rates for men and women aged 35 and over in classes IV and V had either been static or had marginally increased, whereas those for classes I and II showed marked improvement.

You may also have commented on the degree of class consciousness that still exists, among some groups of workers and in single-class communities such as 'Sloane Ranger' Knightsbridge or a mining village. Your life experience may have led you to be intensely aware of having a 'class position': as a stalwart, working class trade unionist perhaps, as an upwardly mobile, successful student, as a comfortably-off middle class child or as a mature student who has known hardship and unemployment. You may identify positively with the culture and lifestyle of the working or middle (or upper) class. On the other hand you may see yourself as a 'free agent' with your own lifestyle, culture and values which are unrelated to class, someone whose appearance, accent and education labels them only as being 'an individual'.

5.4 Class based inequalities and health status

Arguments about class gradients in health are based on the assumption that class exists as a structure of objective material inequality. The members of each class have a similar level of possessions and economic resources – income, occupation, housing, consumer durables, local environment, educational attainment – which marks them out from other classes and which profoundly influences their health status. Not only do different classes have unequal material resources, they also possess unequal social power; hence provision of health services, access, take-up and treatment is uneven across the classes (Townsend *et al.*, 1988). Health inequalities persist over time because class based inequalities persist, even though class boundaries are never clear cut and social mobility is always possible.

The acceptance of class as a structure of 'objective material reality' need not involve the adoption of any particular sociological theory of class. Official statistics about mortality and morbidity have been generated in Britain since the early twentieth century by using occupation as a means of classifying the population. Although the use of the term 'social class' to describe the five classified groupings suggests a leaning towards Weber's ideas about class, the Office of Population Censuses and Surveys (OPCS) – which produces many of the health statistics we currently use – emphasises that social class is being used in their statistics as a reliable measure rather than as a sociological construct.

Measuring health through occupational class

In government statistics, many of which measure differences in terms of social class, occupation is used as the key indicator of class membership. This is because it is considered possible to produce groupings of occupations which are fairly homogenous and which are accepted by the public as being of similar status in terms of the skills and training required. The classification of an occupation reflects its general standing in society; social status, material rewards and educational level are seen as reinforcing each other. The Registrar General's five-fold classification of social class (see Section 1.6), which was first produced in 1911, has continued to be used because it is able to demonstrate inequalities persisting over time. In the cautious language of the Registrar General's office:

The use of Social Class classifications has revealed significant and persisting differences in a wide range of social and economic attributes. It has justified its existence as a variable which highlights important differences that are related to the social position of the individual.

Social Trends (1975)

While official statisticians accept the usefulness of social class classifications, they are not attempting a sociological analysis. 'Social class is treated . . . as a statistical concept for classifying data, not as a means of explaining why or how social differentials exist' (*Social Trends*, 1975).

As a statistical concept social class is not without its problems, and researchers have used different models (see Table 5.3). In the first place, the traditional classifications exclude married women, who are categorised according to their husband's full-time occupation. In fact, the whole household is classified in many statistical calculations according to the occupational class of the 'head of household' – usually the husband as chief wage earner. There is considerable debate among social analysts as to how far married women's social class can be

TABLE 5.3 British Social Mobility Study: social class model. Source: Goldthorpe (1980)

Professionally qualified and high administrative	Managerial and executive	Inspectional, supervisory, and other non-manual higher grade	Inspectional, supervisory and other non-manual	Routine non-manual work	Skilled manual	Semi-skilled manual	Unskilled manual
Lawyer	Headmaster	Colliery engineer	Accountant's clerk	Tax officer	Taxi driver	Bus conductor	Builder's labourer
Doctor	Missionary	Social worker	Shop manageress	Receptionist	Slater	Farm labourer	Railway porter
Surveyor	Nurse administrator	Qualified nurse			Miner (face worker)	Postman	Window cleaner

subsumed in this way. Arber (1991) and others researching health status have demonstrated that different sickness and disability gradients are obtained when women's own social class is measured (see Chapter 7 for a discussion of this). In relation to infant and perinatal mortality, where research has suggested that it is the mother's own nutritional status that is crucial, it may be misleading to rely on social class groupings which are derived largely from male occupational patterns. Retired people are usually classified by their last full-time occupation before retirement, yet many people take a different job at the close of their working lives. The classification, therefore, may not truly reflect their lifetime occupational status. Unemployed people are usually classified in terms of their previous occupation, yet their status and income (and perhaps that of the whole household) may well decline very rapidly after they lose their job.

There are other difficulties which need to be allowed for, arising from the changes in the relative standing of different occupations over time. For example, in 1961 university teachers were reclassified from social class II to I, and aircraft pilots from social class III to II. Conversely, telephone operators were reclassified from III to IV, and 'draughtsmen' from II to III. Partly because of such changes, it has been argued that social class gradients in health are *artefacts* – that is, they are produced by such reclassifications and redefinitions rather than existing as objective categories which express health inequalities (Illsley, 1986). This is discussed further in Sertion 5.5.

Inequalities in income and wealth today

There were very marked inequalities in income and wealth in pre-industrial societies, but their total wealth was modest compared with that accumulated in industrialising societies. It was the enormous scale and speed of capital accumulation by the bourgeoisie that led Marx to predict the growing emiseration of the proletariat, but in fact in the hundred years after the 1840s the industrial working class saw their living standards rise appreciably. Just as important, as we noted earlier, welfare benefits and legislative changes gave them greater protection against sickness and misfortune.

But inequalities in income and wealth have not disappeared, and poverty has remained a significant problem even in industrialised countries. For example, the rising *real income* – that is, the purchasing power of wages, salaries and investment income after allowing for inflation – of the bulk of the working population in Britain has only been partly matched by equalisation of *wealth* – that is, total assets such as land, property, stocks and shares (see Figure 5.2). In 1991 just 1 per cent of individuals owned around 18 per cent of total marketable wealth,

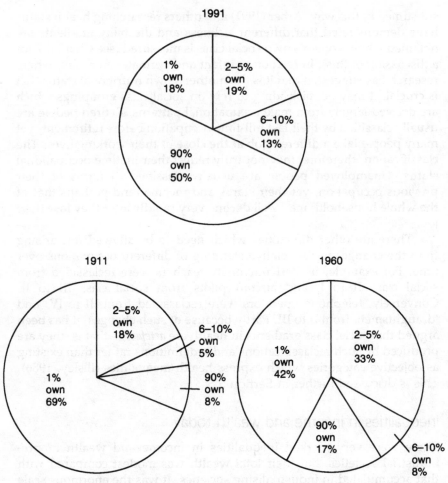

1991

1% own 18%
2–5% own 19%
6–10% own 13%
90% own 50%

1911

2–5% own 18%
6–10% own 5%
1% own 69%
90% own 8%

1960

2–5% own 33%
1% own 42%
6–10% own 8%
90% own 17%

FIGURE 5.2 Wealth holding in the UK. Source: *Social Trends* (1986, 1989, 1994)

whereas the bottom 50 per cent of individuals owned only about 8 per cent of total wealth. Conservative policies during the 1980s, to boost home ownership and share purchase, have had only a small impact on the total pattern of wealth holding. This is partly because the recession of the late 1980s reversed the trend towards home purchase and was characterised by a dramatic fall in house prices. In addition, although share ownership rose from 5 per cent of the population in the late 1970s to 20 per cent by the early 1990s, the total percentage owned by these private individuals remains very small (see Figures 5.3 and 5.4).

In the 1980s the policies directed towards wider distribution of wealth were offset by fiscal measures which widened the earning gap

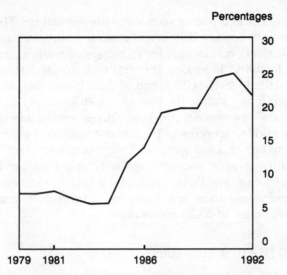

FIGURE 5.3 Shareholders as a percentage of the adult population.
Source: *Social Trends* (1993)

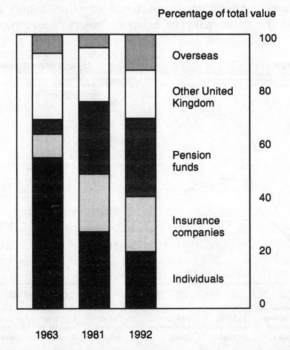

FIGURE 5.4 Shares held in UK companies by sector. Source: *Social Trends*
(1993)

between the richer and poorer sections of the population. The long term trend in twentieth century Britain and other industrialised countries has been towards rising real income for all classes of workers, as individual output (productivity) increased through technological innovation and change. Unskilled, semi-skilled and skilled blue-collar workers have advanced their living standards, though not so markedly as white-collar professional and managerial workers. But since the late 1970s semi-skilled and unskilled workers in particular have seen their wages fall in relation to higher income groups. Other disparities are even more significant; for example, women earn only about 70 per cent of the average male wage (see Figure 5.5). Much larger numbers of women than men earn less than the European Community recommended 'decency level wage' of £3.20 per hour.

Work based health inequalities

The use of class scales based on occupation draws our attention to certain work-related inequalities and their impact on health (although others, as we noted earlier, may remain hidden). It is worth looking more closely at how such inequalities link to health, in order both to provide an example of the persistence of stratification and to give substance to the claim that class exists as 'objective material inequality'.

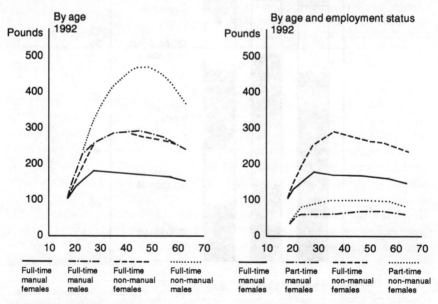

FIGURE 5.5 Disparities between male and female wage levels in the UK. Source: EOC (1993)

TABLE 5.4 Townsend's findings on occupational inequalities. Source: Townsend (1979)

Percentages of men and women experiencing different kinds of deprivation or difficulty at work

	Men	Women
	%	%
The character of the job		
Working mainly or entirely outdoors (inc. transport)	31	4
All working time standing or walking about	57	42
At work before 8 am or working at night	36	15
Working 50 or more hours last week	24	4
Security		
Unemployed more than 2 weeks in last 12 months	5	4
Subject to 1 week's notice or less	44	51
Conditions and amenities		
Working conditions very poor or poor	23	15
Welfare or fringe benefits		
No wages or salary during sickness	37	35
Paid holidays of two weeks or less	56	61
No meals paid or subsidised by employer	76	69
No entitlement to occupational pension	43	61

In the first place, a whole range of well-documented differences exist between the conditions, hours, pay and fringe benefits of the different social classes (see Table 5.4). Workers in social classes IV and V work longer hours and rely on overtime to supplement their low average earnings (Lonsdale, 1985). They are more vulnerable to unemployment; unskilled manual workers (class V) are six times more likely to become unemployed than non-manual workers (classes I and II). In the early 1980s just 3 per cent of the labour force accounted for 70 per cent of unemployment weeks, indicating the existence of a 'large disadvantaged sub-group in the working class' (Lonsdale, 1985). In the 1990s, with unemployment again around three million, vulnerable groups in classes IV and V still bear the main burden of long term unemployment. Regional variations reinforce social class inequalities. Although the shake-out of labour in South East England has been the subject of much comment, it is in the north and west of the UK that high rates of unemployment and high long-term unemployment are most marked. Between 1989 and 1993 unemployment rates in the north of England did not fall below 10.5 per cent, except in 1990, whereas in the South East they did not rise above 7.5 per cent until after 1991.

For those in paid employment patterns of work and conditions have varied greatly, even in the post-war welfare state years. In some ways workplace health seems to have improved; there was a steady fall in the incidence of work-induced injuries and prescribed diseases after the 1950s. The gradual implementation of the Health and Safety at Work Act (1974), which created new and enforceable responsiblities for employers, together with shorter working hours, assisted this fall (Smith and Jacobson, 1988). On the other hand relatively little is known about workplace health and hazards, and there is recent evidence, for example in the construction industry, that accident rates are rising.

A large-scale survey of poverty in the UK revealed significant inequalities in the character of the job itself, in conditions and amenities and in welfare and fringe benefits (Townsend, 1979, and see Table 5.4). For example, nearly half the male workers in routine manual grades (classes IV and V) worked early in the morning, late in the evening or at night, compared with 22 per cent in non-manual grades. Around half of manual workers had no cover from occupational pensions and did not expect to receive payments from employers during sickness. In the 2000 households surveyed, manual workers worked significantly longer hours, had shorter holidays (and less holiday pay entitlement), and only a quarter had a right to a month's notice compared with three-quarters of white-collar workers. Working conditions – heating standards, WC and washing facilities, lighting, security – were substantially worse for manual workers. Fringe benefits followed a similar pattern, with non-manual workers enjoying substantial advantages, such as company cars, medical insurance, occupational pensions, lump sums at retirement, share and loan options. Townsend commented that:

Deprivation arises in different social settings and it needs to be explained and understood in relation to these. Much of an individual's life is spent working – yet conceptions of inequality at work are ill-developed. So the rigidity of the occupational hierarchy – with its disadvantages to national life and purpose is under-rated . . . Inequality at the workplace is systematically related to occupational class . . . Changes in laws, and improvements in employer provision, have prompted some commentators to reach complacent conclusions. But our analysis suggests that inequality at work in recent years has not narrowed between white-collar and blue-collar workers. On the contrary, it appears to have widened.

Townsend (1979)

The survey also noted the range of direct health effects linked to these occupational inequalities, for example higher rates of sickness –

particularly stress, respiratory conditions, back problems, risks of accidents. Beyond this, by highlighting low pay, lack of job security or fringe benefits, poor conditions and unsocial hours, the survey pointed to some of the indirect or hidden ways in which work inequality may influence people's health.

During the 1980s several factors suggest that work inequalities may have widened further. In the first place, skilled manual workers and professional and managerial workers have seen their incomes rise, whereas the bottom one-fifth of wage earners (that is, mainly class IV and V) have seen a reduction in their take-home pay over the decade. In addition, some of the protection enjoyed by manual workers in the 1970s has been removed. For example, until 1986 wages council minimum wage protection (the Whitley Councils) covered nearly 3 million workers in the service sector and in areas of manufacturing such as the clothing industry. The 1986 Wages Act took half a million young workers out of coverage altogether and reduced protection for many adult workers. By the early 1990s the government was planning to abolish wage councils completely, although their claims that freeing wages would 'price workers into jobs' proved entirely wrong and were quietly dropped. The employment legislation of the 1980s gradually extended the period of service required in order to qualify for legal protection against unfair dismissal, a move which disproportionately affected semi-skilled and unskilled manual workers, who experience higher unemployment and more breaks in employment. The Low Pay Unit (1987) estimated that one third of the workforce had lost this right. In the late 1980s unemployment began to rise sharply and – even after 32 changes in the method of calculating unemployment, all except one of which served to reduce the total – by the early 1990s it had reached three million (*The Guardian*, 13 February 1993).

Reflect on patterns of work and employment for social classes IV and V in the 1980s and suggest what implications these patterns might have for health.

You might have mentioned the greater risk of accidents at work, of respiratory diseases such as bronchitis, of stress associated with heart disease and so on (see Figure 5.6). There are also indirect effects arising from poor working conditions or low pay, and some evidence suggests that growing occupational inequalities have produced a rising toll of ill health. The most obvious outcome is the relationship between un-employment and premature death. Platt (1984) found that in each year since 1977 the unemployment rate in Great Britain could be positively and significantly correlated with the total suicide rate: in other words, as long term unemployment grew so did the suicide rate. Another indication has been the rise in industrial injury during the 1980s, particularly among young workers. Between 1981 and 1984, for

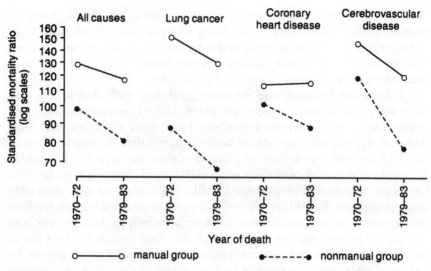

FIGURE 5.6 Social class gradients: selected diseases. Source: Marmot *et al.* (1991)

example, there was a 24 per cent increase in the incidence of fatal and major injuries in manufacturing industry (Smith and Jacobson, 1988).

The evidence that the number of low paid workers is growing is particularly significant for health status, because income is the biggest single influence on housing, diet and environment. Margaret White-head's survey *The Health Divide* (1987) demonstrated that occupational class gradients were becoming steeper for a range of diseases in the 1980s, and that material deprivation – experienced disproportionately by semi-skilled and unskilled manual workers (and their families) – was the dominant factor. Evidence about the contribution of working conditions to ill health, beyond the relatively restricted list of 'prescribed' industrial diseases for which official compensation is paid, is still very hard to find. Although there is increasing evidence that working conditions and practices influence health in complex ways and are likely to damage the health of manual workers disproportionately, it is argued that too little is known for the government to produce any strategy or targets for workplace health:

Non-manual workers are likely to have much lower rates of exposure to chemical and other physical hazards, and so suffer less from both their known and unknown health effects than manual workers. But the distribution of other risk factors, for instance work-related stress, is unknown . . . Only a small proportion of the total mortality resulting from exposure to occupational health hazards is currently identifiable.

Smith and Jacobson (1988)

This section has been concerned with the concept of class as 'objective material inequality' which can be investigated at an empirical level through the collection and interpretation of data about income distribution, wealth holding and (as one example) working conditions, rewards and security. It has also suggested how 'objective material inequality' might influence health and ill health. Obviously this is not a mere 'factual' process. As we noted in Chapter 2, any process of research – although it strives to be absolutely objective and detached – will inevitably construct the 'problem', search for evidence and draw conclusions within particular frameworks of perception and understanding. There is no clear cut distinction between theory and fact, and certainly the interpretation of data leads us straight into theoretical argument. In the section that follows we'll be considering some of the conflicting explanations that sociologists have advanced for the persistence of stratification in contemporary industrialised society and will explore the implications for health of this persistence.

5.5 The debate about class and health

The different approaches to stratification developed by Durkheim, Marx and Weber, and in particular the notion of class as a major form of stratification in industrialised societies have already been noted. Now let's investigate debates about the relationship between class and health in the changing conditions of late twentieth century capitalism. Three aspects will be mentioned: the impact of class on health status, the structuring of health work, and the links between health and class attitudes and values.

Class as a moral consensus

Among sociological theorists the significance attached to class varies. Structural functionalists such as Talcott Parsons (see Section 2.5) have claimed that by the 1940s most Western industrialised societies were well on their way to becoming the type of one-class, moral consensus based society predicted by Durkheim. The transitional, conflict driven stage had given way to mature industrial society based on merit and achievement. Within systems of national education children internalised the 'motivation to achievement' that was the fundamental value in capitalist societies, while the *meritocratic basis* of capitalism allowed the more able to continue their studies and become the highly skilled workers that society needed. What inequality remained was functionally necessary to society; higher rewards and social status reflected the value to society of highly skilled workers as well as ensuring that individuals would continue to accept the long specialised training required of them, for example as a medical student.

This did not mean that social inequality ceased to exist; indeed, Davis and Moore (1945) argued that a degree of institutionalised inequality was a characteristic of all societies. But functional inequality rather than class is the focus of attention:

Social inequality is the [device] by which societies ensure that the most important positions are conscientiously filled by the most qualified persons. Hence, every society, no matter how simple or complex, must differentiate persons in terms of both prestige and esteem, and must therefore possess a certain amount of institutionalised inequality.

Davis and Moore (1945)

○ To what extent do you accept the view that social inequality is functionally necessary in society?

There is a considerable difference between accepting that some form of inequality will probably always exist and arguing that inequality is 'functionally necessary'. The latter involves value judgements about which workers are more valuable and which skills are 'specialist skills'. You may agree that company directors deserve salaries fifty times larger than a cleaner employed by them or – to use a less dramatic example – that family doctors deserve salaries three times larger than their practice nurses. But you may not. Would you argue that nurses are one-third as important to society? Or that only a small pool of potential doctors exists, whom society must offer higher rewards to harness? Or that if salaries were more equal there would be no medical students? This is a difficult case to argue; over the past decades, in fact, we have been told that there is an excess supply of medical students and a chronic shortage of trained nurses.

This view may have a certain resonance with current political arguments about pay and rewards. After all, it has been pointed out that there must be lower taxation and higher rewards for businessmen and executives in order to encourage the risk taking vital for economic growth. Some cynics have commented that the opposite seems to be the case for low earners, who are requested 'not to price themselves out of jobs'. The American economist J.K. Galbraith summarised it like this: 'It holds that . . . the poor do not work because they have too much income; the rich do not work because they do not have enough income.' During the 1980s inequality between high and low income groups has increased: 'the top fifth of wage earners have seen their real salaries increase by 22 per cent since 1979 – six times the increase in wages of the bottom fifth' (Walker, 1987).

You will also need to consider to what extent you accept the functionalist argument that contemporary society functions as a meritocracy, in which – through an open educational system with equal opportunities for all – able individuals can rise to the top. Certainly education presents able children with a ladder of opportunity that scarcely existed in Victorian society. But there are still barriers for working class children to surmount, many of which are to do with material inequalities: lack of access to successful schools, financial hardship, difficult home circumstances (such as overcrowding) and negative subcultural attitudes to education. The expansion in higher education between the mid-1960s and the early 1980s, for example, did not result in a growing proportion of able working class students but a growth in the proportion of middle class children going on to university. Yet widespread intelligence testing has indicated that there is no clear correlation between occupational status and intelligence; this suggests that middle class children disproportionately succeed in the education system because they come from a middle class background with all its attendant material and social benefits – and what A.H. Halsey has called its cultural capital – not because as a group they are intrinsically more able (Halsey, 1980).

Health differences as inevitable

The conceptualisation of class as functional inequality does not deny the existence of inequalities in health but traces them to unavoidable and 'natural' patterns of difference. The language of 'difference' is now creeping into official statements about health. Inequality is not mentioned in *The Health of the Nation* strategy (DoH 1992b), and in some academic literature health is also conceptualised as 'difference' or 'variation' (Ham, 1988). Parsons' analysis of illness does not consider causation in terms of material inequalities, such as pay, working conditions, housing and so on, or in terms of class stratification. Illness is conceptualised as organic dysfunction – incapacity – or, in situations where it is the result of conscious or unconscious retreat from social roles, as deviance; but the social production of illness and disease is otherwise ignored. The presentation of illness to the doctor for diagnosis is Parsons' starting point, because his main concern is with the social control of illness in industrial society, where sick, unproductive workers are a potential threat to the stability of the social system (Parsons, 1951). Thus Parsons does acknowledge the potential for social conflict and disorder created by ill health, but argues that medicine and the health care system effectively neutralise this threat.

Economic class and health

For theorists whose starting point is Marx's analysis of class, the concept does not just describe social groupings with similar material resources or patterns of functional inequality. The class system itself is the product of the fundamental economic relationships arising out of a mode of production, whether it is industrial capitalism or some earlier mode. The driving force behind health inequalities is therefore the requirement of the capitalist class to maximise profit; this has influenced the nature of disease and sickness, the provision of health services and the definition of health itself. Lesley Doyal (1979) commented:

> Patterns of health and illness are to a considerable extent determined by the existence of a particular mode of social and economic organisation, and under capitalism there is often a contradiction between the pursuit of health and the pursuit of profit. Most attempts to control the social production of ill health would involve an unacceptable degree of interference with the processes of capital accumulation, and, as a result, the emphasis in advanced capitalist societies has been on after-the-event curative medical intervention, rather than broadly-based preventive measures to conserve health.
>
> Doyal (1979)

Doyal suggests that this relationship between capitalism, class and health is difficult to disentangle. In particular, since the capitalist class controls the state, why should it sanction the development and maintenance of an expensive and comprehensive health service which freely treats and cares for the working class? One response was to emphasise the 'relative autonomy of the state' in advanced capitalist society, to argue that the state served the overall, long term interests of the capitalist class as a whole rather than particular fractions of that class (Althusser, 1969). Policy decisions safeguarded the fundamental interests of capital even if capitalists were not obviously in control. In this view the establishment of the National Health Service by post-war politicians could be seen as shoring up capitalism and assisting its long term survival, although in the short term it undermined private property and profits.

You may have noticed how this theory assumes that the capitalist system has functional 'needs' which the state will inevitably fulfil. Yet there was no inevitability about the setting up of a nationalised health service; it was preceded by fierce wrangling in which Labour politicians had to give ground to the medical profession or risk the loss of a comprehensive health system (see Chapter 11). In addition, the establishment of the National Health Service was only part of a complex series of post-war deals and political bargaining – within and between political parties, trade unions, professional associations and other organisations – which created a welfare state. It is difficult to accept that this can be easily reduced to a simple satisfaction of the 'needs of the capitalist class'. A major criticism of Marxist theory has been on the grounds of its underestimation of the complexities and contradictions in such political processes and class struggles, which resulted in a *functionalist*-type analysis of class conflict – with the bourgeois state always retaining its control. The theory of *hegemony*, however, has enabled a more conflictual analysis of class politics to be developed, one which notes the divisions between ruling groups and recognises the problems involved in gaining the consent of the mass of society (Gramsci, 1988). Hegemony refers to a situation in which general acceptance of a political or social ideology is achieved, so that people in society come to accept and even take for granted an established social order. The post-war reconstruction in Britain might be seen as a bid for hegemony: an attempt to neutralise class conflict and create secure conditions for capitalism on the basis of collective welfare, citizenship rights and full employment. It is clear that hegemony is difficult to achieve and far from easy to sustain; any post-war consensus about the need for welfare and full employment has since evaporated in Britain. On the other hand the agenda of Thatcherism – market economics, consumer choice, privatisation – constituted a New Right radical bid for a kind of hegemony.

What such theories have in common is that they explain current patterns of ill health and health work in terms of the mode of production in industrial capitalism and the class conflict which this inevitably generates. It is in the interests of employers not to admit the existence of, or compensate their workforce for, work-related diseases, so the process of officially diagnosing disease and mapping industrial hazards has been slow and has underestimated their significance. For example, carcinogenic (cancer forming) substances were widely used in British industry, but the resultant toll of disease remained hidden or was explained in terms of worker carelessness or accidents (Doyal and Epstein, 1983). Diseases such as asbestosis and emphysema have been attributed to smoking, for example, rather than acknowledging the part played by work-related hazards. Community care provides another example of a policy which, it is argued, serves the interests of capital rather than the working class, although it has been packaged as 'social reform' which will 'individualise' care. The shift to community care is seen as an economic necessity for capitalism; as a way of controlling the mounting costs of health care for groups of mainly older, unproductive citizens rather than a progressive attempt to provide more client-centred and sensitive care (Scull, 1983).

Social closure and health work

Weber's elaboration and modification of Marx's theory of economic class, which we discussed earlier, has strongly influenced our view of class in contemporary society. In Section 5.4 we noted that there are still marked inequalities in wealth and income in Britain today; this suggests that economic class – in the Marxist sense of 'ownership of property' and the Weberian sense of 'ownership of marketable skills' – is still of central importance. On the other hand a complex range of status differences and party alliances also influence an individual's class position, and sociologists in the Weberian tradition have developed and adapted his approach to explain contemporary class status and conflict.

Although property represents a major source of power (and foundation for defining class), a whole range of status differences, such as ethnic difference, religion or age, may also be manipulated as sources of power by social minorities (Parkin, 1971). The term *social closure* refers to the process by which groups in society attempt to seize and retain control over resources and to exclude others from access to them. Social closure describes the process of creating some kind of monopoly, where legal and cultural means (as well as wealth or property qualifications) are used to raise entry barriers and create exclusive rights over territory. Groups within the middle class have particular opportunities to effect social closure. Functionalists argue that the professions enjoy higher long term salaries because their long training demanded dedication and initially low material rewards, but this overlooks the ability of some professions to deliberately restrict entry and manipulate training to suit their own ends. Because of controls on entry, standards and conditions of practice within occupations, outsiders could not easily compete, and the insiders created an occupational monopoly. There is no simple correspondence between the length of training prescribed for an occupation and the complexity of the work involved (or the skill in performing it). The occupation's control over its territory helps to determine what the length of training and qualifications are to be.

○   Can you think of any examples of occupations which have successfully controlled entry, standards and conditions of practice in this way?

It is quite likely that you thought of medicine, which is one of the prime examples used by writers in the Weberian tradition to illustrate professional monopoly (Parry and Parry, 1976). Doctors, like lawyers, have been particularly successful at protecting their occupational privileges, and we'll investigate the impact of this on health work relationships in Chapter 11. But many other occupations have achieved varying degrees of social closure, and in many cases the manipulation of educational criteria has been a central weapon. Teachers, for example, have gradually reconstituted teaching (with the assistance of government) as an all-graduate occupation. Nursing is now embarked upon a similar bid to raise its educational standing through Project 2000 and the higher education diploma route; a possible, though by no means self evident outcome could be higher status for nurses as an occupational group, bringing more effective control over their work territory (see Chapters 7 and 12).

Middle class professionals are not the only occupational groups to attempt social closure. Trade unions or other occupational associations might also try to exclude certain groups. For example, many trade unions have successfully prevented women from entering certain grades of skilled work and have colluded with employers to create similar, but distinct jobs with lower rates of pay. Black workers have found similar 'invisible' barriers to their entry into grades of skilled work. Groups may be involved in *dual closure*: that is, they may seek to exclude workers from their ranks whilst at the same time demanding that their group is given greater access to resources – for example more pay, shorter hours, fringe benefits and so on.

Health and social mobility

Social mobility has been highlighted – particularly by structural functionalists – as a key characteristic of mature industrial society. Such mobility is seen most frequently as an upward move by individuals who have taken full advantage of the meritocratic nature of the modern, open society. In the post-war years several studies demonstrated the upward shift of male workers from blue-collar to white-collar jobs and have concluded that this was due to the changing pattern of capitalism, bringing a rising demand for non-manual labour (Bendix and Lipset, 1959). Studies by Goldthorpe *et al.*, (1980, 1986), which have focused on measuring patterns of social mobility in Britain since the 1950s, found quite high levels of upward mobility but also concluded that this was largely related to the expansion of non-manual work. In other words, the chances of 'making it to the top' are in reality very remote, and most social mobility is a product of the shifting requirements of capitalist production. Women, in particular, are likely to find their chances of upward mobility very small indeed.

Related to this is a debate about downward mobility and the extent to which the middle and working classes can be differentiated. All workers in capitalist society are liable to suffer from *de-skilling*: that is, from a continual attempt by capitalists to cheapen the production process and increase profits through labour division, technological change and mechanisation (Braverman, 1974). This has an effect on non-manual as well as manual workers. Both are in danger of finding their work routinised or mechanised, of having their economic position weakened. Marxists argue that this demonstrates the degree to which supposedly 'middle class' workers are in fact part of the working class and are liable to become *proletarianised*.

On the other hand non-manual clerical and administrative workers, although their work has become routinised, have retained higher status and better job security than manual workers (Goldthorpe *et al.*, 1980). Some other groups, particularly part-time workers – many of whom are women – have certainly found their status, job security and pay under pressure in recent years.

Upward (and downward) mobility highlights interesting issues for health workers and for their patients. The *natural/social selection* argument contends that those who are least healthy slip down the social stratification system. Hence, measures of health 'inequalities' are not real measures of this at all; they record the outcomes of health selection (Illsley, 1986). People in good health move up the social scale and people in poor health move down, so some gap between higher and lower groups is inevitable, whatever health initiatives are taken. There is a certain amount of evidence from health studies to support this view, and an OPCS report (Whitehead, 1987) found that taller women were most likely to raise their social class through marriage and shorter women least likely. Of more importance is evidence that serious illness in childhood can affect social mobility: seriously ill boys, whatever their social class, were likely to move down the social scale by their mid-twenties (Wadsworth, 1986). But these are still small numbers, and Whitehead comments:

To sum up, there is some evidence that health selection operates at younger ages, and new evidence for men over fifty that no such selection is evident after this age. Estimates of the size of the selection effect suggest that it accounts for only a small proportion of the overall differential between the social classes.

Whitehead (1987)

Health work itself illustrates some of the contradictory findings about social mobility and de-skilling. Competitive tendering undermined the unemployment rights of many ancillary workers, although the House of Lords ruling in March 1994 that part-timers must have the same redundancy and unfair dismissal rights as full-timers will improve their job security. The pressure towards routinisation of work is evident among administrative workers, and there is evidence of this in nursing too. There are increasing efforts to individualise care – through adoption of the nursing process, for example – but there is an increasing through-put of patients, a growing demand for routine recording of data and the growth of contracts which specify precise tasks and duties.

Class consciousness and attitudes to health

The debate about class consciousness has a particular importance for health. It has already been suggested that class consciousness concerns inter-subjective experiences and relationships and is bound up with feelings about loyalty and solidarity. Class consciousness for Marx was the key to proletarian action, and its essence is well expressed in this comment by E.P. Thompson (1968), in *The Making of the English Working Class*:

Class happens when some men, as a result of common experiences (inherited or shared), feel and articulate the identity of their interests as between themselves, and as against other men whose interests are different from (and usually opposed to) theirs. The class experience is largely determined by productive relations into which men are born – or enter involuntarily. Class-consciousness is the way in which these experiences are handled in cultural terms: embodied in traditions, value-systems, ideas and institutional forms. If the experience appears as determined, class consciousness does not. We can see a logic in the responses of similar occupational groups undergoing similar experiences, but we cannot predicate any law. Consciousness of class arises in the same way in different times and places, but never in just the same way.

Thompson (1968)

It is important to note that here the primary determinant of class consciousness is the shared economic experience (exploitation) of the working class; it is becoming aware of this that creates class as a cultural and institutional experience. Some of the basic ingredients for class consciousness in this form, it might be argued, have withered away; working class solidarity, as the social product of large cohorts of male labour experiencing common economic and social barriers, has been terminally undermined by the decline during this century of the old manufacturing and heavy industrial base of Britain – the coal industry, heavy engineering, shipbuilding and so on. Labour in the 1990s is fragmented and divided by technological change and recession, trade union membership is in decline, and the Labour Party in Britain has been out of office since 1979 – with many of its traditional supporters turning to Thatcherite-style Conservatism.

Critics of class theory, who emphasise the significance of merito-cracy and the modern 'classless' society, suggest that 'working class consciousness' is now a thing of the past. The pursuit of personal 'lifestyle' and the growth of equal opportunity has undermined class solidarity; everyone has become a 'sovereign consumer' in free and open competition. In contrast to this view, numerous studies of 'self rated' class undertaken by opinion research companies as well as sociologists suggest that respondents are aware both of gradations of class in British society and of their own class position in relation to others (for example their parents). Particularly at the lower social levels, it is suggested, class tends to be conceptualised in terms of 'us against them', the 'have nots against the haves'; at the other extreme class is viewed as an unproblematic manifestation of natural hierarchy.

There is little doubt that the nature of class consciousness has changed in the post-1945 period. The vision of working class solidarity that we noted in Chapter 4, of communities such as Bethnal Green in which conviviality, social ritual and a common culture was a marked feature of social life, has faded away. Studies of *social images* of class have suggested that conflicting images existed within the working class itself, influenced by their experience of work and local community life (Lockwood, 1966). Lockwood distinguished between proletarian 'them and us' attitudes, a traditional, deferential 'knowing your place' outlook, and what he termed an *instrumental* attitude. In a study of Luton car workers it was argued that workers' outlook was individualistic and instrumental: that is, work was seen largely in terms of securing a comfortable lifestyle for the particular worker and his family (Goldthorpe *et al.*, 1969). The notion that views about 'what it is to be working class' overlap and even conflict with each other has been emphasised by other theorists; moreover, neither is being 'middle class' (or 'upper class') seen as unproblematic. Following Weber, we can also see that status distinctions will not necessarily follow class lines. A degree of class consciousness may be felt by an individual who also chooses to 'deviate' in some ways from the normal behaviours and attitudes of that class: for example, the middle class 'chip buttie' enthusiast or the factory hand with a passion for opera and classical drama.

The existence of class consciousness – whatever form it may take – raises significant issues for health and for those who work in health care occupations. In the first place, where class is bound up with shared culture and values, it will influence people's lifestyles, their feelings and attitudes towards health and even their health behaviour. Calnan (1987) found four different general concepts of health in his study of 60 women in South East England. The first two categories, health as never being ill and health as being able to carry out routine daily tasks, were more likely to be advanced by working class women. Health as being fit and health as being able to cope were concepts offered mainly by middle class women. Another study in France, by d'Houtard and Field (1984), suggested that working class people offered mainly negative and instrumental responses, whereas middle class respondents viewed health as a positive concept. However, Calnan (1987) warns that we should be wary of jumping to conclusions; when given space to talk in personal terms about health, working class women expressed more complex, multi-dimensional views.

Class attitudes and health encounters

In addition, class consciousness will, to some degree, influence the attitude that members of different social classes adopt towards each other. Given social class gradients in disease, health workers are likely to be in a higher social class (class I or II) than most of their clients and patients; their feelings about the value or otherwise of working class lifestyles and attitudes to health are likely to be bound up with their own, middle class cultural values. You might recall British politician Edwina Currie's now infamous remark about the need to get rid of the 'chip buttie' culture of the working class North, if health was to be improved and the toll from coronary heart disease reduced. This comment illustrated very neatly the attitude of many upper and middle class people towards working class culture as well as highlighting a significant feature of that culture – the famed 'chip buttie'.

Reflect on the extent to which you think a 'consciousness of class' might influence your own and your patients' attitude and behaviour.

There are many possible responses to this question. You might have developed the theme of diet, noting that your own, perhaps middle class, notions of 'healthy eating' might well predispose you to challenge what you see as an inadequate working class diet. You might also have recalled the comments about health behaviour that were made in Section 1.5 and reflected on the extent to which attempts to modify health behaviour may represent assaults on deeper class values and culture. Problems of communication between health professionals and patients may arise if their social background and status are markedly different. Working class patients, in particular, seem to receive a poorer service from doctors, obtaining fewer explanations and getting shorter consultations (Cartwright and O'Brien, 1976; Tuckett, 1985).

Perhaps you were also sceptical about categories such as 'working class' and 'middle class', pointing out that the terms disguise a wide range of different and conflicting attitudes to health (in the same way as Lockwood delineated distinct attitudes to work). Within the middle class, for example, we might highlight various groupings: traditionalists, ecologists, libertarians and so on, all with different philosophies of health (and diet). Even more important, cross-class attitudes and values need to be acknowledged. This is much easier to do within a Weberian style framework which emphasises the importance of status groups as well as social and economic class membership.

5.6 Beyond class?

In recent years market researchers and advertisers of foodstuffs and other consumer products have constructed sometimes very elaborate social and psychological categories which they claim have little to do with social class differences. Techniques of social research such as 'psychographics' have been developed, profiling consumers in terms of attitudes, values, social circumstances, diverse roles and various psychological attributes (K258, 1992). People are classified in terms of an elaborate mapping of their lifestyle and lifecycle positions, to create a segmentation of the market which enables advertisers to target particular groups of like-minded and similarly situated consumers (see Box 5.1).

Is this simply about developing new marketing techniques and controls, or does this mapping of complex lifestyles and values accurately reflect a real and increasing differentiation between people's patterns of living – differences which cannot be wholly captured by a class based analysis? Featherstone (1991) draws our attention to the 'eclipse of a particular coherent sense of culture and associated way of life which was dominant in the Western upper and middle classes which set the tone for the culture as a whole'. In many ways he suggests that this creates a new freedom, a cultural turmoil and incoherence on a global scale in which 'anything goes'. It offers ordinary people the

---

BOX 5.1 Psychographic techniques. Source: K258 (1992)

(A) 'Need-driven people': who buy more out of need than out of choice, and can be subdivided into: 1 'Survivors': who are distrustful and struggling for survival; and 2 'Sustainers': who are hopeful for improvement over time	(B) 'Outer-directed people': who buy with an eye to appearance, and can be subdivided into: 3 'Belongers': who are preservers of the status quo; and 4 'Emulators': who are upwardly mobile and follow the fashions of the rich and successful; and 5 'Achievers': who are materialistic and comfort-loving
(C) 'Inner-directed people': who buy to satisfy their self-expressive, individualistic needs, including: 6 'I-am-me's': who are very individualistic; and 7 'Experiencers': who have intense personal relationships; and 8 'The societally conscious': who are socially responsible and indulge in simple natural living	(D) 'The integrated': rare people who have combined the power of the outer-directed with the sensitivity of the inner-directed.

chance to express their individuality. On the other hand there is the possibility that new dominant groups will emerge to exercise global hegemony over taste and culture.

This eclipse of dominant cultural forms is part of a shift in contemporary society which has come to be known as *postmodernism*, a condition in which the uniformity, imposed coherence and rationality of industrial society is seen as being increasingly challenged by disorder and fragmentation (see Sections 2.8 and 2.9). The postmodernist stance claims not only that diversity and conflict are the central characteristics of contemporary society, but also that overarching structural explanations and explanatory models (such as class) cannot be sustained. Willis (1991) suggests that in contemporary society ordinary people have far more scope to 'be themselves', to express an individualised lifestyle by developing their creativity. Three associated 'revolutions' have transformed and elaborated the map of contemporary culture, he argues, and 'far from degrading everyday life with a thousand cracked mirrors of human potential, commodity and media cultural abundance has massively widened the scope for symbolic creativity'. He points to the 'electronic' revolution, which offers people diverse views and multiple realities and enables them to select and adapt ideas for their own needs. Second, he highlights the 'commodity' revolution, the astonishing range and diversity of consumer products and services from which people are able to select according to their desires (and their income). Finally, Willis notes the 'creative' revolution, the increasing opportunity for ordinary people to 'mix and match', create new patterns, change attitudes and lifestyles during the course of their everyday lives.

This draws us on towards the opposite of an economic determinist view of culture and class. It opens up a view of society about which there is no 'meta-discourse', and no class structure 'out there' determining people's behaviour and attitudes. People create and recreate their lifestyles, constantly bombarded by diverse and conflicting messages, but selecting out those they wish to accept. In Chapter 2 we noted that human agency and 'free-flowing, aesthetic and sensual notions of subjectivity' were central characteristics of postmodernism (Lash and Urry, 1986). In particular, the idea that forms of interaction are essentially 'texts' by which social actors present multiple and conflicting – and constantly changing – accounts of the world to each other, is central to attempts to reconceptualise social theory.

Consider these ideas, in particular in relation to health issues. You might want to review Section 2.8 which deals with postmodernism.

On the one hand the stance of postmodernism offers us the prospect of celebrating diversity and complexity. Health accounts, actions, attitudes can be attended to as important and personal cultural products over which individuals have spent time and trouble, rather than being seen largely as manifestations of 'class consciousness' or class position. Taking ordinary people's views of health and illness seriously, as a crucial part of health work, is a central theme of this book; these new approaches emphasise the creativity of everyday experience. From a health work perspective we might acknowledge that diversity and pluralism may bring benefits, if this means the enlargement of choice and the development of a range of sensitive, patient-focused approaches in place of a monolithic, uniform and highly stratified health service.

On the other hand it is difficult to accept that structural theories of class have no value, since they direct our attention to what are measurable and quantifiable differences and inequalities between social groups. If the class structure does not have a reality beyond our perceptions of its existence, then it is certainly 'real' in its effects. The health differences between those in classes IV and V and those in classes I and II, and the shared patterns of health and illness of people within those classes, are all too apparent (Townsend et al., 1988). Access, take-up and treatment are not uniform across the social classes, and the health gap between rich and poor – particularly between the bottom one-third of the population and the rest – has grown over the last decade.

In Chapter 2 it was suggested that people's everyday transactions and the on-going development and transformation of social structures both needed to be kept in focus, and you may already have opted for some kind of theoretical pluralism. You may also be alert to the limitations of a class based approach on other grounds: namely that it tends to marginalise the significance of other social divisions and inequalities. With this in mind, Chapter 6 investigates poverty and Chapters 7, 8 and 9 consider the significance of divisions based on gender, race, age and disability.

Suggestions for further study

Theories of class are investigated in Cuff et al. Perspectives in Sociology (3rd edn), London, Allen & Unwin. P. Townsend et al. (1988) Inequalities in Health: The Black Report and The Health Divide, Harmondsworth, Penguin, pulls together a great deal of material about social class gradients in health. S. Lonsdale (1985) Work and Inequality, London, Longman, discusses a wide range of issues related to the workplace, and A. Smith and B. Jacobson (1988) The Nation's Health, London, King Edward's Hospital Fund for London, consider occupational and other health risks.

Self assessment questions

1 Explain the concept of social stratification.
2 Argue for and against the statement that 'we are living in a classless society'.
3 What evidence is there that class position influences people's health?
4 How might class attitudes and values influence health work interactions?

Chapter 6

Poverty and health in the welfare state

Contents

Themes and issues

Absolute and relative poverty: subsistence poverty – primary and secondary poverty – the poverty line – relative poverty and deprivation – poverty as social coping

Groups in poverty: health risks – inequalities in health – Health For All strategies

The welfare state: Beveridge system – social security – anti-poverty legislation – full employment – universalism and selectivism – poverty trap – trickle-down theory

Theories of poverty: behavioural/cultural – materialist/structuralist – culture of poverty – cycle of deprivation – cycle of inequality – behavioural change approach and social change approach in health work practice

Learning outcomes

After working through this chapter you should be able to:

1 Suggest why some social groups are vulnerable to poverty.

2 Evaluate the success of the welfare state in solving the problem of poverty.

3 Assess the health effects of poverty.

4 Compare and contrast individualist and structural theories of poverty.

IN this chapter we focus in some detail on a central debate in social welfare which has considerable – some would say crucial – significance for health and health workers: the nature, extent and effects of poverty. Chapter 5 drew attention to the considerable inequalities of wealth and income that still exist in Britain today. This chapter considers the long debate about poverty from a health perspective and evaluates the contribution made by welfare policies and reforms to reducing poverty and ill health.

6.1 Health and poverty

When and how do we draw the line that defines people as 'being in a state of poverty'? What evidence is there that being in poverty or at the margins of poverty damages people's health? And what should be the response of nurses and other health workers to questions about poverty? Debates about poverty and about the relationship between poverty and health are not new. Victorian social reformers such as Edwin Chadwick, the campaigner for public health legislation, and Charles Booth, who documented the extent of poverty in London in the 1890s, accepted that poverty and health status were inter-connected, although they did not agree on the nature of the link. Correlations between poverty and life expectancy were recorded in successive government reports; for example, low paid labourers lived barely half as long as professional men in Britain in the 1840s. Evidence about the extent of poverty and ill health helped to persuade governments in the early twentieth century that some anti-poverty legislation was needed to maintain the efficiency of the nation and to safeguard the nation's population stock.

With the coming of the welfare state in Britain in the 1940s it was thought that poverty would disappear and health chances would gradually be equalised. All citizens gained the right to free, needs based medical treatment in the new National Health Service, and full employment and rising living standards after World War II promised a final end to poverty. But in the late 1960s poverty was 'rediscovered' by researchers such as Peter Townsend (1979), who also found consider-able evidence of its impact on health status.

Research into health inequalities gathered pace in the 1980s, prompted by the Black Report (1980), and once again the issue of poverty became linked to debates about health. Although ruling politicians in Britain (and in the USA and elsewhere) largely ignored the debates about poverty and health inequalities, health professionals have paid them serious attention. A range of initiatives in the last decade, such as the World Health Organisation's Health For All by the Year 2000 and Healthy Public Policy initiatives (WHO, 1981; 1988), and the 'New Public Health' movement in Britian, have openly endorsed anti-poverty measures as a part of their strategy. In the early 1990s the impact of world recession and financial strategy setbacks, with resulting high levels of unemployment, short-time working and cutbacks in benefit levels for social security claimants, once again made poverty a matter of growing public and political concern.

6.2 Defining and measuring poverty

The most brutal way of defining poverty is in terms of life and death. In very poor, famine-hit or war-torn countries today, where poverty and malnutrition (judged by World Health Organisation standards) are the shared experiences of most of the population, *absolute* poverty means not obtaining enough nourishment to avoid starvation. This was the experience of some inmates of Victorian workhouses and prisons, which the novelist Charles Dickens dramatically portrayed in *Oliver Twist* and *Little Dorrit*.

At the other end of the spectrum are models developed by anti-poverty researchers since the 1960s, which endorse a *relative* concept of poverty. Here poverty is measured in terms of people's ability to sustain a basic lifestyle in accordance with the norms and standards of their own society, and researchers attempt to discover the threshold at which individuals and households cease to have the necessary resources for social coping (just 'getting by') or active social participation in that society and instead become isolated and marginalised (George and Howards, 1991). Although opinions vary as to the level of income and resources required to avoid being in poverty, there is agreement that an absolute, life or death view of poverty is inadequate. The poverty or 'deprivation' threshold suggested by Peter Townsend (1979), for example, as one-and-a-half times the level of Supplementary Benefit. Below this, he claimed, there was a sharp decrease in people's ability to participate. Thus, investigating poverty raises questions about tolerable levels of inequality, and suggests that poverty implies a relationship between rich and poor in society.

Subsistence poverty

Over the last century, however, a different definition of poverty has been more widely accepted in Britain: that is, the concept of *subsistence* poverty. This is defined as the level at which an individual or household has not sufficient income or resources to meet a minimum number of basic needs, for food, clothing and shelter. The scientific surveys of poverty carried out at the end of the nineteenth century defined poverty in terms of subsistence, identifying a state of absolute poverty below subsistence level in which survival was threatened by malnutrition, exposure or disease.

An attempt to measure the earnings level required to maintain subsistence was made by Seebohm Rowntree in York in 1899. Rowntree, a Quaker businessman and member of the Rowntree chocolate-making family, was sceptical of the bleak results of Charles Booth's 1892 survey of poverty in London, which indicated that one-fifth of the population were living in absolute poverty (defined by Booth as a weekly income of less than 21s (105p) per week at 1890s prices), and selected York as more representative of urban conditions in Britain.

Rowntree's survey, published in 1901 as *Poverty: A Study of Town Life*, found a similar level of absolute poverty. One-fifth of the York population consisted of families whose total earnings 'were insufficient to obtain the minimum necessaries for the maintenance of merely physical efficiency' (Rowntree, 1901). The subsistence poverty line for a family then was calculated as 21s 8d (109p), and if income after payment of rent fell short of this, the family was deemed to be in absolute poverty. This calculation was made by adding together house rent, minimum sums for fuel, clothing and household goods according to family size, and food costs – arrived at by estimating the average nutritional needs of children and adults and translating these into required foods.

Rowntree's investigation provided important evidence about the relationship between wages and patterns of expenditure. It contradicted contemporary claims that *secondary* poverty – that is, poverty caused by bad money management, fecklessness and drunkenness – was responsible for the large numbers of Victorian poor, rather than low income (or *primary*) poverty. His findings indicated the widespread extent of 'primary' poverty, caused mainly by low wages (52 per cent), family size (22 per cent) and old age, sickness or disability (12 per cent) (Rowntree, 1901).

Here is Rowntree's prescription for subsistence level living in York in 1900. What is your reaction to his regulations?

A family living upon the scale allowed for in this estimate must never spend a penny on railway fares or omnibus. They must never go into the countryside unless they walk. They must never purchase a halfpenny newspaper or spend a penny to buy a ticket for a popular concert. They must write no letters to absent children, for they cannot afford the postage. They must never contribute anything to their Church or Chapel, or give any help to a neighbour which costs them money. They cannot save, nor can they join a sick club or Trade Union, because they cannot pay the necessary subscription. The children must have no pocket money for dolls, marbles or sweets. The father must smoke no tobacco, and must drink no beer. The mother must never buy any pretty clothes for herself or her children, the character of the family wardrobe as for the family diet being

governed by the regulation, 'Nothing must be bought but that which is absolutely
necessary for the maintenance of physical health, and what is bought must be of the
plainest and most economical description'. Should a child fall ill, it must be attended by
the parish doctor; should it die, it must be buried by the parish.

Rowntree (1901)

Compared with today, these requirements seem unbearably harsh and unrealistic. The lack of ability of the Victorian poor to save any money would have meant that, should illness or unemployment strike, the household would have fallen below subsistence poverty into penury and the workhouse. In a large-scale representative survey of public attitudes to poverty in Britain in the 1980s (Mack and Lansley 1991) it was found that well over two-thirds of people interviewed saw public transport, toys for children and the occasional celebration as essentials. This survey was repeated in 1991 and again there was a high level of consensus about items regarded as necessities (Frayman, 1991, and see Box 6.1).

The subsistence approach to poverty has had a considerable impact on policy makers in Britain. It seems to promise a fairly objective measurement of poverty. It established the concept of a poverty threshold and of a basket of goods and services necessary to maintain health at a minimum level. It began the involvement of experts, researchers, and the general public to some degree, in the business of defining and measuring poverty: to determine what an adequate dietary intake was, what minimum necessities were, when income was deemed to be too low.

The 'poverty line'

William Beveridge, an influential civil servant, author of *Full Employment in a Free Society* and the main architect of the 1940s legislation that set up the welfare state, adopted the notion of a poverty line in his proposals for reform. Rowntree's classifications of subsistence helped to determine

BOX 6.1 Items regarded as necessities by at least two-thirds of British adults surveyed for 'Breadline Britain 1990s'. Source: Frayman (1991)

- Self-contained damp-free accommodation with an indoor toilet and bath
- A weekly roast joint for the family and three daily meals for each child
- Two pairs of all-weather shoes and a warm waterproof coat
- Sufficient money for public transport
- Adequate bedrooms and beds
- Heating and carpeting
- A refrigerator and washing machine
- Enough money for special occasions like Christmas
- Toys for the children

the level of National Assistance in the 1940s, although the actual allowances were set lower than either Rowntree or Beveridge recommended.

The concept of a 'poverty line' is still an integral element of the social security system in the 1990s. The cash payments provided by the state (through Income Support and other allowances) define a minimum, so that people who fall below that assistance benefit level are necessarily in poverty. Social security regulations operate a subsistence view of poverty, listing necessities (food, fuel, clothing, travel, cleaning and household items) and the range of extra items which may qualify for loans from the Social Fund.

Decisions about how poverty should be measured inevitably influence judgements about its incidence. For example, until the late 1960s poverty was not a major issue for most politicians because another authoritative poverty study of York in 1950 indicated that it had largely disappeared. A recent re-examination of the data, which had concluded that only 1.5 per cent of the population was in poverty, suggests that researchers had underestimated the extent of poverty. Atkinson (1989) showed that a minimum of 4.9 per cent of family units in York had income levels below National Assistance and that perhaps as many as 9.5 per cent of families fell below that level. Two very different estimates of the numbers in poverty were given in Townsend's (1979) research: 22.9 per cent if judged by his definition of relative poverty, and 6.1 per cent if judged in terms of subsistence. Obviously a great many more people would need assistance, at considerably higher cost to the state, if a relative poverty rather than a subsistence poverty definition was applied.

The starting point for measuring poverty in Britain is the assistance benefit level, the unofficial subsistence 'poverty line' (see Table 6.1). In 1987, 5.3 per cent of people not in receipt of benefits had an income below benefit level, and probably another 1.5–2 per cent on benefit were below this level because of deductions from their benefit (George and Howards, 1991). If poverty is measured less stringently, the numbers deemed to be in poverty will rise. The poverty threshold of 140 per cent of assistance level is the most widely accepted broad measure of 'being on the margins of' or 'at risk of' poverty among researchers in Britain. Judged by this yardstick 20 per cent of people in Britain are at the margins of poverty. There are clearly problems with measuring the extent of poverty by using a scale benefit which is designed to 'solve' poverty through provision of an adequate income for all those that need it. As benefit levels rise, so inevitably do the numbers in and at the margins of poverty; measuring poverty by numbers of claimants doesn't reveal much about levels of household income or real standards of living. We will return to these issues again in Section 6.5. As a

TABLE 6.1 The extent of poverty in Britain 1960–87. Source: George and Howards (1991)

Cumulative proportions of persons NOT receiving assistance benefit with net incomes below and above the assistance level				Proportion of persons in receipt of assistance benefit
Year	Below assistance level	Below 110% of assistance level	Below 120% of assistance level	Below 140% of assistance level	
	%	%	%	%	
1960	3.8*	6.6*	9.0	14.2	
1967	3.5*				
1972	3.4	5.5			7.7
1973	3.0	5.9			7.1
1975	3.0	4.8			6.1
1977	4.0	6.0	7.0		8.2
1979	4.0	6.2	9.0	14.4	7.6
1981	4.9	7.8	11.2	16.9	9.1
1983	5.2	8.5	11.7	19.1	11.4
1985	4.5	7.0	9.3	15.6	12.9
1987	5.3	7.7	10.2	14.9	13.5

* based on household unit and hence underestimates extent of poverty.

comparison with these measures, it is worth noting the European Community approach. It used a different definition in a recent study of poverty, identifying as the poor those whose income was less than half the equivalent disposable income of their country (Wintour, 1989). This is obviously a more generous, relative definition, and on this measurement numbers in poverty in Britain increased from 6.7 per cent of the population in the period 1973–7 to 12 per cent in 1984/85.

Who are the poor?

The groups in the population most likely to find themselves in poverty are not dissimilar to those identified by Seebohm Rowntree in his 1901 study of York. They are older people, the low paid, unemployed people, lone-parent families and people with long-term sickness or disabilities (see Table 6.2). Large families are more at risk of poverty, but not by any means to the same extent as in 1901. Feminist researchers have commented on the increasing visibility of women among those in poverty, and there is some evidence that the 'feminisation of poverty', while not new, has been increasing (Glendinning and Millar, 1987). Another significant change by the mid-twentieth century was the evidence of poverty among black and minority ethnic groups, much of it

TABLE 6.2 The risk of poverty for the various population groups in Britain in the 1980s. Source: George and Howards (1991)

Population group	1981	1985	1987
	%	%	%
I All persons over pension age	12.7	10.6	10.0
(a) Married couples	10.3	8.2	5.6
(b) Single persons	15.3	13.1	15.0
II All persons under pension age by family type	3.8	3.2	4.4
(a) Married couples with children	3.6	2.8	4.1
(b) Single persons with children	6.6	3.4	3.4
(c) Married couples without children	1.6	2.1	2.7
(d) Single persons without children	6.4	5.3	6.9
III All persons under pension age by employment status	3.8	3.2	4.4
(a) Full-time work or self-employed	1.9	1.8	2.9
(b) Sick or disabled for more than 3 months	6.3	4.2	6.4
(c) Unemployed for more than 3 months	13.8	12.1	8.7*
(d) Other	11.9	5.8	
IV All persons	4.9	4.5	5.3

* Includes other

due to discrimination and racism in the job market; occupational class, average wages and employment levels are all markedly lower for black workers (Cook and Watt, 1987).

There is some evidence that the risks of poverty do not vary greatly across the generations, although the reasons for this are hotly disputed, as we'll see in Section 6.5. Nevertheless, there have been significant changes in the proportions in poverty in each of the groups mentioned due to changes in levels of benefit and changing economic circumstances. For example, unemployed people were a very small proportion of those in poverty until the return of mass unemployment in the early 1980s. In the early 1990s unemployment again rose and by 1993, 12.4 per cent of men and 7.5 per cent of women were out of work. Low paid workers with families, on the other hand, have benefited from Family Credit (formerly Family Income Supplement) which was introduced in the 1970s; 420 000 families received Family Credit in 1992/93.

Older people, particularly those living alone, are still at greatest risk of being in poverty: 10 per cent of people over pensionable age were in official poverty (below Income Support level) in 1987, although pensioner incomes have grown at a faster rate than those of the rest of the population since the 1950s (George and Howards, 1991). If poverty is defined as below 140 per cent of benefit level, then over half of all pensioners are in poverty. While most have been helped out of official poverty by welfare benefits and occupational pensions, the very elderly who were in low paid jobs – and elderly women in particular, who live longer, have generally earned less and are least likely to have pension rights – are still highly vulnerable. Also at risk are the one million or so lone-parent families, 90 per cent of which are headed by women, and the long term sick and disabled, especially elderly women with severe disabilities and unmarried and married disabled people with dependent children. Martin and White's study (1988) of the financial circumstances of disabled adults found that, whether measured in terms of income (earnings and benefits), consumer goods, diet or basic social needs, these two groups were especially vulnerable to poverty.

6.3 Debates about relative poverty

Rowntree's research, even though it claimed to be about absolute poverty and bare subsistence, illustrates some of the difficulties of defining poverty except as relative to a particular society in a given historical period.

○ Rowntree's list of essential clothing for a young woman was sparse in the extreme. But which items reflect Victorian social norms rather than 'absolute' needs?

One pair of boots, two aprons, one second-hand dress, one skirt made from an old dress, a third of the cost of a new hat, a third of the cost of a shawl and a jacket, two pairs of stockings, a few unspecified underclothes, one pair of stays and one pair of old boots worn as slippers.

Rowntree (1901)

I would suggest that the 'pair of stays', in particular, is a culturally defined need, just as in contemporary British society a pair of tights might be! Neither is essential for 'physical efficiency', unlike food, but both reflect the fact that defining poverty is also concerned with making a judgement about tolerable inequality and deprivation in a specific social and historical context. Surveys undertaken in the 1930s and in 1950 specifically included non-subsistence elements, such as an allowance for a daily newspaper and a radio license, and were based on his subjective judgements about acceptable standards: 'Rowntree's estimates of costs of necessities other than food were based either on his own or others' opinions . . . Neither in his studies nor in similar studies were criteria of need, independent of personal judgement . . . put forward' (Townsend, 1979).

Poverty can only be defined in relation to particular sets of conditions. Rowntree defined and measured poverty using the norms and standards that were acceptable in 1890s Britain. Judged by the standards of many poor countries, poverty does not exist in contemporary Britain; conversely, UK measures of poverty would be inappropriate for use in the 'third world'. A poor third world country such as Pakistan defines levels of poverty in relation to its own average national incomes, not those of wealthy Western countries, and uses average local dietary intake as an indicator, not World Health Organisation guidelines (Naseem, in George and Howards, 1991). In addition, the term 'relative poverty' suggests that, as social and economic circumstances change, so will views about poverty. The interpretation of subsistence in National Assistance benefit levels in the 1940s was more generous than in Rowntree's 1901 survey. 'Relative' also suggests a relationship between people in a particular society: some individuals or groups are deemed to be in a state of poverty *relative* to the level of material and social resources enjoyed by the majority in society. Rowntree himself made judgements about tolerable inequality, about how far below the living standards of the majority in a population the poor should be allowed to fall. Since the 1960s poverty researchers have been responding to this question by investigating how far a social consensus about poverty exists (Mack and Lansley, 1991) and by exploring the fortunes of specific groups, for example poverty in children (Piachaud, 1979). In general, a poverty threshold of 140 per cent of the Supplementary Benefit scale has come to be accepted as a tolerable minimum level above which people can cope or 'get by' in the wider society, and as a level below which people are increasingly isolated from society.

The concept of 'relative deprivation'

In his book *Poverty in the United Kingdom* (1979) Peter Townsend put forward a concept of relative poverty as 'relative deprivation' within a society, a concept which went some way beyond the idea of coping or 'getting by' towards a notion of adequate social participation. He sought to establish as far as possible an objective measure of poverty, a threshold below which families or groups in the population were clearly excluded, materially and socially, from the society in which they lived:

Poverty can be defined objectively and applied consistently only in terms of the concept of relative deprivation . . . Individuals, families and groups in the population can be said to be in poverty when they lack the resources to obtain the types of diets, participate in the activities and have the living conditions and amenities which are customary, or are at least widely encouraged and approved, in the societies to which they belong. Their resources are so seriously below those commanded by the average individual or family that they are, in effect, excluded from ordinary living patterns, customs and activities.

Townsend (1979)

The research was conducted by means of a representative sample of 2000 households and a complex questionnaire containing 167 questions which covered income (earnings, savings, state and 'fringe' benefits), employment, health and style of living. Levels of social participation were measured using 60 indicators of style of living, including diet, health, education, working conditions and so on (see Table 6.3). There was a clear correlation between income/resource levels and levels of participation, but there was also 'a point in the scale of the distribution of resources below which, as resources diminish, families find it

TABLE 6.3 Indicators of deprivation. Source: Townsend (1979)

Characteristic	% of population	Correlation co-efficient (Pearson) (net disposable household income last year)	
1. Has not had a week's holiday away from home in last 12 months	53.6	0.1892	S = 0.001
2. *Adults only.* Has not had a relative or friend to the home for a meal or snack in the last 4 weeks	33.4	0.0493	S = 0.001
3. *Adults only.* Has not been out in the last 4 weeks to a relative or friend for a meal or snack	45.1	0.0515	S = 0.001
4. *Children only* (under 15). Has not had a friend to play or to tea in the last 4 weeks	36.3	0.0643	S = 0.020
5. *Children only.* Did not have party on last birthday	56.6	0.0660	S = 0.016
6. Has not had an afternoon or evening out for entertainment in the last two weeks	47.0	0.1088	S = 0.001
7. Does not have fresh meat (including meals out) as many as four days a week	19.3	0.1821	S = 0.001
8. Has gone through one or more days in the past fortnight without a cooked meal	7.0	0.0684	S = 0.001
9. Has not had a cooked breakfast most days of the week	67.3	0.0559	S = 0.001
10. Household does not have a refrigerator	45.1	0.2419	S = 0.001
11. Household does not usually have a Sunday joint (3 in 4 times)	25.9	0.1734	S = 0.001
12. Household does not have sole use of four amenities indoors (flush WC; sink or washbasin and cold-water tap; fixed bath or shower; and gas or electric cooker)	21.4	0.1671	S = 0.001

particularly difficult to share . . . in their society's style of living' (Townsend, 1979). The level of income below which the risk of being deprived of one or more of the 'deprivation indicator items' increased rapidly was 150 per cent of the Supplementary Benefit level, and, using this as a threshold, 22.9 per cent of the population of the UK were in poverty.

What do you think might be the main criticisms of this relative deprivation approach to poverty?

You may think that relative deprivation is too broad and too open to attack to be a useful concept. Some critics have argued this and have favoured a more restricted 'social coping' model, in which people are deemed to be in poverty if they are unable to sustain a modest working class style of living (George and Howards, 1991). There has also been some criticism of Townsend's methods and results. For example, Piachaud (1981) found no evidence of a significant deprivation threshold. Although the research tries to measure poverty objectively, the questions asked and the 60 indicators of participation/deprivation selected inevitably derive from the researchers' own interpretation of existing evidence about styles of living and patterns of consumption. You may want to take issue with some of the indicators selected, and certainly the dietary indicators, for example, look rather dated. Health workers might well be critical of the view that a cooked breakfast or meat every other day are needed to avoid relative deprivation. As we noted in Chapter 2, no researchers stand outside the social world which they investigate, and Townsend was measuring poverty in relation to styles of living in the late 1960s, not the 1990s.

The widespread influence of Townsend's research did provoke continued attacks from critics on the political right. In 1989 John Moore, then Secretary of State for Social Security, insisted that 'real' poverty of the absolute, below subsistence kind investigated by Rowntree had disappeared, and that the debate about poverty had re-emerged in the 1960s for political reasons rather than because poverty had once again become a problem:

By the 1960s the gulf in living standards between countries under socialist governments and those with capitalist systems had become glaringly apparent to everyone . . . free enterprise capitalism, so vilified by socialists for creating poverty, was in fact having substantial success in relieving it. Socialism . . . was in danger of being dismissed as serious political ideology. At this point academics came to the rescue.

Moore (1989)

This comment, whether or not you agree with it, is a reminder that the study of poverty is not just a matter for researchers but also the subject of long-standing political debates which have determined the level and character of welfare benefits.

6.4 The welfare state and anti-poverty legislation

When the welfare state was set up in Britain in the 1940s, legislation to eradicate subsistence poverty was an integral feature of it. Victorian Poor Law legislation had been designed to sweep paupers out of sight into workhouses, not to cure poverty (see Table 6.4). The welfare reforms carried out by the Liberal government in the early twentieth century had sought to provide selective benefits for targeted groups of the poor, sometimes at below subsistence level. The 1908 Old Age Pensions Act, for example, gave the over 70s a supplementary pension rather than a subsistence benefit. The government was guided by a concern for 'national efficiency', seeking to ensure that the population was healthy and strong enough to serve the country in wartime and in industrial production.

Review the definitions of health outlined in Sections 1.1–1.3 and suggest which view of health underpins the 'national efficiency' approach.

TABLE 6.4 **Shifting views of poverty**

	'Causes' of poverty (diagnosis of *problem* + perception of needs)	**'Solution'** (policy approach services provided)
Mid 19th century	Fecklessness Misfortune Sickness/death/old age Dependants	Workhouse (deterrent, last resort)
Early 20th century	Misfortune (unemployment) Sickness etc. Fecklessness	National Insurance for at risk groups Workhouse
Mid 20th century	Unemployment Sickness etc. Dependants Fecklessness	'Full employment' policies National Insurance National Assistance → Income Support/Family Credit/ Child Benefit Loss of benefit rules Benefit 'policing' ↑ Workfare?

The 'functional fitness' model in which health is conceptualised as an 'absence of disease' links most closely with national efficiency. The main concern was to produce an efficient workforce for peace and war. This explains measures such as maternity grants, subsidised school dinners and free school medical inspection. Some high risk and low paid groups, such as dock workers, were drawn into social insurance through the 1911 National Insurance Act, which compelled the worker, employer and state to make weekly contributions and entitled the sick or unemployed worker to draw benefit for a limited number of weeks. This was a precursor of the social insurance of the 1940s, but it was designed to meet bare subsistence needs for short periods rather than to eradicate poverty; it supplemented rather than superseded the Poor Law and the workhouse, even though more and more groups of workers came under the insurance schemes after 1918. When unemployment rose to 3 million in the late 1920s many of the unemployed had already run out of benefit entitlement and, to get further relief, were forced to undergo a 'means test' of their household income; penury and the workhouse still threatened.

The welfare state of the 1940s

In *Full Employment in a Free Society* (1944), Beveridge argued that the post-war objective should be a 'determination to make a Britain free of the giant evils of Want, Disease, Ignorance and Squalor' because they were 'common enemies of us all, not . . . enemies with whom each individual may seek a separate peace, escaping himself to personal prosperity while leaving his fellow in their clutches'. The safety net provided by the new welfare state would help to destroy these evils. Disease would be overcome by the work of the new National Health Service and also by the gradual improvement of the population's physical efficiency as want disappeared. Ignorance would be tackled by a National Education Service, set up under the 1944 Education Act. Squalor would diminish as living standards rose and education took effect.

Above all, want would be overcome by establishing compulsory social insurance, which provided adequate, flat-rate benefits for flat-rate insurance contributions, ensuring that no household fell below a minimum standard of living. The National Insurance Acts passed in 1946 covered all full-time workers and any general risk that was involuntary, such as sickness, disability, maternity, widowhood, old age and unemployment. National Assistance (now Income Support) was available for the small proportion who did not qualify for insurance benefits, such as lone-parent households and part-time workers. Family Allowances (now Child Benefit) were paid to all families with dependent children to ensure that child poverty – which Beveridge called the 'worst feature of Want in Britain before the war' – was ended. This legislation, underpinned by 'full employment', was to deliver 'the first blow in the war against Idleness', the fifth giant evil identified by Beveridge.

The insurance principle underlying the welfare state was itself supported by the concept of full employment, which Beveridge defined as a situation in which 'unemployment is reduced to short intervals of standing by, with the certainty that very soon one will be wanted in one's old job again or will be wanted in a new job that is within one's power' (Beveridge, 1944). A policy of full employment would ensure buoyant levels of economic growth as well as taxation receipts that would enable non-contributory benefits such as National Assistance to be easily afforded. It would also prevent the recurrence of inter-war levels of unemployment, which would be politically damaging and, because they would threaten the whole basis of social insurance, financially disastrous.

The framework of welfare today

○ Consider which of the principles embodied in the post-war welfare state still stand in the 1990s and which have been changed.

The most obvious principle which survives is that of social insurance. Those in full-time work still pay National Insurance (NI) contributions and receive benefits. If you have cared for older people in hospital they may have talked about 'paying their stamp' (this referred to NI cards which were stamped for each working week) and 'getting what they've paid for' – their welfare entitlement. The insurance principle has been seen as valuable reinforcement of the virtues of responsibility and saving, even though health services and benefits increasingly came to be paid for out of general taxation rather than weekly contributions.

But the principle of flat-rate contributions and benefits has been modified. Flat-rate contributions could not be raised by enough to cover the rising costs of social security without unfairly squeezing poorly paid workers, so they were made earnings-related. In the 1960s earnings-related benefit supplements were introduced for unemployment, sickness, widowhood and maternity benefits, and in the late 1970s for old age pensions. These were phased out by the Conservative governments of the 1980s, so that in the 1990s people receive flat-rate benefits and pay earnings-related contributions, although the poorest group will qualify for non-contributory state benefits and many of those in work receive private occupational benefits.

Universalism and selectivism
One obvious change to the system has been the relative growth of

selective, means-tested benefits. National Assistance, the 1940s means-tested benefit, still exists in the 1990s as Income Support and Housing Benefit which are paid to households where the breadwinner is unemployed or works less than 16 hours per week. These benefits also 'supplement' other lower level benefits: for example, unemployment pay and the state retirement pension. But as concern about low economic growth rates and high welfare costs grew in the 1960s, there was a gradual shift from a *universalist* system, with comprehensive, general risk coverage, to a *selectivist* system of supplementary benefits (see Box 6.2 and Section 2.4). In general, gaps were plugged by benefits targeted at particular groups, especially those poorly provided for in the 1940s welfare system, such as the growing number of lone-parent households (other than those headed by a widow). An elaborate system of discretionary allowances (now changed to repayable loans from the Social Fund) enabled groups in poverty to meet special needs and purchase major household items, like beds and children's shoes. As National Insurance benefit rates lagged behind Supplementary Benefit rates, old age pensioners and the unemployed also began to depend upon Supplementary Benefit to supplement their insurance-derived income (MacGregor, 1984).

Beveridge had envisaged that National Assistance would support only the small minority who did not qualify for National Insurance, and in 1949/50 only 12.7 per cent of social security expenditure was on means-tested benefits. By 1984/5 this had doubled to 25.6 per cent (George and Howards, 1991). In 1980, when the Supplementary Benefit

BOX 6.2 Universalism and selectivism

Universalism	Selectivism
Providing welfare benefits for all people within a particular category, without making judgements about ability to pay. *Child Benefit*, for example, is provided to all families with dependent children, irrespective of their means. *The National Health Service* is, by and large, a universalist service. It provides most services free at the point of use for all citizens, although there are exceptions (for example prescription charges, dental treatment, sight tests).	Providing benefits only on the basis of certain tests and judgements about an individual's means and ability to pay. These are often called *means-tested* or *targeted* benefits. Weekly income, savings (beyond a certain level) and some other welfare benefits may be included in the calculation about whether an individual qualifies for such benefit. There are cut-off points at which benefit is no longer paid, and some means-tested benefits are included for tax purposes. Selectivism is much less expensive in terms of the total costs of the benefits, but much more expensive to administer.

system was overhauled by the incoming Conservative government, it was accepted as being a mainstay of social security. The overhaul, as the Secretary of State for Social Security Reg Prentice commented at the time, 'would fit the scheme to its mass role of coping with millions of claimants in known and readily definable categories'. There were, however, important omissions from this trend towards means-testing. One example is Child Benefit, a universalist, non means-tested benefit paid to all families with dependent children.

The end of 'full employment'

The other obvious principle which has disappeared from social planning entirely is the commitment to full employment. The Beveridge scheme drew on the ideas of the economist Maynard Keynes, who argued that governments could use their economic and political power to encourage growth, avoid recession and ensure low unemployment. The political right abandoned this policy in the mid-1970s, claiming that attempts to reduce unemployment and stimulate economic revival could not succeed without an accompanying, and even more politically dangerous, upward spiral of inflation. 'Holding down inflation' and allowing sound, non-inflationary economic growth to take place, rather than 'maintaining full employment' through state spending and management of the economy, became the political watchword of the New Right after 1979.

During the recessions of 1981–3 and the early 1990s unemployment again rose above 3 million, but inflation remained low, and as economic recovery followed recession in the mid 1980s, unemployment fell again. In the late 1980s Nigel Lawson, then Chancellor of the Exchequer, spoke of an 'economic miracle'. The new 'monetarism', by stimulating risk taking and wealth creation through market de-regulation and a stable money supply, had delivered growth and signalled the 'death' of Keynesianism. Monetarist policy was also seen as the best anti-poverty strategy. The Conservative government argued that increased wealth and rising incomes, aided by better targeted benefits which reinforced the incentive to work, would cause a 'trickle-down effect', so that the poor also shared in the growing prosperity.

6.5 The current politics of poverty

Two inter-connected debates, therefore, are central to the politics of poverty in the 1990s, one about economic growth and the other about poverty levels. First, has economic growth eradicated poverty, except as unavoidable inequality; has the trickle-down approach of monetarism worked? Second, is there any closer agreement on the extent and definition of poverty?

Economic growth and 'trickle-down'

Claims about the trickle-down effect were given substance by evidence from a new statistical series, Households Below Average Income, which used the household as the unit of measurement of income rather than the individual or family units receiving benefit. It seemed to show that between 1981 and 1985 the real income of the bottom 10 per cent of the population (that is, of over 5 million people) had risen by 8.4 per cent, nearly twice as much as for the population as a whole (Timmins, 1990).

The new series replaced the Low Income Family statistical series, which since the mid-1970s had assessed the numbers of individuals and family units living at or just above Supplementary Benefit level. The Households Below Average Income series, on the other hand, recorded total household income including, for example, that of older relatives or young working adults which might make the collective income and living standards of the household higher than a Low Income Family type assessment would show. The new series did not measure income against the Supplementary Benefit scale but by 'deciles' (tenths). It gave figures for the income of households in the lowest decile of the population, the next decile and so on up to average income.

The new figures were greeted with considerable suspicion, not only by political opponents of the Conservative government, but by the all-party social services committee of the House of Commons and by poverty research agencies such as the Child Poverty Action Group and the Low Pay Unit. Poverty analysts had calculated numbers in poverty from the old figures (generally agreed to be those living below 140 per cent of assistance level, as we saw in Section 6.2). The new figures on household income made it impossible to do this and made assumptions that households would pool and share income and resources, which was far from certain.

In the light of Section 6.4, note down why figures suggesting that numbers in poverty had fallen might be open to question.

In the early 1980s there was a major recession and unemployment rose sharply. In addition, benefit levels had generally lagged behind wages and some benefits, for example those for school leavers, had been cut. Both of these factors might be expected to increase the numbers in poverty between 1981 and 1985. You might also have noted, from your own observation, that growing numbers of people were homeless or sleeping rough in the early 1980s.

John Moore, then Secretary of State for Social Security, greeted the new figures with enthusiasm, pointing out that by 1985, even among the poorest one-fifth of families over 50 per cent had a telephone and central heating, 85 per cent had a washing machine and 70 per cent had colour television (Moore, 1989). In addition, poorer families were helped by better targeted benefits and by rises in some benefit levels. Compared to overall average household income, which:

Rose between 1970 and 1985 by more than a quarter over and above price increases . . . families on Supplementary Benefit did even better than the population as a whole with an increase of 28 per cent. Incomes of pensioners increased still more by 31 per cent.

Moore (1989)

This indicated not only that the poor were not getting poorer; Moore argued that 'they are substantially better off than they have ever been before'. What was called 'poverty' was in reality merely unavoidable 'inequality'; for poverty itself and the poverty lobby it was 'the end of the line' (Moore, 1989).

The political rewards of 'dishing' the poverty lobby were short-lived, however. The social services committee had commissioned its own, independent survey of poverty from the Institute for Fiscal Studies using the Low Income Family format. Its first finding was contentious but not unexpected: that the numbers on less than half average income were reduced from 5.5 million to 4.5 million people by using households as a measure (Institute for Fiscal Studies, 1990). This merely renewed questions about accuracy and equity in measuring poverty: was it best to use actual benefit units, or to make assumptions about shared household income and resources?

But the Institute also found that the real income of the bottom 10 per cent was growing at a slower rate than that of the population as a whole. Government statisticians had made errors in calculating the new figures: in fact, between 1981 and 1985 real incomes for the population as a whole had grown by only 5.4 per cent, those of the bottom decile by only 2.6 per cent – barely more than a quarter of the government's proclaimed rise. As the social services committee commented, the revised figures 'change completely the picture of what has been happening to the position of people living in the poorest households'. More recent figures have tended to tell a similar story: that although living standards have improved during the 1980s, the poorest groups have not benefited from a trickle-down effect at all (see Table 6.5).

Redefining the poverty line?

How does this connect to our second question about poverty? Are we any nearer agreement on the extent of poverty and on the line that

TABLE 6.5 Distribution of disposable household income. Source: *Social Trends* (1994)

	United Kingdom					Percentages
	Quintile groups of individuals					
	Bottom fifth	Next fifth	Middle fifth	Next fifth	Top fifth	Total
Net income before housing costs						
1979	10	14	18	23	35	100
1981	10	14	18	23	36	100
1987	9	13	17	23	39	100
1988–1989	8	12	17	23	40	100
1990–1991	7	12	17	23	41	100
Net income after housing costs						
1979	10	14	18	23	35	100
1981	9	14	18	23	36	100
1987	8	12	17	23	40	100
1988–1989	7	12	17	23	41	100
1990–1991	6	12	17	23	43	100

The unit of analysis is the individual and the income measure is net equivalent household income.

should be drawn between poor and non-poor in Britain today? John Moore's claim that inequality, not poverty, was the hidden agenda of the poverty lobby has had an impact. Peter Townsend's work, as we noted earlier, was criticised by some poverty analysts because the concepts of social participation and 'relative deprivation' blurred the line between poverty and inequality. One response has been to favour a more modest 'social coping' model which allows the basic necessities and a range of social needs to be met at a reasonable level. The necessities and range of social needs are selected on the basis of survey data about current consumption patterns, reflecting to some extent a wider public view as well as the researcher's own judgements about what an acceptable range of necessities and social needs really are:

For public purposes in Britain and the US, there is a strong case for defining poverty in terms of social coping. It is morally unacceptable for governments to define poverty in such affluent societies in terms of either starvation or subsistence. On the other hand, defining poverty in terms of social participation reflecting the living standards of all income groups in society would make it politically impossible for any government in the foreseeable future to commit itself to the abolition of poverty. The social coping definition which sees poverty in relation to only working-class living standards offers both a more realistic approach in terms of public policy and a more justifiable approach in terms of conceptual understanding since the poor are, on the whole, part of the working class.

George and Howards (1991)

○   Take a few minutes to reflect on the ideas about poverty that you have considered so far in this chapter and what you may already know from your own experience or wider reading. Do you agree that a social coping approach is to be favoured?

You might well have accepted the political wisdom of defining and measuring poverty in a restrained way in order to encourage political action. But you might have felt that the larger issue of inequality still lurked behind poverty, because estimates about living 'modestly' and 'coping' still very much involved subjective judgements. That said, much poverty research seems to define being out of poverty as managing to live modestly according to working class standards. Piachaud (1979) adopted this kind of approach in his work for the Child Poverty Action Group on the cost of a child. The cut-off point of 140 per cent of the Supplementary Benefit level as the poverty threshold is still widely used.

A good example of strategic thinking in poverty research is supplied by recent research funded by the Joseph Rowntree Foundation and carried out by Jonathan Bradshaw at York University's family budget unit and researchers at other universities (Bradshaw *et al.*, 1992). It endorses the poverty threshold of 140 per cent of the Supplementary Benefit scale as realistic for the 1990s (see Table 6.6). It also revives the approach used by Seebohm Rowntree in the 1930s, by defining and

TABLE 6.6 Keeping the family on low-cost budgets. Source: Bradshaw *et al.* (1992)

(£ per week April 1992 prices)	Total weekly expenses (excluding rent)	Total benefit
Pensioner		
(owner occupier)	67.06	57.15
Pensioner (local authority tenant)	53.36	57.15
2 adults, 2 children*		
(local authority tenant)	141.40	105.00
Lone parent, 2 children*		
(local authority tenant)	110.72	85.60

All households are assumed to receive the maximum benefits and rent is therefore excluded as it is covered by housing benefits
* Children aged 4 and 10

pricing a basket of goods and services selected to represent a certain standard of living, making it difficult to evade the conclusions by arguing that none of the figures are comparable. The 'low-cost' budget standard selected very much echoes Rowntree's 'subsistence plus limited social needs' calculations of the 1930s. The 1990s equivalents of 6d towards the wireless licence and 7d for a weekly newspaper are allowances for video and TV hire. The budget included essential food at Sainsbury's prices, basic clothing at the cheapest prices in C&A, public transport and hair cuts, but excluded alcohol, cigarettes, cosmetics, a freezer and an annual holiday. The study reported that more than 50 per cent of lone mothers and single pensioners failed to achieve this low-cost budget standard.

Bradshaw and his colleagues also calculated the income needed for what they termed a 'modest-but-adequate' living standard, which was linked far more closely to a relative deprivation and tolerable inequality approach to poverty. Items in this household budget included a five year old car, a one week annual holiday, basic cosmetics and some allowance for alcohol. To reach this standard, a family of two adults and two children under ten would require each week three times the amount of Supplementary Benefit currently received; over a year this was calculated as a gross income of £21 000. Again, lone mothers and single pensioners did worst with only about 30 per cent reaching the budget standard.

The Joseph Rowntree Foundation published the report on the day before the 1992 Chancellor's Autumn Statement was expected to cut back on social security benefits; in the event public sector pay was targeted instead, but the episode neatly demonstrates the complexities of the current politics of poverty.

6.6 Poverty and health

At this point let's take stock of the relationship between health and poverty. We noted in Sections 6.2 and 6.3 that, while absolute poverty had all but vanished in Britain today, there still remained a significant level of subsistence poverty, if 'subsistence' was defined as the basic needs and commodities required for living in Britain in the 1990s. Beyond this, large numbers in the population were living 'at the margins' of poverty, on less than 140 per cent of the benefit level. Measured in 'social participation' terms even larger numbers of people were excluded from full participation in society. In Sections 6.4 and 6.5 we explored the changing response of the state to the problem of poverty and questioned how far the development of a welfare 'safety net' and patterns of economic growth since the 1950s had eradicated poverty. Evidence from the 1980s indicated that, whilst living standards in general continued to rise, the poor were doing relatively badly, and in real income terms the gap between those in or at the margins of poverty and the rest of the population was growing.

○   What do you think are likely to be the main health risks for the groups that are most vulnerable to poverty?

You may have first hand experience of nursing frail elderly people suffering from hypothermia or malnutrition and have strong feelings about the part that you think poverty played in bringing them to such a state. You may also have pointed out that people on low or very low incomes (semi-skilled, unskilled and unemployed workers and their families, in social classes IV and V) suffer more illness and die earlier than higher income groups.

There is no simple correlation between low income and conditions like hypothermia and malnutrition, of course, but lack of adequate heating and serious subnutrition are both more likely in poor households (Blackburn, 1992). There are about 500 deaths from hypothermia recorded each year, the vast majority of them of elderly people, and added to this is the much bigger problem of what is termed 'cold-associated disease'. From the figures of weekly death rates between 1974 and 1984 it has been estimated that there are about 40–50 000 cold-associated deaths in the UK every year (Smith and Jacobson, 1988). Elderly people are the most vulnerable and in severe winters suffer up to 50 per cent excess mortality from respiratory disease and heart disease. A national hypothermia study in the 1970s recommended that effective insulation, an adequate heating allowance and the issue of electric blankets to those at high risk could help to cut death rates (Fox *et al.*, 1973). Being in poverty or at the margins of poverty – with the fear of not being able to pay the heating bill and of getting into debt – is the position in which many elderly people find themselves, and it has a direct impact on their health.

For all groups in poverty inadequate nutrition is likely to be a common feature of their style of life. Although only about 2 per cent of older people suffer serious malnutrition, subnutrition – especially deficiencies of folic acid and vitamin D – are associated with ill health (MacLennan, 1986). The Child Poverty Action Group and the Maternity Alliance, among others, have highlighted the difficulties faced by those on assistance benefits in providing a nutritionally satisfactory diet for themselves or their children. Durward (1984) pointed out that pregnant women on benefit could not afford to eat a diet that conformed to Department of Health official guidelines for recommended nutritional intake during pregnancy:

For a couple on Supplementary Benefit expecting their first child, the woman's food would use up 28% of their income (excluding housing costs) even if she were claiming free welfare milk.

Durward (1984)

The Joseph Rowntree Foundation study of household budgets and living standards calculated that even buying only essential foodstuffs for a family of four would cost 40 per cent more than was available in the £105.00 per week benefit scale (Bradshaw *et al.*, 1992). Research on the actual diets of families in poverty has recorded the monotony, narrow range and undesirable predominance of sugary, fatty foods, which satisfy hunger pangs but do not provide a balanced diet (Burghes, 1980). Medical research on the links between high-fat, high-salt and low-roughage diets and a range of circulatory and digestive tract diseases, such as bowel cancer, has become widely known and incorporated into health education programmes by health workers in recent years (Cole-Hamilton and Lang, 1986). Clearly poverty, as well as 'lifestyle' and cultural influences, plays an important part in determining eating patterns and preventing change.

There are hidden costs for health work here. The rising level of poverty in the UK is associated with increased morbidity and mortality, so a simple prediction would be that the nation's health, far from improving, will deteriorate. In broader terms this might mean that health service costs rise more steeply, as the service attempts to cope with the increased burden of poverty-related conditions which require medical treatment and nursing care. It could be argued, therefore, that at least some of the money which could have been spent to lift individuals out of poverty will be spent on treatment for them as they become sick. This 'prevention' argument is not new; indeed it was widely used in Victorian times to justify expenditure on public housing and sanitation, in the early twentieth century to justify old age pensions and maternity payments and in the 1950s to justify the social security system itself. As we saw in Section 6.5, it is the extent and level of such expenditure, rather than the principle of prevention in itself, that is the focus for debate. Although there are those on the New Right who argue that welfare benefits should be cut back or withdrawn (we shall explore this in Section 6.7), they are still a minority voice. Far more influential are those who point to rises in general living standards and who argue for increasing selective means-tested benefits to those in real need, and for holding down, freezing or cutting back on universal benefits. The 1993 Budget moved further in this direction, while emphasising the need for most people to make greater private insurance provision.

There is some evidence that poverty would be reduced, and health thereby improved, by greater use of selective means-tested benefits. For example, in 1971 Family Income Supplement (now Family Credit) was brought in to supplement the income of low paid workers with children. Although the average wage of low paid workers did not change significantly between 1960 and the early 1980s, the low paid group fell from forming 40 per cent of the total of those in poverty in 1960 to only 23 per cent in 1985 (George and Howards, 1991). But as late as 1984 the take-up of Family Income Supplement was only just over 50 per cent and other means-tested benefits have continued to have quite low take-up rates. In addition, the mesh of income and benefits can cause a *poverty trap*, whereby small additions to income, such as a spell of overtime, result in the withdrawal of benefits to the point where the household is poorer than before (Bradshaw, 1980). The progressive withdrawal of Family Credit at the higher limits results in a poverty 'plateau' which it is difficult to cross. In a similar way, the rather small amount of 'disregarded' income which Income Support claimants are allowed to keep acts as a disincentive to pursue part-time work which might lift people above the 140 per cent threshold.

Low take-up and the existence of the poverty trap have convinced some poverty researchers that a universalist approach is better. They point to other undesirable features: the stigmatising effect of means-testing and the massive bureaucracy required to administer such benefits. The debate about benefits is only one aspect of a wider debate about how to tackle poverty, in which some critics would argue for the return of a comprehensive state-led series of interventions to provide a guaranteed basic income, improved housing and environmental changes to end poverty and reduce inequality. Others see individual lifestyle, personal or family inadequacies or subcultural factors as largely responsible for poverty.

○ The debate about poverty has to some extent been played out within the health arena. What different approaches to reducing poverty and improving health have you noted?

You might have recalled a range of reports, such as the Lalonde Report (1974), the World Health Organisation Health For All targets, the Black Report (1980) and *The Health Divide* (1987), all of which we noted in Chapter 1. They differ to some extent in their emphasis. The Lalonde Report on the health of Canadians, for example, recommended a refocusing of health work on issues of environment and lifestyle. But it was mainly lifestyle factors influencing health – smoking, drinking, drug use – which were picked up by health workers; the counterpart perhaps of the attitude that poverty is linked to inappropriate lifestyles. The Adelaide recommendations on Healthy Public Policy and the New Public Health movement specifically address the need to tackle the causes of poverty, which they see as partly structural and environmental (see Box 6.3).

BOX 6.3 Healthy Public Policy. Source: WHO (1988)

> Healthy Public Policy is characterised by an explicit concern for health and equity in all areas of policy and by an accountability for health impact. The main aim of Healthy Public Policy is to create a supportive environment to enable people to lead healthy lives. Such a policy makes healthy choices possible or easier for citizens. It makes social and physical environments health-enhancing. In the pursuit of Healthy Public Policy, government sectors concerned with agriculture, trade, education, industry and communications need to take account of health as an essential factor when formulating policy. They should pay as much attention to health as to economic considerations.

The study of health inequalities

The Black Report and *The Health Divide* also laid much emphasis on environmental factors, though they did not discount lifestyle issues. In fact, the Black Report arose within the wider framework of concern for welfare needs. In 1977 David Ennals, then Secretary of State for Social Services, echoed the concern of many health professionals by drawing attention to differences in life expectancy between high paid professionals and low paid unskilled workers:

The crude differences in mortality rates between the various social classes are worrying. To take the extreme example, in 1971 the death rate for adult men in social class V (unskilled workers) was nearly twice that of adult men in social class I (professional workers) . . . when you look at death rates for specific diseases the gap is even wider.

Ennals, reported in Townsend et al. (1987)

A working group was set up to examine the issue under the leadership of Sir Douglas Black, president of the Royal College of Physicians. It reported back in 1980, presenting a detailed analysis of health chances based on a wide survey of current research, and pointing to the existence of a growing social class gradient in all the major diseases. In particular it reported that between the 1950s and the 1970s the mortality rates for both men and women aged 35 and over in occupational classes I and II had steadily declined, whereas those in classes IV and V were the same or marginally worse.

The Black Report called for increased spending outside the health service, based on a recognition that social and economic factors like income levels, work, environment, housing, transport, education and 'lifestyle' choices influenced health. It argued that an intersectoral approach and a greater concentration upon vital areas such as child health services were needed. A main feature of its recommendations was a series of measures to end child poverty and 'give children a better start in life' by halting the 'inadequately treated bouts of childhood illness [that] cast long shadows forward' (Townsend et al., 1988).

The Black Report came down firmly on the side of universalist benefits such as Child Benefit as the most effective means of fighting health inequalities. For example, recommendations 24–7 called for the increase of Child Benefit, the introduction of child benefits for older children, an increase in the maternity grant and the gradual introduction of an infant care allowance (see Box 6.4). Other recommendations included the development of comprehensive disability allowances and more state spending on council housing. But its findings, and the call for extra spending, were rejected in favour of a narrower interpretation of individual 'lifestyle' change as the route to better health (Townsend and Davidson, 1982).

In spite of the failure to get its most costly recommendations

BOX 6.4 Black Report recommendations: summary

1 The abolition of child poverty should be adopted as a national goal for the 1980s, by: • Increasing the maternity grant and child benefit • Introducing an infant care allowance for under fives • Ensuring adequate local authority day care for under fives • Providing nutritionally adequate school meals for all • Mounting a child accident prevention programme	2 The introduction of a comprehensive disability allowance for people of all ages.
3 Draw up minimally acceptable and desirable standards of work, security, conditions and amenities, pay and welfare or fringe benefits.	4 Shift resources more quickly towards community care and primary health care, to improve child health services, expand home help and nursing services for disabled people and extend joint care funding and programmes.
5 Set national health goals after consultation and debate.	6 A substantial increase in local authority spending and responsibilities under the 1974 Housing Act.
7 Establish a Health Development Council	8 Improve research and statistical data relating to health, such as statistics on child health, income and health inequalities.

implemented, the Black Report had a profound if gradual effect on the health work field. A study of 'health inequalities' became incorporated into nurse education courses and other health work training programmes. Throughout the 1980s the lines of research highlighted in the report were developed, with many local studies of health and poverty being undertaken in which the impact of poverty on health was revealed. *The Nation's Health*, an authoritative survey of the state of UK health in the late 1980s and a strategic policy document for health into the 1990s commented that:

While we may still lack knowledge of the exact mechanisms through which [risk] factors operate, this does not put their contributory role in doubt . . . Income is clearly associated with health. The evidence is clear that the death rates of old people are affected by changes in the real value of state pensions, and also that as occupations move up or down the occupational earnings rankings they show a corresponding and opposite movement in the occupational mortality rate. The implication is that income – perhaps the major determinant of standard of living and of life-style – has a direct effect on health. It is also clear that health is more sensitive to small changes in income at lower than at higher levels.

Smith and Jacobson (1988)

The impact of income on health is demonstrated by findings from the Health and Lifestyle Survey (Blaxter, 1990) that, as income rises in the lower income groups, the ratio of those suffering from diseases or reporting illness symptoms or poor psycho-social health falls sharply (see Figure 6.1). It is significant that at upper income levels the ratio begins to rise again, suggesting that beyond a certain point wealth does not bring health.

The Nation's Health also documents research which highlights the links between unemployment and health, pointing out that mental ill health is linked to the 'material disadvantages' which unemployment creates. It also pulls together the research into diet, commenting that consumption patterns 'almost certainly reflect income and cost considerations as well as differences in culture or education' (Smith and Jacobson, 1988). In this it reflects one main consequence of a decade or more of research into 'class and health': a more open acknowledgement of the complex interconnections between 'lifestyles' and material, structural 'environmental' factors. The report comes down heavily in favour of a broadly based approach to tackling poverty, pointing out that risk factor reduction may accentuate deprivation unless it takes place within a much wider framework of economic action to increase wealth and redistribute resources, community development to promote autonomy and self esteem, and education of the community.

The Nation's Health, whilst emphasising the importance of reducing 'socioeconomic disadvantage' as a prelude to tackling specific risk

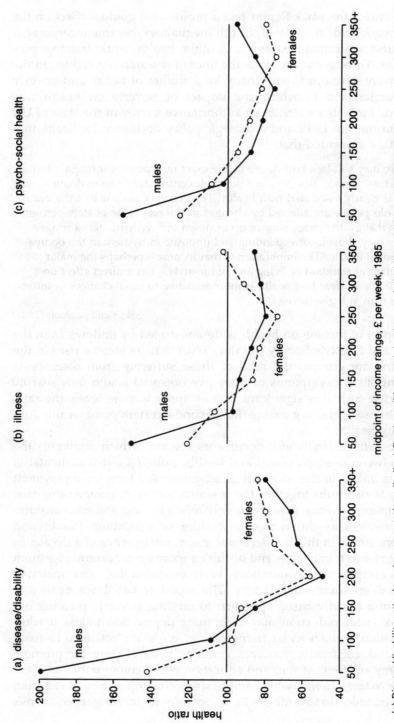

FIGURE 6.1 Age-standardised health ratios in men and women aged 40–59 years in relation to weekly income.
Source: Blaxter (1990)

(a) Disease/disability ratio, based on reported medically-defined conditions and the degree of disability which accompany them, (b) illness ratio, based on reports of symptoms suffered, and (c) psycho-social health ratio, based on reports of psycho-social problems. (All in the age group expressed as 100.)

factors and promoting community action, stops short of including the kinds of non-health sector targets in its recommendations which ensured that the Black Report was sidelined. There is little commitment by government to pursue the kind of broad assault on poverty sought by Black (see Box 6.4, page 234). A survey by Castle and Jacobson (1988) which analysed the strategies and policies of regional health authorities for promoting health and preventing disease concluded that a commitment to the reduction of inequalities in health 'was not prominent'. In addition, Health For All targets, prominent among them targets to reduce inequalities in health, are being only slowly addressed at district health authority level (Beattie, 1990).

6.7 Theorising poverty and health

There are a great many ways of explaining poverty and of interpreting the relationship between poverty and health. The Black Report (1980) distinguished between four theoretical categories: artefact explanations, natural or social selection, materialist or structuralist explanations and cultural/behavioural explanations. The artefact explanation claims that 'health and class are artificial variables thrown up by attempts to measure social phenomena' and that changes in social class composition invalidate comparisons, but the long runs of census data and relative stability of social classes enables the Black Report to dismiss this attack. Natural or social selection claims that health causes allocation to social class, not vice versa. Sickly and frail people drift downwards, the robustly healthy move up; hence the differential morbidity and mortality rates in the social classes. Again, the Black Report finds 'little actual evidence' that this occurs and instead endorses a mix of materialist/structuralist and behavioural/cultural explanations, which we'll explore in more detail below (for a discussion of social selection see Section 5.5).

Other writers on poverty have developed their explanations using different language. For example, George and Howards (1991) in their study of poverty use more overtly sociological categories, distinguishing between functionalist, 'structuralist' and Marxist theories of poverty. Some analysts have used the language of political science and have outlined differences between the ideological 'right' and 'left'. For our purposes it seems best to start by making a broad distinction between theories which explain poverty in terms of *individual* or group deficiencies, and those which focus attention on deficiencies in the *structural* fabric of society. This is not to say that the two explanations are mutually exclusive; it is not helpful to go too far in offering cut-and-dried accounts, but it provides a useful entry point to the debate.

Individualist explanations of poverty

It can be argued that there is some alignment between individualist theories of poverty, selectivist approaches to welfare and a lifestyle/risk factor approach to health. What they share is a preoccupation with explaining the incidence of poverty (or disease) by reference to those groups in poverty (or in sickness), as opposed to looking beyond those groups to their relationship with other sections of society and with the social structures of the whole society.

George and Howards (1991) suggest that the theoretical position of functionalism implies adopting an individualist explanation of poverty. You will recall from Section 2.5 that functionalist theorists argue that, since society needs to ensure that the most able rise to the top, some degree of stratification and inequality are inevitable. In a sense, therefore, poverty must be seen as largely the result of the poor's own deficiencies. However, this need not imply the adoption of any particular policy approach, although in policy terms functionalism has tended to be aligned with the political right. There are in fact several distinct types of poverty theory associated with the ideological right in politics.

Some theorists have focused on genetic inheritance. For example, Eysenck (1971) argued that intelligence is largely inherited and that the poorer educational attainment levels, relative to middle class children, achieved by black children and white working class children could be explained by their relatively lower IQ scores. On these grounds poverty might be viewed as a natural consequence of low intelligence and low attainment. Others are preoccupied with family traits, with the 'pathology' of what are seen as inadequate parents reproducing fecklessness, poverty and poor health habits in an inter-generational spiral. These views have been challenged by several writers who emphasise the importance of environmental influences on intelligence.

Lewis (1965) developed what he saw as a structural explanation of the social isolation and 'culture of poverty' of poor, large families living in slum conditions in capitalist societies. He argued that, faced by a continuous cycle of poverty, poor housing, unemployment and general disadvantage, these families adopted a defensive pattern of socialisation of their children into survival values, attitudes and norms of behaviour which were socially 'deviant', and locked successive generations into a 'culture of poverty'.

A cycle of deprivation

Lewis's work was heavily criticised by those who saw his theories as victim-blaming, but he hit back by arguing that his thesis was 'an indictment not of the poor, but of the social system that produces the

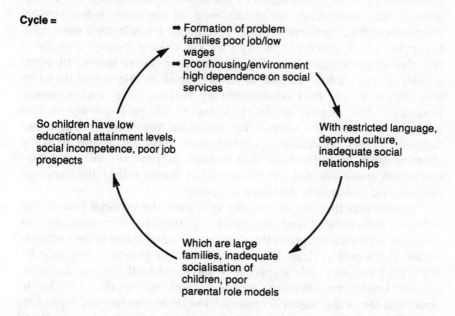

Assumptions: Residual problem
Pathological approach – 'problem families' and
'poor parenting'

Cycle =

→ Formation of problem
families poor job/low
wages
→ Poor housing/environment
high dependence on social
services

With restricted language,
deprived culture,
inadequate social
relationships

Which are large
families, inadequate
socialisation of
children, poor
parental role models

So children have low
educational attainment levels,
social incompetence, poor job
prospects

Solutions: Focus on self help, preparation for parenthood

FIGURE 6.2 Cycle of deprivation

way of life' (Lewis, in George and Howards, 1991). The fact remains that
his culture of poverty theory was adopted by the political right in Britain
to argue that inadequate family socialisation created a *cycle of deprivation*
out of which the poor became unable to escape (see Figure 6.2). Lack of
skills and motivation produced low educational attainment, poor job
prospects and a high risk of poverty: the classic definition of 'problem
families' (Joseph, 1972). Politicians on the right, such as Rhodes Boyson,
argued along somewhat similar lines that defective subcultural values
and norms locked some groups into undesirable modes of behaviour.

How adequate are individualist explanations in explaining the relationship
between health and poverty?

It is difficult to argue that individualist accounts can stand alone in
explaining poverty or health. The evidence we noted earlier – about
structural influences on pay, employment, working conditions – suggests

that poverty is not simply the product of individual lifestyle or intelligence. On the other hand people's attitudes and values cannot be dismissed as merely determined by the wider structures of society. This assumes that individuals are conditioned, or are more or less passive recipients of social influences rather than social actors in their own right. It supposes that, when people say they are making choices, they are in fact the unconscious victims of economic or social forces. In other words, do people who choose to smoke, drink or take drugs do so by free choice, or are they constrained by various social and economic pressures? The answer given by some health professionals is that individual choices are shaped by structural pressures (Ashton and Seymour, 1988). Individualist explanations draw our attention to the characteristics of individuals and groups in poverty, but on closer inspection these are not autonomous but partly reflect the range of options and constraints that exist in society.

Subcultural theories of poverty spill over the artificial boundaries between individualist and structural explanations. For example, the theory of *underclass* proposes the existence of a major line of demarcation within the working class, below which certain groups – in particular black and minority ethnic people – have markedly worse housing, income levels, employment prospects and so on (Rex, 1973). In structural terms the theory focuses on the inter-generational reproduction of this underclass – battered down by continual crises, such as unemployment, incapacity, low wages and large family size into a state of primary poverty and premature death. In this sense it highlights the malfunctioning of the economic system and the need for structural change. On the other hand the theory of underclass has been used by the New Right to highlight the cultural inadequacy and deviance of welfare claimants as a group. These groups, it has been claimed, are locked into a *dependency culture*, in which fecklessness, fatalism and petty dishonesty become a way of life.

A 1988 Department of Employment report (quoted in Squires, 1990) claimed that 'a significant number of benefit claimants are not looking for work. Some are claiming benefits fraudulently while working at least part-time in the black economy. Others seem to have grown accustomed to living on benefit'. Politicians on the New Right argued for a major pruning of benefits to destroy the deviant and dangerous underclass and to free claimants from dependence (Murray, in Squires, 1990). The concern about dependency culture extends to the chronic sick as well. In the late 1980s politicians questioned the findings of the official disability survey (1988), which estimated a total of 6.2 million disabled adults in the UK based on a 10 000 household sample. In 1993 the Conservative government rewrote guidelines for the assessment of disability allowances, claiming that doctors were interpreting them too freely and allowing unemployed people to escape into the niche of chronic sickness and invalidity benefit.

In contrast to this, critics have suggested that the notion of dependency culture has been invented in order to 'blame the victims' and enable governments to undermine the welfare state (Walker, 1990). It obscures the fact that during the 1980s the number of pensioners, one-parent families and unemployed people living on state benefits grew, and at the same time the proportion of these groups living in poverty increased, so that 30 per cent of pensioners, 76 per cent of the unemployed and 30 per cent of those who are sick and disabled were living at or below assistance level.

Even more important, Dean and Taylor-Gooby's study of long-term claimants (1992) indicates that the notion of a separate underclass is a suspect one. The welfare claimants they interviewed shared the attitudes and values of the rest of the population:

The overall conclusion to emerge from our investigation is that any social security policy based on the notion of 'dependency culture' is likely to be counterproductive: first, because the implication that claimants are 'culturally' separate from the rest of society is inaccurate and unhelpful; secondly, because the notion obscures rather than assists our understanding of dependency.

Dean and Taylor-Gooby (1992)

Structural theories of poverty

The other way of viewing poverty and health is by means of theories which focus on the deficiencies of contemporary welfare structures. These are generally associated with the political left, but writers on the ideological right, such as Hayek and Boyson, have advanced 'free market' theories which explain the persistence of poverty in terms of the welfare state structures that were designed to eradicate it. Rhodes Boyson has argued that:

Where poverty remains it is the fault of politicians whose double sin has been to spread benefits too widely and raise taxes on a scale that hinders the increase in the national income . . . We are concerned to point towards a society which will be more efficient on the one hand in abolishing poverty and want because it will give equal priority on the other hand to building up the strength of the individual and the family as good in themselves.

Boyson (1971)

In a similar way, Boyson has argued that the end result of the establishment of a National Health Service to improve the health of the poor has been 'a decline in medical standards below the level of other advanced countries'. Hayek (1944) attributed the persistence of poverty to state interventionism – not just in welfare but across the whole spectrum of economic and social policy. He has argued that a free market system, if unhindered, will increase general prosperity and enable those who lose out – because of skill deficits, technological change and so on – to be helped by 'surplus wealth'. This theory, as you may have recognised from Chapter 2 and from Section 6.5, represented the intellectual force behind Thatcherism in the 1980s, with its emphasis on wealth creation and 'trickle-down', free market economics.

Other structural explanations look not to the dismantling of welfare and state functions to end poverty and promote health, but to the expansion of welfare. Richard Titmuss (1967) saw the welfare state of the 1940s as resolving some of the problems of economic insecurity and poverty, but he recognised that the control exerted by capitalist organisation and privileged institutions acted as a continuing break on any move to a more equal distribution of wealth and power in society.

A cycle of inequality

A dominant theme in structural explanations of poverty has been this emphasis on poverty as a series of unequal relationships between people in society. The implication is that poverty will be swept away only if a strong welfare state can tackle structural inequalities in other areas of economic life: income disparities and gross differences in wealth holding. In contrast to a cycle of deprivation this draws attention to the existence of a cycle of inequality (see Figure 6.3), which reproduces inter-generational poverty by reproducing unequal conditions and opportunities in education, work, employment and family life (Coffield, 1980). Frank Field (1981) has argued that:

Poverty is . . . largely a consequence of the current distribution of income and wealth in society, and while particular individuals may escape from poverty by their own efforts, the structure of earnings and benefits ensures that other individuals will take their place.

Field (1981)

Such critics – we may call them socialist reformers – highlighted the inadequacies of the current welfare system as well as the marked inequalities in income, wealth and power that characterise contemporary society. By the early 1980s several empirical studies had indicated that state welfare was failing to solve the problem of poverty or redistribute income to any great extent. Julian Le Grand's study of housing, education, health and social services (1982) suggested that the middle classes had benefited most from the welfare state, and that redistribution of income took place largely within the working class – from those without children to those with children, from the well to the sick and from younger to older people – rather than from poorer to richer groups. Townsend's study (1979) noted the persistence of

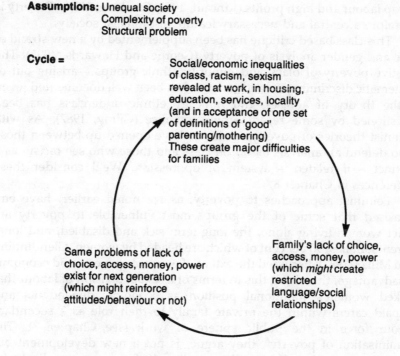

Assumptions: Unequal society
Complexity of poverty
Structural problem

Cycle =

Social/economic inequalities
of class, racism, sexism
revealed at work, in housing,
education, services, locality
(and in acceptance of one set
of definitions of 'good'
parenting/mothering)
These create major difficulties
for families

Same problems of lack of
choice, access, money, power
exist for next generation
(which might reinforce
attitudes/behaviour or not)

Family's lack of choice,
access, money, power
(which *might* create
restricted
language/social
relationships)

Solutions: Major social/structural change, economic change

FIGURE 6.3 Cycle of inequality

poverty, and the Black Report (1980) highlighted social class gradients in health – in spite of a collectivised health system. Other critics drew attention to the deadening bureaucracy and insensitivity of welfare agencies and to their lack of accountability and democracy (Taylor-Gooby, 1991). But it was the New Right, as we noted above, that reaped the political rewards of freeing consumers from the 'nanny' welfare state in policies which forced the left onto the defensive, in spite of evidence that support for state welfare was high (see Chapter 13 for further discussion of these issues).

Another strand in structural accounts of poverty has been the Marxist critique, which looks beyond the piecemeal reform of economic structures and welfare systems to new forms of economic organisation. This theory sees the relationship between rich and poor as rooted in the capitalist mode of production; those who are rich and powerful, even though they might make concessions to maintain their position, require the continued existence of the poor and the powerless as a guarantee of cheap labour and high profits (Kincaid, 1973; Ginsberg, 1979). Poverty is therefore a central and necessary feature of capitalist society.

This class based critique has been supplemented by a new strand of race and gender analysis of poverty (George and Howards, 1991). The relative poverty of black and minority ethnic groups – arising out of systematic discrimination and racism – has been well documented, even if the theory of a black and minority ethnic underclass has been questioned by some recent writers on race (Gilroy, 1987). As with feminist theories of poverty, divisions have opened up between those who defend an analysis based on class and those who see racism as a distinct – if related – system of oppression. We'll consider these differences in Chapter 8.

Feminist approaches to poverty, as we noted earlier, have em-phasised that some of the groups most vulnerable to poverty are older women living alone, the long-term sick and disabled, and lone-parent families, 90 per cent of which are headed by women. Glendinning and Millar (1987) discussed the extent of women's poverty and economic disadvantage, theorising this in terms of a sexual division of labour that linked women's traditional position as economic dependants and unpaid carers within the private family to their role as a secondary labour force in the public sphere of work (see Chapter 7). The 'feminisation of poverty', they argue, is not a new development but employment and welfare policies in the 1980s were more likely 'to increase the extent and depth of women's poverty'.

6.8 Theories and health work practice

The survey of poverty in this chapter is not just an academic exercise. It connects directly to much of the work of nurses and other health workers in community and hospital settings. Many of the people who come as patients to doctors' surgeries, clinics and hospitals suffer not only ill health but also varying degrees of poverty. Indeed it is one of the arguments of this chapter – and, as we have seen, of many recent research studies – that poverty increases the risks of sickness and disease.

If this is accepted, it presents health workers with dilemmas that are far from academic, for the combating of poverty then comes into focus (as in the Black Report and *The Health Divide*) as a major element of health work. In order to make decisions about alleviating poverty and instigating change, health workers need to be able to explain why poverty exists and persists.

Let's look briefly at the logic of this claim. Traditionally health

TABLE 6.7 Health education approaches. Source: Ewles and Simmett (1983)

	Aim	Health education activity
MEDICAL	Freedom from medically defined disease and disability.	Promotion of medical intervention to prevent or ameliorate ill-health.
BEHAVIOUR CHANGE	Individual behaviour conducive to freedom from disease.	Attitude and behaviour change to encourage adoption of 'healthier' life-style.
EDUCATIONAL	Individuals with knowledge and understanding enabling well informed decisions to be made and acted upon.	Information about cause and effects of health-demoting factors. Exploration of values and attitudes. Development of skills required for healthy living.
CLIENT-DIRECTED	Working with clients on the clients' own terms.	Working with clients' identified health issues choices and actions.
SOCIAL CHANGE	Physical and social environment enabling choice of healthier lifestyle.	Political/social action to change physical/social environment.

workers and particularly nurses have concentrated most of their efforts on care and treatment at an individual level. In addition, most of the work on prevention of ill health has been concerned with modifying individual or family behaviour – what have been called the 'behaviour change' and 'educational' approaches (Ewles and Simnett, 1985, see Table 6.7). These can be seen as falling within an individualist theoretical framework, drawing upon either the 'individual respon-sibility' model or the 'cycle of deprivation' model. In either case it is the individual, family (or possible subculture) that is being targeted. Poverty – and poverty-related ill health – is seen as largely generated within these subsystems, in dysfunctional families and communities; so the practical steps taken are to modify and change behaviours by advice and education.

However, if the causes of poverty are seen to lie in wider social and economic structures of inequality, then the potential focus of health work is much broader. A 'cycle of inequality' explanation of poverty points to disparities of wealth and income within society as a whole. Structural factors and a range of social divisions along the lines of class, race, gender and age can be seen as playing a part in the cause and continuation of poverty and ill health. From this structural analysis comes what has been termed a 'social change' approach (Ewles and Simnett, 1985). This is characteristic of recent developments in health promotion and attempts to move towards a social model of health. For example, Sheffield has initiated a Healthy Cities programme in which the health sector, local government, voluntary and private sectors work together on specific projects to improve health (K258, 1992). Some are workplace based, and others are in community and clinic settings. Such intersectoral co-operation for 'healthgain' is becoming a more widespread feature of health work (Ashton and Seymour, 1988). 'Healthy Alliances' at a local level between lay and professional people, and between public and private sectors, are also growing in numbers. However, there are problems in using this approach in health education, and these have sigificance for health work as a whole:

An important difference between the social change approach and the previous ones is that the health education is directed at policy-makers and planners at all levels, as well as at the general public . . . The contentious nature of the social change approach is its chief limitation. Many issues are politically sensitive (eg. unemployment) and the health educator is likely to fall foul of powerful vested interest groups and financial considerations . . . The approach is also contentious because it is markedly different from traditional health education directed at clients.

Ewles and Simnett (1985)

Health promoters have emphasised the need to make use of different approaches, depending on the situation; there is no point in extensive campaigning if essential face-to-face advice and support for those suffering poverty and ill health are neglected. On the other hand a preoccupation with modifying behaviour and offering advice focuses attention on individualist explanations and drives to the margins the structural account of poverty and ill health.

Suggestions for further study

V. George and I. Howards (1991) *Poverty Amidst Affluence*, Cheltenham, Edward Elgar, is a useful survey of poverty in the UK and includes material on the USA and on theories of poverty; J. Mack and S. Lansley (1991) *Poor Britain*, London, Harper Collins, discuss perceptions of the poor. The health risks of poverty are dealt with in P. Townsend (1979)

Poverty in the United Kingdom, Harmondsworth, Penguin, and in C. Blackburn (1992) *Poverty and Health*, Milton Keynes, Open University Press.

Self assessment questions

1 Discuss the difference between an 'absolute' and a 'relative' definition of poverty.
2 Which groups in society are most vulnerable to poverty and why?
3 To what extent has the welfare state succeeded in eliminating poverty in the UK?
4 Outline the main likely health effects of living in poverty.
5 Explain the main differences between 'individualist' and 'structural' theories of poverty.
6 Consider the relevance of theories of poverty to your health work practice with patients and families.

Chapter 7

Gender divisions and health

Contents

Themes and issues

Sex and gender: gender socialisation – divisions of labour – the double shift – production and reproduction

Health status: social conditioning – the impact of social class analysis – women's work and health

Theories of gender: 'malestream' social theory – biological essentialism – possessive individualism – patriarchy and capitalism – social constructionism – contribution of feminist theory

Health work: paid and unpaid work – caring and 'mothering' – good nurse as good woman – gender order in nursing – labelling patients – control of information – empowerment and autonomy

Learning outcomes

After working through this chapter you should be able to:

1 Review and reassess your own beliefs and practices in relation to gender.
2 Describe the main differences between male and female distribution of morbidity and mortality.
3 Outline the theory of 'patriarchy' and suggest why it is relevant to health work.
4 Identify the main features of a 'social constructionist' account of gender.
5 Assess how theories of 'mothering' can help to explain the role of women as paid and unpaid health workers.
6 Identify how gender structures relationships between patients and health care professionals.

THIS chapter investigates how sociologists, in particular feminist writers, have redefined the boundaries of our thinking about sex and gender. It explores how gender has shaped the division of labour in health work and assesses the influence of gender divisions and inequalities on the health of patients, unpaid carers and paid health workers. It suggests that fundamental assumptions about men's and women's bodies and about their 'natural' capacities and abilities continue to exert a powerful influence in contemporary health work.

7.1 Unpacking sex and gender

Sex is a biological term which refers to people's 'biologically given' state, whereas gender refers to their 'socially acquired' psychological and cultural characteristics: their learned masculinity or femininity. With a few exceptions, people are born as biologically male or female. There remain certain, probably irreducible, biological differences between men and women, although they can now be changed, more or less, into their biological opposites and have become increasingly detached, through a process of biomedical innovation, from their 'particular functions' – from production of sperm to production of babies.

Sociobiologists have argued that behaviour differences between men and women derive from their biology, citing the involvement of men in most cultures in hunting and warfare and the less aggressive behaviour of women (Sydie, 1987). But the differences between men and women are fairly small compared with the similarities between them, in terms of body plan, anatomy and function. They are even less marked in childhood and in later years, when hormonal activity is at a low level. Even when testosterone, oestrogen and other hormones are at higher levels, 'maleness' or 'femaleness' cannot be established from the hormone count alone (Oakley, 1985). Some of the characteristics seen as biologically 'fixed' – such as the 'sexual drive' or 'maternal instinct' – could instead be viewed as the product of social conditioning. If we accept that the human body itself is fabricated, and that medicine and psychiatry have influenced how we 'see and know' our bodies, then it seems likely that bodily behaviour is also socially constructed (Turner, 1984). For example, 'sex' – used in the sense of meaning sexuality and sexual intercourse – is not a biological entity but a set of specific (and changing) historical and cultural ideas about how we should feel, think and act, and about what is 'normal' and 'abnormal'.

If most of the behaviours, attitudes, desires and thoughts of men and women arise from social learning experiences rather than biology, there can be no simple assumption that biological 'males' are 'masculine' and biological 'females' are 'feminine'. Although in every known society biological sex is a starting point for ascribing gender, there remains wide variation between cultures about how gender and gender roles are defined. Research findings indicate that children who lack defining (biological) sex characteristics still learn gender identity and role (Oakley, 1985).

This makes the unpacking of gender differentiation a most pressing task. We need to ask how boys and girls learn gender identity, how they are socialised into gender roles and to what extent social institutions and power structures reflect and reproduce gender differentiation and inequality.

○ Review the process of primary and secondary socialisation, which you first encountered in Section 3.4. Suggest how a child might learn to 'act like a boy' or 'act like a girl'.

Children learn gender identity through their early social experiences. Parents, other adults and older children 'teach' gender identity, often quite unconsciously. Even at a very young age girls and boys are treated and handled differently. Girl babies are called 'sweet' and 'pretty' by hospital staff, but boys are 'tough' and 'handsome' (Hansen in Giddens, 1989). A crying girl baby evokes greater concern; if a boy cries, this demonstrates his 'strength' and 'good lung power'. When little boys get hurt, they are told to 'be brave', whereas it is much more acceptable for little girls to cry and show weakness; it has been suggested that women's greater use of health services may – in part at least – be attributed to the effects of this early gender socialisation (Miles, 1991). Gender specific advertising is often used to sell toys, and toyshops arrange toys in boys' and girls' sections. Picture books and media images often project stereotypical masculine and feminine roles: girls have caring roles and keep house; boys get involved in adventures (if girls go along, they often end up needing to be rescued). School teachers treat boys and girls differently in the classroom; in particular, boys are given more attention and more opportunities to contribute to class discussion than girls (Stanworth, 1983). Distinctions made on the basis of gender – from 'lining up for playtime' to stereotyping of girls as 'good and quiet' and boys as 'rough and noisy' – feed into and reinforce already existing differences.

It is difficult to tease out how far these patterns of social conditioning influence children's behaviour, and to determine the contribution made by biology. Ginsberg and Miller (1982), for example, found that boys engaged in riskier types of play and had more frequent accidents than girls. This supports the stereotype of 'adventurous' boys and more 'passive' girls, but does not tell us how far such behaviours are learned – and whether they have a basis in biology. Research findings from kibbutz life in Israel, where men and women experience similar patterns of work, schooling, military service and family life, offer some interesting clues. Differences in mortality rates are demonstrably reduced in circumstances where gender roles converge (Leviathan and Cohen, 1985). Inter-gender differences in life expectancy were about 40 per cent less for kibbutz dwellers than for the population as a whole, although the researchers were careful to point out that no final conclusion could be drawn as to the relative importance of social and biological differences.

7.2 Gender and health status

There are significant differences between the health chances of men and women in Britain, although these appear small in comparison to rates of male and female morbidity and mortality in 'third world' countries. The

TABLE 7.1 Selected causes of death: by sex and age, 1992. Source: *Social Trends* (1994)

United Kingdom							Percentages and thousands
	Under 1	1–14	15–39	40–64	65–79	80+	All ages
Males							
Infectious diseases	4.8	5.1	1.7	0.7	0.4	0.3	0.5
Cancer	1.0	17.3	13.5	34.3	31.6	20.9	28.0
Circulatory diseases[1]	4.0	4.0	10.7	43.6	48.3	47.3	45.5
Respiratory diseases	11.9	5.1	3.4	5.3	10.3	16.7	11.1
Injury and poisoning	17.6	34.2	52.7	6.6	1.3	1.2	4.2
All other causes	60.8	34.2	18.0	9.3	8.3	13.5	10.7
All males (= 100%) (thousands)	1.1	1.3	10.2	58.4	140.9	94.9	306.6
Females							
Infectious diseases	4.3	4.8	1.9	0.6	0.4	0.3	0.4
Cancer	1.5	18.0	33.3	51.8	30.6	14.2	24.3
Circulatory diseases[1]	5.6	4.4	10.7	26.7	46.6	52.3	48.6
Respiratory diseases	10.6	5.6	3.4	5.8	9.2	13.7	11.1
Injury and poisoning	16.8	25.8	28.9	4.0	1.4	1.4	2.2
All other causes	61.3	41.4	21.8	11.1	11.8	18.0	15.3
All females (= 100%) (thousands)	0.7	0.9	4.8	36.4	111.5	169.9	324.2

[1] Includes heart attacks and strokes.

UK mortality rate is higher for males at all ages, in particular in infancy and in late middle age (see Table 7.1). The morbidity rate for some major diseases, such as coronary heart disease, is also higher for men, although women report more longstanding illness and restricted activity than men (see Figure 7.1). Women, for example, suffer more mental ill health and are more prone to some chronic diseases, such as rheumatoid arthitis. In other diseases, for example respiratory conditions, there is no clear gender difference.

○ Suggest why there are differences in male and female rates of mortality and morbidity.

You could have responded to this question in several different ways, emphasising biological data or perhaps looking at social and cultural patterns. The evidence is still far from conclusive, but it seems likely that genetic factors play a part in women's longer life expectancy. Male foetuses are more likely to abort and still birth rates are higher among males. Hormonal differences may be important; for example, oestrogens seem to 'protect' women against cardiovascular disease, a protection that largely disappears when oestrogen levels fall in later life. One of the major threats to women's health – childbearing – has now receded in the UK because of better nutrition, the spread of contraception and safer childbirth, although it remains a main cause of high mortality in other parts of the world.

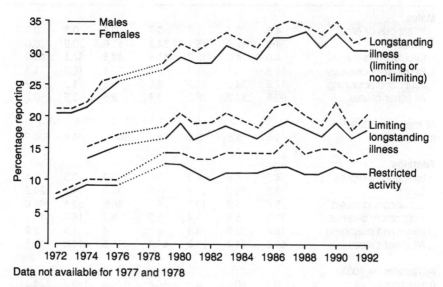

FIGURE 7.1 Morbidity (reported sickness) rates 1972–92: findings from the General Household Survey. Source: GHS (1994)

Socio-economic factors are also important. Male rates of disease and death from industrial hazards have traditionally been greater, because of their higher levels of paid employment in mining and manufacturing. On the other hand it has been suggested that women's proneness to mental illness may reflect the low status and social isolation of domestic labour (Oakley, 1976). Certainly, married women have higher consultation rates for mental illness than single women and single and married men, suggesting that, although marriage works as a protective factor, this operates more effectively for men than for women. In relation to mortality, marriage again seems to offer greater benefits to men than to women (see Table 7.2).

Patterns of gender socialisation produce systematic differences in the behaviour of the sexes which link to health status. For example, men indulge in risk taking behaviour to a greater extent than women: faster driving, higher rates of smoking and drinking and the greater use of dangerous drugs are some key examples of this. This helps to explain their higher rates of accidents, cirrhosis of the liver, lung cancer and coronary heart disease. Women with 'problems' tend to turn instead to (or to be prescribed) tranquilisers, although the rate of smoking (and lung cancer and heart disease) among women has been rising in recent years. Men also make less use of dentistry and other preventive services than women.

There is a lively debate about social and cultural influences on health and how they shape these patterns of disease and death. For example, it has been suggested that the structure of the traditional nuclear family with its gendered division of labour and 'breadwinner' male has influenced the higher incidence of coronary heart disease in men. But evidence that the stereotypical breadwinner man is also a competitive and aggressive 'coronary-prone personality' is lacking; in a similar way, it is unclear that higher rates of mental illness in women are necessarily linked to their domestic role or their 'double shift'. Gender socialisation makes it more acceptable, it is argued, for women to admit

TABLE 7.2 Standardised mortality ratios (SMRs) for women and men by marital status. Source: Fox and Goldblatt (1982)

Marital status	Standardised mortality ratios	
	Males	Females
Single	117	99
Married	96	97
Widowed	109	103
Divorced	123	117

weakness and seek medical help earlier than men, even though young men (5–25 year olds) suffer more serious illness (Whitehead, 1987). Moreover, women are more likely to visit their general practitioner with their children, and to be in part-time work which enables them to fit in visits on their own behalf. Women – the main carers in families – are taught to see themselves as responsible for their children's health, and they also act as unpaid carers of men (Graham, 1984a). Perhaps this is one reason why men visit the doctor less frequently.

Several research reports indicate that the self assessed health of men is better than that of women. The *Nottingham Health Profile* (Hunt *et al.*, 1986) demonstrated that women reported higher rates of illness – another variable which may account for more frequent medical consultations. In the Health and Lifestyle Survey (Cox *et al.*, 1987) men and women respondents were given a symptoms checklist to complete, and the researchers calculated 'illness scores' according to the number of reported symptoms. Again, women consistently reported higher rates of illness than men, both bouts of ill health and pain or discomfort of a chronic non-life threatening kind, which is consistent with their greater use of health services.

Some researchers have drawn attention to the way that statistics are gathered and interpreted, suggesting that an *artefact* may be produced: women may suffer no more illness than men but may notice it more; women may be more willing to undergo treatment and so on. Male general practitioners, when asked to describe a 'normal' healthy person, sketched a 'typically male' profile (Miles, 1991). When asked about patients, they clearly preferred those with treatable, physical symptoms rather than mental problems. Greater numbers of women are diagnosed as needing psychiatric help, but this may well be due to GPs' greater readiness to classify them as emotional or unstable rather than the greater incidence of mental illness in women. Ideological constructs of the 'normal' woman exist in medicine, and women who don't conform are classified as 'deviant' and therefore sick (Graham and Oakley, 1981). In relation to childbirth, for example, women's 'natural' disposition to be maternal, caring, passive and home centred is assumed; their inferiority, instability and lack of emotional control are increased as their biology 'takes over' and they become preoccupied with 'nest-building' and nurturing. Women who don't conform are viewed as selfish, cold and aggressive (see Table 7.3).

○   Note down your reaction to Table 7.3. Does it relate to your own experience as a student nurse or health worker?

There will be many different responses to this table, depending on whether you are male or female, on your own gender socialisation and life experience. Various types of professional health workers – health

TABLE 7.3 'Normal' and 'deviant' women

'Normal' women should be:	'Deviant' women:
Naturally maternal and home centred Caring for/about families and men	Reject/find caring and maternal role difficult: career-oriented
More controlled by their bodies than men are	Do not accept 'natural' limits
Inferior to men	Do not accept inferior position, demand equality
Deferential/submissive	Aggressive, over-assertive
More emotional than men	Unfeminine, cold

'Normal' mothers:	'Deviant' mothers:
Slaves to their bodies, cannot control their bodies	See childbirth as a physically stressful, life-changing event
Emotionally unstable: become essentially 'childish' and present-oriented	Childbirth as emotional and exhausting experience, requiring new skills and hard labour, often with little support
Nest-builders, caring urge	Reject social pressure to give up past life and see motherhood as primary role; demand for partner to share responsibility

Material drawn from: H. Roberts ed. *Women, Health and Reproduction* (1981); A. Oakley *Women Confined* (1980)

visitors, midwives, hospital nurses as well as students – have commented on it in interesting ways. In particular, they have argued that there is great variation in the way that health workers view women, with some doctors and nurses making assumptions about patients on the basis of such stereotypes but others taking a more holistic approach. They also pointed out that stereotypes of men are created at a similar, sub-conscious level. Among the suggested characteristics of male patients were presenting with physical symptoms (whatever the 'real' problem was) and unwillingness to discuss feelings or betray emotion.

Another important artefact effect, as we noted in Chapter 5, is produced by the creation of health statistics using a social (occupational) class classification. Mortality patterns for women follow class gradients similar to those of men when married women are classified according to their husband's occupation. Some researchers argue that a traditional social class analysis based on husband's occupation is still a better predictor of mortality (Marmot *et al.*, 1991). But significant differences appear when women are studied in their own right; since two-thirds of women now undertake paid work outside the home, it is important to assess what contribution this makes to their health. Macintyre (1986) noted that class gradients in some diseases 'disappeared' if women were studied in terms of their own occupations: for example, cancers of the reproductive system were more common among professional women than manual workers.

There is the further problem of trying to measure women's health status in relation to both paid work and unpaid domestic labour – the 'double shift'. Sara Arber (1985) and colleagues used findings from the General Household Survey to examine the self reported ill health of those in paid employment. Women in skilled and unskilled manual jobs or in routine non-manual work, with dependent children, reported greater levels of sickness than did professional or managerial women with dependent children. This suggests that full-time paid work can be health damaging, but this depends on the type of work. Professional women workers often have job flexibility and can afford to pay for cleaning and childcare services, lower grade workers have little support (Arber *et al.*, 1985). Part-time workers, whatever their occupational status, had lower levels of reported sickness than their full-time counterparts.

The 1985 study indicated that housewives with dependent children reported better health than those in low status paid work, but the picture is even more complicated than this. There are tensions and cross-benefits for women arising from their different roles – as paid workers, parents and wives (partners) – which are not fully understood. Arber (1991) has continued to tease out the implications of paid work for women:

The picture is more complex for women. Health status is even more likely to be poor for structurally disadvantaged women than for equivalent men. Health disadvantage for women is associated with non-employment (either being a housewife or unemployed) . . . Employed women report better health, irrespective of housing tenure, marital and parental status. Women who are not in paid employment and have no dependent children report poor health, whereas women with young children report good health irrespective of their employment status. Previously married women without a paid job report particularly poor health.

Arber (1991)

This draws attention to the differences between women which lie concealed beneath an occupational class classification method designed to highlight the differences between paid (mainly male) breadwinners. Arber suggests that future research needs to focus on the inter-relationships between women's domestic labour, paid work and

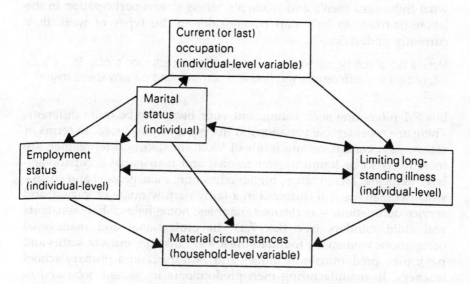

FIGURE 7.2 Key variables associated with women's health status.
Source: Arber (1991)

designated social class status in order to capture in full the complexity of influences on women's health (see Figure 7.2). The sex segregated nature of much paid work (see Section 7.3) means that women are exposed to different types of risks and hazards arising from assembly work, secretarial work, and from service sector jobs as cleaners, cashiers and so on. Common types of reported sickness include musculoskeletal pain in the back, persistent headaches and eye strain and repetitive strain syndrome in VDU operators and supermarket cashiers. This contrasts with hazards common in male dominated industrial occupations: accidents (which rose sharply in the 1980s, especially in the building trade); 'creeping' deafness due to excessive noise levels; contamination from industrial processes or carcinogenic materials, linked to particular occupational diseases such as scrotal cancer, byssinosis, and pneumoconiosis (Webb et al., 1988).

7.3 The gendered division of labour

One of the more visible and fundamental divisions along lines of gender in adult life is the division of labour. There has been fierce debate about what influences men's and women's access to and participation in the labour market, so let's start by considering the types of work they currently undertake.

○   Make a list of ten typical women's jobs and ten typical men's jobs. Study your list, noting any differences you find and commenting on why these might exist.

Box 7.1 offers one such listing, but your own may be quite different. There are considerable variations in the types of jobs listed, in terms of status, pay, conditions and levels of 'skill'. In statistical terms men are most likely to be found in professional and managerial occupations – law, medicine, accountancy, higher education, management and so on – while women are still clustered in a fairly narrow range of 'caring' and service occupations – as cleaners, nannies, home helps, shop assistants and child minders (see Box 7.1). In professional and managerial occupations women are found in the lower ranks (in terms of status and pay): they predominate as nurses and as nursery and primary school teachers. In manufacturing men predominate in 'skilled' jobs and in general unskilled labouring; women become assembly workers in largely female workplaces.

You may also have recalled from Section 3.4 that there is a significant wage differential. Male earnings remain considerably higher, their work is more likely to be defined as 'skilled' or 'managerial' and a greater proportion of them work full-time. In the health service the average earnings of male nurses are higher, because they have moved into higher paid management posts in greater numbers – even though women still form nearly 90 per cent of the workforce (see Section 7.7).

How may such differences be explained? You may have suggested that the sex segregation in work derives from a combination of biological and social factors. In biological terms women have been constrained until quite recently by their reproductive role, so that participation on

BOX 7.1 Ten 'male' and ten 'female' jobs

Male	Female
Doctor	Nurse
Mechanic	Cleaner
Lawyer	Clerical worker
Accountant	Receptionist
University lecturer	Primary school teacher
Bricklayer	Assembly worker
Politician	Secretary
Businessman	Nursery nurse
Bank manager	Dinner lady
Engineer	Shop assistant

equal terms in the labour market has been seen as impossible. You may have recalled from Chapter 3 that this was reinforced by social pressures and gender socialisation designed to restrict women as mothers to the 'private' sphere of the home. In recent years a combination of factors – changing social attitudes, contraception, declining family size, the women's movement – has enabled greater participation by women in the 'public' world of paid work, although not as yet on equal terms. Some of you may feel quite optimistic that, given time, occupational inequalities will largely disappear.

This account raises a number of issues and fundamental problems, in particular about the extent to which biology has shaped men's and women's social roles. Those who have emphasised the importance of biology – of 'nature' as opposed to 'nurture' – have suggested that male and female occupational segregation derives from the essential differences between them. Much skilled work done by women – for example dress making or nannying – has been classified and paid as semi-skilled or unskilled on the grounds that women were natural possessors of 'nimble fingers' or 'maternal feelings'. Women are said to be good nurses because of their inbuilt caring and nurturing qualities, which are derived from their childbearing role. Men are natural managers because of their natural dominance; women become secretaries because they are more co-operative and accept a subordinate position more readily than men and so on. But the definition of skills and aptitudes at work cannot be read off from biology; it has always been profoundly influenced by social and economic factors. In the two world wars, for example, the demand for labour on the home front enabled women to move into a range of better paid and more skilled jobs for which they had hitherto been argued to be unsuitable, on grounds on physical strength, intelligence and femininity (Braybon and Summerfield, 1987).

The argument about biological limitations has been used frequently to prevent the entry of women into male preserves: for example, it was argued that women were constitutionally incapable of becoming doctors (or entering any of the professions). Not only would medicine coarsen their feminine natures, it would also upset their delicate constitutions so that they would become incapable of childbearing. In *The Principles of Biology* published in 1867 Herbert Spencer, who has been called the 'founding father of British sociology', advanced scientific claims about the impact higher education would have on women's biological functions:

Diminution of reproductive power is not shown only by the greater frequency of absolute sterility; nor is it only in the earlier cessation of childbearing, but it is also shown in the very frequent inability of such women to suckle their infants. In its full sense, the reproductive power means the power to bear a well-developed infant, and to supply that infant with the natural food for the natural period. Most of the flat-chested girls who survive their high-pressure education are incompetent to do this.

Spencer, quoted in Doyal (1979)

On the one hand it is clear that women's biological role in reproduction is greater than men's and in the past, at least, fairly continuous child-bearing and breastfeeding restricted women's entry into the job market. On the other hand it was arguably not biological function in itself but the psychological and cultural pressures arising from perceived biological difference which shaped social roles. Categories of 'full-' and 'part-time' work, of 'paid' and 'unpaid' labour, of 'high' and 'low' status jobs, of 'motherhood', the 'breadwinner' and the 'family wage' have been specific (and changing) social and cultural constructions. They have been underpinned by particular organisational structures, such as industrial capitalism with its clear distinctions between 'work' and 'leisure', and 'home' and 'workplace'. In addition, feminist theorists have drawn attention to the predominance of a *male gender order*: that is, the role of male power, male values and the ideology of masculinity and femininity in drawing (and redrawing) the boundaries of work. Game and Pringle (1983) have commented that 'gender is fundamental to the way work is organised; and work is central in the social construction of gender'. Yet as we noted in Section 2.7 mainstream sociological theory paid little attention to issues of gender in relation to the division of labour until quite recently.

7.4 The invisibility of gender in sociological theory

For the founders of sociology the male gender order was natural and therefore largely overlooked in the development of theory; mainstream – indeed all – sociology was also 'malestream' (O'Brien, 1981).

○   Reflect on why sociologists largely ignored issues of gender in sociological research.

We noted in Chapter 2 that founding sociological theories themselves were historically specific: that is, they offered responses to crucial contemporary problems, in particular the demise of 'traditional' social organisation, the rise of 'industrial society' and the problems of modernity. Sociologists have been preoccupied with social order and control in the public sphere of work, the state and the market. Functionalist theorists saw the family as a crucial building block in a stable society, but they did not see it as problematic. Marxist theorists viewed the family as an economic unit exploited by capitalism. The gendered division of labour in industrial capitalism enabled the paid worker to be serviced cheaply and efficiently and the next generation of labour to be raised at little cost to the capitalist. One step towards challenging this, it was claimed, was through women's entry into the labour market, which would promote female independence and liberation.

The private sphere, the domestic domain within which most women were defined, was viewed through the eyes of these male sociologists largely as a 'natural' order, reflecting the childbearing and homemaking roles of women which became more visible as industrialisation sharply demarcated 'working hours' and the 'workplace'. You might have recalled Stacey's (1981) comments about the acceptance of male accounts of the division of labour, originating in the writings of the eighteenth century political economist Adam Smith on the public domain and in the divine origins of Adam's patriarchal power over Eve.

Preoccupation with problems of industrial production and state power drove issues and conflicts over reproduction to the margins. The relationship between production and reproduction was seen as 'natural'. The domain of informal health work, therefore, was seen as natural and unproblematic (Stacey, 1988). Most health work remained ignored and invisible, because only formal paid labour in the public domain was analysed. Unpaid nursing and caring work, the health work undertaken by patients themselves and by families, friends and relatives – which in practice meant women – remained hidden from view. It is only in recent years that informal caring has been theorised in relation to ideologies of familism and possessive individualism (see Section 4.5), and that the inter-relationship of private and public domains has been problematised.

The fact that women had to balance the demands of home and work, in effect doing a 'double shift' of paid and unpaid labour, has had a crucial influence on their range of work opportunities and on their choice of a job. Yet in labour theory women were viewed as being 'just like other workers' when they entered the world of paid work, and the complex connections between part-time work, job status and access on the one hand and mothering and housekeeping on the other remained obscure. A set of underpinning assumptions about the independence of men, as breadwinner workers, and the dependence of women (and children) served to characterise male paid work as 'productive' and female unpaid labour as 'unproductive'. Both these notions fed into the ethic of possessive individualism, which was above all a doctrine of male freedom and individual rights. Women had no rights of their own; their relationship to citizenship and civil rights was via men – until well into the twentieth century (Dalley, 1988).

○   Can you recall how women are classified in occupational class analysis? You might find it useful to reread Section 5.4.

Only unmarried women in paid work figured in the Registrar General's five-fold classification of occupations; otherwise women's social class was derived from that of their husband, the head of household. This provides useful evidence of the invisibility of women in official statistics. The attraction of this traditional classification lies partly in the long runs of data available, and it forms the backbone of the statistical evidence of many reports on health. It also throws up problems in attempting to unravel women's own health status and has led to the development of other classifications, as we noted in Section 7.2.

7.5 The challenge of feminist analysis

In some ways feminist theorists have been concerned, from a very different angle, with issues similar to those tackled by some other types of sociologists. For example, feminists have engaged with postmodern ideas about power and subjectivity and the positioning of 'woman' through discourses about sexuality. They have also been concerned to explore how far 'oppression' can be viewed as 'universal' and how far the range of differences between people – influenced by their lived experience of race, class, gender, disability, sexual orientation, age, ethnicity and so on – makes it impossible to generalise about women as a distinct group. This is analogous to debates in 'malestream' sociology about the universality of class divisions and oppression, or about the experience of racism and imperialism. But feminists have been driven by specific concerns which 'malestream' sociologists have not shared: about 'biological essentialism', the nature of women's oppression and the mechanisms by which this oppression is reproduced inter-genera-tionally.

Many feminist theorists have adopted a 'social constructionist' position, arguing that women's oppression is not fixed in 'human nature' but determined by particular historical, social and cultural factors. Along with many other sociologists, they reject arguments from sociobiology that men's and women's physical attributes and social behaviours are largely determined by a biological imperative (Sydie, 1987). By no means all feminist theorists dismiss essentialism; indeed, as the differences between men and women have been explored, so the temptation to root women's oppression in women's biology has become apparent (see below). Social constructionism itself is a broad-brush term covering several different theoretical frameworks which draw on

Marxist and Weberian approaches, but it moves beyond these approaches – highlighting their failure to deal with gender issues and also putting a much greater emphasis on women's lived experience.

Patriarchy

One central challenge to 'malestream' sociological theory has been made by theories of *patriarchy* and the investigation of patriarchal forms of domination. This has been such a productive and provocative debate and has opened up so many other issues that we'll focus on it here. Although some feminist writers consider the term too problematic to use, it has continued to have great symbolic value, in particular because it emphasises that the social situation of women as a group cannot be explained by reference to other factors, such as social class. Michele Barrett (1988), commenting that her abandonment of the term had provoked strong reaction, acknowledged the importance of patriarchy as a marker of 'the independent character of women's oppression'. Theories of patriarchy offered ways of responding to the problem of why women have been excluded or oppressed in most societies.

At this point, note down your own definition of the term 'patriarchy', introduced in Section 3.7.

In Chapter 3 patriarchy was defined as the domination by older men of women, children and young men. In relation to women this was seen as a systematic organisation of male supremacy, accompanied by exclusion of women from the public domain of economic power and politics. It was characterised by subordination in the home – by means of a sexual and gendered division of labour – and when women entered the sphere of paid work. It was emphasised that feminist theories differed in their use of the term and in their analysis of patriarchy. It originated as an anthropological term meaning the kinship form of male domination, and for this reason some writers have avoided the term 'patriarchy' and used 'male-dominated gender order' instead (for example Stacey, 1988). In general terms, however, the concept of patriarchy focuses attention on the wide range of oppressive and exploitative relations that exist: in sexual relations, parenting, economic power, civil rights, work. It raises questions about whether such oppression has always existed or whether it is the product of particular types of economic organisation and social development. It also raises questions about the ways in which such oppression is transmitted inter-generationally, and how patterns of dominance and subordination are reproduced within the individual psyche, as well as through gender socialisation, a gendered division of labour and male control of the public domain.

Some of the main approaches to the problem of patriarchy were briefly sketched in Section 3.7. Although the central focus is on material exploitation, radical theorists have emphasised the need to grapple with the universality of patriarchy and have identified its origins in women's reproductive capacity and male sexuality. Shulamith Firestone (1971) argued that the root of women's oppression lay in reproduction, because it subordinated women and made them dependent on men. Only if women could be liberated from the biological restrictions of childbearing through technology could they hope to be freed from patriarchal power.

Psychoanalytic theory
Another approach is to investigate how gender is internalised at the psychic level, through an understanding of the unconscious and the early stages of building gender identity. Nancy Chodorow (1978) explored the central role of women in 'mothering' and suggested that some of the different social characteristics of men and women might be explained by reference to their very diverse early experiences: of being able to identify with their mother if they were girls; or having to learn that they were separate and different if they were boys. This represents a reorientation from Freud's concern with the father and male genitalia.

In Sigmund Freud's psychoanalytic theories girls felt most sense of loss (penis envy) and saw mother attachment as second best (see Box 7.2). In recent years his influential psychoanalytic theories of gender development have been criticised and reworked (Chodorow, 1978; Mitchell and Rose, 1982). Feminists have emphasised the historical specificity of Freud's theories – written by a white, Jewish, middle class male patriarch living in central Europe in the late nineteenth century. In particular, they have questioned his preoccupation with the penis and

BOX 7.2 Freud's approach to gender

Sigmund Freud (1856–1939) argued that mental life was marked by a constant struggle between the primary processes in the psyche of biological urges and instinctive drives (the *id*) and the higher, secondary processes of personal reason and sanity (the *ego*), shaped by the power of social constraints (the *super-ego*). Of the instinctive drives, Freud saw sex (the *libido*) and aggression (the *death instinct*) as the most significant in directing and explaining human behaviour.

Freud claimed that the initial learning of gender identity was bound up with the possession (or lack) of a penis – symbolic of masculinity and femininity. He argued that in the Oedipal phase of development (between about four and five years of age) boys suppressed erotic feelings for their mothers (out of an unconscious fear of castration by their fathers) and accepted their male identification with their fathers. Girls suffered 'penis envy', and their identification with their mothers went along with disappointment at their lack of a penis.

its 'natural' superiority. Why should female genitalia be seen as 'not a penis' rather than specialised reproductive parts?

In a similar patriarchal way Freud saw the father as the major influence and authority figure. In contrast to this, Chodorow has argued that the mother is the ever present figure and dominant influence and that patterns of gender socialisation are created and sustained by the primary role of women in early child-rearing. Gender identity is learned earlier, in infancy, and boys and girls are primarily attached to their mothers. Whereas girls can remain openly affectionate and continue to identify with their mothers, boys' gender identity is gained by breaking away from being 'like a mother' and becoming separate. Girls are 'taught' to value close relationships and sharing; boys are 'taught' to be self reliant (not to be 'sissies') and to suppress their emotions. This makes it difficult for them as men to reveal their feelings to others and gives them power over women who seek intimacy and sharing. There has been some reworking of the Freudian theory of 'the law of the father' to argue that patriarchal values are internalised in the individual psyche at an unconscious level, as well as through a process of gender socialisation (Mitchell and Rose, 1982). In other words, the argument of psychoanalytic theory is that patriarchy is very deep-rooted, and its removal is not just a matter of changing laws and transforming organisations.

These ideas have challenged widely held theories about the origins of gender identity. They also highlight the way in which theories – such as those of Freud – which claimed to be objective and scientific might be seen instead as forms of patriarchal ideology. They are very important in suggesting how male dominance can be reproduced at a mainly unconscious level and sustained across generations, although they have been criticised on the grounds that they are *determinist*: in other words, they allow for no adequate explanation of differences between women or women's current struggles for liberation. On the other hand these revisions of Freudian theory, by emphasising the central importance of 'mothering' in the process of gender socialisation, would seem to indicate how women themselves can effect changes in attitudes and practices.

Structuralist and materialist theories
Much of feminist theorising about patriarchy has explored how male power and control was exerted and reproduced through economic and social structures and institutions. One strand in this materialist approach, as we noted in Chapter 3, drew on Engels' 'Theory of the Family' to suggest that it was the rise of private property that marked the emergence of patriarchal relationships: in other words patriarchy had specific historical origins and was tied to capitalist economic

structures. There has been a continuing dialogue between feminists and Marxists, and Heidi Hartmann (1979) and others have explored the difficulties involved in reconciling an analysis based on patriarchy with an economic-derived, class based approach.

○   Suggest why many feminist theorists have found it difficult to reconcile Marx's theory of class with feminist theories of patriarchy. You might find it useful to refer back to Section 5.2 for a summary of 'economic class'.

Theories of patriarchy emphasise the *independent* nature of women's oppression: in other words this oppression cannot be explained by reducing it to other factors. Marx's theory of class, however, asserts the primacy of economic factors in explaining social relationships. It is the economic infrastructure and the economic relationships thrown up by capitalism that largely determine social relationships, such as the structure and role of the family, the division of labour and so on. Most feminist theorists, while they accept that economic factors play some part, assert that family relationships are fundamentally determined by patriarchy. Male supremacy and female subordination are to be found in a range of societies with different economic and social systems, at very different stages of economic development; they may take somewhat different forms, but they cannot be wholly explained away by reference to class.

However, there have been fierce debates within feminism about how patriarchy and capitalism do interconnect. For example, it has been argued that there are two modes of production: the 'industrial' mode of capitalism and the 'family' mode of production, in which women's unpaid labour is exploited by men to reproduce the next generation, to rear children and to undertake domestic labour (Delphy, 1984). But this 'dual systems' theory leaves the relationship between the two modes of production unclear. We still need to tease out how the family mode is penetrated and influenced by industrial production. It also suggests that family relationships are purely economic: men marry only to exploit women's labour, concepts of love, caring and romance do not seem to enter into family life.

One main concern is with the shifting character of patriarchy. In the domestic domain patriarchal power is much less pronounced in the 1990s, even though male violence remains at a worrying level. Most families are not now typical nuclear families of breadwinner father and dependent mother and children, and the domination of the father is not uncontested. Whilst the domestic division of labour is by no means equal, men now take more part in household tasks. Women have equal civil and tax rights and some legal protection against rape and physical assault (see Chapter 3). They are much less ready to endure oppressive relationships: Britain has the highest divorce rate in Europe and a very

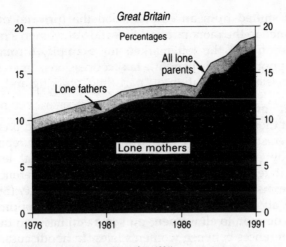

FIGURE 7.3 Families headed by lone mothers and lone fathers as a percentage[1] of all families with dependent children. Source: *Social Trends* (1994)

large number of one-parent families, of which most are headed by women (Figure 7.3). In the public sphere pressure from women and equal opportunity legislation have opened up more areas of paid work to women. The male monopoly of whole areas of work – such as medicine, the law and politics – has disappeared, although women are still clustered in low status, relatively poorly paid occupations. In other words the contemporary face of patriarchy – or the male gender order – is quite distinctive and is shaped more by legislation and public sphere decisions about paid work than by male domination in the home.

This shift from private to more public patriarchal structures has been investigated by feminist theorists (Walby, 1990). Whereas in the nineteenth century women's oppression was mainly reproduced through domestic production – the exploitation of women for childbearing and domestic labour – in contemporary industrialised society, argues Walby, this reproduction takes place mainly in employment and through the state. She identifies six structures of patriarchy: employment, household production, the state, sexuality, violence and culture. By considering their relative contribution in different historical periods she provides a dynamic portrait of patriarchy, although the relation between these structures is not fully worked out. But this allows us to chart how male control has shifted from an emphasis on the (private) ownership of women by men to the more public delineation of women's roles through state legislation and the job market: for example, through levels of Income Support, Child Benefit, tax concessions, maternity leave, nursery provision, designation of 'part-time' working and so on.

The diversity of women's experience

The work of these materialist writers has been criticised on the grounds that it underestimates the contribution made to the reproduction of patriarchy by psychic relationships at the individual level. Just as important, it tends to underplay the important differences between women in terms of class, race, ethnic and sexual identity (Stacey, 1993). The debate about patriarchy, by emphasising that oppression is an experience common to all women, puts less emphasis on the enormous range of differences between women's lives. In her discussion of health and women's healing work Stacey (1988) emphasises that generation, social and economic class and race also influence people's health and help to determine the division of labour in health. Black feminists in particular have argued that the notion of 'universal patriarchy' ignores the substantial differences between black and white women in terms of their experience of racism and imperialism.

Feminist theorists tended to make use of cross-cultural arguments to 'demonstrate' the universality of women's oppression, but in recent years such approaches have been criticised, particularly by black feminists, on the grounds that they obscure the very real differences between black and white women's lived experience:

From questioning the general applicability of particular categories such as 'reproduction', 'patriarchy' and 'the family' to rethinking feminist theories of work, violence, sexuality and parenting, Black feminist work has provided a crucial challenge to the limits and exclusions of white feminist theory . . . Black feminists have also documented their own 'hidden histories' of racism, colonialism and imperialism, which have shaped all our lives in very different ways. Power differentials between women and men are cross-cut by differences in power between women depending on how they are positioned within these histories.

Stacey (1993)

In the health sector, for example, black and minority ethnic women have suffered a double oppression: of being a woman and being black. The gendered division of health labour has helped to keep women in lower status, less well paid, caring working. In addition, racism in the recruitment and selection procedures of the health service have ascribed black women to lower grades and lower levels of nursing (see Section 8.4). The sexual orientation of women, their age, cultural identity and social class position also shape their experience of the male dominated gender order in contemporary British society. Class, it might be argued, represents a third type of oppression for black and minority ethnic women (Doyal, 1979). The divisions between working class and middle class women, or between older, dependent women and young women, are likely to be highly significant. The increasing recognition of this diversity has provoked a challenge to earlier theoretical models of 'patriarchy' as a type of universal oppression and has reinforced a tendency towards fragmentation and celebration of lived experience and human difference.

Postmodern perspectives

One aspect of this fragmentation is the deconstruction of the category 'woman' in postmodern thought. It has been argued that 'woman' and 'man' are not fixed categories, retaining the same meaning over time or from culture to culture. Rather they are social constructs. Woman is a 'shifting signifier of multiple meanings': that is, what we see and know is constantly being reinterpreted because we ourselves are subjects occupying particular but changing positions (Stacey, 1993). Our identities as subjects are problematic; they are produced by discourses – about sexuality, reproduction, medicine and so on – which may be modified and changed. For example, women's reproductive processes have generally been framed in terms of medical discourses which use metaphors of production, implying a similarity to industrial production (Martin, 1987). Indeed, a production line process of managing female reproduction has been evident in health services, and women's own conceptualisations have been marginalised.

How does this relate to our discussion about postmodern theory in Section 2.8?

In Section 2.8 it was suggested that postmodernists were concerned to theorise the human subject 'from outside' as it were, rather than to accept the 'individual' or 'social actor' as an unproblematic 'whole person'. This draws attention to subjectivity, to the body and mind as sites of contradiction and conflict, and to their construction through the weaving of 'texts' and 'discourses'. You may recall the claims about the fabrication of the 'natural body' (as we think of it) by modern medical science (Armstrong, 1983a).

Female bodies, in particular, have throughout history been seen as potentially dangerous, and in traditional societies female sexuality and menstruation have been controlled by taboos and rituals. It has been estimated that around 200 000 people, mostly women, were executed in witchcraft persecutions in medieval Europe. The persecution of (mainly female) witchcraft suspects in sixteenth and seventeenth century Europe, it is claimed, arose not just from fear of female sexuality but from women's reputed healing powers: 'Witches are accused . . . of having magical powers affecting health – of harming, but also of healing. They were often charged specifically with possessing medical and obstetrical skills' (Ehrenreich and English, 1974). Women have variously been conceptualised as 'in league with the devil', 'whores', 'wise women', 'childlike', 'prone to hysteria', 'in touch with nature' and so on.

This suggests that discourses about women and female sexuality are social constructions which illuminate the concerns and priorities of the patriarchal public domain in historically specific social and economic circumstances. Thus in the early nineteenth century, the construction of the 'hysterical woman' in medical discourse reflected the prevailing ideology of women as the 'weaker sex' in need of male protection and regulation (Foucault, 1979). The hysterical woman was characterised as irrational and emotional, and doctors explained this behaviour in terms of specific physical changes in the body; thus one widely recommended cure was hysterectomy (Turner, 1987).

If this account is linked to a materialist analysis of patriarchy, the family and the needs of industrial capitalism, the social value of the construction of the hysterical woman becomes much clearer. It can be seen as part of a process of social regulation designed to bind mainly middle class women to marriage, constant childbearing and domestic labour. If women remained single or sought to pursue a career – in other words to go against their nature – then hysteria might be the result. Turner (1987) has suggested that:

The implication of this medical model was that women could only lead healthy lives in so far as they were sexually connected to a man in a lawful marriage which had the aim of reproduction. Sexual relations outside marriage were associated with another sexual disorder, namely nymphomania. The medical theory of the hysterical woman supported the status inequalities between men and women, supported the medical analysis of the social and psychological values of pregnancy inside marriage, and finally acted as an argument against further education for women on health grounds.

Turner (1987)

Biomedicine conceptualised women as continually in need of medical care and attention. Pregnancy, childbirth, menstruation and menopause were viewed as types of sickness requiring regulation. The strength of this medical construction of women can be seen in the still prevailing stereotypes about women patients, in the medical control of pregnancy and childbirth (though this is receding) and in more recent interventions in relation to reproductive control. Nevertheless, women's lives and roles have been transformed within the shifting social and economic context and modern industrial and post-industrial society. We have already noted the changes in family life (in Chapter 3), in women's legal and civil rights and increasing participation in paid work during two world wars and after 1945. The 'problem' of hysteria declined in the early twentieth century, although other 'diseases' seen as distinctively female complaints superseded it, in particular anorexia nervosa. Although within a functionalist analysis this has been construed in terms of family relationships, it could be seen as symbolic of young women's relative lack of power in the male gender order of contemporary society and as part of the biomedical regulation of women in the interests of men (Turner, 1987).

Applying feminist theory to health

A discussion of patriarchy has raised many of the issues central to the feminist critique of 'malestream' sociology, even if as a theory it hasn't been able to solve all the theoretical problems. It has helped to open up major issues for 'malestream' sociology: about the relationship between production and reproduction, how gender identity is acquired, how male domination is reproduced in the private and public domain and how (whether and, if so, how far) this shifts over time. Moreover, feminists have begun to highlight how class, race and generational inequalities interact with (and perhaps reinforce) gender divisions. In general, feminist critiques have exposed new problems for sociology, areas of social life and contentious issues which cannot be ignored.

But how do these theories illuminate health and health work? What can they reveal about the social distribution of health and sickness and about the social division of health work itself? In the sections that follow we will consider three areas where feminist theory has moved forward debate: in understanding how caring is socially constructed, in an analysis of health work as an occupation and in the investigation of medical practice and power over patients.

7.6 The social construction of caring

This section will draw on theories of 'mothering' and on a materialist analysis of patriarchy and capitalism – dual systems theory – to develop an understanding of the nature of caring and the predominance of women in paid and unpaid caring work.

Informal caring

Stacey (1988) reminds us that paid health work is only one domain of health labour; unpaid carers and the patients themselves also engage in health work. She lists the activities of health work as follows: 'the production and maintenance of health; the restoration of health; the care and control of birth, mating and death; the amelioration of irreparable conditions and care of the dependent'. Unpaid health workers are likely to figure in all these activities:

Using the definition of health work adopted here, it is clear that the entire membership of the society is involved; in market economics this means the unwaged workers in addition to the paid specialists and their waged supporters. In the analysis of the restorative or curative services in such societies all the unpaid workers who help the patient through illness or accident have to be included in the division of labour along with the highly trained salary or fee earners and the waged workers who provide support services. This is true also with regard to the care of the chronic sick and disabled. There are those who are more frequently involved in unwaged health care than others. These are most often women.

Stacey (1988)

There are likely to be considerable differences in the degree to which patients become involved in their own care and, as we noted earlier, one influence on this may be gender, in that men may receive considerable amounts of informal care from women. Moreover, women are the main informal carers for all types of dependants – children, older people, people with physical or mental disabilities, those suffering from chronic, debilitating conditions – so overall the gender imbalance in unpaid health work is considerable. Two-thirds of those providing 20 or more hours of informal care a week are women, and nearly 30 per cent of these also have dependent children. There is also the routine caring of shopping, cooking and cleaning which is mainly done by women (see Chapter 3, page 106, Table 3.2). And since most paid health work is also done by women, the health sector becomes not so much a 'human service' occupation as a 'woman service' one.

○ Suggest how feminist theories can help to explain the predominance of women in caring work.

You may have already noted that caring as an activity was seen as women's 'natural' work, largely to be explained in terms of their role in reproduction, until feminist critics attacked such 'malestream' assumptions. At this point caring began to be analysed as a type of work that was socially constructed, connected to (but by no means fully explained by) women's biology. First, the theory of patriarchy drew attention to male power, exercised within the home and in the public sphere. The exploitation of women as unpaid carers of children, other dependants and male partners was linked to their exclusion from power and authority in the public domain. The social justification for this was found in essentialist arguments about natural, biological roles and functions. Women's caring and informal health work was exposed as patriarchal oppression. But the persistence of caring as women's work within contemporary society – where patriarchal structures have been challenged by women and have shifted considerably – has led to the development of other explanations. Some theories have emphasised the reproduction of mothering at a psychic level (Chodorow, 1978). This positions 'caring' as a part of social learning, but one which happens at an almost unconscious level in early childhood.

Others have investigated the historical specificity of patriarchy and have explored how the state and employment have structured women's oppression in contemporary society (Walby, 1990). In this materialist account women's caring role is sustained and reproduced through specific social structures. The paucity of childcare facilities provided by the state and employers, for example, makes it difficult for women to engage in paid labour when children are small. The benefits system traps lone mothers in poverty. Beyond this, the diversity of women's understanding and experience of 'what caring is' must be explored. Caring takes place within specific contexts which hold different meanings for different people. Caring in a social context in which there are adequate financial resources and social support is unlikely to bear much relation to caring in a situation of poverty, poor housing and social isolation. The needs of black and minority ethnic carers may receive less attention than those of whites; age and gender influence social support as well.

A labour of love?

The notion of caring as women's work has also been problematised by feminist writers in relation to the welfare state. A 'crisis' in caring was initially identified by Moroney (1976) – arising from the growing participation of women in the workforce, declining numbers of spinsters and the changing ratio of younger to older women. This shrinkage in the female 'caretaker pool' was seen as a problem for the state; it was left to feminists to highlight the sexism underlying the analysis and to point out the costs to women of such caring. An analysis of caring for children and other dependants showed that the state made the assumption that women would care for their families. In *Prevention and Health, Everybody's Business* (DHSS, 1976), for example, the need to protect the family's health, to take children for check-ups, to buy 'healthy' food was discussed, but the fact that this burden would largely be carried by women was ignored (Graham, 1979).

The growth of community care policies increased the caring load and was fundamentally incompatible with the equal opportunities legislation designed to open up new prospects for women in the workplace (Finch and Groves, 1980). Moreover, the financial and emotional costs of caring, it was argued, were not calculated by the state. In a classic study of 44 married couples caring for a dependent relative, time diaries were used to investigate the daily distribution of the caring burden (Nissel and Bonnerjea, 1982). Whereas women, whether in paid work or not, spent between two and three hours caring for the dependant, their husbands spent an average of eight minutes. The financial savings to the state of such unpaid caring, calculated in terms of market rates for domiciliary care, were considerable, and the cost to the individual women, in terms of jobs and income forgone, was also high.

Attention then turned to the emotional costs involved. Caring work is largely unseen and unrewarded, the assumption being that it is a 'labour of love' which brings its own rewards (Finch and Groves, 1983). Yet several small-scale ethnographic studies demonstrated the emotional labour as well as the continuous physical toil required. For example, Ungerson (1987) discussed the emotional exhaustion of many of the carers and the grim call of duty 'which so many carers in this sample felt they were trapped by' and which they clearly resented. Like others who have written about caring, she drew both on Chodorow's (1978) analysis of mothering and on a materialist analysis of the relationship between patriachy and capitalism, and suggested that the motivations of carers were very mixed. It may be that some women find that caring gives them a sense of female identity – and Ungerson did find 'joyful' carers in her sample – but many others feel exploited and dehumanised, forced by structural and social pressures into a role they did not seek.

A further issue concerns men who care. Overall about one-quarter of carers are men, and in one study 41 per cent of those caring for a spouse were men (Charlesworth et al., 1984). Data from the 1980 General Household Survey has indicated that in relation to the sample of elderly people with severe disabilities 35 per cent of carers were men (Arber and Gilbert, 1989a). Yet the stereotypical carer is female: 'Men carers have been invisible to researchers, their experience ignored or denied because their unpaid caring contradicts gender norms' (Arber and Gilbert, 1989). While it is true that less is known about the motivations of male carers there is some evidence about them. For example, Ungerson's study included male carers, and she noted not only that they referred to 'love' rather than 'duty' as a motivation but also that they conceptualised caring as a form of 'work', using 'occupational language drawn from the labour market'. These comments by Mr Vaughan, a retired chief accountant caring for his wife, illustrate this approach:

We've tried to be intelligent about it and eliminate inessentials. We've got rid of all our brass ornaments. The other house looked as though a woman lived in it – lots of fussy little bits! I've tried to plan this flat to make it as labour saving as possible . . . She certainly provides me with a reason for living. After so many years of retirement I'd be feeling rather useless by now. If she dies before me I now know so much about caring I'd want to carry on caring for someone else.

Ungerson (1987)

This links to Chodorow's argument that through gender socialisation men learn work values: to become separate, to control feelings and to value rationality. Mr Williams, another carer in Ungerson's study and an active member of the Carers' Support Group, commented that 'a carer must be in charge. I see some of my colleagues there – they're completely under the thumb of their invalid patient'.

7.7 Health work as a gendered occupation

Health work offers a rich and complex example of the gender division of labour. By theorising patriarchy and emphasising how reproduction and production are connected, feminists have demonstrated that the public and private domains have been socially constructed. In Section 7.3 the sex segregated character of professional health work was noted: nursing, midwifery, health visiting, physiotherapy and occupational therapy are overwhelmingly female occupations; medicine and dentistry are predominantly male; some others – such as chiropody – are also largely male. In this section we'll ask why sex segregation still widely exists in health work. Why was the work divided up between men and women in this way? And what prospects are there for the transformation of health work in the future? But before focusing on the professionalised health work, it is important to realise that such an investigation would only provide part of the picture of health labour as a whole.

Note down what other evidence you can find of sex segregation in health-related work.

You probably reported on the evidence of sex segregation in other sectors of health work, for example in subcontracted services such as catering and cleaning – seen as women's work – and in portering – men's work. In health administration most of the routine non-manual workers are women, whereas the middle and upper managers are men. This is reflected in the composition of health authorities, hospital trust boards and in the Department of Health itself. Thus sex segregation works in two different ways to create a gender division of labour in health: women and men are, in practice, largely restricted to certain types of jobs and women are largely confined to the lower levels of health occupations, whereas men climb up the status hierarchy into senior positions. Overall 75 per cent of workers in the British National Health Service are women, and they are grossly under-represented at managerial levels in all professional, administrative and ancillary occupations.

A feminist critique

In view of the predominance of women in health work it is significant to note that until quite recently sociologists have overwhelmingly investigated salaried professionalised health work, and within this small area they have focused on the role of (overwhelmingly male) doctors. This is not just true of 'malestream' sociologists; in 1987 Ann Oakley made a personal confession of 'blindness' about the work of a group of health workers whom she called 'indisputably more important than doctors': that is, nurses:

> In a fifteen year career as a medical sociologist studying medical services I have to admit to a certain blindness with respect to the contribution nurses make to health care. Indeed, over a period of some months spent observing health-care work in a large London hospital, I hardly noticed nurses at all . . . I took their presence for granted (much as, I imagine, the doctors and patients did) . . . If this sounds a bit like Florence Nightingale's definition of a good nurse – an invisible, good woman – then perhaps we should not be too surprised. In many ways, history has defined a good nurse as a good woman, and this can be counted as both the weakness and the strength of nursing as a profession.
>
> *Oakley (1986)*

Throughout the centuries most health work has been done by women. Paid women healers were quite widespread in medieval times and in early modern Europe, although they were increasingly edged out of paid practice as men sought to exploit new, lucrative markets for health care (see Chapter 11). In the case of childbirth, for example, women's area of work was restricted so that only men were allowed to use instruments (Donnison, 1977).

A materialist feminist analysis of changes in the control of reproduction demonstrates how patriarchal control over women as patients and women as health workers has taken new forms in different historical periods. In the early twentieth century midwives were restricted to 'normal' deliveries and required to call doctors to assist in abnormal cases. Childbirth still largely remained in the informal, domestic domain but health workers were themselves becoming defined and professionalised. By the mid-twentieth century professional control over childbirth had grown and increasing numbers of women were giving birth in hospitals (see Table 7.4). The loss of autonomy for female midwives associated with the growth of hospital delivery was

TABLE 7.4 Hospitalisation of childbirth. Source: K258 (1992)

	1927*	1937*	1946*	1957	1968	1973	1984	1990
Hospital	15	25	54	64.6	80.7	91.4	99	99
Home/elsewhere	85	75	46	35.4	19.3	8.6	1	1

Figures are percentages of live births.
* Figures for hospital include hospitals, maternity homes and poor-law institutions.

paralleled by a rise in the status and numbers of male obstetricians (Oakley, 1984). In the 1970s the growth of the women's movement and feminist critiques of the medicalisation of childbirth began to shift opinion inside health work – among midwives and a few doctors, in public debate – particularly among middle class women, and finally in political circles. By the early 1990s government reports were calling for greater choice for women, more midwife controlled deliveries and a shift back to home based delivery (Cumberlege, DoH 1993a). No doubt some of the enthusiasm with which the state has responded to demands for the de-medicalisation of childbirth is bound up with the very high costs of hospital care and medically controlled delivery.

Control of nursing work

Midwifery is perhaps the most dramatic example, but it is not the only area of health work within which patriarchal control has been exerted. Nursing was reconstructed in the mid-nineteenth century as a middle class dominated female vocation to fit the requirements of medical men for disciplined, suitably trained and reliable health workers to carry out the routine, but essential, tasks of monitoring the patient's hour-by-hour condition and of 'nursing the room' to keep it in a sanitary condition. Home nursing, which had been widespread before the nineteenth century (and remained popular for the middle and upper classes into the twentieth century), did not allow the doctor to exercise the same control over subordinate health workers as could be exerted in a hospital setting.

Gendered relationships, in particular patriarchal control over female nurses, was the essential characteristic of the new order that emerged, and the symmetry between the domestic division of labour and paid health work is crucial. Nightingale's goal was to create female controlled nursing hierarchies. Predominantly middle class women, under medical control, became the new cadre of professional nurses, supervising the lower orders of aspirant nurses and auxiliaries, just as in the home such women kept house and supervised their domestic staff under the watchful eye of the Victorian *pater familias*. Nursing was therefore 'natural' work for women because it reproduced patriarchal ideology in the public sphere in the form of the nurse–doctor–patient triad (Gamarnikow, 1978).

It has been argued that medical control in health work was maintained by means of three modes of domination: subordination, limitation and exclusion (Turner, 1987; see Section 11.5). In discussing the process of subordination through the example of nursing, Turner makes use of feminist critiques of profession. Nurses' subordination is characterised by their lack of autonomy – 'nurses in theory merely execute decisions arrived at by doctors' – which is directly linked to the sex-typing of women as mothers and carers. In spite of legislative changes, nursing is still highly gendered and relatively low status work, exemplifying how 'female labour is used to cheapen the costs of production within a capitalist society' (Turner, 1987). On the other hand, this traditional subordination has been challenged by recent militancy and by 'vocabularies of complaint' which criticise medical power and hospital organisation and attempt to unite female nurses against (mainly male) superiors, although these may be symbolic rather than promoting any real change.

As we have noted, materialist analysis explains women's position in the labour force by highlighting how patriarchy as well as capitalism demarcates women's work – the theoretical approach known as 'dual systems theory'. Yet recent work has drawn attention to the difficulties inherent in analysing the precise nature of the inter-connections between patriarchy and capitalism. The impact of patriarchy and capitalism on any 'female professional project', it is suggested, requires grounding in particular historical circumstances (Witz, 1992). In other words, only by studying historically specific examples can we reach a clearer understanding of the precise nature of occupational closure (see Section 5.5 for a discussion of social and occupational closure). In her investigation of nurses' attempt to gain status as a profession through registration, for example, Witz argues that nurses employed particular techniques to resist medical power and hospital control over nurses' working conditions. As a subordinate group they fought back against attempts by doctors to define and limit (demarcate) nursing work by using a *dual closure* strategy of *usurpation* and *exclusion* (see Figure 7.4). They challenged settled gender relations and tried to usurp medical power and hospital control over pay and conditions by demanding a central governing body to control nursing. Linked to this were three types of exclusionary demands, designed to gain nurses autonomy: for a central board (to create an occupational monopoly), for self government (to exclude doctors and hospitals from any control) and for a one-portal system of entry.

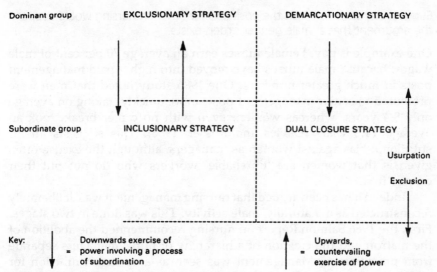

FIGURE 7.4 Strategies of occupational closure: a conceptual model.
Source: Witz (1992)

Nurses failed in this 'female professional project' because, although the Nurses Act of 1919 created a general council, nurses failed to get control of pay and conditions or of the content of examinations. Moreover, one-portal entry covered only the general register, so different entry requirements and conditions of service continued for other groups, such as male nurses, asylum nurses and children's nurses. In these circumstances professionalisation could not be finally achieved. In midwifery, however, dual closure strategies were effective, but at the high cost of accepting demarcation of their work by doctors. Midwives' area of practice was limited to 'normal births', and it was doctors, not midwives, who laid down definitions of 'normal' and 'abnormal' labour (Witz, 1992).

Gender order in contemporary health work

In the 1990s, although relationships between nurses and doctors are more reciprocal and collegial, a male gender order in health work is clearly visible (see Chapters 11 and 12). A predominantly female nursing workforce, carrying hour-by-hour responsibility for the monitoring and care of patients, still has less status and lower material rewards than the medical workforce. Class (and race) significantly influence the hierarchy in nursing, but a theory of patriarchy or male gender order is also crucial to an understanding of the composition of the workforce and the character of nursing as paid work.

○   Suggest any ways in which the position of women in nursing would support
the argument that a 'male gender order' exists.

One example is pay. Female nurses earn an average 70 per cent of male
wages, because male nurses have moved into higher paid management
posts in much greater numbers. One 1986 study noted that men were
promoted to senior management posts more quickly, taking on average
only 8.4 years, whereas women, even with no career break, took an
average 14.5 years (Davies and Rosser, 1986). This suggests an institutional bias against women as managers, although the excuse often
given is that women are 'unreliable' workers who do not put their
careers first.

Indeed it has been argued that nursing management was deliberately
reconstructed as a 'naturally' male activity. This was done in two stages.
First, the 1966 Salmon Report on nursing recommended the abolition of
the matron and the creation of a hierarchy of nurse managers separate
from practitioners. Management was seen as a specialist function for
which a nursing background was not essential. Second, as Carpenter
commented:

The Salmon reform over-emphasised the importance of managerial changes
in job content to the detriment of clinical changes. It created formal structures in
which power, prestige and remuneration increased with distance from the
point of patient contact.

Carpenter (1977)

The result of this was the appointment of male managers, who were
seen as 'natural' authority figures and as career-minded. Women, seen
as 'natural' carers, lost out in the drive towards management control.

Other writers have noted that a male gender order is now emerging
in nursing. Hearn (1987) has argued that nursing, in common with other
occupations such as social work, is showing an increasing tendency
towards domination by men. As these 'semi-professions' push towards
full professional status, male managers and executives take control. The
occupation is reconceptualised in terms of stereotypical male attributes
to which women must either conform or submit. Some empirical data
would support this theory. Although some of this managerial structure
in nursing was pruned back and the role of the clinical nurse given more
prominence, the nursing hierarchy still reflects Salmon's approach. In
the late 1980s men formed 12 per cent of the nursing workforce. A much
greater proportion of male nurses worked full-time (94.6 per cent) and
had SRN qualifications, whereas women (particularly black women)
were heavily clustered in SEN work and nearly forty per cent had part-
time contracts (Hockey, 1993). There is some evidence that these mainly
female part-timers are discriminated against in terms of promotion and
secondment, and other nurses may see them as 'second class' (Mackay,

1989). Yet the major reason women work part-time is to accommodate themselves to unpaid domestic and childcare demands. The structural demands placed on women by family life shape their position in the job market, not just by creating a 'double shift' but by projecting an ideology of women workers as inherently 'not committed' or 'career-minded'.

The rest of health work is heavily gendered as well. For example, 72.3 per cent of ancillary workers, performing the lowest paid work in the health service, are women (DoH, 1992a); 56.1 per cent of them are part-time workers, and many of them have found their hours further cut back (losing sick and holiday pay) by employers who have won contracts for cleaning and catering in the competitive tendering process. In speech therapy, a mainly female occupation, salaries are significantly lower than in equivalent, male dominated professions such as clinical psychology.

In medicine, although women gradually increased their share of medical school places and of junior grades medical posts, they have not made a significant impact at consultant level where 85 per cent of posts are held by men. Only about 25 per cent of doctors are women, and many are clustered in particular specialties, such as community medicine, which offer possibilities for part-time work. In general practice women are more likely to be salaried employees than partners and as part-timers are often steered towards 'women's problems' – contraceptive advice, mother and baby clinics, child welfare (Lawrence, 1987). Research into other health sector occupations, such as administration and medical laboratory work, also indicates that men manage while the organisation depends on women to fill the lower grades (Harvey, 1987).

Caring and curing

The notion of 'the good nurse as the good woman' applies to informal caring as well and reflects an entrenched division between cure and care in health work. Curative work – largely men's work – has high status, high rewards and is characterised by considerable autonomy in working, decision-making and the use of resources (human and financial). Caring work – women's work – has relatively lower status, lower (and sometimes very poor or non-existent) financial rewards and commonly much less control over work patterns and resources.

The status and rewards of curing and caring can usefully be problematised in terms of feminist critiques of 'production and repro-duction', categorisations of 'the social and the natural' and theories of 'public and private' spheres. Caring work in health in some ways reflects and reproduces in the public domain the work of cleaning, cooking, housekeeping, nursing and nurturing performed as unpaid domestic labour in the private domain. Such domestic labour has traditionally been viewed as 'natural' for women: work normally arising from childbearing and its effects. Moreover, this labour is part of reproduction of the next generation of workers rather than being itself productive labour. No finished 'goods' as such – consumer durables, industrial products – are made; no specialised, expensive equipment is required, no large sums of capital are needed.

Compare this scenario with the work of curing. Curative work (as performed by medical personnel) is far removed from domestic labour; indeed a major effort has been made to site all curative work, and even medical work where intervention was rarely required (such as child-birth), in hospitals and clinics away from the home. Large amounts of specialised equipment and expensive technology are used, and demands for more are continually being made. This labour is more obviously defined as productive – getting patients well and back to work – because medical personnel control the diagnosis and treatment of disease and sickness and certify the patient's fitness.

7.8 Gender and medical practice

Feminist analysis of patient–professional relationships in health care has focused mainly on the work of the medical profession. Doctors, with their control over diagnosis and treatment, have most formal authority over patients; it is in medical consultation and intervention that gendered power is most likely to be brought into play. However, nurses as the main paid health carers exert considerable control over patients in hospital and in community settings, and the discussion of gender here will be extended in Chapter 12 by exploring how notions of 'caring', 'women's work' and 'emotional labour' structure relationships between nurses and patients.

Until the 1970s the bulk of research exploring the doctor–patient relationship virtually ignored the gender of the participants. There was a general assumption that doctors were men, but that the rituals and technology of the consultation rendered both doctors and patients 'genderless'. This was reinforced by both the notion of the patient as the 'object' of medical scrutiny and (in the UK) the principle of equality within the National Health Service. Since then a growing number of studies have suggested that doctors do not treat their patients in either a uniform or objective way, and that gender, as well as race and social class, influence medical attitudes and behaviour.

Aspects of patient–doctor interaction

It has been suggested that male and female doctors differ considerably in their behaviour towards patients. Women doctors in general practice appear to spend more time with their patients and are more likely to suggest follow-up consultations, especially for women with sex-specific problems. This may be true of female consultants too, although there is too little evidence to generalise. Wendy Savage (1986), the consultant at the centre of the battle for power between conservative and more holistic obstetricians at the London Hospital, summarised the case for a more equal doctor–patient relationship in the following way:

Over the years I have been practising, I have learnt that women needed to be able to talk as equals with doctors, to be informed of the choices available to them and encouraged to make up their own minds about becoming pregnant, or continuing with a pregnancy. I have realised how important it is for a woman to feel in control of the birth process if she is going to emerge as a confident parent.

Savage (1986)

This view may apply more widely to women doctors. In a survey of literature on interaction Miles (1991) tentatively concludes that 'female doctors may be more willing than male doctors to form egalitarian relationships with patients . . . Especially when dealing with female patients, women doctors may be less likely than male doctors to assume that women are passive by nature, and that they need decisions to be made for them'.

Although until recently most doctors were male, and this might therefore be considered as the 'norm' for medicine, several studies have suggested that women and men prefer same sex doctors, at least in consultations where they are seeking advice about sexual problems or intimate areas of the body. Indeed, the women's health movement and well women centres have been successful partly because women wanted advice and support from other women who understood their experiences (King, in Miles, 1991). Asian women, in particular, wanted female doctors in pregnancy and childbirth (Homans, 1985). In contrast to this, it may be that in relation to psychiatric problems women find it easier to admit their 'weakness' and to talk to male doctors (Roberts, 1985). Miles (1991) suggests that situational factors influence patient preferences; some women in her study found women doctors unsympathetic or unable to appreciate their situation. Indeed, there seems no particular reason why a woman doctor – especially after years of professional socialisation within a strongly male work environment – should be any more understanding of mental illness. As one of Miles' respondents commented, 'women can get very hard when they have a career'.

The evidence about the impact of gender on patient interaction with doctors remains very patchy. We know quite a lot about the impact of class: for example, that working class patients generally have shorter consultations, ask fewer questions and are offered less explanation (Cartwright and O'Brien, 1976). It seems likely that women, of whatever social class, find themselves in a situation similar to that of the working class patient, and that doctors were much more ready to evade questions or provide simplistic, non-technical explanations (Tuckett *et al.*, 1985). However, studies of doctor–patient interaction in maternity care indicate that class as well as gender significantly influence the consultation. Oakley (1980) recorded conversations in which evidence that a woman patient was knowledgeable about childbirth resulted in the male doctor shifting styles and responding in more technical language.

The lack of information is a not uncommon complaint about health services from both men and women, but it seems that the problem may be worse for women. For them the decisions that must be made regarding pregnancy and childbirth open up a large territory in which 'the right to choose' depends on adequate information. This means establishing a relationship with a doctor or nurse in which questions can be asked and are likely to be answered fully and fairly – a circumstance which appears to contradict the views of many doctors that patients do not want, and cannot cope with, much information. For example, Webb (1986) in her research with post-hysterectomy patients found herself caught up in explaining quite basic aspects of their care that had never been made clear: side-effects, the after-effects of treatment, possible complications, even routine procedures had not been explained. As one patient commented, 'if somebody had told me that I might see a lot of blood I would not have been so frightened . . . I think they should tell you that you might have a complication or infection or lose a few drops of blood – then you wouldn't worry so much'. In some situations nurses and other health workers can repair the damage and talk through the issues with patients, but the reluctance of many patients to ask for an explanation still needs to be tackled.

Labelling and stereotyping
The categorisation of patients has been highlighted in research into doctor–patient relationships and also, as we will find in Chapter 12, in nurse–patient interaction.

O   What is meant by categorisation? Suggest some common categorisations of patients in health work.

Categorisation means slotting patients into particular categories on the basis of your judgements about their presenting characteristics. This happens not just in health work but in most areas of life. We use our past experience and judgement – based on our own norms and values – to mentally assign those we encounter to one of a number of types familiar to us. In health work it is very common to assign patients to 'good' and 'bad' categories, and this may carry serious implications in terms of how they are assessed and treated. A particular problem is that personal judgements may colour supposedly 'professional' and 'objective' judgements.

For example, Stimson (1976) found that (mainly male) doctors regarded male patients, who were more likely to present with physical symptoms, as those who 'caused the least trouble'. When asked to describe the type of patient who 'caused the most trouble' they described those presenting with chronic sickness or emotional and psychiatric problems, who were mainly their women patients. Normative and moral judgements about patients, particularly in the area of childbirth and reproduction, have been well documented. Macintyre (1977) noted that in consultations for unwanted pregnancies doctors used their personal value systems to make judgements about the presenting patients, and this influenced diagnosis and treatment. Once labelled as the 'good girl' who 'made a mistake', a patient could expect sympathetic treatment and was more likely to get an abortion than a woman categorised as 'promiscuous' and 'immoral', who was labelled and treated as a 'bad girl'.

It has been argued that male doctors work with stereotypes of women as weak and unstable; as we noted earlier, pregnancy was viewed as exacerbating these already existing 'problem' characteristics of women (Graham and Oakley, 1981). In a classic study of the medicalisation of mental health Chesler (1972) argued that psychiatry controlled the production of 'masculinity' and 'femininity', creating categories of normality which for women involved acceptance of a female role of passivity and dependency: 'Women who reject or are ambivalent about the female role . . . are assured of a psychiatric label and, if they are hospitalised, it is for less "female" behaviours, such as "schizophrenia", "lesbianism" or "promiscuity". This social construction of femininity may hold in relation to physical illness as well. In a study of medical diagnosis Lennane and Lennane (1973) noted that male doctors interpreted pain and nausea, even severe pain, reported by women in menstruation, pregnancy and childbirth as attributable to psychogenic causes, even when there was strong physical evidence for their existence. They argued that this failure to legitimate or investigate women's pain denoted a fundamental sexism on the part of the male doctors. However, although some US studies have endorsed their findings, others have suggested that some women receive more treatment than men for similar conditions. When presenting with common complaints, such as headache, chest pain and back pain, about a third of women were given more extensive checks and prescribed more medication, and this result held true even when age, diagnosis and seriousness of complaints were controlled (Verbrugge and Steiner, 1981).

These studies suggest that the stereotype of the frail and emotional woman patient is responded to in various ways: both by dismissing symptoms and by treating them with (undue?) concern. It is arguably the basis and type of intervention, rather than access to treatment itself, which is problematic. For example, the argument that women's mental health problems are only a construct of medical psychiatry, which Chesler seems to endorse, denies the very real suffering which women experience and which is linked to their roles and lives as women (Busfield, 1989). Women's groups have complained that doctors have not taken women's health issues seriously, pointing out the reluctance of doctors to accept conditions such as pre-menstrual syndrome as legitimate. In her study of hysterectomy Webb (1986) notes that little research has been done into the efficacy of such treatment compared with less invasive techniques, although in 28 per cent of cases laboratory examination of the uterus found no abnormality.

There is widespread criticism of doctors' willingness to prescribe large quantities of anti-depressive drugs and tranquilisers for women – far more than for men (Gabe and Lipchitz-Phillips, 1984). This links back to the social construction of women within modern industrialised society which was noted earlier, in which medical discourse played a significant part in labelling women as inadequate and in controlling their behaviour (Turner, 1987). In this view the expectation that menstruation, pregnancy, childbirth and motherhood – all sex-specific states – will render women emotional, frail and 'trapped by their hormones' will influence the general response of male doctors to women patients. The social categorisation of women as 'natural' patients, whether legitimate or deviant, places them in a relatively powerless position in relation to health professionals. So women's groups have campaigned for more medical research and treatment, but at the same time they have sought to transform the unequal power relations between women and their doctors through self help, well women's centres and information-giving (Williams, 1987).

7.9 Gender and nursing

This chapter has suggested that gender divisions in health, in patterns of interaction between doctors and patients, and in health work itself are significant and persistent. But it also indicates that such divisions are influenced by specific social and historical circumstances. The patriarchal control of nursing as a largely middle class, female, subordinate health occupation – a construction that was resisted by the professional project in nursing, but not successfully resisted – still casts its long shadow over nursing today, helping to define status, conditions and pay. But it would be difficult to argue that nursing has not been significantly transformed since the nineteenth century, both in terms of its much more heterogenous workforce and in relation to medicine. As Chapter 12 will demonstrate, doctors and nurses are engaged in more complex and diverse relationships, and the gendering of these occupations is less clear cut. More doctors are women and more nurses, especially at senior levels, are men. However, a structural analysis of health work, while it must also map class and race, cannot afford to ignore the impact of gender. Similarly, as the composition of the workforce changes, we may expect shifts in the relationships between patients and health workers. As men's and women's patterns of life and work move closer together, their patterns of health and susceptibility to disease are likely to converge. All this means that it is extremely difficult to reach firm conclusions about the impact of gender on health work.

It is important to remember the extraordinary impact of feminist theory on sociology. Feminists have theorised not only the relationship between gender and inequality in paid health work but also in informal caring. This has involved connecting a materialist analysis of the shifts in industrial capitalism with a refinement of theories of patriarchy. In particular, the reproduction of caring as women's work can best be explained in terms of both structural constraints and social pressures, and of psychological theories of mothering. In doing so, feminist theory has challenged the preoccupation of 'malestream' sociology with the public domain and with paid labour. It has exposed the interweaving of private and public, and also of 'the personal and the political'. The wider women's movement has influenced sociological theory by putting 'feelings, experiences, consciousness on the agenda for political action' (Stacey, 1981).

Feminist theory offers a challenge to the expert rationality of medicine, and in doing so raises questions for nurses and other health workers. Some of these relate to the pervasive impact of sex stereotypes of men and women as patients, carers and paid workers in the health service. Increasingly, female health workers are beginning to question aspects of the care offered to women patients. For example, there has been considerable criticism of both the incidence and physical effects of episiotomy and hysterectomy. Webb (1986) has called for research into 'environmental, dietary or other influences on menstruation' and has noted that although hysterectomy is widely used to deal with menstrual irregularities, there is little clinical evaluation of its efficacy. Even more important, accurate information is withheld and women 'must seek and provide it for themselves'. The 'special role' that nurses might play in supporting and informing their patients was not yet appreciated by the majority of nurses in her study.

Another area where medical expertise has been questioned is in childbirth. Here the politics of health provision have moved in favour of lower technology and more woman-focused care. Some midwives have played an important part in evaluating hospital care and demonstrating that some of the medical claims that hospitals are safer and small units and home births inherently unsafe have never been subjected to objective testing (Tew, 1990; Campbell and Macfarlane, 1987). Recent research by midwives has validated the earlier criticisms of women by suggesting that a calm, relaxed environment, helpers who are known to the woman, individual-focused advice and support, and freedom to move around and feel in control will all contribute to a successful and satisfying experience for patients and professionals (Flint, 1991). Some women doctors, the most notable the gynaecologist Wendy Savage, have supported the attempt to provide more holistic care.

Community nurses, particularly health visitors, have played a significant part in the development of community facilities for women, such as crèches, self help groups and well women centres. There is a growing recognition of the advantages of such centres in developing more equal relationships between women patients and health workers, and by 'talking comfortably to other women in their situation . . . [to] give them more insight into their own situation and enable them to believe in their own ability to change things' (Cooke and Ronalds, 1987). However, there is only patchy evidence that, across the health service in general, female nurses see themselves as having any special relationship with their women patients. Nurses are beginning to draw up agendas for action, to get involved in research and evaluation of treatment options and to work in more holistic ways with patients. Jean Orr (1987) has called for the greater utilisation of feminist analysis and research findings on women's lives and women's health to inform practice and education: 'Most urgently, we need to change the nature of the relationship between ourselves and women by moving to a more equal model and giving power and control to those we seek to help'. But it seems that, even if feminist analysis of health and health work has been influential in a few areas of practice, much of the work of empowering patients and developing more equal relationships lies in the future.

Suggestions for further study

A. Oakley (1985) *Sex, Gender and Society*, London, Temple Smith, provides a useful introduction to gender issues, while A. Miles (1991) *Women, Health and Medicine*, Milton Keynes, Open University Press, investigates how gender influences health status and health care. J. Orr (1987) *Women's Health in the Community*, Chichester, Wiley, contains useful insights into gender issues arising in practice settings. Theories of gender can be investigated in D. Richardson and V. Robinson eds (1993) *Introducing Women's Studies*, London, Macmillan.

Self assessment questions

1 Define and distinguish between the terms 'sex' and 'gender'.
2 Describe the major differences in mortality and morbidity between males and females.
3 Discuss the main features of the theory of 'patriarchy'.
4 Why do women undertake most paid and unpaid caring work?
5 Discuss how gender structures relationships in health work.

Chapter 8

Race, ethnicity and health

Contents

Themes and issues

Defining race and ethnicity: prejudice and discrimination – direct and institutional racism – migration

Theoretical approaches: consensus theory and race as 'cultural conflict' – conflict theories: underclass – the relative autonomy of racism – sexism and racism – black people reporting 'in their own voice'

Health status and health chances: cultural and materialist analysis – access and uptake of health services – race, socio-economic class and poverty

Racism in health services: the universalist approach and ethnocentrism – discrimination in the health service workforce

Initiatives in health service practice: the equal opportunities framework – policy guidelines – the task force approach – monitoring

Learning outcomes

After working through this chapter you should be able to:

1 Review and reassess your own beliefs and practices in relation to race.
2 Outline the main patterns of morbidity and mortality in black and minority ethnic groups.
3 Identify and discuss with reference to health the main features of 'consensus' and 'conflict' theories of race.
4 Identify and discuss the different forms that racism may take in health services.
5 Review initiatives to combat racism in health services.

THIS chapter explores sociological debates about race and ethnicity in terms of how they connect to, and what they reveal about, the structure, characteristics, organisational attitudes and practices of health services. Issues about discrimination in health services, it is argued, need to be viewed within a broader framework of ethnocentrism and racism faced by black and minority ethnic groups in the UK. Section 8.1 begins by critically reviewing the language of race and ethnicity, and in subsequent sections we explore issues and problems related to health status, health experiences and health provision for black and minority ethnic groups.

In this chapter (and indeed throughout this book) the term 'black and minority ethnic' has been used to describe those who have a common experience of discrimination and inequality as a result of their ethnic origin, language, culture or religion. This includes anyone who suffers the effects of racism. 'Black and minority ethnic', used in the 1988 Report of the National Association of Health Authorities Working Party on Health Services for Black and Minority Ethnic Groups, encompasses not only people of Afro-Caribbean and Asian (including South East Asian) origin, but also other minority groups who experience exclusion and discrimination, such as refugees and travellers. Since a great deal of the research into black and minority ethnic groups has been concerned with Afro-Caribbean and Asian (Indian, Pakistani and Bangladeshi) people, the phrase 'black people' has been employed when these groups are being discussed, although this runs the danger of overemphasising the commonalities between the experiences of different groups. In some recent literature *race* appears in quotation marks – as 'race' – to distance the term from its biological connotations, but since this issue is explored in Section 8.1, this has not generally been thought necessary. In the following section we will investigate the social construction of race and ethnicity in order to explain how and why these particular definitions – with their emphasis on the shared experience of racism – have been emphasised.

8.1 Thinking about ethnicity and race

Clear thinking about ethnicity and race is obscured not just by emotive language and racial stereotyping – 'lazy blacks', 'stupid Irish', 'miserly Jews' and so on – but by concealment. Kirp (1979) described what he termed 'racial inexplicitness' in education policy: that is, defining 'educational problems posed by the non-white presence in nonracial terms: as reflecting language difficulties or lack of cultural familiarity, or

as an indistinguishable aspect of the dilemmas associated with educational disadvantage generally'. A similar reluctance to confront issues of
race has been evident in the National Health Service. Terms such as
'minority groups', 'ethnic groups', 'cultural minorities' and even
'ethnics' have been used to avoid being explicit about issues of race and
ethnicity. As Pearson (1986) has commented, health research has
frequently reinforced this inexplicitness, for 'it is precisely within a
culturalist framework that data on black people's health have largely
been researched and collected'. This has made it more difficult to
understand how 'race' and 'ethnicity' operate as linguistic and social
constructions and to challenge racism in health services.

Ethnicity

Ethnicity refers to cultural practices and outlooks that characterise a
given group of people and distinguish them from other groups. The
population group feels itself, and is seen to be, different, by virtue of
language, ancestry, religion, a common history and other shared
cultural practices – such as dietary habits or style of dress. Ethnic
differences, in other words, are wholly learned; they are the result of
socialisation and acculturalisation, not of genetic inheritance. There is
no biological foundation, therefore, for the common stereotypes noted
earlier, in spite of efforts by racist researchers and politicians to 'prove'
that blacks are 'inferior' and whites are 'superior'.

Ethnic differences have sometimes led to systematic discrimination
and denial of rights, as in the treatment of migrant gypsies across much
of Europe. But confronted with strange customs, dress and lifestyles,
most people become *ethnocentric*; they value their own culture more
highly than that of the other ethnic group, which is devalued and
belittled. In other words ethnic distinctions are rarely neutral and are
linked, in varying degrees, to patterns of domination and subordination
marked by inequalities of status, wealth and access.

The widespread use of the term 'ethnic groups' in the health service
has helped to disguise and indirectly sanitise *prejudice* and *discrimination*.
Prejudice refers to preconceived attitudes or views held by members of
one group about another, whereas discrimination refers to actual
behaviour towards them. A report by the Policy Studies Institute
(Brown, 1984) demonstrated the existence of ethnic prejudice among
indigenous whites in the UK, rooted in stereotypical thinking about
other cultural groups as inferior, less intelligent and having lower
standards. In a 1985 survey, nine out of ten British whites said that they
believed there is prejudice against black and Asian people, and over a
third admitted to being racially prejudiced themselves (Jowell, 1986).
Some of this has been translated into active discrimination: refusing to

give jobs to members of some ethnic minority groups or discriminating in the field of housing or other social services.

Race

Race might initially be defined as the physical or biological characteristics of individuals: their skin tone, hair colour and texture and so on. However, race as a term has clearly been used to express much more than this. In the past, especially in the nineteenth century, race became a way of dividing humankind which also denoted inferiority and superiority, and which was linked to patterns of subordination and domination. 'Black' and 'yellow' peoples were defined as inferior and more primitive, whereas 'white' or so-called 'caucasian' types were seen as superior and 'born to rule'.

The stigmatising of black races as inferior had long been a convenient justification for the transportation of huge numbers of them from Africa to North America, the Caribbean and South America during the slave trading centuries. Nearly ten million people were taken as slaves between 1601 and 1870. In the eighteenth and nineteenth centuries this manifest subordination of black people was cited to justify further conquest or domination of India, South East Asia and China and the near extinction of the Aborigine people of Australia. Imperialist conquerors and settlers claimed that as white, superior races they brought the benefits of superior culture and civilisation to help educate the black, inferior races.

In other words race acquired a social and cultural meaning beyond mere physical appearance, even though the reading off from biology of inferiority and superiority was being claimed as a scientific enterprise by the mid-nineteenth century. Phrenologists translated details of cranial measurements, shape and other features into a 'scientific' theory which 'proved' white race superiority. Darwin's theory of natural selection, translated into social terms, provided the basis for a 'survival of the fittest' doctrine of race, in which the subjugation and extinction of racial groups 'proved' their inferiority.

Social meanings of inferiority and superiority became attached to sets of physical characteristics, and so they have largely remained. For example, although Victorian pseudo-scientific theories of race are no longer officially endorsed, the notion of distinct 'racial groups' with characteristic biological make-up is still widespread in the popular imagination. Yet there is no basis for this in contemporary science. Apart from the physical details of skin tone or hair texture there are almost no systematic differences between racial groups; indeed there is as much genetic diversity within groups sharing such physical traits as there is between different groups. Geneticists now write of gene pools influenced by population inbreeding and migration patterns rather than of there being distinct 'racial groups'. The prejudice and discrimination which some white UK citizens (including health workers) exhibit and continue to exercise is based on the social meanings attached to race and ethnicity, and this highlights the importance of more recent patterns of political action and immigration.

The significance of immigration

Since 1945 the social meanings attached to race have been reinforced by the migration of quite large numbers of overseas British citizens of the Empire and Commonwealth (see Table 8.1). These mainly black workers were recruited by companies and public services to remedy the post-war labour shortage in the UK. Some of the jobs were skilled, but many were designated semi-skilled or unskilled jobs in the health service, in public transport and in catering and cleaning. Working conditions were (and still are) poor: migrant workers experienced high unemployment and were more likely to work permanent night shifts (see Figure 8.1 and Table 8.2). In the first two decades workers came mainly from the Caribbean, but later also from India, Pakistan, West and East Africa and

TABLE 8.1 UK migration patterns since the 1940s. Source: Layton-Henry (1984), *Social Trends* **(1994)**

Immigration		
1951–60	196 000	
1960–62	289 000	
1963–74	68 900	
1981	59 100	
1992	52 600	

Acceptances for settlement: by category (thousands)		
	1981	1992
New Commonwealth	31.4	27.7
(includes Pakistan)		
Rest of the world	27.7	24.9
Total acceptances	59.1	52.6

Net migration (inflows set against outflows)	
1951–60	+ 12 000
1961–71	−320 000
1971–81	−306 000
1983–87	+ 14 300
1988–92	+ 2 100

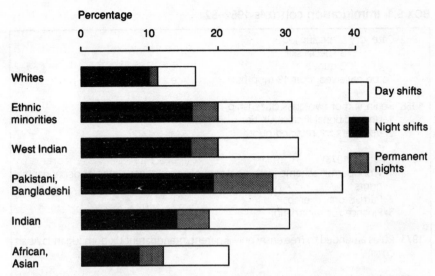

FIGURE 8.1 Percentages of white and black male workers in shift work in the early 1970s. Source: Mares *et al.* (1985)

TABLE 8.2 Unemployment rates by ethnic group, Spring 1993. Source: adapted from *Social Trends* (1994)

(percentages)	Unemployed	Long term unemployed (over 1 year)
White	9	4
Black (Afro-Caribbean and other black)	28	15
Pakistani	30	15
Bangladeshi	13	6

South East Asia. The social meaning of race was perpetuated by images of black people in situations of 'inferiority': unemployed or in low status and therefore poorly paid jobs, living in poor housing conditions and suffering the diseases of the poor, such as tuberculosis.

Look at Table 8.1 which shows UK migration patterns 1951–92. What are its characteristics?

If we look at *net migration* – that is, the overall population gain or loss – it is clear that population loss is the outstanding characteristic since 1945. The slow down in immigration after 1962 was the result of the 1962 Immigration Act, which created three categories for entry: those with a specific job awaiting them (category A) and with a special skill (category B) were differentiated from category C would-be entrants, who had to

BOX 8.1 Immigration controls 1962–82

1962 Category A specific job B special skill C queue To be reviewed after 18 months 1968 Beginning of two-class citizenship 1 Unconditional if close UK ties 2 Vouchers for rest and quota 1971 (enacted 1973) 1 Work permit scheme, with no permanent residence rights or dependants   rights 2 Patrials only exempt 3 Finance for repatriation 1973 Rules amended to free entry only if parent/grandparent UK born (Uganda Asian crisis) 1977 Rules tightened to exclude 'marriages of convenience' 1981 Nationality Act 1 British citizenship rights only for patrials 2 Citizen of dependent territories – no citizen rights 3 British overseas citizen 4 No ban on immigration

join the queue for one of a limited number of entry visas. Since then immigration controls have been further tightened, particularly in 1981 when the Nationality Act redefined 'British citizenship' so that citizenship rights were automatically given only to patrials: that is, those whose father or grandfather was born on UK soil. The category of 'British overseas citizen' was created, with no automatic entry rights (see Box 8.1). It is also worth noting that largely white immigration from the Americas, Australasia and the EC has almost matched that from the Indian subcontinent, and that the latter group are not 'new' immigrants but mainly spouses and children coming to join already existing families.

In spite of the modest numbers of black people who entered Britain – in relation to the total UK population and to EC and 'white Commonwealth' immigration – controversy and conflict have almost exclusively focused on this group. When asked about immigration levels, 15 year old boys in Leicester in 1986 claimed 15–20 million black people (25–35 per cent of the total population) lived in the UK, whereas the actual figure was around 4 per cent, of whom half were born in the UK. The speeches of Enoch Powell in the 1960s, the ambivalence of many leading politicians, the covert hostility of many trade unions (anxious to protect their members' jobs) and the outright racism of far right political groups such as the National Front have signalled to black and minority ethnic groups that they are far from welcome.

Donovan (1986) comments that notions about 'human nature' and the idea of 'natural homes' for different peoples constitute a language in which racism can be represented as 'common sense'. Racism became 'naturalised' and could be claimed as a reasonable, even neutral defence of the 'British way of life', as in the following extract from a speech by Margaret Thatcher:

If we went on as we are now, then by the end of the century, there would be four million people of the New Commonwealth or Pakistan here. Now that is an awful lot and I think it means that people are really rather afraid that this country might be swamped by people with a different culture. And, you know, the British character has done so much for democracy, for law, and done so much throughout the world, that if there is a fear that it might be swamped, people are going to react, and be rather hostile to those coming in.

Thatcher, quoted in Donovan (1986)

Migration as life-history

The pattern of migration to Britain was complex and highly differentiated. Beneath the statistics it is possible to discover the huge variations in migrants' experience and life-history. Through ethnographic research and oral history the lives of some of these people are being made 'visible' to enrich our understanding of the culture and traditions of black and minority ethnic groups.

Asian men arriving in the 1950s and 1960s came alone to the UK from predominantly rural areas, to work in particular industries such as the textile industry around Bradford. They settled in lodging houses and supported each other in dealing with language, work, bureaucracy and racism. Other Asians came as refugees from political troubles in East Africa, bringing with them quite different life experiences and outlooks. Many of the migrants hoped to seek economic advancement, with a view to returning home later on: what Anwar (1979) has called the 'myth of return'. But having worked hard and saved to purchase property, their stake in the UK Asian community grew and they sent for wives and children so that family life and social intercourse could properly be established. By the 1990s half of the Asian population was British born and educated, making it even more difficult to generalise about cultural practices. The experiences of young British Asian people may be as different from that of their parents as that generation's experience was from the one preceding it.

Large-scale Afro-Caribbean migration began after World War II, although groups were already living and working in major cities such as Liverpool and London. Migrants were attracted by the job opportunities at a time of high unemployment and population pressure in the West Indies. There was quite widespread recruitment of Afro-Caribbean people in Barbados and Jamaica by British Rail and London Transport. Like Asian migrants, Afro-Caribbean workers helped each other and tended to settle together in particular areas. Discrimination in housing encouraged migrants to purchase property for themselves and to rent it out to more recent arrivals. In contrast with Asian migrants, single women as well as men came to the UK. Many hoped to return home eventually, having 'made good' in Britain, which as the imperial 'Mother Country' aroused high expectations. Many of these hopes were dashed by low pay and racism (Donovan, 1986).

8.2 Theories of race

Consensus and 'liberal' theories

It is useful to start by making a distinction between *consensus functionalist* and *conflict* theories of race. The consensus functionalist approach has emphasised the disruptive effect of large numbers of immigrants on the host society and has documented how social consensus will be restored through resocialisation and structural integration. The newcomers, with different customs and characteristics, cause temporary disequilibrium – conflict and even racial hatred – but as they settle in and become accepted social order is restored. In crude terms the 'problem of race' is a problem for the immigrants; they must accommodate themselves to the new society, learn the language, adjust their culture and thus become acceptable to their hosts. Once assimilated, the assumption is that civil rights and equal opportunities policies will operate even handedly. Within this consensus approach are found notions of *assimilation* – absorbing the newcomers into mainstream culture and society so that they are indistinguishable from the majority – and *integration* – where the migrants settle in and mix freely with the host society, accommodating themselves to cultural norms and values but not necessarily expunging their own. A more recent goal in a liberal consensus framework is to strive for *cultural pluralism* or *multi-culturalism*: that is, a genuine acceptance of subcultures, norms and values which are different but equal.

Some early studies of the relations between immigrants and hosts used a social consensus framework. In a study of West Indian immigrants in Brixton Patterson (1965) suggested that, although colour was a complicating factor, the main tensions and misunderstandings arose because of their migrant status. She was optimistic that the newcomers would gradually be absorbed – with the help of anti-discriminatory laws and good race relations policies.

Although aware of the increasing complexity of race relations, the Scarman Report (1981) on the riots in Brixton, London, also projected an image of a basically sound 'liberal' society marred by economic misfortune, by policy failures and by 'mischief-making' (Mason, 1982). Scarman explained the Brixton riots primarily in terms of specific economic and political shortcomings, such as high unemployment and urban decay, which he suggested could be remedied by piecemeal adjustments: employment and housing measures, a greater commitment to promoting racial harmony and taking steps to combat racism in the police force. The state would act to ensure a fair deal for all its citizens; the model is of a consensual, basically egalitarian society in which specific problems would be remedied. Other riots in the late 1970s and early 1980s, such as those in Handsworth in Birmingham, St Paul's in Bristol and Toxteth in Liverpool have been explained in similar terms.

Conflict theories

In contrast to this, conflict theories have characterised race relationships in society as part of a continuous struggle between dominant and subordinate groups (Richardson and Lambert, 1985). As we noted in Chapter 2, there are several types of conflict theories, but all reject the fundamental assumption made by consensus functionalists that normative-led co-operation creates a basically integrated and consensual society. Rather, racial conflict is seen as one dimension of conflict between more and less powerful groups in society, and in this case many – though not all – newcomers are forced into this conflict largely because of their physical and cultural characteristics and the significance of these to the host society. They experience *direct racism*: that is, they are discriminated against as individuals on racial grounds. Newcomers do not cause disruption which is then largely overcome; on the contrary, they face continued hostility, and second and third generation immigrants may find acceptance just as difficult. This account also highlights *institutional racism*: that is, systematic and rationalised discrimination against black and minority ethnic people in all sectors of society. This may include maintaining barriers to recruitment and promotion at work, to certain types of housing, social services and to entry to some social and political groups which necessarily discriminate against certain groups. One example of such a barrier in the health service is the long term recruitment of Afro-Caribbean women to enrolled nurse and pupil training because the entry qualifications for SRN training were geared to British education criteria and values (see

Section 8.4). Since such barriers can be seen as 'objective' and since they continue to exist over time, equality of opportunity is never attained. This type of explanation, though it would attach importance to promoting good race relations and legal measures to assist this, would see the root causes of racial hatred as lying in the unequal distribution of economic and social power and control.

Writers in the Marxist tradition have emphasised that to focus on race and race relations is conceptually flawed; they argue that it is the organisation of capitalist production and its attendant class relations which shape racial attitudes and race conflicts (Miles, 1982). The real analysis is, therefore, of how advanced capitalist economies have exploited migrant labour and how the racism and violence is inevitably produced during this process. Black workers were imported to Britain as a 'reserve army' to fill particular gaps in the labour market, one of the largest of which was in the NHS (Doyal, 1979): 'By 1975, 20.5 per cent of all student and pupil nurses in Britain were from overseas and about half had actually been recruited in their country of origin. 5 per cent of hospital doctors and 18.3 per cent of GPs were born outside the British Isles'. By the early 1980s acute non-teaching hospitals in London were heavily dependent on overseas (mainly black) ancillary workers: 84 per cent of domestic and 82 per cent of catering workers came from abroad (Doyal et al., 1981). These workers continued to be used to keep down costs in the health service, leading to resentment and hostility from groups of workers who were attempting to protect their own pay and employment prospects. In this analysis racial hatred and discrimination arise from economic relationships; in the longer term it is the long sequence of economic exploitation and colonialism which has given rise to racist attitudes and theories of superiority and inferiority.

But other writers in the conflict tradition have questioned this *economic reductionism*. They have argued that race cannot solely be explained in economic terms but should be seen as a form of stratification which can operate independently of class. They have drawn attention to the historical specificity of race and racism. From a Weberian standpoint John Rex (1973) has emphasised that social and political influences, as well as economic relationships, need to be studied. Subjective understandings of race, even if they are misguided and wrong, have real consequences. We therefore need to take race seriously and explore how social structures help to create and reproduce racial discrimination and racist beliefs. Rex has argued that it is important to study inter-group conflicts in society as arising not just out of economic forces but also from social and specific historical relationships. Racial conflict and violence results not only from inequality between social groups but also from deterministic belief systems which justify discrimination. In addition, if group characteristics are ascribed (for example by colour), boundaries are fixed, and movement between groups is not possible.

Central to this analysis was the concept of a black *underclass*: a class separate from the working class which develops its own class consciousness and organisation. Rex (1973) argued that, whereas over the last century white workers had won employment and welfare rights from the state, post-war black migrants were denied this protection (and legal protection as well) and found themselves opposed by white workers wanting to protect their own hard won rights. Thus racism is influenced by the imperial past and is built into the structure of post-colonial British society.

Perhaps the most convincing analysis of race and racism in the conflict tradition has come from the work of Hall (1978) and the Centre For Contemporary Cultural Studies (1982); this has emphasised the 'relative autonomy' of race in relation to capitalism and the way in which different historical situations create different types of relationships between race and capitalism. The changing nature of racism and the changing social meanings attached to race influence how class struggle is experienced. In other words, race and racism – as well as capitalism – are constantly being redefined as historical circumstances change. From the 1970s, Hall has argued, growing economic crisis became 'racialised' as state policies portrayed black culture and black communities as a threat to national identity and the 'British way of life'. This threat in turn became a justification for tougher immigration legislation and more violent policing of black communities at the same time as black unemployment and poverty were explained in terms of the cultural inadequacies of black and minority ethnic groups themselves.

At the same time it is important to avoid stereotyping black people as merely 'victims' and the local or central state merely as 'oppressors'. In the early 1980s some local authorities began to introduce equal opportunities policies, including positive action and monitoring and setting up processes of consultation with minority groups. Health authorities began a rather tentative process of defining equal opportunities for patients and workers, even if systems for monitoring lagged behind such statements of intent (see Section 8.5). There is widespread evidence that black struggles over workplace, legal and welfare rights have mobilised local communities to challenge racism and to press for more appropriate services, and in the process have helped to enhance cultural identity. Gilroy (1987) notes how local campaigns, for example for police accountability and for greater opportunities for black schoolchildren, have focused on the need to initiate participation in decision-making and increase democracy at local level.

Several black writers in the conflict tradition have commented on the danger of losing independence and becoming 'neutralised' by accepting state funding of 'ethnic welfare projects, self-help groups, Black women's centres and police monitoring committees' together with 'a whole generation of ethnic workers and race relations experts' (Bryan *et al.*, 1985). On the other hand, as one London based welfare group reported to Bryan, 'the money we receive is ours. It's our taxes and profits from our labour. We want to control the way the money's spent on our own communities. The problem really is how to handle the bureaucrats, to negotiate with local authorities so that we get the money in the first place'. Direct first hand evidence of this kind, gathered through ethnographic studies, oral histories, case studies and biographies, has enabled a richer and more diverse series of pictures of black struggle to be uncovered.

Conflict theories emphasise the complexity and inter-generational nature of racial conflict, noting that racism may persist over time as institutionalised patterns of discrimination become established. Bryan *et al.* (1985) comment on the double oppression faced by many black women; they must battle against sexism in family life and in their relationships with black fellow activists as well as racism within British society. In the early 1990s there has been evidence of the way in which unemployment, poverty and racial hatred reinforce each other. The incidence of racial harassment of inner-city areas, particularly in the East End of London, rose throughout the 1980s, intensifying in the early 1990s (see Table 8.3). The most startling example is the election of a British National Party councillor for Tower Hamlets in September 1993, against a background of claims and counter claims of discrimination in council house allocation and in official financial support for minority groups.

○ Suggest what different implications for health practice might follow from adopting a 'consensus' or a 'conflict' perspective on race.

A consensus perspective on race paints a picture of a basically just and sound society in which newcomers and institutions can work together to seek mutually acceptable accommodations. Although racial problems may occur in the short term, cultural adjustment by the immigrant group

TABLE 8.3 Reported cases of racial harassment in London 1979–93

Year	Number	Source
1979	3827	Layton Henry (1984)
1982	7000	
1990	7500	The *Guardian*, 18 March 1994
1993	8779	

and by the host society will restore stability in the longer term. Here the emphasis is on cultural differences as causing the problem and on various types of cultural adjustment as providing the solution. In health work this would point primarily to the need for health professionals to be informed about minority cultures and to acknowledge that they might have 'special needs' to be met. A related concern would be to overcome barriers to health care experienced by members of ethnic minority groups, including prejudice and discrimination within health work.

A conflict perspective focuses on structures and forms of domination and subordination in contemporary British society. It suggests that racial conflict is one particular dimension of the power struggles between more and less powerful groups. The root causes of racism are seen to lie in systematic patterns of economic exploitation, or in economic, social and political barriers and cultural belief systems. In this approach the emphasis is primarily on recognising the impact of racism and socio-economic inequality on individuals and groups. Understanding other cultures would be one, but not the only or most important, response. Rather than black and minority ethnic groups being pathologised as culturally problematic or abnormal, the concern would be with tackling discrimination and institutional racism in health care systems – in the interests of workers as well as patients.

Researching the experience of diversity

All theorising about race and ethnicity generalises about diverse and divergent experiences. Theories deal with issues at an abstract level and draw on data which aggregates individual experience, teasing out and interpreting common themes and building theory. General theories about race need to be counter balanced by careful attention to the diversity of individual experience. Members of black and minority ethnic groups, while they may collectively experience prejudice and discrimation and while they may be disadvantaged as a group in relation to income, access to health care, employment or housing allocation, do not necessarily have similar experiences of racial disadvantage.

The phrase 'black and minority ethnic' itself, as we noted earlier, is used to describe a huge variety of minority groups of which the two largest in the UK are of Afro-Caribbean and Indian origin, numbering around half a million and three-quarters of a million people respectively. But in the Asian (Indian, Bangladeshi, Pakistani) community of one city, Blackburn, 17 different dialects are spoken and cultural practices vary (Robinson, in Donovan, 1986). Migration patterns and life histories can differ greatly even within a group sharing a common language and culture. In relation to health their needs will vary greatly, even if statistical and theoretical generalisations about health status and disadvantage are soundly based. Ethnographic studies, such as Donovan's (1986) research which is examined in Section 8.3, and case study and autobiographical material, such as that used by Anionwu (1993) and Mares *et al.* (1985), as well as life history, can help to redress the balance by highlighting diversity.

8.3 Investigating the health of black and minority ethnic groups

The colonial legacy

Fear of 'foreign' diseases and, by implication, of alien peoples can be traced back to Britain's imperial past. The main concern of health professionals in colonial territories was to secure the health of white soldiers and settlers, and medical research into exotic diseases such as malaria and leprosy had the intention of providing effective protection for whites. This was a major factor behind the establishment, in 1899, of the London and Liverpool Schools of Tropical Medicine. Whereas sanitary science was widely practised in white settlement quarters of colonial towns, the native populations were characterised as 'insanitary' and beyond the reach of civilised standards, and little public health intervention took place. Control of epidemics was directed towards safeguarding settlers, not natives (Doyal, 1979).

These attitudes influenced health sector responses to post-war immigration. The designation of immigrants from India, South East Asia and Africa as a 'danger' to the health of the native UK population was accompanied by specific concerns about the import of 'exotic' diseases. Tuberculosis, leprosy, hepatitis and rickets, among other diseases, were not only characterised as presenting grave risks to whites but also as constituting a special 'immigrant health problem' (Donovan, 1986). Some health authorities routinely vaccinate all babies born to mothers of Asian origin against tuberculosis and screen specific groups for hepatitis B virus; 'others screen Asian women for hookworm, but do not ask white women whether they have had holidays abroad in places known to have a higher incidence of gastro-intestinal parasites' (Pearson, 1986). This emphasis on the significance of ethnic differences, although it has highlighted points of concern, has also served to pathologise black people and to disguise the extent to which their patterns of ill health reflect those of people in other similar economic circumstances.

The cultural focus and its critics

In the 1980s several special initiatives were aimed at black and minority ethnic groups. The Rickets Campaign, for example, was launched in 1981 to tackle the growing incidence of rickets among British Asians. A major thrust of the campaign was that rickets was an 'Asian problem' and that changes in individual lifestyle, such as eating habits and dress, were appropriate ways of tackling the disease (which is caused by vitamin D deficiency). Suggestions for modifying Asian diets and for exposing the skin to sunlight were made (DHSS, 1980). Critics attacked the double standards involved: changes in sensitive cultural practices were being required from British Asians, whereas protection for the white population came from a government decision in the 1940s to add vitamin D to margarine. Moreover, there was the hidden assumption that rickets was caused by individual lifestyle rather than being a disease of poverty – as it had been originally characterised when it was widespread in poorer, inner-city districts in the early twentieth century (Brent CHC, 1981).

This was followed in 1984 by the Asian Mother and Baby Campaign directed at encouraging earlier take-up and wider use of antenatal services and screening. A central assumption of this campaign was that more antenatal care in general would influence pregnancy outcomes, but this has been questioned. While the emphasis on Asian mothers' health was welcomed, some critics argued that the campaign came close to victim-blaming. The clear message of the campaign was that individual mothers were being irresponsible in not seeking early medical care in pregnancy. Yet research findings indicated that the campaign was underpinned by a stereotyped view of British Asian women and ignored institutional barriers to take-up:

The Asian Mother and Baby Campaign cited Asian mothers as attending antenatal clinics only late on in pregnancy. There seemed no attempt to counter the stereotypes that judged this was because Asian women were submissive, unreliable and not able to cope with situations in which they had to speak English . . . We found that the major reason for the non-attendance . . . was due to up to a four month backlog in notifying pregnant women of their antenatal appointments.

Lone, quoted in Phoenix (1990)

⟩ Suggest arguments for and against organising special campaigns of this kind directed towards black and ethnic minority groups.

These and other initiatives have been defended on the grounds that they raise awareness of health issues and offer extra services to groups with special needs (Veena Bahl, 1985). On the other hand such campaigns have been attacked as racist because, in focusing exclusively on modifying cultural practices in black and minority ethnic groups, they both imply that such culture is deficient and also ignore wider structural deficiences and barriers, including racism: 'Medical ideologies which blame individuals and their cultures for their ill health reinforce racist ideologies which view minority lifestyles as pathogenic and deviant' (Pearson, 1986). One way of overcoming such criticisms is to give members of black and minority ethnic groups themselves a much greater say in the organisation and development of such campaigns. This would involve fewer high profile national campaigns and much more action at a local level (see Section 8.5).

Health counts

An investigation of the health status of black and minority ethnic groups highlights the difficulties involved in ascribing health differences categorically to either 'culture' or to structural and material influences, such as income, occupation and racism. The 1980 Black Report commented on the pattern of economic and social disadvantage experienced by black people, but noted that the invisibility of race in official statistics made any assessment of the impact of this very difficult (Townsend and Davidson, 1982). Little was known about the health of black British born children. On the other hand, since black workers were clustered in low status and less skilled jobs, they and their families were more likely to suffer the cumulative effects of poor housing, unemployment and poverty.

Whitehead's (1987) survey of health and ethnic origin indicated that this was still generally the case, although studies since 1980 had highlighted patterns of morbidity and mortality for adults born abroad. The Immigrant Mortality Study focused on people over 20 born outside England and Wales, thus including British subjects born abroad but excluding British born minorities (Marmot et al., 1984). It found that all immigrant groups had higher mortality than the average (although, except for Ireland, mortality rates were lower than for their country of origin). For particular diseases, such as liver cancer, ischaemic heart disease, strokes and maternal conditions mortality was significantly higher (see Table 8.4). But in general mortality rates for black and minority ethnic groups reflected their concentration in lower social classes and in semi-skilled and unskilled occupations, making them vulnerable to the health disadvantages associated with low income, poor housing and poorer health care facilities and access. Racial and class disadvantage reinforced each other. In terms of morbidity the tradition of investigating exotic diseases had distracted attention from the similarities between black health problems and those found in predominantly white communities: for example, lay concerns about

TABLE 8.4 Summary of main findings of Immigrant Mortality Study (England and Wales, 1970–78). Source: Whitehead (1987)

Mortality by cause	Comparison with death rates for England and Wales
Tuberculosis	*High* in immigrants from the Indian sub-continent, Ireland, the Caribbean, Africa and Scotland
Liver cancer	*High* in immigrants from the Indian sub-continent, the Caribbean and Africa
Cancer of stomach, large intestine, breast	*Low* mortality among Indians
Ischaemic heart disease	*High* mortality found in immigrants from the Indian sub-continent
Hypertension and stroke	*Strikingly high* mortality among immigrants from the Caribbean and Africa – four to six times higher for hypertension and twice as high for strokes as the level in England and Wales
Diabetes	*High* among immigrants born in the Caribbean and the Indian sub-continent
Obstructive lung disease (including chronic bronchitis)	*Low* in all immigrants in comparison with ratio for England and Wales
Maternal mortality	*High* in immigrants from Africa, the Caribbean, and to a lesser extent the Indian sub-continent
Violence and accidents	*High* in all immigrant groups

asthma, back pain, family planning and nutrition. The responses of black and minority ethnic groups themselves indicate that their main health concerns are similar to those of the rest of the population. Only seven of the 3679 calls to a counselling service from British Asians living in London were about rickets, for example, compared with 479 about respiratory and 282 about mental problems – of major importance to white British people as well (see Table 8.5).

One area of medical concern has been infant mortality. A number of studies in the 1980s attempted to explain the much higher rates of infant mortality for babies of mothers born in Pakistan and in the Caribbean (Terry *et al.*, 1980; Gillies *et al.*, 1984). Within this generally high rate there were many differences: for example, stillbirths and perinatal rates

TABLE 8.5 Asian callers' reasons for phoning the counselling service. Source: Webb (1981)

Reason given	No. of questions	Percentage of total
Asthma, hay fever, breathlessness	479	13
Family planning, fertility, infertility, psychosexual problems	408	11
Diabetes	391	11
General nutrition and slimming (not rickets)	288	8
All mental health problems (ranging from mild depression to those receiving hospital treatment)	282	8
Homeopathic treatments/herbal treatments	271	7
Skin complaints	252	7
Back pain	138	4
Child care	100	3
Eye complaints	87	2
Specific gynaecological problems	83	2
Arthritis	82	2
Queries concerning pregnancy	80	2
Mild gastric problems	79	2
Second opinions	79	2
Minor ailments	67	2
Headaches	59	2
Others	323	12
Total	3679	100

were higher for babies born to Bangladeshi, Indian, Pakistani and (to a lesser degree) Caribbean mothers, whereas neonatal rates followed a different pattern (see Figure 8.2). The result of these studies was to identify a number of medical 'risk factors', such as low maternal weight, lower social class, shorter pregnancy intervals, previous perinatal deaths, poor antenatal attendance, anaemia, late childbearing, high number of low birth weight babies, consanguinity and high parity of Asian born mothers (Whitehead, 1987). It was from such identified risk factors that the Asian Mother and Baby Campaign developed, focusing on factors most easily amenable to behavioural change – such as improving clinic attendance and giving advice on pregnancy intervals. Other issues related to social class or poverty, such as those indicated by high rates of anaemia and low maternal weight, were less easy to respond to and were largely ignored.

The case of infant mortality highlights why there has been a

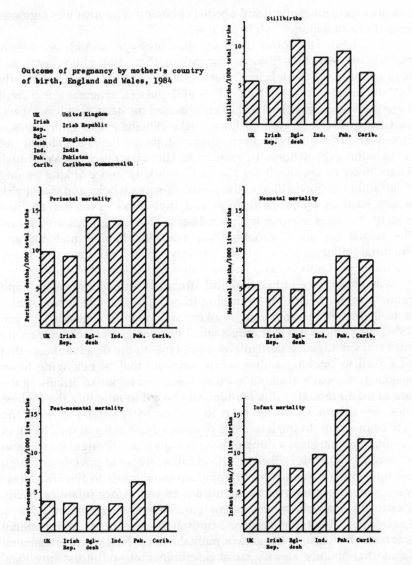

Outcome of pregnancy by mother's country
of birth, England and Wales, 1984

UK	United Kingdom
Irish Rep.	Irish Republic
Bgl-desh	Bangladesh
Ind.	India
Pak.	Pakistan
Carib.	Caribbean Commonwealth

FIGURE 8.2 Outcome of pregnancy by mother's country of birth: evidence in the 1980s. Source: Whitehead (1987)

tendency to focus on cultural and behavioural changes and why this has been viewed as racist. The research identified medical risk factors which differed from those in the British born population; the next stage was to improve health chances by modifying those patterns of behaviour which seemed to 'cause' the health risk. Yet by focusing on a few selected factors it was being signalled that particular customs and cultural practices were inadequate and needed changing. The clear message was to conform to superior 'white' culture.

In relation to some diseases this message would be deeply problematic. In the Rickets Campaign the implication was that vegetarianism was a 'deficient' diet (because vitamin D is found in fatty fish and meat but not in vegetables and pulses), whereas concurrent dietary advice from official bodies emphasised the need to reduce fat and increase fresh vegetable and fibre intake (Sheiham and Quick, 1982). Moreover, other disease patterns demonstrate the limits of cultural and behavioural explanations. In relation to coronary heart disease British Asian lifestyles are 'healthier': rates of smoking and drinking among Asian adults are lower than in the population as a whole, and classic risk factors such as blood cholesterol and high blood pressure are less evident. Yet rates of coronary heart disease in Asian groups are higher. The search for an explanation has now highlighted material and structural influences on health: poverty, poor working conditions, unemployment and stress (Coronary Prevention Group, 1986).

The importance of material and structural influences on black and minority ethnic health are beginning to be highlighted in other studies as well. In her research into smoking and women's health Graham (1990) has pointed out that only a small percentage of black women are smokers, yet 'they are particularly vulnerable to the disadvantages that are linked to smoking among white women': that is, belonging to an unskilled, manual household in a disadvantaged region of Britain. In the case of infant mortality it is perhaps significant to note that the highest rates are still among babies born to women of Pakistani, African and Caribbean origin. In the late 1980s perinatal death rates in the Pakistani community were almost double those in babies of UK origin (Smith and Jacobson, 1988). This is likely to reflect the widespread poverty and high unemployment experienced by Pakistani immigrants to the UK. However, cultural factors may be significant as well, since infant mortality rates for Bangladeshi babies are comparatively low (see Figure 8.3).

Debates about the relative importance of cultural and material factors can be found in the area of mental health. First, there are general claims that 'culture shock', racial discrimination and stress 'produce' more mental disorder among migrant groups (Rack, 1979). In general black people's use of pyschiatric services is lower than in the UK population. At a more specific level British Asian suicide rates and admission rates to psychiatric hospitals are lower than those for whites and for other ethnic minority groups. Rates of affective and depressive illnesses are lower than for the rest of the population among those of West Indian origin, but the schizophrenia rate is much higher (Donovan, 1986). It is a matter of fierce debate how far these are 'real' rates and how far they represent the labelling of some cultures as deficient. For

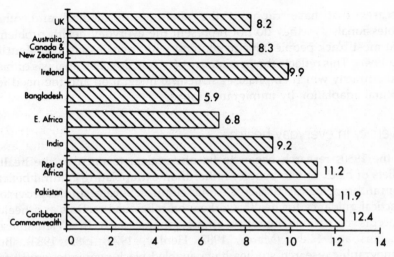

FIGURE 8.3 Infant mortality and mother's country of birth: evidence in the 1990s. Source: Graham (1993) adapted from OPCS (1990)

example, the far greater tendency to diagnose West Indian patients as schizophrenic may be a result of the ethnocentrism or racism of Western trained medical doctors. In a series of studies Littlewood and Lipsedge (1980, 1988) have argued that an episode of schizophrenia or paranoia in a black person may be a defensive reaction to experiences of discrimination and institutional racism in British society. But Fernando (1991) has argued that the export of Western medicine has resulted in the generalisation of Western psychiatric concepts as the only 'objective' and 'scientific' truth instead of being merely one among several culturally specific belief systems. Far from accepting that an international classification of conditions such as schizophrenia can be produced, Fernando calls for an end to the globalisation of Western diagnostic categories and the ethnocentrism and racism which sustain them.

It seems probable that both cultural and material influences on black people's health are important, but the pursuit of 'racial inexplicitness' in relation to the collection of health statistics has made epidemiological research much more difficult. Donovan (1984) reports on the massive racial imbalance in mortality in the USA, where adult death rates from tuberculosis, hypertension and kidney disease in ethnic minority groups were far higher, and infant mortality was nearly twice as high among the black population. These statistics are routinely gathered in the USA, but in the UK the evidence about black people's health is still poorly documented. Donovan's conclusion in 1984 that 'the study of ethnicity and health . . . revolves principally around a few major illnesses and diseases that have captured the attention of medical and other professionals . . . they do not represent the everyday health problems that most black people have to contend with' remains fair comment in the 1990s. This reflects the persistence of a 'functionalist' analysis of race and ethnicity which emphasises structural integration and the need for cultural adaptation by immigrant groups.

Diversity in everyday health

In the 1980s research began to be undertaken to uncover the health beliefs of black British people, rather than extrapolating cultural beliefs from anthropological studies of 'exotic' cultures. Several studies provided practical guidance for health workers on religious practices and health concepts of various minority ethnic groups, such the Vietnamese, Muslims and Sikhs (Mares, 1982; Henley, 1979; 1982; 1983). But ethnographic research studies have enabled black people to 'speak for themselves' about their beliefs and experiences. Donovan (1986) interviewed small groups of Afro-Caribbean and Asian lay people in London and recorded their perceptions of health and illness. Many of their comments demonstrate that they value health as normal functioning and the ability to cope with daily life; illness was seen as a state in which 'you can't carry on to do your work', whereas diseases were what 'you can really die of'. The British Asian women in the sample commented that perfect health was more difficult to attain in Britain because of environmental and social pressures and because of the absence of family and social support. The Asian languages spoken by Donovan's informants had no word for illness as such, but its complexity was appreciated. The causes of ill health were also seen as complex: fate, personal responsibility, 'worries', germs and viruses, heredity and environmental factors were all mentioned.

Other studies of black and minority ethnic groups have indicated that fate – and in particular 'God's will' – are of central importance (for example Currer, 1986). In a secondary analysis of data from the Health and Lifestyle Survey, Howlett et al. (1991) reported that minority ethnic respondents cited improvements in health care and living standards as less important than did white respondents. Much higher numbers of Asian and Afro-Caribbean people reported health as 'a matter of luck' and as having 'a divine purpose' than did matched groups of white people. They suggest that these 'fatalistic' attitudes, which are shared by young and older, better and less well educated black men and women, may be expressive of the impact of racial oppression and a sense of powerlessness.

8.4 Black and ethnic minorities and health services

Concerns about discrimination and institutional racism in health services became more widespread in the early 1980s, as the critique of the 'cultural' approach to black health gathered force. Several reports documented the poor standard of service given to minority ethnic groups in the health service and the lack of response to their perceived health needs (Pearson, 1986; Mares *et al.*, 1985). In addition, black and minority ethnic workers in the health service have reported prejudice and discrimination and the more complex workings of institutional racism. This section will explore the problem of racism in health care, and the section that follows will pay particular attention to health sector initiatives which move toward equal opportunities policies and better practice.

Race and health service patients

The National Health Service was established to provide a comprehensive range of health services to the whole population on the basis of individual need. Everybody had the right to equal treatment, which was paid for out of general taxation and insurance contributions and was free at the point of use. These principles have, perhaps inevitably, created tensions; providing the same service to those who have different needs means that some individuals and groups will be disadvantaged. In relations between black and minority ethnic patients and white staff different cultural and religious practices and language barriers may create misunderstandings and problems which result in ethnocentric and even racist service provision. If staff (whatever their cultural background) make asumptions based on their own cultural norms and values, without taking into account that their patients may not share these values, it will be difficult to deliver good health care. A 'colour-blind' or 'culture-blind' health service, suggest Mares *et al.* (1985), 'is likely to be less effective, and may even prove negligent of the health care needs of minority ethnic patients' (see Box 8.2).

Look at Box 8.2 which is a case study of Mr and Mrs A drawn from Mares *et al.* (1985). In what ways is the health care practice reported here ethnocentric or racist?

There are many points of interest in this case: the culture-bound assumptions made by hospital staff, their (seeming) lack of awareness of the home circumstances or the mother's depressed state, their failure to make earlier use of support staff, such as the interpreter or the social

BOX 8.2 Case study: Mr and Mrs A. Source: Mares *et al.* (1985)

Mr and Mrs A were a Bangladeshi couple living in London. They had two small children and all four of them lived in one cramped room in a Victorian tenement building. They shared washing and lavatory facilities with two other families on the same floor. They did not know any other Bangladeshi families in the area. Mr A worked from early morning till late at night in an Indian restaurant. He spoke little English; Mrs A spoke none. She was very shy and rather nervous and hardly ever went out of their room. She had periods of depression.

Mrs A gave birth to her third child, a boy, in a London teaching hospital. The child was small and weak, and it was thought that he was probably developmentally delayed and possibly deaf. Mrs A became severely depressed after the child's birth and seemed to hospital staff to find it difficult to cope. It was decided that she should go home to her other children and leave the baby in hospital for the time being.

The baby was very lovable and the nurses were extremely fond of him. They gave him as much attention as they could, though they were pressed for time. Mr A came to visit him as often as he was able in his hours off from the restaurant, but Mrs A did not visit him at all. Mr A was keen to take the baby home once he was strong enough, but the hospital staff felt that this was not a good idea; the baby needed all the stimulation he could get and in their view Mrs A was clearly not interested in her child since she never visited him.

The staff at the hospital were not sure that Mr A knew that his son was in any way handicapped. Whenever they tried to explain he said the baby was all right, he was a lovely baby and so on. Whenever Mr A mentioned taking the baby home the hospital staff dissuaded him, saying that the child needed good care and lots of stimulation and play, and was better off in hospital.

By the time her little boy was nine months old Mrs A had only been to see him twice. Each time she had seemed very distressed. The hospital staff loved the baby, and felt very protective towards him. Mr A then came in and said he wanted to take the baby home. He was going to take him back to Bangladesh and leave him there. The hospital staff were appalled at this apparent total rejection and at the prospects the child would face back in Bangladesh with little or no medical care and no chance of speech therapy or other remedial work. They began to apply for a court order to take the child into care.

At this stage the hospital brought in an interpreter to discuss the position with Mr A and to make sure that he understood about the court order and what it would mean. The interpreter explained that because the boy was slightly mentally retarded and deaf he would need the best medical and social care and that this was what the authorities wanted to provide. If the parents didn't feel they could look after him it was in the boy's own interests that he should be taken into care in England.

During the discussion that followed the father said that he knew very well that his son was both mentally retarded and deaf.

He felt that such a child needed as much love and attention as possible. He didn't see, although the nurses were extremely kind and very hardworking, how they could give his son enough attention or stimulus. In fact he usually found him sitting silent and alone in the corner of his cot when he came to visit him and he felt that this was not right.

He knew that life was very difficult for his wife alone with the other two children for most of every day in a small room and he realised that she was probably too depressed and unhappy to cope properly with their third child. The one thing their baby really needed more than anything was love and lots of companionship and playmates. He felt that the baby could get those better than anywhere else at home with his family in Bangladesh. His family were farmers, they lived in a small village, there were lots of other children and adults to look after him and love him. It was warm and sunny, there was lots of space, and children like his son were always loved and protected and looked after. He didn't understand why the hospital wanted to keep his son. He felt that they were trying to be kind but that in fact what they were doing was harming him.

The hospital staff decided not to make any immediate decisions but discuss the whole matter further with Social Services and with Mr A.

worker. The staff judge the situation on face value, reading it off from their own cultural norms and values: 'normal' mothers should love their babies; the baby is better off in hospital with qualified staff than under-stimulated in an Asian family; sending the baby to Bangladesh implied total rejection and consigning it to a 'primitive' existence without specialist health professionals. Clearly the hospital staff think they are acting for the best, yet their views are ethnocentric, and their behaviour is racist; applying to take the child into care implies that they have judged the father to be ignorant and incapable, and that they think a Western 'medical' solution is superior. More than this, the staff are sure of their ability to cope and provide good care, even though they cannot communicate effectively; Mrs A speaks no English, and they are not sure that Mr A understands that his child is handicapped.

The insidious dimension of racism – based on 'treating everyone the same' and a failure to recognise cultural diversity and respond sensitively to different needs – is bound up with wider institutional rules and practices. Health work is organised on a mono-cultural basis, reflecting white, largely middle class priorities. There is a general assumption that patients can understand English, that they can communicate their needs and feelings, that they will follow instructions, that they will submit to physical examination by professional staff (including mainly male doctors) and so on. Cultural practices in hospitals reflect those of the dominant white population: in washing and toileting routines, in attitudes to privacy, in mode of address, in staff expectations about reactions to pain, loss and injury, in attitudes towards professional staff, in the (mainly) English food and English mealtimes. Routine institutional practices, which seem unproblematic to staff, may result in discrimination against black patients:

In one of the antenatal clinics where I work they call out the women's names from the files and if the women don't come forward after the second call, they put the file right back to the bottom of the pile. And quite often the way they pronounce the [Asian] names is completely unrecognisable, and so the women don't go forward and they may wait hours and hours never realising that their names have been called.

clinic worker, quoted in Mares et al. (1985)

In primary health care there is some evidence to suggest that going to see the doctor is 'a last resort' for Afro-Caribbean people in Britain, and that reliance on home remedies is fairly widespread (Donovan, 1984; Thorogood, 1990). Criticism of GPs in the Afro-Caribbean and British Asian groups studied by Donovan focused on concerns about examining and prescribing, in particular the perceived failure of the doctor to get to the root of the problem: 'They could spend more time with the patient, break down the problem, diagnose it better . . . You're in and out before you've had a chance to tell him what's wrong'.

In contrast to reports about hospital services, there was little evidence that racial prejudice or discrimination was a feature of such consultations. Respondents' comments echoed those of white patients: about being rushed through the consultation, about the doctor not listening or only giving pills. Perhaps this is because members of black and minority ethnic groups, like their white counterparts, could exercise some choice over whom to consult. Several of the British Asian women had changed their doctor more than once, and most now attended an Asian general practitioner, because 'he can speak our language, so he can understand our problem'. Most Afro-Caribbean respondents had at some time paid for a private medical consultation.

One of the areas where charges of racism have most frequently been made is family planning. Mares *et al.* (1985) report several accounts of discriminatory treatment of British Asian women. In particular, Asian family size has been viewed by some health workers as problematic, and advice and encouragement have been given to take up family planning aids: the coil, depo-provera and sterilisation:

Because I'm Asian too the other nurses get at me. When an Asian women comes in to have her fifth or sixth baby they are so rude to her, especially if she doesn't speak English. They say terrible things right to her face, like, 'I'd do something to your husband if I could' or 'This one should be sterilised' . . . They say [to me], 'She's one of yours, tell her it's revolting to have so many children. Somebody should do something to her husband'.

Mares et al. (1985)

Medical decisions to prescribe depo-provera have been hotly contested. Critics have condemned its use among ethnic minority women and pointed out that it stereotypes them as ignorant and incapable of remembering to take a daily pill. Moreover, it has too often been prescribed without real consultation with the woman involved (Savage, 1986). Brent Community Health Council (1981) reported that half the prescriptions in its health area were for black women. On the other hand, male cultural norms may make it the only practical form of birth control for Asian women who wish to limit their family size (Stacey, 1988).

In 1988 a report by the working party established by the National Association of Health Authorities (NAHA, now NAHAT) commented on the extent of direct and indirect racial discrimination in the NHS. It highlighted 'inconsistent standards of care', 'lack of integral planning' for the needs of minority groups and the 'limited NHS response to health issues which particularly affect black and minority ethnic groups'. In particular, it drew attention to barriers to equality of access deriving from health service staff's ignorance about cultural differences and the lack of information and support for black and ethnic minority patients. It questioned the existing models and theories operating in mental health services, giving an example of 'a devout Muslim patient, aged 69 [who] was diagnosed by a community psychiatric nurse as having a severe mental disorder. The patient wished to continue his religious practices including praying five times a day, facing towards Mecca, whilst kneeling on a prayer mat. This was interpreted as abnormal behaviour'.

The report also commented on particular areas of deficiency in NHS services, for example the absence of accurate data on genetic conditions such as sickle cell anaemia and thalassaemia major and the lack of genetic counselling, screening and treatment. Increased awareness of these conditions is mainly due to the work of the Sickle Cell Society, a self help group formed by black people themselves in the early 1980s to spread knowledge of the condition and provide support (Prashar et al., 1985). In spite of the fact that the molecular sickle cell anaemia was known in 1956, that it mainly affects those of African, Asian, East Mediterranean and Middle Eastern origin, and that a fairly simple blood test could detect those at risk, it was seen by GPs, paediatricians and obstetricians as of little significance (Anionwu, 1993). Very few black families were referred to the genetic counselling services, and the individual experiences documented by the Sickle Cell Society have been very distressing (see Box 8.3).

In relation to black older people stereotypical views of their culture and health needs are widespread (Fennell et al., 1988). It is assumed that black elders live in extended families and that care and support is readily forthcoming. A study of community services' work in Birmingham revealed that, although health workers thought they knew what services were needed, there was a considerable mismatch between their

BOX 8.3 Case study: sickle-cell anaemia. Source: Anionwu (1993)

The following is an extract of a taped interview in 1981 with a mother of an affected child when she visited the Brent Sickle Cell Counselling Centre, the only such service in existence in Britain at this time.

'It started just over a year ago, when Julie was about two years of age. She had a temperature and I took her to the doctor. He said, "It's natural for a child of her age to have a temperature." But I insisted that she should have a blood or urine test. So he sent me down (for the blood test) and he diagnosed sickle-cell anaemia. He said, "It's sickle cell, which the majority of coloured people, black people have; and there is no cure." He just told me that. He said, "They can't do anything about it, but if she gets any funny symptoms I should try giving her Junior Disprin or aspirin and try to keep her warm; and that's about it." But she keeps on going in (to hospital) very often, with swollen legs and hands and pain in her tummy, which I couldn't understand, which they didn't really explain.

Sickle-cell anaemia can cause great pains and it's all different ways. She's off her food, she has pains in her joints and she gets urine infection pretty regular, or sometimes she passes blood with her urine. These are her symptoms. When she is getting the attack she goes very quiet, doesn't play with her sister; she just lies and wants to go to sleep and sometimes she wants water. Just water all the time. She doesn't want to eat or anything. Then the temperature begins and I know she's going funny.

(Before that) I had never heard anything about sickle-cell anaemia. It was only after the diagnosis that I was reading in the West Indian World paper about your Sickle Cell Centre in London. So my sister here in London advised me to come and get more advice about it and I put it off. I said, I can't do anything because here is Dr G telling me one thing and different people tell me another. Finally they persuaded me: if I didn't come to London my child would probably die on me and I would probably be blamed by the Welfare for not taking care of her. They should explain better how you can deal with it and where you can get advice. The doctor says there is nothing to worry about, but you do worry. You could scream. You could feel like hitting them over the head, if you know what I mean, but when you have the child 24 hours and they "Oh, Mummy, I'm this and that," it really gets you down.

I have had to come 60 miles to hear more about it (from the Sickle Cell Centre), which I don't think is right. I think it should be the GP that you turn to really.

No I'm going to go and see my doctor and have a word with him. I know you don't really think about these things until your child is ill but it's really terrible. You say "It couldn't be me because I'm never ill" and my husband says it couldn't be him: and we're blaming each other, but there is none of us to blame really, it's just traits; we can't help it'.

perceptions and the expressed needs of black older people (Cameron *et al.*, 1989). One district nurse commented that 'Asian families tend to look after their own. They tend to live as extended families in a single household, and they respect their elderly people far more than we do. They don't usually need us'. In fact the study confirmed other research suggesting that low take-up of services was in part due to a widespread lack of knowledge that domiciliary health and social services existed. In a study in Coventry researchers found that 80 per cent of Asian older people had not heard of services, apart from day centres (Holland *et al.*, 1987). Black older people were not being asked about their needs for community support, so those needs remained hidden from view.

Racism and health sector workers

The NAHA Report did not just draw attention to deficiencies in services, but also to the lack of equal opportunities for members of black and minority ethnic groups in NHS employment. It commented that to point to mere numbers employed by the NHS was to avoid the issue; black workers were clustered 'in low status jobs and low grades, on the least popular shifts and in less favoured specialties. They are rarely represented in management positions'.

This cannot be understood in isolation but must be related to the history of migration to the UK that we noted earlier in Section 8.2. Doyal notes that British immigration policies, though designed to restrict the entry of black migrants, specifically encouraged the entry of qualified overseas doctors and nurses under the 1962 voucher scheme to work in the least popular sectors of the health service (Doyal, 1981; 1985). In 1972, 9 per cent of all NHS nurses came from overseas, but they formed 20 per cent of the total number of SENs working in the NHS. This represents an army of low paid and exploited workers who helped, over the years, to keep down labour costs in the health sector:

Over the past thirty years the NHS has got – and is getting still – a huge captive, low-waged Black women's labour force . . . For many Black women who joined the NHS with the intention of becoming nurses, this was to remain an elusive goal. Relegated to the hospitals' kitchens and laundries, or trudging the wards as tea-ladies, cleaners and orderlies, we were to have first-hand experience of the damning assumptions which define our role here. The patients saw it as fitting that we should be doing Britain's dirty work and often treated us with contempt.

Bryan et al., *1985*

A small-scale study in the early 1980s revealed that Afro-Caribbean nurses were less likely than either Irish or 'English' nurses to have reached ward sister, nursing officer or senior nursing officer grade (Doyal *et al.*, 1985).

In addition, black and minority ethnic women who had passed the General Nursing Council examination for entry to nurse training found themselves enrolled on State Enrolled Nurse training courses rather than on courses for State Registered Nurses. Unfamiliarity with the system in Britain resulted in many who were qualified for SRN training losing out in career prospects and the opportunity to return home, since the SEN was not recognised in most countries outside Britain:

On the plane over, I got chatting to a woman who I found out was a nurse over here. I told her about the hospital I was going to, and she asked me whether I was going to be a pupil nurse or a student nurse. Well, I hadn't registered any difference at the time. Then she explained that SEN pupils were lower than SRN students and that Trinidad didn't even recognise the SEN qualification. She told me I could change when I got here, since I'd passed the General Nursing Council exam at home. I wasn't worried then, but she did drum it in that I should tell them I wanted to change as soon as I got here . . .

The next day, before I could see the matron, I had to be fitted for a uniform. Of course, the lady in the sewing room started measuring me up for an SEN uniform. She handed me this old, patched up uniform, and I thought, 'Have I come from Trinidad for this?' I told her no, I would be getting the starched, green uniform and she said, 'But all the coloured girls are pupils'. That really got me going. I went to see Matron and demanded to change. They were taken aback, but there was nothing they could do about it because I'd passed the test. I didn't realise then that they thought that if you were Black, you were stupid. You learn quickly though.

Bryan et al. *(1985)*

Such discrimination and institutional racism is by no means confined to the past, and the increasingly high entry qualifications demanded by nursing colleges, together with the widespread under-attainment of Afro-Caribbean pupils at school, are in some ways making matters worse. The Swann Report (1985) on the British education system indicated that Afro-Caribbean children are systematically under-achieving at school, and critics have argued that racial stereotyping and racism have played some part in this process (Chavannes, 1989). This means that young Afro-Caribbean school leavers will have less access to RGN/Diploma and degree studies in nursing. It may well be that the NHS today is in danger of creating a divided workforce of high status registered general nurses and low status health care assistants which compounds the SEN/SRN division of the past.

In addition, there are the difficulties faced by nurses currently working in the health service. These include cultural concerns, such as dress, religious practices, dietary taboos and inevitable misunderstandings between nurses from different cultural backgrounds thrown together in nurse training (Mares *et al.*, 1985). Several cases involving recruitment or employment in the health service have been referred to the Commission for Racial Equality (CRE). They include discrimination on racial grounds: for example, the rejection for overtly racist reasons of Yim Chong, a RMN British trained staff nurse who had lived in the UK for 12 years by Sister Dora School of Nursing in the West Midlands. This case was referred to the CRE, and Walsall Health Authority admitted discrimination and paid compensation (CRE Employment Report, 1983).

Another aspect of institutional racism is the under-valuing or marginalisation of black and ethnic minority staff. Black nurses working on a hospital ward can come to be viewed as the 'ethnic specialist' because of their colour, pulled from their work to act as translator or provide support to black and minority ethnic patients. Health workers providing specialist services to black clients in community settings can become viewed as 'a second-class health worker providing a service to a second-class community . . . or else you find that every problem relating to patients from that community is automatically referred to you, whether it's necessary or not' (Mares *et al.*, 1985).

8.5 Equal opportunity and anti-racist strategies in the health sector

The legislative basis for equal opportunities is somewhat ambiguous. Under the 1966 Local Government Act, Section 11, money has to be made available to local authorities to provide educational support services; as we noted earlier, the funding was aimed at the 'special needs' – mainly linguistic – of migrants and in doing so conceptualised them as culturally problematic. But in 1993 Section 11 funding was drastically cut back. In 1976 the Race Relations Act, in particular Sections 20, 35–38 and 71 outlawed direct and indirect racial discrimination and allowed for promotion of equal opportunities programmes. 'Positive Action', as the Act defined this, enabled health authorities to encourage members 'of particular racial groups' to seek employment and offer them access to training to enable them to take up particular posts, and enabled them to meet special welfare needs. Health authorities as employers or providers have used this legislation to provide backing for special services in a fairly restricted way. Much of the emphasis has been on black groups pressuring for funding rather than health authorities initiating change. However, Section 20 of the Act has enabled some health workers who have suffered direct discrimination or institutional racism to seek legal redress.

What responses have there been to the data documenting inadequacies in service delivery and prejudice and discrimination in the health sector? As we noted earlier, the Department of Health (formerly the DHSS) launched several initiatives in the 1980s: the Rickets Campaign, the Asian Mother and Baby Campaign, and funds to support several innovative projects. Out of these has emerged a working group on Asian health care and an Ethnic Minority Health Advisor at the centre, and link-worker schemes in several health authorities.

The reports from the National Extension College in the early 1980s (some with the collaboration of the Health Education Council) not only documented deficiencies and problems in health services but also highlighted existing good practice and offered detailed guidelines and support for generalising this across the NHS (for example, *Providing Effective Health Care in a Multi Racial Society*, 1984). In a study of maternity care inappropriate services were listed, including failure in shared care, overlong waiting times, use of male doctors,inappropriate diets, insensitivity over cultural rites (Pearson, 1985). But in addition a range of initiatives was discussed: the use of outreach and link workers, the benefits of continuity of care, organising services so that female staff could examine Asian women patients, providing better information for patients and staff and improving staff recruitment and training (see Box 8.4). In a similar way, McNaught's (1987) study, while documenting evidence of neglect and discrimination, emphasises the positive steps that can be taken to improve access to and uptake of health services.

Indeed it has been a feature of research into black and ethnic minority health needs that improvements and initiatives, as well as deficiencies, have been highlighted. Some of this work has been done by

BOX 8.4 Recommendations for improving staff recruitment and training in maternity care. Source: Pearson (1985)

STAFF RECRUITMENT AND TRAINING
There should be positive action to promote recruitment of black and ethnic minority staff at all levels.
The employment of outreach workers from the local communities with strong community and professional support to mediate between the service and the local population whilst also acting as advocates for patients would:
☐ Improve access to services.
☐ Promote continuity of shared care.

Sufficient fully trained interpreters should be employed by the health authority:
☐ All staff should be trained in how and when to use them.
☐ They should be trained to cope with particularly difficult situations such as still or malformed births.

There should be enough female doctors or midwives able to undertake physical examinations.
All staff should receive training in:
☐ Racism awareness and communication skills.
☐ The use of English as a Second Language.
☐ Different naming systems.
☐ Religious and cultural practices and beliefs surrounding childbirth.
☐ The importance of asking patients their preferences.

Staff responsible for history taking should be trained in:
☐ Interviewing skills and the importance of taking time.
☐ The importance of explaining the purpose of questions and procedures such as tests of blood or urine samples.

'professional' researchers, but a great deal of it has been the result of self help by black people themselves. One long-standing project, the Brent Sickle Cell Counselling Centre, developed information and support services for affected families with little encouragement and no financial assistance from the NHS. As a result of constant pressure for specialist services, and the impact made by black parents and sufferers questioning professional advice and demonstrating their knowledge of sickle cell (which was sometimes considerably greater than that of health professionals), by the early 1990s there were 20 health authorities with haemoglobionopathy counselling services (Anionwu, 1989; Baxter, 1992).

There are many other initiatives among black and minority ethnic groups, ranging from voluntary services organised by black community and church groups to city-wide initiatives to involve black people in pressuring for improved services (Baxter, 1992). In the Brent Black Mental Health Befriending Scheme, for example, volunteers befriend black patients diagnosed as being mentally ill, supporting them in hospital or in the community. In other projects – such as the long-standing Black Health Workers and Patients Group in London – black health workers and users work together to monitor racism, support black workers and patients and press for improvement to services.

In 1986 a task force was set up jointly by the Department of Health and the King's Fund to help health authorities to implement equal opportunities policies, and in the following year the King's Fund produced a 'model policy' for health sector employment (King's Fund Equal Opportunities Task Force, 1987). The then DHSS also issued advice to health authorities concerning equal opportunities in employment, stating that:

Authorities should do more than seek to secure bare compliance with the provisions of race relations legislation. Employment policies and practices should include effective positive procedures to ensure equality of opportunity for members of minority groups. This can best be achieved by developing a policy which is clearly stated, known to all employees, has and is seen to have the backing of senior management, is effectively supervised, provides a periodic feedback of information to senior management, and is seen to work in practice.

DHSS (1986b)

The 1988 NAHA Working Party reported that there was great diversity in policy, with some health authorities producing comprehensive equal opportunities policies with systematic monitoring, but that overall progress was slow. It recommended several changes and initiatives: at the Department of Health, in the health education authorities (HEAs), in regional and district health authorities (RHAs and DHAs) and family practitioner committees (FPCs, now FHSAs), in community health councils (CHCs) and in the voluntary sector. In general, the NAHA Report regarded planning and systematic monitoring as crucial and called on the Department of Health to set up a central resource unit to provide advice, consultation and support, including a database on ethnic minorities. It also called on the HEAs to set up databanks of health education information. It proposed that all regional health authorities should establish working parties to consider the health needs of black and minority ethnic groups, ensure wider representation of members from these groups in RHAs and DHAs and consult with CHCs on the needs of local communities. FPCs were envisaged as the agency for collecting statistical data on epidemiological trends and ethnic composition for their areas. The report also called on national training bodies such as the UKCC to incorporate a multi-racial and multi-cultural dimension into professional training (NAHA, 1988). Finally, it set out its own model of guiding principles and objectives to assist DHAs in moving ahead (see Table 8.6).

○   Check on whether an equal opportunities policy exists in your health authority, and whether this incorporates the guiding principles shown in Table 8.6. Note down any gaps or problems you think might exist in the NAHA guidelines.

In the mid-1990s there are still marked variations in the responses of health authorities to the call for equal opportunities initiatives. For example, many health authorities still have sketchy information on the distribution and needs of black and minority ethnic groups. Ethnic monitoring of health service staff is not being uniformly carried out, with the result that it is still difficult to assess recruitment, drop-out and completion patterns among, for example, student nurses. On the other hand, the emergence of DHAs as 'purchasers' of health care for their populations has given them a real opportunity to ensure that provider trusts take equal opportunities issues seriously. The DHAs themselves can take the health needs of black and ethnic minority groups fully into account when assessing overall health needs. Plans for an effective system of monitoring and evaluation of services can be written into the provider contracts. Since hospital and community trusts are now autonomous corporate providers, however, with a remit from the Department of Health to control recruitment and decide staff wages and conditions, equal opportunities in staff employment may be much more difficult to monitor. Moreover, provision of services for particular groups, such as genetic counselling and screening services, may not be a high priority if money is tight; financial considerations have already undermined some staff training programmes.

To what extent have the NAHA Report's recommendations been carried out at national level? Here the response has been encouraging.

TABLE 8.6 NAHA guiding principles and objectives. Source: NAHA (1988)

A model of guiding objectives and principles

The objectives listed are intended as a guide. Each health authority should adapt the model after consultation with relevant users of the service, and in view of the varying conditions in which they operate locally.

Community consultation in this report means the delegation of power of decision making to community groups.

To achieve the major programme of change, it is important that health authorities integrate the model into all future short- and long-term plans. The strategic planning guidelines currently being prepared, offer an ideal opportunity to begin this work.

Realistic objectives

The objectives are not necessarily comprehensive, neither are they impossible or unrealistic. Most of the initiatives mentioned are predominantly funded from sources outside health authorities' budgets. The Working Party strongly recommends that health authorities do not rely on alternative short-term funding but rather recommends that such initiatives are maintained through mainstream budgets.

Objective	Action programme
(1) To identify the health needs of black and minority ethnic groups; to decide on action and to employ staff to implement plans.	(i) Establish a black and minority ethnic working party involving authority members and officers. (ii) Employ development officers in fields of equality of opportunities in employment and service provision.
(2) To ensure effective monitoring and evaluation of services in promoting equality of opportunity for service provision.	(i) Ensure effective monitoring and evaluation of services in promoting equality of opportunity for service provision. (ii) Assess all services through staff, CHC and consumer surveys.
(3) To ensure that all authority plans and policies are formulated with an awareness of black and minority ethnic groups.	(i) Publish a document setting out the health authority's policy on equality of opportunity on service provision. (ii) Establish mechanisms for ensuring that policy statements consider the multi-racial and multi-cultural perspective.
(4) To improve information on health care to ensure accessibility to black and minority ethnic groups.	Encourage black and minority ethnic groups to use health services by supplying information about services, in relevant languages.

TABLE 8.6 *Continued*

Objective	Action programme
(5) To ensure that members/officers and health staff undertake training in promoting equality of service provision.	Establish in-service training courses for all staff.
(6) To ensure that racial and cultural differences are reflected in all health promotional material.	Provide information on general health care in appropriate languages and culturally relevant.
(7) To ensure continuing availability of services of particular relevance to black and minority ethnic groups.	Allocate resources for specific services, eg, screening/counselling facilities and health facilitators, mental health services relevant to black and minority ethnic groups.
(8) To ensure equality of communication between health authority staff and black and minority ethnic groups.	(i) Ensure availability of a wide-ranging interpreting service. (ii) Encourage further development of link-worker schemes. (iii) Encourage development of advocacy schemes.
(9) To ensure the availability in hospitals and clinics, of food appropriate to black and minority ethnic groups.	Produce guidance for catering staff on the dietary needs of black and minority ethnic people.
(10) To ensure equality of opportunity with respect to complaints procedures in hospitals and in the community.	(i) Make complaints procedures simple and clear and have information on these procedures translated into relevant languages. (ii) Staff handling complaints must have training to appreciate individual prejudices.

Several national bodies have developed initiatives or recoginsed the need to collect data: for example, the English National Board for Nursing has commissioned research into the training of nurses and midwives to meet 'ethnic minority health needs' (ENB, 1993). In August 1993 the Department of Health set up an ethnic health unit to respond to the health needs of black and minority ethnic groups, drawing attention in particular to their high rates of schizophrenia, heart disease, stroke and diabetes (*The Guardian*, 12 August 1993). Issues of access were highlighted, such as lack of knowledge of what services exist, lack of information and too few female doctors at all levels. The unit is highlighting existing good practice in reaching and treating these minority groups by monitoring health authorities and hospitals and identifying areas where further research is needed to improve services. It is also making links with local and voluntary groups and supporting their work with grants; in 1993, in addition to existing grants of £800 000, the department gave an extra £500 000.

At regional and local level the response has been more patchy. Many health authorities have produced statements of equal opportunities and some have developed detailed guidelines and anti-racist training, but effective monitoring and evaluation of policies is not generally in place. There is not yet routine monitoring of recruitment, promotion and wastage patterns of NHS workers in health authorities or trusts, nor is training in health and race issues widespread. It is not clear that the health sector has moved beyond the fashionable trend, noted in the late 1980s, for pledging itself to equal opportunities but doing too little to implement them (GLARE, 1987). One major discussion point in health policy, as we have noted, concerns the extent to which a service based on principles of equity and universalism should make provision for special treatment for particular groups. It is interesting to note that in both *The Health of the Nation* strategy and in 'The Patient's Charter' there is no mention of black and ethnic minority groups as such. Indeed 'The Patient's Charter' focuses on the individual's existing rights to choice and how these may be monitored through standard setting. The assumption is that choice may be exercised equally by all; the possibility that material, structural, cultural (or behavioural) barriers to choice may exist and that all individuals do not have an equal opportunity for choice is not discussed.

8.6 The significance of race in health care

Issues of race and ethnicity are central to health care. For black and ethnic minority workers in health services discrimination and institutional racism hamper recruitment and adversely influence career patterns and promotion. For black and ethnic minority patients in need of health services structural and cultural barriers – racism, poverty and unemployment as well as language, customs and values – interact to deny them an equal service or sometimes to prevent access to needed health services altogether. As the NAHA Report (1988) comments, 'it is sometimes argued that discrimination can be resisted by ensuring that inequalities are reduced by treating everyone the same, no matter what their background and culture. Treating everyone the same, however, often results in everyone being treated as 'white' and thus results not in equality but inequality'.

It is also argued, in the 'cultural adjustment' approach to race, that once initial fears are dispelled and adjustments are made at an individual and societal level, the 'problem' of race will disappear. In this consensus view a socially just society such as Britain will act to redress grievances and ensure fair play. You will need to decide how far you accept this account or incline to a conflict approach, which locates race and racism within a broader framework of structural and material inequality. Moreover, should the emphasis for health work practice be mainly on developing a greater sensitivity towards minority cultural practices or on challenging institutionalised racist and discriminatory practices in the health services? The argument of this chapter is that both are necessary; there is still widespread evidence of ignorance about cultural practices among health workers and too little knowledge among black and minority ethnic groups of the scope, character and purposes of health services. But a health policy which only tackles cultural barriers will not redress the structural inequalities that undermine attempts to provide an equal, comprehensive and needs based health service. The problems that black and ethnic minority groups face – racial harassment, lower incomes, higher levels of unemployment and poor housing – continue to exist over time and continue to influence their health chances, both as patients and as health service workers.

Suggestions for further study

P. Mares et al. (1985) Health Care in Multi Racial Britain, London, Health Education Authority National Extension College, is a sound anti-racist study providing unrivalled practical guidance for health workers. J. Richardson and J. Lambert (1985) 'The Sociology of Race', in Haralambos, M. Sociology: New Directions, Ormskirk, Causeway, offers a clear discussion of different theories of race. The National Association of Health Authorities (NAHA, now NAHAT) (1988) Action Not Words is a useful resource for continuing to challenge and change practice. A. Beattie et al. (1993) Health and Wellbeing: A Reader, London, Macmillan, also has several articles relating to aspects of race and health, by Anionwu, Thorogood and Fernando.

Self assessment questions

1 Check your understanding of the terms 'race', 'ethnicity', 'prejudice', 'discrimination' and 'direct' and 'institutional' racism.
2 Identify the main features of 'consensus' and 'conflict' theories of race and comment on their relevance to health care.
3 Describe the main patterns of morbidity and mortality in black and minority ethnic groups.
4 Identify and discuss the different forms that racism may take in health services.
5 Review initiatives to combat racism in health services.
6 Review and reassess your own beliefs and practices in relation to race.

Chapter 9

Dependency: age and disability

Contents

Themes and issues

Dependency: social construction – physical and economic dependency – welfare and dependency culture

Disability: 'handicap' – the individualisation of disablity – medicalisation – total institutions – normalisation – mental handicap and nursing – social death and social barriers models

Age and generation: social construction of childhood and old age – old age as a burden – ageism – lay views of ageing

Theories of old age: functionalist and conflict theories – disengagement – activity theory – life history – structured dependency – postmodern accounts

Health and old age: rectangularisation and the compression of mobility – health inequalities – health work and scientific discourse – empowerment

Learning outcomes

After working through this chapter you should be able to:
1 Review your own attitudes and values in relation to dependent groups you may care for.
2 Explain how dependency is socially constructed.
3 Discuss how far the medical model of dependency has been modified and challenged in recent years.
3 Describe the main influences on the health of older people.
5 Compare and contrast consensus and conflict theories of old age.

THIS chapter will explore how contemporary social debates about age and disability connect to health and consider what questions they raise for those engaged in health work practice. In particular, we will investigate changing notions of dependency and note how these have influenced the care and treatment of client groups, such as people with mental health problems, those with physical disabilities and with learning difficulties.

The chapter will then review how the framing of older people as 'dependants' in expert discourse has served to structure their experience of health and health care. This focus on older people reflects their significance in contemporary society and in health work; they now make up some 21 per cent of the total UK population and consume over half of the health care budget. These facts also colour our view of older people; they are seen as 'dependent', and governments have viewed the 'burden of dependency' of an ageing population with some alarm (Bond *et al.*, 1993). Yet only a minority are dependent in a physical sense, needing hospital treatment or residential care; 93 per cent live in private households, although some of these rely on domiciliary help and nursing care. The label of dependency sticks because most older people have retired from paid work and are 'unproductive' in an economic sense. It is these two related meanings of dependency – as a physical state and an economic state – that form the starting point of this chapter.

9.1 Unpacking dependency

What is meant by the notion of *dependency*? In social policy the term has been widely used to refer to those individuals or groups who are not able to live 'independent' lives. In *health* terms we think of dependent groups as those who are unable to function independently and whose care needs to be provided by others. Thus, frail elderly people, or those who have a long term illness, or physical or mental handicaps or mental health problems are generally viewed as dependent. Together they form around 18 per cent of the total population. They are the main groups, as we noted in Chapter 4, for whom community care provision is made.

But it is clear that in welfare policy dependency has been defined more broadly than this. For example, children, even if they are well, are defined as requiring care from others – not just the family but state workers such as health visitors, school nurses and teachers. In addition, as we noted in Chapter 6, large numbers of individuals and families are dependent on social security benefits. Only some of these people will have chronic health problems; for many in this group it is not their health status that defines them as being dependent, but their *economic dependence* on state benefits. Underpinning this view is a philosophy of possessive individualism which, as we noted in Chapter 3, is associated in particular with industrial capitalism and with patriarchal power. As Dalley (1988) pointed out, 'whole' individuals have been seen as men, the 'breadwinners' whose rights to call themselves independent are confirmed by their roles as productive paid workers.

Dependency culture?

The widespread and growing reliance on welfare benefits, as we noted in Chapter 6, has given support to arguments about dependency culture. In the 1980s in particular, it was claimed that state claimants formed an underclass of dependants, whose character, habits and sense of morality were different from those of most of the population. Irresponsibility, dishonesty and fatalism were seen as characteristic of dependency subculture. A 1988 Department of Employment report (quoted in Squires, 1990) claimed that 'a significant number of benefit claimants . . . seem to have grown accustomed to living on benefit', and political pressure on welfare 'scroungers' – the chronic sick as well the unemployed and single mothers – was intensified. Doctors were reprimanded for allowing too many unemployed people to be re-classified as 'chronic sick' with more generous benefits.

Critics have seen the attack on dependency culture as a deliberate policy of victim-blaming which has justified attacks on welfare benefits and disguised the rising incidence of poverty. They have argued that welfare claimants share the attitudes and values of the rest of the population (Dean and Taylor-Gooby, 1992). Crime may be widespread in areas of high unemployment, but this is because these areas are the most poverty-stricken and wretched; structural factors and government policies rather than personal failings are the root cause.

The debate about dependency culture feeds into a larger debate about the purpose of welfare, to which we will return in Chapter 13. At this point it is important to note how misleading it is to suggest that there is a clear distinction between states of 'dependence' and 'independence'. Many people in work receive benefits; many retired people have private occupational pensions and savings; and the state pensions, attendance allowances and other benefits that individuals receive are paid for out of taxes to which almost all citizens have contributed. A more useful concept is that of *interdependency*, which highlights the idea that all of us are, to some extent, dependent on each other. This has been discussed in recent writings on social welfare (Doyal and Gough, 1991; Johnson, 1993).

The dependency burden?

Within health work dependants are conceptualised as 'individuals with impaired abilities to function independently. Their common characteristic is their resistance to curative treatment, their potential cost as long-term users of medical and social services and their multiple needs which are not the responsibility of a single profession' (Illsley, 1981). This definition is a widely accepted tenet of health policy making, but it also raises several interesting questions for those in health work. How are those with 'impaired abilities' defined and selected? What marks the boundary between the 'normal' and the 'impaired'? Who gets to define 'multiple needs'? Why is the whole definition couched in the rather negative terms of cost and resistance? Unearthing some answers takes us beneath the edifice of current social policy to consider the foundations on which it was built.

Above all, those defined as dependent are those who are not 'owners of themselves', who are unable to operate as productive workers and who therefore constitute a 'burden' to society (Allsop, 1984). Such notions help to delineate the boundary between the 'normal' and the 'impaired': between those who are not independent, 'whole individuals' in Dalley's (1988) sense of the phrase. This boundary is patrolled by doctors, social workers and other agents of the state, who are responsible for defining their needs and providing services, paid for mainly out of public taxation. Entitlement to Attendance Allowance, Invalidity Benefit, Sickness Benefit (beyond the first few days), domiciliary support and hospital treatment is only conferred after official medical or social care assessments have been made. Such assessments are influenced by political decisions which categorise claimants, regulate entitlement and define benefit levels. In this sense we can say that dependency is *socially constructed*: that is, it has been shaped by political, social and economic processes even if it is perceived by most people as a largely 'common sense' definition.

The social construction of dependency?

A further point to note is that dependency is a shifting term, and that what was defined as constituting dependency in the past, or in the 1990s, will not necessarily remain the same in the future. In other words, dependency is not an objective state 'out there' waiting to be discovered; it has been brought into being (or in Foucault's terms 'fabricated') by human activity. Like other knowledge, knowledge about dependency, indeed dependency itself as a state, has been socially constructed. One main question which we need to answer, therefore, is why and how dependency came into being.

A related issue concerns the part played by language. Much of this construction of common sense categories and understandings proceeds through language. Language conveys the symbolic meanings and images which influence our understanding and responses (see Chapter 2). The language of dependency that is used here – impairment, burden, multiple needs – depicts dependants as less than complete individuals.

○   Bearing in mind these points, define what you understand by the terms 'the elderly' and 'childhood'.

You may have used your knowledge of nursing to delimit the elderly into different categories: the 'frail elderly', the young old, the oldest old and so on. These are socially constructed categories; in the past these groups were not differentiated, nor was old age seen as a period of retirement from paid work. The term 'the elderly' today encompasses all those past retirement age, and most have access to particular benefits such as pensions, bus passes and other subsidised services. Beyond this they may have little in common with each other. Yet the category 'the elderly' or 'old age' suggests a homogenous group with characteristics (and possibly also attitudes and values) in common. In a similar way 'childhood' conveys particular meanings and images: of a period of dependence on adults in which certain rights are withheld – voting, driving a car and so on – and of common categories of experience – school, family life, socialisation. Once again these rights and experiences will change over time. The meanings and images of childhood held by an older person, aged 75, and a middle aged person, aged 45, will reflect their own, probably very different experiences of childhood. In a more general sense popular Victorian notions of childhood as a time to 'be seen and not heard', of unquestioning obedience to parental authority, when to 'spare the rod' was 'to spoil the child', suggest how differently it was viewed in the past.

In relation to disability Oliver (1993) notes that 'definitions . . . are relative rather than absolute'; in other words, they are specific to particular societies and historical contexts. Disability is socially constructed not just through 'individual meanings', 'the activities of powerful groups and vested interests' or public policy, but through language which is heavily influenced by ideology. The result in the UK is that disability is conceptualised as individual disadvantage rather than as an issue about disabling barriers or social attitudes. Disabled young people are socialised into the idea that their disability makes them a victim, a burden, someone who should be grateful and remain passive. Stereotypes of the 'cheerful' sufferer, the 'heroic' winner against the odds or the ungrateful disabled person with a 'chip on their shoulder' are commonplace.

Social and economic policies have influenced our perceptions of disability. Industrialisation hastened the exclusion of disabled people from paid labour (Ryan and Thomas, 1987). They were increasingly perceived as slower and less productive, and this categorisation was sustained in the workhouse era and in early welfare legislation, which reinforced the notion of disabled people as 'helpless' and in need of 'care'. In addition, health and welfare professionals have often presented themselves as the 'experts' on disability who 'know best' what such people need. The creation of the 'dependent individual' is thus a complex inter-weaving of ideological and structural fibres.

9.2 The shifting category of the 'disabled person'

Two of the main 'dependent groups' as defined in contemporary society are those with physical and mental disabilities. It is in these groups, particularly among the mentally disabled, that perhaps the greatest challenges to definitions have occurred. Their social construction as a 'problem' group in modern times was linked to the emergence of biomedicine in the early nineteenth century. The notion of therapeutic intervention to restore 'normality', which was a prominent feature of the medicalisation of the 'insane', was less significant in relation to those with mental and physical handicaps. The growing sophistication of medical processes of delineating and diagnosing 'mental defectives' was not matched by therapy. The number of asylums in Britain increased from 400 in 1850 to over 2000 by 1914 as more and more people were classified as 'handicapped' in some way.

Institutional care

Long term institutional care was largely custodial, carrying with it the removal of citizenship rights and the subjection of the individual to the rigours of the total institution (Goffman, 1961). At its best the institution gave some protection and limited training to individuals rejected by their families and shunned by society; at its worst it was a holding operation designed to control vast numbers of inmates (nearly 40 000 by the 1930s) and to provide minimum standards of care: 'Given the isolation of the institutions and the absolute power of their medical superintendents, the regime actually experienced by patients varied a great deal depending on the character and beliefs of the individual doctor in charge' (Dingwall et al., 1988).

Between 1900 and the 1950s the largest group of people with

disabilities were children. There were nearly half a million physically disabled children in Britain, many of them living at home but a significant proportion segregated in institutions or in special schools for 'the blind', 'the deaf', 'cripples' and so on (Humphries and Gordon, 1992). The medical confusion of physical and mental disability – and the general assumption that children whose appearance was not normal were 'abnormal' – led to children with cerebral palsy and severe physical disabilities being classified as 'imbeciles'. The accounts of physical, emotional and sensory deprivation in many of the institutions, where children were given numbers instead of names and where contact with parents was strictly limited, make harrowing reading. In 1935 Mary Baker, a 12 year old girl with a dislocated hip, was sent to the Halliwick Home for Crippled Girls. Her mother had died, and the authorities decided the father would be unable to bring up the children:

When I first arrived at Halliwick the nurse took me into this bathroom and she stripped me off completely. She cut my hair short, right above the ears. And then I was deloused with powder of some description. Then they put me in a bath and scrubbed me down with carbolic soap . . . I was dressed in the Halliwick uniform . . . and taken up into the dormitory . . . I had entered a different life . . . The next morning you were given a number and you had to remember it. My number was twenty-nine and when I went up to wash, my towel and flannel had my number on them . . . We were hardly ever called by our first names, only by the other girls. And if matron wanted you she called you by twenty-nine or whatever number you had.

Humphries and Gordon (1992)

The de-medicalisation of mental handicap

The shifting construction of disability can be demonstrated in changing linguistic categories: from 'mental defectives' and 'idiot' in the nineteenth century to 'educationally subnormal' and 'mentally handicapped' in the 1950s, to 'people with learning difficulties' in the 1990s. In a similar way, 'physical handicap' has been replaced in much of the literature by the phrase 'people with physical disabilities'. The emphasis on disabilities and difficulties rather than handicap reflects a clear linguistic challenge, in that handicap conveys personal inadequacy whereas disability directs attention to the disabling environment and to the reasons why the individual is 'disabled', which might be more to do with the design of buildings, roads, consumer durables and so on than with any particular personal disability.

These shifts in language were linked to, and themselves symbolise and give meaning to, shifts in practice from institutionalisation to community care (see Chapter 4). From the 1960s a planned reduction of institutional care was underway, although this was to be a painful

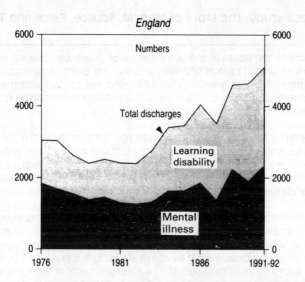

FIGURE 9.1 Discharges from mental illness and learning disability hospitals and units: stays of five or more years. Source: *Social Trends* (1994)

process. In spite of considerable evidence of chronic understaffing (and low morale and low pay) the closure of mental handicap hospitals was much slower than of mental hospitals. A government White Paper, *Better Services for the Mentally Handicapped* (DHSS, 1971), criticised the tradition of custodial nursing which permeated mental handicap nursing, and subsequent reports emphasised the need for domiciliary support workers and social care for patients in local residential units (Jay Report, DHSS, 1979). By the 1980s, although the pace of change was still slow, a decisive shift away from long term institutional care had been carried through (see Figure 9.1). For mental handicap this marked a new stage in the de-medicalistion of the specialty. Many patients – with varying degrees of disability – learned to live 'an ordinary life' with a fair degree of independence (see Box 9.1).

Read Box 9.1, which is one ex-patient's account of her resettlement in a local residential home. What strikes you as significant about this account?

Perhaps the most moving aspect of Mary's story is that the very basic, everyday routines and journeys were possible for the first time. She could get up when she wanted, choose her clothes, help with everyday domestic tasks, do her own shopping. She was living an ordinary life and exercising some choice rather than following a set routine. It is valuable to compare her story with accounts from Ryan and Thomas (1987) about

BOX 9.1 Case study: the story of Mary M. Source: Felce and Toogood (1990)

Mary moved into the house in the second week of November. She moved from an environment which had aspects of prison security – for example, being confined to a locked dormitory from early evening until morning. Her contact with the outside world was non-existent. She did have disruptive behaviour, the reason for her initial transfer there . . .

Mary was severely mentally handicapped with few self-help skills. She ate using a spoon and her fingers, could drink unassisted but with considerable spilling, and dressed (given that she wore loose tops and elasticated trousers) with help. She was fully ambulant but with a lopsided gait. She was basically continent but did not wash even her hands herself . . .

In the first six months after moving in [to the group home], Mary received a greater than proportionate share of the clothing budget in order to obtain a suitable range to her wardrobe, a new top coat, dresses and shoes. As well as looking right, it was found that more fashionable adult women's shoes with a slight heel in fact helped her to walk with a more normal gait. She had appointments at the hairdresser's and chiropodist's and began a course of dental treatment which was to lead to the provision of dentures. She was proud of her appearance, liked having her hair done and enjoyed brushing it herself. Apart from a slight awkwardness in movement, in time Mary's appearance became such as to give little indication of handicap . . .

The new opportunities for Mary on moving to the house within the general context of staff support led to fairly rapid development. She quickly learnt to use a knife and fork at meal times. She was so thrilled at this new accomplishment that for a period of a few weeks she chose to eat even her toast and marmalade at breakfast by that means. In hospital, she had been described as taking food from others' plates and as being terribly messy, but now she learnt to follow the normal conventions of waiting for others to finish before taking more, offering serving dishes (when prompted) to others and using language to express preferences and wants. Proficiency at feeding herself improved enormously. She participated in the routine domestic tasks of the house: clearing the dining table, putting the things on the kitchen hatch, wiping surfaces and sweeping or hoovering the floors. She went shopping almost daily. Of course, the majority of these things would be done with staff instruction and direct guidance, but through regular practice and some specific teaching she increased considerably the part she played and the level of independence she showed . . .

As Mary became familiar with joining in more and learning simple domestic tasks such as emptying the dishwasher or pegging out the washing, her agreement to follow requests became easier to obtain. Once occupied, she participated with good grace, enjoying the social situation . . . Mary liked to celebrate her achievement by saying, 'I done it' and returning to the living room to sit down. Care had to be given to allow her the opportunity to be pleased with doing what she had been asked to do; the breaks between activities did not have to be prolonged.

life on a mental handicap ward, where the custodial model of care was predominant. Inmates had little or no privacy, few personal possessions, wore ill-fitting, institutional clothes and were largely regarded as ineducable by the staff, who spent more time having coffee and smoking in the office than attending to the patients.

But life in long-stay institutions was not inevitably of such poor quality, nor is living outside the institution necessarily easier. The security and sense of community which characterised the better long-stay hospitals have not been achieved in the sometimes hostile localities into which patients have been discharged. Community care has not delivered the same kind of choice and independence to all former inmates, as we noted in Chapter 4. Patients have been moved into the community with too little preparation and have sometimes found themselves living in threatening neighbourhoods, on low incomes and with little social support (Flynn, 1989). Families of those with learning difficulties, who would in the past have been relieved of the work of caring, have found themselves coping, with two little professional support. However, it does seem that people with learning difficulties, even though their quality of life in the community may be fairly poor, prefer independent living to hospital and hostel care (Booth *et al.*, 1990).

The 'de-construction' of mental handicap as a state of medicalised dependency has not taken place without conflict. The philosophy of *normalisation* that underpins de-institutionalisation is that services should enable each person with learning difficulties to live as independ-ent, normal and full a life as possible, but this is open to different interpretations (Wolfensberger, 1972). There has been some resistance from hospital consultants, on medical and professional grounds. Mental handicap nurses working in hospitals did not welcome the recom-mendation of the Jay Report (DHSS, 1979) that mental handicap patients should be cared for wholly in the community. In particular, suggestions that the small residential units created should be staffed by a new group of 'care workers', and that training and certification should be within social work, were resented. However, mental handicap training was modified and reoriented in the early 1980s to train nurses to work in community settings under the revised (1982) Registered Nurse, Mental Handicap syllabus. More recently mental handicap has been drawn into Project 2000 courses, where students undertake a common foundation programme with other nursing students.

Another major problem has been finance. Local authorities have been reluctant to enter joint-funded schemes with health authorities because, after the early years, they become wholly responsible for running costs. Regional health authorities have differed in the degree to which they were willing to give local authorities per capita 'dowry' payments for patients being transferred to community settings (Hardy *et al.*, 1990). Consequently the speed and effectiveness of transfer has varied greatly. The meanings attached to de-institutionalisation and 'normalisation' have differed as well. In some health authorities the priority has been for community provision in 'ordinary homes'; in others small-scale institutions and buildings in hospital grounds have been used.

Changing views of physical disability

Although many poor older people with physical disabilities were treated in long-stay poor law institutions in the nineteenth century, suffering a similar kind of custodial regime which increased their levels of dependency, younger people were less likely to be confined in this way. Nevertheless, it was only after the break-up of the Poor Law in the 1940s that any special provision was made to enable disabled people of working age to engage in paid work. In the first half of the century the employment prospects for disabled people were very poor. In 1936, for example, 35 000 out of a total blind population of 40 000 were unemployed. It was World War II and the acute labour shortage that followed conscription which transformed employment opportunities for disabled people. By the early 1940s, 310 806 disabled men and women – hitherto mainly classified as 'unemployable' – were working in industrial and commercial jobs.

Employment legislation in the 1940s instituted a 'quota' system by which larger employers agreed to accept a minimum number of disabled workers (to form 6 per cent of the total workforce). The quota system was never properly policed, and many employers simply ignored its demands, but some firms did take on less severely disabled workers (Lonsdale, 1985). The severely disabled – for example blind workers – had little chance of employment. It was only through voluntary sector organisations, such as the National Institute for the Blind, that these groups gained any independence through paid employment.

A considerable proportion of the registered disabled are currently dependent on social security benefits and, as means-tested benefits (such as Income Support) and new supplementary benefits (such as disability and attendance allowances) have been introduced to fill the gaps in the welfare state, the numbers of dependants have grown (see Table 9.1). The ageing of the population has meant that larger numbers of older people are swelling the ranks of the physically disabled. At the last full national survey of disability in the UK, 5 per cent of the population were found to have a severe disability, though many more had more minor problems. Levels of dependency are rising, 'created' – that is to say recognised and legitimated by the state – through welfare benefits.

The government's current view is to apply tests of disability more stringently in an attempt to reduce the numbers receiving disability benefits. However, disabled people (and to some extent older people)

TABLE 9.1 Main targeted benefits for long term sick, injured and disabled people (non-contributory benefits)[1]. Source: adapted from *Social Trends* (1994)

Type of benefit	Recipients ('000s)			
	1976–7	1981–2	1991–2	1992–3
Severe Disablement Allowance	105	180	305	320
Attendance Allowance	230	350	975	765
Disability Living Allowance[2]	–	–	–	935
Disability Working Allowance	–	–	–	5
Mobility Allowance	30	210	665	–
Industrial Injuries Disablement Benefit	–	–	295	295
War Disablement Pension	415	345	280	310

[1] Invalidity benefit is also payable to those who have been entitled to Statutory Sick Pay (that is, those in employment) for the first 28 weeks of sickness. It is made up of Invalility Pension and supplements. This is a contributory benefit, that is, it is only paid to those who have enough contributions through national insurance.

[2] In 1992 Disability Living Allowance replaced (a) Attendance Allowance for those disabled before the age of 65 and (b) Mobility Allowance.

are now much more visible. They are living in community settings instead of being tucked out of sight in institutions. They are also increasingly vocal and, as their numbers grew, able – in theory at least – to influence policy making.

The challenge to 'dependency'

Large-scale institutional care for disabled people has declined, but until recently smaller-scale residential homes for disabled people have been seen as a 'sensible solution'. This view was challenged by Miller and Gwynne's (1972) study of residental homes which concluded that 'by the very fact of committing people to institutions of this type, society is defining them as, in effect, socially dead'. The role of the home, they noted, was to help the residents 'make the transition from social death to physical death'. This began a long debate about how such segregation could be successfully challenged and whether independence and autonomy were possible, given the tremendous power exercised over disabled people's lives by welfare systems and professional providers. In particular, Mike Oliver (1990) has sought to challenge conceptions of disability as 'personal tragedy' and to demonstrate how it is culturally and socially constructed. The ideology of dependency, underpinned by medicalisation and possessive individualism, is seen as rooted in contemporary capitalism and its preoccupation with production.

Finkelstein (1993) has examined how the 'social death' model of

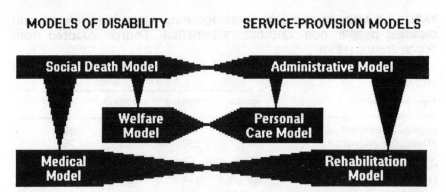

FIGURE 9.2 The 'social death' model of disability. Source: Finkelstein (1993)

disability reinforced the dominance of the 'administrative model' of service provision in which disabled people had little choice or control. He argues that the 'social death' model is underpinned by the medical model of health, in which able-bodiedness is seen as the norm. Disability is seen as dysfunctional and therefore as requiring expert intervention. Welfare experts administer personal care services; medical experts provide rehabilitation (see Figure 9.2). Wider acceptance of a 'social barriers' model of disability, which 'emphasises the social and attitudinal barriers constructed by a world built for able-bodied living', would enable service provision to be transformed (see Figure 9.3). Neither health nor welfare professionals would be front-line decision makers if an 'integrated living support model' was adopted. Instead, disabled people themselves would negotiate with planners and policy makers to create 'enabling environments'. The focus would be on 'barrier removal': that is, on challenging not only the medical model and

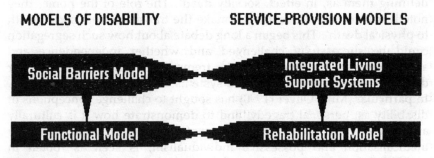

FIGURE 9.3 The 'social barriers' model of disability. Source: Finkelstein (1993)

institutional care but also the power of professional service providers in the community.

The greater visibility of those with physical and mental disabilities has been matched by changing attitudes and organisation. From the organisations *for* disabled people that were a feature of the 1960s and early 1970s there has been a shift to organisations *of* disabled people: a significant growth in voluntary, and in particular self help, groups engaged in various types of action. Drawing inspiration from the women's movement of the 1970s, local groups have campaigned on issues to do with health and with safety and access. Their emphasis on raising consciousness, hard campaigning and direct action stresses the rejection of dependency and the celebration of social and political independence. The London based Campaign for Accessible Transport, for example, organised a mass 'sit-down' by wheelchair users in Oxford Street, blocking traffic for an hour and 'making news'. One of the organisers has commented:

I think that for those of us who've taken part in it, it's been more than just about transport, although it's partly about that. It's also been a sense of actually testing our own power, and it's amazing what you can do with thirty people sitting in the middle of Oxford Street.

Ruth Bashall, quoted in K258 (1992)

Equal opportunities initiatives in local government and other public services, including the health sector, have expanded employment opportunities to some extent, but people with disabilities still face disabling barriers to a normal life. These include structural and material barriers, such as social isolation, unemployment, poverty, inadequate transport and lack of access. Some of the major problems for people with disabilities arise from planning, roads, shopping and housing schemes which are built with only the able-bodied in mind. Many older people have minor disabilities – such as difficulties in walking up stairs or declining strength in joints – which are exacerbated by local environments and household appliances designed for the 'normal' adult.

Nevertheless, the extent to which disabled people are all equally disadvantaged has been questioned. Class, race and gender act as powerful influences on disability. Disabled women suffer from stereotyping as passive and particularly dependent and from the gender bias in care services (Lonsdale, 1990). Far more disabled women are likely to be living in poverty. Only a small proportion receive employment rehabilitation training or are entitled to national insurance benefits.

There are also cultural barriers. Public perceptions of those with disabilities are changing slowly, but stereotyping of them as 'the handicapped' and the 'subnormal' has not disappeared. Community care, as well as holding out the promise of normalisation and an ordinary life, threatens people with disabilities or learning difficulties with the prospect of living among unsympathetic or even hostile local residents.

9.3 Age and generation

Age refers to chronological age – being four or perhaps 40 years old – whereas *generation* refers to commonalities, public events and patterns of social change which bind age cohorts together. For example, children too young to participate in World War II were termed the 'post-war generation', and it has been suggested that their freer attitudes and values were threatening to their parents' generation, who had fought in the war, endured privation, evacuation, rationing and the post-war 'austerity' years. Cohen (1981) has argued that the castigation of youth culture as decadent, materialist and violent – epitomised in the press by the sensationalist reporting of 'Mods' and 'Rockers' clashes on south coast beaches in the 1960s – represented a 'moral panic' of the wartime generation against the alien values of the young.

○ Suggest some examples of generational influences in relation to health provision.

You might have contrasted attitudes towards the National Health Service expressed by many older people, who grew up before a comprehensive health service was created, with the attitudes of younger people whose only experience is of the NHS. Younger people often have more awareness of what services are available and are more willing to use them, whereas older generations were socialised into 'suffering in silence'. Most women now in their retirement years will have given birth in their own homes and will have experienced childbirth in a domestic social setting. For most succeeding generations, however, childbirth is a medical event that takes place in a hospital. The experiences of these different generations will be quite distinctive. A final example might relate to the experiences of those with mental health problems. Earlier generations will have been incarcerated in long-stay institutions, whereas most young adults will have experienced only fairly short periods of hospitalisation in acute psychiatric wards.

Childhood

Age, it might be thought, is a fairly straightforward concept, but in contemporary society it has become problematised in new ways. First, chronological age has been increasingly used to signal entitlement or responsibilities: to attend school, to vote, to drive a car, to receive a pension. Second, the lifespan has been rigorously divided up into 'childhood', 'youth', 'adulthood' and 'old age'. Third, as we noted earlier, these categories are historically and culturally specific social constructs.

Before modern times 'childhood' as a concept had little meaning; children from the age of about seven were regarded as small adults in terms of expectations of behaviour, dress and attitudes (Aries, 1973). The creation of childhood as a distinct phase of life, in which moral and physical health must be instilled through discipline, schooling and hygiene, is seen by Aries as a product of seventeenth and eighteenth century bourgeois culture. Other writers, however, have emphasised the importance of capitalism in changing views of childhood, because of its demarcation of home and work, dependant and worker (Thane, 1982). In the growing concern to accumulate wealth and protect inheritance and property rights, the middle class increasingly trained and controlled their children – an approach generalised in Victorian times throughout society.

The legislative protection of children from market forces and adult exploitation dates initially from the 1830s and 1840s, when child labour became outlawed in the mines and regulated in factories. The extension of childhood into the teenage years only began in the late nineteenth and early twentieth centuries, as compulsory schooling removed young children from the labour market. Childhood thus gradually became a time of 'dependency', when parents were required to provide food, clothing and shelter. The torrent of advice and warnings about child-rearing is a nineteenth and twentieth century phenomenon (Rex Stainton Rogers, 1993). Experts from medicine and the social sciences established 'truth claims' about child-rearing, attempting to establish it as a science by uncovering its 'laws'. There has followed over a century of theorising about childhood which revealed a great deal about the issues and problems which researchers saw as 'important' and rather less about what parents should actually do (see Box 9.2). The state has also played an increasing part in defining childhood, not just through the extension of the school leaving age but through legislation such as the Children Act (1989) which recast the responsibilities of parents and emphasised rights of children.

Old age

We have noted that *old age* is used to define the later part of life, the post-retirement years, yet like childhood it is a shifting concept, given meaning through the cultural context within which the term is used. In the centuries before old age pensions came into existence, older people

BOX 9.2 Conflicting theories of child-rearing. Source: R. Stainton Rogers (1993)

The theories		Children are:
• Childhood masturbation is a cause of untold physical and psychological damage	• Childhood masturbation is harmless	• Biological blue-prints unfolding through maturation
• Too much cuddling damages children's adjustment	• You cannot cuddle your child too much	• Almost infinitely flexible receptacles of specific socialisation practices
• Young children should never leave their mothers	• Nursery education is positively beneficial	• A seething mass of unconscious sexuality and aggression
• 'Mongoloid idiots' are ineducable and best institutionalised	• 'Down's children' thrive in families and can be integrated into mainstream schooling	• Elaborated puppies undergoing house-training
• 'Mothers are always to blame'	• 'Mother-blaming' is a patriarchal conspiracy	• A set of inner traits of disposition and ability
• Children are fragile and irreversibly damaged by aversive early experiences	• Children are hardy and capable of overcoming adversity	• A mind striving for knowledge – a biological computer

did not legally 'retire'; they worked until their feebleness drove them to the workhouse or to parish relief, or until they were cared for by relatives or until they had saved enough to stop working. Macintyre (1977) has discussed how state policies in the nineteenth and twentieth centuries reconstructed old age as a 'social problem'. On the one hand the state sought to minimise the 'burden on society' of large numbers of old people requiring support through organisational means. This was attempted by means of the Poor Laws of 1834 which created workhouses with their attendant philosophy of 'less eligibility' (see Chapter 6). On the other hand, particularly through welfare state legislation from 1908 onwards, the state sought to ease for the older individual the 'personal burden' of disadvantage, illness and dependency. The old age pension, therefore, both freed old people (to some extent) from absolute poverty and simultaneously made them a permanent burden on society.

The meanings that are now commonly associated with old age, which include frailty, dependence and senility, reflect the social construction of old age in the twentieth century. Older people themselves (and of course many younger people too) do not accept this terminology uncritically. In a Scottish study of 70 people aged 60 or over Williams (1990) noted that respondents offered five distinctive types of accounts of old age:

1 Early old age as liberation: 'I am free to follow my interests'
2 Early old age as a setback: 'My interests and social connections are reduced' and/or 'If I encounter the younger generation I may have trouble'
3 Early old age as a repairing of defences: 'I keep my interests going'; 'I keep up my social connections'
4 Late old age as resistible: 'If I keep active, I will always keep real old age at bay'
5 Late old age as surrender: 'If I become really old, I may legitimately give up my activities'.

Williams (1990)

How do these accounts of old age compare with your own views?

Much will depend on what age you are and what experience you have of living with or caring for older people. If you have a dearly loved grandparent or a cheerful elderly neighbour, then your views of old age may be very positive. As a health work student you may already have worked with frail elderly patients on hospital wards or in a nursing or residential home, and this will have influenced your views. For many young people being over 30 seems like being 'ancient', so to contemplate old age brings out all the negative images of decay and senility. Some conditions associated with old age, such as Alzheimer's disease, may be remote but are also frightening, adding to the vision of decay. Bytheway (in K256, 1993) has noted that dictionary definitions reflect, and help to shape and reproduce, particular views of old age. Whereas old age itself was defined as 'the later part of life', 17 other associated terms – such as antique, decrepit, dotage, senile and second childhood – were defined by using the term old age, thus firmly investing it with negative connotations. For example, senescent was defined as 'verging on old age', senile as 'showing the decay or imbecility of old age' and dotage as the 'childishness of old age'.

Ageism

Ageism refers to discrimination against people on the grounds of their age. Many types of categorisation already occur through state legislation – as in compulsory schooling between five and 16 years, voting rights at 18 and the driving test at 17. In the world of work being made redundant over the age of 50 (or in some cases 40) makes it unlikely that the worker will be offered another job, yet the equal opportunities policies of private companies and the public sector usually have nothing to say about discrimination by age. It is this general acceptance that employment and other rights diminish as people get older that makes ageism such an insidious and pervasive type of discrimination: 'In particular, ageism "legitimates" the use of chronological age to mark out classes of people who are systematically denied resources and opportunities that others enjoy, and who suffer the consequences of such denigration, ranging from well-meaning patronage to unambiguous vilification' (Bytheway and Johnson, 1990).

Also bound up with ageist attitudes are assumptions about physical decay: 'the ageing process' which conjures up a vision of steady and irresistible decline which is 'natural' and 'normal'. While women, in particular, are encouraged to 'stay young' and 'keep in shape', the effort to look young if you are older is largely ridiculed through phrases like 'mutton dressed up as lamb'. These two components – the social and the physical – reinforce each other to create a society in which (unlike racism and sexism) ageist attitudes and regulations are not widely challenged.

In the women's movement, for example, the main preoccupations have been with the domestic division of labour and the double burden of childcare and paid work carried by mothers. The concerns of older women went largely unresearched, and assumptions about solidarity and sisterhood disguised the real differences between younger and older women (Fennell *et al.*, 1988). One feminist writer has recorded her realisation of the strength of ageist attitudes among younger women and her own ageist assumptions:

Slowly, I began to see that the fear of the stigma of age, and total ignorance of its reality in the lives of older women, flow deep in myself, in other women I know, in the women's movement. That our society breeds ignorance and fear of birth, ageing and death. That the old woman carries the burden of that stigma, and with remarkable, unrecognised, unrecorded courage. I begin to see that I myself am ageing, was always ageing, and that only powerful forces could have kept me – from self-interest alone – from working to change the social and economic realities of older women.

Macdonald and Rich (1984)

On the other hand there is still room for discussion about what constitutes ageism. For example, 'concessions' of various kinds, such as cheap bus passes, cheap entry tickets or special offers, mark out 'senior citizens' as different. Many senior citizens welcome these because they offer valuable savings and this prompts the question: Are such policies ageist? After all, students (and sometimes nurses) are also given concessions of this kind. But these 'hand-outs' are attractive to older people largely because they are among the poorest groups in UK society (see Section 9.5). If the bus pass is seen as a concession to those too poor to travel freely otherwise, then the issue becomes one about adequate income in old age. The stigma attached to the take-up of the concession derives from the designation of old people as poor and dependent. Most students, by contrast, can expect to find jobs and become economically independent; they are merely 'slumming it' for a few years and can get credit and run up overdrafts because their income is likely to rise.

9.4 Theories of old age

There has been a long-standing tendency for those researching in social gerontology (the sociology and social policy of old age) to avoid broader theoretical questions, working instead from normative assumptions 'with implicit or explicit judgements being made about the lives of older people' (Fennell *et al.*, 1988). Instead of grounding studies of old age in a wider structural and cultural analysis, the focus has often been on 'individual adjustment'. Thus the application of consensus functionalist role theory to gerontology was mainly concerned with adjusting elderly people themselves to a situation of compulsory retirement in a post-war, rapidly changing, socially mobile industrial society.

Consensus functionalist theories of old age

Role theory explained the position of older people in terms of adjustment from valued social roles, in particular the male 'work role'. Retirement was conceptualised as a crisis point, the normative assumption being that loss of work left the individual 'in a peculiarly functionless situation, cut off from participation in the most important interests and activities of the society' (Parsons, quoted in Fennell *et al.*, 1988). Retirement was viewed as a potentially depressing state of social isolation from the mainstream of functioning society, although it was acknowledged that for some it might be a release. Successful adaptation to retirement was linked to taking up new activities and leisure pursuits, and emphasis was placed on the need for role flexibility and role adjustment. Much of the focus was on men; women were assumed to experience less of a crisis because their 'housekeeping role' did not change.

Disengagement theory supported and extended the work of role theorists by exploring the ageing process in more detail from the standpoint of social pyschology. It was claimed that during ageing people gradually withdrew or 'disengaged' from certain types of roles and interactions, retaining a more limited and intimate circle of friends and activities. This was conceptualised as a 'natural' and 'normal' process: a 'quiet closing of doors' as it has sometimes been described. The exclusion of older people from the workforce, it was suggested, met their interests as well as meeting the demands of society for an active and alert workforce:

A key assumption made in the theory is that 'ego energy' declines with age and that as the ageing process develops, individuals become increasingly self-preoccupied and less and less responsive to normative controls. The socio-logical premise, taken as self-evident, is that, since death occurs unpredictably and would be socially disruptive if people 'died in harness', there is a functional necessity to expel from work roles any older person with a statistically high risk of death. This illustrates a common criticism of functional-ist theories, that they simply provide a convenient rationalisation for unequal power relationships.

Fennell et al. *(1988)*

In contrast to this, *activity theory* is based on research into older people who have continued into their old age activities and lifestyles associated with middle age. It suggests that the secret of 'successful ageing' lies in the maintenance of patterns of activity rather than in gradual dis-engagement and increasing passivity (Havighurst, 1954). In some cases it is possible for interests to be pursued into old age – social networks, leisure activities and voluntary work are often taken up in middle life. But social and economic constraints such as enforced retirement disrupt activity patterns, and physical constraints may make it impossible for older people to be very active in old age. Like disengagement theory, but from a very different perspective, activity theory propounds an idealised model of ageing which takes little account of the structural and biological realities confronting many older people.

The other major criticism that can be levelled at functionalist theories is that, on the whole, they ignore the complexity of structural, material and cultural influences on ageing. There is no acknowledge-ment that ageist attitudes may stereotype older people or coerce them into unwanted roles. Nor is there an appreciation of diversity in experiences of ageing; people age in very different ways and although some may withdraw, others will not. It may be that disengagement is prompted by changing circumstances – loss of spouse, poor health, the difficulties of forming new friendships if work relationships disappear – rather than an ageing process itself. Finally, the general application of disengagement as the 'normal' way of ageing has been challenged by studies of other cultures and historical periods (Crawford, 1981).

Conflict theories of old age

Criticism of consensus functionalist theories of ageing have come from both interactionists and neo-marxists. *Interactionism*, in rejecting a general theory of old age, has emphasised diversity and individual experience. Johnson (1976) went beyond this in discussing the insights to be gained by taking a biographical approach, which was able to take into account the particular life-history of the person: their age, cultural background, class, generational, domestic and work experiences. *Life-history* has become a powerful interpretive approach in gerontology and provided a necessary corrective to the over-socialised view of older people advanced through functionalist theory (Bornat, 1989).

Conflict theorists have also challenged functionalism by exploring the social construction of dependency. Biographical studies demonstrated not only the diversity of ageing but also pointed to its reconceptualisation as dependency in twentieth century society. Theorists in the Marxist and Weberian tradition have linked this emerging language of dependency – burdens, problems, unproductive members of society, demographic pressure – to the economic, political and social crisis of late industrial capitalism (Phillipson and Walker, 1987). The resultant 'political economy' analysis attempts to relate contemporary social attitudes and policies towards older people to the economic and ideological crisis of the welfare state, to shifts in the national and international labour market and to social and cultural change. It is argued, for example, that the experience of old age is heavily influenced by social divisions of class, race and gender, which create and reproduce inequalities through the lifecycle. The poverty and exclusion facing many elderly people is not a 'natural' result of their retirement and withdrawal from active life, but has been socially constructed through the social and economic policies of the state.

Structured dependency

Within this approach there are different emphases and theoretical concerns, but a shared interest in how the state and other institutions have constructed old age. In particular, the role of welfare systems in creating dependency has been investigated. It has been argued that dependency has been 'structured'; in particular, the state and employers have marginalised older workers and pushed them out of the labour market, forcing them to become dependent (Walker, 1990). In one such study Walker notes the systematic inequalities encountered by women in the labour force. He asks why the incidence of poverty is greater among older women than in any other group, including elderly men, and responds:

It would be wrong to conclude that it is simply because women live longer than men. We have already seen that even within age cohorts women are more likely to experience poverty and low incomes. An adequate explanation of the greater incidence of poverty amongst women in old age must reflect on the social and economic status of women before as well as after retirement and, therefore, the systems of distribution which determine status and access to resources. Chief among these are employment and, linked to it, the occupational pension system and social security. Inequalities forged or reinforced in the labour market are carried into retirement . . . Thus the poverty of elderly women . . . rests on the social production and distribution of resources in relation to the combination of social class, age and gender.

Walker (1987)

The notion of 'structured dependency' has been contested. Johnson (1993) has argued that the theory rests on a misguided notion of workers as 'powerless pawns' and of the state and employers as a homogenous category. Moreover, since it assumes that state benefit signifies dependency, work is conceptualised as 'independence'. Yet for many older people pensions offer a security (and therefore an independence) which did not exist in the past. It is also not clear how far workers were pushed out of jobs or whether they chose retirement (Macnicol and Blaikie, 1989).

It may be that theories of 'structured dependency' have over-simplified the complex inter-relationship between older people, the job market and state legislation. But they have also highlighted the necessity of taking into account wider political and social influences when exploring the lives of older people. They have drawn attention to the significance of broader social divisions of class, race and gender in structuring the experience of old age. Such influences, as we will see in the next section, help to shape the health chances of the elderly.

Postmodern perspectives on ageing

Postmodern theorists have explored the fabrication of 'ageing' and 'old age' within rationalist, scientific discourse. They have pointed to the breakdown of this discourse and to the increasing 'de-differentiation' of the life course in postmodern society. This is characterised by the blurring of boundaries between different age groups and by an emphasis on creating 'designer' lifestyles, an important aspect of which is 'body maintenance' to control personal appearance. Postmodernists highlight the historical and cultural specificity of age and ageing practices and suggest that in contemporary industrialised societies middle life and old age are being socially reconstructed (Featherstone and Hepworth, 1989).

A postmodern approach, therefore, emphasises fluidity and diversity, suggesting that current concepts of 'age' are not fixed and immutable but highly volatile. Far from medical science having uncovered the objective truth about ageing and the lifecycle, these are both seen as relativist social constructs subject to change. Predominantly negative images are currently associated with old people, reflecting their loss of economic and cultural capital, social power and cognitive, emotional and bodily control. In a similar way, youth has lower status than adulthood because it is symbolised by lack of power, capital and control. But as new cohorts enter old age, so a new language and conception of ageing may be developed.

9.5 The health of older people

There is conflicting evidence about the health of older people. In Western industrial nations each successive age cohort reaching old age seems to be a little healthier and with an improved life expectancy, although shifting social and cultural influences may change this (Fennell *et al.*, 1988). In consensus functionalist theories retirement was seen as a time of crisis in which loss of role might precipitate mental and physical ill health. Conflict theorists argued that loss of resources and poverty, rather than retirement alone, provoked anxiety and disorientation. But other researchers have found retirement to be of minor importance in influencing health status. For example, Crawford (reported in Phillipson, 1990) found that, although there were tensions and anxieties concerning retirement among the couples she studied, there was no evidence of a link to mental ill health. In a survey by Long and Wimbush in the mid-1980s respondents reported a slight improvement in health after retirement: 'There was no doubt that many did miss some of the satisfactions they had derived from their work, but there were also the benefits of lower levels of stress and pressure, and much in their retired life-styles provided its own satisfactions' (Long, 1989). Physical or mental ill health has been much more important in provoking retirement among older workers, in particular among semi-skilled and unskilled male workers. The part played by ill health in causing early withdrawal from the labour market recalls the arguments of the structured dependency theorists that the situation of elderly people needs to be related to wider structural patterns. Let's look briefly at some of these trends.

Britain, like much of the industrialised world, is characterised by an ageing population. In 1971, 13.3 per cent of the population were aged 65 or over and by 1981 this had grown to 15.1 per cent. By 1991 the figure was nearly 16 per cent, which represents over ten million people of pensionable age. This is projected to rise steadily until 2031, when the population of pensionable age will exceed 16 million (see Figure 9.4). At the same time the population aged under 16 will remain fairly stable. Thus the *dependency ratio* – the combined number of children and pensioners for every 100 people of working age – will rise, from 63 in 1991 to 79 by 2031.

○ What is the reason for the increased numbers of older people in the population?

Your response was probably to cite the steady fall in child mortality. The fact that more children have been surviving into adulthood means there are larger age cohorts of people to grow older. Increased average life

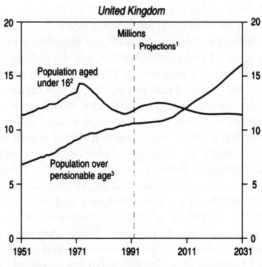

1 1991-based projections.
2 Data for 1951 to 1971 relate to population under 15
    (the school-leaving age was raised in 1972).
3 Males aged 65 and over, females aged 60 and over.

FIGURE 9.4 Dependent population by age. Source: *Social Trends* (1994)

expectancy has largely come from the fall in child mortality rather than people dying at a more advanced age.

Within this ageing population certain characteristic patterns have emerged. More women than men survive into old age, reversing the trend of earlier centuries when childbearing and tuberculosis were

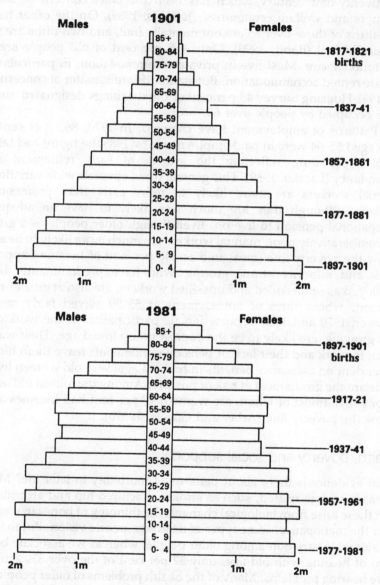

FIGURE 9.5 Age and sex structure of the British population, 1901 and 1981. Source: Jefferys (1989)

responsible for higher female mortality. Among elderly people the numbers of those over 75 and of the 'oldest old' – those aged 80 and over – have grown most dramatically (see Figure 9.5). 'It is the implications of the changing age structure of the population of pensionable age and the likelihood of a continuation of that trend into at least the first decade of the twenty-first century which has been the chief concern of social planners and welfare economists' (Jefferys, 1989). On the other hand four-fifths of those over 85 are not mentally frail, and two-fifths are not physically frail (Bond, 1990). Only 4–5 per cent of old people are in institutional care. Most live in private accommodation, in particular in private rented accommodation. But standards are a matter of concern; in the 1981 Housing Survey 43 per cent of the dwellings designated 'unfit' were occupied by people over 65.

Patterns of employment have changed. In 1970, 86.7 per cent of men aged 55–64 were in paid employment; by 1985 the figure had fallen to 57.5 per cent, reflecting the growth of early retirement and redundancy (Laczko, 1989). This general trend conceals wide variations. Manual workers are more likely to retire early than professional workers, although they are much less likely to have an adequate occupational pension to live on. Even though older people as a group are comparatively poor, manual workers are much more likely to be at or below the poverty line (measured as 140 per cent of Income Support). Black and minority ethnic groups, who have predominantly been employed as semi-skilled and unskilled workers, are also at greater risk. Women, whose rates of employment at 55–59 stayed fairly steady between 1970 and 1985 because female participation in the workforce was growing, are likely to be the poorest group in old age. Their wages when in work and their lack of pension entitlements leave them highly dependent on assistance benefits in frail old age; very old women living alone are the group most at risk of poverty. Among the 'oldest old' aged 80 or above (most of whom are women) 47 per cent had incomes at or below the poverty line (Arber and Gilbert, 1989b).

Health, poverty and social support

What evidence is there about patterns of morbidity in later life? Many diseases are age-related, such as strokes, fractured hip and arthritis. In part these arise from biological changes: the thinning of bones in women after the menopause, some types of deafness, poorer vision. But there is considerable variation among older people; whereas we associate being hard of hearing with old age, only 32 per cent of the over 65s actually have hearing problems. Many of the health problems of older people are similar to those of younger age groups – cancers, respiratory conditions, circulatory diseases – but the incidence of such diseases increases.

Among the younger old chronic illness and disability are much less common than among the over 75s, and the prevalence of disability increases from 12 per cent (for 65–69 year olds) to 80 per cent (for the over 85s) (Briggs, reported in Bond *et al.*, 1993). Various surveys of the mobility and capacity of older people have demonstrated the difference between the young and oldest old (see Table 9.2). Nevertheless, the striking aspect of such research is the confirmation that most older people are active and capable. A few tasks such as toenail cutting, climbing stairs, cleaning windows and washing paintwork become too difficult, but most people are also to cope even when they are in their 80s (Victor, 1991).

There has been considerable debate about the pattern of morbidity in old age and indeed about mortality trends. It has been argued by some that morbidity is becoming compressed into the last years of life, and that this tendency will become more pronounced as average life expectancy evens out and the 'natural lifespan' is attained by most

TABLE 9.2 Inability to undertake mobility, self care and domestic tasks. Source: Bond *et al.* (1993)

| | Age | | | | | |
	65–69	70–74	75–79	80–84	85+	All 65+
Walk out of doors	5	7	14	24	47	13
Getting up and down stairs and steps	4	5	10	17	31	9
Getting around the house on the level)	1	1	2	3	6	2
Getting to the toilet	1	1	2	2	7	2
Getting in and out of bed	1	1	3	2	7	2
Cut toenails	16	24	34	48	65	29
Bathing, showering, washing all over	4	5	10	16	31	9
Brushing hair (females), shaving (males)	1	1	1	3	7	2
Washing face and hands	0	1	1	1	2	1
Feeding	0	1	0	1	2	1
Household shopping	7	10	16	29	56	16
Wash paintwork	8	13	24	34	62	20
Clean windows inside	9	13	21	34	63	19
Clean and sweep floors	5	7	13	20	45	12
Job involving climbing	17	25	36	52	76	31
Wash clothing by hand	4	5	9	12	32	8
Open screw-top jars	7	7	11	15	29	10
Cook a main meal	4	4	9	13	29	8
Use a frying pan	2	2	5	8	19	5
Make a cup of tea	1	1	3	3	8	2
Numbers in survey	1062	1025	788	395	240	3510

people (Fries, 1980; Fries and Crapo, 1981). In this 'rectangularisation of mortality' and 'compression of morbidity' theory it is claimed that increasing numbers of older people are reaching 'natural death' because the 'medical and social task of eliminating premature death is largely accomplished' (Fries, 1980). In this situation the task of health services is to operate preventive policies and encourage older people to live healthier lives so that chronic illness is postponed. Whereas many researchers were predicting the growing need for care and treatment services because of this, Fries was arguing that individual responsibility – 'use it or lose it' – was the way forward.

This account has been challenged on several grounds (Bury, 1988). First, there is no real evidence that mortality has reached a plateau; on the contrary, mortality has continued to fall – although not consistently – and to fall most sharply for the oldest old. Second, the notion that morbidity has become compressed into old age has been questioned, not least because measuring health status is problematic. There is no evidence of 'age-specific decline' in conditions such as hip fracture or cancers (Marmot and McDowall, 1986). Third, the link between 'healthy lifestyles' and enhanced health status in old age is challenged, and the dangers of a simplistic endorsement of this approach are noted. Bury (1988) argues that little account is taken of structural constraints on health choices in Fries' analysis, leaving the way open for a victim-blaming approach in health policy.

In fact, the evidence linking poor health among older people to poverty and low social class is very strong. Workers in social class V are less likely to reach retirement age: two-and-a-half times as many unskilled workers die before retirement than workers in social class I (Phillipson, 1990). Of those manual workers who do survive into old age many will find themselves on the borders of poverty, and many other old people, as we noted earlier, will have to adjust to considerably reduced incomes. Victor (1989), while emphasising the 'substantial range of income amongst older people', has highlighted the poverty of households headed by women, the very old and those from lower social classes. These groups had greater need of health and social support services and were more likely to have disabilities. Whitehead's *The Health Divide* (1987) demonstrated the social class gradients which exist actoss the lifespan, not just in mortality but for all limiting long-standing illnesses (see Figure 9.6).

Exploring patterns of health by means of the General Household Survey, Evandrou and Victor (1989) noted how social class differentiated the experience of old age. In particular, housing tenure was a clear demarcator; homeowners were the most materially advantaged, and they experienced better health than did either council tenants or those in private rented accommodation (see Table 9.3). For example, 43 per cent

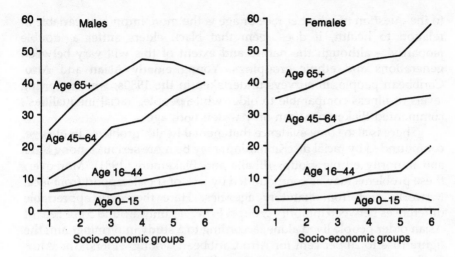

FIGURE 9.6 Social class gradients in mortality and chronic illness. Source: Whitehead (1987)

TABLE 9.3 Housing tenure and health status. Source: Evandrou and Victor (1989), in Bytheway

| | Degree of disability[1] | | | |
	None	Slight	Moderate	Severe
Owner occupier	53	47	40	45
Rented:				
From local authority	32	38	46	42
From housing association				
(or co-operative)	2	3	3	2
From relative	1	2	2	2
Privately – furnished	1	0	0	0
Privately – unfurnished	11	10	9	9
Total (= 100%)	2139	1124	762	337

[1] Using the index of 'personal incapacity' of Townsend and Wedderburn (1965).

of retired people who reported their health as 'good' were owner occupiers whereas 29 per cent were council tenants; 53 per cent of retired people who had no disability were owner occupiers compared with 32 per cent who were council tenants.

Blakemore (1989) reported that the relatively low employment status and poor pay of black and minority ethnic groups created 'multiple hazards to health' in later years. Whilst there is no final answer to the question of whether race or age is the more important variable in relation to health, it does seem that black elders suffer a 'double jeopardy' – although the nature and extent of this will vary between generations and ethnic groupings. Young elderly Asian and Afro-Caribbean people, in surveys undertaken in the 1980s, were reporting levels of illness comparable to older white people; 'racial inequalities', commented Blakemore, 'can only widen with age'.

There is also some evidence that mental health problems in old age, compounded by racial discrimination, may be more serious among black and minority ethnic groups (Bhalla and Blakemore, 1981). Moreover, these problems may be compounded by lack of social support from local networks and from statutory agencies. Here there are appreciable differences between minority groups. Whereas only around 5 per cent of Asian older people lived alone, according to a study in Birmingham, the figure rose to 20 per cent for Afro-Caribbean 'young' elders. The Afro-Caribbean people were more likely to live in rented accommodation, to move around, to be further away from the centres of their communities and to see relatives less than once a week (Blakemore, 1987). Other researchers have found social networks to be of importance in relation to the health of older people (Wenger, 1989; Long, 1990). For example, in a recent study very elderly people with low levels of social support reported less 'life satisfaction' than those with larger social networks (Bowling, 1993).

In relation to statutory support services recent studies of black older people have confirmed that 'they are under-represented among those receiving community and health services' (Cameron et al., 1989). In their large-scale survey of black older women's needs in Birmingham Cameron et al. found that community care services were in touch with relatively few of these women and that services which were provided were often inappropriate.

9.6 Health work and dependency

What implications for health work arise from this investigation of 'dependent' groups? Perhaps the first and most important is the need to recognise how biomedicine and the 'medical model' have themselves contributed to the social construction of dependency. Modern scientific medicine is one important aspect of the rationalist, scientific discourse which divided up and categorised the human 'lifespan'. Medical specialties such as paediatrics and geriatrics have institutionalised age as a factor of significance. Age-related tables of 'normal functioning' have formed the basis for making judgements about rights to benefit. The medicalisation of mental handicap, as we noted earlier, arose within a scientific discourse about normality. Nurses and other health workers need to be aware of the powerful images and stereotypes conveyed by medical language and to avoid using terms which demean and dehumanise their patients. Nursing models and theories, which have deliberately eschewed medical language and terminology, have sought to place the active patient centre stage (Roper *et al.*, 1980). Another concern is about social, cultural and racial stereotyping, which may or may not be reinforced through medical language. For example, the district nurse in the Cameron *et al.* (1989) survey who commented that 'Blacks have a lower pain threshold' was disguising her stereotyping of black clients by framing it within a formal 'scientific' discourse.

Another issue concerns the promotion of independence. To some extent 'structured' dependency in the health sector is receding. People with mental and physical disabilities are no longer so likely to be patients in long-stay institutions cared for by nurses; they are (to a larger extent) residents in a local community. Older people are now more likely to be cared for at home, through domiciliary services and respite care, rather than on long-stay care of the elderly wards – although during the 1980s the numbers in private residential homes grew sharply (see Chapter 4 and Figure 9.7). The exchange between care provider and the cared-for person in a domestic setting offers a greater opportunity for negotiation and power-sharing than did routinised care delivery in an institution. There is a greater possibility of effective communication with older people and of promoting their independence. A broader understanding of socio-economic influences on health in later life can assist health workers to use a social model of health in the assessment of their older patients. Greater emphasis on 'holistic' health care, it might be argued, should shift the focus away from stereotyping and routinised care to individual needs assessment. But it does not follow that, in itself, community care will deliver flexible and holistic care. The danger of caring for dependent people without really treating them as 'whole individuals' is a real one:

Too often we do not listen to people who tell us about their problems, especially when they are no longer able to look after themselves. We do not spend time finding out what is on their minds. Often with dependent people we are too busy 'caring' for them to care. We assume that we know from the limited facts available to us how they feel, that we know best what they should do, and that our idea of what is 'right' or 'wrong' should determine what other people decide to do.

Scrutton (1989)

Recent accounts by writers with physical disabilities have made similar points about the tyranny of caring. Ken Davis (1993) notes that linguistic

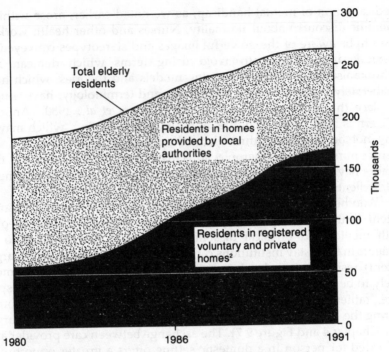

FIGURE 9.7 Elderly people in residential accommodation[1]. Source: *Social Trends* (1993)

[1] Residents aged 65 and over in homes for elderly people and homes for the younger physically handicapped. Figures for Wales also include residents in homes for the blind.
[2] United Kingdom up to 1988. Figures for 1989, 1990 and 1991 exclude Northern Ireland.

adjustments – for example using 'client' instead of 'patient', or 'community care' – have implied that there is equivalence in choice and control (or at least negotiation) between disabled people and professionals. Yet, he argues, 'our lives are still substantially in their hands. They still determine most decisions and their practical outcomes . . . The carefully crafted, mechanical embrace of "care" ' is a product of professional power, and it demands, to a great extent, patient acquiescence. Beyond this any real shift from dependence to independence needs to go beyond the model of 'physical independence' held by many professionals to embrace the notion of decision making and autonomy (Oliver, 1993). This approach sees independent living as being about quality of life, risk taking and equal partnership in determining priorities and services.

Using theory

It is important to recognise the limits of a positivist 'scientific' approach to age and disability. You will recall from Chapter 2 that, while such analyses can be very powerful, much can also be learned from phenomenological studies using ethnography and other approaches.

○ Read the case study of Sarah in Box 9.3, noting how social influences and personal biography are interwoven in her health status and life-history. How do such personal accounts add to our stock of knowledge?

Sarah's story illuminates the struggles, hopes and beliefs of black people in Britain. Quantitative surveys of health in old age can reveal much, but they also conceal much of the richness and variety of people's experiences which ethnographic research has documented. There is great diversity amongst older people, not simply because of the

BOX 9.3 Case study: Sarah. Source: K258 (1992)

Sarah, who is 67, came to London from Jamaica in 1960 to join her sister. For over 20 years she worked on the London buses as a clippy, a job she thoroughly enjoyed. Her ties with her family are very strong and, although the pay was not good, she was very careful with her money and always put some aside to pay for visits to Jamaica. She lives in a one bedroom flat on a very large but run-down London council estate. The local crime rate is extremely high, but Sarah is not worried and is very happy with her flat. She has an exercise bike and grows fresh vegetables in containers on her balcony.

She has strong views about health: 'If you notice some of these older people [from the West Indies], they are living to 110. The thing is that in them days they didn't have these chemicals. That's destroying the human body, you know these chemicals they put in the food. You don't know what to eat . . . I guess that's why there's so much sickness. The people in the West Indies, they live to such a good age; they didn't know anything about these chemicals – we always had pure, fresh food, lots of fresh fish and vegetables, nothing was added to it.'

Sarah has arthritis. She does attend physiotherapy sessions, but does not take the pills prescribed by her doctor, preferring her own remedies: 'When people take all these tablets, it's rotting your system. What I do, I get up in the morning and turn on the hot tap and soak the rag in it and put it on it [her shoulders], and sometimes I spray it when I remember and I rub it with olive oil.'

Sarah does voluntary work and sings in two church choirs: 'I like meeting people, seeing people. I like being among people because when I retired my sister said do dressmaking. I said, oh no, I couldn't sit down at a machine all day. I'm like a bird, to be out in the air that's me. I like to be out.

'Good health? Well I think good health is when you can laugh and make people laugh . . . you can still go about, the limbs are alright, and you can make someone happy.'

influence of class, race, generation and gender, but because of the specific nature of their past experiences – of their own particular 'life course'. The health state of an old person represents the complex sum of all these influences. So while it is necessary to be aware of health and social influences on the lives of patients, it is also important to see the 'person'.

In this respect postmodernism has challenged medicine by helping to deconstruct old age as one of a series of discrete 'normal' and 'natural' stages in life. It has challenged the idea that ageing and old age have any universal significance and explored how both are social constructs. Together with the structured dependency approach this has highlighted the need to study old age within a wider social framework. Many recent discussions of age (for example Fennell *et al.*, 1988) attempt to keep in focus both personal experience and structural analysis. But it is important to grapple with theories of how old age is structured in contemporary society. Such analyses can have considerable impact on practice, by highlighting that 'a fully effective service response to the needs of the black community would necessitate a fundamental shift in the wider political, ideological, economic, and social structure' (Cameron *et al.*, 1989).

In a similar way, the deconstruction of disability – and in particular the challenge to scientific, medical truth claims to define and categorise it – has highlighted the importance of the structured dependency account. Having pointed out how health and welfare services and service providers have helped to reinforce and extend dependency, Oliver (1993) suggests that structural changes are needed to promote autonomy: 'anti-discrimination legislation, freedom of information and the proper financial and other support of organisations controlled and run by disabled people themselves'. He argues that the combination of legal backing, supported by the right to look inside 'the locked medical cabinets', and the vesting of control in the dependent groups themselves would decisively shift the balance of power from professionals to disabled people. By contrast, a 'supermarket' consumer model, such as that envisaged in current government policy reforms, would not serve the needs of those with difficulties 'in reaching the shelves'.

Suggestions for further study

J. Bond, S. Peace and P. Coleman's (1993) *Ageing in Society*, London, Sage, provides a comprehensive introduction to health and welfare issues related to older people. J. Swain, V. Finkelstein, S. French and M. Oliver's (1993) *Disabling Barriers, Enabling Environments*, London,

Sage, is a challenging and thought-provoking discussion of disability. A. Brechin and J. Walmesley (eds) (1990) *Making Connections*, London, Hodder and Stoughton, is a varied collection of articles written from a number of different perspectives.

Self assessment questions

1 What are the different meanings of the term 'dependency'?
2 In what ways do you understand dependency to be 'socially constructed'?
3 What are the possible advantages and drawbacks for people with disabilities in the shift from institutional to community care?
4 Outline the main influences on the health of older people.
5 How can health workers challenge prejudice and discrimination in relation to 'dependent' groups?

Chapter 10

Health beliefs and health action

Contents

Themes and issues

Socio-cultural production of health and illness: the triumph of Western biomedicine – the fabrication of the body

Ancient and contemporary 'alternative' medical thought systems: Chinese medicine – homeopathy – Ayurveda

Health accounts in anthropology: internalising and externalising systems – the Gnau and the Amhara

Accounting for lay illness behaviour and action: structural and interactionist models – lay referral systems

Theorising illness: Talcott Parsons and sick role theory – the patient career: acute and chronic illness – open and closed institutions – labelling theory

Learning outcomes

After working through this chapter you should be able to:

1 Review your own beliefs about health and illness in the light of lay accounts outlined in the chapter.
2 Explain the main differences between biomedicine and alternative and non-Western health belief systems.
3 Discuss the main social factors which may influence an individual's response to illness.
4 Compare and contrast structural and social action theories of illness behaviour.

I N Chapter 1, Health in a social context, several distinctive ways of defining health and illness were noted. It was seen that *lay* definitions of health overlapped and were extended by various types of *official* definitions, such as those originating in medical circles or in the World Health Organisation. Helman (1986), for example, indicated that 'folk' beliefs about colds and fevers flourished among patients in his London general practice and that health professionals, for various reasons, adopted this explanatory mode (and thus helped to perpetuate it) when dealing with patients. It was also noted that 'public' definitions of health, given by people in response to researchers' enquiries, might differ considerably from 'private' explanations given to family, friends and neighbours.

This chapter picks up and develops these observations about the diversity and the competing claims of contemporary accounts of health and illness and considers how far pluralism and conflict characterise the health scene today. It reviews research into lay belief systems and sets against this various types of official or 'expert' account from modern biomedicine and from 'alternative' medicine. It considers how such accounts – not excluding biomedicine itself – have been shaped by cultural change and by social structures and ideology.

The second theme of this chapter is health action. In Chapter 1 we noted that people's statements about health, whether expert or lay, were influenced by a range of cultural and social factors – by age, gender, social class, ethnicity and so on. In subsequent chapters we have explored the nature of the complex inter-connections between health and these major social divisions and inequalities. In this chapter we'll apply this analysis to a consideration of the process of becoming a patient. How and why do people identify themselves as ill and when and why do they seek out medical treatment? How do they make decisions about what treatment to seek? In what ways do social factors influence their behaviours and actions? And what social relationships do they enter when they become 'patients'?

10.1 Understanding health and illness

Health and illness may seem to happen to us as individuals, but all of us experience and make sense of them by drawing on a stock of current health beliefs, ideas and practices of various types, both lay accounts and expert theories. This observation is an essential starting point in any discussion about health beliefs. First, it acknowledges that people's attitudes are greatly influenced by expert or official ideas about what health and illness are (and are not) and how they may best be dealt with.

We noted in Chapter 1 that 'sickness' and 'disease' rather than a subjective state of 'illness' are the main focus of concern of official health agencies; they exist primarily to treat presented sickness and to uncover, explain and cure specific disease states. In everyday life this is often converted into a normative, social and moral pressure to 'keep going' and avoid 'going off sick', which owes much to a medical notion of health ·as 'absence of disease'. On the other hand several official definitions of health are currently in circulation. 'Absence of disease' has been joined by 'a complete state of wellbeing' and 'adequate resources for living' to create a set of distinctive approaches, each with a different philosophy, focus and set of objectives. While modern biomedicine has established itself on a basis of scientific objectivity and hypothetico-deductive research methods, the 'social model' of health – implicit in notions of wellbeing and resources for living – expands this to encompass qualitative criteria and measurement as well. Here already is evidence that official accounts are not monolithic, unchanging or one-dimensional, and that people will inevitably find themselves making choices about which official explanation to believe.

Second, (as Chapter 1 also began to demonstrate) the concept of a stock of health beliefs draws attention to the idea that people's beliefs about health and their accounts of health and illness are woven together from personal and shared experiences, folk beliefs and stories, not just from public traditions and theories. Official, publicly approved explanations have never been simply swallowed wholesale by the masses. People have sifted and selected what made sense to them, although it has usually been necessary to conform outwardly to official pronouncements about 'what health is' and how it may be attained. In recent surveys (for example Cox et al., 1987) many respondents volunteered the 'right' responses to questions about their health, acknowledging the importance of 'cutting down fat intake' and 'getting more exercise', but it is doubtful whether they practise, and they may not even privately believe, such prescriptions.

○ Can you think of any other examples of conflict between 'official' pronouncements on health matters and ordinary people's attitudes and responses?

A number of examples exist, the most recent being the contrast between Department of Health warnings and medical advice about the spread of HIV/AIDS in the heterosexual population and the widespread evidence of continuing 'unsafe' sexual behaviour among young people. At a more fundamental level, compare the damning indictment of alternative medicine and therapies by the British Medical Association (1986) with evidence of rapidly growing consultation rates among the general public for all kinds of alternative practitioners: acupuncturists, homeopaths, chiropractors and so on. In past centuries (and today) the widespread use of charms, folk remedies, herbal medicines or consultations with the local 'wise woman' or 'witch' – despite official disapproval and often heavy penalties – is testimony to the persistence of popular beliefs about the causes of and cures for ill health. Throughout history, although officially sanctioned accounts of health and disease have been prominent in shaping ordinary people's ideas, they have never remained unchallenged.

Third, it is important to ask questions about the origins and character of the stock of current health beliefs, ideas and practices which is drawn upon. Why do some ideas receive official sanction and support whereas others are marginalised? Why do ideas about health and ill health change over time and between different cultures? Why are some once widely accepted ideas now stigmatised as 'non-scientific' or 'quackery'?

'History as progress' and its critics

There are various types of response to these questions, but you may be most familiar with the 'history as progress' account. In this view doctors and scientists have gradually discovered more and more about the structure and functioning of the human body through a rational, empirical and scientific approach that has enabled them to convince others (rival theorists, the public, governments, religious bodies and so on) of the objective truth of their discoveries. As Paul Unschuld (1986) puts it, the traditional explanation is that:

Surrounded by a sea of ignorance and irrationality, some scholars, working over centuries, have brought together more and more precise knowledge of how the human body is structured and how it functions under normal conditions or under conditions of illness. Progress of this kind, it is argued, has led unerringly from the early beginnings of medicine among primitive tribes, and later among the Greeks, to the astonishing results of the present.

Unschuld (1986)

The logic of the 'history as progress' view points to the inevitable triumph of modern biomedicine as the one true account of health and disease, knocking to the floor – conceptually and methodologically – less robust and convincing types of explanations. This is substantially the position adopted in most history of medicine and nursing texts. But there are problems with this account. While Unschuld fully acknowledges the enormous growth of 'successful medical interventions', he points out that historically and in contemporary society:

Mutually exclusive and contradictory systems often co-existed, not merely in divergent cultures but even within one and the same culture . . .

'Outdated' and 'mistaken' concepts live side-by-side with those of 'scientific truth', not only among the uneducated strata of society but also among those which may be regarded as educated. There is also the unresolved question of why modern medical concepts are convincing and acceptable for some parts of society while those same concepts are rejected or even bitterly opposed by some other social groupings.

Unschuld (1986)

We have noted these features in passing already, in relation to the different emphases in official accounts and in the variety of alternative approaches – lay and expert – that co-exist in contemporary society. In the sections that follow we'll consider these ideas in more detail.

The 'history as progress' approach has been criticised on much broader grounds as well, as you might recall from Chapter 2 where we considered the ideas put forward by Michel Foucault about the socio-cultural 'fabrication' of the body in scientific medicine.

○   Note down how the ideas of Michel Foucault about the 'fabrication' of the body relate to this discussion.

Social constructionists have argued that, far from being a fixed biological entity waiting to be discovered by scientists, the body as we know it only came into being when the 'clinical gaze' of doctors constructed it and when health personnel were trained in the use of the 'anatomical atlas' of the body – by means of which they could 'see' what they were looking at. This insight directs our attention away from focusing simply on the linear march of science and medicine and towards a broader analysis of the shifting cultural and social basis of medicine. It suggests that our current conceptualisation of the human body simply represents one way of looking at it. We have learned to see and know it and to intervene in relation to its management and treatment in a particular way, but there have been, and may be in the future, other ways of seeing (Foucault, 1973). This prompts debate about how and why this new view of the body became acceptable, and under what circumstances another shift of view might take place (see Section 11.2).

Explanations as social and cultural products

If we return to the questions posed earlier – about why some scientific ideas receive official sanction and support whereas others are marginalised; why ideas about health and ill health change over time and between different cultures; and why some once widely accepted ideas are now stigmatised as 'non-scientific' – at least two types of response can now be made.

○   Check your own understanding of how 'history as progress' supporters and critics of this view would respond to these questions.

The 'history as progress' approach would point to the superiority and objectivity of scientific knowledge. Scientific ideas receive official sanction and wide social approval because they offer more convincing explanations; herein lies the explanation of the world-wide success of modern biomedicine. The shifts in thought are conceptualised in terms of the onward march of medical science and the consequent discrediting of non- and pre-scientific ideas, which become stigmatised and marginalised. By contrast, critics point out that in many societies conflicting and mutually exclusive accounts co-exist, even though at certain times some may be much more powerful and persuasive than others. It might be argued, for example, that in the early twentieth century biomedicine became the predominant world mode of thought and model of intervention, but as the end of the century approaches its continued domination is more doubtful.

Social constructionists have emphasised that all production of medical knowledge takes place within societies and cultures, not outside them, and is therefore influenced by (and itself helps to create) changing ideologies and social practices. The rise of clinical medicine with its treatment regimes and positioning of the patient (or rather the patient's disease) as the 'object' of medical scrutiny was underpinned by a changing conceptualisation of the body and its relation to society. Modern medicine both reflected this shift and helped in the process of 'reconstructing' the body. So an alternative view is to argue that some scientific ideas receive offical sanction and support because they 'fit in' with other ideas and practices of the time, projected by powerful groups in a society. Ideas about health and medicine must be studied in relation to the wider belief systems and social practices of the societies in which they operate: they are *relative* concepts. As other ideas and practices change, ideas about health and ill health shift too; hence, once widely accepted ideas may become unacceptable. In other words, explanations of health, illness, disease and sickness are specific social and cultural products rather than universal objective 'truths'. This directs our attention to concepts of health and disease as arising from people's changing perceptions and motives and not just from their empirical observations of the natural world.

10.2 Health belief systems in non-Western societies

Anthropologists have long been interested in how official and lay explanations of health and sickness are deeply embedded in the social ideologies and structures of non-Western societies. Indeed there is a long tradition of anthropological research into exotic cultures and 'primitive' peoples. Until very recently:

A search in a good anthropological library in Britain would reveal more about the everyday health beliefs of (say) African, Asian or South American countries than could be discovered in any library in Britain about the everyday health beliefs of the peoples of the British Isles.

K258 (1992)

Traditionally such anthropological research highlighted the *cultural specificity* of ideas of health and illness. It drew attention to the correspondence between their subjects' views about health and medicine on the one hand, and their life experiences, social patterns, customs and ideas on the other. Paul Unschuld (1986) comments that the study of 'rather undifferentiated civilisations within which each member shared the worldview of all the others' encouraged anthropologists to make generalised claims about cultural specificity in relation to complex societies, ignoring the issues of social and historical change.

In some research racist assumptions were made both about the innate superiority of Western beliefs and medical systems and about the primitive, undifferentiated nature of non-Western cultures. Such assumptions sometimes led to questionable interpretations, but recent anthropologists are much more aware of the dangers of ethnocentrism and cultural imperialism: that is, of imposing their own meanings on the particular cultural practices they are studying. Two examples of the fascinating research that has taken place in non-Western societies are briefly sketched below: the work of Gilbert Lewis among the Gnau of New Guinea and of Allan Young in Ethiopia. Having noted some of their findings, we'll move on to draw some conclusions about the significance of such studies.

The Gnau of New Guinea

Gilbert Lewis (1986) studied the health beliefs and healing practices of the Gnau peoples of New Guinea and was amazed to discover that they held different and conflicting views when asked whether birds and some animals die:

I treasure the feeling of discovery I had then . . . I had presumed that something was as obvious to them as to me, and I was wrong. Yet I had lived with them more than two years without finding out so great a difference in the answers we would give to that question.

Lewis (1986)

Through this discovery Lewis became aware that the Gnau had two conceptions of life: 'consciousness, being able to move, purpose guiding action' and life as a contrast to death 'as a passage of time, a span with a beginning and an end'. Whereas they were clear that plant life was of the latter type, there were differences of opinion about whether animals and birds had 'consciousness'.

Lewis noted that the Gnau had one undifferentiated word – *wola* – for 'undesired', which covered 'ill', 'bad' and also 'forbidden' and 'dangerous'. *Neyigeg*, 'to be sick', referred to illnesses of the whole person but not chronic states, or frailty in old age or external ailments. Health was implicitly defined as 'accumulated resistance to potential dangers' which in a normal life 'waxes and then wanes'. 'The Gnau rules on correct behaviour, proper food, the dangers in objects, animals, trees, represent an ordering, or a collection of precepts which one should follow to achieve the ideal normal life' (Lewis, 1986).

Explanations of illness varied, and sometimes none was offered. Some illnesses just came – *neyigeg gipi'i*, 'he is sick nothingly' – and death might just happen too. Lewis gives the example of breast abcesses, which were very painful but were seen as a 'natural event' and women continued with their everyday life. Where illness was seen as 'caused', it was explained in terms of spirits, magic or sorcery, or breaking a taboo, but Lewis found no consistent connection between symptoms and explanations in the Western sense of this. He cites what he diagnosed as 25 cases of pneumonia or bronchopneumonia: of these seven were attributed to 'named great spirits'; 11 to 'undifferentiated spirits'; six to dead individuals; five to broken prohibitions; four to sorcery. Some were attributed to several causes and some to no cause.

Lewis also reported that the Gnau had no particular specialist practitioners or systematised knowledge regarding ill health. Anybody might offer the sick comfort or assistance. Ill people made decisions themselves about adopting a 'sick role'; they shut themselves away or lay apart from the group, rejected some foods and covered themselves with dust and ashes to trick the illness-bearing spirits into thinking that they had triumphed. Meanwhile the main task of relatives and friends was to help to defeat the spirits, although they also comforted the sufferer and perhaps applied herbal remedies. He concluded that the Gnau lacked a medical system 'in the sense of lacking a special department of coordinated knowledge and practice concerned specifically with the understanding and treatment of illness' (Lewis, 1986). But they clearly have well-established beliefs about the causes of illness and about the appropriate way to restore the sufferer to health.

The Amhara of Ethiopia

Unlike the Gnau, the Amhara are concerned to identify the body's internal organs; the heart and pulse and the stomach and digestive process, in particular, are attended to because over- or under-activity of these organs/systems signals danger to health. In the stomach, *wosfat* (worms) digest the food, but if they quarrel or over-multiply this results in pain and nausea. Over-pulsing of the heart endangers the intellect, which is thought to reside in the heart. Health is defined as *tena*, a state of wellbeing resulting from harmony and equilibrium in the body. Young (1986) identified five categories of pathogenic agents which could upset this equilibrium: excess of everyday foods/activities; corrosive substances – *likift* – which irritate or interfere with bodily function; poisons; *wer-hyenas*, humans with spirit aspects – *buda* – which enter and upset the body; sickness-stuff, *bashiyta*, caused by contagion or the acts of demons, which give rise to influenza and other acute conditions (see Figure 10.1).

The Amhara examine the sick person, but rely quite heavily on subjective descriptions of symptoms by the sufferer. Their therapeutic interventions are much more elaborate and systematic than those of the Gnau, carried out by a variety of specialist healers. Some healers (*habesha hakiym*) attend to body parts or processes, for example bone setters and removers of diseased body parts; others, in particular herbalists, treat several conditions with infusions, emetics and diet therapy. Spirit healers, on the other hand, treat the whole range of illness by intercession with the spirit and the use of expelling agents – purges,

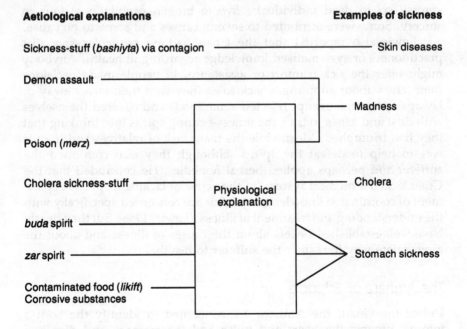

FIGURE 10.1 The Amhara health belief systems. Source: Young (1986)

emetics, fumitories and so on. The growth of these specialist healers, although their bodies of medical knowledge are mainly pragmatic, parallels the much greater division of labour and the existence of differentiated legal and political institutions, in contrast with the simple, homogenous Gnau society.

Drawing conclusions

One useful way of beginning to make some sense of these anthropological findings is to distinguish between 'internalising' and 'externalising' medical belief systems (Young, 1986). Young suggests that internalising systems use physiological explanations as their starting point: that is, 'images or analogies which make it possible for people to order events within the sick person's body from the onset of symptoms to the conclusion of the sickness episode'. For example, heat pulse and breathing are observed, and hunger, thirst and evacuation reveal internal changes. Young suggests that the most widely used image in this approach is that of the 'disturbed natural equilibrium', common to European, Chinese and Hispano-American traditions.

Externalising systems focus on developing aetiological explanations: that is, on assigning a cause (or several causes) for illness that lies outside the sufferer's body. They are concerned to identify where the search for cause should start and to explain the complex process through which the sufferer came to be afflicted. Responsibility for ill health may or may not be seen as the fault of the sufferer, depending on what the search for cause reveals; for example, lack of care on the part of sufferers – due to ritual lapses, disturbed spirits, deviant lifestyle and so on – may result in their sickness being seen as illegitimate.

Look back to the brief accounts of Gnau and Amhara health beliefs and suggest whether they are, in Young's terms, 'externalising' or 'internalising' systems.

Gnau health beliefs clearly fall into the 'externalising' category presented by Young. The Gnau see illness as being caused by external events or agents, and the response of undifferentiated lay helpers is not to examine the sufferer and try to trace the internal pathways of disease but to outwit the 'evil spirit'. Amhara medical beliefs, as Young reports them, lean more towards the 'internalising' system; they emphasise the importance of internal body organs and systems working together to ensure balance and harmony, and they elaborate how pathogenic agents disturb and endanger the body. They also have a considerable range of specialist healers. On the other hand, this approach does not exclude *buda*, or the existence of those *habesha hakiym* who operate as spirit healers, treating the whole range of sickness.

Young suggests that many medical belief systems employ both kinds of explanation. Even Western biomedicine, for example, which Young sees as unambiguously associated with internalising systems, could be claimed to offer aetiological explanations rooted in 'deviant lifestyles'. However, having reflected on the relationship between medical beliefs and the larger cultural and social systems of which they form a part, he suggests that 'structurally simple, tribal societies tend to rely on externalising systems of medical beliefs', whereas 'internalising systems . . . are characteristic of the structurally complex, literate state societies of Asia, Europe and North Africa' (Young, 1986).

The different systems reflect the different modes of socio-cultural explanation that exist in these types of societies. In Gnau society each individual sickness episode denotes a fundamental disruption of relations between people and spirits who reflect (and invert) the 'moral order of society', so the observation and investigation of the sick body and specialist treatment of it are of low priority. Everyone's efforts are directed towards appeasing the angry spirit. Internalising systems develop as specialisation and complexity develops in the social and political system; then the sick body needs to be decoded in order that the disruption and deviance associated with sickness can be legitimised and controlled. This is very much the way in which Foucault (1973) discussed the preconditions for the emergence of biomedicine.

We have tended to use the findings of anthropologists to reinforce our own sense of superiority; how 'primitive', we say, to fail to make the connection between particular clinical signs and symptoms and specific (or cluster) causes. But a more even-handed and imaginative use of such research is to enable us to identify the underlying assumptions and implicit belief systems of our own society.

○ Think back to the ideas of Foucault about the rise of clinical medicine. Can you see any connection between these ideas and the Gnau and Amhara belief systems?

Both modern Western medicine and Gnau and Amhara health beliefs advance accounts of health and illness and offer explanations; both represent a search for some order or reason in events, so that an effective response can be made. They all try to make sense of the world around them. It is usual to contrast 'scientific' biological medicine with 'magical' (sometimes supernatural) beliefs like those of the Gnau. But Foucault drew attention to modern medicine as a magical system; the body, far from being a natural object described by medical scientists, was brought into existence for us by the clinical gaze and anatomical atlas.

Robin Horton (1970) has argued that explanations which are mystical or magical and scientific accounts have more in common than we like to think. On the other hand he sees Western thought as 'open' whereas that of, say, the Amhara or the Gnau is 'closed'. But this has been questioned for at least two reasons. First, because most of us have to believe rather than actually understand science and biomedicine: 'most people in the West are in much the same position in relation to scientific knowledge as are the Amhara and other adherents of mystical systems' (Stacey, 1988). Specialist knowledge creates a great gulf between expert and lay people. Second, the openness of Western science has been questioned, because the process of production of scientific knowledge does not seem to encourage deviance, challenge and doubt so much as conformity to dominant paradigms and 'truths' (Kuhn, 1970).

10.3 The emergence of biomedicine as a belief system

In Chapter 1 it became clear that the model of health and disease which came to dominate Western thinking after about 1800 – the 'medical model' as it has been termed – was grounded in biology and other sciences. Overriding importance was given to learning about anatomy and physiology, in particular to understanding mechanisms such as the heart, arteries, nerves, brain and so on. The body was conceptualised as a machine in which all the parts functioned together to ensure health; if some parts broke down, clinicians intervened to limit and treat the damage. This model offered us a distinctive way of 'seeing' and understanding our bodies, a set of guidelines about relating to them and about dealing with them – to groom, nurture and exercise them, for example. Normal functioning, normal parameters of size, shape, distribution became reified as 'health'; or rather, deviation from these norms became viewed by the medical profession as pathological.

But how did this view of health and disease, with its beliefs about normal bodily form and function, come into being? The theories of Michel Foucault and the insights of Paul Unschuld and Allan Young suggest that specific features of the social and cultural system in the West – the growth of specialisation and the division of labour, the increasing complexity and sophistication of political and legal systems and so on – were paralleled in medical belief systems. Health beliefs and medical intervention shifted in concert with shifting ideologies and changing socio-economic organisation. Among the structural changes that influenced the development of biomedicine were the growth of capitalist enterprise, the expansion of Europe overseas to exploit new territories and the beginning of industrialisation in Europe, all of which emphasised the dominance of humans (particularly Western men) over the natural world. The parallel fragmentation in religious beliefs encouraged by the Reformation led to the emergence of a more questioning and experimental attitude to science and nature (see Section 11.2).

In many different ways changing social forms and cultural practices created a framework within which new ideas about health and the body could flourish. Although biomedicine has shifted its ground and incorporated new theories and technologies during the last century or so, many of its fundamental assumptions remained unchanged – because it has been so successful at establishing its claims to truth. There are several dimensions to this:

1 the denunciation and marginalising of 'non-scientific' and alternative health beliefs;
2 the association of medicine with scientific methods, in particular the hypothetico-deductive experimental approach and its claims that all other health belief systems should be tested using scientific methods;
3 the success of doctors in finding cures and treating disease;
4 the emergence of doctors as a very powerful professional group defining health and illness and largely controlling the organisation and division of labour in health care.

It is points 1 and 2 that mainly concern us now (3 and 4 will be discussed further in Chapter 11). How far have 'non-scientific' and alternative health beliefs been driven to the margins as biomedicine established itself in the West (and increasingly all over the world) as the predominant account of health and illness? What lay and alternative beliefs exist today, and how much impact do they make? How far can these traditional, lay or alternative accounts claim that they should be evaluated on their own terms, rather than being tested using scientific methods such as 'double blind' trials?

10.4 Alternative accounts of health and illness

It is useful to distinguish between various types of *alternative* accounts: some were (at various times and in different societies) official, widely accepted public accounts; others have always existed on the margins. Humoral theory is one example of an alternative account which was very popular. It proposed that nature, represented by the key elements of earth, air, fire and water, was mirrored in the human body by the four humors: phlegm, blood, yellow bile and black bile. These fluids created

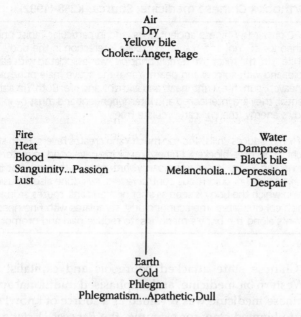

FIGURE 10.2 The theory of humors. Source: K258 (1992)

the temperament of the individual. Throughout Western Europe and beyond humoral medicine enjoyed high status as a widely accepted set of beliefs about health until after 1700 (see Figure 10.2). Thereafter notions of a correspondence between the individual (microcosmos) and the universe (macrocosmos) continued to have (and still have?) symbolic power, but faded in importance as a way of seeing and explaining health and illness.

Chinese and Indian cultures have some of the earliest recorded health accounts which for centuries were officially sanctioned and publicly influential. Yet in the twentieth century they were nearly eclipsed, at a formal and official level at least, by Western biomedicine and were in danger of being relegated to the ranks of alternative medicine. Orthodox Chinese medicine developed as a complex mix of philosophical theories and practical treatment regimes, combining acupuncture and herbal medicines, diet and exercise therapies, emphasising the need for balance and harmony and honouring the contemplative life (see Box 10.1). In the nineteenth century these hitherto official beliefs began to be eroded by Western biomedicine, and the two systems jostled for power: one symbolising Chinese traditional values and ways of life; the other projecting not just a new concept of health, disease and the body but also distinctive values derived from industrial capitalism. But in the cultural revolution of the 1960s and

BOX 10.1 Orthodox Chinese medicine. Source: K258 (1992)

From 3000 BC onwards, Chinese ancient texts, and in particular Taoist philosophy, developed theories of 'Yin' and 'Yang' to explain interaction in the body, in nature and in social life. Yin, the receptive female principle, was associated with earth, water, darkness, cold, and with sorrow and death. Yang, the active male principle, became linked with heaven, sun, fire, light, heat, and with joy and life. Both Yin and Yang are seen as essential; they are interlocked and interdependent and must be in balance so that the body's energy (the *chi*) can circulate freely.

An excess of Yin produces chills, and too much Yang creates fevers. Both states cause the body's chi to become blocked. Chinese medicine developed to restore health by rebalancing Yin and Yang. This is done partly through diet therapy. Hot foods counteract excessive Yin; cold foods control fevers. It is done also by using acupuncture in which the body is seen as a set of meridians, routes around the body through which chi circulates. The acupuncturist stimulates with fine needles particular points along the body's meridians, to reduce pain and promote healing.

1970s the Chinese state attacked bourgeois and capitalist elements, including Western biomedicine, and emphasised traditional approaches. Ancient Chinese medicine was revalued as a source of knowledge equal or superior to biomedicine; for example, the *Barefoot Doctor's Manual* of the Revolutionary Health Committee of Hunan Province (1974) has Western and traditional accounts side by side.

In India, since independence from British rule, a similar revaluing of traditional Ayurvedic health beliefs and practices has taken place. Ayurveda, with its linking of the individual body and lifespan with the universe and the changing seasons, and its emphasis on diet and meditation (see Box 10.2), continued to exert a major influence at a popular level, but during the British colonial period biomedicine, with its curative powers, formal training, specialisation, powerful hierarchy

BOX 10.2 Ayurvedic health beliefs. Source: K258 (1992)

Hindu theories of Ayurveda (*ayur* = life, *veda* = science) date back to 1000 BC at least and are some of the very earliest health accounts we have.

The universe is seen as being composed of five elements: earth, air, fire, water and ether, corresponding to three '*dosha*' in the body. These '*dosha*', a person's qualities or humors, vary naturally according to the season and time of life. The *dosha* are phlegm, linked to earth, springtime and the growing season; bile, linked to water, the rainy season and middle age; and wind, linked to dryness and old age. The body is seen as being composed of seven tissues, the '*dhatus*', which have to be in balance to assure good health, but the changing seasons and the individual lifespan and habits create tensions and problems for health. Notions of hot and cold in diet exist in Ayurvedic tradition and diet therapies are important. Unbalanced diets may impair the *dosha*, and produce disease in the *dhatus* of the body.

and mechanistic approach to the body, symbolised Western scientific 'progress'. Now training in Ayurvedic medicine is funded by the Indian government and the two systems co-exist.

Today both Chinese medicine and Ayurveda accounts form part of a stock of *alternative* medicine available in the West and are becoming increasingly popular, but not recognised or sanctioned within bio-medicine. (Although doctors are beginning to take courses in acupuncture, they do not subscribe to the philosophical approach underlying it.) They are two of a growing number of health accounts or therapies which co-exist with biomedicine and to varying extents present a challenge to its claim to be the 'one true system' for dealing with disease and restoring health.

○ Can you suggest any other alternative health theories and therapies which people in Britain make use of today?

There are several well-known types of alternative medicine, for example homeopathy, aromatherapy, reflexology, osteopathy and chiropractic. Some, such as chiropractic, can be seen as complementary to orthodox biomedicine because they specialise in particular conditions and types of healing – although underlying osteopathy and chiropractic practice is the theory that many diseases are linked to deformations or problems around the spinal column. Other approaches, such as homeopathy, run directly counter in theory and practice to biomedicine and are utterly rejected by it. The main grounds are that the minute dosages prescribed in homeopathy are too small, scientifically speaking, to have any effect (British Medical Association report, 1986). *Homeopathic* cures start from the principle that diseases can be cured by means that cause similar symptoms in healthy persons, whereas biomedicine is *allopathic* – seeking to cure diseases by oppositional treatment. Homeopathy works with the lowest possible dosage, seeking to restore the self healing potential of the person. From this it follows that a total diagnosis of the person – their habits, personality, way of life as well as physical symptoms – is essential (see Box 10.3). In 1989, 11 per cent of people in Great Britain consulted a homeopath, and 37 per cent had seriously considered using one (*Social Trends*, 1994).

C.W. Aakster (1986) explores some of the other unofficial, non-scientific therapies that exist, for example naturopathy – 'restoring or stimulating the ability of the person to heal himself' – paranormal medicine (spiritual healing), and mental therapies – bioenergetics, Gestalt therapy, bio-release, rebirthing and so on. He suggests that they share similar concepts of health and illness which are profoundly different to those of biomedicine and which emphasise a whole-person approach (holism), balance and harmony between the person and the environment (see Table 10.1). Health, which in biomedicine is seen as an

BOX 10.3 Homeopathy. **Source: Homeopathic Development Foundation (1988)**

To select a remedy correctly:

1 Consult the Index of Ailments to find the medicines recommended for your principal symptoms.
2 Study the description of the medicines in the List of Medicines.
3 Select the medicine which most closely matches your total symptoms picture and, where mentioned, the appearance and temperament.

The following example will show how this is done.

Consider a young lady, fair haired, blue eyed, of a gentle, emotional nature suffering from catarrh. Looking under 'Catarrh' in the Index of Ailments she finds four medicines indicated, namely Calc. Fluor., Euphrasia, Kali. Bich. and Pulsatilla. On consulting the full medicine descriptions she soon discovers that Pulsatilla is the best choice for the following reasons:

● It is the medicine which is suited to her appearance and temperament.
● It describes her actual catarrh which gives a yellow-green thick discharge.
● She notices that there is an indication – 'worse from eating rich or fatty food' – and remembers that she too had experienced this.

This example is taken from real life and resulted in a complete cure of catarrh. It clearly illustrates the simple and logical method of selection. It should be understood that it isn't necessary to experience all the symptoms listed under a medicine for it to be the correct one.

TABLE 10.1 Concepts in conventional and alternative medicine. **Source: Aakster (1986)**

Concept	Conventional interpretation	Alternative interpretation
Health	Absence of disease	Balance of opposing forces, internally as well as externally
Disease	Specific, locally defined deviations in organ or tissue structures	Body language indicating disruptive forces and/or restorative processes
Diagnosis	Morphological	Functional
Therapy	Combating destructive forces	Strengthening constructive forces
The patient	Passive recipient of external solutions	Active participant in regaining health

absence of disease, is framed as a positive concept involving balance. Disease is viewed in alternative accounts as the result of a general state of disruption and dysbalance in the human organism, rather than as a specific, localised set of abnormalities. The patient is viewed as the active, central participant in alternative accounts as opposed to the (mainly) passive recipient of medical treatment and advice.

Look at C. W. Aakster's summary (Table 10.1) of the different concepts underpinning conventional and alternative medicine. From your own knowledge of the two systems, consider how far you agree with his classification.

You may have agreed with Aakster's ideas, or you may have wanted to take issue with them. As a health work student you may have questioned his depiction of biomedicine as still lacking a concept of health or as still demanding passive patients. What about Health For All 2000 and the World Health Organisation campaigns of the 1970s and 1980s to shift the balance towards health promotion and illness prevention? In addition, there are a growing number of health professionals who endorse what is now termed a *holistic* approach, in which the relationship between people and their environments is seen as central. This may take the form of patient-focused care or be expressed more broadly in terms of a social model. Patrick Pietroni (1988) argues that:

The holistic attitude to health care eschews the dogma of the one true religion as much as it decries the tyranny of the one true science. We are body and mind enthused with spirit. We form only one species in this world and rely on plants, winds, the sea, the atmosphere, as well as the existence of other species to survive.

Pietroni (1988)

On the other hand it is important to remember that, although these trends to broaden the base of biomedicine are evident, an overwhelming share of human and financial resources is still used to treat disease in sick (and largely passive) patients. At least some of the talk about holism is (well-intentioned) rhetoric which is helping to move on debate, but which isn't at present so successful in shifting resources.

Thought-provokingly, in view of Section 10.2 on non-Western health beliefs, Aakster invites us to view biomedicine as a particular ideology or religion, which because of its success in explaining and treating disease demands that all other theories and systems should be evaluated on its terms, using scientific, biomedical measures. He suggests that in overvaluing the rational, the quantitative and the 'masculine' we have ended up with 'a strong, dominating, "aggressive", medical technology', and he argues that this needs to be challenged by developing intuitive, qualitative and 'feminine' values in health. Part of this process may be to assess the value of alternative medicine on its own terms; many alternative practitioners would claim that being tested using scientific methods, such as 'double blind' trials, is inappropriate and that seeking the views of patients and their relatives would be a more obvious starting point (West, 1984).

Ruth West (1984) has argued that it is not so far-fetched to see the fate of alternative medicine as bound up with the future, not only of health care in general, but of the wider economy and society. She suggests three possible futures in which alternative medicine may have a place:

In one, we continue much as we are. The economy survives; material well-being is maintained; and the health services are extended, modified and improved to cope with an increasing population that is weighted towards old age. In a second, disaster strikes, and we are in a life-boat economy. Alternative medicine takes up a 'bare-foot' doctor role in the struggle to provide any kind of health care. In the third, society is transformed. People change from being 'outer-directed', looking for the achievement of material goods, to becoming self-explorers, seeing inner growth as the way forward. Alternative medicine takes its place as a resource for self-care, leading to health, wellbeing and personal development.

West (1984)

West writes as a proponent of alternative medicine and director of the Koestler Foundation which undertakes research into unorthodox areas of science. Other writers, such as Rosalind Coward (1990), have seen alternative therapies as a fantasy or snare distracting people from taking action and campaigning for social change and directing them instead into self absorption and self blame. She surveyed the enormous and still growing range of popular writing issuing from the alternative health movement. Coward argues that for alternative health the crucial aim 'is that the individual should feel better, less in conflict and less dragged down by the horrors of modern life'. The ultimate goal of alternative health, she continues, is that:

The individual will be able to do better, achieve more, and live in greater ease in society. Very often the aims are almost explicitly conservative. They are aims of harmony, order, balance, the end of struggle, strife, and 'unproductive' conflict . . . The healed individual is one who can have and be everything in the existing society.

Coward (1990)

On the other hand research by Ursula Sharma (1990) into alternative medicine suggests that patients who seek it do so for particular reasons, in particular because conventional medicine has failed to cure or alleviate their complaint, but also often because of dissatisfaction with their doctor. Sharma provides some evidence that people are actively rejecting the 'passive patient–expert doctor' scenario and are seeking to be actively involved in recovering their health. Her respondents put a high value on the more equal, informed relationship with their therapist and on the holistic approach which considered 'the personal context of illness'. What she did not find was evidence that medical stereotyping of these patients as inadequate, freaks or deviants was at all accurate. In fact, patients went on consulting orthodox practitioners for some complaints and alternative therapists for others; they 'shopped around' to find the best buy.

Reflect on your own views about alternative medicine. Do you welcome the growing popularity of such therapies – perhaps as a sign of pluralism in health? Or are you dubious about their claims?

The health sector in general has not welcomed alternative practitioners within its ranks. In a few health centres, such as the Marylebone Health Centre in London (in which Dr Patrick Pietroni is a partner), acupuncturists and homeopaths are associated members, but in most cases alternative practitioners exist on the fringes of or more often completely outside orthodox medicine. In the rest of Europe, by contrast, which works mainly on a mixed state and occupational health insurance basis, the patient has more freedom of choice, and alternative practitioners can be consulted on the same basis as orthodox practitioners. You may see the exclusion of alternative therapists as welcome, at least until they can 'prove' in a scientific that their treatments work. You may, like Coward, be alarmed at the self absorption and conservatism of the alternative health movement; on the other hand you may be more sympathetic to arguments about the need to revalue the mystical, qualititative and 'feminine' dimension of health (and human existence).

10.5 Lay beliefs about health and illness

In recent years, as we noted earlier, lay accounts of health and illness have become more visible, but this does not mean that long-standing folk traditions have not always existed, challenging expert discourse. In Section 1.4 we noted Cecil Helman's (1986) account of lay beliefs about colds and fevers in an English suburb and his classification of them in terms of 'hot' and 'cold', 'wet' and 'dry'. These link to much older beliefs about health and the body, in particular to ideas of *correspondence* between the individual human being and the universe: of a natural world reflected in human physical and mental characteristics. To varying degrees ancient Chinese medicine, Indian Ayurvedic beliefs and humoral medicine all emphasise how nature – the cycle of life and death, seasonal change and so on – influences human health. Properties and characteristics of nature, such as wind, water and heat, are viewed as properties of human bodies which need to be kept in balance if health is to be maintained.

Helman's pioneering research was undertaken in the mid-1970s, but several writers record much earlier, and more fleeting, lay testimony (Seabrook, 1973). Janet Woodward (1977) traced the widespread and persistent circulation of popular ideas about reproduction in nineteenth and early twentieth century Britain. These pamphlets and popular books dealing with sexual practices and reproduction were edited translations of Aristotle's *Works* and *The Masterpiece*; in other words, ancient Greek ideas, once 'official' knowledge, had become absorbed into a folk tradition frowned on and belittled by the increasingly powerful medical profession. The 'dirty books' – as they were viewed by the authorities (and possibly by the public too) – were passed from hand to hand, and Woodward argues that 'until attacked by some members of the medical profession in the 1930s, and earlier, the compilation had long been possibly the most popular source of information on sexuality and childbirth'.

In a different vein, Jeremy Seabrook has written of the superstitious and complex links made by a working class bootmaking community between signs and portents in nature and the course of ordinary human life. He suggests that:

The world had for them a wholeness and coherence which it has since lost . . . Everything had meaning . . . There was a profound connection, not always pleasant or beneficient, between human life and the most insignificant wild flower or the smallest insect. Corn-poppies induced sleep and blindness, drooping blossoms introduced into the house presaged death. I remember as a child my mother's sudden, bewildering anger one day when I picked up some trampled daffodils on the muddy cobbles from a market flower-stall: 'Pick up a flower, pick up sickness', and she thrust them vigorously from me into the gutter. My grandmother, seeing a solitary crow perched on the clothes-line, would prophesy a death before the week was out.

. . . Ellen Youl, like everyone else of her generation, knew that the moon shining on the face of a sleeping child was likely to cause madness. When her children had warts, they could be charmed away by being rubbed with some meat that afterwards had to be buried. As the meat rotted in the earth, so the warts would disappear . . . There was a vast and complicated network of relationships between apparently unconnected events and phenomena: if you deliberately killed a spider, you would never 'live and thrive' . . . Cow dung used as a poultice cured boils and abcesses, a potato under the mattress was proof against rheumatism.

Seabrook (1973)

Seabrook suggests that this mass of prohibitions, rituals and beliefs created order and meaning in the lives of these bootmakers, but it also prevented them from choosing freely and thinking independently. The weight of the traditions, 'shreds of superstition, half-understood aspects of Christianity, fragments of ancient ritual and custom', kept them in thrall. For this reason, we may argue, it operated effectively as a health belief system that precluded any other way of living.

The uncovering of contemporary lay beliefs about health and illness has focused on classifying people's accounts, pointing to their diversity and to the conflicts between them. Seabrook (1973) noted that the accounts he recalled were inconsistent and sometimes contradictory, and this is an important theme in recent research. It is not just that different groups of people make different responses – for example working and middle class people, men and women, young and older people. It is also that the same person may use several distinctive explanations or stories to make up a complete account.

Claudine Herzlich (1973) investigated the beliefs of mainly middle class people in Paris and Normandy and identified three different conceptions of health:

1 'health in a vacuum' – the lack or absence of illness;
2 'reserve of health' – a quality someone has, making them able to resist illness;
3 'equilibrium' – which she calls 'real' health, in which someone is active and aware of their body.

In relation to illness she found that heterogenous categories emerged, and that her respondents saw illness both as external and as caused by undesirable behaviours, such as not eating properly or lack of hygiene (although being over-hygienic also endangered health). Illness was seen as being caused by their modern, unnatural 'way of life', which included external threats – stress, pollution, traffic and so on – and by people's own lack of resistance, their own weakness. The notion of illness as related to the 'toxicity' of the modern way of life was particularly marked in the responses of Parisians. Illness was conceptualised in three main ways:

1 as 'destructive' – here the illness was seen as destroying someone's life;
2 as 'a liberator' – enabling someone to retreat into a sick role and escape from a stressful life;
3 as 'an occupation' – here the sick person was seen as a victim, but allowed to be so because of chronic illness. The illness became the new mode of production for that individual, the new occupation, as it were.

○   Decide which (if any) of these explanations of health and illness you
    would adopt, and why.

You might well have been reluctant to settle on a single definition of
health or explanation of ill health. Like Herzlich's respondents, you may
think that both external and internal factors (say, smoking and
atmospheric pollution) bring about disease. Herzlich's findings have
been echoed to varying degrees by other researchers; in particular, the
notions of health as a reserve of strength (the result of a good
constitution or inner strength or fitness), as capacity to function fully
and as 'absence of disease' have been recorded by Williams (1983) and
Blaxter and Paterson (1983). In Blaxter's (1990) discussion of the Health
and Lifestyle Survey undertaken in 1987 she delineates ten conceptualisations of health (see Box 10.4) and discusses how age, sex and social
class appear to influence people's responses. She also comments that 'it
is the individual's own perceived health status which appears to
determine the way in which health is defined, rather than the reverse'.
    In a similar way to Herzlich's respondents, Blaxter recorded a
widespread belief about 'the unhealthiness of modern living'. People
referred to factors beyond their control, such as heredity, to factors in
the external environment and to psycho-social influences, especially
stress. Yet there was also considerable emphasis on personal behaviour
as the major cause of disease. People mentioned smoking and drinking
as significant factors in lung cancer, heart attacks, chronic bronchitis and
other conditions. Blaxter makes the point that lay health beliefs are by
no means unitary, one-dimensional or simplistic: 'It is obvious that a
"positive" attitude to health as something within one's own control, and
a "passive" attitude which implies that illness is imposed by outside
forces, do not provide an easy dichotomy'. She does, however, note the
difficulties in getting at the complex private beliefs that people have
about their health through survey techniques. People may be giving
researchers the answers they think they want to hear rather than

BOX 10.4 Ten conceptualisations of health. Source: Blaxter (1990)

• Health as never thinking about being healthy or ill	• Health as energy, vitality
• Health as not ill, not going to the doctor	• Health as social relationships
• Health as absence of disease, or health *despite* disease	• Health as the ability to function, to 'do things'
• Health as a reserve of strength, vitality, inheritance	• Health as psycho-social wellbeing
• Health as behaviour, as 'the healthy life'	

uncovering their private thoughts about health and illness. Blaxter comments on why certain responses may predominate in research surveys:

There is a high level of agreement within the population that health is, to a considerable extent, dependent on behaviour and in one's own hands . . . at the least it is recognised that these are the 'correct' or 'expected' answers to give.

Blaxter (1990)

Stainton Rogers (1991) also acknowledges the difficulties in trying to uncover lay beliefs about health and illness. As a social psychologist she became increasingly critical of the predominant model used in psychology to explore health beliefs: 'health locus of control' (HLC) theory and its 'multidimensional health locus of control' (MHLC) variant. HLC classified people as 'internals' – autonomous individuals in control of their own behaviour – or 'externals' – fatalists who thought in terms of luck and chance. In health terms internals controlled their own health, whereas health and illness 'happened' to externals. Wallston *et al*. (1978) added a third category, 'powerful others', such as health professionals or family members who were seen as influencing health and illness.

Stainton Rogers argued that such models were simplistic and misleading, viewing people's accounts as easily classifiable and their lives as one-dimensional and homogenous – whereas both were complex, fragmentary, changing and often conflicting. You may want to add that your accounts often make use of external and internal locus of control simultaneously: for example, explaining a bout of flu in terms of both 'bad luck' and 'stress'. Stainton Rogers argued that people should be seen as weavers of stories making 'artful use of language to make sense of the world' and drawing on rich and varied experiences and insights. In her own research she identified eight such accounts which differed considerably from each other in their approach, priorities and types of explanations (see Box 10.5).

Examine the eight accounts of health and illness described by Wendy Stainton Rogers. Do your own views about health and illness fit with one or more of these 'stories'? What links can you find between her accounts and those of Herzlich and Blaxter?

You may well have decided that (as Stainton Rogers reports of her research subjects) you adopt more than one of these accounts; how you weave your stories depends on your state of health, outlook, circumstances, your audience and so on. You may also have thought of some other possible accounts. It is interesting to compare Stainton Rogers' mapping of accounts with that of Blaxter (1990) and Herzlich (1973). All three researchers distinguish between the conventional medical view of

BOX 10.5 Alternative accounts of health. Source: W. Stainton Rogers (1991)

1 The 'body as machine' account, in which illness is accepted as a matter of biological fact and modern biomedicine is seen as the only valid type of treatment	**2** The 'body under siege' account, which sees the individual as under constant threat from germs, diseases, stresses and conflicts of modern life
3 The 'inequality of access' account, which accepts modern bio-medicine but is concerned about unequal access and treatment	**4** The 'cultural critique' of medicine account, which highlights how Western biomedicine has oppressed women, minority groups and colonial peoples and which emphasises its 'social construction'
5 The 'health promotion' account, which emphasises the importance of a healthy lifestyle and personal responsibility although it also sees health as a collective responsibility	**6** The 'robust individualism' account, which emphasises the individual's right to live a satisfying life and their freedom of choice
7 The 'God's power' account, which views health as righteous living and spiritual wholeness	**8** The 'willpower' account, which emphasises the moral respon-sibility of individuals to use their will to maintain good health

health and illness – the 'body as machine', 'health-in-a-vacuum', and 'health as never ill, no disease' – and more positive concepts. These may be about deep personal feeling – as in 'equilibrium', 'psycho-social wellbeing' and 'willpower', for example – or more concerned with various types of external influences such as 'the modern way of life', 'external environment' or 'body under siege'. There are also links between Herzlich's category of 'reserve of strength', Stainton Rogers' 'robust individualism' and the 'functional' approach cited in Blaxter. In addition, all three have emphasised the multiple dimensions and shifting combinations of lay ideas.

Some researchers have put much greater emphasis on how stories about health and illness are embedded in and grow out of people's everyday lives and experiences. Nicki Thorogood examined a folk model of health, illness and human anatomy used by British Caribbean women in London and noted that it co-existed with a regular use of orthodox biomedical treatment. The women's conceptualisation of their bodies and widespread use of a variety of herbal remedies is linked to a shared culture and history. Thorogood comments that this knowledge:

About the way the body works and the sources of risks and dangers to it (symbolic and actual) . . . has grown out of the historical experiences of these women . . . [It is] an expression of their culture, their history, and their current experiences as black women.

Thorogood (1990)

In Jocelyn Cornwell's work health is not directly addressed at all by her respondents (an interest in health as such being seen as morbid), but as their stories are told it is clear that social circumstances have a profound influence on their state of health. Mick Chalmers, a drayman, acknowledged that his work was hazardous but commented that:

I find I haven't got a lot of choice really . . . I don't feel all that great now at thirty-nine, but I can imagine in twenty years' time how I'm going to react to this job. I'd hate to think the job is doing me back in so that in the end I'm going to suffer. I can put me hand to roughly anything if I have to. But there isn't actually a lot of work about.

Cornwell (1984)

This (all too realistic) assessment of how health and illness arise from everyday life and work finds echoes in other experiences recorded by researchers such as Blaxter and Paterson (1982) and Calnan (1987). It not only provides a graphic reminder of the difficulty of unravelling ideas about health and illness, but also points to the complexity of people's motivations. It is a useful starting point from which to begin to explore the other concern of this chapter: how and why people take action on illness, and at what point (if any) they enter the 'sick role'.

10.6 Taking action on illness

To fall ill and enter the sick role is a social process and not just a matter of biochemical imbalance or physical abnormality. It is not only that we need to understand the social dimensions of ill health – how people behave, feel and act, what kinds of language they employ, what explanations they offer, cultural and social influences – by age, gender, social class, ethnicity and so on; it is also that the whole process of becoming ill is fundamentally a social state of affairs. The recognition, response and decision making process is rooted in social life, influenced by a complex range of social and psychological (and biological) variables. To begin thinking about illness as a social process, let's review an everyday example: 'going down with the flu'.

Think back to your last bout of flu. Note down how you organised and negotiated this period of illness. For example, did you carry on in spite of your illness, or did you take time off work or studies? Did you seek medical help? What factors influenced your responses?

You probably concluded that a range of different factors influenced your response to illness. For example, you may have weighed up work pressures – in paid work or/and in family life – against physical and mental feelings of discomfort – aching head, high temperature, feelings of stress and so on. If you were a full-time 'carer' you may have been unable to take time off; if you were in paid work with sickness entitlement it will have been easier (but this may have been hindered by a dominant personal or professional 'work ethic'). You were probably influenced by past experience of having flu, by reports from other sufferers, by the attitude of your family and friends. Barely acknowledged or unconscious motivations – the desire for a 'breathing space' or concerns about self esteem, perhaps – may have played some part too. Your wider social experiences, early socialisation and cultural and generational values will have influenced your general expectations of health and framed your attitude to this illness. In other words, a whole range of factors – from immediate influences such as your degree of discomfort, past experience of treatment, mental state and family circumstances, to more 'hidden' influences such as age, gender, cultural background and so on – form the 'evidence' from which you pieced together your response to being ill. A decision about whether or not to consult your doctor will probably have been influenced less by illness symptoms than by an elaborate 'weighing up' of the costs and benefits in seeking professional help at various stages of your sickness, which included consideration of practical issues (transport, childcare), economic concerns (cost, loss of pay) and social factors (support networks, past experience of treatment). Several conditional decisions were probably sketched out, such as: 'If I don't feel any better by tomorrow, then I'll go to the doctor' or 'I can't take time off this week but I'll book an appointment for next Monday'.

Social divisions and responses to sickness

In reviewing this particular episode of illness you may well have been reminded of some of the wider inter-connections between people's health and social differences and divisions that we explored in earlier chapters. An exploration of systematic variations in the ways that people perceive, evaluate and act in relation to health and illness has been a major theme in health research since the 1960s, when Mechanic (1962) first used the term 'illness behaviour'. An important element in the differential response of people towards illness arises from their social circumstances, and researchers within a structural tradition have highlighted common features in the ways in which groups with shared cultural and social experiences react to ill health. For example, the Black Report (1980) noted that social classes IV and V were less likely to consult their doctor at an early stage of illness or to make use of preventive services than the higher social classes, and that a higher proportion of working class patients were likely to be admitted to hospital. The report concludes that:

This pattern of unequal use is explicable not in terms of non-rational response to sickness by working-class people, but of a rational weighting of the perceived costs and benefits to them of attendance and compliance with the prescribed regime. The costs and benefits differ between the social classes both on account of differences in way of life, constraints and resources, and of the fact that costs to the working class are actually increased by the lower levels and perhaps poorer quality of provision to which many have access.

reprinted in Townsend and Davidson (1982)

Subsequent studies (for example Blaxter, 1984) have confirmed that people in lower occupational classes make less use of preventive services, but the evidence on take-up of GP and acute services is less clear. Some studies indicate a very small degree of difference in consultation rates between the classes while others seem to confirm the Black Report's comments about non- or late presentation of sickness. For example, Bucquet and Curtis (1986) used the Nottingham Health Profile (see Box 10.6) with respondents from manual and non-manual classes to chart self reported sickness against health service usage and to identify what types of illness led people to take up health services. They found that, although manual groups were more prone to tiredness, sleep

BOX 10.6 The Nottingham Health Profile

This was developed by Hunt *et al.* (1984, 1986) to measure how lay people themselves feel when they experience various states of ill health. It is a simple self report questionnaire, which has been widely used to assess patients' perceptions of their health status before and after treatment. People's views are sought about their physical mobility, sleep, pain, energy, emotional reactions and social isolation.

There are two parts. Part 1 measures current subjective health status through yes/no responses to 38 simple statements, for example:

'I'm tired all the time'
'Things are getting me down'
'I have pain at night'

Part 2 asks whether people's present state of health is causing problems with their work, social life, home life, sex life, hobbies and so on, for example:

'Is your present state of health causing problems with your:
    job of work?'
    social life?'
    looking after the home?'

disturbance, pain and emotional distress, this did not lead to higher consultation rates.

One of the problems in trying to unravel people's responses to illness is, as we noted above, that a cluster of different factors may influence their response. There are significant differences, as Chapter 7 reported, between the response of working class women to illness and those of working class men. Women of all social classes consult their doctors proportionately more than men, and some studies have suggested that female consultation rates for acute and chronic sickness are not systematically related to social class at all (Whitehead, 1987). Some, at least, of the difference in response to illness of men and women has been related to sex-role socialisation in childhood and to contingent medical stereotyping of male and female patients (Miles, 1991). In relation to preventive and maternity services systematic social class differences do appear to exist; for example 'late booking' for ante-natal care is much more prevalent among working class women. Hilary Graham (1984a) has drawn attention to the range of physical, financial and practical difficulties that contribute to late booking and low levels of attendance antenatally.

There is also a growing body of evidence about black and minority ethnic groups' attitudes towards, and take-up of, health services, as we noted in Chapter 8. Cameron et al. (1989) found that, although British Asian elders identified a range of felt needs for community health services, community nurses did not perceive such needs because they assumed that the immediate or extended family would provide sufficient care and support. This suggests that under-utilisation of some health services may be quite marked. On the other hand it has been demonstrated that in particular areas racist stereotypes and ethnocentric assumptions about black people's 'problems' and 'needs' have resulted in a disproportionate referral of Afro-Caribbean people to psychiatric services (Littlewood and Lipsedge, 1986).

The case of mental illness demonstrates that the relationship between the level of ill health in society and the use of health services is not straightforward or easy to explain. People's perceptions of, and reactions to, illness are influenced by class, gender and age as well as by their personal experience. In turn, the treatment of disease is influenced by diagnostic frameworks and changing conceptualisations of health work, by the attitudes and values of health professionals. For example, mental illness admission rates indicate that overall more women than men are treated each year and that women are more prone to depression. In self report studies women report more psychological distress (Blaxter, 1990). A classic study by Brown and Harris (1978) investigated the pathway from vulnerability to depressive illness, noting the range of social circumstances and life events that influenced

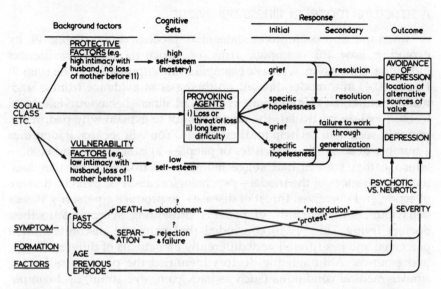

FIGURE 10.3 The social origins of depression. Source: Brown and Harris (1978)

outcomes for women. Experiencing social isolation and lacking a confiding relationship increased women's chances of becoming depressed (see Figure 10.3).

All this suggests that women are more prone to mental illness. Yet how far are women *really* more vulnerable – as opposed to *seeing* themselves as more vulnerable, or being categorised (or stereotyped) as such? How far has women's mental illness been socially constructed by shifts in medical knowledge and practice? In the nineteenth century, for example, fewer women were diagnosed as mentally ill; it remains unclear whether the rise in admissions in the twentieth century is 'real' or a result of changing diagnostic practice (Busfield, 1989; Pilgrim and Rogers, 1993). In a similar way, the designation of Afro-Caribbean men as more prone to schizophrenia cannot be accepted unproblematically as a 'real' rate. We noted in Chapter 8 that the institutional and inter-personal experience of racism – denial of citizenship, threat of exclusion and demands for 'proof' of entitlement – has implications for the health of black and minority ethnic groups. But it can also be argued that the construction of minority groups within medical discourse as problem-atic, threatening and 'alien' itself helps to create the category of the 'schizophrenic' black person' (Fernando, 1991; Pilgrim and Rogers, 1993).

A structural model of illness behaviour

A structural approach investigates the process of becoming ill by exploring how this complex array of structural factors influences individual behaviour. A classic example of this approach can be seen in Figure 10.4, in a model devised on the basis of evidence from a large number of (largely) United States studies of 'illness behaviour' (Kasl and Cobb, 1966). In particular, the model sought to explain why people do, or don't, seek medical help for their illness. You will see that it identifies a number of social characteristics of people – age, sex, race and so on – which earlier studies had suggested were associated with the three mediating factors of the model – psychological distress, perceived value of action and perceived threat of disease – to produce a person's 'illness behaviour'. In one study of patients presenting symptoms to their doctors Irving Zola (1975) concluded that pain and discomfort were perceived and interpreted very differently by patients of different ethnic backgrounds. Although the doctors identified the patients as having similar medical conditions (such as back pain, eye strain) and compa-

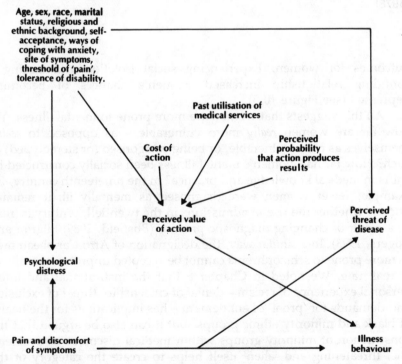

FIGURE 10.4 Relationships between symptoms and illness behaviour.
Source: Kasl and Cobb (1966), adapted by Bond and Bond (1986)

rable levels of discomfort, the patients themselves expressed widely different feelings. For some the discomfort was unbearable, whereas for others it was barely noted; some saw pain as engulfing them, and others dismissed it. Those of Irish descent were dismissive of physical symptoms, whereas those of Italian descent described pain and discomfort as gripping their whole bodies (see Table 10.2). The 'social

TABLE 10.2 Culture and symptoms. Source: Zola (1975)

Diagnosis	Question of interviewer	Irish patient	Italian patient
1 Presbyopia and hyperopia	What seems to be the trouble?	I can't see to thread a needle or read a paper.	I have a constant headache and my eyes seem to get all red and burny.
	Anything else?	No, I can't recall any.	No, just that it lasts all day long and I even wake up with it sometimes.
2 Myopia	What seems to be the trouble?	I can't see across the street.	My eyes seem very burny, especially the right eye . . . Two or three months ago I woke up with my eye swollen. I bathed it and it did go away but there was still the burny sensation.
3 Pharyngitis	Is there any pain?	No, maybe a slight headache but nothing that lasts.	Yes, I have had a headache a few days. Oh, yes, every time I swallow it's annoying.
4 Presbyopia and hyperopia	Do you think the symptoms affected how you got along with your family? Your friends?	No, I have had loads of trouble. I can't imagine this bothering me.	Yes, I have had a headache, I'm very irritable, very tense, very short-tempered.
5 Deafness, hearing loss	Did you become more irritable?	No, not me . . . maybe everybody else but not me.	Oh, yes . . . the least little thing aggravates me . . . and I take it out on the children.

profile' and past experience of the individual will influence how (and to what degree) disease and distress are responded to, and therefore determine the nature of the illness behaviour.

○   At this point study the Kasl and Cobb model carefully. Note down any strengths and weaknesses of the model in the light of your earlier investigations into your own 'illness behaviour'.

The Kasl and Cobb model offers useful insights into why 'illness behaviour' may vary, and why people may or may not decide to seek professional help. It enables us to link social characteristics to the particular and immediate circumstances of the illness episode. It is clear that different people react in different ways and that levels of psychological distress in response to pain and discomfort vary according to individual psycho-social characteristics. You may have noted that aspects of your own social background or life experience, for example, influenced your perceptions and tolerance of pain and discomfort.

The model also acknowledges the complex cost-benefit type analysis that people usually make in deciding how to respond. Kasl and Cobb indicate that the illness behaviour that people engage in and the extent to which they make use of health services may vary widely due to the interplay of these various factors.

The model also acknowledges the complex cost-benefit type analysis that people usually make in deciding how to respond. Kasl and example, many of you may have ignored your illness and carried on regardless, an outcome that is not developed in the model. The process of weighing up costs and benefits of action is frequently a much more complex process than the model can indicate, undertaken at various stages or as illness symptoms change. Interaction with others is only hinted at, yet consultation with family, friends and colleagues – 'lay referral' as it has been termed – is generally a first step in dealing with illness. In the model 'illness behaviour' suggests a conditioned response to stimuli – social and psychological – in which freedom of action is limited. Yet the negotiation of an illness episode, even a (generally) self limiting illness such as flu, is difficult to explain without some reference to personal biography (as, for example, a decision to wait and see the doctor next week because of work pressures this week). Finally, the Kasl and Cobb model does not explain why people with similar social backgrounds and experiences may respond to symptoms of flu (or any other illness symptoms) in distinctive ways.

Illness action and lay referral

Illness behaviour is complex, and a number of studies have demonstrated that most episodes of illness are handled by the sufferer without recourse to medical help. Freidson (1961) noted the widespread existence of a 'lay referral system' in cases of illness, by which he meant that people will consult close relatives, friends and trusted colleagues to get advice and support. Hannay (1979) identified a 'symptom iceberg' among a Glasgow population in that nearly a quarter of respondents 'had at least one physical, mental or behavioural symptom for which they did not seek professional advice, although they said the pain or disability was severe, or they thought the symptom was serious'. A large, and growing, number of conditions are self treated by lay people through the use of medicines from the chemist. In a 1972 survey Dunnell and Cartwright found that the consumption of self prescribed medicines was twice as great as that of prescription medicines, and this trend towards self treatment has continued (Sharma, 1990). In addition, media coverage of illness and disease has increased, and the growth of self help groups and of health awareness among women's groups, black and minority ethnic groups and others has increased the resources available to lay people to know about and take action on their illness.

In these circumstances researchers have begun to use the term 'illness action' rather than 'illness behaviour', in order to emphasise that lay people are active participants in the whole process of dealing with their own (and others') illnesses. Of course, a structural approach does not ignore that people are also actors in their own illness drama, but its main interest is in the stable and predictable social patterning of that action. In contrast to this, interactionists have highlighted how people are conscious decision makers and purposive agents at the centre of webs of complex negotiations.

An interactionist model of illness action

Robert Dingwall (1976) developed an 'illness action model', drawing on research findings from acute and chronic illness and from a study of childbirth, all of which demonstrated the active role of lay people in decision making (see Figure 10.5). Dingwall used the term 'disturbance' rather than illness symptoms, to signal that change in the external environment might give meaning to signs and symptoms which already existed, but at an unconscious level or in an uninterpreted state. He suggested the perception and interpretation of the disturbance could come about through medical screening (for example a cervical smear or blood pressure check) or through the acquisition of new health information. Media information about the prevalence of flu, for example, might persuade you to make a connections between a number of hitherto disparate symptoms, or indeed to become aware of them for the first time.

The 'interpretive work' that takes place, on the part of the sufferer and others, is to determine the nature and degree of seriousness of the

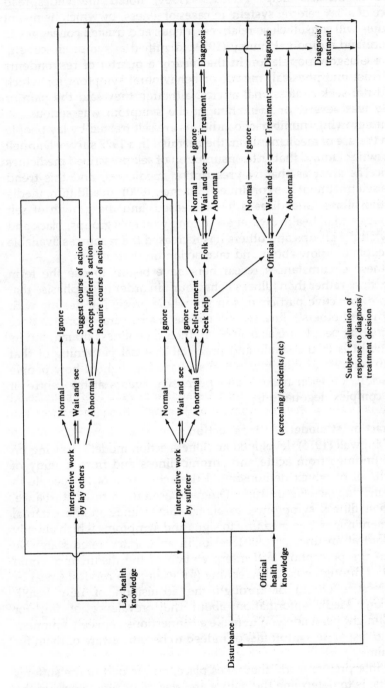

FIGURE 10.5 An illness action model. Source: Dingwall (1976)

disturbance. In the case of flu, for example, the symptoms might be ignored at first, but if new information was acquired (say from colleagues at work who experienced similar symptoms) or if the symptoms persisted, action might be required. Dingwall suggested that in the case of chronic disease the disturbance will take the form of some exacerbation of the existing condition which is seen as 'normal'. In the case of asthma, for example, it might be greater breathing difficulties or extreme tiredness that would alert the sufferer to disturbance and provoke some interpretive action.

As you can see, Dingwall suggested three possible 'pathways', only one of which brings the sufferer into contact with 'official' health care services. The other two pathways involve the sufferer in lay referral or in negotiations with self, and in both situations a range of possible alternative routes are indicated.

○ Compare Dingwall's illness action model with the Kasl and Cobb model of factors influencing illness behaviour and comment on the main differences of emphasis.

In the Kasl and Cobb model we get a strong sense of how wider social forces shape individual illness behaviour, whereas in Dingwall's model there is little sense of the social context of the individual sufferers. Dingwall's concern is with the social process of negotiation and choice in which sufferers engage when they become aware of disturbance, but he makes no comment on the differential extent to which people might become aware of that disturbance – because they take up preventive services to a greater or lesser extent, because they read less about health matters, because of their occupation and so on. These differences lead us back to consider the influence of education, age, social class, gender and other structural factors. On the other hand it seems that in pulling structural factors into focus, the complex negotiations involved in coping with disturbance are neglected.

The contrast between these two models reflects some of the broader concerns of this chapter about conflicting approaches to the investigation and explanation of health and illness. In particular, the dominance of expert accounts of health and illness and of abstract and quantitative research studies has tended to push lay accounts and explanations to the margins. The Kasl and Cobb model arises from a focus on medical concerns: that is, on why people do or do not present when they have signs and symptoms of illness. It is a powerful quantitative model in which one objective is to predict how sufferers will behave. It tends to assume that 'illness symptoms' are unproblematic, that they have a objective existence and are easily discoverable by the sufferer.

Dingwall's model draws attention to the uncertainties surrounding 'disturbance of equilibrium'; it implies that people may not recognise disturbance, may initially recognise and then ignore it, and may not move along a clear pathway to the doctor. In this model illness symptoms are socially negotiated constructs; the courses of action that the model predicts are not clearly delineated pathways but matters of individual perception and interpretation. To a greater extent, therefore, Dingwall's model takes into account lay beliefs and explanations of health and illness. Within its framework we can incorporate the folk traditions which Helman (1986) researched, and the findings of Herzlich, Blaxter and others about lay interpretation of illness. We can also incorporate changing patterns of official help and advice. Consider the growing role of pharmacists, for example, in supporting self treatment by lay people. In a study of mothers' use of pharmacists in relation to child illnesses, Cunningham-Burley and Maclean (1990) reported that mothers who consulted pharmacists made less use of their family doctors.

10.7 Illness action and 'sick role' theories

Increased understanding of the variety and complexity of lay action has led to even greater criticism of accounts which propose a straight-forward relationship between patients' symptoms and the route to medical treatment, indicating that when people fall ill they 'normally' enter the 'sick role', and hence that not to do so is to be 'deviant'. But as we noted in Chapter 1, the medical profession does exert considerable control over popular concepts of health and illness, it defines disease and sickness and it makes the final decisions about who should be treated. It might be argued that what is important to a society is the maintenance of a fairly clear boundary between sickness and health, so that it can continue to operate and the potentially disruptive effects of illness are contained. In this sense lay referral systems and self help might be seen as efficient ways of screening illness so that only the most pressing concerns reach the doctor. The problem with this theory, as Hannay's (1979) study and others have indicated, is that those who do not consult may have just as much pain and suffering as those who do visit the doctor.

Talcott Parsons' sick role theory

Parsons' classic theory of the 'sick role' was developed in the 1950s (see Chapter 2) from an empirical study of the medical profession in Boston, USA. One of his main concerns in developing the concept was to counter the biomedical model by highlighting the social dimensions of

TABLE 10.3 Parsons' 'sick role' theory: a summary

Patient: sick role	Doctor: professional role
1 Exempted from responsibility for sickness; seen as being unable to get better without professional help	1 Must be objective and remain detached, not impose own values
2 Can legitimately withdraw from normal activities and social responsibilities, for example paid work, family duties, housework	2 Must not act in self interest (for example for money, career) but in interests of patient; must obey professional code of practice
3 Must seek competent treatment from a professional health expert	3 Must apply a high degree of knowledge and skill to treat the patient
4 Under a social obligation to get better as quickly as possible	4 Given right to examine patient intimately, prescribe treatment and exercise professional authority; granted wide autonomy in medical practice

the sick role. His approach was that of a structural functionalist, and the sick role was viewed in terms of the contribution it made to the maintenance of the social system in general, and to the profession of medicine in particular (see Table 10.3). In Chapter 11 we'll consider Parsons' theory of profession, but at this point let's focus on his conceptualisation of the role of the patient.

Parsons did indeed argue that the social control and regulation of sickness were necessary because any society needed to maintain equilibrium and achieve its general goals; too great a burden of sickness threatened social order. The sick role regulated patients' conduct while 'sick' and created a set of conditions governing entry to and exit from the role. There were four component parts:

1 The sick person is exempted from responsibility for their sickness; they are regarded as being unable to get better without professional help. It is sickness, not the sick individual, that is deviant.
2 The sick person can legitimately withdraw from normal activities and social responsibilities, such as employment, housework and family duties into a sick role.
3 The sick person must seek competent treatment from a professional health expert and have their sickness diagnosed and recorded.
4 The sick person is under a social obligation to get better as quickly as possible. This is the main justification for creating the sick role.

○   Review these dimensions of the sick role in the light of your own experience of 'being sick', the discussion in Section 10.6 and any wider professional experience you have as a health worker or health work student. What is your assessment of this typology?

There are several useful aspects of the sick role which Parsons draws attention to: in particular, the social framing of sickness, the processes of social negotiation involved and the potentially disruptive effects of being sick – for the individual, for others and for society in general. You may have noted that it emphasises a widely used definition (that we encountered in Chapter 1) of health as an ability to function normally, fulfil work and family obligations, be a productive worker. It also points to health care professionals (especially doctors) exercising a social control function for society by regulating and controlling the production of sickness. Underlying the sick role is the notion of a 'competence gap' between doctors and patients: patients consult, are diagnosed, follow advice and treatment, become passive patients. To what extent does your own experience of becoming sick bear this out?

Over the years Parsons' typology has been quite widely criticised. One problem with an 'ideal type' of patient behaviour is that the patient role isn't universal; acute and chronic sickness, for example, may give rise to distinctive patient roles. Whereas an appendicitis sufferer may fall easily into the patient role that Parsons discusses, a sufferer from some long-standing complaint, such as migraine, asthma, rheumatism or depression, may come to know almost as much as their doctor or other health worker about their condition. This may produce negotiation and bargaining about diagnosis and treatment, and it may lead to non-compliance and even to open conflict between doctor and patient, with the doctor's authority being challenged. In the case of 'new' diseases or uncertain conditions, such as pre-menstrual stress syndrome (PMS), post-viral fatigue syndrome or tenosynivitis (repetitive strain injury – RSI), sufferers may not be admitted into the sick role by some doctors; the signs and symptoms may be viewed as unproven and the demand for patient status seen as illegitimate.

You may have noted some other interesting features of this typology arising from the earlier discussion in Section 10.6. By no means all patients move into the sick role, yet Parsons assumed the interpretive work and pathway to the doctor had been satisfactorily undertaken; 'Parsons' analysis of the patient role therefore tends to be rather a narrow slice of the total character of illness behaviour and help-seeking behaviour' (Turner, 1987). Certainly there is an emphasis in health service literature in Britain on consulting the medical expert rather than treating yourself in serious illness, but the dividing line between serious illness and 'trivia' is unclear. Parsons views the decision as being taken by the patient within a normative social framework: that is, the patient's motivation for seeking treatment and trying to get well is the weight of social obligation. If this social pressure did not exist, the voluntary character of health care might endanger social order. In fact, as you may have experienced yourself, some people do not, or cannot hope to, get well, and Parsons acknowledged that this 'deviancy' was de-stabilising for society. Although he accepted that there would be some for whom sickness became a way of life (much as Herzlich's respondents characterised 'illness as occupation'), this also confirmed that sickness was a form of social deviance, which every society had to find ways of regulating and controlling.

Although Parsons' typology has been criticised as characterising the sick role only in modern American society, Turner (1987) comments that this is in fact precisely what Parsons set out to analyse. He continues:

To be sick in American society was to be inactive and withdrawn from the competitive race of a society which gave an emphasis to moral individualism. Parsons had suggested that different social structures would produce different sick roles and he was particularly concerned to provide a contrast between sickness in state socialist societies and sickness in competitive capitalist society.

Turner (1987)

The sick role is a form of social withdrawal which is widespread in human cultures, and Turner offers examples from the Middle East, North American Indians and Japan to demonstrate how it is used to justify deviation from social norms and customary behaviour patterns. He suggests that whereas in all these societies 'sickness and health are criteria of social membership and engagement', the particular forms that the sick role may take vary very considerably. Indeed, we have already noted in Section 10.2 that the retreat into the sick role of the Gnau of New Guinea takes a very different form to the sick role prescribed among the Amhara of Ethiopia, or the social pressures which may be experienced by the sick person in contemporary Britain. This is not just a difference between Western industrialised societies and 'non-Western' societies. In Japanese culture the sick role is one in which 'positive vacation and recreation' is emphasised, characterised by peace, quietness and unusually lengthy periods of hospitalisation. In addition, the continuing solicitude and support of close relatives is an important feature; 'a ritualised system of visitation' and the sharing of food are characteristic of this.

10.8 Becoming a patient

Once patients have presented their symptoms for diagnosis by health professionals, whether in primary care or at the accident and emergency

TABLE 10.4 Open and closed institutions. Source: Goffman (1961)

Closed/total	Open/permeable
1 High degree of control of activities, routines, whole life of inmates and staff; whole life of inmates (sleeping, eating, work, recreation) takes place within single location	**1** Low degree of control by institution/ staff of activities; clients may enter/exit at will
2 All activity is planned and controlled to achieve organisation's official goals	**2** Activity is programmed, but goals of institution accept need for flexibility/ change
3 Clear division exists between staff and inmates/clients; clear authority of all staff (even most junior) over inmates (even senior); hierarchy of staff and often inmates; staff controlled from top, accountability upwards	**3** Lack of clear division between staff/ clients; co-operation, non-hierarchical, organic and client-centred
4 Sharp division made, for inmates (and staff), between 'outside' behaviour, language, attitudes, networks, self image and that seen as appropriate 'inside'; outside norms and values broken and replaced (disculturalisation)	**4** Continuity of norms and values
5 Entry procedure for inmates (and staff) is sudden, clear-cut, harsh, to emphasise the break (= the mortification process, in which the self is reshaped); similar rituals at exit	**5** Absence of rituals, mystique; acceptance of client's social 'self'

department, they can be said to have embarked upon a *patient career*. Some possible aspects of the patient career have been noted in earlier chapters, for example labelling, dependency and institutional care. In writing about patients in long-stay psychiatric hospitals Goffman (1961) characterised the career of the patient as a series of status passages, including initial diagnosis, admission procedures, treatment regimes and eventual outcome (Table 10.4). These status passages are accompanied by various rites or rituals, which together create the patient's career as both a social, psychological and normative experience.

'Closed' and 'open' institutions

As Table 10.4 indicates, the rituals that Goffman observed in long-stay hospitals were elaborate and in many cases highly oppressive. They were deliberately concerned with the removal of the previous identity of the individual and the creation of the new identity of 'the patient'. Bathing, medical inspection, the removal of personal belongings and the donning of hospital clothing formed a 'mortification process' which de-personalised the entrant. Life within a total 'closed' institution involved not just treatment but the transformation of the patient's self image: a reconceptualisation of self derived from diagnosis, treatment and new relationships with other patients and health professionals. Within the closed intitution there was wide control over the activities and behaviour of the inmates (and staff) within a rigid hierarchy. In contrast to this we can characterise as 'open' institutions those organisations in which the clients' social self is accepted and there is no sudden break with the outside world. In clinics and day centres, for example, and in some residential homes, clients are free to come and go at will, and health professionals share power and consult with clients about treatment.

Labelling theory
Interactionists have suggested that some patients may learn to view themselves in terms of the diagnostic label attached to them by health workers and patients: 'the schizophrenic', 'the psychotic' and so on. For interactionists the whole creation of deviance is an essentially social act. They point out that, although many people in society deviate from the behaviour expected of them and fail to fulfil allotted roles, such acts of *primary deviance* – or rule breaking – may pass unnoticed. For example, the behaviour of people with drink problems or incipient schizophrenia may be ignored or rationalised by family and friends. The stage of *secondary deviance* is reached when such symptoms are diagnosed and the sufferer is labelled as deviant and takes on a deviant role. By 'policing' sickness – an aspect of the medical role which Parsons also highlighted – doctors help to determine what should constitute deviance (see Figure 10.6).

Medical diagnostic categories, as we have noted, are not fixed and immutable but shifting and subject to change. Whether they are applied or not depends on a number of complex variables involving, among other factors, the social background of the doctor and the patient. Once an act of diagnosis has attached a label to a patient, the subsequent reaction of the patient to this label, the attitudes of other patients and health professionals and the reaction of the patient to these expressed or implied attitudes 'amplify' the deviance. The patient is marked out as 'different', stigmatised by the diagnostic category (Lemert, 1972). Now the patient's perception of self reflects the social and psychological impact of the diagnostic label, and any real identity has disappeared. At the extreme the patient sees him/herself, and is viewed, merely as a set

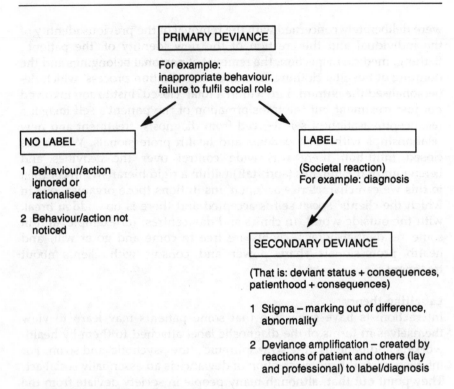

FIGURE 10.6 Labelling theory

of symptoms requiring a set of treaments. Labelling theory has been criticised for ignoring the issue of primary deviance; after all, it is deviant behaviour which sparks off the labelling process. Nor does labelling theory take into account the way in which class, race and gender influence attitudes and responses to deviant behaviour (Pilgrim and Rogers, 1993).

Clearly, most patients do not experience either the repercussions of this extreme form of labelling or the processing and degrading of self in a long-stay institution. Many patients do not even enter hospital; many with acute symptoms may stay for only a few days. Even patients with chronic sickness are much less likely to be treated in hospital, although they may find themselves in a residential or nursing home in a community setting that has some of the characteristics of a 'closed' institution. But most treatment settings, whether in hospital or in the community, are 'permeable': rituals are much less intrusive, and contact between patients and the outside world is maintained and encouraged.

● Suggest some 'rituals' and 'rites of passage' that do still exist in hospitals. Are they all, in clinical terms, necessary? If not, why are they maintained?

You may have suggested admissions procedures such as taking the patient's history. Patients admitted for more than one day still usually remove their everyday clothes and dress in pyjamas or nightdress, dressing gown and slippers. Visiting hours are much relaxed now, but in some wards there are still restrictions on hours and numbers of visitors. Meals are served at set times, and other aspects of care such as washing may be carried out within a fixed routine. There are a number of reasons why rituals survive: in particular, the expectations of the patients and the comfort derived from rituals by the staff are both very important. For example, nursing students have reported that patients in wards where activity is expected and day clothes are generally retained often expect and want to 'go to bed' and 'have a rest'.

The diversity of patient experience

People are likely to have very diverse attitudes to their roles as patients. An ideal type of patient career, in which the patient is diagnosed and treated and in which a specific outcome – cure, alleviation, remission, death – is produced, can only be a generalisation which highlights some central issues (see Figure 10.7). Many people with chronic sickness, for example, may know nearly as much about their condition as the specialist – and rather more than other health workers. In one classic study patients with tuberculosis in a long-stay hospital setting entered into complex negotiations with the medical staff, drawing on the experiences of other patients to argue the case for a status passage to the next stage of treatment (Roth, 1978). In Goffman's (1961) study of the asylum, patients learned to work the system and gain more control over their situation. They evaded rules and 'psyched out' staff: that is, they outwardly conformed to staff expectations in order to gain favour but participated in a covert institutional 'underlife'.

More to the point, many patients know a great deal about their particular condition in terms of how it affects them as individuals. Older people, for example, are likely to be aware of new symptoms, of the impact on their bodies of changing medication and so on. In this sense patients are active workers in the health care process. As Stacey (1988) has commented, 'rather than being a consumer of health care, the patient should be considered a partner in the health-care team and a producer as much as a consumer of health care'.

| Symptoms | ➡ | Medical consultation | ➡ | Diagnosis | ➡ | Treatment – hospital – community – home | ➡ | Outcomes – cure – alleviation – death |

FIGURE 10.7 'Ideal type' of patient career

The changing status of the patient

The conceptualisation of patients as active 'partners' in the health care process might have reminded you of earlier discussions about the 'social construction' of identities (Section 2.8). The human sciences have played an important role in analysing – and thereby constructing – identities and relationships in health care. Sociology, like science, does not stand outside the social world, observing and recording relationships in a detached way. It is inevitably actively involved in the making and remaking of social identities and relationships. Consider, for example, the theories of Talcott Parsons about the role of the patient in the doctor–patient relationship. In these theories, developed in the 1940s and 1950s, the patient role was characterised by withdrawal from everyday activities and acceptance by others of the legitimacy of the sickness – providing the patient sought medical advice, followed it and demonstrated the desire to get better as soon as possible. The patient was active only in seeking medical treatment and was subsequently limited to complying with medical instructions.

The largely passive role of the patient discussed in Parsons' sick role theory reflects the social construction of the patient in traditional biomedicine as the 'object' of medical scrutiny. This notion of the docile patient and the dominant doctor (who diagnosed, treated and expected to be obeyed) also fits in with the 1960s textbook view of the nurse–patient relationship: the patient was the largely passive recipient of nursing care, the nurse was the active manager (see Section 12.2).

Since the 1950s Parsons' analysis has been subject to extensive criticism and reformulation (Gerhardt, 1989). New theories about patients have emphasised their status as social actors, active participants and manipulators. In Section 10.6 we noted the research on the complexity of patient behaviour and the dynamics of patient action. Today health workers are encouraged to see patients as 'bio-psycho-social wholes'. Armstrong (1983b) has commented on the shifting nature of the concept of the patient both in medical discourse and in the nursing literature. He highlights the relativism of the concept; just as the earlier model of the patient was socially constructed, so too is this new 'active patient'. The passive body surveyed by the clinical gaze becomes the active body of the extended or community gaze. In the future some new interpretation of the patient might be seen as equally valid. Moreover, the notion that patienthoood as a category is not fixed and can be reconstructed to 'fit' with a changing social context can equally well be applied to our concepts of 'the nurse' and 'the doctor'.

10.9 Beliefs, action and health work

We have explored health and illness as social processes from the perspective of the individual member of society and, in broader terms, as sets of distinctive and variable socio-cultural norms and customs. Health and illness, it has been argued here, are social products which develop and change over time and between different societies as a result of negotiation and conflict between different groups in a society. Definitions of health and illness arise within societies and are connected to other aspects of the belief system; the triumph of a biomedical account of health and illness in Western society was part of a fundamental socio-cultural and economic reconceptualisation of the natural world and of the place of human beings within that world.

What are the messages here for nurses and other health workers? First, the obvious ones about the need for sensitivity to patients' 'stories' about their illness, for an informed understanding of the diversity of health beliefs and open-mindedness as regards the biomedical approach. Second, we can emphasise that accounts (ways of seeing, knowing and doing) of health and illness in different societies and cultures will be bound up with, and will reinforce, different values. This also indicates the potential for change over time, as negotiation and/or conflict about who should define health and illness, about the legitimate parameters of the sick role and about the proper relationship between health care workers and their patients (customers? clients? users?) intensifies. Nurses and other non-medical health workers, although hitherto often neglected in discussions about such matters – by doctors, lay people, sociologists and others – are in fact key players in this unfolding drama.

A major part of nurses' work lies in the area of negotiation about health and illness accounts and practices. Nurses are intermediaries between medical and lay belief systems: they interpret doctor's 'messages' to patients and patients 'messages' to doctors. Implicit in their practice is a very different set of values to those held by most doctors, values which are closer to those of their patients: the importance of caring and emotional support, the contextualising of sickness within everyday life and the sick role as a continuous process of negotiation. Although nurses and other health workers have often aligned themselves with doctors and a medicalised approach to sickness, their reorientation towards the user perspective, patient advocacy and quality issues has been marked in recent years. As Ann Oakley (1986) commented, 'an alliance between nurses and health care users is a strategy that could drastically improve the health care scene'.

Since nurses make up such a large proportion of health sector staff, we'll be using the example of nursing to focus on health care as a series of intimate and interactive processes (see Chapter 12). But first we need to set nursing work within the broader framework of the rise of professional health work. So in Chapter 11 we'll consider the implications of changing ideologies and shifting structures on the delivery of health care and on nursing as an occupation.

Suggestions for further study

C. Currer and M. Stacey (1986) *Concepts of Health, Illness and Disease*, Oxford, Berg, contains a varied collection of useful articles about concepts of health and different health work systems. C.W. Aakster (1993) 'Concepts in Alternative Medicine' in A. Beattie *et al.*, *Health and Wellbeing: A Reader*, London, Macmillan, is a useful summary of the debate about alternative medicine. M. Blaxter (1990) *Health and Lifestyles*, London, Tavistock, discusses the major survey of health beliefs and attitudes undertaken in 1987. Sick role theory is thoughtfully reviewed in B. Turner (1987) *Medical Power and Social Knowledge*, London, Sage, and different theories of the state of illness are explored in U. Gerhardt (1989) *Ideas about Illness*, London, Macmillan.

Self assessment questions

1 Review how your own beliefs about health and illness relate to the lay accounts outlined in this chapter.
2 In what ways can health and illness be viewed as social products?
3 Explain the main differences between internalising and externalising health belief systems and give examples of each.
4 Review the social factors which may influence an individual's response to illness in the light of your own practice experience.
5 Discuss the main strengths and weaknesses of structural and social action theories of illness behaviour.

Chapter 11

Power and control in health work

Contents

Themes and issues

Early health theories: humors – supernatural beliefs – lay and professional healers

Biomedical theories: biological base – scientific methods – concepts of function, normality, aetiology – the clinical gaze and medical truth claims – shift in cosmologies – germ theory

The social organisation of modern medicine: rise of the hospital – public health movement – health division of labour – health service bureaucracy – the emergence of the National Health Service – restructuring in 1974 – Griffiths and general management

Medical dominance: capitalist critiques – medical imperialism – the medicalisation of everyday life

Learning outcomes

After working through this chapter you should be able to:

1 Explain why biomedicine became established as the major health belief system in modern industrial society.
2 Discuss the main characteristics of the health division of labour in professionalised health work.
3 Outline the main problems and issues facing the National Health Service in Britain by the 1980s.
4 Apply theories of organic and bureaucratic organisation to explain contemporary health work structures and practices.
5 Critically examine the claim that modern medicine has become too powerful and invasive in society.

IN most of the Western world the health care system as we know it
today – with its biomedical focus, its hierarchy of trained health
professionals and complex primary, secondary and tertiary facilities for
cure and care – came fully into being only in the twentieth century. In
Britain some health occupations, such as health visiting, only came into
existence after 1900, and the idea of a national, co-ordinated service to
treat illness was a product of the 1940s. The notion of a single medical
'profession', with a virtual monopoly over medical practice, dates from
the later nineteenth century in Britain; in the USA monopoly status for
doctors came much later. It was only in the 1880s that 'germ theory'
began to be accepted, and it took another 30 years for it to become the
orthodox way of thinking about disease among professional health
workers in Europe. Finally, it was about two hundred years ago in the
West that people began to think about bodies as collections of discrete
cells and membranes rather than mainly undifferentiated 'flesh' and
organs (Jewson, 1976).

In other words, the ways of thinking about and organising health
care that we take for granted are actually quite 'new' and distinctive. If
we go back in time it becomes apparent that not only the organisation of
health work but also the conceptualisation of health and disease was
very different. So how and why did the contemporary health work
system emerge? Why were older ways of seeing the body and thinking
about health discarded, and what are the implications of this for health
workers and patients? What is the relationship between the health work
system and broader social and economic changes? What are the social
characteristics of the health work system of the 1990s? In this chapter we
will briefly review older ways of working for health, before exploring the
circumstances in which biomedicine triumphed as the new orthodoxy in
Europe and beyond and health professionals came to dominate the
production of health care. A critical evaluation of professional power
will be followed by an exploration of the shifting patterns of power and
control in the contemporary health system. This leads on to Chapter 12,
which explores and assesses the care and control exercised by nurses –
the biggest group of health service workers yet one which has been in
many ways 'invisible'.

11.1 Pluralism in early health work

Health beliefs

Health beliefs, like health work, were pluralist in character. Highly
elaborate theories of health and disease existed alongside widespread
belief in supernatural powers and in natural causes. The theory of

humors, for example, synthesised by the Greek physician Galen, continued to be widely applied by physicians until well after 1700 (see Chapter 10, page 379, Figure 10.2). This proposed a 'correspondence' between people and the natural world. Just as an ideal state in nature was the peaceful co-existence of the four elements, so positive health depended on holding a balance between the bodily fluids. Blood-letting was one widely practised therapy linked with humoral medicine. Rival theories, such as those of Paracelsus, combined more empirically based work on physiology with astrology and even alchemy (Webster, 1979).

There was also general endorsement of a different order of beliefs about disease: that is, of the existence of witches, apparitions and supernatural powers, which could protect or harm people. Both religious and secular authorities as well as lay people of all classes, accepted demons and other supernatural beings as powerful actors in the battle between good and evil. Witch-hunts, which some feminist writers have seen as a major attempt to persecute and eliminate women healers, were widespread throughout this period. It is unclear how many 'witches' were put to death, but witch trials remained – from the authorities' point of view – a useful check on the influence of unauthorised healers (Ehrenreich and English, 1974). Co-existing with this belief in the power of the supernatural, however, was a belief in environmental causes of disease and in other natural explanations.

Health workers

Health work, before recent times, largely took place in the private domain and most of it was carried out by women. As well as providing lay nursing care, many of the village herbalists, midwives and 'wise country people' who treated the sick would have been women. Some hospital treatment for travellers and the local community was provided in the sanitoria of monasteries and nunneries; in Catholic Europe these continued to provide a focus for health care into modern times whereas in Protestant countries, including Britain, they were closed down. In London five royal 'chartered' hospitals were founded to fill the gap. In some urban areas 'infirmaries' – voluntary hospitals for the poor – were established by public subscription and city authorities supervised 'lazar houses' for the sick poor. But most people were treated and cared for by female relatives at home. This contrasts with contemporary health work, most of which is focused in the public sphere of the hospital, clinic and health centre. However, as we noted in Chapter 7, women, paid or unpaid, are still the main health workers and some health work still takes place in the home (Graham, 1984a).

People in the sixteenth century could call on the services of apothecaries, who offered advice and produced a range of medicines, and of 'barber-surgeons', who carried out limited surgical procedures. Most common folk relied on 'empirics' – a numerous group of health practitioners without formal training, who included midwives, bone setters and village herbalists, as well as more esoteric categories of 'cunning men' and 'wise women'. Only the small upper class, the gentry and aristocracy, could afford to consult learned physicians. In some town records women figured as formal health workers – for example as surgeons and apothecaries – as well as empirics. Pelling's (1982) study of sixteenth century Norwich gives a ratio of one practitioner for every 200 citizens, a remarkable figure but perhaps not surprising given that average life expectancy was around thirty years.

○   Now compare the health beliefs and health work system described here with those of non-Western societies discussed in Section 10.2. What common features are there?

These beliefs may well have reminded you of the health beliefs of the Amhara, who emphasise internal bodily balance and harmony but also acknowledge external agents of sickness. In addition, the Amhara have a range of specialist healers and *habesha hakiym* who work as spirit healers. There are clearly some similarities between early modern European health systems and those of non-industrialised non-Western societies. This is also apparent if we consider health practices and the underlying notion of an *undifferentiated* individual as under attack by disease: that is, of the whole person, body and mind, falling sick.

Health practice

The plurality of health workers in early modern times enabled patients with funds to be selective and critical in their dealings. Treatment was a matter of bargaining over cost and diagnosis; patients remained in active negotiation with their chosen healers and 'shopped around' for the most likely cure.

Jewson (1976) has argued that 'bedside medicine' – in which the sick person was a major participant and not just a passive recipient of treatment – was the dominant mode of health work before about 1800. For several reasons, he suggests, the 'sick man' remained as the central point of reference and the source of information and inspiration for practitioners. It was a sensible precaution, after all, to listen to clients who were paying for your services, and to take their views into account in suggesting treatment. There were so many different possible treatments, and so many rival theories, that the wealthy client who could pay well for medical services was in an ideal position to demand complete all-round attention.

More important, in most of these varied theories (and therapies), some grounded in experience and empirical knowledge and others highly abstract and theoretical, disease was seen as striking the whole person, body, mind and spirit. Relatively little was known about anatomy and physiology or the course of disease through the body. The battery of therapies – from blood-letting and diet therapy to herbal remedies – was designed to restore the whole, undifferentiated individual to spiritual and physical health. Even where it was evident that a treatment or surgical intervention was efficacious, the restoration of health to the individual remained a more complex matter of restoring balance and harmony to body and spirit. Ambroise Paré, a sixteenth century French surgeon, commented: 'I dressed the patient, but God healed him' (Cartwright, 1977).

11.2 The rise of biomedicine

For the last 150 years biomedicine has dominated our thinking about health and disease. Its scientific approach and its conceptualisation of the body as a machine have constituted a distinctive way of 'seeing and knowing' which has been highly successful and influential (Foucault, 1973). 'Modern' nursing work, which we investigate in Chapter 12, emerged in the shadow of biomedicine, specifically charged with 'nursing the room' so that strict hygienic principles were maintained, and with undertaking the arduous, hour-by-hour scrutiny of the patient's condition. The medical profession established itself at the apex of the health work hierarchy, entrenching its own position and increasingly able to direct and control the whole division of labour in health. The 'truth claims' of biomedicine have been successfully projected at the expense of older ways of thinking about health and disease.

Note down the characteristic features of a biomedical approach to health and disease.

You may have included some of the following features of the biomedical approach, and perhaps others not included below:

- Biomedicine explains health in terms of biology, attaching supreme importance to learning about body structure (anatomy) and systems (physiology).
- It rests on an assumption that all causes of disease – mental disorders as well as physical disease – can ultimately be understood in biological terms.

- It explains disease and sickness in terms of specific or multiple aetiology (theory of cause), tracking the cause and course of disease as it affects particular parts of the human body.
- It draws heavily on scientific knowledge in general and emphasises its association with scientific method and objectivity (the hypotheco-deductive method).
- Disease and sickness are seen as deviations from normal functioning, and health is seen in largely mechanical terms, as a state where all parts of the body function 'normally'.

Economic and social transformations

How did this view of health and disease, and the pattern of medical dominance associated with it, come into being? The triumph of biomedicine over other, rival ways of conceptualising health and illness has been associated with complex cultural and economic transformations in Europe, which encouraged the growth and acceptance of a scientific approach to the natural world. The Protestant Reformation of the sixteenth century resulted in the fragmentation of religious beliefs and the gradual decline of a homogenous culture and shared morality in Europe. Over the succeeding centuries religious authorities were less able to censor and police new ideas, especially when the invention of the printing press enabled new knowledge to be made more widely accessible. The rise of the nation state created new political priorities and shifting legislative frameworks, which to some extent encouraged the secularisation of society.

From around 1500 onwards, as European nations began to expand overseas to colonise and exploit new territories, a growing awareness developed of the possibility of controlling and harnessing the power of the natural world. In the seventeeth and eighteenth centuries learned societies sponsored expeditions and investigations to discover more about the 'secrets of nature'. Together with this went increased confidence in the ability – and, it was argued, the God-given right – of Europeans to become the masters of 'inferior' conquered peoples.

Linked to this were economic changes, in particular the growth of capitalist enterprise and organisation, stimulated by the growth of overseas trade. It has also been argued that the new Protestant religions, in particular Calvinism, encouraged wealth making by putting an enhanced value on wordly success as evidence of God's favour (Weber, 1948). Together these factors underpinned one of the most important conceptual shifts: the gradual reassessment, in the West, of the position of human beings in the universe.

Enlightenment thought and the rise of science

The growth of *Enlightenment* thought in the late seventeenth and eighteenth centuries was of great importance in the rise of biomedicine. Investigation of the natural world, encouraged by economic expansion and cultural change, suggested the existence of a rational universe. Enlightenment philosophers and mathematicians, such as René Descartes and Isaac Newton, emphasised that the natural world, including human beings, could be classified and ultimately explained through the application of human reason. Newton theorised the universe as a mechanical clock keeping perfect time and, like a clock, able to be dissected and understood.

Descartes' pronouncement 'I think, therefore I am' drew attention to the primacy of the intellect. Philosophers argued that it was the human mind which made humans superior to nature and able to control and harness its power: this was the divine, spiritual part of 'man'. By contrast, the human body was a separable, 'natural object'. It began to be claimed that human bodies could be investigated and ultimately understood using similar methods to those employed to explore and uncover the other secrets of the universe. Human beings could, as it were, stand outside their bodies and investigate them in an objective way, using the tools of the new science.

There was an increasing emphasis on natural explanations of health and disease, which in part reflected the growing secularisation of society but also the preoccupations of social reformers in Enlightenment Europe. By the mid-eighteenth century the beginning of industrialisation and the rapid growth of cities had put new pressures on municipal authorities to act, particularly against epidemic diseases which struck at both rich and poor. In many European cities active campaigns to clean up filth led to street paving and lighting and to experiments with piped water and waste disposal. In an attempt to halt the spread of epidemic diseases such as cholera quarantine regulations were introduced at European ports, and hospitals were built to isolate the sick (Riley, 1987).

So in many different ways changing social forms and cultural practices created a framework within which new ideas about health and the body could flourish. Theories about the operation of the universe, about gravity, mechanics and hydraulics, offered convincing explanations of the operation of human bodies and challenged traditional religious and expert beliefs. Religious taboos about anatomical investigation and human dissection lost some of their force, opening up the possibility of developing new theories of how bodies were constructed.

The clinical gaze

Central to this theory building was a particular process of observation and interpretation, which Michel Foucault (1973) has characterised as the 'clinical gaze' (see Section 2.8). In his view this reconceptualisation of the body was the driving force in the rise of biomedicine. It involved viewing the signs and symptoms of disease and tracking the course of disease within the human body. Disease was diagnosed by building up concepts of normality and abnormality through the study of corpses and sick patients. Above all, it meant using dissection to look beneath external lesions and uncover the internal impact of disease. The French doctor Xavier Bichat commented:

For twenty years, from morning to night, you have taken notes at patients' bedsides on affections of the heart, the lungs, and the gastric viscera, and all is confusion for you in the symptoms which, refusing to yield up their meaning, offer you a succession of incoherent phenomena. Open up a few corpses: you will dissipate at once the darkness that observation alone could not dissipate.

Bichat (1801)

Disease, which had previously been seen as striking the whole person, began to be spatialised and individualised. Patients were carefully examined, and signs and symptoms were increasingly monitored, not just on the surface of the human body but within it. Dissection and medical inspection 'revealed' the mystery of the body. Foucault (1973) suggests that doctors questioned their patients in new ways; instead of asking 'What is the matter?' they began to ask 'Where does it hurt?'. An interest in the whole suffering patient was replaced by an interest in the site of disease. With the rise of the medical examination came a new classification of disease (see Box 11.1).

BOX 11.1 The birth of the clinic: the 'mutation in medical knowledge'. Source: Foucault (1973)

From:	To:
Mass of organ/area	Discrete elements and tissue
Botany of symptoms	Grammar of signs
Nosological tables (cataloguing exact quality of disease)	'Linear series of morbid events' (mapping course of disease)
Disease possessing person as a whole	Disease affecting physical body, part of body tissue
What is the matter with you?	Where does it hurt?

Doctors believed that it was the 'natural order' of the body itself which was being revealed. In other words, they argued that they were *merely describing what they saw*, in the same way as botanists described the structure of a plant. Biomedicine could therefore align itself clearly with the methods of observation of science, as opposed to supernatural explanations. But Foucault (1973) and others have argued that a new 'anatomical atlas' came into being, without which the 'natural order' of the body could not have been 'read'. The clinical gaze, therefore, was not merely empirical but analytic; it recorded symptoms and observed signs, and in doing so it also interpreted signs and predicted symptoms. Far from being a fixed biological entity which awaited discovery by accurate observation, the body as we know it only came into existence when defined by the anatomical atlas.

○ Read the following quotation from David Armstrong (1983a), which records his growing awareness of the 'clinical gaze' and the 'fabrication' of the body. Make notes on how Armstrong's ideas about 'the body' changed over time.

I doubt if it ever occurred to me or my fellow medical students that the human body which we dissected and examined was other than a stable experience. It was therefore with considerable surprise that years later I learned that it was only since the end of the eighteenth century that disease had been localised to specific organs and tissues, and that bodies had been subjected to the rigours of clinical examination.

At first it seemed strange to me how the apparent obviousness of disease and its manifestations inside the body had eluded scientific discovery for so long. How had pre-Enlightenment generations failed to see clearly differentiated organs and tissues of the body? Or failed to link patient symptoms with the existence of localised pathological processes? Or failed to apply the most rudimentary diagnostic techniques of physical examination? My disbelief grew until it occurred to me that perhaps I was asking the wrong questions: the problem was not how something which is so obvious had remained hidden for so long, but how the body had become so evident in the first place. In dissecting and examining bodies I had come to take for granted that what I saw was obvious. I had thought that medical knowledge simply described the body. I argue in this book that the relationship is more complex, that medical knowledge both describes and constructs the body as an invariate biological reality.

Armstrong (1983a)

As a student Armstrong saw bodies as solid, unchanging natural objects. But later on he learned that before the eighteenth century people saw bodies in a different way. He concluded that bodies can only be seen in terms of how we learn to look at them. You have encountered these ideas before, in discussing postmodernism. In this approach it is argued that modern medicine created a new reality through an epistemological shift: knowledge and the meaning of language were reconceptualised. Our view of the body is therefore *socially constructed*, and it is theoretically possible that at some future time we might come to hold a different view of it. Foucault suggested that our current conceptualisation of the human body, the way we have learned to see and know it and to intervene, is 'only one way, in all likelihood neither the first, nor the most fundamental – in which one spatialises disease. There have been, and will be, other distributions of illness' (Foucault, 1973). Note that it is shifts in cultural perceptions, in ways of 'seeing and knowing' not just socio-economic forces, that are emphasised in this analysis.

Just as important, the 'clinical gaze' of doctors represented not only knowledge and truth claims but also the exercise of power. The acceptance of this new discourse about the body and about health and disease in general gave doctors much greater power in relation to patients and to other health personnel, who had to be trained in the use of the 'anatomical atlas' – by means of which they could 'see' what they were looking at. This insight directs our attention away from focusing simply on the linear march of science and medicine and towards a broader analysis of the shifting cultural and social basis of medicine. This prompts debate about how this new view of the body became acceptable – and under what circumstances another shift of view might take place.

The rise of the hospital

Fundamental to doctors' success was their ability to convince other people, including other health workers, to share their new way of 'seeing and knowing' about health, with its implications for 'doing' through new patterns of treatment. And crucial in this process was the role of the hospital, the focus of clinical medicine. The hospital or *clinic*, with a mass of patients who could be observed, diagnosed and subjected to supervised and carefully regulated treatment regimes, provided an ideal environment in which doctors could amass the knowledge and develop the theories to establish beyond doubt their truth claims. Examining 20 livers in succession revealed a great deal about what a 'normal' liver looked like, and therefore what an 'abnormal' liver was. Examining 20 cases of 'hysteria' enabled the mapping of common features and the development of specialised treatments and routines. The general and (increasingly) emerging specialist hospitals tended to attract only poorer, working class patients unable to afford treatment elsewhere. This eased the problem of experimentation; the bodies of the poor provided the training ground for the clinical gaze, while the middle classes continued to receive treatment from doctors in their own homes throughout the nineteenth century.

As we have noted, the increasingly complex patterns of treatment created a role for a reliable assistant to the doctor: the nurse. And in time clinical medicine gave rise to a veritable army of paramedics. The whole regulatory enterprise of observing, categorising, segregating, pre-scribing, treating and so on engulfed and reconstructed existing groups of health workers and created new groups: radiographers, health visitors, district nurses, specialist clinicians such as obstetricians and paediatricians and so on.

Other institutions, such as workhouse hospitals and insane asylums, also developed in the nineteenth century as a response to new social and economic pressures. The emergence of the secular nation state and the rise of industrial society had led to the need for new methods of social regulation of growing urban populations which had been cut adrift from traditional social ties and religious practices. As Durkheim and others noted, severe social tensions and considerable public order problems were thrown up by industrialisation and rapid urbanisation. The principles underlying the eighteenth century asylum movement – of replacing punishment by a 'moral regime' and rehabilitating the inmate to live in normal society – all but disappeared as pressure of numbers caused overcrowding and squalor. Conditions in the overcrowded workhouses were often appalling as well. For most of the century these institutions remained under lay control, and the main aim was to keep costs down; only later on did medical men gain a key position of power in diagnosis and treatment.

The hospital and mental institution became increasingly important as places where the 'unproductive' and 'deviant' – the sick, insane or feeble-minded – could be safely segregated from the mass of 'normal' society and gradually restored to health. Thus clinical medicine not only became more important in the treatment of sickness in the overcrowded, poorly housed, malnourished urban poor; clinicians themselves became of increasing value to the state as regulators of the urban masses. The clinical gaze enveloped not just the individual body as an object of scrutiny but whole populations (Foucault, 1973). Modern biomedicine, with its emphasis on increasingly complex forms of medical surveillance and on segregation of the diagnosed physically and mentally sick and handicapped, fitted in well with the requirements of the state for an amenable, docile population (Armstrong, 1983a).

The disappearance of the 'sick man'?

Perhaps the most important shift was in the patient's role. Think back to our discussion of the active role of the patient in early health work. Jewson (1976) has argued that this role was transformed in hospital medicine in Europe so that patients lost their autonomy and became the passive objects of medical enquiry (see Table 11.1).

TABLE 11.1 Changing modes of production of medical knowledge. Source: Jewson (1976)

	Patron	Occupational role of medical investigator	Source of patronage	Perception of sick man	Occupational task of medical investigator	Conceptualisation of illness
Bedside medicine	Patient	Practitioner	Private fees	Person	Prognosis and therapy	Total psycho-somatic disturbance
Hospital medicine	State; hospital	Clinician	Professional career structure	Case	Diagnosis and classification	Organic lesion
Laboratory medicine	State; academy	Scientist	Scientific career structure	Cell complex	Analysis and explanation	Biochemical process

○   Look at Table 11.1, which is taken from Jewson (1976) 'The disappearance of
the sick man in medical cosmology'. Comment on his ideas about how
medical knowledge and practice in Europe have changed since the early
eighteenth century.

Jewson suggests that medical theory in Europe shifted from the concept
of a 'whole' person to be treated to a notion of people as collections of
differentiated parts. In 'bedside medicine' the patient, who held the
purse-strings, was the patron of the doctor, and the patient's illness was
conceptualised as a 'total psychosomatic disturbance'. But in 'hospital
medicine' the patient became a medical case, admitted for treatment if
the hospitals agreed or if the state provided funding. The conceptualisation of the patient's illness was no longer of total disturbance but of
'organic lesion'. Note that Jewson delineates a third shift, to 'laboratory
medicine', in which a conception of illness as a 'biochemical process'
further diminishes the patient's control over the process of being ill.

There are several comments you might have made about this. First,
consider the language he uses. From being a 'sick man' the patient
becomes a medical 'case'. The 'whole person' disappears from view, as it
were. You may have noted that the term 'disturbance', which Jewson
uses to describe the patient's illness, has been used by Dingwall and
other interactionists in illness action theory. Armstrong (1983a) has cast
doubt on this unproblematised use of language and offered a social
constructionist interpretation. The 'sick man' didn't disappear in about
1800 as clinical medicine triumphed; he is an 'invention' of the 1970s.
The category of the 'sick man' – the whole, undifferentiated person of
pre-clinical medicine – is a social construction which reveals the
preoccupations of social scientists and others in this era. Armstrong has
suggested that the category emerged as part of the concern to refocus on
the 'patient as subject' which came from some doctors, interested in new
ways of treating patients, and from social scientists who were critical of
professional power.

Second, it is interesting to note that in Jewson's view, as in
Foucault's, it is the changing perception of what constitutes medical
knowledge that is seen as crucial, and Jewson generalises this across
Europe. Their views have been criticised by medical historians on the
grounds that they pay too little attention to the historical specificity of
the development of ideas and institutional frameworks for medicine.
Porter (1979), for example, suggests that there were variations in the
nature and timing of medical changes, and that in England state and
medical power was less well established than in France. Unlike France,
where the clinical gaze is seen as dominant from around 1800, no
bureaucratised medical profession emerged in England until later in the
nineteenth century. It has also been suggested that Jewson overestimated the role of patronage as the basic type of medical transaction

in the eighteenth century (Pelling, 1987). Most of the population could not afford to consult physicians; moreover, as we noted earlier, the urban poor already had some access to institutional care through the infirmaries.

11.3 The consolidation of medical power

Why were doctors able to consolidate their power and gain exclusive rights to practise medicine? Part of the explanation we have already noted: the powerful analytic and predictive power of the new bio-medical approach, and its construction as a 'clinical gaze' which reconceptualised the body and projected a radical new view of health and disease in the institutional setting of the hospital. In addition, doctors were increasingly viewed as valuable agents of the state in the matter of segregating and controlling urban masses. In 1858 the Medical Registration Act was passed, giving the medical profession – or, more accurately, the hospital elite – control of medical education and specialist services. Only those who had passed through a recognised system of medical training were now allowed to join the professional register and call themselves 'qualified medical practitioners'. In Section 11.4 we'll explore the emergence of medicine as the predominant 'profession' in the health division of labour. But before we begin it is worth noting the relative weakness of biomedicine as a healing system in the nineteenth century. Medical registration was not granted because of the curative success of the clinical gaze; one might almost say that it was granted in spite of its lack of success.

Despite the gradual acceptance of the 'truth claims' of biomedicine as the only correct way of thinking about health, there is little evidence that doctors were successful in solving the major health problems of the nineteenth century. Up to the 1870s hospital regimes included several forms of medical therapy, such as bleeding the patients (leeching and cupping) and using powerful purgatives and dietary management, which had been employed for centuries. The clinical gaze, although it could reveal much more about the localisation and course of disease, was not able to cure cholera, tuberculosis, typhoid fever, venereal disease, diarrhoea or the many other epidemics or common causes of death. Nor was there common agreement among medical men about the causes of epidemic disease, such as cholera. Some doctors supported 'contingent contagion' theories – that disease spread by direct contact – and wanted tough quarantine and isolation measures. Others espoused different versions of contagion theory, of which the best known is *miasma*: that is, epidemic disease was caused by foul air from decomposing organic matter, such as cesspools, slums and a dirty environment. In addition, there was a power and status struggle between the hospital elite who controlled medical education in the specialist hospitals and other less prestigious groups: the emerging general practitioners, public health doctors and state hospital employees. It was the resolution of these intellectual and power struggles which finally enabled medical power to be consolidated.

The Victorian public health movement

Miasma theory provided the impetus for the public health movement, but its main supporters were not the medical elite. The pressure for public health measures – sewage systems, proper drainage, a supply of pure water, street paving and through ventilation in slum housing – came from the reforming middle classes, some general practitioners (such as Dr John Snow) and was supported by the state. Above all, it was prompted by the fear of cholera and typhoid fever. The 1848 Public Health Act demanded action from local councils in areas with a high death rate, and Edwin Chadwick, Secretary to the General Board of Health between 1848 and 1858, pressed for extensive powers to intervene. In his 1842 report on sanitary conditions among the working classes Chadwick called for 'drainage, the removal of all refuse of habitations, streets, and roads, and the improvement of supplies of water'. 'It would be good economy', he added, 'to appoint a district medical officer . . . to initiate sanitary measures and reclaim the execution of the law' (Chadwick, 1842).

Chadwick argued that the moral elevation of the poor required that their filthy habits and noxious environment be improved: physical contamination bred social disorder; public health would create social order as well as health. Such ideas remained influential well into the twentieth century, presenting something of a challenge to medical power. Control of public health policy making remained firmly in lay hands; the new medical officers of health were employed by local councillors, and environmental measures rather than clinical interventions were seen as of fundamental importance.

What evidence exists today of the influence and achievements of the Victorian public health movement?

You might have mentioned that the whole sewage, drainage and water system in the UK is the product of Victorian public health activity, although it is no longer owned by municipalities. Street lighting, paving, refuse collection, swimming pools and parks all provide evidence of the preoccupation with physical order and moral elevation in the poor. Health visiting developed under the control of the medical officer of health to support and educate mothers in childcare and wifely duties (Davies, 1988). Moreover, as public health has moved higher up the political agenda, the public health functions of 'community physicians' have been emphasised.

The impact of germ theory

By the late nineteenth century the theory of miasma and the whole public health approach was challenged by the germ theory of disease, derived from microscopic research by Louis Pasteur, Marie Curie and Robert Koch, among others. Germ theory propounded that disease was caused by bacteria and that a specific micro-organism would be present in every case of a particular disease: the doctrine of specific aetiology. Pasteur demonstrated the existence of micro-organisms, which could be killed by sterilisation or made to multiply rapidly in suitable media. This theory refocused attention on the host (body) and invading organism, the individual and the specific aetiology, the immediate cause of disease rather than the wider local environment. It gave the medical profession a powerful, predictive theory with which to tackle human disease.

The significance of the wider social environment in causing disease was subsequently viewed in a new way: in terms of a concern about individuals, their inter-personal contact, personal hygiene and possible role in the transmission of disease (Armstrong, 1993). Public health in the sense of large-scale intervention to improve the local environment gave way to public health as a medically controlled enterprise which involved study, guidance and control of the patient. Germ theory provided the ammunition for a medical attack on personal filth – spitting, lice, scabies, dirty bodies, as well as poor housekeeping – but provided little constructive commentary on the social conditions which made such problems widespread in working class districts. For example, John Robertson, the Medical Officer of Health in Birmingham from 1903, argued that 'want of knowledge and want of care in the methods of feeding and looking after infants [was] almost entirely' the cause of infant deaths from diarrhoea; he continued:

There is now little hesitation in saying that dirt in various forms is the exciting cause of the disease – dirty milk, dirty feeding bottles, dirty clothes, dirty floors, dirty comforters and, in fact, anything dirty with which the baby or young child comes into contact, is likely to set up diarrhoeal diseases.

Robertson, quoted in Jones (1993)

Although health work in the inner-city areas made clear the complex inter-connections between disease and poverty, medical officer of health reports emphasised individual behaviour as the key to ill health and medical surveillance and health education as the main solutions.

11.4 Professional power in health work

As we noted earlier, British medicine became a registered and regulated occupation after 1858, an occupation (along with law) that is often seen as the quintessential *profession*. But how have sociological theorists analysed the concept of profession and the process of professionalisation in health work? And in what terms have they conceptualised the resultant division of labour between doctors and other health workers? In this section we'll consider a range of conflicting theories, highlighting in particular their relevance to nursing.

Professions in health work

The sociology of professions in health work was founded on Talcott Parsons' (1951) use of medicine as a test case of utilitarian economics and on Weber's analysis of the bureaucratic foundations of authority in industrialised societies (Dingwall and Lewis, 1983). Weber viewed 'professions' as anachronistic features of the social order which would be superseded by bureaucratic control. In contrast, Parsons argued that professions represented an alternative form of social organisation and acted as a stabilising force in industrialised society by projecting non-profit oriented values. Professions shared certain features: functional control of specific tasks, the creation and restriction of a domain of power, the application of impersonal standards and a shared ethic of disinterested service, which contradicted the simple maximisation of income and self interest assumed by economics to be the driving force motivating every individual. Members of a profession upheld a set of standards and acted in the best interests of their clients. Parsons' analysis became simplified and standardised as 'trait' theory, so called because it claimed to define the nature of profession from the characteristic features of particular occupations such as law and medicine (see Box 11.2).

○ Comment on the 'traits' listed in Box 11.2 and suggest what problems there might be in viewing professions in this way. (You might find it useful to look again at Parsons' doctor–patient relationship model in Chapter 10, page 403, Table 10.3).

One main problem is that trait theory leads us into analysing a profession on its own terms: that is, we implicitly accept the notion of ethical conduct, altruism and impersonal standards which the profession claims to uphold. Another difficulty is that logic demands that we call all groups with these traits 'professions', but there are clearly differences in power and status between groups which might qualify in

BOX 11.2 'Trait theory' of professions

1 Theory of knowledge underlying and informing the practice of the profession	**2** Code of ethics (accepted rules) regulating practice
3 Control of entry to the profession, through tests, training and so on, and through disciplinary powers	**4** Professional authority over the layman, based on specialist knowledge
5 Confidential nature of the professional–client relationship	**6** Existence of a professional culture: that is, an agreed way of behaving, which may be designed to exclude/impress

trait analysis as professions, for example between doctors and social workers. Moreover, trait analysis suggests that if all traits are fulfilled profession will be achieved, yet it is doubtful whether, say, nursing will rank as equal in status terms with medicine – even though its knowledge base is being refined through nursing theory and higher education.

Medical dominance

Freidson (1970), following Weber, redirected attention to profession as a particular type of occupation, different only in that it had 'assumed a dominant position in the division of labor, so that it gains control over the determination of the substance of its own work' and persuaded others that this special status was justified. In Section 5.5 we encountered the notion of *social closure*, which refers to the process by which groups in society gain a monopoly over territory and resources and erect cultural and legal barriers to keep out intruders (Parkin, 1971). Medicine was able to effect social closure by gaining a monopoly of medical practice and by subordinating and regulating related occupations such as nursing, but in doing so it upheld the ethos of self interest and division of labour of capitalist society. Freidson (1983) developed the idea of a 'market shelter', provided by legislative controls, which protected the profession from open competition. This highlighted the more specific historical determinants of professions such as medicine, a point developed by Johnson (1972) in his study of the relationships between 'professionals' and 'clients'.

This Marxist analysis focused on the relationship between specific socio-economic changes and specific occupations. In the case of medicine Johnson (1972) argued that, whereas in pre-industrial society physicians were relatively powerless and their wealthy clients exercised control, industrial capitalism and class formation (in particular the rise of the middle class) in nineteenth-century Britain enabled doctors to develop institutional means of controlling their occupational activities. Using the backing of the state, for whom they acted as agents of control, doctors were able to practise on working class patients who had little control over their treatment. Medical knowledge was esoteric – that is, specialised and mystifying – and served to distance doctors from their patients. Johnson suggests that in advanced capitalist societies 'collegiate control', as practised in Victorian Britain, has given way to 'mediation' in which a third party (in this case the state) intervenes to regulate relations between producers and consumers (see Box 11.3). In this view the power of professions has been eroded by state control.

In some ways this is not a very convincing account. After all, we have noted that only the wealthy could operate a patronage system; the poor were already dependent on public and voluntary services in the eighteenth century. Moreover, it does not reveal much about the occupation of medicine itself: how it was organised, how it established its claims against other health work occupations, how it gained higher social status. In the early nineteenth century, for example, there were class divisions within medicine between general practitioners and higher status physicians; the increasing cohesion of medicine came largely from the physicians' success in subordinating other groups. A growing occupational consciousness led doctors to push for registration, which would limit entry and enhance doctors' financial rewards. In other words, the changing occupational organisation of medicine was important as well as its relation to the class structure (Parry and Parry, 1976).

BOX 11.3 Typology of producer–consumer relationships. Source: Johnson (1972)

1 **Patronage** 'in which the consumer defines his own needs and the manner in which they are to be met'	2 **Collegiate control** 'in which the producer defines the needs of the consumer and the manner in which these needs are catered for'	3 **Mediation** 'in which a third party mediates in the relationship between producer and consumer, defining both the needs and the manner in which the needs are met'
Example: Pre-nineteenth century physician–patron relationship	Example: Nineteenth century professions	Example: The mediating role of the state after 1945 in defining who was to receive medical services

More recent discussions of professions and of the process of professionalisation have emphasised the need to combine Weberian and Marxist insights: that is, to consider both strategies for occupational closure and the relationship of occupations to the class structure. Turner (1987) defines medical dominance as:

A set of strategies requiring control over the work situation, the institutional features of occupational autonomy within the medical division of labour, and finally occupational sovereignty over related occupational groups. This medical dominance further involves a privileged location within the general class structure of society.

Turner (1987)

This medical dominance is maintained, he argues, by means of three modes of domination: subordination, limitation and exclusion. Subordination characterises the relationship of nursing and midwifery to medicine, whereas dentistry and pharmacy are characterised by limitation – to a specific part of the body (dentistry) or a specific therapy (pharmacy). Exclusion means that rival occupations are marginalised or excluded from health work; Turner gives the example of the clergy's exclusion from psychological counselling.

The gendered division of labour in health

In general, the sociology of the professions has overlooked gender relations, or has seen gender as an unproblematic notion which defines 'normal' male and female social roles. In response to this feminists have discussed how women were deliberately excluded from medicine and other higher status health work by men, and that a patriarchal ideology of 'good nurses as good women' underpinned the entry of women into public domain health work (see Section 7.7). The effects of this are still potent in the 1990s. Speech therapy, for example, became characterised as women's work whereas an equivalent type of health work, clinical psychology, came to be dominated by men. Only in the mid-1990s were speech therapists able to establish, through the European Court, their claim to be given equal pay. Before then they were paid at rates about 60 per cent lower than their male counterparts.

The use of feminist theory offers a much richer, more historically grounded analysis of gendered occupations in health work. In particular, it draws attention to the fact that the professionalisation of medicine represented not just the triumph of a middle class occupational group but the gendering of power and privilege within health work. It was the institutionalisation of male dominance that ensured, in some form, female subordination. Women did not 'just happen' to become nurses, nor did they 'just happen' to be paid less, accorded lower status and less autonomy than doctors. The gender influences on women entering the health service (such as mothering ideologies, male definitions of work, double shift, childcare responsibilities) continued to shape relations between (mainly male) doctors and (mainly female) nurses, midwives and community nurses in the workplace. We'll explore these issues in relation to nursing in the next chapter.

11.5 Medical control of health work

During the early twentieth century the medical profession consolidated its control of the division of labour in health work. Established work, such as nursing and midwifery, and newer occupations such as health visiting remained under medical control although they were influenced by changing medical practices. For example, the shedding of routine tasks like temperature taking gave nurses wider scope to practise, but did little to alter the power relationships between doctors and nurses. The medical profession also became entrenched as the monopoly providers of medical care and knowledge: whether as general practitioners, specialist hospital clinicians or public health doctors. The rise of 'laboratory medicine', as Jewson (1976) termed it, did not detract from the status of the doctor; on the contrary, it was the doctor (or several specialist doctors) who controlled medical input to the patient. On the other hand medicine itself was increasingly influenced by central state regulation – for example the 1911 National Insurance Act – and by local authority provision of child welfare and hospitals.

The shifting nature of medical knowledge

During the nineteenth century, as we noted earlier, doctors had relatively little to offer in terms of curative interventions for epidemic disease. A few medical therapies, such as vaccination for smallpox, may have been effective. In the hospital surgical interventions saved some lives, but these must be balanced against loss of life from bacterial infection and the trauma of surgery. The new knowledge about bacteriology and the introduction of antiseptics and aseptic techniques by the end of the century made surgery much safer. It has been argued that well into the twentieth century doctors made little impact on the rate of death from scarlet fever, measles and tuberculosis (McKeown, 1976). Although the tubercle bacillus was identified by Robert Koch in 1882, for example, it was only in 1947 that an effective therapy, streptomycin, became available. BCG immunisation started in the UK in 1954. However, between 1838 and 1900 there was a 57 per cent decline in the rate of death from tuberculosis (see Figure 11.1).

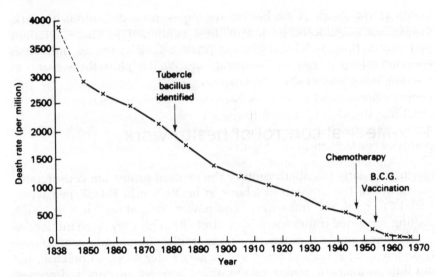

FIGURE 11.1 Respiratory tuberculosis: death rates (England and Wales).
Source: McKeown (1976)

○   Suggest why death rates for diseases such as tuberculosis, typhoid and
cholera fell in the period 1848–1901.

The achievements of the public health movement – provision of clean
water, adequate drainage and sewerage and (to some extent) improved
working class housing – played a significant part in preventing the
spread of epidemic disease (Woods and Woodward, 1984). Improved
methods of, and knowledge about, birth control may also have been
important. In the 1880s the birth rate began to fall and this may have
influenced maternal mortality rates. But it has been argued that rising
living standards, in particular improved nutrition, were the major
reason for falling death rates (McKeown, 1976). It may be that the
virulence of some diseases such as cholera decreased, but it was the
increased resistance of the host that was crucial. Better nourished people
(especially adults) were able to fight off infection.

The general acceptance of germ theory enhanced the ability of
health workers to offer palliative or curative treatment to patients.
Bacteriological research highlighted the importance of cleanliness inside
the hospital and elsewhere. We noted in Section 11.3 that the focus in
public health shifted to an attack on personal and household 'filth'.
Health visitors, under the control of medical officers of health, were
given particular responsibility for the support and education of mothers.
Lewis (1980) has argued that the campaign to 'raise the standard
of motherhood' became narrowly victim-blaming. Medical officers

assumed 'the existence of dirt to denote women's responsibility for it'. Preventive medicine and 'health education' – focused not on sick patients but on risky behaviours and personal hygiene in 'well' people – became an increasing part of medical work in the twentieth century.

The foundation and elaboration of this 'extended medical gaze' into people's homes and daily lives has been traced in Armstrong's (1983a, 1993) investigation of the shifting orientation of medical literature. The gaze now extended beyond the body and its interior parts to 'exterior points of contact' and into the 'undifferentiated space between bodies'. The adoption of germ theory also resulted in the 'reconstruction' of diseases such as tuberculosis:

> Tuberculosis, which had, until the closing decades of the nineteenth century, been primarily a disease of individual bodies and of environmental neglect, became a disease of contact and social space . . . The danger now arose from people and their point of contact . . . Might not health, Newman (Chief Medical Officer of Health) argued, be promoted 'by maintaining a clean mouth and clear breathing, and by abstinence from spitting, sneezing, coughing and shouting at each other.
>
> *Armstrong (1993)*

This growing preoccupation with people and points of contact – the new 'social' surveillance of twentieth century medicine – also resulted in a changing view of patients in medical literature. Whereas the clinical gaze had construed the patient largely as a medical case, the extended medical gaze depended to some extent on the active participation of the patient. Medical staff in hospital settings and in general practice were told to encourage patients to 'tell their story', not just their medical history but their feelings and anxieties. Beyond this, the whole process of social surveillance of those 'at risk' and of the health of communities required the more active co-operation of patients, their families and wider social networks.

○ To what extent do you agree with Armstrong's account of the reconceptualisation of the patient in medicine – from a 'medical case' to a more 'active participant'?

As students of health work some of you might argue that the construction of the patient as an 'active participant' is still very much controlled by the doctor. Patients are not always encouraged to tell *their* story so much as respond to medical enquiry. It is very difficult for some patients to ask questions and to get answers; nurses, for example, still act as interpreters for the patient. Although the conceptualisation of the patient may have changed in medical literature, this does not ensure it has changed in medical practice.

Yet clearly there has been a shift in perceptions; patients are now subjects, not objects. In nursing literature they are bio-psycho-social individuals meriting 'holistic' assessment, even if task-oriented practice is still widespread (see Section 12.5 for a discussion of the changing nurse–patient relationship). As Armstrong (1993) has noted, the human sciences have played a part in creating patients as subjects: 'Sociologists, in close alliance with medicine, opened up areas of the health experience of "ordinary" people through surveys of health attitudes, of illness behaviour, of drug taking and of symptom prevalence'.

Advances in scientific knowledge greatly increased the range of therapies available to doctors. X-rays were first made in 1895, vitamins were 'discovered' in 1911 and insulin treatment was available from 1922. A huge expansion in pharmaceutical research and production characterised the mid-twentieth century: sulphonomide drugs were in use from the 1930s; by the 1950s so were antibiotics and mood-changing drugs (tranquilisers and anti-depressants); immunisation for tuberculosis, whooping cough and other diseases became widespread in the 1950s. Germ theory itself became much more sophisticated during the twentieth century as further research revealed the significance of co-factors and host state, as well as invading organism. In place of the doctrine of specific aetiology, scientists emphasised multiple aetiology. This led to calls for a 'new medical model' which fully acknowledged multi-causality (Engel, 1977). It also, as we have just noted, directed attention to the complex interactions of physical, behavioural and social circumstances which in medical language are termed 'risk factors'.

The organisation of medical practice

Although the National Health Service did not come into existence until after World War II, the state played a growing role in the organisation of medical practice in the earlier twentieth century. Increasing concern about 'national efficiency' – the genetic and physical health of the nation's population stock – was one of the influences on the emergence of health visiting as a statutory service and on the creation of registers of qualified practitioners of nursing and midwifery. The Liberal government's legislation before 1914 included welfare services for children – such as school medical inspection and subsidised school meals – and help for older citizens and for the sick or unemployed (see Box 11.4).

The 1911 National Insurance Act provided a lifeline to general practitioners, many of whom had only remained in practice by contracting to work for commercial or voluntary sector 'sick clubs' or by working part-time for local authority Poor Law services (Stacey, 1988). They found this lay control over their work distasteful and initially opposed the 1911 Act, which set up a system of insurance for low paid workers (to which employer, employee and state contributed) and of

BOX 11.4 Liberal welfare reforms, 1906–14

1906 Act – to permit local authorities to provide subsidised school meals for the poorest children

1908 Old Age Pensions Act – providing 5s a week for old people over 70, or 7s 6d for married couples

1909 Budget – reduced income tax rates for parents of young children; introduced a new 'supertax' and capital gains tax on land

1909 Trade Boards Act – set up boards to set wages for the most vulnerable groups of workers

1909 Act – established Labour Exchanges

1911 National Insurance Act – created a contributory unemployment insurance scheme for some groups of workers, for example dock workers, and a more comprehensive sickness insurance scheme which was geared to the working population but included a small maternity benefit

designated general practices to provide free, non-specialist medical care. In fact general practitioners benefited from the scheme; it raised their average incomes and, since they elected to be paid by capitation fee, they became subcontractors rather than employees of the state. This, of course, became the generalised relationship between the general practitioners and the state in 1948.

Another area of increasing state involvement was in the provision of local health and welfare services, arising from pre-war Liberal legislation and from the Maternity and Child Welfare Act of 1918. In most local authorities health visitors and mainly female medical officers (under medical officer of health direction) set up mother and infant welfare clinics, training classes and home visiting. They also took over voluntary sector services such as infant feeding centres and pure milk depots. The thrust of this activity, as we noted earlier, was 'national efficiency' through improving the 'quality of motherhood' (Lewis, 1980). It was not about providing all-round care or treatment; indeed general practitioners successfully prevented clinic workers from diagnosing or treating illness, which had to be referred to the GP.

A third example of increasing state intervention in health care can be found in the hospital sector. Here there was a diversity of provision: local authority-run Poor Law hospitals and asylums, general and specialist voluntary hospitals and after 1918 a growing number of local authority-funded general hospitals. In spite of massive fund-raising in the voluntary sector it was the municipal hospitals, financed from the local rates, which increasingly dominated the scene (Webster, 1988).

They had more modern facilities and equipment and treated a growing number of patients by the 1930s, while the voluntary sector was in decline. Webster suggests that, even if World War II had not made central state support and rationalisation of the hospital sector essential, some restructuring would have been necessary to maintain hospital care.

It is thought-provoking to contrast this growing involvement of the state in medical practice, which partly stemmed from a concern for 'national efficiency' (and in the inter-war years a fear of social unrest), with the increased specialisation in medicine. It was in the interests of hospital doctors who remained outside the 1911 National Health Insurance Act to develop special expertise to ensure their livelihoods. Moreover, the expansion of scientific and medical knowledge made specialisation almost essential. Psychiatry, orthopaedics, opthalmology, dentistry and so on became recognised specialties, and in each case doctors moved to subordinate, limit or exclude potential and actual rivals (Turner, 1987, and see Section 11.4). Psychiatrists fought to exclude lay practitioners, including psychotherapists; in several cases – such as radiography and dentistry – the process of occupational closure subordinated and de-skilled women (Larkin, 1983; Witz, 1992). Together, scientific research and medical specialisation increased decade by decade the costs of medical care and treatment. New technology, drugs, routines and surgical interventions were not only costly but created a spiralling dependence – on the part of doctors as well as patients – although this was not fully evident until the 1950s.

The National Health Service

By the time the National Health Service (NHS) was established in 1948, the power relations and hierarchy in health work and many of its organisational features were already in place. As Allsop (1984) has pointed out, the structure and organisation of the NHS represented a political compromise – between the demand of Labour Minister of Health Ernest Bevan for a national, comprehensive and equitable service free at the point of use and the desire of the medical profession to maintain or enhance its autonomy, control and income.

Some Labour politicians, in particular Herbert Morrison, wished the new health service to be put under local government control, providing democratic accountability and also recognising the major part in providing health care played by local authorities. But general practitioners and hospital doctors had no intention of allowing themselves to be controlled by local councillors. Bevan recognised the need to compromise in order to establish a national system; in the case of the hospitals this meant direct accountability to central government, and in the case of general practitioners it meant accepting capitation fees and subcontractor status. Commenting that he had 'stuffed their mouths with gold', Bevan agreed a generous package of appointments, promotion and merit awards, which allowed hospital doctors to continue their private practice, and gave the teaching hospitals direct funding from the Department of Health. The other hospitals were to be under the control of hospital boards, controlled by consultants and by former voluntary hospital governors; nurses, paramedics and ancillary workers scarcely figured on the boards (Webster, 1988). Community health services remained under the control of local authorities until 1974 (see Figure 11.2).

Nurses and other health workers were almost invisible in all these negotiations. 'In general it seems to have been assumed that nursing policy questions would be considered along with those relating to health policy in general and that nurses would accommodate themselves to whatever arrangements were made . . . What is also striking is the lack of evident action by nursing organisations on policy questions'. (Dingwall *et al.* 1988).

○ Study Figure 11.2, which shows the main features of the National Health Service in 1948. Suggest what strengths and weaknesses existed in this system.

The main strength of the 1948 settlement was that it represented a fairly workable solution. It did create a national service for health, funded from taxation and based on universalist principles: equity, collective

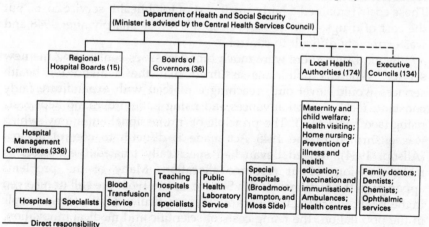

Fig. 1. Organisation of the National Health Service in England and Wales 1948–74.
Note: The Ministry of Health became the Department of Health and Social Security in 1968.

FIGURE 11.2 Organisation of the NHS in England and Wales 1948–74. Source: Allsop (1984)

responsibilty, free access and comprehensive health cover. The main problems lay in what has been termed the 'tripartite' structure of the National Health Service, in particular the relationships between the sectors. There was no co-terminosity (common geographical boundaries) between hospital catchment areas and local authorities, who provided community welfare services (such as housing and social services) as well as community health services. Nor was there any rational pattern of general practices, although a committee was established to try and get a fair distribution of GPs (Allsop, 1984). Since GPs were self employed they made the decisions about services and standards. Patients might receive excellent care, but they might equally find little or no co-operation between hospital, local authority and GP services over admission, discharge or community support. Problems of inter-agency co-operation and variation in general practice standards and services have not entirely disappeared!

Another central problem concerned finance. Overall financial control lay with the Department of Health, but year-on-year spending was largely determined by calculating past spending plus growth money. Thus prestigious, high spending hospitals (in particular the London teaching hospitals) received disproportionately large resources compared to hospitals which, historically, had low levels of funding (such as former Poor Law hospitals). Inequalities within the hospital sector were institutionalised. General practitioners were paid on a capitation fee (fee per patient registered), but they were also given fees for service (such as maternity checks) and reimbursed for expenses. These costs remained a fairly small part of total health service costs, but the cost of drugs – for GPs and hospitals – rose sharply after 1948 and was extremely difficult to control.

Beyond this, there were much broader issues confronting the new service. Whereas politicians assumed that the demand for health services would 'level out', reaching a plateau with expenditure fairly constant, technological advances and rising patient demand kept costs rising (see Table 11.2). The principle of 'professional autonomy' which was enshrined in the 1948 Act made it difficult to control doctors (Allsop, 1984). Indeed Bevan had specifically trusted the doctors to make decisions about resource allocation. Many of the problems apparent in the National Health Service by the 1960s are still unresolved in the 1990s: the rising numbers of older, particularly frail elderly people in the population, the rising costs of scientific and medical innovation, the seemingly insatiable demand for health services and the proper limits of professional autonomy. Above all, the National Health Service was (and still is) primarily concerned with the treatment of patients in hospitals. This is where two-thirds of the funding went, and this is what has led to the service being termed 'the National Sickness Service'.

TABLE 11.2 National Health Service expenditure UK 1949–88. Source: Ham (1992)

Year	Total £m	Total NHS cost at 1949 prices £m
1949	437	437
1950	477	477
1951	503	466
1952	526	499
1953	546	452
1954	564	459
1955	609	477
1956	664	489
1957	720	509
1958	764	515
1959	826	549
1960	902	590
1961	981	623
1962	1 025	628
1963	1 092	655
1964	1 190	695
1965	1 306	728
1966	1 433	769
1967	1 556	816
1968	1 702	861
1969	1 791	875
1970	2 040	929
1971	2 325	950
1972	2 682	997
1973	3 054	1 054
1974	3 970	1 171
1975	5 298	1 229
1976	6 281	1 271
1977	6 971	1 258
1978	7 997	1 288
1979	9 283	1 324
1980	11 914	1 434
1981	13 720	1 498
1982	14 483	1 479
1983	16 381	1 584
1984	17 241	1 581
1985	18 412	1 602
1986	19 690	1 670
1987	21 488	1 737
1988	23 627	1 797

Recent reorganisations of the health service have been largely directed towards overcoming the structural and organisational weaknesses of the 1948 settlement. In 1974, for example, the service was

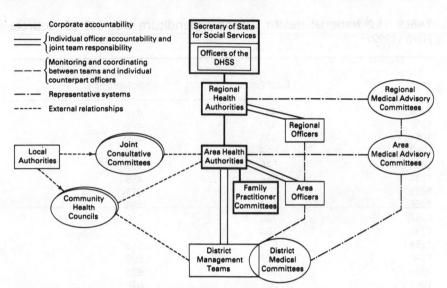

Corporate accountability

Individual officer accountability and joint team responsibility

Monitoring and coordinating between teams and individual counterpart officers

Representative systems

External relationships

Secretary of State for Social Services

Officers of the DHSS

Regional Health Authorities

Regional Medical Advisory Committees

Regional Officers

Local Authorities

Joint Consultative Committees

Area Health Authorities

Area Medical Advisory Committees

Family Practitioner Committees

Area Officers

Community Health Councils

District Management Teams

District Medical Committees

FIGURE 11.3 Organisation of the NHS 1974–82. Source: Allsop (1984)

reorganised on a unitary basis with regional, area and district level tiers of authority (see Figure 11.3). The introduction of consensus based management in these authorities provided an opportunity for other health work occupations, such as nursing, to have a voice in planning and resource allocation. Regional health authorities controlled strategic planning and resource distribution. Area health authorities had boundaries co-terminous with local authorities; they were a new tier, designed to plan and provide a comprehensive health service (including former local authority-run health services), and they had links with local authorities. General practitioners kept their subcontractor status but were accountable to the areas through family practitioner committees. A Resource Allocation Working Party (RAWP) was set up to try and equalise resources across the regions. More recent changes have included abolition of the area health authority tier in 1982 (see Figure 11.4), the Griffiths Management Enquiry reforms of 1984 (discussed below) and the massive restructuring of health care since 1990 (see Chapter 13).

11.6 The health service as an organisation

The National Health Service which emerged in the 1940s was a massive, unwieldy organisation, difficult to control and to change. Doctors, for example, had their own beds in the hospital to which they could admit

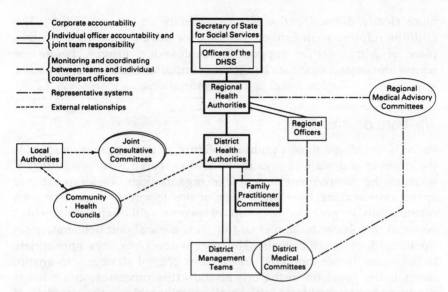

FIGURE 11.4 Organisation of the NHS 1982–90. Source: Allsop (1984)

patients (Stacey, 1988). They formed a professional elite with functional autonomy, controlling diagnosis and treatment of *their* patients. They could exert influence over the boards of governors. Nurses were grouped in wards under the control of a sister, who was initially responsible to the hospital matron for the entire running of the ward. In many senses, therefore, the health service did not correspond to the average large-scale commercial organisation. In particular, the doctors' influence over hospital resources and practices was disproportionately great and the management structure much less well-developed. There were parallel hierarchies of doctors, nurses and administrators. The hospital administrators (not managers) occupied a role as enablers and regulators in the system:

A massive edifice of administrative lore became the underlying structure of the NHS organization but it was always built around the assumption of medical autonomy and expertise. The health service administrative tradition was established to enable a service to run rather than to run it.

Cox (1991)

A main thrust behind the successive reorganisations of the health service between the 1960s and 1990s was to create a more rational – and thus a more efficient, effective and accountable – organisational structure by modelling the service more closely on other large-scale enterprises. The 1974 reforms were consciously bureaucratic and 'managerialist' in arguing for a rationalised corporate structure and more clearly defined paths of accountability and responsibility. The Griffiths reforms went further, pushing for management leadership in place of administrative support for professional groups. Before we review the impact of these changes it is important to be aware of some important sociological insights into organisations.

What are organisations?

Perhaps the single most significant feature of contemporary society is the number and scale of organisations. Compared with pre-industrial societies the involvement of people in organisations is widespread: we spend our working lives and much of our leisure time in them. An organisation is not just a group of people, although relationships between people are fundamental to it; it is a social unit deliberately set up to achieve specific goals. The organisation employs appropriate technologies (work methods) and creates control strategies to ensure that what is going on in the organisation (the processes) and what is produced by the workforce (outcomes) actually achieves the stated goals (Figure 11.5).

○   Spend a few minutes thinking about the NHS in these terms. What are its goals? What work technologies are used and how is the workforce controlled? What are the outcomes and do they match the goals?

The goals in health work, we might suggest, are to cure and alleviate pain and sickness or to enable people to die with dignity, to prevent disease and to promote health. Some work technologies commonly used by nurses are task allocation, patient-focused nursing care, care plans,

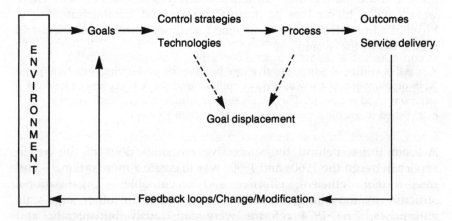

FIGURE 11.5 Organisations: a simple model

home visits and so on. Control of the nursing workforce is through line management. The outcome should be a dignified death, cured or alleviated patients or healthier people.

Of course, once we start describing the health service in this way it becomes clear that the real life of the organisation is far more complex. In broad terms the goal of alleviating sickness, for example, may conflict with allowing patients a dignified death. There has often been conflict over priorities and resources: for example between acute and preventive medicine or between services for children and for those with mental health problems. Priorities set within specialties – which result in rationing access to kidney dialysis or to coronary by-pass surgery and so on – may conflict with the overall goal of alleviating or curing sickness. There may be power struggles and cultures within the organisation which create 'goal displacement': that is, employees are so busy in-fighting or following routines that the aim of caring for the patient becomes secondary. Rigid task allocation strategies might produce goal displacement.

Control strategies

Work technologies can also operate as control strategies. Task allocation, for example, has not just been used to 'get through the work' but also to exercise control over the nursing workforce. Student nurses who were taught in school to spend time talking to patients found on the ward that this was not valued as nursing work, and they were seen as 'not pulling their weight' (Melia, 1987). Control strategies are needed in any organisation because most work has to be delegated – carried out by employees who don't necessarily share the interests of the managers.

Weber defined organisations in terms which also emphasised their role in controlling people: 'The vesting of domination or power of command in the individual or the office, a set of offices constituting the organisation. It should be noted that the claim to an authoritarian power of command is ultimately a coercive claim' (Weber, in Andreski, 1979).

As you may recall from Chapter 2, Weber argued that rational-legal authority would come to predominate in modern industrialised societies, and he saw the characteristic organisational form of this as the *bureaucracy*. Although bureaucratic organisations could take many forms, Weber identified certain key features common to them all. These included a hierarchy of authority – 'a clearly established system of super- and sub-ordination in which there is a supervision of the lower offices by the higher ones'; a specialised division of tasks undertaken by officials; a standardised set of rules governing activities and procedures; a formalised system of record keeping and files; and officials who are appointed to posts on the basis of merit and paid according to their rank

BOX 11.5 Ideal type of a bureaucracy (from Max Weber)

1 Business conducted continuously
2 Bureaucrats are employees, appointed to a specific office/role in organisation
3 Bureaucrats' authority derives from, and loyalty belongs to, employer; accountable to employer and regulated in work by contract
4 Specific office has established and defined sphere of authority and responsibility, based on impersonal formal rules, regulations (and contract), as opposed to bureaucrat's personal judgements, discretion or client needs
5 Business conducted in writing; great deal of paperwork, records and files
6 Characterised by high degree of division of labour, specialisation of roles and departments
7 Hierarchies of unequals in which command is downward from the top and accountability is upward; orders flow down, information/response flows up

Note: This is an 'ideal type' of a bureaucratic organisation; it does not mean that all organisations conform exactly to this model.

and responsibility. Thus bureaucracy was a continuous activity in that personnel came and went, but the rules, files and structure remained intact (see Box 11.5).

○   What features of bureaucratic organisation can you identify in today's health service?

The National Health Service has many bureaucratic features, some of which may be among the things that most annoy you! Specialisation in health work is very evident, and regulation of the workforce and hierarchical control, in the shape of increased centralisation, are on the increase (we'll discuss this later on in the section). You may already be feeling swamped by records and files, not only patients' records but also requirements to account for health workers' time and performance. Community nurses, for example, have far more paperwork than in the past, and the nursing process has been widely criticised for the amount of form-filling that is demanded.

People tend to react negatively to the concept of bureaucracy, conjuring up images of 'red tape', endless files, secret records, written job contracts resulting in an unwillingness to take risks by going outside one's area of responsibility and so on. Bureaucracy has been seen as deadening to initiative and creativity, and some writers on the health service have seen medical dominance as preferable to managerial power. Weber himself acknowledged the potentially stifling effects of bureaucracy on individuals, but he also argued that rational-legal authority secured impersonal and efficient organisational control. In time professions would be subsumed under these new structures.

It is clearly not the case that professions have been neutralised in health work, but we must distinguish between occupations which call themselves professions but have relatively little independent power, and those which have retained a significant degree of autonomy. The acknowledgement of the professional standing of some groups can itself be viewed as a control strategy. For example, the nursing leadership emphasised that nurses were professionals and frowned on 'unladylike conduct', unionisation and industrial action; one result was that nurses remained low paid and experienced poor working conditions and long hours (Dingwall et al. 1988).

Nursing, health visiting and midwifery are subject to bureaucratic and professional regulation, but their professional freedom of action is heavily circumscribed. Doctors, by contrast, retain considerable professional power to make and enforce decisions because of their pivotal role in the diagnosis and treatment of patients: 'The hospital authority structure is fractured around the difference between the rational bureaucratic system and the professional autonomy of the doctor through a system of medical domination' (Turner, 1987).

Clearly, organisations are not all the same, and sociologists have identified very different types of control strategies. Burns and Stalker (1961) made an initial distinction between 'organic' and 'mechanistic' structures of control. *Mechanistic* structures are characterised by hierarchic control and precisely defined rights, tasks and obligations, whereas *organic* structures emphasise collective responsibility, lateral communication, shared tasks and knowledge and a network structure of control. These distinctions reflect those observed between regimes in total and open institutions (Goffman, 1961, and see Chapter 10, page 406, Table 10.4). Mechanistic structures are appropriate if the environment of the organisation is stable and simple, but organic responses work better if the environment is complex and variable. Different organisations (or parts of organisations) at different times may exhibit these organic or mechanistic features to different degrees. The challenge for those in control is to determine which response (and where and when) will be most effective.

A negotiated order?

When control strategies and technologies are in place we still need to explore what actually happens: the *processes*. The health care organisation is complex and delivers a huge range of different types of services; success depends on different groups of workers with diverse skills negotiating with each other and securing each others' co-operation or consent (Klein, 1983). In health work action theorists have suggested that 'negotiation' rather than classic bureaucratic control has been more evident. Sociologists have been criticised for their lack of interest in the organisation of health care, which has led to the too ready adoption of simplistic bureaucratic organisational models by health service reformers (Hunter, in Cox, 1991). The distribution of power cannot be assumed to match patterns of formal authority; instead we need to study organisations as 'politically negotiated orders'. Nurses, doctors, groups of paramedic and ancillary workers, social workers, volunteers and many other groups do not share a common training or social background. Their professional education and socialisation is varied, their status within health work differs radically, and they each bring with them different personal values and assumptions. Although in theory bureaucracies can rely on rules and regulations to keep control, in practice employees may not know or may not apply the rules. Nor does it follow that the application of hierarchical authority will solve all problems; individuals or groups quite low down the hierarchy can sometimes exert considerable influence and even subvert control. Negotiations may range from amicable 'give and take', through bargaining and diplomacy to outright conflict.

○ Note down some examples of 'negotiation' between workers in health care that you have observed or read about.

You may have observed many kinds of negotiations between doctors and nurses over the treatment and care of patients, ranging from hard bargaining to gentle persuasion. Medical power is more frequently challenged in today's health service, even if nurses do not usually employ methods of frontal attack (Porter, 1991, and see Section 12.4). In the past in the NHS there has sometimes been open conflict between managers and front line workers, unionised ancillary workers and nurses (Carpenter, 1980). Tactics such as working to rule, boycotts and 'go-slows' have been used. More hidden conflicts may occur in relations between different specialisms and departments, as some teams or areas try to 'empire-build' at the expense of others. 'Shroud-waving' by specialists to get extra resources is not unknown. The power of professional groups in health work, especially of the medical profession, is still considerable.

Strauss *et al.* (1963) wrote a classic study of the hospital as a 'negotiated order' in which co-operation, informal bargains, personal contacts, by-passing the system and so on represented the real life of the organisation, rather than the formal rules and regulations. They suggested that specialisation in medicine and the growth of specialist teams have meant that the hospital resembles a collection of 'workshops' rather than being a rational, unified structure. The theory of negotiated order was derived from studies of two psychiatric hospitals in which conflicts between psychiatrists over how to treat patients created ripple effects throughout the organisation. In particular, the researchers discovered that covert tactics were used by staff lower down the formal hierarchy – such as transferring patients between wards without the consultants' knowledge.

Strong (1979) has suggested that negotiation is also the characteristic pattern of interaction among staff, and between staff and patients in other clinical settings. However, he argues that patient–practitioner interaction in health work takes a particular form which he terms 'bureaucratic' in the sense that it is formal, regulated and purposive rather than expressive. In other words, the social actors engage with each other as instances of a type – 'the psychiatrist', 'the neurotic' and so on – in a fairly anonymous way. Their concern is with the clinical negotiation and not with other aspects of their lives.

The notion of a set of highly formalised structures which are subverted by an informal subculture of backstairs negotiations and deals is presented in Goffman's (1961) work on total institutions. On the one hand Goffman offers us a picture of a 'total' closed institution in which inmates become institutionalised and to an extent dehumanised. The status of the most senior inmate remains lower than that of the most junior member of staff, but staff as well as patients are subject to the intricate formal rules and regulations of the institution. Admission procedures involve a 'mortification of self', a stripping away of the old identity and taking on the status of the patient. This may involve creating files, removing clothing, cleansing procedures, all signalling a loss of personal control.

On the other hand, patients develop an informal culture which enables them to survive and which may be an informal part of the therapeutic regime. They 'psych out' what is required and, through a process of 'secondary adjustment', outwardly conform whilst actually retaining a degree of independence. In a similar way and in spite of bureaucratic pressures staff become involved in negotiations with each other and with patients, particularly 'back stage' in the institution, where norms and customs regulate the work.

The point that interactionists have made most strongly is that in the complex organisations found in health care a bureaucratic model will not explain social relationships fully. Yet social action theories, because they tend to focus on inter-personal negotiation at the micro level, can be argued to marginalise or ignore relationships between the organisation and the wider society. The power and authority of doctors and other health workers, the social order of the hospital, the role of the hospital in contemporary society in part derive from influences beyond the hospital itself: shifting cultural patterns and values, economic transformations and structural constraints such as state legislation. In this sense, as Turner (1987) comments, Weber's concept of bureaucracy is a powerful and apt analysis of a process of modernisation: 'We may conceptualise the modern hospital as the social vehicle for the rationalisation of medical practice, the specialisation of medical knowledge and the division of health-care systems into specialised units'. This process, as we have already noted, was discussed by Foucault (1973) in terms of a reconceptualisation of medical knowledge about the body leading to the positioning of patients within the 'clinical gaze' as hospital cases. From this follows the modern rationalisation and institutionalisation of health work.

11.7 The search for effective control

The 1974 reorganisation of the National Health Service was one of a number of attempts to strengthen its formal bureaucracy by implementing a 'managerialist' strategy. The emphasis was on creating greater efficiency and effectiveness through changing the structure, strengthening management and introducing a planning system. Clearer lines of accountability upwards to the Department of Health and a clearer delegation of responsibility downwards to the health authorities would result in a better, tighter managed service with more effective control at the centre (see Figure 11.3, page 442). However, developing a degree of democratic control was also an issue; this was done partly through the establishment of community health councils, but also by the creation of consensus management, in which all members of the management assumed responsibility for decisions. This was part of an on-going strategy of controlling costs through curbing the professional autonomy of hospital doctors. Indeed the Cogwheel reports of the late 1960s had attempted to persuade clinicians to play a greater part in managing resources and co-operating in decision making (Allsop, 1984).

The imposition of managerialism reached a new stage with the 1984 Griffiths Management Enquiry. Cox (1991) has commented that sociologists have generally been distrustful and dismissive of managerialist initiatives and at times have seemed to defend a traditional 'organic' model of health care organisation built on medical dominance. In contrast, Griffiths' introduction of the concept of 'general management' was intended to transform the old style NHS admininstrator into someone prepared to take overall responsibility for the running of the service – even against the wishes of clinicians. Ethnographic evidence from Strong and Robinson (1988) reveals how the new NHS managers were inspired by the Griffiths gospel of reform. Griffiths provided 'a philosophy, a paradigm, a doctrine' rather than an exact science:

The recurring themes of Griffiths' managerialism are action, effectiveness, thrust, urgency and vitality, management budgeting, sensitivity to consumer satisfaction and an approach to management of personnel which would reward good performance and ultimately sanction poor performance with dismissal.

Cox (1991)

These approaches, borrowed from the private sector from which Sir Roy Griffiths had been drawn (he was Chief Executive of Sainsbury's, the food retail chain), were not unique to health care. Thatcherism was already emphasising market solutions and 'value for money' initiatives. The reforms took place against a background of rising private sector provision for health, internal scrutinies of expenditure (by Lord Rayner of the Marks and Spencer chain) and competitive tendering of ancillary services (see Chapter 13).

The introduction of general management was not just designed to put in place managers prepared to manage, but also to change NHS culture by drawing in substantial numbers of private sector managers and by involving doctors in clinical budgeting (see Box 11.6). In fact, at all levels in the service around 60 per cent of managers were ex-administrators, but there were significant numbers of private sector and

BOX 11.6 The 1984 Griffiths Management Enquiry Report: selected recommendations

Budgeting/performance reviews	Recommendations
• The Review process needs to be extended beyond Districts to Units of Management, particularly the major hospitals, and it should start with a Unit performance review based on management budgets which involve the clinicians at hospital level. Real output measurement, against clearly stated management objectives and budgets, should become a major concern of management at all levels	• We therefore propose the identification of a general manager to harness the best of the consensus management approach and avoid the worst of the problems it can present. The general manager would be the final decision taker for decisions normally delegated to the consensus team, especially where decisions cross professional boundaries or cause disagreements and delay at present
• Above all, of course, lack of a general management process means that it is extremely difficult to achieve change	• In identifying a Unit general manager we believe that the District Chairman should go for the best person for the job, regardless of discipline. The main criterion for appointment should be the ability to undertake the general management function at Unit level and manage the total Unit budget.

TABLE 11.3 Analysis of NHS general managers: by background. Source: Ham (1992)

	Adminis-trators	Doctors	Nurses	Other NHS	Outside NHS	Total
Regional general managers	9	1	1	1	2	14
District general managers	113	15	5	17	38	188
Unit general managers	322	97	63	16	44	542

military appointees. Only 2.3 per cent of regional and district managers and 10 per cent of unit managers were nurses, and nurse influence (which had been wielded by chief nursing officers at regional level) diminished (see Table 11.3). Griffiths made little reference to nursing, but the outcome of his reforms has been considerable restructuring in the nursing hierarchy (Strong and Robinson, 1988). His main concern was to bring the doctors under managerial control by involving them in resource discussions, monitoring clinical activity and developing a budgeting system which held clinicians to account. But there is little real evidence that managers are as yet succeeding in controlling consultants. The 1990 changes in health service structure do give managers more say in consultants' appointment and contracts, and in the monitoring of their work. On the other hand the creation of market-driven hospital trusts may enhance consultants' power (see Chapter 13).

11.8 Critiques of medical power

Sociologists have become increasingly critical of medical power. In the 1960s there was a backlash against Talcott Parsons' theory of the role of medicine. His analysis of doctors as a mediating force in capitalist society, who helped to underwrite social order by maintaining impersonal standards and exhibiting altruism, was questioned. Neo-Marxists, for example, attacked the role of health care in the social control of the workforce and saw the medical profession as the willing allies of the state (Navarro, 1978; Johnson, 1977). Other critics employed neo-Weberian theory to explore how medical dominance was achieved through occupational closure and control of the division of labour in health (Freidson, 1970; 1986). Interactionists produced a blistering analysis of total institutions in health care (Goffman, 1961). Feminist critics explored the gendering of power in health work and drew attention to the relative powerlessness of (particularly) women patients when negotiating with doctors (Oakley, 1980; 1984; Graham and

Oakley, 1981). They were joined by other writers who criticised medical dominance on libertarian and religious grounds (Illich, 1976).

There was considerable common ground among the assailants, in particular in their criticism of medical power. To some extent the modern health care system itself was on trial; it was seen as not having delivered better health but predominantly medical treatment within a sickness-focused service in which patients remained relatively power-less and needs, resources and services were largely defined and controlled by doctors. We have noted that Foucault's theory projects power as a relationship between groups; disciplinary power produces a new reality, a new way of 'seeing and knowing', it is essentially productive. In a similar way the 'whole individual' as a bio-psycho-social being is only produced by means of the extended medical gaze (Armstrong, 1983a). But this account is challenged by a structural definition of power as concerned with domination and control. Implicit in this analysis is a 'zero sum' definition of power (Lukes, 1977). In the case of health work this implies that the power and control exercised by the medical profession inevitably undermined and reduced the power of other groups – whether groups of paid health workers or patients.

Lukes identified three dimensions of power held by groups or individuals: the ability to 'modify the conduct of others', to 'control the issues on the agenda' and to 'prevent people . . . from having grievances by shaping their perceptions in such a way that they accept the existing order of things'. While this last dimension of power might remind you of Foucault's notion of the clinical gaze which creates 'reality', it is important to note that Lukes emphasises the oppressive nature of power which obliterates people's legitimate grievances. Allsop (1984) argued that all these dimensions of power have been used by the medical profession to secure their position since the 1940s. They have influenced NHS organisation, protecting their own autonomy and controlling the agenda for change so that curative medicine and hospital treatment predominated, and have persuaded others of the truth of their conceptualisation of 'health'.

It is important to note, as we consider critiques of medical power more closely, that nurses have always been closely involved in carrying out medical orders. While they have generally been in a position of weakness in relation to doctors, they have themselves exerted consider-able control over patients. Any consideration of medical power needs to include acknowledgement of nursing's role in the support and extension of that power as well as in mediating between doctors and patients. With this in mind, let's investigate two contrasting and very influential critiques of medical power: the first focusing on its relationship to capitalism, the second on the extension of medical power into everyday life.

Medical power and capitalism

How should we view medical power? As a productive force helping to create contemporary social 'reality' or as a repressive force controlling and constraining us? From a Marxist viewpoint medical power, the health work system and the very nature of health and illness are produced by the fundamental economic relationships arising out of industrial capitalism (see Section 5.5). You will recall Doyal's (1979) comment that the emphasis on curative medical intervention rather than broadly based preventive measures serves the interests of capitalism by disguising how ill health is socially produced. In the USA it has been claimed that, while the role of medical power is repressive, doctors have little real autonomy; their position as professionals has been increasingly eroded with the growth of the medical industrial complex. The logic of capitalism has penetrated deep into health care. Health has become *commodified*: made into just another product for sale (McKinlay, 1984). It might be argued that a similar pattern of commercial medicine and market values is emerging in the UK.

Navarro (1979) has argued that doctors act as servants of the capitalist state by ensuring that health and illness are conceptualised in individualistic terms. They emphasise diet, lifestyle and exercise rather than the part played by industrial processes and capitalist production. They regulate sickness and contribute towards the productivity of capitalism by treating and returning workers to the workforce. He has suggested that the establishment of the National Health Service in Britain consolidated medical power in health work, with the result that doctors as a dominant group supported a version of health care which focused on upper class and professional groups at the expense of working class health. Inequalities are not an unfortunate by-product of health work but an integral part of the logic of provision. The medical model reinforces the notion of health as a commodity and conceptualises illness as an individual responsibility. Moreover, if expenditure cuts have to be made it is patients and ancillary and lower status health workers who feel the pinch rather than the highly paid doctors.

This account can be criticised on several grounds. There is little evidence that most disease is rooted in capitalist processes, even though it is clear that industrial diseases are a significant – and often overlooked – part of the disease burden. Neither is there evidence that in socialist societies health is better; indeed in terms of mortality and morbidity it appears to have been worse, particularly in the exposure of workers to harmful industrial processes. In Britain and most other Western countries the health work system has expanded in recent years, the cost of maintaining it has risen and the numbers taking sick leave or undergoing hospital treatment have grown significantly. This suggests that doctors have raised the costs for capital and increased rather than reduced sickness (Hart, 1985). The notion of doctors as the agents of capital sits uneasily with the evidence of their power to influence popular thinking about health and illness (including political parties' manifestos) and to direct resources into health work. As we noted earlier, the idea that health care meant 'entitlement to medical treatment' was accepted by the Labour politician Bevan in the 1940s and has proved difficult for politicians since then to resist. Successive attempts to control spending and restrict medical power by expanding managerial control have as yet failed to work.

The medicalisation of everyday life?

Another, more persuasive analysis of medical power focuses on its spread: the so-called 'medicalisation of everyday life'. There is certainly considerable evidence to suggest that in contemporary society medicine operates as an 'institution of social control' (Zola, 1972). But it does not follow that this is the result of the use of repressive force or a drive for professional 'imperialism'. Instead, Zola suggests, the explanation lies 'in our increasingly complex, technological and bureaucratic system – a system which has led us down the path of the reluctant reliance on the expert'. Medicine is the 'new repository of truth where absolute and often final judgements are made by supposedly neutral and objective experts . . . in the name of health' (Zola, 1972). Such judgements go far beyond the diagnosis of disease to influence people's daily lives: their working, eating, sleeping and eating.

Zola then explores the process by which medicine came to occupy such a position. He considers the role of doctors in the definition of sickness, their role in de-stigmatising human and social problems by explaining them in terms of physical or mental disorder rather than immorality or illegitimacy and their increasing applications of the labels 'healthy' and 'ill' to ever expanding areas of peoples' lives. Thus medicine has laid claim to deal with any area which can be conceptualised in terms of health and illness, whether or not its interventions are effective. Zola lists four ways in which this control is growing:

- The expansion of what in life is deemed relevant to the good practice of medicine: this refers to the expansion of medicine into new areas, involving surveillance of well people.
- The retention of absolute control over certain technical procedures: this refers to the right to do surgery and prescribe drugs, a right which has expanded due to medical specialisation and the huge expansion of the pharmaceutical industry.
- The retention of near absolute access to certain taboo areas: this refers

to the right of intimate access to patients' bodies and minds, even in situations (such as childbirth and ageing) which were considered natural processes.

- The expansion of what in medicine is deemed relevant to the good practice of life: this refers to the use of medical evidence and rhetoric to advance any cause.

Zola argues that the level of patent medicine consumption and growing preoccupation with 'healthy lifestyles' is evidence of how health is a paramount value and therefore how potentially controlling the medical profession has become. The danger lies partly in the fact that 'not only is the process masked as a technical, scientific, objective one, but one done for our own good'.

In a rather similar way, but from the very different perspective of liberationist Catholic theology, Ivan Illich (1978) produced a theory of 'iatrogenesis' and 'medical nemesis'. In writing of *iatrogenesis* he is referring to the damage inflicted by doctors at the level of clinical misjudgement and negligence and to hospital-induced disease and injuries. A second stage identified is 'social iatrogenesis': that is, increased dependence on medical expertise leading to the medicalisation of aspects of life, blind belief in medical progress and the institutionalisation of medicine as an industry which commodifies and sells 'health'. The final stage, 'structural iatrogenesis', refers to the stripping away from human culture of ways of coping with birth, pain and death and their replacement by a sanitised, technological medical intervention against which individuals and societies are unable to fight back. People stop relying on and trusting each other and depend only on medical intervention: 'Health, or the autonomous power to cope, has been expropriated down to the last breath. Technical death has won its victory over dying. Mechanical death has conquered and destroyed all other deaths' (Illich, 1978).

Although they share common ground in being profoundly concerned about the power of medicine in contemporary society, these two accounts emphasise different aspects of medical control. For Illich it is the dehumanising of people in the face of medical technology, the sanitising of pain and death and suppression of natural human emotions, that is of most concern. For Zola it is the fact that the medicalising of daily life wrests control from patients 'for their own good' and vests it in experts who are increasingly required to have all the answers.

○ Reflect on these two critiques of medical power. Would your observations of health work lead you to endorse these views?

Your experience of health work in different settings may have prompted a range of responses. For example, the growth of the hospice movement and of 'community care' support for dependent groups has shifted the focus away from the medicalisation of death and from institutionalisation of people with mental and physical disabilities, mental health problems and chronic disease. This suggests a de-medicalising of some groups hitherto viewed as 'patients'. Childbirth is also becoming reconceptualised in official reports as a 'natural event' with recommendations that it should move from hospital settings towards care by midwives in the community, although this process is only just beginning (Cumberlege Report, DoH, 1993a).

On the other hand the importance attached to medical risk factors, the Health of the Nation strategy (1992) and the rise of health promotion would suggest that daily life is becoming subject to greater medical surveillance and control. Doctors have been asked to provide health checks, screening, advice and counselling. The 'community gaze' extends well beyond the hospital (Armstrong, 1983a). You may recall how Finkelstein (1993) has argued that, while de-institutionalisation of patients with disabilities is to be welcomed, there can be no real autonomy if community and welfare 'experts' still exert control over people's lives. Social workers, counsellors, fitness trainers, alternative practitioners are increasingly working from health practices under a 'health' banner.

How far does this influence lay people in their everyday lives? Certainly health claims are used to sell a huge range of products and medical endorsements are highly prized, but it is unclear how far this influence extends. Blaxter (1990) pointed out that, when questioned about health, people responded with stock 'official' answers concerning the importance of exercise, diet, smoking and alcohol. But this didn't necessarily have an impact on their own behaviour (see Chapter 10). Does the growth in the consumption of patent medicines by self medication signify growing medical control over people's lives or a healthily independent attitude towards seeking medical advice?

Medical power in health work

This chapter has focused on power and control in health work and, perhaps inevitably, on the power of organised medicine. In spite of recent attempts to exert managerial control over doctors, their virtual monopoly over medical diagnosis and treatment has remained intact and, as we have seen, has even expanded through their growing role in monitoring 'at risk' and 'well' people. What significance does this have for nursing work? On the one hand nursing has from its origins been intimately associated with organised medicine and has played a not inconsiderable part in the growth of medical power. In its (sometimes reluctant) acceptance of the 'handmaiden' role the nursing leadership allied itself with medicine as an expert and professional group which was entitled to exert control over patients. Of course, for many nurses the reality of health work was quite different: low status, long hours, poor conditions, endless drudgery and probably a greater identification with the patient and their social background rather than with an ethic of vocation or profession (Dingwall et al., 1988). But the ideological and organisational alliance between nursing and medicine cannot be overlooked.

On the other hand doctors have resisted attempts to allow nurses formal powers to prescribe a limited range of drugs and dressings, for example, even though nurses often have more knowledge of what is needed and the 'doctor's signature' is just a formality. In maternity care midwives perform most of the routine antenatal work with women, yet doctors are reluctant to give up their (often cursory) medical examination of women at the clinic – not least because it is a valued 'fee for service'. Practice nurses, as employees of the doctor, may be asked to perform a wide range of duties some of which may stray into medical territory, but their status and pay remain those of a nurse. Similarly, in hospitals nurses are being asked to take on more and more quasi-medical responsibilities – for intravenous injections, for example – but medical control remains intact.

As far as patients and lay people in general are concerned it is very difficult to see medical power as simply repressive. From the evidence all around us of patients ignoring medical advice, refusing treatment, forgetting or discarding drugs and directing (for better or worse) their own daily lives, it seems clear that the twentieth century expansion of medical power – where it has happened – has to some extent been productive. The extended medical gaze has reconceptualised the passive patient as a 'whole' subject, and in doing so the patient has become an active participant: with a growing voice in his/her health care, with increasing rights of refusal and with greater choice.

But part, at least, of the explanation of this lies in the increasing regulation of medicine by the state and in its pivotal role as mediator of health work relationships. In other words, medicine has been refocused not simply by some internal conceptual transformation but also because of external cultural, social and economic pressures. Some pressures have worked to 'liberate' the patient and transform relationships within health work. Nursing has increasingly emerged as an autonomous type of caring-focused work which implicitly rejects a narrow medical, technical model of health and treatment, and we'll explore this in Chapter 12. Other pressures have operated to reinforce a technologically-driven, treatment-focused and increasingly commodified health care system of the kind regarded with suspicion by Zola, Illich and others. The most recent round in the reconceptualisation and reconstruction of health care organisation and practice and its implications for the future of health work and nursing will be the focus of Chapter 13.

Suggestions for further study

D. Armstrong's article 'From clinical gaze to regime of total health' in A. Beattie *et al.* (1993) *Health and Wellbeing: A Reader*, London, Macmillan, is a good starting point for reflecting on shifts in medical power. Those who want to explore the professionalisation of medicine more fully should look at B. Turner (1987) *Medical Power and Social Knowledge*, London, Sage. The debate about the medical contribution to decreased mortality is raised in T. McKeown (1976) *The Role of Medicine: Dream, Mirage or Nemesis*, London, Nuffield Provincial Hospitals Trust. Earlier changes in the health sector are well covered by J. Allsop (1984) *Health Policy and the National Health Service*, London, Longman, and developments in nursing are discussed in R. Dingwall *et al.* (1988) *An Introduction to the Social History of Nursing*, London, Routledge.

Self assessment questions

1 Note down the main characteristics of 'modern scientific bio-medicine'.
2 Explain what is meant by the concept of 'the clinical gaze' of modern medicine.
3 Discuss the main features of the health division of labour as it emerged in professionalised health work.
4 To what extent was the medical profession able to control the organisation and development of the NHS in Britain?
5 Outline the main recommendations and results of the Griffiths Enquiry into health service management.
6 From your own health work experience, suggest arguments for and against the notion of the 'medicalisation of everyday life'.

Chapter 12

The work of nursing

Contents

Themes and issues

The character of nursing: women's work – caring – emotional labour – bodily management and control

Nursing ideologies: vocation and professionalism – the social construction of nursing and the nurse–patient relationship – occupational socialisation – students and workers – nursing as 'doing'

Division of labour in nursing: the doctor–nurse game – interaction with patients: negotiated order – the use of emotions – routines – categories and stereotypes

Learning outcomes

After working through this chapter you should be able to:

1 Appraise the concepts of 'women's work, 'caring' and 'emotional labour' in relation to your own health work practice.

2 Review your own experience of professional socialisation, using ideas and concepts from this chapter.

3 Assess the significance of class, race and gender divisions in nursing.

4 Explore changing concepts of the 'nurse–patient relationship' in relation to your own area of health work practice.

IN this chapter nursing work will be explored as a complex series of intimate, interactive processes and interventions which not only influence health and illness states but are also charged with symbolic meaning for health workers, patients and lay people. We will explore how far sociological theories and concepts can shed light on the development and contemporary character of nursing work and consider what they have to say about the relationships between nurses and other health professionals, in particular doctors. The nursing workforce is the largest in the health service, and a case study of nursing work provides a useful illustration of the major issues and conflicts noted in Chapter 11. While nursing is a particular occupation, it also has characteristics, knowledge frameworks and underpinning values which are common to other groups in health work. Nurses' changing experiences of caring work and relationships with patients, their professional culture and socialisation, their occupational struggles and bid for autonomy will find echoes in the experience of other health work professionals, such as physiotherapists, occupational and speech therapists, radiographers and chiropodists.

In general, sociological (and other) studies of health work have focused on the development and contemporary role of the medical profession and have assumed that nursing and other health work 'fitted in' with this framework. Medical sociologists studied what doctors did, hardly noticing nurses at all (Oakley, 1986). In Chapter 11 we explored how health work became professionalised and how the division of labour was created and reproduced. Here it is primarily nursing work which is problematised and explored; the medical profession is referred to in order to explain aspects of nursing work, such as intra-professional relationships. The first part of this chapter explores the social construction of contemporary nursing as *women's work* and as *caring work*, drawing on some of the theories discussed in Chapters 5, 7 and 8. The professional socialisation of nurses is explored as well as the changing nature of the 'nurse–patient' relationship. We will examine the social dimension of interactions with patients and clients in contemporary hospital wards, clinics and community settings and in different stages of illness. The chapter also highlights issues of power and control in health work, through an analysis of the nurse–doctor relationship; this draws on discussion of the health division of labour in Chapter 11.

12.1 Nursing as a particular type of work

This section begins to explore some of the main features of nursing and other non-medical health work in the light of sociological theories and concepts and suggests that its characterisation as 'caring work' and 'women's work' is problematic. Questions are raised about the extent to which bodily management and 'control', as well as care, are central aspects of nursing, and about the significance of 'emotional labour'. These themes and problems are revisited as the chapter develops.

Nursing as 'women's work'

Nursing and much other non-medical health work has been firmly identified as *women's work*: that is, work which is deemed more suitable and appropriate for women to undertake: about 75 per cent of the total health labour force is female but – in spite of recent changes – a disproportionate number of managers are men. Female workers continue to provide the vast bulk of 'hands-on' care in every setting, whether this is nursing care, domestic or catering work or unpaid lay caring (Finch and Groves, 1983).

O   What types of arguments have been advanced over the years to justify the notion of 'women's work' and reinforce a sexual division of labour in health?

Notions about women's inbuilt qualities of caring and nurturing, often ascribed to their childbearing role, are influential in sustaining a sexual division of labour, not least in health work (Sections 7.3–7.6). 'Women's work' draws on the notion of a core of female skills and abilities which are peculiar to women, or at least more pronounced and widespread in them as a social group. It cuts across cultural, generational and class boundaries, in that women of any social status, age or ethnic origin are assumed to possess these qualities. They are universal and intrinsic, built on the foundations of women's biology. This approach to women's work has been challenged not only for its biological determinism but also because it ignores the dynamics of social and cultural change. In particular, the exclusion of women from certain types of work and their segregation within a narrow range of occupations has arguably been more to do with men's attempts to control wages and conditions than with women's ability to perform particular types of work (Braybon and Summerfield, 1987).

However, the notion of nursing as 'women's work' is also embedded in nursing's history. Florence Nightingale defined a good nurse as a 'good woman'. She saw nursing as a caring occupation and as proper work for women, but not all women were suitable; only those with a good character, appropriate social background and high standards were to be admitted. Nineteenth century ideologies of nursing distanced the modern 'trained' nurse from the disreputable, untrained nurse of the past and also used Nightingale to make claims about nursing as a fit and proper activity for 'gentlewomen'. On the other hand the Nightingale legend has been used to project several distinct ideologies of nursing for students. Whittaker and Olesen (1978) noted in the United States that traditional schools of nursing and university nursing departments in the 1970s emphasised very different aspects of Nightingale's life. Whereas the traditional school praised her femininity and heroic self sacrifice, the university celebrated her contribution to scientific knowledge and her role as an innovator. In Britain in the climate of the 1980s, as nursing began to move into mainstream higher education, the writings of other nurses – such as Mrs Bedford-Fenwick, who emphasised the need for a highly educated nurse cadre – have been revalued. In other words, within nursing itself the notion of 'women's work' is problematic.

Central to the ideology of nursing as women's work is the concept of femininity: the idea that there is a cluster of characteristic and distinctive behaviours and outlooks which are particular to women. As we noted in Chapter 7, some feminist writers such as Chodorow come close to a biological essentialist view by emphasising how women transmit gender socialisation through their pivotal role in early child-rearing: for example, she suggests that girls are taught to value intimacy and expressiveness, whereas boys are taught self reliance. It is certainly clear that a whole range of behaviours has been viewed as typically 'feminine' by nurses and doctors at various times, and that women's work has been framed in terms of these supposed behaviours. For example, nursing has been viewed as women's work on the positive grounds that women's qualities of tenderness, compassion, expressiveness, empathy and so on are central requirements of the job. On the other hand women have been viewed as fit only for nursing on the negative grounds that they are naturally submissive or deferential, manipulative, emotional, irrational and so on. Both these ideologies of femininity have been used at various times to equate nursing and women's work.

Exclusion of women from the medical profession and their strict subordination to male doctors were defended in earlier decades not just in terms of the need to preserve women's biological femininity – that is, their reproductive capacity – but also on the basis of the gender stereotypes noted above. In Victorian times the 'natural' order of the hospital reproduced the 'natural' order of the home. The ideological triad of father–mother–child in the private family was translated into the doctor–nurse–patient triad in the public sphere of the Victorian hospital (Gamarnikow, 1978, and see Figure 12.1). As in the home, so in the hospital the doctor had patriarchal control over the nurse, to whom was delegated responsibility for aspects of the patient's care. Nurses were expected to be submissive and accommodating to doctors and compassionate towards patients; their presumed emotionality and irrationality could be held in check by strict training and by patriarchal control.

Nursing as women's work also draws attention to the significance of 'mothering'. Basic nursing care has sometimes been seen as 'good mothering' reproduced in the paid public sphere: it involves personalised care, hard manual and sometimes 'dirty' labour, long hours, some

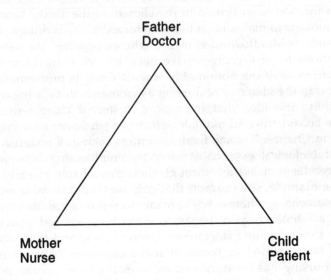

Father
Doctor

Mother   Child
Nurse   Patient

Figure 12.1 Gender order in the Victorian home and hospital

degree of organisational skill and accommodation to (usually male) authority. This draws us on to consider a second, closely related concept in nursing: that of 'caring'.

Nursing and caring

Like mothering, *caring* is often viewed as a normal and natural part of being a woman. The domestic labour of child-rearing and housekeeping is still largely undertaken by women, even though men contribute to a much greater degree than in the past. Caring work straddles the private and public spheres, whereas every effort has been made to locate *curing* work firmly in the public arena (as we noted in Section 7.7). Since much caring work takes place in the home, and many women who engage in paid labour are clustered in female dominated occupations in caring and servicing work, there is assumed to be an equivalence between them. Caring work can thus be viewed as 'common sense' labour which needs needs no lengthy training and merits no high rewards.

Melia (1987) noted a tendency among the student nurses she studied to distinguish between 'talking', 'basic nursing care' and 'theory'. It was 'theory', by which the students meant medical knowledge and information about disease states, that gave them status as professional nurses, whereas there was a tendency to view 'basic nursing care' and 'talking' as common sense routines which auxiliaries (trained on the job) could equally well perform. This may be less widespread in the mid-90s, at least as far as students are concerned, because of the impact of Project 2000; on the other hand the rise of the health care assistant may sharpen the distinction between theory and basic nursing. It has been a real problem for nurses that there seemed to be no definitive body of nursing work and knowledge which could be separated from caring work undertaken by non-nurses. The development of nursing models and theories, such as those of Roper, Roy and Orem, which identify a distinctive arena of activity, approach and value system, has been one response to this situation.

A useful distinction can be made between 'caring about' and 'caring for', which helps to illuminate the position of nursing (Graham, 1983). 'To care for' another describes the process of tending, 'to care about' describes a relationship. Yet it is commonly expected that, in relation to her child or to family responsibilities, a woman will normally exhibit both. As Gillian Dalley (1988) comments, women are considered deviant if they do not care *about* as well as *for* their babies; handing over the care of dependants on other than a temporary basis is widely seen as 'unnatural' in a woman, though understandable in a man:

This blurring of boundaries between functions typifies woman's universe. In the domestic sphere, the menial tasks of family life are wrapped up and presented as part and parcel of her role as mother, and given the same affective values as the feelings she has about the family members for whom she is performing these tasks . . . It is a short step to transfer the same values to the tasks involved in servicing and tending family members outside the everyday cycle of family routine.

Dalley (1988)

We might add that another 'short step' lands women in full-time caring as a paid job. We can see these pressures at work in the occupation of nursing: indeed in some ways these two aspects of caring are now closer together than in the past. If 'caring for' the sick has always been the hallmark of nursing, 'caring about' them at an affective level has been discouraged in the past. Nurses were taught to control and hide their emotions and not to get involved with patients; being a 'professional nurse' meant remaining detached and formal.

○ Suggest what changes in the orientation of nursing have transformed this image of the detached 'professional nurse'.

There has been a shift in nursing towards patient-oriented care; you may have mentioned the development of the nursing process and of patient allocation systems with individualised care. The system of patient allocation, in which a nurse undertakes the total care of named individual patients on the ward, is one in which building affective relationships is seen as an important part. In a sense this approach collapses 'caring for' and 'caring about' into one. In some situations, such as in hospice nursing, a 'family care' model which emphasised intimacy and warmth and familiarity was deliberately introduced (James, 1992). There are obvious benefits, to nurses and patients, of building closer relationships, but there may also be dangers. Several recent writers have noted that nurses may need greater knowledge and support in handling these more intimate and higher risk relationships with patients (Melia, 1987; Smith, 1991). We'll consider aspects of communication between nurses and patients in Section 12.5.

Another neglected aspect of nursing as caring concerns the nature of the caring work itself. As we noted in Chapter 7, the reality of caring is often far from the romantic image of it; it is more to do with 'the daily grind' (Bayley, 1973). The caring work of the families whom Bayley studied was onerous, emotionally very demanding and often not very rewarding in that the 'mentally subnormal adult children' could not reciprocate by showing much gratitude or by helping with their care. The physical labour involved in nursing is emphasised in studies of hospice care, where the completion of physical tasks resulted in a sense of 'control' over the environment – in contrast to the heavy emotional demands which could not be easily regulated (James, 1992; James and Field, 1992). Even if you are just beginning your health work training you may agree that 'daily grind' characterises much of paid caring work.

A study of nurses' work in care of the elderly settings indicates that the burden of physical caring that was required resulted in the widespread adoption of a 'warehousing' model of care (Evers, 1981). Patients were physically tended, but no steps were taken to rehabilitate them. On some wards, however, a 'horticultural' model of care was adopted, in which patients were actively encouraged to become more independent.

Nursing and emotional labour

A third, closely related aspect of nursing lies in its deployment and management of emotion. The term *emotional labour* highlights the way in which much of the work of servicing and caring for people in human service organisations involves formal and ritualised intimacy which is not 'natural' but socially constructed (Lewin and Olesen, 1985; Harre, 1987). Human service workers – from supermarket cashiers and lawyers to residential care workers – have to learn to manage both their own emotions and those of their customers, clients and patients. For example, health workers (except perhaps doctors) are expected to be polite, calm and relaxed; however harassed they feel inwardly, they are taught to make time for the patient and respond cheerfully to his/her needs. They may need to work, therefore, both to conceal their own 'real' feelings, to suppress those feelings and to stimulate positive feelings in themselves. For example, by forcing themselves to be cheerful and attentive to particularly irritating or demanding patients, nurses may persuade those patients to moderate their demands or at least present them in a more acceptable way. They may also influence other patients' attitudes and responses or elicit peer group pressure – perhaps to censor the over-demanding patient. In other words, nurses work to produce (and control) emotions in themselves and others, and their manipulation of their own emotions may often be designed to elicit particular responses from their patients.

○ Can you think of any episodes of performing 'emotional labour' of this kind in your own practice or life experience?

If you are a student of nursing or health work you will probably be all too aware of the need to 'manage' your feelings in relation to patients (and to other health workers!). In one sense it can be said that people are always manipulating and managing emotions in social interaction. Through processes of primary and secondary socialisation, as a child and adult, we learn to see ourselves through the 'looking glass', to view ourselves with other people's eyes and to present ourselves in (mainly) acceptable ways (see Section 3.3). As social actors we work long and painstakingly on the business of presenting 'ourselves' in everyday life (Goffman, 1959). In a study of airline cabin staff in the United States Hochschild (1983) identified three aspects of emotional labour (see Box 12.1). Her airline workers not only had face (or voice) contact with the

BOX 12.1 Three types of emotional labour. Source: Hochschild (1983)

1 **Contact with the public**: (for example patients) in a face-to-face relationship or through voice contact	2 **The management of emotion**: both of the producer (for example nurse) and the recipient (for example patient); this entails the 'induction or suppression of feeling in order to sustain an outward appearance that produces in others a sense of being cared for . . .'	3 **The social production of emotion**: through training processes and supervision of the workforce (for example through nurse training programme and management supervision)

public and laboured to produce particular (positive) feelings in others, but their own emotions were regulated by their employers through training, occupational socialisation and managerial supervision.

Some jobs, such as nursing, have a high emotional content, constituting a significant part of this as formal, paid labour. Nurses work to control their actions as well as their reactions. Their work involves not just physical but a high degree of emotional labour and individualised care – spending time with patients, listening, becoming involved – which may compete with other work (Smith, 1992). In hospice care, for example, where patients are dying and this type of labour is crucial, there may be tensions between organisational demands and the individual care model (James, 1992). This may result in individual care being undermined by a more routinised approach, so that order can be maintained:

The labourer is expected to respond to another person in a way which is personal to both of them but like other aspects of care it develops from the social relations of carer and cared-for and is shaped by the labour process.

James (1992)

You may recall particular episodes in training in which you were taught communication skills, techniques for coping with your own feelings and ways of handling patients. Perhaps there were even questions at interview which were designed to screen out unsuitable students, by checking attitudes towards 'people work', feelings about caring, emotional control and so on. We will develop this concept of emotional labour in relation to nursing in Section 12.3.

Bodily management and control

Exercising control is an important aspect of nursing practice, but in many respects a hidden one. 'Caring for', especially when linked to 'caring about', emphasises health work as 'tender, loving care' – a crucial component of the healing process. Yet historically and still today health workers wield a considerable amount of *control* over people through routines and rituals associated with being a patient, whether this takes place in a hospital or community setting. To some extent the emphasis on the physical labour of 'doing' things for patients – clinical interventions, management and nursing care tasks – can be seen as ways of keeping control, whereas intimacy and involvement threaten the social order of the ward or clinic.

The control which may be exerted over patients in long-stay institutions has been discussed in earlier chapters. Elaborate rules and rituals distanced inmates from their previous life outside the institution and enabled often quite small numbers of staff to control very large groups of patients. Extra sanctions, such as solitary confinement, could be used in difficult cases. Although the long-stay mental institution represents an extreme example of health worker control over patients and institutional control over both patients and staff, some regulation of patients (and staff) is apparent in all health work settings. As we noted in Chapter 11, much of this control is focused on managing the patient's body. The fabrication of our modern view of the 'body as object' in the clinics and hospitals of nineteenth century Europe was accompanied by the development of routine interventions and treatment regimes for the medical surveillance of the individual sick body as well as for 'sick' populations (Foucault, 1973). At the level of populations this involved the segregation of the 'sick' from the 'well' in hospitals and other institutions. At an individual level nurses had a key role in carrying out the processes of treatment prescribed by doctors, a role which included a high degree of control over patients' physical movements, bodily functions, nutritional intake and local environment. Whether in the mental institution, the general hospital or in community settings health workers have undertaken the active management and control of the patient's body (in whole or in part), in order to help in its recovery of health. Whilst many of the rigid routines of hospitals have disappeared – for example, visiting hours are now much freer and bath and oral hygiene 'rounds' have given way to more individualised patient care – management and control of the patient is still a central part of the work today. Health workers may consult patients much more and may encourage patients to participate actively in their own care but – in the interests of the patient's own health – they also expect compliance with treatment, regularly monitor the patient's body and restrict activities.

○ Suggest two or three activities undertaken by nurses or other health workers today which 'actively manage and control' the patient's body.

You may have mentioned the drug round, temperature taking, checks on dietary intake and excretion, timings of meals, baths and bedtime and so on. This kind of control is usually associated with that of the parent over the child; adults are normally expected to make such decisions themselves, unless they are patients (or are characterised as 'disabled' due to a mental health problem or perhaps extreme age).

12.2 The social character of nursing

To a large exent 'modern' nursing is a product of mid-nineteenth century changes in the nature of medicine, which opened the way for a new group of trained and reliable medical auxiliaries. While doctors kept control of diagnosis and treatment, they welcomed the assistance of nurses in the laborious task of monitoring patients and carrying out prescribed interventions. Nurses were therefore centrally involved in bodily management and control, as well as in providing much of the hands-on care that would have been carried out by unpaid carers if the patient was at home. Nursing drew on a sizeable pool of unmarried middle class women, who became the matrons and lady nurses maintaining the hygienic ideal, and working class women, who carried out the more menial tasks under the former's authority and moral leadership. Thus from the start the occupation of nursing was characterised by a division of labour based on gender and class. It was women's work, but it also reproduced the hierarchy of the middle class home in the workplace: mistress and servants, nurses, maids and orderlies in a carefully graded structure. It reproduced the domestic division of labour in the workplace, as well: the classes of women together carried out the 'women's work' of caring, cleaning and cooking while male doctors maintained a distant control over the whole process.

Ideologies of nursing

Gamarnikow (1991) argues that nineteenth century nursing was based on notions of ideological equivalence between nursing, femininity and women's work, but suggests that doctors and nurses interpreted this equation differently. Doctors used the concept of femininity to argue that nursing was women's natural work; in other words, to set boundaries between female and male territories in health work. Nurses emphasised that their subordination was professional – flowing from doctors' role in diagnosis – rather than gender based. Nurses obeyed because they were nurses, not because they were women. In practice, however, nurses were advised by teaching manuals and journals to use devices of manipulation and accommodation – associated with feminine stereotypes – to gain their ends:

At the interpersonal level, nurses gendered professional subordination to encompass the traditional power resource available to women – manipulating the powerful to internalise the outlook and perspective of the powerless.

Gamarnikow (1991)

The ideology of 'vocation' was employed by nurses to purify and uplift what were essentially dirty jobs, such as washing, feeding, clearing away bodily excretions and 'nursing the room': that is, ensuring that hygiene was maintained at all times. But Williams (1978) has commented that 'professionalism' and 'custodialism' emerged as alternative ideologies. The former was based on the shedding of more menial aspects of nursing and the acquisition, from doctors, of higher status tasks such as the use of thermometers or – much more recently – the giving of injections. The ideology of custodialism was most pervasive in mental institutions and geriatric nursing, where the helpless adult was seen as a 'regressed child'. These were also institutions which admitted male nurses, who were specifically excluded from general hospitals.

Clearly, the role and tasks of hospital nursing have changed considerably since the nineteenth century. The Salmon Report (1966) introduced a managerial model into nursing, and the power of the matron was broken. The all-female hierarchy of the hospital was undermined by the incorporation of management structures drawn from industry and the definition of posts in functional terms. The unwritten assumption was that female nurses could not be 'real' managers (Carpenter, 1977). After Salmon there was a rapid rise in the number of male nurse managers, drawn from pyschiatric and mental handicap nursing, where there had always been male nurses. The more recent regrading exercise and the widespread changes in National Health Service structure and organisation have begun to reverse this trend and to put a higher value on clinical nurses and nurse specialists working at ward level in closer contact with patients.

In terms of its composition and character there are still points of contact between Victorian ideologies of nursing and nursing today. The most obvious similarities are the predominantly female workforce and the class basis of nursing – still recruiting middle class as well as working class young women. In the mid-1980s the small pool of 18 year old women with five 'O' levels or two 'A' levels was providing well over 40 per cent of all recruits to nursing, although the management consultants Price Waterhouse calculated that there would be a growing shortfall in recruitment from this group from then, stretching on into the twenty-first century (UKCC, 1987). Until the end of the 1980s prestigious training schools attached to teaching hospitals, such as those in London, could attract middle class female students while other, smaller schools had a much more heterogenous intake. One study of a London nursing school reported that teachers seemed to prefer middle class females, and that men and black and minority ethnic students were poorly represented in the mid-1980s (Smith, 1991). In the years that followed the study, however, the gender and racial composition began to change as the traditional pool of recruits dried up. Project 2000 can be seen as part of a new professional ideology which aims to attract and retain middle class students by upgrading nursing to diploma level, so it will be instructive to see if the class basis of nursing shifts in the future. The development of professionalism as an ideology has already been explored in Chapter 11.

The shifting basis of nurse–patient relationships

Underpinning this analysis of the scope and character of nursing is the notion of 'social construction' which we encountered in Chapter 2. In other words, nursing has not unproblematically developed over time as a discrete occupation; the meanings attached to the work, as well as the nature of the work itself, have been continually fought over and reinvented. It is not just that many of the jobs that doctors once performed – blood pressure checks, temperature taking, injections – are now defined as nursing tasks. It is also that the whole notion of 'being a nurse' has shifted in ideological and personal terms and is still on the move. Nursing has always been a contested activity between different ideologies of care and control and between notions of femininity and professionalism.

In contemporary health work, as we shall see, there are conflicting ideologies of nurse training and socialisation and of the nurse–patient relationship. Notions of patient participation and empowerment do not always mean, in everyday health practice, that the patient's voice will be heard. But the whole idea of 'the patient's voice' is itself the product of a particular way of thinking about and 'seeing' the patient. It was only in the 1930s and 1940s that the medical profession began to pay serious attention to patients' accounts and to persuade them to 'tell their stories'.

The relationship between nurses and their patients has shifted over time, even though it has always been seen in manuals and training programmes as a fundamental part of the nursing task. We noted earlier that task allocation characterised earlier types of nursing intervention, whereas today the emphasis has shifted to patient allocation. In the past 'caring for' as a prescribed sequence of tasks was the core of nursing work; in most contemporary health work, affective relationships are seen as integral and the 'therapeutic gaze' is seen as a central aspect of nursing (May, 1988).

It has been suggested (Armstrong, 1983b) that the use of the term 'relationship' to describe interactions between nurses and patients has misled us into assuming that empathy and intimacy were always present. In fact manuals of nursing up to the 1970s, whilst identifying the patient as 'an individual human being and not a case', emphasised the need for formality and detachment. The main focus was on the patient's physical needs:

The nurse's chief role was described as gaining the trust of the patient . . .
It is clear that the relationship was not construed as something dynamic, that led to problems of communication, of meanings and misunderstandings, of emotions and feelings. The nurse plays a part; the patient watches and hopefully is impressed. The passivity of both actors in the relationship is

confirmed by the role assigned the patient: he 'will abide by instructions and will cooperate in the carrying out of the treament'.

Armstrong (1983b)

By the end of the 1970s nursing theorists such as Kratz (1979) and Roper (1980) were emphasising that 'helping the patient to communicate', establishing an atmosphere of trust and intimacy and being aware of one's own emotional needs and anxieties were essential elements in nursing. Put another way, 'emotional labour' began to be viewed as a central aspect of nursing work. This shift followed that within medicine, which was from a conception of the patient as passive object to the patient as active subject. Nurses were now being asked to engage with and monitor the world of the patients' thoughts and feelings (and their own): 'From a simple concern with the care of the patient's bodily functions, nursing has started to become a surveillance apparatus which both monitors and evinces the patient's personal identity: in doing so it helps fabricate and sustain that very identity' (Armstrong, 1983b). By means of an academic discourse of subjectivity, drawn from the behavioural and social sciences, nurses as well as patients were 'fabricated'. The image of what the caring nurse should be – one which permeates nursing theory today – is thus highlighted as a recent invention. This notion of nursing as a discourse – embodying complex and shifting ways of conceptualising and practising nursing work – can be usefully applied to illuminate the whole history of the occupation.

We noted in Section 2.8 that the human sciences have played an important role in analysing – and thereby constructing – identities and relationships in health care. Sociology, like science, does not stand outside the social world, observing and recording relationships in a detached way. It is inevitably actively involved in the making and re-making of social identities and relationships. Consider, for example, the theories of Talcott Parsons (1951) about the doctor–patient relationship (see Section 10.7). His notion of the docile patient and the dominant doctor – the other party to the relationship, who diagnosed, treated and expected to be obeyed – fits with the 1960s textbook view of the nurse–patient relationship: the nurse is the active manager, the patient is the largely passive recipient of nursing care. You may also recall that Parsons' analysis has been subject to extensive criticism and reformulation since the 1950s. Much of this has focused on what is seen as his one-dimensional view of the patient, and there is now a growing body of research on the complexity of patient behaviour and the dynamics of patient action (see Sections 10.5 and 10.6). This in turn fits with the current view of patients as 'bio-psycho-social wholes' and with nursing as a set of intimate, emotionally complex, patient-focused, holistic interventions.

12.3 Becoming a nurse

Are nurses born or made? The ideology of nursing as an occupation emphasises the inherent virtues of character and spiritual values that make up 'the good nurse'. In reality nursing has always employed a heterogenous workforce. For example, in spite of the projected ideology of nursing in late Victorian times as a 'vocation', a majority of those who entered nursing came from other jobs, such as nannying, domestic service or factory work (Maggs, 1983). Women seem to have moved fairly freely in and out of nursing, undermining the claims of matrons that it was a unique, selfless and devotional occupation which entrants must view in vocational terms.

In recent times the job opportunities open to women have become much wider, and nursing has had to compete for entrants with industrial and commercial sectors, which often offered higher rates of pay. Wastage has been high, with qualified nurses leaving the occupation at a higher rate than new recruits entered it, although this trend showed signs of changing in the early 1990s. Entry to nursing still needs to be viewed in relation to broader social and industrial factors, for example the availability of other types of work. Recruitment levels may reflect attitudes in the wider community and the degree of isolation of that community, unemployment levels and general levels of educational attainment. These factors may not only influence recruitment but also shape trainees' attitudes to their work (Clarke, 1978).

However, the heaviest recruitment has traditionally been among school leavers, and for many of these young entrants nursing is seen as a long-desired career move rather than 'just a job'. One study of two groups of first year learners in a health authority reported that just under half of the recruits had wanted to nurse since childhood, although for one-fifth the decison to nurse was only taken in the year or so before starting training (Mackay, 1989). Almost all those interviewed had contact with a relative or friend who was a nurse. When interviewed, the students acknowledged the extent of hard work involved in nursing and commented on the need for dedication, but only a small minority spoke of having a vocation. This led Mackay to see vocation as being an ideology constructed through the student nurse training programme rather than as pre-existent in the minds of new entrants. Through training students were taught to believe that they were 'a breed apart', to accept that nurses were born not made and that if someone was born to be a nurse, this would show through in training:

The notion of vocation is weak amongst recruits and . . . is instilled during training. As the learners come into contact with demanding and trying situations their ability to 'take it' may be linked to the depth of their vocation for nursing. In other words, if you can't take it, you do not have a vocation for nursing. And if you can take it, you have obviously got a vocation.

Mackay (1989)

○ Consider the reasons for your own entry into nursing or another area of health work. To what extent did you feel you had a vocation?

A higher proportion of school leaving entrants report a long-standing interest in nursing as a career than older entrants, but there is little evidence that a widespread 'vocation to nurse' exists. On the other hand most entrants respond to the question 'Why do you want to be a nurse' by talking about wanting to 'care for people' and ease their suffering, which may be seen as a secularised version of a religious ethic. New entrants bring with them popular stereotypes of the job – from 'emptying bedpans and mopping up vomit' to 'being a Florence Nightingale'. They are also influenced by media images of what nurses are like, which run the whole gamut from 'angels' to black-stockinged temptresses (Salvage, 1985). There are fewer stereotypes of other health work occupations, although a popular image persists of dentists and opticians as 'failed doctors'. From my (unrepresentative) sample of health care students over the years the most widespread responses have been interest in the work and a wish to 'help people'.

Occupational socialisation

Most early accounts of occupational socialisation focused on medical education and were concerned with how occupations became professions. The functionalist approach to occupational socialisation has been preoccupied with the transmission of professional knowledge and culture to students, so that they learn in full the 'professional role' they will be required to enact. Merton *et al.*'s (1957) study of medical education assumes a coincidence of interest between the student and teacher – the teacher propounds and upholds the professional role which the student aspires to learn. Professional socialisation is seen as the relatively unproblematic acquisition of knowledge, skills and values, a view which fits with 'trait' theory (see Chapter 11, page 430, Box 11.2).

Interactionist critiques of this analysis have focused on what happens to students themselves during professional training, rather than on 'taking on the professional role'. These studies again tended to focus on medical students, but two early explorations of nurse training in the USA drew attention to important occupational characteristics. Olesen and Whittaker (1968) noted that the skills and attitudes learned during training may be quite different to those influencing qualified nurses. In training students need to survive by learning to cope with the demands of their tutors and with the different practice situations that they encounter; such skills are not required in the very different environment they move into after training is successfully completed. This directs our interest to the experiences of the students themselves, and to how they learn to cope and to survive.

A classic interactionist study in the 1970s drew attention to the process of change that occurred as students passed through training programmes; this was termed *doctrinal conversion* to signify that it involved students in internalising a completely new set of beliefs and attitudes about the activity of nursing (Davis, 1975). Davis developed a six stage model of status passage from 'initial innocence' to 'stable internalisation' (see Table 12.1). Since American nursing has been college based and academically oriented for much longer than in the UK, many of the stages may be familiar. For example, 'initial innocence' describes how new entrants bring with them the lay image of nursing as a 'secular . . . ethic of care, kindness and love for those who suffer'. Instead of being able to care in a practical way or being taught practical skills which will enable them to act like a 'real nurse', they are asked to observe and to learn to communicate with patients. In stage 2, 'labelled recognition of incongruity', this mismatch between their expectations of

TABLE 12.1 Model of nurse socialisation. Source: Davis (1975)

Student stage	Characterised by
Initial innocence on entry	Emphasis on doing/caring ethic
Labelled recognition of incongruity (first few weeks)	Clash between values of student (caring) and college (observing) makes students feel inadequate
Psyching out	'Putting on a front'; working out/ responding to teachers' demands and college 'doctrines' (that is, correct attitudes, values, behaviour)
Role simulation	Producing acceptable performances of the 'nurse' role to please staff; playing at being a nurse
Provisional internalisation (years 2 and 3)	Gradual shift from playing the part of a nurse to entering the role; shift from questioning to internalising the 'doctrine'
Stable internalisation	Professional self image created and doctrinal conversion complete

nurse training and the demands made on them by teaching staff leads some to consider leaving and others to stage 3 – the 'psyching out' of their teachers to discover what attitudes and behaviour are required to get through the course. In stage 4, 'role simulation', the students self consciously adopt the new role of being a nurse required by their teachers, in spite of their feelings of inadequacy and embarrassment at their own performance. As others accept and respond to this play-acting, however, the students become more accepting of the teachers' version of what a nurse is like. Davis suggests that this stage is reached by the end of year one of training; over the next two years the students move from the 'provisional internalisation' of institutionally sponsored and approved attitudes, behaviour and skills to their 'stable internalisation'. By this final stage students' lay images of nursing have been completely erased and so have the negative models they encountered in clinical settings. It is the college teachers' version of nursing that is accepted, and doctrinal conversion is complete.

○   Make notes on your own nurse (or other health work) training, indicating to what extent Davis' model is useful in identifying changing attitudes and values at different stages of training.

After trying this exercise with nursing and other health work students over many years, it is clear to me that many – both pre-registration students and qualified health workers reflecting on their training – do experience the stages of initial innocence and labelled incongruity. In Mackay's study (1989) half the learners had considered leaving in their first year. On the other hand many entrants have had some direct contact with nurses and many have undertaken voluntary or paid caring work, so they are not entirely 'innocent'; this seems to be particularly the case in mental handicap nursing. The development of a strong student subculture, in which there is a clear recognition of the need to satisfy the demands of the teachers and in which 'psyching out' and role simulation are undertaken collectively, is widespread too. In psychiatric nurse training this has been referred to as a 'social world' shared by students on the ward (Towell, 1976). Some qualified nurses have commented that it was only after having qualified that they felt able to move beyond mere play-acting to the stage of provisional internalisation. One reason for this may be that students are continually 'passing through', moving from ward to ward and encountering different models of nursing.

Until recently in the UK nursing was not college based to any extent, and nurses learned in hospital schools of nursing which were in close touch with clinical areas. Students spent relatively brief periods in the school and from the start of training spent substantial blocks of time as learners and assistants on the wards. Many nurses have reported that the real conflict was not between students' own image of nursing and that of their tutors, but between the ideology of nursing propounded on the ward and that in the school. Whereas in the US colleges the influence exercised over students by teachers was much stronger, in the UK it was undermined by their role as workers on the ward; the ward staff had greater influence, and the apprenticeship model of learning from staff in clinical settings was more prominent.

In the 1990s, as Project 2000 courses become the dominant mode of training, it is possible that Davis' model will become more appropriate. Students are spending increasing amounts of time in college or school, on academic studies, and once on the wards (after an initial period observing 'healthy people' in the community) they are acting as observers and assistants, learning techniques and communicating with patients rather than operating as 'pairs of hands'. They have supernumerary status until the last stages of training and are increasingly regarded by ward staff as students rather than as apprentices.

Learning and working

Nursing students have always found themselves caught between two worlds: the world of 'the school' and that of 'the ward'. After undertaking an initial, short block of 'theory' in the nursing school, students on traditional training courses went out on to the wards to encounter the 'practice' of ward staff. Much has been written about the confusion and 'cognitive dissonance' suffered by nursing students as they grappled with the sharply contrasting priorities and expectations of nurse tutors and ward staff. Kramer (1974) used the term 'reality shock' to define the situation in which students become aware of the gulf between the model of nursing presented in the school and the reality of work on the ward. In one study of three nurse education centres in South Wales, for example, the students drew clear distinctions between the 'school way' and the 'ward way' (Wilson and Startup, 1991). This reflected the gulf that was seen to exist between 'theory' and 'practice', whereby research based teaching about issues such as pain control or pre-operative fasting were directly contradicted by ward practices and norms 'written on tablets of stone'.

A mid-1980s study of occupational socialisation explored the experiences of students from two Scottish colleges of nursing who were eight, 18 and 30 months into their training (Melia, 1987). For these students, at whatever stage of training, a major feature of their accounts was the division between 'the idealized version of work as it is presented to new recruits and the work as it is practised daily by members of the occupation' (Melia, 1987). At one level this is about the conflict between, for example, the school-taught methods of lifting or bathing and the more unorthodox techniques used on the ward. At another, such conflicts are part of a struggle between the education side and the service side over priorities. At a fundamental level, as Melia suggests, the conflicts reflect segmentation in the occupation of nursing, of which the two main segments are 'service' and 'education', each projecting its own particular version of what nursing is, that is:

An historic compromise between the provision of a nursing service and the education of nurses. This compromise makes student nurses both learners and workers. The compromise is rooted in the way in which the nursing service operates in Britain, that is by employing large numbers of students who work under the direction of a much smaller number of qualified staff.

Melia (1987)

In the 1990s, as we have noted, Project 2000 courses have moved nurse training onto a new basis, with a more academic, college based start to training, supernumerary status and the expansion of the health care assistant role to provide the hands-on labour once undertaken by students. But this process will be a slow one, and it is by no means certain how far traditional conflicts between 'school' and 'ward' will be neutralised. One recent study of the implementation of Project 2000 in a Midlands health authority reported a degree of conflict between traditionally trained nurses and Project 2000 students, as well as some scepticism about the new-style training among trainers and managers (Elkan and Robinson, 1991).

○ Reflect on your own training for nursing (or for another type of health work) and note down whether conflicts existed between education and clinical staff. Suggest why they did or why not.

It is very difficult to generalise about nurse education let alone about health work in general because it is still in the process of change, so the comments here must be seen as provisional. As a teacher involved in one of the early pilot scheme courses for Project 2000, it is clear to me that cultural conflict between the college and the clinical area will not magically disappear; their priorities and rationale are, and will remain, very different. For example, for clinical staff adequate cover, appropriate care and maintaining efficiency are central concerns, whereas tutors hope to provide a sound educational experience for their students; many also hope to change ward practices and norms. There is a great risk that students are being seen as the catalysts of change in the clinical area, when it is really hospital structures and qualified personnel who need to be transformed. Leonard and Jowett (1990) have argued that students cannot be expected to change the existing nursing culture, since they are also seeking to be accepted into that culture: 'Without an adequate support structure, the vulnerability of their situation as novices, and their dependence on personal acceptance for achieving integration into the teams they have to work with, can make a role as catalyst for change untenable'.

Moreover, there has already been some revision of the conditions and extent of supernumerary status: for example, the notion of acting as 'observers' is not unambiguous and may actually create difficulties for students in their relations with clinical staff. Willmott's (1990) study of the views of traditional RGN and undergraduate nursing students suggests that the latter group – who had been supernumerary for many years – perceived disadvantages as well as advantages in this status (see Table 12.2). It is also possible that the NHS trusts will exercise more, not less, control over nurse education in the future. As colleges bid for contracts they will have to satisfy trusts that their programmes of study will produce nurses who are trained appropriately.

Whether students are observers or participants in clinical areas, it seems likely that the process of 'learning to be a nurse' will remain problematic. Wilson and Startup (1991) note how students' values and priorities in their first year of training differed from those of qualified staff and tutors. Whereas students valued empathy and communication

TABLE 12.2 Perceived advantages and disadvantages of supernumerary status. Source: Wilmott, in Elkan and Robinson (1991)

Advantages	Frequency*
Able to observe procedures on and off the ward	9
Able to leave the ward for lectures	5
Able to fulfil set aims and objectives	5
Weren't used as 'pairs of hands'	4
Able to question accepted practices	3
More time to learn	3
Could arrange 'off duty' to make most of learning opportunities	2
Only given responsibility related to level of experience	2
Gained a holistic impression of patient care	1

Disadvantages	Frequency*
Not included in ward team	10
Misused due to misunderstanding of the course by ward staff	8
Discriminated against/excluded due to supernumerry status	7
Resented by ward staff and GSNs (General Student Nurses, ie traditional RGN student nurses)	4
Seen as an elitist group	3
Seen as different as worked different hours	3
Had to fight to gain acceptance	3
Were undervalued	2
Didn't get enough experience of high pressure work	1
Lack of agreement on whose job it was to teach us	1

*Sample size = 13

highly – aspects of 'emotional labour' that we have seen coming to the fore in nursing texts – these were less valued by qualified staff and tutors and by students at the end of their training. By contrast, dedication became seen as more important as training progressed. Above all, qualified and teaching staff valued 'mixing well and having a pleasant personality', qualities which became increasingly valued by students as they moved through the course: 'This was the item most often referred to as an attribution of a good nurse by teaching staff as well as by sisters and charge nurses' (Wilson and Startup, 1991). This puts another slant on the notion, discussed above, that nurses are 'born, not made'.

'Getting through the work'?

We noted earlier (in Section 12.2) that the conceptualisation of nursing has not remained constant; in the 1970s a new emphasis on communication skills, empathy and patient-focused care entered nursing textbooks, and the notion of nursing as a series of tasks to be completed fell out of favour (Armstrong, 1983b). Nursing models and theories emphasised nursing as 'process-oriented' work which involved systematic observation, planning, implementation and evaluation of care. It was part of an attempt to create a knowledge base which was independent of medicine, which conceptualised nursing as an autonomous activity and which could claim to be scientific in its approach. Project 2000, with its academic orientation, diploma award and student status, represented the generalisation of this conception of professionalised nursing in nurse training.

In order to consider how far nursing practice has been redefined 'on the ground' as well as being reconceptualised at a theoretical level it is useful to explore the attitudes and experiences of students, because they straddle the two domains of education and clinical practice. Clarke (1978) used the phrase 'getting through the work' to characterise the attitude to their work of nurses (psychiatric and enrolled nurses, auxiliaries and students) in a large nursing home. Constant activity was seen as the appropriate response, and nursing was defined in terms of physical tasks. Studies in the late 1980s indicate that there was no general institutional shift in the hospital sector towards process allocation, even though the nursing process was in general use in hospitals by this time. The extent to which this had become bureaucratised as a series of form-filling tasks is a matter of debate, but Melia's (1987) study in Scotland and Wilson and Startup's (1991) study in Wales reach very similar conclusions about the dominance of traditional concepts of nursing and their acceptance by students. For example, it was clear that students welcomed the emphasis on routines; they 'like sameness and routine . . . they feel secure as they know what to do' (Wilson and Startup,

1991). Although students entered the clinical area valuing process and communication skills, they shifted towards putting more emphasis on tasks.

In a similar way, the students in Melia's (1987) study accepted the 'unwritten rules' of the wards – often learned from nursing auxiliaries – that getting through the work, working quickly, pulling your weight and looking busy were the most highly valued qualities. By contrast, talking was not seen as working on many wards; where it was valued, some students spoke of being 'allowed' to talk to patients, suggesting that they had internalised the notion that physical labour was more important. The importance of routines and task allocation can be appreciated in clinical situations where keeping ahead, in case a crisis should arise, is of real importance and where understaffing is often a problem (Mackay, 1989). Nonetheless, it does suggest that students on the wards may have learned to disregard the patient allocation approach (Melia, 1987). Until we have more studies of the impact of Project 2000 it is difficult to tell whether a shift in these values will occur.

On the other hand these approaches were cross-cut with other categories signifying the status of the work undertaken. Here students ranked physical tasks lower, as 'just basic nursing care', and valued 'theory', by which they meant learning about diseases and medical knowledge, more highly. 'Real nursing' was identified as technical or surgical, whereas care of the elderly was seen as 'not really nursing' (Melia, 1987). It is unclear how far Project 2000 will reinforce or undermine such categorisations and approaches to the work. On the one hand students should be given more guidance and support to sustain the 'ideal model' of nursing when they enter the clinical area. On the other various doubts have been voiced about the practical capability of the new nurses, the 'over-academic' emphasis of the new courses and the danger that nursing, instead of valuing 'holistic nursing care', will create qualified nurse practitioners who are substitute (and much cheaper) doctors.

Nurse education is a battleground, not just for different models of nursing – those of the college and the clinical area – but for broader struggles about what nursing should be. 'Becoming a nurse' is not a stable experience, but one which has shifted over time as changing beliefs and values have redefined the role of both the nurse and the patient. Nursing as an occupation is 'socially constructed'; the knowledge and skills projected as desirable in a 'good nurse' today are markedly different from those of 30 years ago. In this sense nursing is responding to shifts in social and economic conditions, which have altered the position of women in the workforce and made nursing a less attractive career. The Project 2000 strategy, in transforming the curriculum and attempting to cut high wastage and falling recruitment, represents both a conceptual and a strategic attack aimed at reversing the decline of nursing.

12.4 The social organisation of nursing work

Nursing work is carried out in a wide range of settings and by many different types of nurses. Until very recently student nurses performed most of the hands-on care in hospitals, together with nursing auxiliaries. Now the latter group, working with health care assistants, will provide this basic care. But nursing does not take place only in hospitals but in a range of community settings. For example, domiciliary care is delivered by midwives, health visitors and community nurses; community psychiatric and mental handicap nurses provide day-care and hostel visits; growing numbers of trained and untrained health workers provide care in private residential and nursing homes. Within hospital settings 'nursing' can mean very different things, for example in an intensive care unit, in an accident and emergency department and in a care of the elderly ward. Although much of the basic nursing care remains the same, the types of interventions and the social character, structuring and organisation of the work will differ considerably.

For this reason the analysis will both focus on common themes and issues in nursing work and try to illustrate some of its diversity. This section will consider social aspects of work organisation and control, and Section 12.5 will consider relationships with patients in terms of the elaboration of nursing as 'women's work', 'caring', 'emotional labour' and 'bodily management'.

The division of labour in contemporary nursing

Class, race and gender divisions characterise the contemporary health service, reproducing, as Lesley Doyal (1979) has commented, 'the class, sexual and racial divisions in the wider society'. Nursing, in which a minority of qualified SRN nurses, health visitors and midwives direct the work of SEN nurses, students, auxiliaries and health care assistants, also reflects this social division of labour. Nearly 90 per cent of its workforce is female (see Table 12.3), but male nurses hold many key managerial jobs. A disproportionate number of low paid auxiliaries and SEN nurses are black women, while white women form the overwhelming proportion of SRNs and above in the general hospital sector. By contrast, in sectors dealing with mental illness, mental handicap and subnormality, and geriatrics – where long-stay hospitals have now been largely closed down – there has been a heavy

TABLE 12.3 Nursing and midwifery staff: by sex and specialty, 1989 (England). Source: DoH (1990)

Hospitals	Female	Male	Males as % of females
General	179 920	10 420	5.8
Care of the elderly	46 910	1 920	4.1
Mental illness	44 540	18 660	41.9
Midwifery	21 690	60	0.3
Mental handicap	26 910	8 400	31.2
Paediatrics	11 540	270	2.3
Maternity	11 540	30	0.3
Education	5 390	1 880	34.9
Primary health care	50 500	830	1.6

representation of nurses born overseas. Writing in the 1970s, before the long-stay hospital closure programme gathered speed, Doyal argued that overseas nurses have been used:

To compensate for the shortage of British recruits into notoriously underpaid and often unpleasant work. Their role as a reserve army has recently been demonstrated with particular clarity by the fact that because of high levels of unemployment among British nurses, overseas nurses are increasingly being refused a renewal of their work permits.

Doyal (1979)

Black and minority ethnic recruits, as we noted in Chapter 8, have suffered considerable discrimination and harassment since the first recruits entered the new National Health Service in the 1950s. It is not just that Afro-Caribbean entrants were too often shunted off into enrolled nurse training rather than being allowed onto registered nurse training courses (GLARE, 1987). In addition to this, as Smith (1991) noted in her study of a London teaching hospital school of nursing, black and minority ethnic candidates have found it difficult to gain admission to higher status registered nurse courses – at least until the increasing shortage of school leavers in the mid-1980s made recruitment a problem. The ideologies of nursing, whether they projected nursing as a vocation or profession, can be seen to contain hidden racist assumptions about the desirability of selecting white – as well as middle class – candidates. By contrast, where the ideology of custodialism was predominant (in psychiatric, mental handicap and prison hospitals) considerable numbers of black and minority ethnic staff – particularly men from South East Asia – were recruited.

Feminist theorists have highlighted nursing as gendered work, in which stereotypes of what is 'natural' and 'normal' combine together to delineate women's role. We noted in Section 12.1 that the cluster of skills associated with nursing conveniently 'matches' the skills it is claimed that women possess: caring, nurturing, empathy and so on. Feminists have argued that women's work, such as paid and unpaid caring, has long been downgraded as instinctive or biological, whereas it should be recognised as skilled and of equal or greater value to society than men's work. Applied to nursing, this has resulted in the highlighting of women's exploitation as paid carers, but there has been less recognition of the position of men in nursing, of black nurses and of class difference and status.

In the health sector the use of migrant and female labour has helped to keep costs down. At the same time class and racial divisions in the workforce have helped to keep nursing divided. In the 1990s Project 2000 seems more about creating a professional elite in nursing than about improving the conditions for all those who provide nursing care. It may well serve to create a top tier of Project 2000 nurse practitioners and managers, underneath which is a new hierarchy of RGN nurses, SENs, nursing auxiliaries and health care assistants. Indeed some critics argue that the introduction of health care assistants will prove to be a return to the old SEN grade nurse, which the nursing professional bodies have pledged to get rid of by using conversion courses (Elkan and Robinson, 1991).

Men have also been subject to stereotyping – in particular as being effeminate or gay – if they entered nursing. Their employment in more custodial roles in mental and mental handicap hospitals and their recruitment from predominantly working class backgrounds (with a strong trade union orientation) created conflicts and tensions between psychiatric and general nursing which have not been entirely overcome (Colledge, 1979). Male students report that gender stereotyping on the ward is not uncommon, with male nursing students in their white coats being seen as more important and knowledgeable than females. Other professional staff also expect males to be more competent and confident (Wright and Hearn, 1993).

The place of nursing in health work

Medical sociology, preoccupied with the role of doctors, has only belatedly interested itself in nursing work. Nursing was seen as confined to assisting doctors, and the nursing role was seen as largely unproblematic. Whereas doctors had 'functional autonomy' – that is, 'a position of legitimate control over work' – nurses and most other health workers did not exercise such control; they were in a position of *subordination* (Freidson, 1970). As Gamarnikow (1978) has pointed out,

Nightingale's conception of the nurses' role was to assist the doctor, much as the wife might help her husband. The subordination of nurses was both patriarchal and technological. It was doctors who defined sickness, prescribed treatment and regulated the relationship between experts and patients. It was the medical profession that controlled the health division of labour, taking the lead in determining the work to be undertaken by nurses, physiotherapists, radiographers and so on.

The subordination of nurses to doctors in formal terms has – until quite recently – been reinforced by social and sexual politics. Nursing textbooks advised nurses to co-operate with doctors and to maintain a united front in face of the patient. The result has been that 'the traditional dominant-subservient relationship between doctors and nurses remained unchallenged for many decades. Rooted as it is in status differentials, the position of women in society, differences in education and remuneration, and the tendency of nursing to be an adjunct to medicine, this relationship has become deeply entrenched (Dingwall and McIntosh, 1978).

The doctor–nurse game

Research by Stein (1978) appeared to confirm the formal subordination of nurses, yet at the same time highlighted the very considerable degree of informal influence and power exerted by them over medical staff. Not surprisingly, nurses' knowledge of patients' needs and treatment is likely to be useful since they provide 24-hour care and get to know patients more intimately whereas doctors (particularly junior ones) rotate fairly swiftly round the specialties. Stein examines the process whereby nurses transmit advice and make suggestions regarding treatment without violating what he terms 'the rules of the game':

> The cardinal rule of the game is that open disagreement must be avoided at all costs. Thus, the nurse can communicate her recommendation without appearing to be making a recommendation statement. The physician, in requesting a recommendation from a nurse, must do so without appearing to be asking for it.
>
> Stein (1978)

Stein suggests that the origins of the game lie in the training for 'omnipotence' undertaken by the doctor and the training for 'subservience' of the nurse. The reward for playing the game well is not only an efficient doctor–nurse alliance, but mutual respect and admiration and the maintenance of the formal status quo (see Box 12.2). It continues because the work culture and power relationships – including sexual politics – reinforce it.

○   Consider how far Stein's notion of the doctor–nurse game can be related to your experiences of health work. The extract in Box 12.2 will give you a taste of one such negotiation.

BOX 12.2 The doctor–nurse game. Source: Stein (1978)

This is Dr Jones.	*An open and direct communication*
Dr Jones, this is Miss Smith on 2W. Mrs Brown, who learned today of her father's death, is unable to fall asleep.	*This message has two levels. Openly, it describes a set of circumstances, a woman who is unable to fall asleep and who that morning received word of her father's death. Less openly, but just as directly, it is a diagnostic and recommendation statement; Mrs Brown is unable to sleep because of her grief, and she should be given a sedative. Dr Jones, accepting the diagnostic statement and replying to the recommendation statement, answers . . .*
What sleeping medication has been helpful to Mrs Brown in the past?	*Dr Jones, not knowing the patient, is asking for a recommendation from the nurse, who does know the patient, about what sleeping medication should be prescribed. Note, however, his question does not appear to be asking her for a recommendation. Miss Smith replies . . .*
Pentobarbital mg 100 was quite effective night before last.	*A disguised recommendation statement. Dr Jones replies with a note of authority in his voice . . .*
Pentobarbital mg 100 before bedtime as needed for sleep, got it?	*Miss Smith ends the conversation with the tone of the grateful supplicant . . .*
Yes I have, and thank you very much doctor.	

Many qualified nurses have recognised this representation of relationships only too well, in spite of the fact that Stein was writing about nursing in the USA. They are much more forceful than Stein about the gendering of power. They have suggested that the game is played in several different ways, more and less covertly depending on the care setting. In some areas, such as psychiatry, there is more of a team relationship between health professionals, whereas in others, such as general medicine or surgery, there may be a more hierarchical structure. Students have reported most conflict in accident and emergency wards, where junior doctors often have great responsibility but little knowledge when they start, and where nurses build up considerable specialist skill.

More recent research has substantially modified the rather one-dimensional game model (Porter, 1991; Hughes, 1988). Here situational factors are seen to be crucial determinants of how and to what extent the game is played. In the British casualty department studied by Hughes the volume of admissions, rapid turnover of medical staff and high proportion of overseas doctors (whose different cultural background made communication and diagnosis difficult) all increased the power of the nurses. Their involvement in decision making was overt and deliberate, although formal diagnostic control remained with the doctor. Porter's (1991) study of an intensive care unit (ICU) in Ireland found a range of versions of the doctor–nurse game, from what he termed 'unproblematic subordination' through to 'informal overt decision making' (see Box 12.3). In this latter category nurses in ICU actually made and implemented medical decisions (such as the decision to stop giving morphine). But the 'formal overt decision making' power of nurses via the nursing process and the care plan was 'profoundly underused': 'It seems as if it functioned more as a legal document than as an aid to nursing care' (Porter, 1991). His general conclusion is that gender inequality is losing some of its power in nurse–doctor relationships, but that gender conflict may be growing in other areas of health work, for example in the relationship between male nurse managers and female workers (Porter, 1992).

12.5 Health worker–patient interaction

A range of social and structural factors influences the way that health workers and patients relate to each other. The nature of the illness and its duration, the type of treatment and level of technology, the place of treatment, all influence interaction. The organisation of the health care institution, if care takes place in an institutional setting, and the hierarchies of control that exist may encourage or discourage intimacy. It is much easier for patients to talk freely and disclose intimate information if they feel at ease, in their own surroundings rather than in the formal and institutional setting of the hospital clinic. Part of the antagonism felt by some women towards hospitalised maternity care has stemmed from their experience of dehumanising hospital antenatal clinics and routinised care during childbirth (Oakley, 1984; House of Commons Health Committee Report, 1992). As we have noted in earlier chapters, the social class background, cultural affiliations, gender, age and political views of the individual patient and health worker may also operate to enable or to inhibit interaction. The particular circumstances

BOX 12.3 Typologies of doctor–nurse relationships. Source: Porter (1991)

Unproblematic subordination

Unproblematic subordination is the traditional interpretation of nurse–doctor interaction and involves nurses' unquestioning obedience of medical orders, and the complete absence of nursing input into the decision-making process. Instances where a medical order was given without prior consultation or explanation, where nurses carried out that order without further negotiation and where no alternative explanation could be posited for their apparent subservience, were classified as belonging to this type.

Informal overt decision making

Informal overt decision making involves breakdowns of nursing deference and the overt involvement of nurses in decision making. Interactions where this occurred and where nurses' involvement was not sanctioned by the use of the nursing process were categorized as belonging to this model.

Informal covert decision making

Informal covert decision making involves the pretence of unproblematic subordination, whereby nurses show respect for doctors and refrain from open disagreement with them or making direct recommendations or diagnoses, while at the same time attempting to have an input into decision-making processes. Situations where nurses made recommendations without appearing to do so by using statements about patients' conditions as substitutes, where doctors requested or accepted recommendations in the same fashion and where there was no other feasible explanation for their actions, were classified as belonging to this type.

Formal overt decision making

The nursing process, with its stages of data collection, diagnosis, planning, treatment and evaluation, has officially been implemented throughout the north of Ireland. Every patient admitted to hospital is the subject of a nursing care plan, whereby all the stages cited above are formulated, written up and subsequently revised daily. Needless to say, if such a system was working in the fashion proposed by its progenitors, nurses would have attained a major decision-making role.

of their meeting and what meanings they attribute to it and to each other's contribution will be important too.

This section examines some common themes in discussions of patient and health worker interaction and highlights the influence of social factors, roles and statuses. Relationships of various kinds exist between health workers and patients, and these are distinctive and different from other types of relationships. This does not mean that all health work relationships are the same. That between nurse and patient will differ from that between doctor and patient; moreover, the relationship between an individual nurse and patient will be particular and will have unique features. In fact, because of the ambiguity of 'relationship' most research has focused on more observable – or at least less elusive – interaction between health workers and patients.

Medical sociologists have conceptualised health professional–patient interaction in a variety of ways. We noted in Section 12.2 that Armstrong's (1983b) analysis of the nurse–patient relationship draws attention to its shifting epistemological basis: that is, to how the whole nature of the nurse–patient relationship becomes reconceptualised in nursing literature in the 1960s and 1970s, although the continued use of the term 'relationship' implies that its meaning remained stable. This social constructionist account draws attention to the way in which the social sciences themselves have 'fabricated' the nurse–patient relationship; we noted how Parsons' (1951) conceptualisation of doctors and patients was primarily focused on the professional role. In functionalism the patient role was largely to be obedient and responsive – in ways that the doctor required and controlled. Interactionist sociologists and ethnomethodologists, on the other hand, have emphasised negotiation and conflict; they have played an important part in creating the 'active patient', the subject rather than the object of study. In their research patients are individuals who negotiate their social world. Their motivations and their actions are complex, and it is the role of interpretive sociology to tease out, construct and sustain the personal identity of each individual actor.

○   Suggest how the terms 'health behaviour' and 'health action' (see Section 10.6) reflect differences between studying patients as objects or as subjects.

Health behaviour focuses on people's socially predictable responses to illness, whereas health action emphasises the complexity and diversity of individual actions taken in situations where a 'disturbance in equilibrium' is perceived (Dingwall, 1976). Studies of health behaviour accumulate quantitative data which aggregates individual responses into numbers and percentages; they tend to view people as objects, as the raw data from which, after analysis, statistically valid conclusions can be drawn. In contrast to this, interactionist and other interpretive accounts are concerned to expose and sustain the subjective identity of the individual person. Carried to its logical conclusion, it would become very difficult to make any kind of generalisation, because of the unique nature of each individual.

A negotiated order

Interactionists have interpreted how people make sense of social situations through the use of various techniques and models which try to explain interactions, while acknowledging the unique character of each. For example, Goffman (1974) developed the theory of *frame analysis* to interpret the complex and seemingly infinite array of social actions that occur. He suggests that people rely on a range of 'primary frameworks' in order to locate, identify and label situations. Each social actor frames the situation, based on past socialisation, social experience and understanding, and actors work together to establish its structure and scope. For example, when patients visit the practice nurse at the health centre they act in ways which are framed by both the nurse's and their own shared view of the appropriate form of this type of interaction. This may involve the use of particular kinds of language, gestures and verbal interchanges, such as formalised greetings and farewells or asking standard questions. Nurse and patient negotiate within a largely taken-for-granted 'primary framework', which enables the actors to be aware of and to interpret social experiences and which structure and define those experiences. Having said this, Goffman also emphasises the uniqueness of each encounter; it is not just as nurse and patient that individuals negotiate, but as people, as subjective beings. Inter-subjective negotiation takes place within many different frames, and within each framework a whole range of different factors will be significant.

Understanding of primary social frameworks, which are accumu-lated on the basis of past experience, enable people to act appropriately and comfortably. In difficult and intrusive work, such as health work, this can defuse potentially hazardous situations. For example, health professionals use particular forms of language and procedures in relation to intimate physical examinations of patients, and these operate to keep sexual readings out of the frame.

○ Suggest some examples of situations you have encountered where special procedures are used to 'defuse' the situation.

There are a numbers of situations in health work where rituals and defined procedures are used, some of which we will investigate below. Part of nursing work, in particular, involves touching of intimate parts of the patient's body or helping the patient to carry out basic bodily tasks which are usually undertaken in privacy. You might have mentioned ritualised admission procedures, or learning special routines for bed-bathing or special procedures for the 'laying out' of dead patients.

In relation to dying, health workers can be seen to operate within primary frameworks which on the basis of clinical judgement and past experience encapsulate the patient's likely career. This is not unlike the 'dying trajectory' which Glaser and Strauss (1968) have argued that staff construct for each patient. Predictions are made about the speed and probable character of the dying process and about when 'nothing more can be done' to change the outcome. Problems can occur for inexperienced ward staff when this trajectory alters, leaving them unprepared at 'critical junctures': for example, with inappropriate treatment continuing, the patient unprepared or relatives not alerted (Strauss, 1993). A study of the social organisation of dying in two large North American hospitals suggested that patients are labelled as 'dying' only if they satisfy certain criteria, and that younger patients were much less likely to be so labelled (Sudnow, 1967). Such labels act as signals to health workers, so that before 'clinical death' has taken place 'social death' may already have been signalled. The patient may no longer be given medical treatment, personal belongings may be tidied away and the relatives may be prepared. In Sudnow's study one nurse was found trying to close the eyes of a patient before death because it was sometimes difficult to achieve afterwards, and she knew that this would distress the relatives. Dying, therefore, is a socially constructed process which involves complex negotiations between health professionals, the patient and their relatives.

The idea of health professional–patient interaction as 'negotiated order' is fundamental in interpretive sociology. Obviously the degree to which negotiation is possible will vary greatly; think of the different circumstances in which the unconscious patient in intensive care and the chronically sick person in their own home are cared for. Women giving birth in their own homes were treated by midwives more as partners in care and could be more assertive than women undergoing hospital confinements. There was much more 'give-and-take' over procedures, with women successfully resisting routines which were commonplace in hospitals (Kirkham, 1983). Strong's (1979) account of the 'ceremonial' order of the clinic suggests that the degree of negotiation possible depends stongly on situational variables. Children, for example, were in some ways better able to break through conventions than adult patients, from whom a standardised 'patient role' was expected.

Aspects of emotional labour

Contemporary nursing lays great emphasis on communication and negotiation between nurses and patients, through the nursing process, patient allocation systems and nursing theory. Health workers of all types are being urged – by social and behavioural scientists as well as by professional tutors – to become actively involved in building positive relationships with patients. Psychology, sociology and communication are on the curriculum; the affective components of nursing – subjectivity and emotions – are emphasised. Although the rhetoric of the nursing process is largely about individualised care and emotional labour, we have noted how assumptions of a coincidence between 'caring for' and 'caring about' have given affective relationships a low status compared with medical knowledge and technical care (see Section 12.1). Smith (1991) commented in her study of a London teaching hospital school of nursing that students 'described the nursing process as a work method rather than in conceptual terms related to its underlying framework of living activities, communication and affective/psychological patient care'.

Several recent studies have highlighted some of the problems as well as advantages in incorporating more sensitive 'emotional labour' into health work. Consider the sensitive area of touch, for example. Therapeutic touch is part of a long tradition of healing in health work and is still quite widely used in alternative medicine (Pietroni, 1990). The touching of patients by nursing staff is inevitable, given the wide range of physical interventions involved in caring for very sick people: bathing, toileting, bed-making and so on. Yet research indicates that, in relation to elderly patients at least, touch is rarely used as a therapeutic device. McCann and McKeown (1993), in a study of elderly patients, found that over 95 per cent of touches by nursing staff were 'instrumental': that is, almost all touching was in order to deliver physical care rather than to offer comfort or demonstrate intimacy. Two similar studies of elderly patients found that four-fifths or more of touches were instrumental, and less than one-fifth could be classified as 'expressive' (Le May and Redfern, 1987; Oliver and Redfern, 1991).

Certain tentative conclusions can be drawn: students used expressive touch rather more than other staff, suggesting that expressive dimensions were valued more highly by them than by trained staff. Since we have already noted that students put a higher value on talking to patients, perhaps this is not surprising. Does the increasing value placed on 'getting through the work' as responsibilities mount squeeze out these potentially therapeutic elements of nursing? Another important issue to consider is the cultural significance of touching. The studies reported that some patients were uneasy when expressive touching took place, and it would clearly be unwise to assume that expressive touching was necessarily 'a good thing'. Savage (1987) deplores the unfortunate 'moves within nursing to attempt some sort of standardisation in the use of expressive touch', commenting that, while it is useful, 'it cannot become a tenet of nursing that the nurse should touch or hold patients according to some preformulated plan. Expressive touch arises from empathy and from a genuine regard for the person one is moved to touch'. We need to know far more about patients' attitudes to touch; for some social groups and subcultures touch is deeply significant or problematic, whereas for others it may be more acceptable. It may be that students were less aware of the problematic side of touching than other staff.

Some of the challenge of emotional labour in health work may be illustrated by considering issues related to sexuality. 'Expressing sexuality' is one of the twelve activities of living described in Roper *et al.*'s (1980) model of the nursing process. But there is still a tendency to regard patients as somehow asexual – as if when people become sick these needs can be safely ignored. Webb (1985) discusses how some nursing staff find it difficult to deal with sexuality, both in terms of sharing information and offering support about the effects of specific surgical or medical treatments, and in a more general sense of maintaining patients' self concept and self esteem. Nursing has a history 'fraught with sexual repression and stereotyping', and patients find difficulties as well:

Talking about sexuality is hard for many people because social mores are not conducive to frank discussion of personal, intimate and possibly threatening subjects, even in families or between sexual partners. It can be easier to 'open up' about feelings or reveal a lack of understanding to a sympathetic stranger, and nurses who are skilled communicators and present a warm and non-judgemental manner can act as facilitators for patients.

Webb (1985)

Webb comments on the wide range of advice and information that health workers in particular specialist areas might require and the variable degree to which it is actually given. In gynaecology wards, for example, where her own research was carried out, women were sometimes given only brief hints after hysterectomies that they should 'take it easy' and no advice about resuming sexual activity was offered (Webb, 1983). In a follow-up study of gynaecology patients Webb (1986) found herself supplying a considerable amount of information about very basic aspects of the operation and its effects. In Chapter 8 we noted that British Asian mothers having their third or fourth baby in hospital were treated negatively by nursing staff who held ethnocentric or racist views about 'correct' family size. Similar judgemental attitudes about teenage pregnancies and repeat abortions have been expressed by health workers (Macintyre, 1977).

Dealing with issues of sexuality is an aspect of emotional labour which has not featured much at all in the nursing curriculum; in this it reflects traditional attitudes of secrecy about sex. The students interviewed by Savage (1987) reported the difficulties experienced by tutors in teaching about sexuality, which was felt by some students to be inadequate. Although nursing theories proposed that nurses should be sexually at ease with themselves in order to assist their patients, there was little open discussion of sexual orientation. Tutors and ward staff made assumptions that all nurses and patients were heterosexual.

Students also noted the lack of support for nurses on the ward when trying to implement what might be very stressful patient-focused care in sexual matters.

From a feminist perspective health workers have viewed greater emotional involvement with clients as encouraging a democratisation of the professional role, and as an essential part of the creation of the patient as a subject rather than the object of study (Roberts, 1981a). Becoming more involved with patients means listening to them, respecting their wishes and acting as their advocate, even when this undermines professional authority and is painful or difficult. Meeting patients' emotional needs may involve some personal cost. When district nurses have formed close and supportive relationships, the withdrawal of treatment – and of their visits – may be distressing for both parties (Twomey, 1986).

A recent large-scale research study in eight clinical areas of a city hospital in Canada indicated that 'the relationship that is established between the nurse and the patient is the result of interplay or covert negotiations until a mutually satisfying relationship is reached' (Morse, 1991). It concluded that not only is building relationships a matter of establishing trust, which may be time-consuming and difficult, but also that there is no 'model' of an ideal affective relationship. The research findings suggested four main types of relationships, ranging from a 'clinical relationship', where the patient has a minor illness and contact is brief, to 'over-involved relationships', where 'the nurse is committed to the patient as a person, and this over-rides the nurse's commitment to the treatment regime, the physician, the institution and its need, and her nursing responsibilities toward other patients. She is a confidant of the patient and is treated as a member of the patient's family' (Morse, 1991). In between lie the 'therapeutic nurse–patient relationship', a fairly short term interaction in which the nurse views the patient within the 'patient role' first and only secondarily as a 'person', and the 'connected relationship', in which this order is reversed, largely because a longer term interaction takes place (see Table 12.4).

○ Comment on these four types of relationship in the light of your own experience of nursing or other health work. Which do you think is the most appropriate as an 'ideal type' of health worker–patient relationship?

The four main relationships point up some of the problems of an increased emphasis on emotional labour in health work today. First, the through-put of patients is now so great in many British hospitals that many relationships will neccessarily remain at the clinical level. The second type of relationship – the therapeutic nurse–patient relationship – Morse suggests is seen as 'ideal' by Canadian managers and educators. The nurse does not get involved with the patient as a person to any

TABLE 12.4 Four types of nurse–patient relationship. Source: Morse (1991)

Characteristics	Types of relationship			
	Clinical	Therapeutic	Connected	Over-involved
Time	Short/transitory	Short/average	Lengthy	Long-term
Interaction	Perfunctory/rote	Professional	Intensive/close	Intensive/intimate
Patient's needs	Minor Treatment-oriented	Needs met Minor–moderate	Extensive/crisis 'Goes the extra mile'	Enormous needs
Patient's trust	Nurse's competence	Nurse's competence Tests trustworthiness	Nurse's competence and confides Consults on treatment decisions	Complete: 'puts their life in the nurse's hands'
Nurse's perspective of the patient: patient's perspective of own role	Only in patient role	First: in patient role Second: in patient role	First: as a person Second: in patient role	Only as a person
Nursing commitment	Professional commitment	Professional commitment Patient's concerns secondary	Patient's concerns primary Treatment concerns secondary	Committed to patient only as a person Treatment goals discarded

extent, and limits her/himself to meeting 'normal' psycho-social needs, for example for reassurance before surgery. Yet it seems that nursing theories are encouraging nurses to move beyond these confines toward the connected relationship, seeing the patient first and foremost as a person. Morse describes such a relationship, in which a woman gave birth to an anacephalic baby and the nurse 'bent' the rules by responding to the mother's plea to be allowed out of bed to nurse the baby in a rocking chair in its brief hour of life.

Most nurses will enter all four types of relationships at some point in their careers; negotiating the level and nature of involvement depends on personal attitudes and situational factors, such as length of stay, shifts and specialisation, which might disrupt established inter-action. Learning to build trust, give support and balance commitment to an individual as person and as patient may be a long process: 'Wise nurses, experienced nurses learned painfully, by trial and error, how to find the right level of involvement in a relationship' (Morse, 1991).

Routines and procedures

Whether health work takes place in hospitals, in the home or in 'community' settings, patients are likely to encounter routines. These have several functions: to exert control over staff themselves; to enable health professionals to control the flow of work in the most convenient way; and to socialise patients into a patient role, which involves accommodating themselves to waiting, providing information, obeying instructions and so on. For example, pregnant women at their first visit to the antenatal clinic undergo a standardised examination – both physical and in question form. This subtle form of *bodily management* reduces the woman to a 'pregnant patient' as her only status; she becomes the object of the professional gaze, which operates to control her actions and responses. Although Kirkham (1986) comments that 'a great deal is learnt at antenatal clinic and these checks should be a source of information for the woman herself and not just for her file', complaints about lack of information or opportunities to ask questions are still widespread (House of Commons Health Committee Report, 1992). A conveyor belt approach, with long queues and impersonal interventions, is a feature not just of antenatal clinics but of many hospital clinics and indeed of some doctors' surgeries.

Clearly, history taking is an important source of information for nurses and medical staff, but patients frequently find themselves asked to provide the same information several times over. The convenience of the staff generally seems to outweigh the needs of the patient, although the nursing process has threatened to bury nurses themselves in paperwork and in some cases is downright masochistic. In one Irish hospital, for example, Porter (1991) observed that little use was made of the nursing care plan, despite the fact that 'on admission of each patient, several hours were spent listing each of their problems and what was to be done about them. Much of this took the form of a mundane routine, with the same formulae being painstakingly written out in long hand on every occasion'.

Routines can provide safeguards for staff, ensuring that all the required work is covered and thereby that the same high standard of care is offered to all. Routinisation of care may take the form of task allocation, in which 'doing the baths' and 'doing the drug round' enable the work to be divided up and allocated efficiently: the more complex tasks to senior staff, the simpler, 'dirty' jobs to juniors (Melia, 1987). But routines can also insulate staff from real contact with patients and enable them to keep control. Such control may be exerted over patients as well as over staff, and patients lose any real possibility of exercising choice. Asking for a bath or for pain relief other than at the set time becomes a direct challenge to ward authority. More subtle forms of routinisation concern control of information. Bond (1986) reported that 'what nurses tell cancer patients about their treatment and condition is reduced to a number of routine explanations appropriate to the categories defined by the nature of the patient's diagnosis, and type and stage of treatment'.

Midwives may divert questions by telling women to 'ask the doctor', although they are often in the situation of explaining to patients 'what the doctor means'. This is frequently the role of nurses in hospital wards; they interpret medical information about treatment procedures for patients when doctors have left the ward. Oakley (1986) describes her experience as a cancer patient when, after failing to understand the 'mystifying technical-medical language' of the doctor, she lay in bed with a radioactive implant stitched into her tongue:

A young nurse came into the room to fetch the remains of my lunch, and she saw that I was distressed. Instead of taking my lunch tray away, or offering me drugs for the pain I was in, she sat down on the bed and held my hand and talked to me. I told her how I felt and after a while she went away and read my notes and came back and told me everything that was in them, and that, in her of course unmedical view, I would probably be all right . . . I never saw this nurse again after I left hospital, but I would like her to know that she was important to my survival.

Oakley (1986)

The purpose of routines and procedures is complex, and they are by no means only defensive – or indeed only confined to the health sector. They are, to some extent, a necessary part of the bureaucratisation of all large organisations, as we noted in Chapter 11. In spite of efforts to shed routines and hand control to the patient, even the best intentioned health workers encounter problems. Twomey (1986) discusses a feminist approach to district nursing, an important aspect of which she sees as encouraging patient autonomy. She notes that 'control cannot simply be handed back without any changes in the system which generates the inequality . . . I very much control the nature of relationships that are built up with most patients'. The processing of large numbers of people quickly and efficiently from the organisational point of view, whether in the hospital clinic or in patients' own homes (or in the job centre), is perhaps incompatible with individualised care.

Categorising patients

Another dimension of routinisation of care is *typification* or *stereotyping*: that is, categorisation of individuals into types which then become a major determinant of how they are subsequently dealt with. The individual patient is viewed as a type, slotted into a category or made to fit a pre-existing stereotype, and this is what is responded to rather than the individual. Several studies have highlighted how health professionals categorise people into 'good' and 'bad' or 'problem' patients, depending on the particular norms and objectives of the clinical area (Stockwell, 1972). Staff also judge patients against an ideal of patient behaviour which reflects Parsons' (1951) categorisation of patient behaviour: that is, seeking medical advice, being unable to recover voluntarily, following doctors' orders, wanting to get well. For example, Rosenthal *et al*. (1980) comment that 'ideally, from a nurses' perspective, all patients should be sick when they enter hospital, should follow eagerly and exactly the therapeutic programme set up by the staff, should be pleasant, uncomplaining, fit into ward routines, and should leave the hospital "cured" '. Those who did not fit this ideal type, who were unco-operative, demanding and ungrateful, for example, were seen as 'problem patients' or – if they were neurotic or not felt to be genuinely sick – as 'career patients'. A discussion of the problem patient in psychiatry suggested that a key factor in nurses' judgements about patients concerned the degree to which patients legitimate the nursing role by recognising nurses' therapeutic competence and professional authority and responding appropriately (May and Kelly, 1982).

Perhaps because they offer such a rich variety of patient 'types', accident and emergency departments have been the subject of several studies in professional attitudes and values. Jeffery (1979) and Dingwall and Murray (1983) explored mainly medical typifications of casualty patients as legitimate (good) or deviant in some way. Good patients allowed staff to practise their skills and tested their 'general competence and maturity'; they 'make demands which fall squarely within the boundaries of what the staff define as appropriate to their job' (Jeffery,

1979). 'Bad' patients – normal 'rubbish' as the staff termed them – included 'trivia', 'drunks', 'overdoses' and 'tramps'. 'It's a thankless task, seeing all the rubbish, as we call it, coming through', commented one casualty officer. Jeffery suggests that 'rubbish' broke the 'unwritten rules', which turn out to be remarkably similar to Talcott Parsons' categorisation of the 'sick role'. Unlike good patients, they were responsible for their illness, they delayed in seeking medical help, they were unco-operative and did not wish to get well. The mental categorisations of patients as 'rubbish' influenced their subsequent treatment. Staff employed various tactics to try to deter such patients: increasing their waiting time, verbal hostility, threats to call the police and vigorous handling, for example in the treatment of overdose cases.

The *labelling theories* of interactionists, which we noted in Section 10.8, offer valuable insights into typification and stereotyping. They interpret deviance as a process of interaction between deviants and non-deviants, between those who hold power and represent authority and those who do not. Deviance is defined, and labels are generated, by the powerful. Applied to health work, we can see some of the dangers in labelling. In the hospital health professionals are in authority and patients are not. Diagnosed deviance – such as coming to casualty with a trivial complaint – results in the allocation of the patient to the 'rubbish' category, a *label* which influences subsequent interaction and treatment and from which the patient is unable to escape. Should the patient visit casualty on a future occasion, the label is likely to be reapplied, and perhaps a 'legitimate' complaint will not be detected.

However, Dingwall and Murray (1983) suggest that categories are not always so fixed, and that initial typifications of patients (such as children) as conforming or deviant did not apply or were reassessed on examination. Patients who started off as 'deviant' might be reclassified as clinically 'interesting'.

○   Note down your reactions to such typifications. To what extent do you see categorisation as a necessary part of dealing with large numbers of patients?

Nursing students who have read Jeffery's study have often been shocked by what seem to be the rather brutal reactions of the staff, but having worked in a casualty department they evince greater understanding. Mackay (1989) noted that qualified nurses rarely mentioned (to outsiders at least) 'the specific idiosyncrasies of the patients', whereas students were more open in their reactions and more likely to categorise patients as good or bad.

It is very difficult to avoid categorising people (not just patients) on the basis of prior experience. Faced with a mass of new students at the beginning of the year, teachers fit students into categories: as conforming or deviant, interesting or routine and so on. The category into which students are mentally slotted is just as likely to influence future interactions with them. At what point does categorising become rigid stereotyping, in which – however diversely the subjects behave – the view of them remains fixed? Categorising patients may not prevent health professionals from treating them as individuals and providing patient-focused care, but it does make this more difficult. We need to ask how far the goal of treating every patient as an individual is, in fact, a realistic goal, given the fast turnover of patients in hospitals today and the increasing workloads of community nurses and health visitors.

12.6 Nursing in the future

It is difficult to generalise about nursing work because it takes place in so many different settings; the character, pace and style of work vary, resulting in distinctive work cultures and values. In some specialties, such as midwifery and health visiting, health workers have long-standing claims to be independent practitioners and to have professional autonomy, although in the case of midwifery the hospitalisation of childbirth severely undermined freedom of action. In other areas, particularly in hospital nursing, there is a long tradition of being a handmaiden to the doctor. In hospital clinics, for example, nurses may see their job as helping the doctor by moving patients through as efficiently as possible rather than enabling patients to articulate their concerns. Graham and Oakley (1981) report a not uncommon complaint of patients:

The nurse says, 'Now do you want to ask the doctor anything?' and more invariably than not you say 'No', because you just don't feel you can. The way they ask you, 'Right, do you want to ask the doctor anything?', you think, 'No'. All you want to do is get up and get out.

Graham and Oakley (1981)

The reconceptualisation of nursing – signalled by the shift to Project 2000 training, the substitution of a student based curriculum in place of an apprenticeship system, the move from task to patient allocation and from rote learning to academic study – has as its goal the demise of the 'handmaiden' and the creation of the independent 'nurse practitioner'. This project has a number of implications for nursing work in the future. Even if it is successfully carried through, it will still leave the majority of day-to-day hands-on caring to be done by low paid women workers. There will also be new problems and stresses for nurses, as 'emotional labourers' and 'managers of embodiment' in the system of patient allocation and the nursing process. Some, at least, of the routines and rituals associated with 'traditional' nursing are linked to the processing of large numbers of people in any type of organisation, and it is an open question how far 'individual-focused care' can be achieved.

In particular, the 'new nursing' approach associated with Project 2000 and the emerging discourse of the professional, autonomous practitioner can be viewed in different ways. To some extent they represent a liberation of nursing from medicine and a shift from a medical to a holistic model of care. They also offer nursing a professionalised future, with primary nursing developed in centres such as Burford providing a vision of autonomous practice. Yet another important strand is the claim of the new nurse to be the patient's advocate, to empower patients to make their voices heard (see Box 12.4).

There are problems in reconciling these alternative visions. Salvage (1992) points out that 'students would have to rebel against the [nurse education] system in order to build partnerships with patients'. The drive to professional status may be incompatible with the empowerment of the patient. The shift to a holistic model may be resisted by those who continue to see technical 'scientific' procedures as superior to 'care'. Moreover, there may be continued reluctance on the part of management to allow further experiments in primary nursing. After all, the Oxford Nursing Development Unit was closed down in 1989. In the new era of the NHS trusts such innovations may be encouraged; on the other hand the likely prospect at present is staffing cuts, increasing skill mix and more 'efficiency' savings.

BOX 12.4 Nursing in the future

Traditional nursing	'New' nursing
Task orientation	Process orientation
School of nursing	College/university based
Routines	Problem-solving
Patient as object	Patient as active subject
Biomedical model	Holistic model
Science focus	Care emphasis
Nursing as medically derived	Nursing as unique, autonomous activity
Emotional distance	Emotional attachment
Physical labour	Physical and emotional labour
'Warehousing'*	'Horticultural'*

*See page 466.

Suggestions for further study

P. Smith (1992) *The Emotional Labour of Nursing*, London, Macmillan, offers a useful discussion of the complex nature of nursing and to some extent all caring work. L. Mackay (1989) *Nursing a Problem*, Milton Keynes, Open University Press, provides some thought-provoking commentaries from nurses themselves about their work and outlook. S. Porter (1992) 'Women in a women's job: the gendered experience of nurses', in *Sociology of Health and Illness*, Vol. 14, 4, comments on shifts in the gender balance of power. For a well-focused summary of changes in the occupational structure of nursing see R. Dingwall *et al.* (1988) *An Introduction to the Social History of Nursing*, London, Routledge.

Self assessment questions

1 Explain why nursing has been seen as 'women's work'.
2 Comment on the relevance of the concept of 'emotional labour' for your own health work practice.
3 Make notes on what you see as the key stages in your own professional socialisation. If possible, compare your ideas with a colleague.
4 To what extent are tensions between the 'ward' and the 'college' way and between 'practice' and 'theory' inevitable in health work?
5 From your own experience, comment on the significance of class, gender and race divisions in health work.
6 Discuss the relevance of Morse's (1991) models of nurse–patient relationships for your own health work practice.

Chapter 13

The contemporary politics of health care

Contents

Themes and issues

Welfare principles: the fiscal and ideological crisis in welfare – the New Right challenge to collectivism and the social – the crisis of the state – market principles: privatisation – contractualism – consumer sovereignty – quasi-markets

The rise of managerialism: market principles in health – purchaser–provider split – fundholding – issues of democracy and accountability

Evaluation: NHS founding principles – measuring outcomes – QALYs – problems of evaluating social model approaches – rationing in health care – the sovereign consumer – the patients' charter – health futures: a disease or a health service?

Learning outcomes

After working through this chapter you should be able to:

1 Explain what is meant by the 'ideological crisis in welfare' and how it applies to the health sector.
2 Outline the key features of the shift from professional autonomy to managerial control.
3 Discuss the merits and drawbacks of the purchaser–provider split in health services.
4 Make an assessment of the current impact and likely future outcomes of the NHS internal market for your area of health work.
5 Outline and assess the merits of different approaches to measuring and evaluating health.

THIS final chapter will explore recent changes in health care within the broader framework of the contemporary crisis in welfare. The health sector was one of the last to be affected by the ideological and fiscal 'crisis of welfare', yet health care and health work have now been profoundly reconceptualised and reshaped. What are the consequences of this transformation for patients and for health workers? Do market and consumer models provide an adequate basis on which to develop health care in the future? In the sections that follow the contemporary reconstruction of health and health work will be evaluated using several different measures of 'success', and the relative value of these will be explored. Finally, using the sociological insights developed in the book so far, we will consider likely futures for health and health workers. Will a comprehensive 'health service' survive? What will be the future position of nursing in health work? To what extent will dependent groups and 'lay voices' be able to influence health care provision in the future? How far will the reduction of disease and the promotion of health, rather than the treatment of disease and sickness, become the main focus of health work?

13.1 The crisis in welfare

The welfare state was established in Britain in the 1940s, as we noted in Chapter 6, to provide a safety net of benefits against what Beveridge termed 'the giant evils of Want, Disease, Ignorance and Squalor'.

○ Note down the main underlying principles of the welfare system of the
   1940s. You'll find them discussed in Section 6.4.

The welfare legislation was characterised by the *insurance principle* and underpinned by a commitment to *full employment* which, it was argued, would defeat idleness – the fifth 'giant evil'. In its origins the welfare system was planned as a *universalist* response to poverty and un-employment. In other words, it was designed to provide minimum standards of living for all citizens by means of benefits or services designed to meet a range of contingencies: unemployment, sickness, retirement, housing needs, education, the support of dependants, the birth and upbringing of children. The National Health Service, for example, provided comprehensive health care on a collective basis which was free at the point of use. The national education system provided free schooling for all children up to the age of 15. A massive expansion in public sector house building was planned to provide housing for people of all classes who wished to rent from their council.
    As the cost of welfare mounted, it began to acquire an increasingly

selectivist character. Gaps in the welfare system were plugged by the introduction of means-tested benefits such as Family Income Supplement which, since they were targeted at particular, limited low income groups, were less costly than universal benefits – although they were far more expensive to administer. By the early 1970s a combination of economic factors – principally sluggish economic growth, the oil crisis, rising unemployment and high inflation – placed greater than ever pressure on the welfare system. The welfare state began to be considered by those on the political right as an increasing burden; in particular, there was a growing disinclination to support the Keynesian policy of full employment (see Box 13.1). By the later 1970s the retention of full employment was being seen as of secondary importance compared with the fight against inflation. On both the right and left in British politics any further expansion (and to some extent retention) of the welfare state began to be linked more and more closely with economic recovery and growth.

A fiscal crisis?

Much of the criticism of the welfare state in the late 1970s and early 1980s centred on the supposedly excessive state spending on social security, education and health. In fact there is little evidence that social expenditure in the UK was rising faster in real terms than in the rest of Europe. It was certainly rising, but not uniformly. In the recession of the early 1980s unemployment levels pushed up social security expenditure, whereas public sector housing experienced real cutbacks; in education,

---

BOX 13.1 Keynes and full employment

Keynes argued that the control of policies influencing credit and investment should be in the hands of the government rather than in private hands. Then government could take steps in a recession to stimulate employment by a combination of low interest rates and public sector investment in programmes of public works. This would give unemployed people spending power which they would use to purchase goods and services, thus stimulating output and aiding recovery. The result of state investment would be to create a 'multiplier' effect through the economy, stimulating spending and new investment and creating jobs.

Keynes' proposals were based on the theory that employment was determined by people's propensity to invest and to consume, rather than by the level of wages. People's preferences were influenced by the supply of money and credit. If the banking system increased the supply of money and credit, people were encouraged to invest. If the supply was low, people were less likely to invest or to consume: this hit at industry and commerce, causing unemployment levels to rise. The policy solution, therefore, was for the government itself to spend to aid recovery.

where pupil numbers were falling, there was a small decline in real terms.

The argument was less about expenditure as such than about efficiency and productivity. The public sector was conceptualised as extravagant and unproductive, as parasitic on tax-paying citizens and on a productive private sector. All through the 1980s, as the battle over welfare raged, welfare expenditure as a proportion of total government expenditure held steady or expanded (see Table 13.1). There was no drastic switch in public sector borrowing levels, in taxation or in the percentage of Gross National Product spent on welfare. The debate focused not on what was or wasn't spent, but on what *should* or *should not* be spent and on *where* it should be spent: in other words, the debate was primarily ideological and political rather than fiscal.

Other observers agree that, although the crisis of welfare was framed as a fiscal crisis in which an intolerable burden of increasing dependency was seen as threatening to overwhelm the taxpayer and stifle the spirit of individual enterprise, behind this critique lay a more

TABLE 13.1 Social expenditure in relation to UK government expenditure 1981–92. Source: *Social Trends* (1994)

United Kingdom	Percentages			
	1981	1986	1991	1992
Defence[1]	10.8	11.8	9.2	9.7
Public order and safety	3.7	4.2	5.6	5.5
Education	12.2	11.9	12.9	12.7
Health	11.4	11.8	13.7	13.8
Social security	26.6	30.8	32.3	33.1
Housing and community amenities	6.1	5.0	4.0	4.3
Recreational and cultural affairs	1.4	1.5	1.7	1.6
Fuel and energy	0.3	−0.7	−1.5	−0.6
Agriculture, forestry and fishing	1.4	1.3	1.2	1.1
Mining, mineral resources, manufacturing and construction	3.0	1.2	0.7	0.5
Transport and communication	3.6	2.3	3.0	2.5
General public services	3.9	3.9	4.9	4.8
Other economic affairs and services	2.5	2.5	2.0	2.0
Other expenditure	13.1	12.7	9.4	9.1
Total expenditure (= 100%)(£ billion)	117.1	162.3	228.3	254.1

[1] Includes contributions by other countries towards the United Kingdom's cost of the Gulf conflict – £2.1 billion in 1991.

fundamental questioning of welfare state principles. Deakin, writing in 1987, commented:

There is now widespread uncertainty, covering all shades of opinion, about the future of welfare and the objectives that it should be seeking to achieve . . .

Some of the questions opened up . . . are about tensions between rival objectives for social policy, exposed by the decline in the economy and the changing relationship between social policy and the broader objectives set by government, and the purposes that the state's presence in the field of welfare are intended to serve and whether it is capable of securing them. Some are about means: whether welfare can be better provided through the market or informally . . . Others are about ends: whose interests welfare is intended to serve and who has really benefited from its expansion.

Deakin (1987)

An ideological crisis

Debates about the purpose and character of welfare provision have never been entirely absent, but in Britain from the mid-1970s such debates came to reflect deeper ideological and philosophical un-certainties about the legitimacy and desirability of state-run welfare provision. The most dramatic of these conflicts, though by no means the only ones, were between supporters of comprehensive, universalist welfare services and those on the New Right who espoused market-led, commercially based solutions.

Hayek (1944), the guru of the New Right, had argued that collectivism could only destroy freedom and oppress the citizen; the main role of the state was to safeguard the freedom of the individual, not to provide welfare services which could be better obtained through free market competition. In economic terms this constituted a neo-liberal approach in which rational producer and consumer choices would ensure that supply balanced demand, and therefore that a free, self regulating market could deliver all and any commodities that were required, from tooth paste to palliative care. Hayek and the New Right utterly rejected the Keynesian approach with its commitment to delivering and sustaining full employment through state intervention in macro-economic policy (see Section 2.4).

Underpinning the New Right position was a profound general distrust of the state and a belief that state intervention – except to secure property, protect individual freedom and regulate at the margins – was wrong and dangerous. This linked to a philosophy of 'possessive individualism' which we noted in Chapter 3 as a central plank of familism, and which Dalley (1988) defined as 'the single-minded pursuit of self-improvement, both in material and spiritual terms: the deter-mination that the family, under the guidance of the head of the family –

the husband/father, should be autonomous in thought and action'. By
the late 1970s the philosophical argument for possessive individualism
had become firmly linked to the socio-economic argument that the
welfare state had tried and failed to deliver either equity or efficiency.
Those on the New Right argued that it was necessary for the survival of
family values that the family, and its individual members, should be
freed from dependence on the welfare state and taught to 'stand on their
own feet'. This was the celebrated return to 'Victorian values' of self
help, thrift and entrepreneurship. The welfare state was seen as
incompatible with wealth creation and the preservation of personal
freedom; in fact it was seen as fatally undermining enterprise and
initiative.

Although the radical rethink of welfare is now associated with the
New Right and Thatcherism, it is important to realise that some of the
ammunition for their attack on state welfare came from critics campaigning for the restructuring and democratisation of welfare services. For
example, in 1975 Donnison had warned other reformers that 'the
commitment of professional groups to the development of their work
and status has repeatedly led them to demand more and better social
services – larger and more expensive services, too, which may not be
best for the consumer'. The sociological critique of the monopoly power
and control exerted by health professionals, in particular doctors (see
Section 11.5), was used by the New Right to support their case for
reforming health services. The analysis of the 'poverty trap' effect in
social security (Bradshaw, 1980) could be used by the right to
demonstrate that the welfare state was keeping in poverty those it was
meant to help (Minford, 1984). The argument advanced by critics on the
left that the welfare state was failing to deliver equity and equality of
opportunity in health or other services could be turned on its head to
demonstrate the futility of attempting to 'legislate for equality'.
Inequality was an inevitable, indeed 'natural' result of differences
between individuals, argued the New Right. Some people were
'energetic, successful and thrifty' whereas others were 'idle, the failures
and the feckless'. It was wrong (morally wrong, but also wrong in
practical terms) for the state to try and equalise these differences
through welfare:

The present welfare state, with its costly universal benefits and heavy taxation,
is rapidly producing . . . economic and spiritual malaise among our people.
Planned, introduced and encouraged by good men who believed that state
intervention would bring both economic and spiritual returns, the end-product
is completely different.

The National Health Service was introduced by men of compassion who
wished to improve the health of the poor and to remove the worry of medical

bills. The end result was been a decline in medical standards below the level of other advanced countries because people are not prepared to pay as much through taxation on other people's health as they would pay directly on their own and their families'. Long queues in surgeries, an endless waiting-list for hospital beds, and the emigration of many newly-trained doctors are among the unexpected results. Small wonder that more and more people are looking for some form of private insurance to give them wider choice in medicine and surgery.

Boyson (1971)

○   What is significant about the argument that Rhodes Boyson put forward to demonstrate that state welfare is wrong?

Boyson argued that the health and other welfare services set up in the 1940s to make economic and moral progress possible have had the reverse effect, and he implied that the 'good men' who planned these services – and all other sensible citizens as well – would repudiate them by seeking greater choice and higher standards in the market place. In other words, collectivism has been tried and has failed. Those on the political left, by contrast, have argued that a tradition of *reluctant collectivism* has dominated in state welfare: that is, hesitant and fragmented progress towards a welfare state for the first half of the twentieth century and a marked reluctance to extend social planning further after the 1940s. They argue that more collective action rather than less is what is needed: 'The goal is equality with participation. This means structural change and not piecemeal reform. Thus a first step must be to establish social planning' (Walker, 1984).

As the debate over welfare developed it became apparent that to make clear cut, fixed distinctions between 'individualism' and 'collectivism', or between Thatcherism and various types of socialism on the left, served to obscure the complexity of the debate and the fundamental nature of the issues at stake (Deakin, 1987, and see Figure 13.1). Many on the political left as well as the right were highly critical of the inability of the welfare system to become more accountable and client-oriented, of its bureaucratic remoteness in the face of the poorest and weakest people in society.

For example, two right-wing 'think-tanks' – the Institute of Economic Affairs and the Institute for Policy Studies – produced an array of literature from academic and policy experts criticising the shortcomings of the welfare state. At the same time policy analysts on the left, such as Le Grand (1984), argued that the existence of a welfare state was no guarantor of equity and equality of access. Through an examination of selected welfare provision he demonstrated that the middle class reaped disproportionate benefits from education and health services. Field (1982) detailed the extent to which welfare, when broadly interpreted to include tax benefits (such as mortgage relief) and

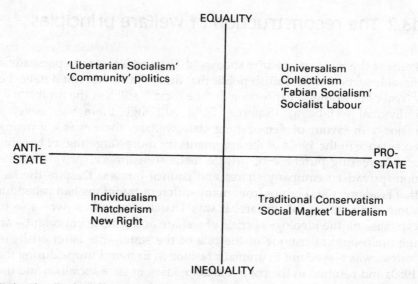

Note: The diagram indicates the complexity of the politics of welfare and how political parties may shift over time between quadrants.

FIGURE 13.1 Mapping traditions in social welfare. Source: Adapted from Lee and Raban (1983); see Chapter 2, FIGURE 2.3

employer concessions (such as company cars for which employers could also claim tax relief), had overwhelmingly benefited the middle classes. Le Grand (1984) also pointed out that cuts in welfare in the early 1980s tended to safeguard services from which the middle classes were net beneficiaries, while dismantling those, such as state housing, which had to some extent redistributed income to the working class.

Disillusioned with the remoteness and bureaucracy of state-provided welfare, a range of academic critics associated with the political left, right and centre have argued for protection for citizens through various kinds of local-level, locally accountable service provision and greater voluntary sector participation. For example, Hadley and Hatch (1981) advanced the case for a local 'patch' system in social services, in which greater use was made of voluntary and informal caring systems, and Hoggett and Hambleton (1987) argued for decentralisation and lay and voluntary sector participation in local government. There is considerable overlap between the position these writers advance and the arguments of the New Right for a 'social market' approach which emphasises 'consumer sovereignty' and greater choice (Willetts, 1987). The position of the liberal democratic centre has also been to support a safety net of welfare benefits whilst encouraging individuals to be thrifty and self reliant.

13.2 The reconstruction of welfare principles

Perhaps the most spectacular success of Thatcherism was to persuade a sizeable section of the British public that the welfare state could never be a 'real or meaningful expression of "the social", still less the protector of individual well-being' (Squires, 1990). Although there was never a majority in favour of demolishing state welfare, there was a growing acceptance in the 1980s of the arguments for more 'targeting' of benefits and increasing purchase of private medical insurance, private education, privatised company shares and council houses. Despite the fact that academics and critics from many different traditions had called for some restructuring of welfare, it was Thatcherism which was able to capitalise on the ideological crisis of welfare and – more important – on the philosophical critique of the role of the state. This latter crisis, of course, was played out in dramatic fashion in Eastern Europe during the 1980s and resulted in the complete demolition of state socialism and the fatal weakening of the collectivist concept. As Jacques (1988) commented, while the left was seen as 'profoundly wedded to the past, to 1945 . . . the Right has glimpsed the future and ran with it . . . It is the Right which now appears modern, radical, innovative and brimming with ideas about the future'. Meanwhile the public sector and state 'welfarism' were increasingly being equated with 'serfdom', authoritarianism and a culture which encouraged idleness and 'welfare dependency':

> The public sector was henceforth redefined by the New Right as the home of control, queues and coercion; of means-tests and state supervision; of ill-fitting National Health spectacles and overcrowded classrooms; of barrack-like council estates with few amenities and high-rise blocks with broken lifts; of buses that were often late, town halls ignorant of choice and impervious to criticism and bureaucracies as paternalistic as anything the Victorian philanthropists might have created.
>
> *Squires (1990)*

The rise of market principles

The ideological and political commitment to 'roll back' the 'nanny state' has been at the heart of New Right welfare philosophy and owes a great deal – as we noted earlier – to theories of neo-liberalism and individualism. In espousing this cause it was argued that Thatcherism was returning Britain not merely to the 'Victorian values' of self help, thrift and self reliance but also to basic moral and religious principles which gave support to wealth creation and success – providing spiritual duties and voluntary endeavour were not neglected (Thatcher, 1988). In practical terms this meant asserting *market principles*: freeing enterprise from the stultifying effects of nationalisation and over-regulation by moving to privatisation, competitive tendering and contractualism; and freeing citizens from dependence and bureaucracy by lowering taxes, trimming back welfare benefits and promoting consumer sovereignty. Before we turn to a more detailed investigation of what this has meant in the health sector it is worth clarifying what these policy approaches involve.

Privatisation refers to the removal of hitherto public sector enterprises, such as British Gas or the national water boards, into private sector ownership and management, with government appointed regulators to oversee pricing policy. In some cases a private monopoly has been created – as with British Gas; in others competition has been introduced – as with British Telecom, where Mercury competes for business but uses British Telecom technological infrastructure. In both cases hitherto exempt agencies are becoming subject to the operation of *market principles*: in other words, segments or whole parts of what were state bureaucracies or nationalised companies are being forced to operate as if they were in a commercial market.

Competitive tendering refers to the process by which local authorities and other agencies, including the health service, have been required to put service contracts out to tender. In some cases the local authority workforce or some other direct labour force has secured the contract; in other cases it has been won by a newly formed or already established commercial firm. This growth of *contractualism* means that the main job of local authorities and other public service agencies is increasingly to negotiate and monitor contracts in the interests of the public (the 'sovereign consumers'). Their directly employed workforce may become very much smaller (Mulgan, 1991). Contractualism, you might recall, has been brought into community care provision through the 1990 National Health Service and Community Care Act. This required social services departments, through key workers, to develop 'packages of care' for dependent people in the community. This takes the form of a contract, which is monitored, between the dependent person, the care providers and the key worker. The local authority social services department purchases but does not necessarily provide any of the contracted care (see Section 4.5).

Contractualism and competitive tendering exemplify the application of *market principles* to the public sector. The objective is to create an *internal market* – that is, a market within each remaining public agency – that will operate as far as possible like an open, competitive market. Le Grand and Bartlett (1993) have used the term 'quasi-markets' to describe this situation, arguing that for a number of reasons the markets created are not conventional ones. First, although there is competition for customers between productive enterprises or service suppliers 'these organisations are not necessarily out to maximise their profits; nor are they necessarily privately owned. Precisely what the non-profit organisations do have as their objectives is often unclear, as is their ownership structure'. There are also differences on the demand side, because consumer purchasing power does not take the form of money as it does in a conventional market:

Instead either it takes the form of an earmarked budget or 'voucher' confined to the purchase of a specific service allocated to users, or it is centralised in a single purchasing agency. Also, it is important to note that, in most cases, it is not the direct user who exercises the choices concerning purchasing decisions; instead those choices are often delegated to a third party.

Le Grand and Bartlett (1993)

Welfare cuts and tax cuts are associated with the rise of *consumer sovereignty*. The declared objective in cutting direct taxes and targeting welfare benefits has been to 'put money back into people's pockets' so that they can determine, as individual consumers, their priorities and choices. Sovereign consumers, through these measures and through the expansion of market principles, will be handed back power and responsibility for their own lives; personal freedom and autonomy will thus be increased.

These policies are, of course, the focus for heated debate and controversy by social policy analysts and others. For example, politicians of all parties make loud claims to be the true representative of 'the consumer'. It is still an open question how far market principles can really deliver consumer choice as opposed to a limited range of predetermined, profitable options; it is equally unclear whether the rise of a contractual market model of service agencies responsible to sovereign consumers will provide adequate protection for any but the most 'street-wise' citizens. For example, Mulgan (1991) has argued that the contractual model assumes that consumers can be readily identified and have perfect information, that consumers and producers have equal power and that every relationship can be reduced to a 'transaction'. But consumers often have little information and no real power over contracts. Public sector work often benefits the community as a whole and not just individual consumers, yet contractual theory cannot allow for the possibility of altruism and a public service ethic. Writers on the political left have argued that a genuine public sector pluralism would need to include not only diversity of provision and co-operation between public, private and voluntary sectors, but also collective provision, community participation and empowerment and democratic accountability (Mulgan, 1991; Wilding, 1992). Le Grand and Bartlett (1993) comment that 'the quasi-market reforms are in their infancy and it is too early to predict their long-term consequences'. However, they remain rather sceptical about the claims made for these market principles, both on the grounds of their ability to deliver greater efficiency and equity and because of the huge transition costs involved in setting them up.

Critics who have challenged the social programme of Thatcherism have not rejected the 'mixed economy of welfare' or even 'market principles' as such; what they have rejected has been the increased central control and decreased local democratic control (or transformation of control) that has characterised this programme. For example, local management of schools (LMS) has strengthened the position of school governors and (in theory at least) the position of parents, but in doing so it has dismantled local democratic control over many schools via local government. At the same time central political and bureaucratic control has been considerably strengthened through the imposition of a national curriculum for education.

Much of the debate about welfare has been fought on the messy middle ground between the two extremes of comprehensive state-led welfare and free market consumerism for other reasons too: because in practice Thatcherism has steered an uneasy course between the two. As we noted earlier, state spending continued to rise in the 1980s. Opposition political parties, out of office for a decade and a half, cannot reverse the significant legislative and structural changes of the 1980s and early 1990s. Some sectors, such as public sector housing, have been severely cut back; others, such as education and social security, have undergone almost continuous review and restructuring. The onward march of contractualism has forced academics and politicians alike to rethink the relationship of the state and the market.

13.3 The crisis in health care

In this section we will be applying the analysis of the 'crisis in welfare' to the health sector. The fiscal and ideological roots of the crisis in welfare have been quite deliberately sketched in first, in order to develop an understanding of the relationship between health policy developments and broader trends in state policy and welfare provision. Since health had always had a privileged position as the 'jewel in the crown' of British welfare services, and since the health sector remained relatively stable until after 1990, it has been all too easy to argue that questions of politics and ideology are irrelevant to the work of nurses and other health care professionals. This is now a dangerous argument. The growth of managerialism, of hospital trusts and practice budgetholders and of a purchaser–provider split in health not only has significant effects in terms of how health care is delivered but is influencing the social organisation, working conditions and status of all groups within the health sector: patients as well as health care workers.

The rise of managerialism

We'll begin by reviewing some of the changes in health care organisation over the last decade or so, and in the next section their impact on patients and on health workers will be assessed. In Sections 11.5 and 11.6 the 1974 health service reorganisation and 1984 Griffiths Management Enquiry were discussed as two distinctive attempts by the government to gain greater control over health priorities and expenditure. In particular, Griffiths' concept of 'general management' was designed to put in place managers prepared to manage, to control clinicians and shake up the health sector by setting objectives and promoting business principles (see Table 13.2).

○ Look at Table 13.2, which shows some of the shifts in National Health Service priorities. Suggest why changes in priorities might be difficult to achieve.

One of the main obstacles to achieving this shift in priorities has been the power and prestige of senior medical personnel, in particular established hospital consultants who hold regional contracts. Their main concerns – to protect and develop their specialty, define patient needs and secure treatment for their patients – sit uneasily with tighter managerial control, cost-cutting and market principles. The key shift was from a principle of 'professional autonomy' to one of 'managerial control'. The other changes in emphasis, it was hoped, would flow from this: for example, medical demands for 'adequate' resources could be

TABLE 13.2 The rise of managerialism

Professional autonomy	→	Managerial control
Clinical freedom	→	Clinical budgeting, generic drugs list
'Adequate' resources	→	Efficiency savings Competitive tendering Performance indicators
Medical power	→	Planning, performance review, quality control, new contracts
Consensus management, professional influence	→	General management function

countered by managerial concern for 'efficiency savings' and 'value for money'. Rising costs, fuelled in part by professional autonomy, could be contained by improving information and planning systems and by quality control. Clinical freedom would be tempered by involving clinicians in budgeting and performance reviews.

But managers have had to work with overlapping 'empires' of professional staff – doctors, nurses, a range of therapists and para-medics – whose priorities were not making profits, 'breaking even' or even efficiency but treatment of patients. Clinicians showed little interest in issues of cost-effectiveness, medical audit and clinical effectiveness. The evidence gathered by researchers in the late 1980s suggested that, while 'the frontier of control between government and doctors has shifted a little, in favour of the former, there is as yet little evidence that managers have secured greater control over doctors' (Harrison et al., 1990). Although general managers were appointed to put in place a series of top-down, central government-led controls and initiatives, it remained difficult to gain real central control over the vast and complex NHS organisation. The most recent changes in the NHS, the result of the 1990 Act (see below), have strengthened the position of managers by involving them in the appointment of clinicians and in the discussion of their annual job descriptions and merit awards (Cox, 1991). It has also enabled managers to improve patient services in some cases. For example, the Churchill/Radcliffe Hospital in Oxford now has 24-hour consultant cover for its accident and emergency department, a change facilitated by the ability of trusts to employ more consultants and set their own contracts (NAHAT, 1994, personal communication).

The rise of market principles

During the 1980s market principles began to be applied to the health sector, initially in the form of information gathering and evaluation of performance and then through competitive tendering processes. Examples of the former include the 'scrutinies' of health authorities' performance in particular areas, carried out by Lord Rayner after 1979, and the development of regional reviews, performance indicators, audit and 'value for money' studies. Competitive tendering was introduced in 1983.

○ Review the earlier discussion of competitive tendering and note down some examples in the health service.

Domestic, catering and laundering services were all candidates for competitive tendering. In other words, health authorities' in-house direct labour was forced to bid for contracts against private external contractors. Health authorities are spending over £1000 million a year on these services, which were euphemistically renamed 'hotel' services – presumably to distance them from the 'legitimate' health care business of treating patients. About 85 per cent of contracts were awarded in-house, with a loss of 30 per cent of directly employed labour. This suggests that not only are staff working more intensively and for longer shifts, but that standards may have fallen. As Harrison *et al.* (1990) have commented, health authorities have not been allowed to specify rates of pay or conditions of service when they draw up the contracts, and even with the fairly small proportion of external contractors savings are calculated at around £120 million a year.

Until 1991 the onward march of market principles in the health service was fairly slow. Health authorities were required to establish cost improvement programmes (CIP) from 1984, and each authority was expected to deliver at least 1 per cent of their cash allocation each year through the CIP (Harrison *et al.*, 1990). Hospitals were encouraged to generate extra income from commercial activities, from the sale of land and property, from creation or extension of pay beds and private wards and from deals with the private health sector. The private health sector itself was stimulated through changes in planning regulations, tax relief on insurance payments by older people and changes in consultants' contracts which enabled them to undertake more private work (Griffith *et al.*, 1987).

A far more extensive application of market principles followed the 1990 National Health Service and Community Care Act, which established quasi-markets in health and community care. The plans for the restructuring of health care were floated in the government White Paper *Working For Patients* (DoH, 1989a), which claimed that 'the organisation of the NHS – the way it delivers health care to the individual patient – also needs to be reformed'. Arguing that costs were rising too fast and standards and costs were too variable across the country, the White Paper proposed delegating to the local level 'as much power and responsibility as possible'. This would involve establishing NHS 'Hospital Trusts' with self governing status within the health service and encouraging general practitioners in the larger group general practices to become 'fundholders' with control over their own budgets. Health authorities and GP fundholders would become purchasers of health care for their populations, with the NHS trusts and general practices as the providers of services. Thus some general practioners would become both purchasers and providers of care, but elsewhere a purchaser–provider split would emerge (see Box 13.2).

○   Look at Box 13.2, which summarises the 1989 White Paper proposals for health care. Suggest what aspects of market principles are being advanced here.

BOX 13.2 1989 White Paper on the NHS: main proposals. Source: DHS (1989a)

Key changes

The Government is proposing seven key measures to achieve these objectives:

First: to make the Health Service more responsive to the needs of patients, as much power and responsibility as possible will be delegated to local level. This includes the delegation of functions from Regions to Districts, and from Districts to hospitals. They include greater flexibility in setting the pay and conditions of staff.

Second: to stimulate a better service to the patient, hospitals will be able to apply for a new self governing status as NHS Hospital Trusts. This means that, while remaining within the NHS, they will taker fuller responsibility for their own affairs, harnessing the skills and dedication of their staff.

Third: to enable hospitals which best meet the needs and wishes of patients to get the money to do so, the money required to treat patients will be able to cross administrative boundaries. All NHS hospitals, whether run by local authorities or self governing, will be free to offer their services in different health authorities and to the private sector.

Fourth: to reduce waiting times and improve the quality of service, to help give individual patients appointment times they can rely on, and to help cut the long hours worked by some junior doctors, 100 new consultant posts will be created over the next three years.

Fifth: to help the family doctor improve his service to patients, large GP practices will be able to apply for their own budgets to obtain a defined range of services direct from hospitals. Again, in the interests of a better service to the patient, GPs will be encouraged to compete for patients by offering better services. And it will be easier for patients to choose (and change) their own GP as they wish.

Sixth: to improve the effectiveness of NHS management, regional, district and family practitioner management bodies will be reduced in size and reformed on business lines, with executive and non-executive directors.

Seventh: to ensure that all concerned with delivering services to the patient make the best use of the resources available to them, quality of service and value for money will be more rigorously audited.

The most obvious aspect of market principles is the creation of a quasi-market in health care, rooted in competitive tendering and contractualism. The other central market principle adopted is consumer sovereignty. The NHS was to stay as a public sector organisation – it was not technically being privatised – but power and responsibility were to be delegated downwards by the breaking up of the service into different constituent parts. This would enable the service to be more responsible to consumers (point 1). One part, the health authorities – the new purchasers of health care through contracts – would be reformed along business lines, with slimmed down, non-representative management bodies and a reduced workforce. Family health services authorities, who manage general practitioners, would also be reformed on business lines (point 6). The other parts of the quasi-market were to be NHS trusts providing community and hospital care (point 2) and general practices providing primary care (point 5). Competition in this quasi-market was to be achieved by allowing the money to 'follow the patients' across administrative boundaries and by allowing hospitals to compete for patients (point 3). Quality control and value for money would be achieved through medical audit (point 7).

By the time the first wave of NHS trusts was established in 1991, the passing of the 1990 Act and vigorous debate and clarification had given the initially somewhat sketchy quasi-market more substance. Competitive tendering and contractualism would sustain this quasi-market. Health authorities, funded by central government on the basis of their population, were to draw up contracts for the types of health care they required for their populations and these would be put out to tender. NHS hospital trusts (and community and other trusts), directly managed units (DMUs, ordinary NHS hospitals which were not yet trusts), NHS community units (which were not yet trusts) and private hospitals would be able to bid, as appropriate, for the contracts. The position of general practitioners was somewhat different because, as continuing providers of primary health care to the patients on their lists, they were not required to compete for contracts. Statutory changes have made it administratively easier to change GPs and make a complaint, but there is little evidence yet that people are exercising these rights (Williams and Calnan, 1991). General practice fundholders are also purchasers of hospital care on behalf of their patients and can 'shop around' to get the best deal. Consumer sovereignty, it was assumed, would be advanced by competition between providers and by the work of the purchasers – which would enhance patient choice.

The new structure of the NHS in the 1990s was considerably different from that of 1974 (see Chapter 11, page 442, Figure 11.3). The NHS trusts became free floating businesses within the health sector, detached from district control and accountable only to the NHS Management Executive (see Figure 13.2). District health authorities planned for population needs and purchased the care; family health services authorities oversaw the work of GPs, dentists, opthalmists and pharmacists. Regional health authorities remained, for the time being at least, the strategic planning level, although in late 1993 it was announced that they would be phased out over the next two years. Several were amalgamated, bringing the total number of RHAs down to eight.

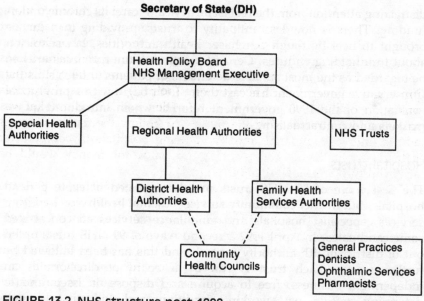

FIGURE 13.2 NHS structure post-1990

13.4 Evaluating market principles in health care

How successful have the changes in the National Health Service been? One problem to face is that, as Le Grand and Bartlett (1993) commented about quasi-markets in general, it is too early to come to any final conclusions. It is also clear that the 1990 reforms exposed and accelerated trends in health care already apparent in the 1980s. The decline in acute beds, for example, was a marked feature of the 1980s, fuelled by changes in medical technology which increased minimally invasive surgery and day surgery. Any judgement about the 1990 reforms must acknowledge that rapid change was already taking place in health care. It must also acknowledge that market principles have not been allowed free rein in the health service, and that government direction and control of the market is still very evident.

Before you read through this section, reflect on your own reaction to the rise of the 'internal market in health'. Try to gather information about its impact on the organisation you work for (or hope to be employed by in the future) and compare this with the comments below.

On the political left the creation of NHS trusts and general practice fundholders was met with deep scepticism and seen as a way of

distracting attention from the real issue in health care: its chronic under-
funding. There is now less antipathy to trusts, providing they can be
brought to heel by tough purchaser health authorities, but suspicion
about fundholding endures. General practioners are not necessarily to
be regarded as the most suitable defenders of patients' interests, as the
Conservative government has cast them. Let's begin with a provisional
evaluation of the 1990 government reforms which introduced quasi-
markets and contractualism.

Hospital trusts

The first wave of 57 NHS trusts mainly consisted of acute general
hospitals, but district community services, mental health and handicap
services, specialist hospitals and ambulance services all contributed
some candidates. In April 1992 a second wave of 99 NHS trusts opted
out of district health authority control, and this has been followed by
further waves. Each trust is run by a board of directors as an
independent business, free to acquire and dispose of assets and to
determine staffing, pay, working conditions and skill mix, although
output levels are negotiated with purchasing authorities (Bartlett and
Harrison, 1993). The cost of trust status – the board, staffing, business
planning and so on – is high, estimated at between £500 000 and
£750 000 a year for acute trusts and £250 000 for community trusts. Most
of these costs would have been met regionally or centrally before 1990.
The high costs of trust status and the high fixed costs of running
hospitals, together with rapid technological change, have made acute
trusts vulnerable in the new internal marketplace. The loss of even small
contracts, when fundholding GPs or purchaser district health authorities
(DHAs) decide to move business elsewhere, can mean the difference
between breaking even and running at a loss. Of the first wave of 57
trusts eight failed to achieve the required return on capital and two did
not manage to break even (Newchurch, 1993).

  To date most of the contracts that have been negotiated by the
DHAs with the trusts have been for *block contracts*: in other words, a
contract in which the purchaser agrees to pay the provider trust an
annual amount in return for using a broad range of agreed services.
Only a minority of NHS trusts have become involved in *cost-per-case
contracts*, in which prices are set for each type of treatment (NAHAT,
1993a). This is mainly because very little information currently exists
about the cost of individual treatment (Bartlett and Harrison, 1993).
However, this type of contract is widely used in the United States and
undoubtedly will be adopted here. It would have the effect of making
health care costs more transparent and would enable the construction of
competitive 'league tables' of costs of treatments in different trusts – a

process which the New Right would claim as extending consumer sovereignty. The extension of cost-per-case contracts will also put acute trusts under greater pressure to cut costs, resulting in mergers and in the disappearance of some trusts altogether.

Mergers between acute hospital trusts are already a marked feature of health care in the 1990s, and the drive to reduce costs by lowering labour costs has been evident. The impact on staffing has been significant, with redundancies and changes in skill mix threatening nursing in particular. But the mergers and closures are not just cost-cutting exercises. They are also evidence of the impact of technological change, in particular the rapid rise in day surgery, in new surgical techniques which are less traumatic and do not require long hospitalisation, and in out-patient care. In Birmingham, for example, 43 per cent of planned surgery is already done on a day-case basis. It has been argued that even with the loss of far more acute beds the average district general hospital will be able to serve a population 50–100 per cent bigger by the end of the 1990s (Newchurch, 1993), and projections are that as few as 28 high-technology hospitals, supported by locality hospitals for day cases, could provide all UK secondary and tertiary care (The *Guardian*, 3 January 1994). It was on this basis that the Tomlinson Report (DoH, 1993b) recommended rationalisation of hospitals and a shift of funds to primary and community health services in London, but such changes are now being planned over all Britain. They will not, however, get through without enormous difficulty, partly because of public distaste for hospital closure but also because waiting lists have soared above one million and bed crises and treatment failures hit the headlines daily. It is difficult to justify closing hospitals which are breaking even and treating more patients than ever before, and where the level of need is evidently high. Hospital staff, faced with transferral or redundancy, have made common cause with patient and consumer groups to resist closures. Behind all this is the fear that freed resources will not be transferred into primary care but seen as 'efficiency savings' which must be used to meet NHS running costs.

General practice and community trusts

Community trusts have lower management costs, but the entry costs for newcomers are much less and competition between the trusts is getting fierce. This may be one area where the private sector will make inroads in the 1990s. Technological and policy change is rapidly expanding the range of services that will be delivered by these trusts – through 'hospital-at-home' schemes, local treatment options and the extension of domiciliary care. They are coming under some pressure from GP fundholders, who have been encouraged by the new legislation to expand from being small businesses into larger-scale enterprises and who want a flexible and responsive community trust to fit in with practice requirements. Some new models of primary–community linkage are emerging, such as the Lyme Community Care Unit model (Ham *et al.*, 1993). In this instance two non-fundholding GP practices took over the management of community health services staff for their area and provided services for 8000 patients under contract to Dorset.

GP fundholding involved nearly 20 per cent of GP practices and over 20 per cent of the population by 1993, and single-handed practitioners and smaller practices are being encouraged to form consortia and move into fundholding on a joint basis. Fundholders have real power in the market, not just as purchasers of care packages for their patients but as strategic players in the shift to primary-focused health care. An increasing number are contracting into their practices new services such as chiropody and occupational therapy and are undertaking some surgical procedures. Practice nurses' roles are being expanded and may engulf some of the work of the community nursing services hitherto carried out by health visitors, whose numbers are being cut back (*The Guardian*, 6 October 1993). Caversham practice in Reading, Berkshire, one of the first wave of GP fundholders with six partners and 12 000 patients, rethought its strategy; instead of focusing on where to send patients it began to ask, 'Why not treat them here?'. Over the first two years the practice moved to providing in-house physiotherapy, psychology and counselling services. It has reduced waiting times for in-patient and out-patient treatment substantially. Its 1993–4 priorities are to improve community nursing services; in particular, it seeks to integrate these nurses with their own practice nurses and is critical of health visitor bureaucracy and information systems. The practice wants its own integrated nursing team, although it claims to 'prefer to contract from them than employ' (Smith, presentation at IHSM Conference, June 1993). In general, increasing co-operation between GP fundholders and DHAs has enabled services to be de-centralised, although this is still in its early stages. A recent study concluded that 'GPs appear to have replaced hospital doctors and managers as the key advisers to DHAs' (Ham *et al.*, 1993). Important initiatives are the use of GP surgeries for minor surgery and as centres in which to locate secondary care services. Physiotherapy, audiology, dermatology, child psychiatry and dietetics are specialties now being offered in some GP practices in some DHAs, such as Stockport, Dorset, Hampshire and Wirral (NAHAT, 1993a).

There seems to be a real possibility that community nursing could wither away as the opportunities for practice nurses expand. The result could be that community nurses are integrated into general practice, working under GPs. This may be hastened by the process of competitive tendering, in which the local community nursing service may not necessarily be awarded the contract to provide the local nursing service. If the link between nurses and the local community is broken, it will be very tempting for doctors to develop comprehensive, in-house nursing services. Added to this is the issue of community nurse identity in the future, in particular whether district nurses, health visitors and practice nurses should continue to be trained for distinct occupations. Some observers have highlighted the need for 'radical changes in working practices' and the 'removal of intra-professional boundaries' – which are linked with the need to reduce labour costs – as major priorities for the 1990s (Newchurch, 1993).

Evaluating the purchaser–provider split

Perhaps the biggest shake-up of all has taken place in the purchaser DHAs, squeezed by spending cuts and rising demands for health care. By 1993 mergers between DHAs were becoming commonplace, bringing economies of scale and aiding the drive to develop coherent health strategies based on significant populations. In Oxford Region, for example, the number of DHAs fell from nine to five, in North East Thames from 15 to seven, in Yorkshire from 16 to seven, in East Anglia from eight to a projected five by April 1994. This has resulted in increasing co-terminosity (shared boundaries) between DHAs and family health services authorities (FHSAs), such that enabling legislation has been called for to allow DHAs and FHSAs to merge (Ham et al., 1993). This would mean that one body performed all the work of purchasing, in association with GP fundholders, and could overcome some of the current fragmentation. Even without legislation a few DHAs and FHSAs have begun to work in close co-operation, just as DHAs and GP fundholders are forming new alliances to plan purchasing (see Figure 13.3). In Dorset, for example, an FHSA and DHA set up the Dorset Health Commission in 1992, a joint body which aims to assess health needs more comprehensively and guide the development of primary, community and hospital health services (Ham et al., 1993).

However, this trend is quite recent and the multi-functional character of the FHSAs may inhibit faster change – they are not primarily purchasers but providers of family health services and managers of the fundholding scheme. In spite of such innovations the general picture is of much slower changes to traditional working relationships. Bartlett and Harrison's (1993) study of the introduction of the quasi-market in health in Bristol and Weston Health Authority indicates that it 'will fail to operate in a competitive fashion in many local areas':

The absence of a range of suppliers, and the likelihood of services being purchased almost exclusively by a single purchaser, suggests that competition

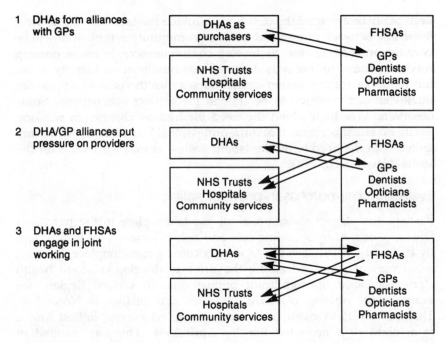

1 DHAs form alliances
   with GPs

2 DHA/GP alliances put
   pressure on providers

3 DHAs and FHSAs
   engage in joint
   working

FIGURE 13.3 Purchaser alliances in the new NHS. Source: Ham et al. (1993)

does not exist in any real sense of the word. The potential for altering these conditions rests in part with the DoH and regional health authorities, but at a local level it may be argued that it is equally important for the purchasers of services to be willing to stimulate a range of suppliers, as to draw up well-structured contracts for the purchase of services.

Bartlett and Harrison (1993)

From other studies, which looked at the potential for competition, it seems that quasi-markets may be able to operate, but this will depend on a number of factors such as population density and the readiness of patients to travel further (Appleby *et al.*, 1991; Le Grand and Bartlett, 1993). GP fundholders are better placed to use a range of providers than health authorities, but the question remains whether this will benefit their patients. The creation of alternative suppliers is not likely to come about in the short term, and it is arguably not an efficient use of resources to spend money on creating competitors rather than improving existing services. To date there is a lack of evidence that trusts have enhanced patient choice. It is not patients who get to make choices about which hospitals are used, but GPs or health authority purchasers.

The development of comprehensive needs assessment strategies for their populations by DHAs, however, may enable them to improve standards of health care in the longer term and to shift the balance towards prevention and health promotion. As DHAs develop their purchaser role, the potential for shaping health services to meet the real needs of service users is beginning to be recognised, and some health authorities are developing tools for evaluating population needs. Targets for shorter waiting lists and more flexible, consumer-oriented services could be some of the output requirements written into contracts. Le Grand and Bartlett (1993) conclude that further de-centralisation of purchasing may improve the operation of quasi-markets by making them more efficient and responsive and by enhancing choice. On the other hand they acknowledge that 'cream-skimming' by GP fundholders – that is, being more selective in choosing patients so that the old and chronic sick are excluded – is difficult to control and would lead to greater inequity in health care. They also note the large transition costs and, we might add, the considerable growth in health service bureaucracy – an estimated 40 per cent increase since 1990.

Accountability

The lack of democratic accountability that now characterises the new NHS, from government-appointed regional chairs through to the boards of hospital trusts and the role of the GPs, is perhaps the most worrying aspect of the changes. Until 1990 there was some representation on regional and district health authorities from local authorities and communities, but now there is none. Regional health authorities themselves are being phased out, with regional offices of the NHS Management Executive taking over their residual functions. Until 1984 consensus management did ensure that occupational groups had some representation on health authorities, but now they have no necessary access. Until 1974 community health services and public health were under the control of democratically elected local authorities. Now there is no accountability at local level, apart from such monitoring as the community health councils (CHCs) are able to do. The NHS, the biggest employer of labour in the world with over a million workers, is of course democratically accountable to Parliament, via the Secretary of State for Health. The minister can be questioned, and the running of the NHS is scrutinised by the Select Committee on Health, the Public Accounts Committee and the Audit Commission. But this is the same minister who agrees the appointment of the chairs of the DHAs and FHSAs, appoints the chair and non-executive directors of the NHS trust boards and has until now been appointing the chair and non-executive members of regional health authorities – who in their turn have overseen the appointment of district chairs and managers. The opportunity for patronage in the health service, and for making 'political' appointments, has enormously expanded.

This has given rise to a fierce debate about accountability. While some have argued that DHAs should be brought under the control of local authorities (Harrison *et al.*, 1990) others have pointed to the successive decisions by politicians over the last 50 years to keep the NHS under national and central control (NAHAT, 1993b). They point to the difficulties there would be in persuading FHSAs and GPs to work under local authorities and the problems inherent in any realignment of the purchaser–provider split. On the other hand the safeguards for the public in the present quasi-market system (apart from accountability to Parliament and CHC monitoring) rest almost entirely on the extent to which DHAs and trusts are prepared to allow their work to be scrutinised. NAHAT (1993b) has called for openness in board selections and dealings, for ethical behaviour and for links with the local community. But in a market system, where trusts are in increasing competition for patients and funding levels are not growing fast enough, it seems unlikely that widespread consultation with local residents and open door access to meetings and committees will be seen as a priority unless there is overwhelming pressure to do so. Local authority control of purchasing for health, set beside its already existing control of purchasing for community care under the 1990 NHS and Community Care Act, could bring about greater local democratic control, and central control over funding, health objectives and overall strategic planning could still be retained. However, it is worth noting that the current fierce debates about hospital closures would probably be more difficult to handle if local authorities controlled purchasing. The popular demand for local hospitals to remain open would be difficult to resist, encouraging local authorities to make contracts with local trusts rather than with the most cost-effective providers.

Evaluating the restructured health service

Beyond this, what criteria may be used to evaluate the restructured health service? Le Grand and Bartlett (1993) developed four criteria against which the reforms can be judged and which they drew from current government thinking as expressed in the 1989 White Papers and recent government speeches:

- Efficiency . . . crude efficiency . . . which minimises the total costs of service delivery, [and] productive efficiency [which] relates the costs of the service to the quantity and quality of service provision.
- Responsiveness . . . responding flexibly and sensitively . . . to local needs and preferences (1989 White Papers). [Le Grand and Bartlett develop this

separate category, but suggest that it is a component of productive efficiency.]
- Choice . . . diversity and choice (Bottomley, 1992) between the kinds of services received . . . and between several providers. There is [also] the question as to whose choice is the focus of concern . . . Voice mechanisms [allowing individuals to complain, user groups to comment and so on] may on occasion be preferable . . . to exit mechanisms.
- Equity . . . an equitable service [is] one where use is determined primarily by need [resource requirements] and not by irrelevant factors such as income, socio-economic status, gender, or ethnic origin.

Le Grand and Bartlett (1993)

Judging the current restructuring against these criteria, Le Grand and Bartlett came to interesting conclusions about health, social care and housing and education. As we have already noted, the quasi-market in health gets a mixed rating: GP fundholding offers more prospect of achieving gains in efficiency, choice and responsiveness but at some sacrifice of equity; on the other hand it is equity, rather than the other three criteria, which is more likely to be satisfied if a health authority is involved. A similar pattern pertains in community care, measuring social services department provision against the care-management reforms of the 1991 Act, and in housing and education reforms 'prospects for real improvements' exist.

It is, of course, still very early to make any final judgements, and the authors reach only very tentative conclusions. But this early investigation suggests, as many critics have argued, that equity and equality could be endangered by the restructuring of health and community care (see Chapter 4). The spectre of a 'two-tier' service developing in health care – as represented in the United States by an impoverished public sector and an immensely wealthy, highly expensive and interventionist private sector – is not a reassuring one.

On the other hand those on the New Right would argue that greater efficiency, effectiveness and choice can be promoted without damaging equity; indeed the New Right philosophy of personal freedom and natural inequality rests on the assumption that choice and equity are closely related. The notion of the sovereign consumer, you will recall, proposes that individuals make free and untrammelled choices in the marketplace of health or social care; since supply will balance demand, everyone – in theory – gets what they want. The fact that different entry points, resources and opportunities mean that everyone doesn't get a fair share is seen as natural and inevitable. The market provides a better way than any other of ensuring that everyone gets closest to gaining an equitable share. Critics of this view point to the inefficiencies of the free market in regulating the economy and argue that too high a price must be paid by some – through unemployment, poverty and lack of access –

for the choice and personal freedom gained by others (Wilding, 1992). The assumption that everyone can participate in the free market of health care is mistaken; for example, most users lack the knowledge and information on which to base informed choices about their treatment and care.

13.5 Issues and problems in health care

This section will step back from a concern with current structural and organisational changes to examine broader dilemmas and conflicts in contemporary health care: about how to evaluate health care, how far a sovereign consumer model in health is feasible and desirable and what the prospects are for reorienting health services from a disease model to a health focus. By asking how health care should be measured – by numbers of people treated, or numbers cured, or prevented from becoming ill, or experiencing an enhanced quality of life – we are also asking what we value about health. This connects to the contemporary debate about what kind of health care system we should have and what we want health care to achieve. This will lead on to the final section which considers what implications there are for nurses and other health workers in the various 'alternative futures' being proposed for health care.

Medical evaluation

Health care can be measured and assessed in several distinctive ways, and these will influence future priorities in health. In the early 1970s there was a call for more widespread use of a medical tool for evaluation: the *randomised controlled trial* (Cochrane, 1971).

○   Briefly explain what is meant by the randomised controlled trial (RCT).

The RCT was an experimental design for testing the efficacy of treatments. People were allocated to one of two groups at random; one group then received the new treatment being tested while the other was given the old treatment or a placebo (non-active therapy). Since the groups were similar in all respects except for their treatment, differences in outcomes could be measured and the treatment thus evaluated. Although this was seen at the time as the key to a more 'rational' health service, ethical and practical objections have restricted the use made of the randomised controlled trial. Some doctors objected to the employment of scarce resources in this type of evaluation, others felt that it would be difficult to control for all possible other variables which might influence outcomes – such as the impact of the placebo on the control group. More important, was it right to deliberately withhold a new therapy from a group or, conversely, to use a group as 'guinea pigs' to test new treatments?

A range of other approaches has been used to measure outcomes. As you might expect from a discipline which is heavily dependent on science, most of these have been largely quantitative and experimental, although they have in general attempted to circumvent ethical problems by starting from a basis of voluntary participation. This has meant that the scientific strength of random allocation has been weakened, even if such experiments attempt to control for potentially influential variables.

In reality evaluating health care goes far beyond using RCTs to assess new treatments, although this is one significant part of evaluation. For example, clinicians have used various types of medical audit to check on the efficacy of different types of treatment: reviewing case-notes of selected patients and peer review – where one group of doctors assess their colleagues' work. This type of evaluation does result in changes in treatment or the adoption of treatment protocols, a particular approach with consensus backing. However, as Savage (1986) has noted, case-note and peer review takes place within particular social settings, in which power and control are unevely distributed. The weight of an orthodoxy backed by senior colleagues can result in the minority view being challenged, whether or not it represents 'better' treatment. On the other hand initiatives such as the Confidential Enquiry into Peri-operative Deaths (1987), although it remained entirely confidential, represented an important step in assessing treatment (Harrison *et al.*, 1990). Whilst the investigation was anonymous, voluntary and aimed to take no action against individuals, it did suggest that avoidable deaths could be related to doubtful practices and inexperienced clinicians.

Medical audit has now been supplemented by new managerial measures of success. Clearly the measurement of effectiveness in health care goes beyond treatment alone. In these circumstances Illsley (1980) has argued that instead of searching for the perfect experimental method and conditions – which are not likely to be found anyway – health workers should concentrate on 'successive partial evaluations and reforms' which assess and modify the complex processes involved in health work. In particular, it seems a rather dubious course to assess a clinical intervention without taking into account the nursing and other health worker contribution to the patient's recovery.

The QALY

As we have noted, measures are being sought by those in the field of medicine and epidemiology which will answer questions about the economy, efficiency and effectiveness of different types of treatment and of medical intervention. Among the findings which are being used to make such decisions are those from the field of health economics, which has emerged as an influential discipline in health care in the last two decades. Clinical budgeting, management budgeting and optional appraisal are all financial decision making systems which have been designed to enable clinicians and managers to operate more efficiently. Clinical budgeting, for example, in which health authorities allocated resources to each major area of clinical activity rather than on a functional basis, was an attempt to involve hospital clinicians and charge nurses in annual resource allocation. The objective was to encourage health professionals to increase efficiency and achieve a more 'rational' use of resources by providing them with information about the cost components of their clinical area.

QALYs – quality adjusted life years – are the most contentious and potentially comprehensive of these recent initiatives. They have come into prominence not just because cost-containment is seen as increasingly important in the health sector, but also because they seem to offer a more 'rational' and equitable way of rationing health care, one which focuses on 'quality of life' rather than disease. Health economists have argued that the range and cost of health interventions demands that new methods of rationing should be used, which weigh costs and benefits against the quality of life that can be expected for various types of patients.

The QALY attempts to do this by applying a cost-benefit analysis, expressed in monetary units, to every form of treatment. The costs of any treatment are set against the benefits, which are defined not simply as 'added years of life' but in terms of the 'quality' of that year of life. Thus, a 'well-year' is 'the equivalent of a year of completely well life, free of dysfunction, symptoms and health-related problems' (Fallowfield, 1990). In other words, QALYs attempt to go beyond merely measuring relative *financial* costs of various treatments to take into account the human, *quality of life* dimension. If a particular treatment leaves someone immobile or in pain for one numerical year after it is carried out, for example, that person will have experienced less than one 'well-year'. In QALY analysis this can be expressed in numerical terms.

The York health economists developed the QALY by classifying eight levels of states of illness and disability and four levels of distress (see Table 13.3). Particular states of illness or disability were then ranked according to the matrix formed by putting the disability and distress classifications together (Rosser and Kind, 1978). The original ranking was carried out by 70 people: experienced SRN nurses, senior doctors and patients from medical wards and psychiatry plus 20 'healthy volunteers' (Fallowfield, 1990). You can see the valuation matrix produced from the original ranking in Table 13.4.

○ Look at Table 13.3, which gives the disability and distress classifications, and at Table 13.4, the valuation matrix. Comment on the results. What are your views about the results and the process?

TABLE 13.3 Classification of states of illness. Source: Fallowfield (1990)

Disability
(Extent to which patient is unable to pursue activities of normal person at time which classification is made.)
1 No disability
2 Slight social disability
3 Severe social disability and/or impairment of performance at work. Able to do all housework except heavy tasks
4 Choice of work or performance at work severely limited. Housewives and old people able to do light housework only but able to go out shopping
5 Unable to undertake any paid employment. Unable to continue any education. Old people confined to home except for escorted outings and short walks and unable to do shopping. Housewives only able to perform a few simple tasks
6 Confined to chair or to wheelchair or able to move around home only with support from an assistant
7 Confined to bed
8 Unconscious

Distress
(Describing patient's pain and/or mental disturbance and/or reaction to disability.)
A No distress
B Mild
C Moderate
D Severe

TABLE 13.4 Valuation matrix. Source: Fallowfield (1990)

Disability rating	Distress rating			
	A None	B Mild	C Moderate	D Severe
1 None	1.000	0.995	0.990	0.967
2 Slight	0.990	0.986	0.973	0.932
3 Some impairment of performance	0.980	0.972	0.956	0.912
4 Performance severely limited	0.964	0.956	0.942	0.870
5 Unable to undertake employment	0.946	0.935	0.900	0.700
6 Confined to chair, etc.	0.875	0.845	0.680	0.000
7 Confined to bed	0.677	0.564	0.000	1.486
8 Unconscious	−1.028	not applicable		

Fixed points: healthy = 1; dead = 0.

Comments on this process and on the matrix were sought from students who tested this material for an O.U. course (K258, 1992). They found few problems with the ratings at each extreme of the matrix – obviously it was better to have a slight impairment than to be confined to bed or unconscious – but the rest they found problematic. The testers were also dubious about the idea of trusting someone else's judgements. Fallowfield (1990) commented that there was no consensus among the original assessors; in particular, doctors, medical patients and medical nurses disagreed, whereas pychiatric patients and nurses tended to agree in their rankings. Doctors saw distress as a greater problem than the other groups. If you rebelled against the whole idea of the QALY, it is worth remembering that doctors (and nurses and managers) have always made rationing decisions about access to health care. Is it a less equitable system than the professional judgement that has been exercised in the past?

Academic commentators from the social sciences, whilst acknowledging the potential of the QALY and similar 'rational choice' systems, have expressed doubt about whether health economists' concept of rationality in health and of the 'rational conduct' of the consumer or producer of health services bear much relation to the socially complex, often irrational, constructed world of health (Ashmore et al., 1989). In a different vein, Weale (1988) points out that the use of the QALY will tend to favour some categories of patients more than others. Older people, for example, whose quality of life is already poor before a particular intervention, will find themselves discriminated against even if their health improves. He argues that the QALY confuses the concept of need with the notion of ability to benefit:

This fails to offer any weighting to favour those whose needs stem from great misfortune – especially, in our context, medical misfortune – over those whose 'needs' consist simply of a capacity to benefit.

Weale (1988)

Managerial measures of success

As we noted in Section 13.3, the rise of managerialism in the health service has resulted in the development of new methods of quality assurance for measuring process and outcomes. These have mainly consisted of scrutinies of spending, performance reviews and performance indicators. One of their most contentious contributions has been the development of *performance indicators*: routinely collected statistics about specific activities, such as hospital admissions rates, bed stay, bed occupancy rates and so on (see Table 13.5). This enables services in particular sectors to be compared across the country,

TABLE 13.5 Performance indicators. Source: Davey and Popay (1993)

	National average	Coventry average
Gynaecology day cases for people aged 16–64, expressed as a percentage of what would be expected given national rates	100	121.7
Hospital day-case episodes for people aged 65+ concerning gynaecology, expressed as a rate per 1000 people in the population (national or district)	0.450	0.660
Cervical cancer annual SMR for females aged 16–64	99.6	171.5
Average length of hospital episodes for gynaecology (days)	2.5	2.45
Number of patients awaiting admission for gynaecology, per 1000 people in the population (national or district)	4.75	7.03
Number of gynaecology consultants per 100 000 people in the population (national or district)	3.02	2.28
Number of women aged 35–64 who have had a cevical smear in the last 5.5 years, divided by the number of women in the population (national or district)	68.21	85.37

but has created a positive minefield in interpretation. It is possible to know a great deal about activity within the health service and yet not be able to determine clearly what should be changed to influence outcomes. Moreover, the scheme was introduced hurriedly and did not link to other evaluation measures; although managers have made use of it, doctors and other health workers remained sceptical (Harrison *et al.*, 1990). Nothing has yet emerged to reverse the general view of performance indicators as a limited measure of top-down assessment of a very narrow range of criteria. Managers themselves are measured and evaluated through individual performance review and performance-related pay, and they have now begun – as we noted earlier – to apply this to clinicians.

○ Suggest some other approaches to evaluation used by managers of health services.

Increasingly, managers are also using patient satisfaction surveys and investigations to evaluate health service performance. The somewhat crude measures of through-put can be supplemented by various evaluations of the quality of the service received by patients (see Figure 13.4). Many of these are simple questionnaires developed for easy assessment by computer, but a few are fairly sophisticated, qualitative studies. Some managers have made use of the wide variety of health survey methods generated by epidemiologists and social scientists, which are considered below. Finally, there is some evidence to be

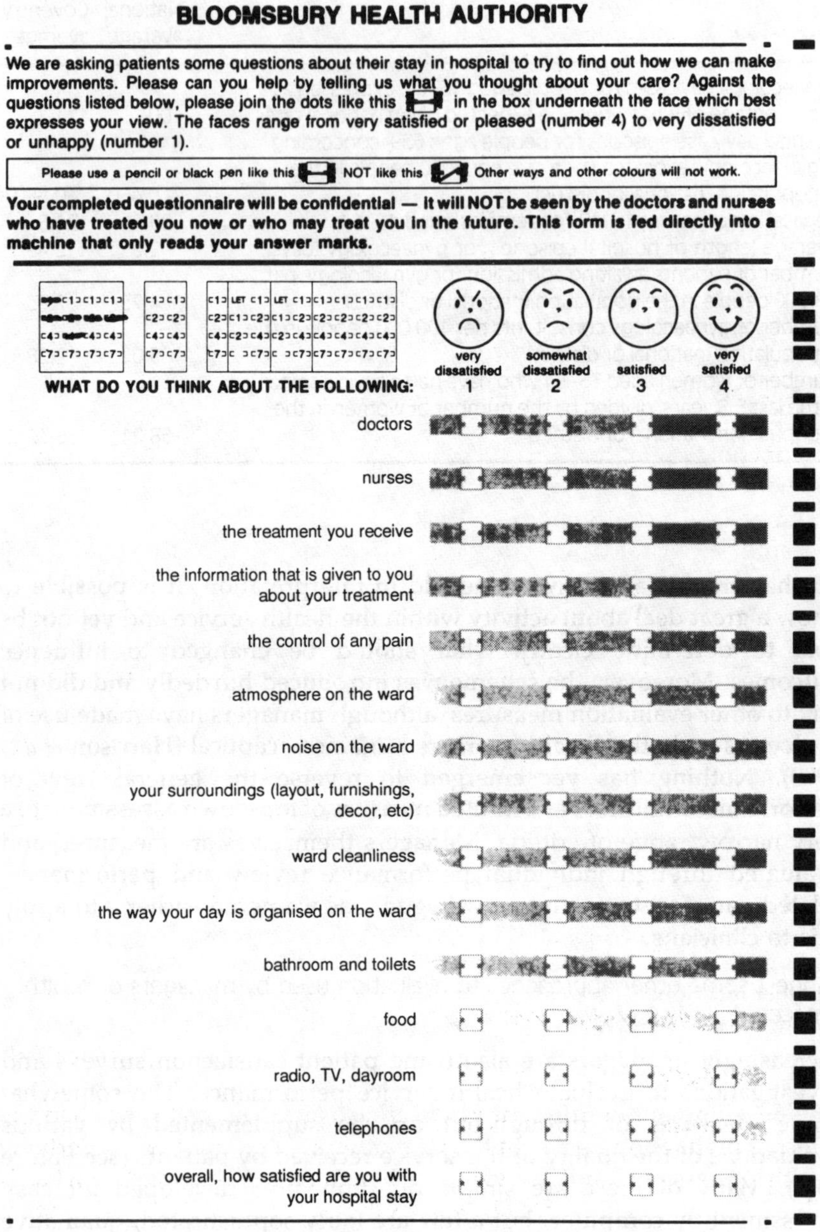

BLOOMSBURY HEALTH AUTHORITY

We are asking patients some questions about their stay in hospital to try to find out how we can make improvements. Please can you help by telling us what you thought about your care? Against the questions listed below, please join the dots like this ▬ in the box underneath the face which best expresses your view. The faces range from very satisfied or pleased (number 4) to very dissatisfied or unhappy (number 1).

Please use a pencil or black pen like this ▬ NOT like this ▨ Other ways and other colours will not work.

Your completed questionnaire will be confidential — it will NOT be seen by the doctors and nurses who have treated you now or who may treat you in the future. This form is fed directly into a machine that only reads your answer marks.

WHAT DO YOU THINK ABOUT THE FOLLOWING:

	very dissatisfied 1	somewhat dissatisfied 2	satisfied 3	very satisfied 4
doctors				
nurses				
the treatment you receive				
the information that is given to you about your treatment				
the control of any pain				
atmosphere on the ward				
noise on the ward				
your surroundings (layout, furnishings, decor, etc)				
ward cleanliness				
the way your day is organised on the ward				
bathroom and toilets				
food				
radio, TV, dayroom				
telephones				
overall, how satisfied are you with your hospital stay				

FIGURE 13.4 Quality of service evaluation. Source: CASPE (1988)

gleaned from 'exit behaviour': that is, people's choices about which services to avoid or to use. It has been argued by some on the New Right that exit choice should be the main market mechanism of health provision. If consumers do not like the services that are provided, they will not use them or will demand better services.

Measuring health and quality of life

Over the last decade or so a great deal of research effort has gone into measuring health. A wide variety of questionnaires and ratings schedules have been devised to assess people's feelings about their health state and quality of life. Some of these have been developed by health economists, and we have explored one ambitious attempt to measure and value quality of life – the QALY. Ann Bowling (1991) has critically reviewed a wide range of quality of life measurement scales which are increasingly being used to measure health outcome: in terms of functional ability, health status, psychological wellbeing, social networks and social support and in terms of measures of life satisfaction and morale. These attempt to take into account what the patient feels, to measure social and psychological aspects of health rather than just physical ones.

There are many problems in devising and using such measures: How is health defined and who is defining it? Should health outcome be defined in functional or wider social terms? How are classifications about illness or disability states arrived at? Part of this is the question about who gets to do the research, what research gets done, and how far academic researchers are really able to represent the views of lay people through gathering such data. Bowling (1991) comments about quality of life measures that:

While a number of self-rating scales exist . . . few indicators attempt to measure patients' perceptions of improvements or satisfaction with level of performance; yet it is this element which is largely responsible for predicting whether individuals seek care, accept treatment and consider themselves to be well and 'recovered'.

Bowling (1991)

The development of different kinds of measurement scales has had the effect of highlighting some of the very different assumptions underlying health professional and lay views of health and illness, and of what is valued about quality of life. For example, one study used several different scales to investigate whether assessments of quality of life of cancer patients by health professionals are meaningful and reliable. It compared the assessments made by patients and by professionals and found wide variations between those of doctors and patients, suggesting that doctors did not accurately assess patients' quality of life (Slevin *et al.* reported in Bowling, 1991). A very broadly based local needs assessment survey in Kirkstall, Leeds, found that lay and professional

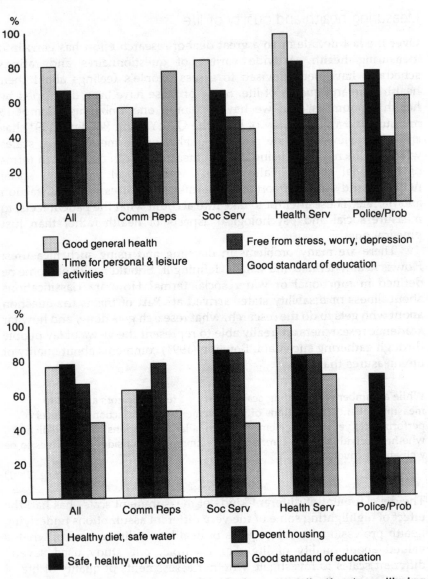

FIGURE 13.5 Perceived importance of factors contributing to wellbeing and quality of life. Source: Percy-Smith and Sanderson (1992)

groups valued aspects of physical and mental health differently and attached different degrees of importance to factors underpinning health status, such as a non-hazardous physical environment, economic security and appropriate health care (Percy-Smith and Sanderson, 1992). The study also found that different professional groups interviewed had differing views, and that community representatives' views about people's needs did not necessarily reflect those expressed by 'ordinary local people'. This suggests that, if the NHS is going to rely on consumer surveys as a way of enabling ordinary people to make their voices heard, then such studies will need to be extensive and sophisticated rather than quick and simple questionnaire-style surveys (see Figure 13.5). Differences between the interests and outlook of health and social care workers, police and probation officers and lay people, as well as between the priorities of different groups of reseachers, are likely to continue.

Health service principles and practice

We also need to find ways of assessing health services as a whole. One approach is to consider the principles underpinning the health service. What were and are its guiding principles? What were the main priorities in setting up the service and are they still important in the 1990s? Allsop (1984) has suggested that five principles underpinned the National Health Service when it was established in the 1940s (see Box 13.3). Have these founding principles been upheld in the half century or so since the NHS was established? Alongside this, it would also be appropriate to ask whether these founding principles are still valid, whether they reflect the priorities and concerns of the 1990s. Clearly any assessment

---

BOX 13.3 Founding principles of the NHS. Source: Allsop (1984)

- *The collectivist principle* of centralised state organisation and responsibility for the health needs of all citizens, with central government control of finance and policy. Democratic accountability is envisaged as being achieved through this collectivist approach.
- *The comprehensive principle* of access for all citizens to all types of health services: primary secondary and tertiary care and treatment from dentists, pharmacists and opticians.
- *The universal principle* of providing health services which were free for the whole population at the point of use, on the basis of doctors' determination of health need, and which were paid for through National Insurance contributions and general taxation.
- *The principle of equality* of providing health services which were as nearly as possible of a uniform standard.
- *The principle of professional autonomy* which meant that GPs and hospital doctors had complete clinical freedom in relation to their patients and thus had considerable influence over resource allocation.

based on these principles would have to be provisional, but it is a useful starting point.

○   Reflect on Allsop's (1984) founding principles of the NHS. Consider whether they are still in place and how far they are still valid.

If nothing else, this exercise should demonstrate that any discussion of evaluating health care is bound up with values and beliefs. Any reflection on how far the founding principles are, and should be, in place today involves some consideration of the rights and wrongs of the NHS when it was established in the 1940s and of the situation in health care today: in other words, we run into an ideological and political minefield. However, there may be a consensus on some issues. For example, the universal principle still seems largely intact. Health care is still mainly free at the point of use, and health professionals still determine individual patient needs through consultation and diagnosis. However, charges were introduced in the 1950s, and now an increasing number of charges for services are being made – for example for prescriptions, dentistry and opthalmic services. The comprehensive principle is still in place, and it could be argued that coverage is improved because the range of services has grown considerably since the 1940s (to embrace specialist tertiary care services, for example). In a similar way, concern for equality has been a feature of health service policy since the 1940s. Inequalities in access to primary and hospital care have been tackled, though the problems are not solved, and standards of treatment are more uniform than in the past. On the other hand evidence of an inverse care law of class related health inequalities and of racial discrimination and ageism in the delivery of health services is a reminder that the NHS has not fully realised its principle of equality (Tudor Hart, 1971; Townsend et al., 1988).

How far do you think the collectivist principle is still in place? Interestingly, the shell of collectivism in the NHS is still in evidence, in spite of one-and-a-half decades of New Right attacks. Centralised state organisation of health has been deliberately undermined by the quasi-market restructuring, but central control over policy, resources and appointments is now arguably greater. It is the rhetoric of collectivism that has been most strongly challenged; in place of 'state responsibility for health' individual responsibility – to develop a healthy lifestyle, to care for dependants, to take out private health insurance – is now emphasised. But as we noted in Section 13.4, democratic accountability is arguably less now than in the 1940s when part of the service was under local authority control and there was local representation on hospital boards.

Finally, the principle of professional autonomy has been deliberately confronted and attacked (see Section 13.4). Managerialism has been developed as a way of controlling clinicians and reducing the freedom to determine treatment and thereby influence resources. Other measures, such as the generic drug list for hospitals and new GP contracts, have chipped away at medical control. But it is possible that the emergence of quasi-markets in health will enhance the power of doctors; certainly GPs are being given the opportunity to build up their businesses (although through the 1990 GP contracts their work is being more closely prescribed). Cox (1991) suggests that trust status, clinical budgeting, revenue earning and so on could lead to 'new forms of autonomy' for consultants.

The 'four Es'

To some extent Allsop's principles have been refined and extended. For example, the widely used evaluative categories of the 'four Es' – economy, efficiency, effectiveness and equity – offer a more specific mechanism for evaluating health care but are not unrelated to Allsop's guiding principles. *Equity* – the notion of fairness – carries with it a commitment to providing equality in service provision, but also the recognition that to achieve fairness of treatment might require positive action and special types of services, for example for black and minority ethnic patients. *Economy* – keeping down costs – has been a concern of the NHS since just after its inception when it was realised that demand for health care would not 'plateau out'. Many of the recent structural changes, as we have noted, have been driven by the desire to contain costs. *Efficiency* – ensuring that the service is efficiently run and getting value for money – goes further than control of costs towards providing a service that is 'fit for purpose'. The debate about the character and appropriateness of NHS structure and organisation to deliver this service has already been reviewed. Finally, *effectiveness* is about delivering a service that is not only economic and efficient, but actually reaches the people it should be serving and provides them with the types of services they need and can use. If the four Es are in place, Allsop's first four principles of collectivism, universalism, equality and comprehensiveness are likely to be underpinning the service. On the other hand the professional autonomy principle might contribute little towards achieving the four Es.

13.6 The future of health and health work

To move beyond the more focused (but also more restricting) medical, economic and policy measures of health care and health outcome is to enter a conceptual minefield. Judgements about health and health care are inevitably bound up with deep-seated values and beliefs. The different approaches we have investigated in Sections 13.4 and 13.5 are bound up with different conceptions of 'what health is'; in Foucauldian terms, what we would suggest are distinctive 'ways of seeing' and 'ways of knowing' (Foucault, 1973). In other words, as these contrasting approaches are considered, it is important to remember that health and illness are 'socially constructed'; they are developed and sustained through the disparate and sometimes conflicting accounts that are given by health professionals, official sources, service users, lay people and so on. In the late twentieth century there is no single health 'discourse' to which everyone subscribes (Beattie *et al.*, 1993).

A disease model or a health model?

Having said this, there are some promising avenues to explore beyond the medical model. One approach is to take much more seriously lay people's expressed views about their own health and illness. As we noted in Chapter 10, there is now more interest in personal stories and lay accounts, even if it is still mainly researchers who get to do the reporting back. Ann Bowling (1991) notes that 'researchers are increasingly inclining towards self-ratings of present health; personal evaluation of physical condition; feelings of anxiety, nerves, depression; feelings of general positive affect; and future expectations about health'. But people's thoughts and feelings about health and illness, and about the quality of health care, are not just expressed through research. As we noted in earlier chapters, new social movements, community activities, self help groups and pressure groups of all kinds are demonstrating their views about health and illness through action. Some health service managers and health professionals are finding that user groups and voluntary sector organisations can offer new (and sometimes controversial) insights.

At a more formal level several frameworks for individual understanding and perceptions of health in its broadest sense have been developed, as for example in health promotion models and theories (see Seedhouse, 1985). But a major temptation here, as we noted in Chapter 1, is the tendency to conceptualise health as an object rather than viewing it, as the World Health Organisation (1984) has suggested, as a 'resource for living'. Hughes' (1990) framework for beginning to assess aspects of quality of life is a fluid and suggestive model (see Figure 13.6). It draws attention to the relationship between the 'conditions of life' – such as housing and income – and the 'experiences of life' – such as satisfaction and a positive self image. Whereas conditions can be more objectively assessed, she suggests, experiences

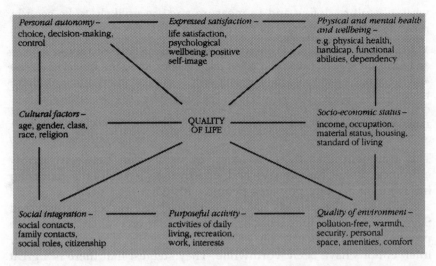

FIGURE 13.6 A conceptual model of quality of life. Source: Hughes (1990)

are more subjective; however, conditions often influence experiences, and (it might be added) our experiences colour our perceptions of conditions to some extent. By combining objective and subjective dimensions into a single framework Hughes begins to map the broader view of health and health care as a 'quality of life'.

A social model?

Health promotion constitutes the most ambitious programme for transforming health and health care. The UK Health of the Nation strategy (DoH, 1992a) derives from a medical model, although it also offers opportunities to move beyond this. Evaluation of the progress made towards better health in this strategy is largely to be measured through assessment of the extent to which the mortality and morbidity toll from various diseases – cancers, stroke, cardiovascular disease and so on – has been reduced (see Chapter 1, page 10, Table 1.2). The World Health Organisation 1985 Health For All (HFA) strategy (see Chapter 1, pages 25–6, Table 1.5) and the 1987 Healthy Public Policy strategy represent much bolder attempts to chart objectives and guiding principles within an all-embracing social model of health. An evaluation within this model encompasses not just disease reduction but assesses a wide range of other, positive health indicators – such as an increase in 'healthful behaviour', in community participation, change in local environments to make 'healthy choices easier choices' and shifts towards more 'healthy' public policies. These changes, as health promoters acknowledge, are very difficult to define and to measure and are unlikely to be seen by most health professionals as representing value for money:

> Most academic approaches to evaluation are limited to a time scale of several years and focus on specific cause and effect relationships; the germ model of disease and the magic bullet solution of an antibiotic or surgical intervention continues to dominate scientific thought. Within health systems there is a strong emphasis on value for money and on measures of efficiency – effectiveness is rarely addressed.
>
> *Ashton and Seymour (1988)*

The argument that there is likely to be tension between narrow efficiency (value for money) and effectiveness (whether a particular intervention actually provides people with what they need, want and are able to make use of) has been highlighted earlier. Ashton and Seymour argue that little work has yet been done on evaluation in health promotion, in particular on enabling lay people to assess whether interventions have been worthwhile. They suggest that there is a great need to develop positive indicators which are qualitative, not just quantitative, which focus on contexts as well as people and which are bottom-up and broadly based. These characteristics will, of course, make evaluation much more difficult. As we have noted, the HFA targets have been adapted by health promoters and campaigners involved in the Healthy Cities movement in the UK, by those developing HFA 2000 initiatives and involved in the New Public Health movement, but health promotion as an activity remains on the fringe of health work.

○ Look back at the Health For All targets (WHO, 1985) Table 1.5 on pages 25–6. Suggest why this approach is still fairly marginal to the health sector.

These 38 targets are very wide-ranging, encompassing not just health in the physical or medical sense of the term but 'health as a resource for living'. Ill health is seen to arise from all aspects of the environment: from work, housing, the conditions of everyday life. Improving health is seen as partly about reducing risks and the incidence of disease and about providing appropriate health care of those who are ill, but it is also about making everyday life safer and 'healthier'. The Healthy Public Policy approach is concerned with promoting structural changes which will make health a higher priority on wider policy agendas: housing, environment, transport and so on. The territory of health, it seems, has been redefined as bound up with the whole of life. In this context the work of health professionals is never ending – concerned with changing public attitudes, transforming public policies and encompassing people's everyday lives. Evaluation of health and health care interventions becomes very difficult. Perhaps it is not surprising that most health professionals prefer to work within a more restricted medical model.

It should be noted that the whole health promotion approach has also attracted criticism both on the grounds that it is regulatory and repressive and also as individualistic and elitist. The New Right has attacked health promotion on the grounds that it attempts to extend the 'nanny state'; under the guise of promoting health it seeks to control people's lives and limit their personal freedom (Green, 1990). Within sociology conflict theorists have questioned the extent to which health promotion can hope to set a new agenda for health and health care and have noted that the dominant values in much of contemporary health education and health promotion remain individualist and elitist (Rodmell and Watt, 1986). Although health promotion programmes claim to promote structural change and empower lay people, they operate within the boundaries of the health sector and may have a rhetorical rather than a real commitment to 'empowerment'. In a different vein, social constructionists have noted how the reconceptuali-sation of health and 'caring for health' has expanded into a potential surveillance of all aspects of daily life. You will recall that Armstrong (1983a, 1993) has argued that the 'clinical gaze' became a 'community gaze' – a surveillance not just of sick people in hospitals but of healthy people who were potentially 'at risk' in the whole community. He sees this as a productive process in which the extended gaze assists in the construction of new identities and subjectivities (see Chapter 11). But others have emphasised the negative aspects of the social regulation of lives and bodies (Crawford, 1984).

The future of health services

The rolling back of the welfare state, although it has been the rhetorical centrepiece of New Right philosophy, has been more apparent than real. There is, of course, a real possibility that this could change. For example, targeting and means-testing in social security could develop further, with the removal of certain categories of claimants such as the short term unemployed. In the health service the rationing of treatment could become more explicitly linked to patient characteristics such as attitudes, health behaviour and age. The open refusal of treatment to patients who refuse to give up smoking or to follow medical advice may mark the beginning of the end of a commitment to NHS founding principles of universalism, comprehensiveness and equality. Whatever happens, it is clear that the health sector will no longer be a protected, universalist-oriented system but will be open to the same pressures that operate in other parts of the welfare state.

In theory, the announcement of the coming demise of regional health authorities and the development of regional offices of the NHS Management Executive (NHSME) clears the way for a full internal market in health care. District health authorities and GP fundholders will be the purchasers; strategic planning for health care needs will be done at the level of the local population – or perhaps at the centre by the NHS Management Executive. In a free market, it might be argued, strategic planning is not required at all; the laws of supply and demand will deliver the appropriate mix of health care. Trusts will be the providers, regulated only by stipulations about accident and emergency provision and the requirement to write an annual business plan for the Department of Health. In practice it is not entirely clear that a full market system will emerge. In one sense control by the NHSME brings ministerial and political intervention closer, and as protests and public pressure grow, the temptation to make political rather than market decisions will be greater.

It is an open question whether such a system will continue to deliver a relatively comprehensive, equitable and universalist health care service and whether standards will improve or decline. What is likely is that private health care and private health insurance will grow faster in the future. Private hospitals will win more contracts to carry out the types of cold surgery – hip replacements, cataract operations – that are relatively unproblematic and cost-containable. The growth of private health insurance, already beginning to recover after the recession years, reflects increasing public awareness that ward closures and rationing in the NHS will have an impact on their health unless they make separate provision. Even if universalism, collectivism and equality remain formal NHS principles, they could be fatally undermined by growth of the private sector.

This suggests that the major issues for health care in the future are creeping privatisation, cash constraints and the danger of a two-tier health system. The market structure and the freedom of manoeuvre of the trusts mean that mergers and deals with the private health sector are not to be ruled out. Could a few major public-private hospital chains replace the multiplicity of present NHS trusts? Will government step in to prevent mergers or will it, as in other sectors, allow a few major providers to dominate the health market? A related issue is the question of funding. Will the current wave of ward closures and unemployed health professionals continue? Or will purchasers and providers learn to work the internal market so that these teething troubles are overcome? Perhaps the market will move towards dialogue rather than more competition, with much closer relationships developing between fund-holding GPs, FHSAs and DHAs to share information, research needs and develop contracts – perhaps case contracts – that have much tighter specifications. If this happens, the prospects for improving health services will be much greater.

Finally, what is the likelihood of a two-tier health service emerging?

Critics on the political left argue that this is already apparent, with queue jumping by privately insured patients, preferential treatment in private wards and a privileged position in relation to access to treatment being enjoyed by patients of fundholding GPs. These may be seen as minor hiccups in an emerging system; on the other hand the growth of private health care will reinforce the differences between patients, particularly for access to non-urgent treatment.

Lay voices in health care

Williams (1992) has argued that the real challenge for welfare in the 1990s is to develop a strategy that combines both universality in provision and a sensitive regard for diversity in needs and interests, which new social movements – such as survivors' groups, black women's groups and disability rights groups – have increasingly articulated. She suggests that the notion of citizenship could become the vehicle which 'combines in creative and imaginative ways universal entitlements to basic provisions in income, health and social welfare to the collective articulation and active pursuit of specific welfare needs'. This envisages a future in health services in which lay voices are increasingly heard and responded to and in which service users have a growing part to play in helping to set priorities and principles in health care.

But how realistic is this scenario? Increasingly consumer choice is being seen as a major way of moving forward and evaluating health care, but it is being developed in ways which are not necessarily connected at all to active participation in health, let alone notions of citizenship. The Patient's Charter (1991) outlines ten rights and nine national standards, which include the right to be given detailed information on health services, to be treated within two years of being put on a waiting list and to have any complaints fully investigated (see Box 13.4). Consumers, it is claimed, will be free to change doctors, to 'vote with their feet' or to complain if national standards are not met.

○ Thinking back to the earlier discussion of the sovereign consumer, what issues and problems are raised by consumer choice in health care?

First, consumers cannot choose health care in the same way as they choose goods in a supermarket. In fact, it is GP fundholders and purchaser health authorities who choose which services they will get. Second, not all consumers have equal knowledge or social status. For some it will be relatively easy to make a complaint, for others it will be impossible. Third, it is unclear who the consumer really is: is it only the current user of health services, or should the views of all taxpayers and potential patients be heard too? If so, how should this be effected: by

BOX 13.4 The Patient's Charter: selected extracts. Source: DoH (1991)

Seven existing rights	Three new rights from 1 April 1992
Every citizen has the following established National Health Service rights:	
1 To receive health care on the basis of clinical need, regardless of ability to pay	**1** To be given detailed information on local health services, including quality standards and maximum waiting times
2 To be registered with a GP	**2** To be guaranteed admission for treatment by a specific date no later than two years from the day when your consultant places you on a waiting list
3 To receive emergency medical care at any time, through your GP or the emergency ambulance service and hospital accident and emergency departments	**3** To have any complaint about NHS services – whoever provides them – investigated and to receive a full and prompt written reply from the chief executive or general manager.
4 To be referred to a consultant, acceptable to you, when your GP thinks it necessary, and to be referred for a second opinion if you and your GP agree this is desirable	
5 To be given a clear explanation of any treatment proposed, including any risks and any alternatives, before you decide whether you will agree to the treatment	
6 To have access to your health records, and to know that those working for the NHS are under a legal duty to keep their contents confidential	
7 To choose whether or not you wish to take part in medical research or medical student training	

responding to 'exit choices', by listening to patient representatives, by increasing the representation of local people in the health service? Winkler (1987) has argued that a 'supermarket model' of health, with the consumer's main job being to make a selection of goods, cannot deliver equity and is being used by managers mainly to control clinicians. On the other hand perhaps there is potential for local voices to be heard in the new health service, if managers develop patient satisfaction surveys beyond merely the assessment of 'hotel services'. In 1992 the NHSME, in its paper *Listening to local voices in the NHS*, argued that purchasers should listen to local people's views and take them into account in making decisions about priority services and rationing in health care (Sykes *et al.*, 1992). It envisaged developing much more sensitive indicators of patient response as well as consultation with patient groups and representatives. But there is still the question of why NHS trusts should give such work any real priority.

The future of nursing within health work

What will be the role of nursing in the health service of the future? The most evident trend at present is the absolute decline in the number of qualified nurses in employment. Nursing students reaching the end of their training are being told that there are no jobs for them, wards are closing and trusts are signalling that there are no funds to continue treating patients. The cutback in nursing numbers has hit Project 2000 diplomates as well as traditionally trained nurses, but in the medium term nursing diplomates and nursing graduates are likely to win in competition with traditional RGN qualifiers.

In trusts, and to a lesser extent in community nursing, the crucial new dimension is skill mix. The emergence of the health care assistant to fill the gap left by giving supernumerary status to student nurses has considerable implications for the future of nursing. The freedom of trusts to set their own salary rates and their own terms and conditions of employment offers great opportunities for extending skill mix. It also suggests that qualified experienced nurses will increasingly become supervisors of care-giving rather than hands-on care-givers themselves. Other professional groups allied to medicine, for example speech therapists and occupational therapists, are also finding that trusts are not always willing to pay for their services.

The new community care and fundholding arrangements will inevitably have a profound effect on nursing in community settings. Certain groups of nurses, such as community mental handicap nurses, are being phased out altogether in some health authorities and replaced by social services department employees (for example in Somerset RHA). Many nurses feel uneasy about the juxtaposition of 'social care' and 'health care' in the Griffiths Report (DoH, 1988), feel threatened by the emergence of social workers as 'key workers' in the delivery of community care and concerned that 'holistic' care will not be achievable if skill mix is extended in domiciliary care. As fundholding GPs gain more power in the NHS quasi-market, they may well decide to initiate a closer and more supervisory relationship with community nursing services. Moreover, there is continued uncertainty about whether local community nursing teams will win their bids to provide a service to their localities. These trends, together with the fact that many GPs are developing the role of their practice nurses, may mean that community nursing is pulled in the direction of general practitioner services. Certainly the possibility of developing the autonomous nursing service proposed by the Cumberlege Committee Report (DHSS, 1986a) seems to have receded for the present.

The work of nursing, although it continues to attract male students and their participation is increasing on Project 2000 courses, will remain a predominantly female occupation, but the class, race and gender composition of the workforce may well change. It has been noted that Project 2000 upgrades the work of nursing by offering students a recognised and transferable higher education award. This upward movement in qualifications, manifested also in the rising number of nursing degrees, is likely to create a new class structure in nursing. The future nursing elite is likely to be composed of predominantly white, middle class, female (and male) nurses and managers and working class male managers. This elite will supervise and control a white, working class core of qualified RGN nurses and a solid phalanx of semi-qualified and unqualified SENs, auxiliaries and health care assistants, a disproportionate number of whom will continue to be recruited from black and minority ethnic groups. In other words, class, race and gender barriers – although they may be overcome by women in middle and upper nursing management – will still limit opportunities for other groups. Indeed nursing seems to be more concerned to create a professional elite training equivalent to medical training than to improve conditions and opportunities for the ranks of semi-qualified and unqualified health workers.

In some ways the shifts in service structure and the new strategic approach to health – for example in the Health of the Nation strategy (1992) – offer exciting prospects for nurses to become change agents for health. Within trusts and in GP practices the obvious advantanges of using nursing labour where possible to replace the much more expensive medical labour are already well known. There is the possibility of involving nurses in medical procedures and in prescribing a limited range of drug therapies and treatments – some of which already happens *de facto* in hospital wards and in the district nursing team. One detailed study of the implications of the Griffiths Management Enquiry for nurses also suggested that, after a painful process of adjustment, nurses were becoming highly skilled middle managers and 'will be in an excellent position to be the general managers of the future, having both expert knowledge and enhanced management skills' (Owens and Glennerster, 1990).

Should nurses welcome this shift or not? How ready are they, in terms of training and attitudes, to take on such responsibilities or to play a broader strategic role – for example in health promotion? Part of the answer depends on the adequacy of the new Project 2000 education programmes. But part also depends on the extent to which nurses (and other health workers) can retain and extend their autonomy. In the latest round of changes in the NHS, as in the Griffiths Management Enquiry of 1984 and in previous reorganisations of the NHS since its inception, nurses have been conspicuous by their absence from the inner policy making circle. Although profoundly influenced by the changes, nursing has had little input into the development of quasi-markets. It seems that the power of clinicians may be enhanced by the changes, but the position of nurses – apart from those who have succeeded in the field of NHS management – looks more uncertain.

Alternative futures for health

Finally, nurses and other health workers will be operating in an increasingly complex health market. This does not only include trusts, fundholders and health authority purchasers, but private charitable and commercial providers and a growing number of independent alternative practitioners. As we noted in Chapter 10, alternative medicine forms an increasingly respectable and popular part of health provision, and in a quasi-market situation, if consumer demand continues to grow, GPs and health authorities may start to purchase some of the more 'acceptable' therapies, such as acupuncture, for certain categories of patients. We might reach a situation, as in continental Europe, where such therapies are widely accepted and more freely available.

This growing diversity in health care provision reflects a deeper pluralism in health beliefs. There is now no longer such unquestioning acceptance of traditional biomedical explanation and practice. The intractable nature of many contemporary diseases, such as cancers, and the rising evidence of the side effects and dependency-inducing character of many treatments and drugs have encouraged a loss of faith and a search for new, more gentle and 'natural' therapies. At the same time, of course, the power of medicine over people's lives may be said to be advancing; in many areas of life – taking out an insurance policy, getting a new job, qualifying for a mortgage and so on – medical inspection and certification are required. The power of 'magic bullet' medicine is enormous, and people give large sums to causes like cancer research. Medicine itself is changing, incorporating new therapies and adopting a holistic style with the active participating patient at the centre.

It is possible that biomedicine will regroup and extend its control over the whole of the new health market, embracing and neutralising the threat from alternative therapy in the same way as in the past it colonised pharmacy or radiography. Although the quasi-market in health care was claimed as a triumph for the sovereign consumer, it is at present doubtful whether the consumer's voice will make itself heard. In spite of recent attempts to control it, the medical profession still looks the most likely candidate to dominate the new market. However, an alliance of purchasers and consumers – not just 'sovereign consumers' but patients' groups, self help and pressure groups, community health councils, health and community projects in which lay and professional people work together – could prove strong and resilient champions of the felt needs and concerns of ordinary users of health services. Nurses and other health workers, if they are searching for new roles beyond the 'professional' model, would do well to endorse this type of participative and enabling approach to health work.

Suggestions for further study

N. Deakin (1987) *The Politics of Welfare*, London, Methuen, is a thoughtful survey of the 'crisis in welfare' of the 1980s. B. Davey and J. Popay (1993) *Dilemmas in Health Care*, Book 7 of the Health and Disease series, Milton Keynes, Open University, contains several useful articles on evaluation, choice and health management. J. Gabe *et al.* (1991) *The Sociology of the Health Service*, London, Routledge, has useful chapters on recent health sector changes, although nursing is only addressed in the chapter by David Cox on health service management.

Self assessment questions

1 Explain what is meant by 'market principles', 'contractualism' and 'consumer sovereignty'.
2 Suggest why managerial control was seen as important in the health sector from the 1980s.
3 What evidence is there that the 'ideological crisis in welfare' has spread to the health sector?
4 Debate the merits and drawbacks of the internal market in the health service from the viewpoint of:
   a) a patient
   b) a health professional (make your choice)
   c) the Secretary of State for Health.

5 Assess the merits of quantitative and more qualitative approaches to measuring and evaluating health.
6 Make a set of predictions about the character and role of health services by the year 2000. Justify your claims.

List of references

Aakster, C.W. (1993) 'Concepts in alternative medicine', in Beattie, A., Gott, M., Jones, L.J. and Sidell, M. (eds) *Health and Wellbeing: A Reader*. London, Macmillan.

Aakster, C.W. (1986) 'Concepts in alternative medicine', *Social Science and Medicine*, 22, 2, pp. 265–73.

Abrams, P. (1977) 'Community care: some research problems and priorities', *Policy and Politics*, 6, 2, December 1977.

Allsop, J. (1984) *Health Policy and the National Health Service*. London, Longman.

Althusser, L. (1969) *For Marx*. London, Allen Lane.

Anionwu, E. (1993) 'Genetics – A philosophy of perfection?', in Beattie, A., Gott, M., Jones, L.J. and Sidell, M. (eds) *Health and Wellbeing: A Reader*. London, Macmillan.

Anionwu, E.N. (1989) *Ethnic Factors in Health and Disease*. London, Wright.

Anwar, M. (1979) *The Myth of Return, Pakistanis in Britain*. London, Heinemann.

Appleby, J. *et al.* (1991) *Implementing the Reforms: a Survey of Unit General Managers in the West Midlands Region* Monitoring Managed Competition, Project Paper No. 5, Birmingham, NAHAT.

Arber, S. (1991) 'Opening the 'black box': inequalities in women's health', in Abbott, P. and Payne, G. (eds) *New Directions in the Sociology of Health*. Basingstoke, Falmer.

Arber, S. and Gilbert, G.N (1989a) 'Men: the forgotten carers', *Sociology*, 23, 1, pp. 111–18.

Arber, S. and Gilbert, G.N. (1989b) 'Transitions in caring: gender, life course and the care of the elderly', in Bytheway *et al. Becoming and Being Old*. London, Sage.

Arber, S., Gilbert, G.N. and Dale, A. (1985) 'Paid employment and women's health: a benefit or a source of role strain?', *Sociology of Health and Illness*, 7, 3, pp. 375–400.

Aries, P. (1973) *Centuries of Childhood*. London, Peregrine.

Armstrong, D. (1993) 'From clinical gaze to regime of total health', in Beattie, A., Gott, M., Jones, L.J. and Sidell, M. (eds) *Health and Wellbeing: A Reader*. London, Macmillan.

Armstrong, D. (1983a) *Political Anatomy of the Body*. Cambridge, Cambridge University Press.

Armstrong, D. (1983b) 'The fabrication of nurse–patient relationships', *Social Science and Medicine*, 17, 8, pp. 457–60.

Ashmore, M., Mulkay, M. and Pinch, T. (1989) *Health and Efficiency: a Sociology of Health Economics*. Milton Keynes, Open University Press.

Ashton, J. and Seymour, H. (1988) *The New Public Health*. Milton Keynes, Open University Press.

Atkinson, A.B. (1989) *Poverty and Social Security*. London, Harvester Wheatsheaf.

Atkinson, J.M. (1978) *Discovering Suicide: Studies in the Social Organisation of Sudden Death*. London, Macmillan.

Audit Commission (1986) *Making A Reality of Community Care*. London, HMSO.

Bahl, V. (1985) Interview given in U205 television programme 'Rickets: the English Disease'.

Baldwin, S. and Parker, G. (1989) 'The Griffiths Report on community care', in Brenton, M. and Ungerson, C. (eds) *Social Policy Review 1988–9*. London, Longman.

Barclay Committee (1982) *Social Workers: Their Role and Tasks*. London, Bedford Square Press.

Barrett, M. (1988) *Women's Oppression Today: Problems in Marxist Feminist Analysis*. London, Verso (first published 1980).

Barrett, M. and McIntosh, M. (1982) *The Anti-Social Family*. London, Verso.

Barrow, J. (1982) 'West Indian families: an insider's perspective', in Rapoport, R.N., Fogarty, M.P. and Rapoport, R. (eds) *Families in Britain*, London, RKP.

Bartlett, W. and Harrison L. (1993) 'Quasi-markets and the National Health Service reforms', in Le Grand, J. and Bartlett, W. (eds) *Quasi-Markets and Social Policy*. London, Macmillan.

Baxter, C. (1992) 'Significance of black and minority ethnic health initiatives in redefining health knowledge', in K258 *Health and Wellbeing*, Workbook 1, Part 1. Milton Keynes, The Open University.

Bayley, M. (1973) *Mental Handicap and Community Care*. London, RKP.

Beattie. A, Gott, M., Jones, L.J. and Sidell, M. (eds) (1993) *Health and Wellbeing: A Reader*. London, Macmillan.

Beattie, A. (1991) 'Knowledge and control in health promotion: a test case for social policy and social theory', in Gabe, J., Calnan, M. and Bury, M. (eds) *The Sociology of the Health Service*. London, Routledge.

Beattie, A. (1990) *A Picture of Health (For All?) – a Review of the First Cohort of Reports on Public Health*. London, Faculty of Public Health Medicine.

Becker, H.S. (1963) *Outsiders: Studies in the Sociology of Deviance*. New York, Free Press.

Bell, C. and Newby H. (1971) *Community Studies: An Introduction to the Sociology of the Local Community*. London, Allen & Unwin.

Bendix, R. and Lipset, S.M. (1967) *Class, Status and Power. Social Stratification in Comparative Perspective*. London, RKP (first published 1959).

Berger, P. (1966) *Invitation to Sociology*. Harmondsworth, Penguin.

Berkman, L.F. and Syme, S.L. (1979) 'Social networks, host resistance and mortality: a nine year follow-up of Alameda County residents', *American Journal of Epidemiology*, 104.

Beveridge, W. (1944) *Full Employment in a Free Society*. London, George Allen & Unwin.

Bhalla, A. and Blakemore, K. (1981) *Elders of the Ethnic Minority Groups*. Birmingham, All Faiths for One Race.

Black, N. *et al.* (eds) *Health and Disease: A Reader*. Milton Keynes, Open University Press.

Blackburn, C. (1992) *Poverty and Health, Working with Families*. Milton Keynes, Open University Press.

Blakemore, K. (1989) 'Does age matter?', in Bytheway, W., Keil, T., Allatt, P. and Bryman, A. (eds) *Becoming and Being Old*. London, Sage.

Blaxter, M. (1990) *Health and Lifestyles*. London, Tavistock.

Blaxter, M. (1984) 'Equity and consultation rates in general practice', *British Medical Journal*, 288, pp. 1963–7.

Blaxter, M. and Paterson, E. (1982) *Mothers and Daughters: A Three Generational Study of Health Attitudes and Behaviour*. London, Heinemann.

Bloor, M. and McIntosh, J. (1990) 'Surveillance and concealment: a comparison of techniques of client resistance in therapeutic communities and in health visiting', in Cunningham-Burley, S. and McKeganey, N. (eds) *Readings in Medical Sociology*. London, Routledge.

Blumer, H. (1969) *Symbolic Interactionism: Perspective and Method*. New Jersey, Prentice Hall.

Bond, J., Coleman, P. and Peace, S. (eds) (1993) *Ageing in Society: An Introduction to Social Gerontology*. London, Sage.

Bond, J. (1990) 'Living arrangements of elderly people', in Bond, J. and Coleman, P. (eds) *Ageing in Society: An Introduction to Social Gerontology*. London, Sage.

Bond, J. and Coleman, P. (1990) 'Ageing in the Twentieth Century', in Bond, J. and Coleman, P. (eds) *Ageing in Society: An Introduction to Social Gerontology*. London, Sage.

Bond, J. and Bond, S. (1986) *Sociology and Health Care*. London, Churchill Livingstone.

Booth, T., Simms, K. and Booth, W. (1990) *Outward Bound: Relocation and Community for People with Learning Difficulties*. Buckingham, Open University Press.

Bornat, J. (1989) 'Oral history as a social movement: reminiscence and older people, *Oral History*, Autumn 1989, pp. 16–23.

Bowling, A. (1993) 'Changes in life satisfaction among very elderly people', *Social Science and Medicine*, 36, 5, pp. 641–55.

Bowling, A. (1991) *Measuring Health: a Review of Quality of Life Measurement Scales*. Milton Keynes, Open University Press.

Boyson, R. (ed.) (1971) *Down with the Poor*. London, Churchill Press.

Bradshaw, J. et al. (1992) *Household Budgets and Living Standards – Findings*. York, Joseph Rowntree Foundation.

Bradshaw, J. (1980) 'An end to differentials?', *New Society*, 9 October.

Bramley, G., Le Grand, J. and Low, W. (1989) *How Far is the Poll Tax a Community Charge?* WSP/42. London, Suntory Toyota International Centre for Economics and Related Disciplines.

Braverman, H. (1974) *Labour and Monopoly Capital: The Degradation of Work in the Twentieth Century*. New York, Monthly Review Press.

Braybon, G. and Summerfield, P. (1987) *Out of the Cage: Womens' Experiences in the Two World Wars*. London, Pandora.

Brechin A. and Walmesley, J. (eds) (1990) *Making Connections*. London, Hodder and Stoughton.

Brent Community Health Council (1981) *Black People and The National Health Service*. London, Brent CHC.

British Medical Association (1986) *Report on Alternative Medicine*. London, BMA.

Brown, C. (1984) *Black and White Britain: The Third PSI Survey*. London, Heinemann.

Brown, G. and Harris, T. (1978) *Social Origins of Depression*. London, Tavistock.

Bryan, B., Dadzie, S. and Scafe, S. (1985) *The Heart of the Race: Black Women's Lives in Britain*. London, Virago.

Bucquet, D. and Curtis, S. (1986) 'Socio-demographic variation in perceived illness and the use of primary care: the value of community survey data for primary health care planning', *Social Science and Medicine*, 23, 7, pp. 737–44.

Bulmer, M. (1987) *The Social Basis of Community Care*. London, Unwin Hyman.

Burghes, L. (1980) *Living from Hand to Mouth: A Study of 65 Families Living on Supplementary Benefit*. London, Child Poverty Action Group/Family Services Unit.

Burns, T. and Stalker, G.M. (1961) *The Management of Innovation*. London, Tavistock.

Bury, M. (1988) 'Arguments about ageing: long life and its consequences', in Wells, N. and Freer, C. (eds) *The Ageing Population: Burden or Challenge?* London, Macmillan.

Bury, M. (1986) 'Social constructionism and the development of medical sociology', *Sociology of Health and Illness*, Vol. 8, pp. 137–69.

Busfield, J. (1989) 'Sexism and psychiatry', *Sociology*, 23, 3, pp. 343–64.

Byrne, D.S., Harrison, S.P., Keithley, J. and McCarthy, P. (1986) *Housing and Health*. London, Gower.

Bytheway, W. (1993) in K256 Open University Course Team, *An Ageing Society*. Milton Keynes, The Open University.

Bytheway, W. and Johnson, J. (1990) 'On defining ageism', *Critical Social Policy*, pp. 27–39.

Bytheway, W., Keil, T., Allatt, P. and Bryman, A. (eds) (1989) *Becoming and Being Old*. London, Sage.

Calnan, M. and Gabe, J. (1991) 'Recent developments in general practice: a sociological analysis', in Gabe, J., Calnan, M. and Bury, M. (eds) *The Sociology of the Health Service*. London, Routledge.

Calnan, M. (1987) *Health and Illness: the Lay Perspective*. London, Tavistock.

Cameron, E. *et al.* (1989) 'Black old women, disability and health carers', in Jefferys, M. (ed.) *Growing Old in the Twentieth Century*. London, Routledge.

Campbell, R. and Macfarlane, A. (1987) *Where to be Born: The Debate and the Evidence*. Oxford, National Perinatal Epidemiology Unit.

Carpenter, M. (1980) *All For One: Campaigns and Pioneers in the making of COHSE*. London, Confederation of Health Service Employees.

Carpenter, M. (1977) 'The new managerialism and professionalism in nursing', in Stacey, M. *et al.* (eds) *Health and the Division of Labour*. London, Croom Helm.

Cartwright, F.F. (1977) *A Social History of Medicine*. London, Longman.

Cartwright, A. and O'Brien, M. (1976) 'Social class variation in health care and the nature of general practitioner consultations', in Stacey, M. (ed.) *The Sociology of the National Health Service*. Sociological Monograph, 2, University of Keele.

Castle, P. and Jacobson, B. (1988) 'The health of our regions: an analysis of strategies and policies of regional health authorities for promoting health and preventing disease'. *A Report for the Health Education Council*. Birmingham, NHS Regions Health Promotion Group.

Centre for Contemporary Cultural Studies, Birmingham (CCCS) (1982) *The Empire Strikes Back*. London, Hutchinson.

Chadwick, E. (1842) *Report on the Sanatory Condition of the Labouring Population of England*, Vol. 26. London, HMSO.

Challis, D. and Davies, B. (1986) *Matching Resources to Needs in Community Care*. Aldershot, Gower.

Charlesworth, A., Wilkin, B. and Durie, A. (1984) *Carers and Services: A Comparison of Men and Women Caring for Dependent Elderly People*. London, Equal Opportunities Commission.

Chavannes, M. (1989) 'Underachievement in school children', *Health Visitor*, 62, pp. 304–5.

Chesler, P. (1972) *Women and Madness*. New York, Doubleday.

Chodorow, N. (1978) *The Reproduction of Mothering*. Berkeley, University of California.

Cippolla, C. (1973) *Cristofano and the Plague: A study of Public Health in the Age of Galileo*. London, Collins.

Clarke, M. (1978) 'Getting through the work', in Dingwall, R. and McIntosh, J. (eds) *Readings in the Sociology of Nursing*. Edinburgh, Churchill Livingstone.

Clinical Accountability, Service Planning and Evaluation (CASPE) (1988). London, King's Fund.

Cochrane, A. (1971) *Effectiveness and Efficiency: Random Reflections on Health Services*. London, Nuffield Provincial Hospitals Trust.

Coffield, F. (1980) *A Cycle of Deprivation?* London, Heinemann.

Cohen, S. (1981) *Folk Devils and Moral Panics*. London, Martin Robertson.

Cole-Hamilton, I. and Lang, T. (1986) *Tightening Belts: A Report on the Impact of Poverty on Food*. London, London Food Commission.

Colledge, M. (1979) 'The place of men in nursing', in Colledge, M. and Jones, D. (eds) *A Reader in Nursing*. Edinburgh, Churchill Livingstone.

Commission For Racial Equality (1983) *Employment Report on Sister Dora School of Nursing, Walsall*. London, CRE.

Cook, J. and Watt, S. (1987) 'Racism, women and poverty' in Glendinning, C. and Millar, J. (eds) *Women and Poverty in Britain*. Brighton, Harvester.

Cooke, M. and Ronalds, C. (1987) 'The Manchester experience III: Rusholme well woman clinic' in Orr, J. (ed.) *Women's Health in the Community*. Chichester, Wiley.

Cornwell, J. (1984) *Hard-Earned Lives*. London, Tavistock.

Coronary Prevention Group (1986) 'Coronary heart disease and Asians in Britain'. London, Coronary Prevention Group and Confederation of Indian Organisations.

Coward, R. (1990) *The Whole Truth: The Myth of Alternative Health*. London, Faber & Faber.

Cox, B.D. *et al.* (1987) *The Health and Lifestyle Survey: preliminary report*. London, The Health Promotion Research Trust.

Cox, D. (1991) 'Health service management – a sociological view: Griffiths and the non-negotiated order of the hospital', in Gabe, J., Calnan, M. and Bury, M. (eds) *The Sociology of the Health Service*. London, Routledge.

Crawford, M. (1981) 'Not disengaged: grandparents in literature and reality', *Sociological Review*, 29, pp. 499–519.

Crawford, R. (1984) 'A cultural account of 'health'; control, release, and the social body', in McKinlay, J.B. (ed.) *Issues in the Political Economy of Health Care*. London, Tavistock.

Cuff, E.C. and Payne, D. (1979) *Perspectives in Sociology* (3rd edn). London, Allen & Unwin.

Cunningham-Burley, S. and Maclean, U. (1990) 'The role of the chemist in primary health care for children with minor complaints', *Social Science and Medicine*, 24, pp. 371–7.

Currer, C. (1991) 'Understanding the mother's viewpoint: the care of Pathan women in Britain', in Wyke, S. and Hewson, J. (eds) *Child Health Matters*. Milton Keynes, Open University Press.

Currer, C. (1986) 'Concepts of Mental well- and ill-being: the case of Pathan mothers in Britain', in Currer, C. and Stacey, M. (eds) *Concepts of Health, Illness and Disease: A Comparative Perspective*. Oxford, Berg.

Dalley, G. (1988) *Ideologies of Caring: Rethinking Community and Collectivism*. London, Macmillan.

Davey, B. and Popay, J. (1993) *Dilemmas in Health Care*, Book 7 of U205 *Health and Disease*. Milton Keynes, Open University.

Davidoff, L. and Hall, C. (1987) *Family Fortunes: Men and Women of the English Middle Class, 1780–1850*. London, Hutchinson.

Davies, C. (1988) 'The health visitor as mother's friend', *Journal of the Society for the Study of the Social History of Medicine*, Vol. 1.

Davies, C. and Rosser, J. (1986) 'Gendered jobs in the health service: a problem for labour process analysis' in Knights, D. and Willmott, H. (eds) *Gender and the Labour Process*. Aldershot, Gower.

Davis, F. (1975) 'Professional socialisation as subjective experience: the process of doctrinal conversion among student nurses', in Cox, C. and Mead, A. (eds) *A Sociology of Medical Practice*. London, Collier Macmillan.

Davis, K. (1993) 'The crafting of good clients', in Swain, J., Finkelstein, V., French, S. and Oliver, M. *Disabling Barriers, Enabling Environments*. London, Sage.

Davis, K. and Moore, W.E. (1945) 'Some principles of stratification', *American Sociological Review*, Vol. 10, pp. 242–9.

Deakin, N. (1987) *The Politics of Welfare*. London, Methuen.

Dean, H. and Taylor-Gooby, P. (1992) *Dependency Culture*. Hemel Hempstead, Harvester Wheatsheaf.

De la Cuesta, C. and Pearson, M. (1993) 'Social Control or revolution at the fringes? Ideologies and health visiting practice', paper delivered to Conference on Nursing, Women's History and the Politics of Welfare, 21–24 July, Nottingham University.

Delamothe, A. (1991) 'Social inequalities in health', *British Medical Journal*, 303, pp. 1–9.

Delphy, C. (1984) *Close to Home: A Materialist Analysis of Women's Oppression*. London, Hutchinson (first published 1977).

Department of Health (1993a) *Changing Childbirth: Report of the Expert Maternity Group chaired by Baroness Cumberlege*. London, HMSO.

Department of Health (1993b) *The Tomlinson Report on London's Hospitals*. London, HMSO.

Department of Health (1992a) *Health and Personal Social Services Statistics for England*. London, Crown Copyright.

Department of Health (1992b) *The Health of the Nation*. London, HMSO.

Department of Health (1991) *The Patient's Charter*. London, HMSO.

Department of Health (1990) *NHS Workforce in England*. London, HMSO.

Department of Health (1989a) *Working For Patients*. Cmnd. 555, London, HMSO.

Department of Health (1989b) *Caring For People*. Cmnd. 849, London, HMSO.

Department of Health (1988) *Community Care: Agenda For Action*. London, HMSO.

Department of Health and Social Security (DHSS) (1987) *Promoting Better Health*. London, HMSO.

DHSS (1986a) *Primary Health Care*. London, HMSO.

DHSS (1986b) *Promoting Better Health*. London, HMSO.

DHSS (1986c) *Neighbourhood Nursing: a Focus for Care*. Cumberlege Committee Report. London, HMSO.

DHSS (1986d) *Circular HC (78) 36 (19)*. London, HMSO.

DHSS (1984) *Griffiths Management Enquiry*. London, HMSO.

DHSS (1981) *Growing Older*. Cmnd. 8173, London, HMSO.

DHSS (1980) *Rickets and Osteomalacia, Report of a Working Party on Fortification of Food with Vitamin D*. Committee on Medical Aspects of Food Policy. London, HMSO.

DHSS (1979) *Report of the Committee of Inquiry into Mental Handicap Nursing and Care* (The Jay Report). London, HMSO.

DHSS (1976) *Prevention and Health: Everybody's Business*. London, HMSO.

DHSS (1971) *Better Services for the Mentally Handicapped*. London, HMSO.

DHSS (1968) *Seebohm Committee on Local Authority and Allied Personal Social Services*. Report. Cmnd. 2703, London, HMSO.

Derricourt, N. (1985) 'Strategies for Community Care', in Loney, M., Boswell, D. and Clarke, J. (eds) *Social Policy and Social Welfare*. Milton Keynes, Open University Press.

d'Houtard, A. and Field, M.G. (1984) 'The image of health: variations in perceptions by social class in a French population', *Sociology of Health and Illness*, Vol. 6, pp. 30–60.

Dingwall, R, and Robinson, J. (1990) 'Policing the family?', in Gubruim, J.F. and Sankar, A. (eds) *The Homecare Experience: Ethnography and Policy*. London, Sage.

Dingwall, R., Rafferty, A.M. and Webster, C. (1988) *An Introduction to the Social History of Nursing*. London, Routledge.

Dingwall, R. and Lewis, P. (1983) *The Sociology of the Professions, Introduction*. London, Macmillan.

Dingwall, R. and Murray, T. (1983) 'Categorisation in accident departments: 'good' patients, 'bad' patients and children', *Sociology of Health and Illness*, 5, pp. 127–48.

Dingwall, R. and McIntosh, J. (1978) *Readings in the Sociology of Nursing*. Edinburgh, Churchill Livingstone.

Dingwall, R. (1977) *The Social Organisation of Health Visiting*. London, Croom Helm.

Dingwall, R. (1976) *Aspects of Illness*. London, Martin Robertson.

Donnison, D. (1979) 'Social policy since Titmuss', *Journal of Social Policy*, Vol. 8, No. 2.

Donnison, D. (1975) *Social Policy and Administration Revisited*. London, Allen Lane.

Donnison, J. (1977) *Midwives and Medical Men: A History of Inter-Professional Rivalries and Women's Rights*. London, Heinemann.

Donovan, J. (1986) *We Don't Buy Sickness, It Just Comes*. Aldershot, Gower.

Donovan, J. (1984) 'Ethnicity and health: a research review', *Social Science and Medicine*, 19, 7, pp. 663–70.

Doyal, L. and Gough, I. (1991) *Towards a Theory of Human Needs*. London, Macmillan.

Doyal, L. (1985) 'Women and the National Health Service: the carers and the careless', in Lewin, E. and Olesen, V. (eds) *Women, Health and Healing*. London, Tavistock.

Doyal, L. and Epstein, S. (1983) *Cancer in Britain: the Politics of Prevention*. London, Pluto.

Doyal, L., Hunt, G. and Mellor, J. (1981) 'Your life in their hands: migrant workers in the National Health Service', *Critical Social Policy*, 1, 2, pp. 54–71.

Doyal, L. with Pennell, I. (1979) *The Political Economy of Health*. London, Pluto Press.

Dubos, R. (1979) *Mirage of Health*. New York, Harper.

Dunnell, K. and Cartwright, A. (1972) *Medicine Takers, Prescribers and Hoarders*. London, RKP.

Durkheim, E. (1970) *Suicide: A Study in Sociology*. London, RKP (first published 1897).

Durkheim, E. (1964) *The Rules of Sociological Method*. New York, Free Press (first published 1895).

Durward, L. (1984) *Poverty in Pregnancy: The Cost of an Adequate Diet for Expectant Mothers*. London, Child Poverty Action Group.

Edholm, F. (1982) 'The unnatural family' in Whitelegg, E. *et al.* (eds) *The Changing Experience of Women*. Oxford, Martin Robertson.

Ehrenreich, B. and English, D. (1974) *Witches, Midwives and Nurses: A History of Women Healers*. London, Glass Mountain Pamphlet No. 1.

Ekblom, P. (1986) 'Community policing' in Willmott, P. (ed.) *The Debate about Community*, papers from a seminar on Community in Social Policy. London, Policy Studies Institute.

Elkan, R. and Robinson, J. (1991) *The Implementation of Project 2000 in a District Health Authority: the Effect on the Nursing Service*, Nursing Policy Studies No. 7. University of Nottingham, Department of Nursing Studies.

Elkin, T., McLaren, D., with Hillman, M. (1991) *Reviving the City: Towards Sustainable Urban Development*. London, Friends of the Earth.

Engel, G.L. (1977) 'The need for a new medical model: a challenge for biomedicine', *Science*, Vol. 196, pp. 129–36.

English National Board for Nursing (1993) *Research Proposal*. London, ENB.

Equal Opportunities Commission (1993) 'Men and Women in Britain'. London, EOC.

Evandrou, M. and Victor, C. (1989), 'Differentiation in later life', in Bytheway, W. *et al.* (eds) *Becoming and Being Old*. London, Sage.

Evers, H. (1981) 'Care or custody? The experiences of women patients in long-stay geriatric wards', in Hutter, B. and Williams, G. (eds) *Controlling Women: the Normal and the Deviant*. London, Croom Helm.

Ewles, L. and Simnett, I. (1985) *Promoting Health*. London, Wiley.

Eysenck, H. (1971) *Race, Intelligence and Education*. London, Temple Smith.

Fallowfield, L. (1990) *The Quality of Life: the Missing Measurement in Health Care*. London, Souvenir Press.

Featherstone, M. (1991) *Consumer Culture and Postmodernism*. London, Sage.

Featherstone, M. and Hepworth, M. (1989) 'Ageing and old age: reflections on the postmodern life course', in Bytheway *et al.* (eds) *Becoming and Being Old*. London, Sage.

Felce, D. and Toogood, S. (1990) 'Mary M.', in Brechin, A. and Walmsley, J. (eds) *Making Connections*. London, Hodder & Stoughton.

Fennell, G., Phillipson, C. and Evers, H. (1988) *The Sociology of Old Age*. Milton Keynes, Open University Press.

Fernando, S. (1991) *Mental Health, Race and Culture*. London, Macmillan/MIND.

Field, F. (1982) *Poverty and Politics*. London, Heinemann.

Field, F. (1981) *Poverty and Inequality*. Harmondsworth, Penguin.

Figlio, K.M. (1982) 'How does Illness Mediate Social Relations? Workmen's Compensation and Medico-Legal Practices 1890–1940', in Wright, P. and Treacher, A. (eds) *The Problem of Medical Knowledge*. Edinburgh, Edinburgh University Press.

Finch, J. and Groves, D. (1983) *A Labour of Love: Women, Work and Caring*. London, RKP.

Finch, J. and Groves, D. (1980) 'Community care and the family: A case for equal opportunities?', *Journal of Social Policy*, 9, 4, pp. 487–511.

Finkelstein, V. (1993), 'Disability: a social challenge or an administrative responsibility', in Swain, J., Finkelstein, V., French, S. and Oliver, M. *Disabling Barriers, Enabling Environments*. London, Sage.

Firestone, S. (1971) *The Dialectic of Sex: The Case for Feminist Revolution*. London, Cape.

Fitzgerald, T. (1985) 'The New Right and the family', in Loney, M., Boswell, D. and Clarke, J. (eds) *Social Policy and Social Welfare*. Milton Keynes, Open University Press.

Flint, C. (1991) 'Continuity of care provided by a team of midwives – the know your midwife scheme', in Robinson, S. and Thomson, A.M. (eds) *Midwives, Research and Childbirth*, Vol. II. London, Chapman & Hall.

Flynn, M. (1989) *Independent Living for Adults with Mental Handicap: A Place of My Own*. London, Cassell.

Foucault, M. (1979) *The History of Sexuality*, Vol. 1. London, Allen Lane.

Foucault, M. (1973) The *Birth of the Clinic: An Archaeology of Medical Perception*. London, Tavistock.

Foucault, M. (1971) *Madness and Civilisation*. London, Tavistock.

Fox, A.J. and Goldblatt, P.O. (1982) *OPCS Longitudinal Study: Socio-Demographic Mortality Differential 1971–75*, Series LS No. 1. London, HMSO.

Fox, R.H. *et al.* (1973) 'Body temperatures in the elderly: a national study of physiological, social and environmental conditions', *British Medical Journal*, 1, pp. 200–6.

Frayman, H. (1991) *Breadline Britain 1990s*. London, Domino Films/London Weekend Television.

Freidson, E. (1986) *Professional Powers: A Study of the Institutionalisation of Formal Knowledge*. London, University of Chicago Press.

Freidson, E. (1983) 'The theory of professions – state of the art', in Dingwall, R. and Lewis, P. (eds) *The Sociology of the Professions*. London, Macmillan.

Freidson, E. (1970) *Profession of Medicine: A Study in the Sociology of Applied Knowledge*. New York, Dodd Mead.

Freidson, E. (1961) *Patients' Views of Medical Practice*. New York, Sage.

Fries, J.F. (1980) 'Aging, natural death and the compression of morbidity', *New England Journal of Medicine*, 303, 3, pp. 130ff.

Fries, J.F. and Crapo, L.M. (1981) *Vitality and Ageing: Implications of the Rectangular Curve*. San Francisco, Freeman.

Gabe, J. and Lipchitz-Phillips, S. (1984) 'Tranquillisers as social control?', *The Sociological Review*, 32, 3, pp. 524–46.

Galbraith, J.K. (1958) *The Affluent Society*. Harmondsworth, Penguin.

Gamarnikow, E. (1991) 'Nurse or woman: gender and professonalism in reformed nursing 1860–1923', in Holden, P. and Littlewood, J. (eds) *Anthropology and Nursing*. London, Croom Helm.

Gamarnikow, E. (1978) 'Sexual divisions of labour: the case of nursing' in Kuhn, A. and Wolpe, A.M. (eds) *Feminisim and Materialism*. London, RKP.

Game, A. and Pringle, R. (1983) *Gender at Work*. London, Allen & Unwin.

Garfinkel, H. (1967) *Studies in Ethnomethodology*. New Jersey, Prentice Hall.

General Household Survey (1985). London, OPCS.

George, V. and Howards, I. (1991) *Poverty Amidst Affluence*. Cheltenham, Edward Elgar.

Gerhardt, U. (1989) *Ideas about Illness. An Intellectual and Political History of Medical Sociology*. London, Macmillan.

Giddens, A. (1989) *Sociology*. London, Polity Press.

Giddens, A. (1982) *Profiles and Critiques in Social Theory*. London, Macmillan.

Giddens, A. (1979) *Central Problems in Social Theory, Action: Structure and Contradiction in Social Analysis*. London, Macmillan.

Gillies, D.R.N. *et al.* (1984) 'Analysis of ethnic influences on stillbirths', *Journal of Epidemiology and Community Health*, 38, 3, pp. 214–17.

Gilroy, P. (1987) *There Ain't No Black in the Union Jack*. London, Hutchinson.

Ginsberg, H. and Miller, S. (1982) 'Sex differences in children's risk-taking behaviour', *Child Development*, 53, pp. 426–35.

Ginsberg, N. (1979) *Class, Capital and Social Policy*. London, Macmillan.

Gittins, D. (1985) *The Family in Question*. London, Macmillan.

Glaser, B.G. and Strauss, A.L. (1968) *Time For Dying*. Chicago, Aldine.

Glendinning, C. and Millar, J. (eds) (1987) *Women and Poverty in Britain*. Brighton, Harvester.

Goffman, E. (1974) *Frame Analysis: An Essay on the Organisation of Experience*. New York, Harper & Row.

Goffman, E. (1964) *Stigma: the Management of Spoiled Identity*. Eaglewood Cliffs, Prentice Hall (Penguin edition 1968).

Goffman, E. (1961) *Asylums: Essays on the Social Situation of Patients and Other Inmates*. New York, Anchor (Penguin edition 1968).

Goffman, E. (1959) *The Presentation of Self in Everyday Life*. New York, Doubleday (Penguin edition 1969).

Goldthorpe, J.H. and Payne, C. (1986) 'Trends in intergenerational class mobility in England and Wales, 1972–1983', *Sociology*, Vol. 20.

Goldthorpe, J.H., Llewelyn, C. and Payne, C. (1980) *Social Mobility and Class Structure in Modern Britain*. Oxford, Oxford University Press.

Goldthorpe, J.H. *et al.* (1969) *The Affluent Worker in the Class Structure*. Cambridge, Cambridge University Press.

Graham, H. (1993) *Hardship and Health in Women's Lives*. Chichester, Wheatsheaf.

Graham, H. (1988) 'Women and smoking in the United Kingdom: implications for health promotion', *Health Promotion*, 3, 4, pp. 371–82.

Graham, H. (1986) 'Caring for the family', Research Report No. 1. London, Health Education Council.

Graham, H. (1985) 'Providers, negotiators and mediators: women as the hidden carers', in Lewin, E. and Olesen, V. (eds) *Women, Health and Healing*. London, Tavistock.

Graham, H. (1984a) *Women, Health and the Family*. London, Health Education Council/Wheatsheaf.

Graham, H. (1984b) 'Surveying through stories', in Bell, C. and Roberts, H. (eds) *Social Researching: Politics, Problems, Practices*. London, RKP.

Graham, H. (1983) 'Caring: a labour of love', in Finch, J. and Groves, D. *A Labour of Love: Women, Work and Caring*. London, RKP.

Graham, H. and Oakley, A. (1981) 'Competing ideologies of reproduction', in Roberts, H. (ed.) *Women, Health and Reproduction*. London, RKP.

Graham, H. and McKee, L. (1980) *The First Months of Motherhood*. London, Health Education Council.

Graham, H. (1979) 'Prevention and health: every mother's business', in Harris, C. (ed.) *The Sociology of the Family*. Keele, University of Keele.

Graham, H. (1976) 'Smoking in pregnancy: the attitudes of expectant mothers', *Social Science and Medicine*, 10, pp. 399–405.

Gramsci, A. (1988) *A Gramsci Reader* (ed. D. Forgues). London, Lawrence & Wishart.

Greater London Association for Racial Equality (1987) *No Alibis, No Excuses*. London, GLARE.

Green, D.G. (1990) *Equalising People*. London, Institute of Economic Affairs Health and Welfare Unit.

Griffith, B., Iliffe, S. and Rayner, G. (1987) *Banking on Sickness: Commercial Medicine in Britain and the USA*. London, Lawrence & Wishart.

Hadley, R. and Hatch, S. (1981) *Social Welfare and the Failure of the State*. London, Allen & Unwin.

Hall, C. (1989) 'The early formation of Victorian domestic ideology', in Burman, S. (ed.) *Fit Work for Women*. London, Croom Helm.

Hall, S. (1978) *Policing the Crisis*. London, Macmillan.

Halsey, A.H. *et al.* (1980) *Origins and Destinations*. Oxford, Clarendon.

Ham, C., Scholefield, D. and Williams, J. (1993) *Partnerships in Purchasing*. Birmingham, NAHAT.

Ham, C. (ed.) (1988) *Health Care Variations: Assessing the Evidence*. London, King's Fund Institute.

Hannay, D.R. (1979) *The Symptom Iceberg: A Study of Community Health.* London, Routledge & Kegan Paul.

Hardy, B., Wistow, G. and Rhodes, R.A.W. (1990) 'Policy networks and the implementation of community care policy for people with mental handicaps', *Journal of Social Policy*, 19, 3, April.

Harre, R. (1987) *The Social Construction of Emotions.* Oxford, Blackwell.

Harris, R. and Selden, A. (1979) *Over-ruled on Welfare.* London, Institute of Economic Affairs.

Harrison, S., Hunter, D. and Pollitt, C. (1990) *The Dynamics of British Health Policy.* London, Unwin.

Hart, N. (1985) *The Sociology of Health and Medicine.* Ormskirk, Causeway.

Hartmann, H. (1979) 'Capitalism, patriarchy and job segregation by sex', in Eisenstein, Z.R. *Capitalist Patriarchy and the Case for Socialist Feminism.* London, Monthly Review Press.

Harvey, J. (1987) 'New technology and the gender divisions of labour', in Lee, G. and Loveridge, R. (eds) *The Manufacture of Disadvantage.* Milton Keynes, Open University Press.

Havighurst, R.J. (1954) 'Flexibility and the social roles of the retired', *American Journal of Sociology*, 59, pp. 309–11.

Hayek, F.A. (1944) *The Road to Serfdom.* London, RKP.

Hearn, J. (1987) *The Gender of Oppression: Men, Masculinity and the Critique of Marxism.* Brighton, Wheatsheaf.

Heath, C. (1981) 'The opening sequence in doctor–patient interaction', in Atkinson, P. and Heath, C. (eds) *Medical Work: Realities and Routines.* Aldershot, Gower.

Helman, C. (1986) 'Feed a cold, starve a fever: folk models of infection in an English suburban community, and their relation to medical treatment' in Currer, C. and Stacey, M. (eds) *Concepts of Health, Illness and Disease: A Comparative Perspective.* Oxford, Berg.

Henderson, P. and Armstrong, J. (1993) 'Community development and community care', in Bornat, J., *et al.* (eds) *Community Care: A Reader.* London, Macmillan.

Henderson, P. and Thomas, D.N. (1987) *Skills in Neighbourhood Work.* London, Unwin Hyman (2nd edn).

Henley, A. (1983) *Caring For Hindus and their Families.* Cambridge, National Extension College (for HEC).

Henley, A. (1982) *Caring For Muslims and their Families.* Cambridge, National Extension College (for DHSS).

Henley, A. (1982) *Caring For Sikhs and their Families.* Cambridge, National Extension College (for DHSS).

Henley, A. (1979) *Asian Patients at Hospital and at Home.* London, Pitman Medical Library.

Herzlich, C. (1973) *Health and Illness.* London, Academic Press.

Hill, M. (1992) *Health Policy in Britain.* London, Macmillan.

Hobsbawm, E. (1964) *Labouring Men.* London, Weidenfeld and Nicholson.

Hochschild, A.R. (1983) *The Managed Heart: Commercialisation of Human Feeling.* Berkeley, University of California Press.

Hockey, J. (1993) 'Women and health', in Richardson, D. and Robinson, V. (eds) *Introducing Women's Studies.* London, Macmillan.

Hoggett, P. and Hambleton, R. (eds) (1987) *Decentralisation and Democracy: Localising Public Services*. Bristol University, School for Advanced Urban Studies.

Holland, B. and Lewando-Hundt, G. (1987) *Coventry Ethnic Minorities*. Coventry, City of Coventry Ethnic Minorities Unit.

Holmes, B. and Johnson, A. (1988) *Cold Comfort*. London, Souvenir Press.

Homans, H. (ed.) (1985) *The Sexual Politics of Reproduction*. Aldershot, Gower.

Homeopathic Development Foundation Ltd (1988) *Homeopathy for the Family*, 8th edn. London, Wigmore.

Horton, R. (1970) 'African traditional thought and western science', in Warwick, M. (ed.) *Witchcraft and Sorcery: Selected Readings*. Hardmondsworth, Penguin.

House of Commons Health Committee (1992) *Maternity Services*, Vol. 1. London, HMSO.

Howlett, B., Ahmad, Wl-U. and Murray, R. (1991) 'An examination of Asian and Afro-Caribbean people's concepts of health and illness causation', paper presented at the Annual Conference of the British Sociological Association, Manchester, 25–28 March.

Hoyes L. and Means R. (1993) 'Quasi-Markets and the reform of community care', in Le Grand, J. and Bartlett, W. *Quasi-Markets and Social Policy*. London, Macmillan.

Hughes, B. (1990) 'Quality of life', in Peace, S. (ed.) *Researching Social Gerontology: Concepts, Methods and Issues*. London, Sage.

Hughes, D. (1988) 'When nurse knows best: some aspects of nurse/doctor interaction in a casualty department', *Sociology of Health and Illness*, 10, 1, pp. 1–22.

Humphries, S. and Gordon, P. (1992) *Out of Sight*. Plymouth, Northcote House.

Hunt, S.M., McEwen, J. and McKenna, S.P. (1986) *Measuring Health Status*. London, Croom Helm.

Illich, I. (1976) *Limits to Medicine: The Expropriation of Health*. London, Marion Boyars (Penguin edition 1977).

Illsley, R. (1986) 'Occupational class, selection and the production of inequalities in health', *Quarterly Journal of Social Affairs*, 2, 2, pp. 151–65.

Illsley, R. (1981) 'Problems of dependency groups: the care of the elderly, the handicapped and the chronically ill', *Social Science and Medicine*, 15A, 3, Part 2.

Illsley, R. (1980) *Professional or Public Health?* London, Nuffield Provincial Hospitals Trust.

Institute for Fiscal Studies (1990) *Poverty in Official Statistics*. London, IFS Commentary No. 24.

Jackson, B. (1982) 'Single parent families', in Rapoport, R.N., Fogarty, M.P. and Rapoport, R. (eds) *Families in Britain*. London, RKP.

Jackson, S. (1993) *Family Lives: A Feminist Sociology*. Oxford, Blackwell.

Jacques, M. (1988) 'New times', *Marxism Today*, October, p. 3.

James, N. (1992) 'Care = organisation + physical labour + emotional labour', *Sociology of Health and Illness*, 14, 4.

James, N. and Field, D. (1992) 'Routinisation of hospice: charisma and bureaucracy', *Social Science and Medicine*, 34, pp. 1363–75.

Jeffery, R. (1979) 'Normal rubbish: deviant patients in casualty departments', *Sociology of Health and Illness*, 1, pp. 90–107.

Jefferys, M. (ed.) (1989) *Growing Old in the Twentieth Century*. London, Routledge.

Jewson, N. (1976) 'The disappearance of the sick man from medical cosmology, 1770–1870', *Sociology*, 10, pp. 225–44.

Johnson, M.L. (1993) 'Dependency and interdependency', in Bond, J., Peace. S. and Coleman, P. (eds) *Ageing and Society*. London, Sage.

Johnson, M.L. (1976) 'That was your life: a biographical approach to later life', in Munnichs, J.M.A. and Van Den Heuval, W.J.A. (eds) *Dependency or Interdependency in Old Age*. The Hague, Martinus Nijhoff.

Johnson, T. (1977) 'The professions in the class structure', in Scase, R. (ed.) *Industrial Society: Class, Cleavage and Control*. London, Allen & Unwin.

Johnson, T. (1972) *Professions and Power*. London, Macmillan, Studies in Sociology Series.

Jones, L.J. (1993) 'The individualist paradigm in infant mortality'. Conference on Health, Women's History and the Politics of Welfare. Nottingham, 21–24 July.

Joseph, K. (1972) 'The cycle of deprivation', speech at Conference of Pre-School Playgroups Association, 29 June.

Jowell, R. (1986) *British Social Attitudes*. Aldershot, Gower.

Kasl, S.V. and Cobb, S. (1966) 'Health behaviour, illness behaviour and sick-role behaviour', *Archives of Environmental Health*, 12, pp. 246–66, 531–42.

Kincaid, J. (1973) *Poverty and Equality in Britain: A Study of Social Security and Taxation*. Harmondsworth, Penguin.

King's Fund Equal Opportunities Task Force (1987) *A Model Policy for Equal Opportunities in Employment in the NHS*. London, King's Fund.

Kirkham, M. (1983) 'Labouring in the dark: limitations on the giving of information to enable patients to orientate themselves to the likely events and timescale of labour', in Wilson-Barnet, J. (ed.) *Nursing Research: Ten Studies in Patient Care*. Chichester, Wiley.

Kirp, D. (1979) *Doing Good by Doing Little, Race and Schooling in Britain*. Berkeley, University of California Press.

Klein, R. (1983) *The Politics of the National Health Service*. London, Longman.

Kramer, M. (1974) *Reality Shock: Why Nurses Leave Nursing*. New York, Mosby Books.

Kratz, C.R. (ed.) (1979) *The Nursing Process*. London, Balliere Tindall.

Kuhn, T.S. (1970) *The Structure of Scientific Revolutions*. Chicago, University of Chicago Press.

K258 Open University Course Team, *Health and Wellbeing*. Milton Keynes, The Open University.

Laczko, F. (1989), in Jefferys, M. (ed.) *Growing Old in the Twentieth Century*. London, Routledge.

Lalonde, M. (1974) *A New Perspective on the Health of Canadians*. Ottawa, Ministry of Supply and Services.

Lambert, H. and McPherson, K. (1993) 'Disease prevention and health promotion', in *Dilemmas in Health Care*, Book 8, U205 *Health and Disease* series. Milton Keynes, The Open University.

Larkin, G. (1983) *Occupational Monopoly and Modern Medicine*. London, Tavistock.

Lash, S. and Urry, J. (1986) 'Dissolution of the social?' in Wardell, M.L. and Turner, S.P. (eds) *Sociological Theory in Transition*. London, Sage.

Laslett, P. and Wall, R. (1972) *Household and Family in Past Time*. Cambridge, Cambridge University Press.

Lawrence, B. (1987) 'The fifth dimension: gender and general practice', in Spencer, A. and Podmore, D. *In a Man's World*. London, Tavistock.

Layton Henry, Z. (1984) *The Politics of Race in Britain*. London, Allen & Unwin.

Lee, P. and Raban, C. (1983) 'Welfare and ideology', in Loney, M., Boswell, D. and Clarke, J. (eds) *Social Policy and Social Welfare*. Milton Keynes, Open University Press.

Le Grand, J. and Bartlett, W. (1993) *Quasi-Markets and Social Policy*. London, Macmillan.

Le Grand, J. (1984) 'The future of the welfare state', *New Society*, 7 June, pp. 385–6.

Le Grand, J. (1982) *The Strategy Of Equality*. London, Allen & Unwin.

Le May, G. and Redfern, O. (1987) 'A study of non-verbal communication between nurses and elderly patients', in Fielding, P. (ed.) *Research in the Nursing Care of Elderly People*. Chichester, Wiley.

Lemert, E.M. (1972) *Human Deviance, Social Problems and Social Control*. Eaglewood Cliffs, Prentice Hall.

Lennane, J.K. and Lennane, R.J. (1982) 'Alleged psychogenic disorders in women – a possible manifestation of sexual prejudice', in Whitelegg *et al*. *The Changing Experience of Women*. London, Martin Robertson.

Leonard, A. and Jowett, S. (1990), in Elkan, R. and Robinson, J. (1991) *The Implementation of Project 2000 in a District Health Authority: the Effect on the Nursing Service*, Nursing Policy Studies, No. 7. University of Nottingham, Department of Nursing Studies.

Leviathan, U. and Cohen, J. (1985) 'Gender differences in life expectancy among kibbutz members', *Social Science and Medicine*, 21, 5, pp. 545–51.

Levitt, R. (1980) *The People's Voice in the NHS*. London, King Edward's Hospital Fund.

Lewin, E. and Olesen, V. (1985) *Women, Health and Healing*. London, Tavistock.

Lewis, G. (1986) 'Concepts of health and illness in a Sepik society', in Currer, C. and Stacey, M. (eds) *Concepts of Health, Disease and Illness: A Comparative Perspective*. Oxford, Berg.

Lewis, J. (1980) *The Politics of Motherhood*. London, Croom Helm.

Lewis, O. (1965) *La Vida: a Puerto Rican Family in a Culture of Poverty*. London, Panther.

Lipset, S.M. and Bendix, R. (1959) *Social Mobility in Industrial Society*. Berkeley, University of California Press.

Littlewood, R. and Lipsedge, M. (1988) 'Psychiatric illness among British Afro-Caribbeans', *British Medical Journal*, 296, pp. 950–1.

Littlewood, R. and Lipsedge, M. (1980) 'Ethnic minorities and psychiatric services', *Sociology of Health and Illness*, 2, pp. 194–201.

Llewelyn Davies, M. (1978) *Maternity: Letters From Working Women*. London, Virago (first published 1915).

Lockwood, D. (1966) *The Blackcoated Worker: A Study in Class Consciousness*. London, Unwin.

Loney, M. (1983) *Community Against Government*. London, Heinemann.

Long, J. (1990), in Bond, J. and Coleman, P. (eds) *Ageing in Society: An Introduction to Social Gerontology*. London, Sage.

Long, J. (1989) 'A part to play: men experiencing leisure through retirement', in Bytheway, B. *et al.* (eds) *Becoming and Being Old*. London, Sage.

Lonsdale, S. (1990) *Women and Disability*. London, Macmillan.

Lonsdale, S. (1985) *Work and Inequality*. London, Longman.

Low Pay Unit (1987) Annual Review. London, Low Pay Unit.

Lukes, S. (1977) *Power: A Radical View*. London, Macmillan.

Macdonald, B. and Rich, C. (1984) *Look Me in the Eye: Ageing and Ageism*. London, Women's Press.

MacGregor, S. (1984) *The Politics of Poverty*. London, Longman.

Macintyre, S. (1986) 'The patterning of health by social position in contemporary Britain', *Social Science and Medicine*, 23, 4, p. 393ff.

Macintyre, S. (1977) *Single and Pregnant*. London, Croom Helm.

Mack, J. and Lansley, S. (1991) *Poor Britain*. London, Harper Collins.

Mackay, L. (1989) *Nursing a Problem*. Milton Keynes, Open University Press.

MacLennan, W.J. (1986) 'Subnutrition in the elderly', *British Medical Journal*, 293, pp. 1189–90.

Macnicol, J. and Blaikie, A. (1989) 'The politics of retirement', in Jefferys, M. (ed.) *Growing Old in the Twentieth Century*. London, Routledge.

Maggs, C. (1983) *The Origins of General Nursing*. London, Croom Helm.

Mares, P., Henley, A. and Barker, C. (1985) *Health Care in Multi Racial Britain*. London, Health Education Authority/National Extension College.

Marks, L. (1988) *Promoting Better Health? An Analysis of the Government's Programme for Improving Primary Care*, Briefing Paper 7. London, King's Fund Institute.

Marmot, M., Kogevinas, M. and Elston, M.A. (1991) 'Socioeconomic status and disease', in Badura, B. and Kickbush, I. (eds) *Health Promotion Research. Towards a New Epidemiology*, WHO Regional Publications No. 37. Copenhagen, WHO.

Marmot, K.G. and McDowall, M.E. (1986) 'Mortality decline and widening social inequalities', *Lancet*, 2 August, p. 274.

Marmot, M. and Bulusu, L. (1984) *Immigrant Mortality in England and Wales 1970–1978*. OPCS Studies No. 47. London, HMSO.

Martin, E. (1987) *The Woman in the Body. A Cultural Analysis of Reproduction*. Milton Keynes, Open University Press.

Martin, J. and White, A. (1988) *The Financial Circumstances of Disabled Adults Living in Private Households*. London, HMSO.

Marx, K. (1933) *Capital*, Vol. 1. London, Dent (first published 1867).

Mason,D. (1982) 'After Scarman: A note on the concept of institutional racism', *New Community*, Vol. 10, 1.

May, D. and Kelly, M.P. (1982) 'Chancers, pests and poor wee souls: problems of legitimation in psychiatric nursing', *Sociology of Health and Illness*, 4, pp. 197–220.

Mayall, B. (1990) 'The division of labour in early child care – mothers and others', *Journal of Social Policy*, 19, 3, pp. 299–330.

McCann, K. and McKeown, H.P. (1993) 'Touch between nurses and elderly patients', *Journal of Advanced Nursing*, 18, pp. 838–46.

McKeown, T. (1976) *The Role of Medicine: Dream, Mirage or Nemesis*. London, Nuffield Provincial Hospitals Trust.

McKinlay, J.B. (1984) *Issues in the Political Economy of Health Care.* London, Tavistock.

McNaught, A. (1987) *Health Action and Ethnic Minorities.* London, Bedford Square Press.

Mechanic, D. (1962) 'The concept of illness behaviour', *Journal of Chronic Diseases*, 15, pp. 189–94.

Medawar, P. (1985) *The Limits of Science.* London, Tavistock.

Melia, K. (1987) *Learning and Working: the Occupational Socialisation of Nurses.* London, Tavistock.

Merton, R.K., Reader, G. and Kendall, P. (eds) (1957) *The Student Physician: Introductory Studies in the Sociology of Medical Education.* Cambridge, Harvard University Press.

Miles, A. (1991) *Women, Health and Medicine.* Milton Keynes, Open University Press.

Miles, R. (1982) *Racism and Migrant Labour.* London, RKP.

Miller A. and Gwynne G. (1972) *A Life Apart.* London, Tavistock.

Mills, C. Wright (1970) *The Sociological Imagination.* Harmondsworth, Penguin (first published 1959).

Minford, P. (1984) 'State expenditure: a study in waste', *Economic Affairs*, April–June.

Ministry of Health and Department of Health for Scotland (1966) *Report of the Committee on Senior Nursing Staff Structure* (The Salmon Report). London, HMSO.

Mitchell, B.R., with Deane, P. (1962) *Abstract of British Historical Statistics.* Cambridge, Cambridge University Press.

Mitchell, J. and Rose, J. (1982) *Female Sexuality.* London, Macmillan.

Moore, H. (1988) *Feminism and Anthropology.* Cambridge, Polity Press.

Moore, J. (1989) 'The end of the line for poverty', speech delivered by the Secretary of State for Social Security, 11 May. London, DHSS.

Moroney, R.M. (1976) *The Family and the State: Considerations for Social Policy.* London, Longman.

Morse, J.M. (1991) 'Negotiating commitment and involvement in the nurse–patient relationship', *Journal of Advanced Nursing*, 16, pp. 455–68.

Mulgan, G. (1991) 'Power to the people', *Marxism Today*, May 1991, pp. 14–19.

Naidoo, J. (1986) 'Limits to individualism' in Rodmell, S. and Watt, A. (eds) *The Politics of Health Education.* London, RKP.

National Advisory Committee on Nutritional Education (NACNE) (1983) *Nutritional Guidelines for Health Education in Britain.* London, Health Education Council.

National Association of Citizens' Advice Bureaus (NACAB) (1991)

National Association of Health Authorities (NAHA, now NAHAT) (1988) *Action Not Words.* Birmingham, NAHA.

National Association of Health Authorities and Trusts (NAHAT) (1993a) *Purchasing for a Healthy Population.* Birmingham, NAHAT.

National Association of Health Authorities and Trusts (NAHAT) (1993b) *Securing Public Accountability in the NHS.* Birmingham, NAHAT.

Navarro, V. (1979) *Medicine under Capitalism.* London, Croom Helm.

Navarro, V. (1978) *Class Struggle, the State and Medicine: An Historical and*

Contemporary Analysis of the Medical Sector in Great Britain. London, Martin Robertson.

Newchurch & Company (1993) *Strategic Change in the NHS. 1. – Unleashing the Market.* London, Newchurch & Company.

Nissel, M. and Bonnerjea, L. (1982) *Family Care of the Handicapped Elderly: Who Pays?* London, PSI.

Oakley, A. (1986) *Telling the Truth about Jerusalem.* Oxford, Blackwell.

Oakley, A. (1985) *Sex, Gender and Society.* London, Temple Smith.

Oakley, A. (1984) *The Captured Womb. A History of the Medical Care of Pregnant Women.* Oxford, Blackwell.

Oakley, A. (1980) *Women Confined: Towards a Sociology of Childbirth.* Oxford, Martin Robertson.

Oakley, A. (1976) *Housewife.* London, Martin Robertson.

O'Brien, M. (1981) *The Politics of Reproduction.* London, RKP.

O'Donnell, M. (1981) *A New Introduction to Sociology.* Walton-on-Thames, Nelson.

Olesen, V. and Whittaker, E.W. (1968) *The Silent Dialogue: A Study in the Social Psychology of Professional Socialisation.* San Francisco, Jossey Bass.

Oliver, M. (1993) 'Disability and dependency: a creation of industrial societies?', in Swain, J., Finkelstein, V., French, S. and Oliver, M. *Disabling Barriers, Enabling Environments.* London, Sage.

Oliver, M. (1990) *The Politics of Disablement.* London, Macmillan.

Oliver, S. and Redfern, S. (1991) 'Interpersonal communication between nurses and elderly patients: refinement of an observation schedule', *Journal of Advanced Nursing*, 16, pp. 30–8.

Orr, J. (1987) *Women's Health in the Community.* Chichester, Wiley.

Orr, J. (1986) 'Feminism and Health Visiting', in C. Webb (ed.) *Feminist Practice in Women's Health Care.* Chichester, Wiley.

Owens, P. and Glennerster, H. (1990) *Nursing in Conflict.* London, Macmillan.

Pahl, R.E. (1981) 'Employment, work and the domestic division of labour', in Harloe, M. and Lebas, E. (eds) *City, Class and Capital.* London, Edward Arnold.

Parkin, F. (1971) *Class Inequality and Political Order.* London, Paladin.

Parmar, P. (1988) 'Gender, race and power: the challenge to youth work practice', in Cohen, P. and Baines, H.S. (eds) *Multi-Racist Britain.* London, Macmillan.

Parry, N. and Parry, J. (1976) *The Rise of the Medical Profession: A Study of Collective Social Mobility.* London, Croom Helm.

Parsons, T. (1964) *The Social System.* London, RKP (first published 1951).

Parsons, T. and Smelser, N. (1959) *Economy and Society, a Study in the Integration of Economic and Social Theory.* London, RKP.

Parsons, T. and Fox, R. (1952) 'Illness, Therapy and the Modern Urban Family', *Journal of Social Issues*, 8, pp. 31–44.

Patterson, S. (1965) *Dark Strangers.* Harmondsworth, Penguin.

Pearson, M. (1986) 'Racist notions of ethnicity and culture in health education', in Rodmell, S. and Watt, A. (eds) *The Politics of Health Education: Raising the Issues.* London, RKP.

Pearson, M. (1985) *Racial Equality and Good Practice.* London, HEC.

Pelling, M. (1987) 'Medical practice in the early modern period: trade or profession?', in Prest, W. (ed.) *The Professions in Early Modern England*. London, Croom Helm.

Pelling, M. (1982) 'Occupational diversity: barber-surgeons and the trades of Norwich, 1550–1640', *Bulletin of the Society for the Study of the Social History of Medicine*, 56, pp. 484–511.

Percy-Smith, J. and Sanderson, I. (1992) *Understanding Local Needs*. London, Policy Studies Institute.

Phillipson, C. (1990) 'The Sociology of retirement', in Bond, J. and Coleman, P. *Ageing in Society: An Introduction to Social Gerontology*. London, Sage.

Phillipson, C. and Walker, A. (1987) *Ageing and Social Policy: a Critical Assessment*. Aldershot, Gower.

Phoenix, A. (1990) 'Black women and the maternity services', in Garcia, J., Kirkpatrick, R. and Richards, M. (eds) *The Politics of Maternity Care*. Oxford, Clarendon.

Piachaud, D. (1981) 'Peter Townsend and the Holy Grail', *New Society*, 57, pp. 419–21.

Piachaud, D. (1979) *The Cost of a Child*. London, Child Poverty Action Group, Poverty Pamphlet 3.

Pietroni, P. (1990) *The Greening of Medicine*. London, Gollancz.

Pietroni, P. (1988) 'Alternative medicine', *Royal Society of Arts Journal*, Vol. 136, No. 5387, October, pp. 791–801.

Pilgrim, D. and Rogers, A. (1993) *A Sociology of Mental Health and Illness*. Buckingham, Open University Press.

Pill, R. (1990) 'Change and stability in health behaviour: a five year follow-up study of working-class mothers', in Health Promotion Research Trust *Lifestyle, Health and Health Promotion*, pp. 63–79. Cambridge, Health Promotion Research Trust.

Pill, R., and Stott, N.C.H. (1982) 'Concepts of illness causation and responsibility: some preliminary data from a sample of working-class mothers, *Social Science and Medicine*, Vol. 16, No. 1, pp. 43–52.

Platt, S. (1984) 'Unemployment and suicidal behaviour: a review of the literature', *Social Science and Medicine*, 19, pp. 93–115.

Pollitt, C.J. (1988) 'Bringing consumers into performance measurements: concepts, consequences and constraints', *Policy and Politics*, 16, 2, pp. 77–87.

Porter, R. (1979) 'Medicine and the enlightenment in eighteenth century England', *Bulletin of the Society for the Study of the Social History of Medicine*, 25, pp. 27–40.

Porter, S. (1992) 'Women in a women's job: the gendered experience of nurses', *Sociology of Health and Illness*, 14, 4.

Porter, S. (1991) 'A participant observation study of power relations between nurses and doctors in a general hospital', *Journal of Advanced Nursing*, 16, pp. 728–35.

Prashar, U., Anionwu, E. and Brocovic, M. (1985) *Sickle Cell Anaemia: Who Cares? A Survey of Screening and Counselling Facilities in England*. London, Runnymede Trust.

Qureshi, H. and Walker, A. (1989) *The Caring Relationship*. London, Macmillan.

Rack, P. (1982) *Race, Culture and Mental Disorder*. London, Tavistock.

Rapoport, R.N., Fogarty, M.P. and Rapoport, R. (eds) (1982) *Families in Britain*. London, RKP.

Read, C. (1991) *Air Pollution and Child Health*. London, Greenpeace.

Revolutionary Health Committee of Hunan Province (1974) *Barefoot Doctor's Manual*. London, RKP.

Rex, J. (1973) *Race, Colonialism and the City*. London, RKP.

Richardson, J. and Lambert, J. (1985) 'The sociology of race', in Haralambos, M. (ed.) *Sociology: New Directions*. Ormskirk, Causeway.

Riley, J.C. (1987) *The Eighteenth Century Campaign to Avoid Disease*. New York, St. Martin.

Roberts, H. (1985) *The Patient Patients: Women and their Doctors*. London, Pandora.

Roberts, H. (1981a) *Doing Feminist Research*. London, RKP.

Roberts, H. (1981b) (ed.) *Women, Health and Reproduction*. London, RKP.

Roberts, R. (1951) *The Classic Slum*. Harmondsworth, Penguin.

Robertson, J. (1993) 'Possible futures for work', in Beattie, A., Gott, M., Jones, L.J. and Sidell, M. (eds) *Health and Wellbeing: A Reader*. London, Macmillan.

Rodmell, S. and Watt, A. (1986) 'Conventional health education: problems and possibilities', in Rodmell, S. and Watt, A. (eds) *The Politics of Health Education*. London, RKP.

Roper, A., Logan, W. and Tierney, A. (1980) *The Elements of Nursing*. Edinburgh, Churchill Livingstone.

Rose, R.B. (1972) *The Relief of Poverty, Studies in Economic and Social History*. London, Macmillan.

Rosenthal, C.J., Marshall, V., Macpherson, A.S. and French, S.E. (1980) *Nurses, Patients and Families*. London, Croom Helm.

Rosser, C. and Harris, C. (1965) *The Family and Social Change: A Study of Family and Kinship in a South Wales Town*. London, RKP.

Rosser, R.M. and Kind, P. (1978) 'A scale of valuations of states of illness: is there a social consensus?', *International Journal of Epidemiology*, Vol. 7, 4, pp. 347–58.

Roth, J. (1978) 'Ritual and magic in the control of contagion', in Dingwall, R. and McIntosh, J. (eds) *Readings in the Sociology of Nursing*. Edinburgh, Churchill Livingstone.

Rowbotham, S. (1973) *Hidden From History*. Harmondsworth, Penguin.

Rowntree, S. (1901) *Poverty: A Study of Town Life*. York.

Ryan, J. and Thomas, F. (1987) *The Politics of Mental Handicap*. London, Free Association Books (2nd revised edn).

Salvage, J. (1992) 'The new nursing: empowering patients or empowering nurses?', in Robinson, J., Gray, A. and Elkan, R. (eds) *Policy Issues in Nursing*. Milton Keynes, Open University Press.

Salvage, J. (1985) *The Politics of Nursing*. London, Heinemann.

Savage, J. (1987) *Sexuality and Nursing*. London, Heinemann.

Savage, W. (1986) *A Savage Enquiry: Who Controls Childbirth?* London, Virago.

Scarman Report (1981) *The Brixton Disorders, 10–12 April, 1981*. London, HMSO.

Scrutton, S. (1989) *Counselling Older People: A Creative Response to Ageing*. London, Age Concern.

Scull, A. (1983) *Decarceration. Community Treatment and the Deviant: a Radical View*. Cambridge, Polity Press (first published 1977).

Seabrook, J. (1973) 'The underprivileged: A hundred years of their ideas about health and illness', in Currer, C. and Stacey, M. (eds) *Concepts of Health, Disease and Illness: A Comparative Perspective*. Oxford, Berg.

Seedhouse, D. (1986) *Health: the Foundations for Achievement*. Chichester, Wiley.

Sharma, U. (1990) 'Using alternative therapies: marginal medicine and central concerns', in Abbott, P. and Payne, G. (eds) *New Directions in the Sociology of Health*. Basingstoke, Falmer Press.

Sheiham, H. and Quick, A. (1982) *The Rickets Report*. London, Haringay CHC.

Shorter, E. (1975) *The Making of the Modern Family*. London, Collins.

Slavin, M. (1992), paper delivered to the Transport and Health Study Group, Coventry (unpublished).

Smith, A. and Jacobson, B. (1988) *The Nation's Health*. London, King Edward's Hospital Fund for London.

Smith, P. (1992) *The Emotional Labour of Nursing*. London, Macmillan.

Smith, P. (1991) 'The nursing process: raising the profile of emotional care in nurse training', *Journal of Advanced Nursing*, 16, pp. 74–81.

Smith, Dr. R. (1993) 'Secondary to primary care: General practitioner fund holding as the lever', paper delivered to the Institute of Health Services Managers Annual Conference, 9–11 June, Birmingham.

Social Trends 24 (1994). London, HMSO.

Social Trends 23 (1993). London, HMSO.

Social Trends 15 (1975). London, HMSO.

Spencer, J. (1982) *Survey of Nurses' Smoking Behaviour*. Institute of Nursing Studies Research Unit, Hull, University of Hull.

Squires, P. (1990) *Anti-Social Policy. Welfare, Ideology and the Disciplinary State*. Chichester, Harvester Wheatsheaf.

Stacey, J. (1993) 'Untangling feminist theory', in Richardson, D. and Robinson, V. (eds) *Introducing Women's Studies*. London, Macmillan.

Stacey, M. (1988) *The Sociology of Health and Healing*. London, Unwin.

Stacey, M. (1986) 'Concepts of health and illness and the division of labour in health care', in Currer, C. and Stacey, M. (eds) *Concepts of Health, Disease and Illness: A Comparative Perspective*. Oxford, Berg.

Stacey, M. (1981) 'The division of labour revisited or overcoming the two Adams', in Abrams, P. and Deem, R. (eds) *Practice and Progress: British Sociology 1950–1980*. London, Allen & Unwin.

Stacey, M. (1969) 'The myth of community studies', *British Journal of Sociology*, Vol. 20, 2, pp.134–47.

Stainton Rogers, R. (1993) 'The social construction of child-rearing', in Beattie, A., Gott, M., Jones, L.J. and Sidell, M. (eds) *Health and Wellbeing: A Reader*. London, Macmillan.

Stainton Rogers, W. (1993) 'From psychometric scales to cultural perspectives', in Beattie, A., Gott, M., Jones, L.J. and Sidell, M. (eds) *Health and Wellbeing: A Reader*. London, Macmillan.

Stainton Rogers, W. (1991) *Explaining Health and Illness: An Exploration of Diversity*. London, Harvester Wheatsheaf.

Stanworth, M. (1983) *Gender and Schooling: A Study of Sexual Divisions in the Classroom*. London, Hutchinson.

Stein, L. (1978) *Readings in Sociology of Nursing*. Edinburgh, Churchill Livingstone.

Stimson, G. (1976) 'General practitioners, 'trouble' and types of patient', in Stacey, M. (ed.) *The Sociology of the National Health Service*. Keele, University of Keele Monograph, 22.

Stimson, G. and Webb, B. (1975) *Going to See the Doctor*. London, RKP.

Stockwell, F. (1972) *The Unpopular Patient*. London, RCN.

Strauss, A. (1993) 'Dying trajectories, the organisation of work and expectations of dying', in Dickenson, D. and Johnson, M. (eds) *Death, Dying and Bereavement*. London, Sage.

Strauss, A. (1963) 'The negotiated order', in Cox, C. and Mead, A. *A Sociology of Medical Practice*. London, Collier Macmillan.

Strong, P.M. and Robinson, J. (1988) *New Model Management: Griffiths and the NHS*. Warwick, Nursing Policy Studies Centre.

Strong, P.M. (1979) *The Ceremonial Order of the Clinic*. London, RKP.

Sudnow, D. (1967) *Passing On: The Social Organisation of Dying*. Eaglewood Cliffs, Prentice Hall.

Swann Report (1985) *Education For All*. London, HMSO.

Sydie, R.A. (1987) *Natural Women, Cultured Men*. Milton Keynes, Open University Press.

Sykes, W. *et al.* (1992) *Listening to Local Voices in the NHS*. Leeds and Salford, Nuffield Institute for Health and PHRRC.

Taylor-Gooby, P. (1991) *Social Change, Social Welfare and Social Science*. Hemel Hempstead, Harvester Wheatsheaf.

Terry, P.B. *et al.* (1980) 'Analysis of ethnic differences in perinatal statistics', *British Medical Journal*, 281, pp. 1307–8.

Tew, M. (1990) *Safer Childbirth? A Critical History of Maternity Care*. London, Chapman & Hall.

Thane, P. (1982) *Foundations of the Welfare State*. London, Longman.

Thatcher, M. (1988), address to the General Assembly of the Church of Scotland (reprinted in Raban, J. (1989) *God, Man and Mrs Thatcher*. London, Chatto & Windus).

Thompson, E.P. (1968) *The Making of The English Working Class*. Harmondsworth, Penguin.

Thornley, P. (1987) 'The development of well women clinics', in Orr, J. (ed.) *Women's Health in the Community*. Chichester, Wiley.

Thorogood, N. (1990) 'Caribbean home remedies and their importance for Black women's health care in Britain', in Abbott, P. and Payne, G. (eds) *New Directions in the Sociology of Health*. Basingstoke, Falmer Press.

Thunhurst, C. (1985) 'The analysis of small areas samples and planning for health', *Statistician*, 34, pp. 93–106.

Timmins, N. (1990) 'Fixing the poverty line', in *Search*, 6, pp. 14–16. York, Joseph Rowntree Foundation.

Titmuss, R. (1968) *Commitment to Welfare*. London, Allen & Unwin.

Towell, D. (1976) *Understanding Psychiatric nursing – a Sociological Study of Modern Nursing Practice*. London, Royal College of Nursing.

Townsend, P., Davidson, N. and Whitehead, M. (1988) *Inequalities in Health: The Black Report and The Health Divide*. Harmondsworth, Penguin.

Townsend, P., Phillimore, P. and Beattie, A. (1987) *Health and Deprivation: Inequality and the North*. London, Croom Helm.

Townsend, P., and Davidson, N. (1982) *Inequalities in Health: The Black Report*. Harmondsworth, Penguin.

Townsend, P. (1981) 'The structured dependency of the elderly', *Ageing and Society*, 1.

Townsend, P. (1979) *Poverty in the United Kingdom*. Harmondsworth, Penguin.

Trades Union Congress (1981) *The Unequal Health of the Nation: a TUC Summary of the Black Report*. London, TUC.

Tuckett, D. *et al.* (1985) *Meetings Between Experts*. London, Tavistock.

Tudor Hart, J. (1971) 'The inverse care law', *Lancet*, 1.

Turner, B. (1987) *Medical Power and Social Knowledge*. London, Sage.

Turner, B. (1984) *The Body and Society: Explorations in Social Theory*. Oxford, Basil Blackwell.

Twomey, M. (1986) 'A feminist perspective in district nursing', in Webb, C. (ed.) *Feminist Practice in Women's Health Care*. Chichester, Wiley.

Ungerson, C. (1987) *Policy is Personal*. London, Tavistock.

United Kingdom Central Council for Nursing, Midwifery and Health Visiting (UKCC) (1987a). *Report on Nurse Recruitment* (by Price Waterhouse). London, UKCC.

United Kingdom Central Council for Nursing, Midwifery and Health Visiting (UKCC) (1987b). *Project 2000: A New Preparation for Practice*. London, UKCC.

Unschuld, P. (1986) 'The conceptual determination (Uberformung) of individual and collective experiences of illness', in Currer, C. and Stacey, M. (eds) *Concepts of Health, Disease and Illness: A Comparative Perspective*. Oxford, Berg.

Verbrugge, L.M. and Steiner, R.P. (1981) 'Physician treatment of men and women patients: sex bias or appropriate care?', *Medical Care*, 19, 6, pp. 609–18

Victor, C. (1991) *Health and Health Care in Later Life*. Milton Keynes, Open University Press.

Victor, C. (1989) 'Income inequality in later life', in Jefferys, M. (ed.) *Growing Old in the Twentieth Century*. London, Routledge.

Wadsworth, M.E.J. (1986) 'Serious illness in childhood and its association with later-life achievement', in Wilkinson, R.G. (ed.) *Class and Health: Research and Longitudinal Data*. London, Tavistock.

Walby, S. (1990) *Theorising Patriarchy*. Oxford, Basil Blackwell.

Walker, A. (1993) 'Community care: from consensus to conflict', in Bornat, J. *et al.* (eds) *Community Care: A Reader*. London, Macmillan.

Walker A. (1990) 'Poverty and inequality in old age', in Bond, J. and Coleman, P. (eds) *Ageing in Society: An Introduction to Social Gerontology*. London, Sage.

Walker A. (1987) 'The poor relation: poverty among older women', in Glendinning, C. and Millar, J. (eds) *Women and Poverty in Britain*. Hemel Hempstead, Harvester Wheatsheaf.

Walker, A. (1986) 'Community care: fact and fiction', in Willmott, P. (ed.) *The Debate about Community*. London, Policy Studies Institute.

Walker, A. (1984) *Social Planning. A Strategy for Socialist Welfare*. Oxford, Blackwell.

Wallston, K.A., Wallston, B.S. and De Vellis, R. (1978) 'Development of the multidimensional health locus of control (MHLC) scales', *Health Education Monographs*, 6, pp. 161–70.

Watkins, S. (1987) *Medicine and Labour: the Politics of a Profession*. London, Lawrence & Wishart.

Weale, A. (1988) *The Search for Efficiency. Cost and Choice in Health Care: the Ethical Dimension*. London, King's Fund.

Webb, C. (1986) 'Women as gynaecology patients and nurses', in Webb, C. (ed.) *Feminist Practice in Women's Health Care*. London, Wiley.

Webb, C. (1985) *Sexuality, Nursing and Health*. Chichester, Wiley.

Webb, C. (1983) 'Hysterectomy: dispelling the myths', *Nursing Times, Occasional Papers*, 79, 30, pp. 52–4 and 31, pp. 44–6.

Webb, P. (1981) 'Health problems of London's Asians and Afro-Caribbeans, *Health Visitor*, 54, April.

Webb, T., Schilling, R. and Jacobson, B. (1988) *Health at Work? A Report on Health Promotion in the Workplace*. London, Health Education Authority.

Weber, M.(1979) *Max Weber on Capitalism, Bureaucracy and Religion*, a selection of texts edited by S. Andreski. London, Allen & Unwin.

Weber, M. (1948) *The Protestant Ethic and the Spirit of Capitalism*. London, Unwin (first published 1904).

Webster, C. (1988) *Problems of Health Care: The British National Health Service Before 1957*. London, HMSO.

Webster, C. (1979) 'Alchemical and Paracelsian medicine', in Webster, C. (ed.) *Health, Medicine and Mortality in the Sixteenth Century*. London, Croom Helm.

Weeks, J. (1989) *Sexuality and its Discontents*. London, Routledge.

Wenger G.C. (1989) 'Support networks in old age', in Jefferys, M. (ed.) *Growing Old in the Twentieth Century*. London, Routledge.

West, R. (1984) 'Alternative medicine', in Black, N. *et al.* (eds) *Health and Disease: A Reader*. Milton Keynes, Open University Press.

While, A. (ed.) (1989) *Health in the Inner City*. Oxford, Heinemann.

Whitehead, M. (1987) *The Health Divide*. London, Health Education Council.

Whittaker, E.W. and Olesen, V. (1978) 'The faces of Florence Nightingale: functions of the heroine legend in an occupational sub-culture', in Dingwall, R. and McIntosh, J. (eds) *Readings in the Sociology of Nursing*. Edinburgh, Churchill Livingstone.

Wilding, P. (1992) 'The public sector in the 1980s', in Manning, N. and Page, R. (eds) *Social Policy Review 4*. London, Social Policy Association.

Willetts, D. (1987) 'The price of welfare', *New Society*, 14 August, pp. 9–11.

Williams, A. (1987) 'Making sense of feminist contributions to women's health', in Orr, J. (ed.) *Women's Health in the Community*. Chichester, Wiley.

Williams, F. (1992) 'Somewhere over the rainbow: universality and diversity in Social Policy', in Manning, N. and Page, R. (eds) *Social Policy Review 4*. London, Social Policy Association.

Williams, F. (1989) *Social Policy: A Critical Introduction*. Cambridge, Polity Press.

Williams, K. (1978) 'Ideologies of nursing: their meanings and implications', in Dingwall, R. and McIntosh, J. (eds) *Readings in the Sociology of Nursing*. Edinburgh, Churchill Livingstone.

Williams, R. (1990) 'Images of age and generation', in Bryman, A. and Bytheway, B. (eds) *Life Cycle Perspectives*. London, Macmillan.

Williams, R. (1983) 'Concepts of health: an analysis of lay logic', *Sociology*, 17, 2, pp. 185–204.

Williams, S. and Calnan, M. (1991) 'Key determinants of consumer satisfaction with general practice', *Family Practice*, 8, 3, pp. 237–42.

Willis, P. (1991) *Towards a New Cultural Map*. National Arts and Media Strategy Discussion Paper 18. London, Arts Council.

Willmott, P. (1989) *Community Initiatives: Patterns and Prospects*. London, Policy Studies Institute (PSI).

Willmott, P. and Thomas D. (1984) *Community in Social Policy*. London, PSI.

Willmott, P. and Young, M. (1973) *The Symmetrical Family*. London, RKP.

Wilson, A. and Startup, R. (1991) 'Nurse socialisation: issues and problems', *Journal of Advanced Nursing*, 16, pp. 1478–86.

Winkler, F. (1987) 'Consumerism in health care: beyond the supermarket model', *Policy and Politics*, 15, 1, pp. 1–8.

Wintour, P. (1989) 'Numbers in poverty up to over three million', *The Guardian*, 28 April.

Witz, A. (1992) *Professions and Patriarchy*. London, Routledge.

Wolfenden Committee Report (1977) *The Future of Voluntary Organisations*. London, Croom Helm.

Wolfensberger, W. (1972) *The Principle of Normalisation in Human Services*. Toronto, National Institute on Mental Retardation.

Woods, R. and Woodward, J. (eds) (1984) *Urban Disease and Mortality in Nineteenth Century England*. London, Croom Helm.

Woodward, J. (1977) 'Popular theories of generation', in Wood, J. and Richards, D. *Health Care and Popular Medicine in Nineteenth Century Britain*. London, Croom Helm.

World Health Organisation (1988) *Adelaide Recommendations on Healthy Public Policy*. Adelaide, WHO.

World Health Organisation (1984) 'Report of the Working Group on Concepts and Principles of Health Promotion'. Copenhagen, WHO.

World Health Organisation (1985) *Health For All by the Year 2000*. Geneva, WHO.

World Health Organisation (1974) *Alma Ata Declaration*. WHO.

Wright, C. and Hearn, J. (1993) 'The 'invisible man' in nursing', paper delivered to the Conference on Nursing, Women's Health and the Politics of Welfare, 21–24 July, Nottingham University.

Wright, P. and Treacher, A. (1982) *The Problem of Medical Knowledge: Examining the Social Construction of Medicine*. Edinburgh, Edinburgh University Press.

Young, A. (1986) 'Internalising and externalising medical belief systems: An Ethiopian example', in Currer, C. and Stacey, M. (eds) *Concepts of Health, Illness and Disease: A Comparative Perspective*. Oxford, Berg.

Young, M. and Willmott, P. (1957) *Family and Kinship in East London*. Harmondsworth, Penguin.

Zola, I. (1975) 'Culture and symptoms', in Cox, C. and Mead, A. (eds) *A Sociology of Medical Practice*. London, Collier Macmillan.

Zola, I. (1972) 'Medicine as an institution of social control', *The Sociological Review*, 20, 4, pp. 487–504.

Author index

Subject index